CITIZEN OF THE WORLD

—

CITIZEN

OF THE

ALFRED A. KNOPF CANADA

JOHN ENGLISH

WORLD

THE LIFE OF PIERRE ELLIOTT TRUDEAU

VOLUME ONE: 1919–1968

PUBLISHED BY ALFRED A. KNOPF CANADA

Copyright © 2006 John English

All rights reserved under International and Pan-American Copyright
Conventions. No part of this book may be reproduced in any form or by any
electronic or mechanical means, including information storage and retrieval
systems, without permission in writing from the publisher, except by a reviewer,
who may quote brief passages in a review. Published in 2006 by Alfred A. Knopf
Canada, a division of Random House of Canada Limited, and
simultaneously in Quebec by Les Éditions de l'Homme, Montreal.
Distributed by Random House of Canada Limited, Toronto.

Knopf Canada and colophon are trademarks.

www.randomhouse.ca

Pages 545 to 546 constitute a continuation of the copyright page.

Library and Archives Canada Cataloguing in Publication

English, John, 1945–
Citizen of the world : the life of Pierre Elliott Trudeau / John English.
Includes bibliographical references and index.
Contents: v. 1. 1919–1968.

ISBN-13: 978–0–676–97521–5 (V. 1)
ISBN-10: 0–676–97521–6 (V. 1)

1. Trudeau, Pierre Elliott, 1919–2000. 2. Canada—Politics and
government—1968–1979. 3. Canada—Politics and government—1980–1984.
4. Prime ministers—Canada—Biography. I. Title.
FC626.T7E53 2006   971.064'4092   C2006–902597–5

Text design: CS Richardson

First Edition

Printed and bound in Canada

This book is printed on ancient-forest friendly, 100% recycled,
100% post-consumer waste paper.

2 4 6 8 9 7 5 3 1

To Hilde, without whom this book and so much else
would never have been possible

CONTENTS

—

PREFACE

ierre Trudeau is the prime minister who intrigues, enthralls, and outrages Canadians most. Remarkably intelligent, highly disciplined, yet seemingly spontaneous and a constant risk-taker, he made his life an adventure. The outline of the story is well known. Born into a wealthy French-English family in Montreal, he was educated in the city's best Catholic schools and at university in Montreal, followed by graduate work first at Harvard, then in Paris and in London. When he returned to Canada in the late forties after an extensive journey through Europe, the Middle East, and Asia, he spent the next decade and a half seemingly as a dilettante, writing articles for newspapers and journals, driving fast cars and a Harley-Davidson motorbike, escorting beautiful women to concerts and restaurants, travelling the globe whenever he wished, founding political groupings that went nowhere, and finally getting a teaching position at the Université de Montréal. Then, suddenly, or so it seemed, in 1965 he stood as a Liberal candidate in the federal election, won his seat, and quickly gained national attention as a constitutional expert and an innovative minister of justice. Three years later, he became leader of the Liberal Party of Canada amid a media frenzy usually reserved for rock stars, not politicians. How did it all happen?

This first volume of *The Life of Pierre Elliott Trudeau* offers a key to this mystery. Soon after Trudeau's death, his executors asked me if I would be interested in writing a definitive biography, based on unique, full access to his papers and including both his personal and his public life. I had doubts, knowing how private Trudeau had been and how little he had revealed of his life in his memoirs, even though his public career ranks among the most influential in Canada. While I admired Trudeau, supported him during his political career and after, and shared many mutual friends and acquaintances, I had met him only a few times, nearly always in political settings, where sometimes he was superb but, at other moments, visibly uncomfortable.

Yet the enigma of Trudeau intrigued me. Moreover, when I learned from some of his executors—Alexandre Trudeau, Jim Coutts, Marc Lalonde, Roy Heenan, and Jacques Hébert—that he had kept a huge trove of letters and personal documents in his famous Art Deco home in Montreal, I realized I had a rare opportunity and agreed to accept their challenge. These papers, which are now mostly housed in the ancient Tunney's Pasture research centre of Library and Archives Canada, provide an extraordinary record of his private life. I am the only biographer who has had full access to these papers and to the closed room in which they are preserved. In addition, through the Trudeau family and others, I have had access to other papers that have been ignored, restricted, and absent to earlier scholars. Together these papers form an extraordinary collection that reveals the private hopes, fears, loves, and loathings of Trudeau from his earliest years until his death.

The personal papers, which were assembled by Grace Trudeau and by Trudeau himself, give a detailed record of his early life. Until the 1960s Trudeau, a literary perfectionist, drafted every letter he wrote and kept most of the drafts—in some cases several drafts of the same letter. In this sense, Trudeau's papers are more complete than those of Mackenzie King, his only rival in maintaining a full record of his life. Moreover, Grace Trudeau was even more diligent than Isabel King in saving the school records of her favourite son. Virtually every report card, school notebook, award notice, and school essay was preserved. Trudeau also kept materials in his papers that were highly controversial, notably the evidence of his nationalist and secret activities during the early 1940s.

In reading Trudeau's own words, I came to realize that the seeming contradictions in his life were more often consistencies, and that this man of reserve to his male colleagues and friends was astonishingly open and honest with women. I uncovered youthful allegiances he hoped to keep secret, yet saw how completely he changed from a socially conservative Catholic to Catholic socialist once he was exposed to different ideas and influences at Harvard and the London School of Economics. I also discovered that his move into political life in middle age was no surprise at all, but something he had planned since his adolescence. He had merely been waiting for the right moment to make it happen. And the playboy who was photographed with one stunning blonde after another had, I found, enjoyed deeply rewarding relationships with a few extraordinary women. His letters to his female friends and his mother are the most frequently quoted in this volume, not because they are sensational but because they reveal most fully the private self that Trudeau quietly cloaked.

As a youth, Trudeau wrote in his journal that mystery was essential to defining identity and that he wanted to be a friend to all but an intimate to none. It was an intention he held to for the rest of his life. Although he read through many of his papers in his later years, he did not use them in his own brief memoir published in 1993. Nor did he succumb to the temptation to edit or destroy them. Fortunately, he chose the course of integrity and truth, and he retained controversial or intimate items in his archive. Once I had read through the collection, many of his close friends who are still alive generously agreed to discuss these letters with me, and, as we talked, they told me more of their memories of Pierre (I thank them in specific detail in the Acknowledgments to this book). As a result of their generosity and support, my text in several instances revises and even contradicts Trudeau's own account of his life and other earlier biographies of him. Trudeau, as he emerges in these pages, is a far more complex, conflicted, and challenging character than we have ever known before.

The first volume of this biography takes Trudeau through the crucial formative years, from his birth in 1919 (a year of disappointment in Canada) to the Liberal leadership convention of 1968 (a year of abundance and promise in the nation he was soon to lead). The second volume will cover his fifteen controversial years as prime minister, his role as husband and devoted father, and his often tumultuous public and private life until his death in the opening year of the twenty-first century.

CHAPTER ONE

—

TWO WORLDS

T he Great War was over; the times tasted bitter. Influenza came back with the soldiers and killed more at home than had died in the trenches. Like the war, it preferred the young to the old. Death usually came quickly as the victims suffocated in a blood-tinged froth that sometimes gushed grotesquely from their faces.[1] As winter became spring in 1919, theatres stayed empty. Men and women entered public places warily, concealing their faces behind gauze masks. The plague invaded private spaces, compelling isolation and reflection. What, then, did Grace Elliott Trudeau and her husband, Joseph-Charles-Émile, think when she learned she was pregnant in Montreal in mid-winter 1919? Pregnancy was dangerous in normal times, but the influenza surely terrified her as her body began to swell with her second child.

The twentieth century had so far been a great disappointment—especially for francophone Canadians. There was some excitement and hope when it began with Canada's first French-speaking prime minister, Wilfrid Laurier, in power, and an increasingly prosperous economy. The great transformation of Western society that occurred as electricity, steamships, telephones, railways, and automobiles upset the balance of the

5

Victorian age profoundly affected the world of the young Trudeaus. In Quebec, as elsewhere, people were in motion, leaving the familiar fields of rural life and traditional crafts for the cities that were exploding beyond their pre-industrial core. In Montreal, the population rose from 267,730 in 1901 to 618,506 in 1921. The rich had clustered together, initially in mansions in the "Golden Square Mile" along Sherbrooke Street and north up the southern slope of Mount Royal, while the poor spread out below them and in the east end. It was said in 1900 that the Square Mile contained three-quarters of Canada's millionaires. Stephen Leacock, who knew them well, commented, "The rich in Montreal enjoyed a prestige in that era that not even the rich deserve."[2]

Unfortunately, the rich were nearly entirely English; the poor, overwhelmingly French. When the French lived mainly in the villages, the gap was less obvious. In the city, it sowed the seeds of deep discontent. And, as new immigrants, mainly Jewish, flowed in from continental Europe, new tensions emerged in the more diverse city.[3]

Even before the war, foreign visitors sensed trouble. In 1911 the Austrian writer Stefan Zweig, after a visit to Montreal, said that all reasonable men should advise the French to abandon their resistance to assimilation. They were fast becoming simply an episode in history.[4] Among francophones in Quebec, the challenge of the new century brought an increasingly nationalist response, particularly when English-Canadian politicians became entangled in the British imperialism that marked the years before the Great War. By then there was a new prime minister, Robert Borden, and the voice of French Canada in the federal government became faint. And in 1914 the war divided the country as never before between the French and the others.

Once again, it seemed that a bargain had been broken.

Now leader of the official Opposition, Wilfrid Laurier supported the war, along with the French Catholic Church. Even Henri Bourassa, who had founded the nationalist newspaper *Le Devoir* and become the vocal spokesperson for francophone rights throughout Canada, kept his silence. He and the bishops went along because Borden promised there would be no conscription, but, three years later, conscription was proclaimed, accompanied by vitriolic attacks in English Canada on the French in Quebec. In the bitter and violent Canadian election in 1917, francophones voted overwhelmingly for Laurier's Liberals, who opposed conscription, while anglophones responded by backing a coalition composed of English-speaking Liberals and Conservatives. There were riots in Montreal and deaths in Quebec City. In 1919 Laurier died, then depression struck, while, at Versailles, the victors divided the spoils even as the world began to understand that the war to end all wars had not done so.

In their modest but comfortable row home at 5779 Durocher Avenue in the new suburb of Outremont, the Trudeaus could find some comfort. Outremont was neighbour to Mount Royal and, in population, split between residents of French and British origin, along with a substantial number of Jews. They lived far from the crowded tenements of the city below the hill, where death often came for both mother and child during pregnancy.[5] Charles and Grace had married on May 11, 1915, and she had become pregnant soon after with an infant who did not survive.[6] In 1918 she gave birth to a daughter, Suzette. Charles already had good reason not to enlist and, after the *Military Service Act* became law in 1917, to avoid conscription.

When the Trudeaus married, Grace, in common with other Quebec women of the time, acquired the same legal rights as minors and idiots. Her husband owed her protection in return for her submission.[7] Yet Grace had her own sources of strength. Her father, a substantial businessman of United Empire Loyalist stock, had sent his daughter to Dunham Ladies' College in the Eastern Townships, where she had acquired an education in literature, classics, and etiquette that few girls in Quebec possessed. She knew French, her mother's tongue, as well as English, which she and Charles chose to speak most often at home. Like Charles, she was Roman Catholic and devout.* Though not wealthy in the first years of their marriage, the Trudeaus had the means to hire country girls to help with household tasks.

Assisted by a midwife at home, Grace gave birth to Joseph-Philippe-Pierre-Yves-Elliott Trudeau on a warm fall day, October 18, 1919.[8] The parents immediately chose Pierre from his multiple names, though he, later, took a long time to make up his mind which name he favoured. His mother probably reflected the original intention when she wrote in his "Baby Book" Joseph Pierre Yves Philip Elliott Trudeau. Years later, when he was quizzed about it, Trudeau himself could not recall the correct order.[9] He weighed eight pounds four ounces and, from the beginning, suffered from colic. The crying finally stopped when he had an operation for adenoids in May

---

* Grace's mother was a Catholic and, in the practice of the day, she took her mother's religion. She also spoke fluent French, even though her mother died when she was ten years old. Trudeau later explained, "Obviously she always spoke French too because otherwise she wouldn't have met the gang that my father was hanging around with in the time of his studies in Montreal." Trudeau also said that they met at a church attached to Collège Sainte-Marie, adding, "It's a good place to meet, I suppose, at least in the stories you tell your kids." Interview between Pierre Trudeau and Ron Graham, April 28, 1992, TP, vol. 23, file 3.

1920. Along with Pierre's physical health, Grace recorded his spiritual growth in a diary. It began with his baptism, followed by the moment in October 1921 when two-year-old "Pierre made the sign of the cross." In December he began to say his prayers alone and "blessed Papa, Mama, Suzette etc."[10] Six months later the proud mother recorded that her precociously bilingual child knew "Sing a Song of Sixpence," "Little Jack Horner," "Au clair de la lune," and "Dans sa cabane." She continued dutifully to collect mementos of Pierre's life—school essays, marks, news clippings, and letters—until he finally left her home in the 1960s as a middle-aged man.

Grace kept only a few documentary fragments revealing the lives of herself and her husband. We have one intriguing letter from Charles in 1921, when he was working in Montreal and Grace, pregnant with Charles Junior (nicknamed "Tip"), was with Pierre and Suzette at Lac Tremblant, where the family had a cottage. He began with an apology for not being in touch but claimed that his daily tasks were overwhelming. Then his emotions flowed freely as he anxiously asked after the children in a hastily written letter:

> How are the "babies"? Always watch them most attentively; and I urge you not to think of me but of them. Watch their steps, their games, their fights, their health. It appears that the little brother [Pierre] is on the right path. This should make you happy, enjoy it; but you must remember that the two of them, the couple, are young and an accident can always happen. If we had to lose one . . . They are so sweet, so nice—both of them—and you know the proverb: "if you are too nice, you'll die young." These words are so true that they make me frightened for those two; a third, and a fourth etc. . . . would be very welcome if only the good Lord would provide more like those we

have. I believe now that I am a "garage man" I can use the
expression: more of them would make good "spares."

After this lame attempt at humour in which he referred to
the service stations he had recently purchased, Charles returned
to his didactic style, telling Grace to watch their children's character closely and to correct their faults. Such correction, he
urged, was always for the children's good. After a few more hom-
ilies, he closed with kisses and hugs to all: "Salut à Madame, un
bon baiser à toi et des caresses aux petits" [Bye Madame, a good
kiss for you and hugs for the little ones].[11]
Affectionate obviously, hierarchical certainly, Charles
has remained elusive, even in the descriptions given by his
children and friends.[12] He moved outside the familiar categories
of his time and place, much as his son would later do. In the
beginning, however, his path was familiar. Like most nineteenth-
century francophones in Quebec, he grew up on a farm. His
father, Joseph Trudeau, was a semi-literate but fairly prosperous farmer at St-Michel de Napierville, south of Montreal. He
was a descendant of Étienne Truteau, a carpenter from La
Rochelle, France, who had arrived in 1659. Three years later,
according to a now vanished plaque that was once affixed to
a building on the corner of La Gauchetière and St-André in
Montreal: "Here Truteau, Roulier, and Langevin-Lacroix resisted
50 Iroquois, May 6, 1662."[13] By the time of Charles's birth in
1889, the challenge to the French presence came not from the
Iroquois or the British soldiers who had conquered Quebec but
from the impersonal forces arising from the transformation of
a commercial and agrarian society into one that was urban
and industrial.
Charles's parents, especially his mother, Malvina, a
mayor's daughter and a doctor's sister, knew that their world
of the farm, parish, and family would soon be lost. They were

determined that the boys among their eight children would have a chance in the new world they faced. They sent Charles to Collège Sainte-Marie, an eminent classical college in Montreal established by the Jesuits in 1848, once the previously banned powerful religious order was allowed to return to Canada. Although situated in the heart of the city, the college was—at least in the later view of some students—a place apart. Its discipline, beginning in the morning with prayers at 5:30, followed by study at 6:00 and Mass at 6:30, took the students "away from the daily realities and the concerns of the day."[14]

Paradoxically, by stepping out of the world, these boys became part of a privileged elite that would eventually dominate the fields of law, politics, religion, and medicine in twentieth-century Quebec. Those areas, however, were the traditional ones for francophones in the province, and, in the new industrial age, they increasingly brought fewer material rewards than did the world of finance and industrial capitalism, where the English dominated. Moreover, politics seemed increasingly beholden to wealth, and the francophone politicians of the time catered to the English capitalists. Just as some leading Quebecers, especially in the Roman Catholic Church, developed a critique of modern capitalism, others came to terms with its needs—including Charles Trudeau.

A few notebooks survive from Charles's years at Collège Sainte-Marie, and they cast a faint light on his education and personality. Warned by his parents that failure meant a return to the farm, he was diligent. In his final year, 1908–9, he wrote and defended his thesis in Latin in a class on philosophy given in that language. He also copied out quotations to memorize and reflected negatively on the issues of the early years of the twentieth century—revolution, alcoholism, and war. "War kills the arts, the sciences, the civilization," he wrote and then transcribed quotations supporting that cryptic declaration. On the key question of imperialism, he was not yet a stern critic of Britain. One of his quotations suggests it would be dangerous to separate from "Albion": "We would be incomparably weaker, isolated as we are in a nation of five million facing an immense country of sixty million." Moreover, Quebec needed foreign investment. But he had some doubts: "The authority of the mother country and the decisions of the Privy Council are not sufficient protection for the rights of Catholics in a province." The seeds of nationalism had taken root. After Charles left the college, where he won many prizes despite a reputation as a troublemaker, he studied law for three years at the Montreal campus of Laval University (which became the University of Montreal in 1919).[15]

Charles seems to have been a good student: his notes are impressive in their organization and detail; he wrote in a fine and even elegant hand; and his classical education provided a strong intellectual base. Yet, in the accounts of those who knew him later, he changed radically at this time. He became an extrovert who loved games, gambling, and the high life. At home, though, it was different. In interviews, both Suzette and Pierre recalled him as a strict father who, though often absent, was intense and dynamic when present. He taught Pierre boxing, shooting, and even wrestling tricks. He also made him independent. Trudeau later told how disappointed he was that his friend Gerald O'Connor was put in the second grade and he in the first. He complained to his father, begging him to ask the principal to promote him. "No!" his father said. "It's your problem. Knock on his door and ask him yourself." Pierre did—and he happily joined Gerald in the second grade. In the seventies George Radwanski described how, when Trudeau spoke of his father, his eyes lit up and his gestures became more animated. He got "the impression of a child who may have been unknowingly overawed by an exceptionally dynamic father, perhaps in ways that contributed to his childhood sensitivity, insecurity, and later self-testing and rebellious."[16]

Trudeau himself wrote more openly about how his father was "very extroverted. He spoke loudly and expressed himself vigorously. His friends were the same."[17] On weekends at Lac Tremblant, he invited guests, sometimes as many as twenty, and expected Grace to cook for them. "They liked to get involved in our games," Trudeau recalled; "they liked to play cards, and they liked to drink and feast." Sometimes the parties were organized in the basement of their Montreal home, but normally, he explained, "the only time in the whole day that we got to enjoy his company" was when Charles came home for dinner, took a quick look at the children's schoolwork, and disappeared into the night to work or play. Although Pierre credited his father with teaching him sports, he claimed, despite visits from the flamboyant Montreal mayor, Camillien Houde, that they did not discuss politics: "I never asked my father any questions on the subject, and he for his part made no attempt to arouse my interest." But, at the very least, he did so indirectly.

Others have painted a darker picture of Charles as "Charlie" or "Charley," the bon vivant who played poker with rough-edged friends. Stephen Clarkson, co-author with Christina McCall of a study of Pierre Trudeau, has speculated that Charles was sometimes abusive towards Grace. They quote a family friend who said that Charles was brutal with his own friends and made things difficult when he came home drunk.[18] There is no documentary evidence to support these suggestions. The family strongly denies the rumours of abuse towards Grace, though not of loud partying late in the night.

A small, wiry man, Charles's energy and drive for success soon made him tire of petty legal affairs in his reasonably prosperous three-person law firm, Trudeau & Guérin, on St. James Street.

In the fashion of the times, Charles-Émile Guérin was a Liberal, while Charles and his brother Cléophas were identified as *bleus,* or Conservatives. He took big chances; his son's papers contain an undated notebook detailing his gambling wins and losses, nightly sums that often exceeded the yearly earnings of a Montreal worker. But in 1921, with two children and another, Charles, on the way, he completely changed course. He had noticed how automobiles were increasingly common on city streets and wondered who fixed and fuelled them. In 1910 there were only 786 automobiles in Quebec; in 1915, 10,112; in 1920, 41,562—and, within five years, there would be almost 100,000. By the 1920s, roads had become the largest item in the Quebec budget.[19] Sensing the future, Charles opened a garage near his home, and soon he owned several others offering gasoline as well as the maintenance so often needed by the automobiles of the time—a "garage man," as he had described himself to Grace—and he called his operation the Automobile Owners' Association, with offices at 1216 St-Denis. The business quickly succeeded, and he ingeniously expanded the association into a club in which car owners signed on for an annual fee in return for guaranteed service.[20]

By the early 1930s the association had approximately 15,000 members, and Charles owned thirty garages. Imperial Oil noticed his success and offered him $1.2 million for the business in 1932. He accepted and then invested the funds in mining (mainly Sullivan Mines), Belmont Park (a large amusement park in Montreal), and even the Montreal Royals baseball team, of which he became the vice-president. Mining and entertainment were the best investments for the 1930s, and the stock market moved briskly upward immediately after Charles received his funds. Charles's fortune was, Pierre Trudeau wrote modestly later, a sum that was "quite respectable for the time." He became a member of the Cercle Universitaire, the Club Canadien, and several golf clubs. In truth, their affluence brought financial security for Grace and her children for the rest of their lives.[21] They became and remained members of the *haute bourgeoisie* of Quebec.

Perhaps what impressed Pierre about his father was the way in which he so cleverly beat the English at their own games. His father had left law early, although he did tell Pierre that it was a "useful" degree. More interesting and rewarding was business, and his extroverted personality fitted it well. Charles had an excellent Jesuit and French education, but he was determined to learn English, and he insisted that his children write to him in that language. He even signed some of his letters to them "Papa Charley." He knew they must learn English to succeed in the Quebec of that time, and he sent them to French schools only after he was certain they were fluent in English. Although Pierre later recalled that the workers in his garages were French, the company name on its stationery was in English alone, and probably the majority of customers were anglophones.[22]

Yet Charles was committed to the French presence in Quebec. He chose to live in Outremont, not Westmount—his wealth would have gained him easy entry. His club was the St-Denis, the "French" club founded in the 1870s; and his office on St-Denis was far from the centre of bourgeois wealth in Montreal. He was generous to many French Catholic charities, particularly the hospitals. His politics were Conservative and nationalist. Very tellingly, his newspaper was the nationalist bible *Le Devoir*, and he was even a member of its operating board. Unlike many Quebec francophones of the day, Charles relished modern times and its wonders. The family's increasing prosperity brought a move from the row house on Durocher to a more substantial Outremont home at 84 McCulloch (sometime McCullough) Street, with a large veranda and rooms for the maid and the chauffeur, Elzéar Grenier. It was also near the great park on Mount Royal, away from the city's slums, and close to the best schools for the children. The brick house, while not pretentious, was impressive in its three storeys, large rooms, stately furnishings, and easy access to the verdant surroundings on the mountain.

When Charles was not at his garage or his club, he travelled sometimes to Europe and often to the United States. In one letter that Pierre sent to his father, Grace added a postscript: "Will write you in Los Angeles—at Biltmore Hotel. I don't know of any other."[23] Clearly, Charles was always difficult to follow, a trait his son inherited, yet his presence was strong, sentimental, and loving with, or away from, his family. On September 28, 1926, he sent a postcard with a photograph of an airplane to Pierre and wrote over the picture: "There I was for nearly 3 hours." On the back he informed his young son: "Whatever you do when you grow to be a man, Pierre, don't be an aviator. Your Papa would be too much afraid. 3000 feet high, a speed of 125 miles an hour for 3 hours. Gee that's long!" From New York City in May 1930 he sent another postcard, with a cartoon of a young boy who is being rebuked by his mother for spitting on the floor: "Hello there, Pierre! Are you the papa at home just now? Tell them they have to take orders from you. Love & kisses, Pa." He wrote from San Francisco a few months later, "My own Pierrot," and told him, "Glad to see that you can do anything when you want."[24]

Pierre was equally warm in his letters to his father—which were normally written in English. He wrote in the summer of 1929, when the children and Grace were at their summer home at Old Orchard Beach in Maine:

Dear Papa
How are you? We are having a good time. We are doing our exercises three times a day. Tippy [brother Charles]

is learning how to swim pretty good. I can float and I like it. We went on a picnic yesterday afternoon—ten kids. We played around and when it was time to eat we had to open our bottles on a barbwire fence! There were lots of mosquitoes so we came home. I would like to have my bike down here and Tippy would his also. Did mamma tell you about it? Hope you come back soon.

> Your loving son, Pierre
> (P.S.) don't forget the bike.

Pierre's plea was gently rebuked. On July 19 Charles replied to "Mon cher petit Pierre":

I am very glad to see that you're having a good time, that you are doing your exercises and you are good "kids" because Mamma told me so in her last letter . . .

Being the oldest I hope you are showing Tippy how to swim and you yourself are watching him: the biggest brother should always do that.

I like to see that you have learned how to float and I bet you have also improved your swimming. Now, is Suzette doing her exercises good and is she practicing swinging? I wish I had an eye on her too and show her how to get strong and healthy and wise.

Yes, Mamma told me about your "bike," Pierre and you may be sure Mamma does not forget anything when she thinks it can please her "kids" but my opinion is that out there you don't need the "bike" because you can play all sorts of games on the beach, have all sorts of exercises etc., which is much better, I think, than promenading on the streets with a "bike." Never mind, Pierre, if the other guy gets one: he won't be any better off and then you have things that he does not have and besides there are very few boys that have a bike over there. In fact I don't think I saw one.

Now tell Suzette that I expect a letter from her by return mail and I don't see why she has let you write before her.

Tell Tippy too that he can at least write a postal card and sign his name.

Tell Mamma that I'll write tonight or tomorrow. Keep on having a good time and be good. Don't forget your exercises and your swing and listening to Mamma and by doing all that you'll be working as hard as your papa and work is what makes a man out of one.

Kisses to all, Papa Charley

There would be no bikes on Old Orchard Beach that summer.[25]

Charles's frequent absences brought a flow of postcards, and ten-year-old Pierre responded with banter and warmth. In an undated letter of the late 1920s he assured his father that he did "not mind staying till half past five every afternoon" at school because, when he got home, he had all his homework done. After saying that he had not missed his 5BX exercises, a military calisthenics drill, and had missed piano practice only once, he concluded: "I have nothing more to say so I will close up my letter giving lots of xxxxxx and love." In the summers they went to the Laurentians, followed by a long stay at Old Orchard Beach. In their Lac Tremblant cottage, the children "would listen for the faraway sound of tires on the bridge across the outlet of the lake that would mean [Charles] was arriving." Pierre often became playful in his signoff, once declaring himself J P E Trudeau and another time mimicking the end of radio programs: "We are now signing off. Please stand by for station announcement. Your loving son, Pierre."

In 1933 Charles decided to take the entire family and

Grace's father to Europe. Sixty years later, Pierre said that he retained "a thousand vivid images of it" in his mind. For the first time, he said, they (presumably the children) "experienced the remarkable feeling of being almost totally out of our element." He enjoyed that feeling and always would. He developed an abiding wanderlust. One story that Trudeau retold many times was how his father stopped the car in front of a German hotel and said, "Pierre, rent us the rooms." Faced with the challenge and possessing limited German, the thirteen-year-old lad nevertheless made the deal.

Although Charles gave his older son adult tasks, Pierre retained a childlike tone when dealing with his father in his early teenage years. He wrote to his father from Old Orchard Beach in the summer of 1934. He and Tippy, who seems to have become the subordinate younger brother, had just enjoyed the Marx Brothers in *Duck Soup*, and he reported on the arrival and departure of friends and relatives. The latest group did not "interest me much as there are only girls in both families," he said, but the complaint was almost certainly a fib. Beach photographs from the period suggest that Pierre's already penetrating eyes were constantly fixed on the girls, who were often grouped around him. Once again he reported on his exercises and concluded: "I hope you come up and see us sometime soon. Now I must be signing off as everybody is on the beach and I must go too. Kisses (xxx), Pierre."[26] Pierre treasured these summer months and yearned for his father's presence.

On March 30, 1935, he complained to his parents, who were then vacationing in Florida as the Montreal Royals began their spring training, about the "disagreeable" winter season in Montreal. He eagerly awaited the coming Easter vacation, but even more the summer holiday that was only three months away. At school he had received a "Bene," but the most interesting event of the month was the visit of "Antoni, the famous

Canadian magician," who had mystified the students with his extraordinary tricks. His mother returned from the South on April 8, and Pierre immediately wrote to his father:

> Dear Papa,
> As Maman has decided to send you my report card [from Brébeuf] which came today, I've decided to add a few words:
>   When I got home this evening, Maman told me you were ill and I hasten to wish you a speedy recovery. I'm relieved to know it is apparently nothing serious.

He expressed hope that his father would write soon, noted that he had obtained another "Bene," and suggested that the results of his essays should also please him. Then he concluded:

> Don't stay away too long and try to be with us for Easter at least!
>   We're all well here. Goodbye!
>   Your loving son,
>   Pierre

But Charles did not come home for Easter.

The pneumonia that had not been "serious" had caused a heart attack. When Grace heard that Charles's condition was quickly worsening, she and Suzette flew down to Florida, leaving Tip and Pierre with an aunt. Before Pierre could send his letter, the telephone rang. From the landing in the stairwell, he saw his aunt turn towards him. "Your father is dead, Pierre," she said.[27] "In a split second," he recalled later, "I felt the whole world go empty. His death truly felt like the end of the world." And forty years later he said: "It was traumatic, very traumatic . . . I still can't go to a funeral without crying."[28] Death had come quickly for Charles, who was only forty-six, and it traumatized the whole family.* Grace told Suzette: "I'll never be able to bring up the boys alone."[29] Pierre himself recalled that, at fifteen years of age, "all of a sudden, I was more or less the head of a family; with him gone, it seemed to me that I had to take over."[30] Brébeuf's rector wrote to him: "Poor little one! But you are a little Christian, Pierre, and you have the consolation of our beautiful Catholic faith."[31] It helped, but the distraught boy tore up the letter he had written to his father.

When Grace came home, she found its pieces in the wastebasket, along with a draft of the earlier letter he had sent to his parents in Florida. She carefully pasted the pages together. They were among the documents she kept until her death, when they passed to Pierre—and into his collection of papers. He preserved another item too. In the celebrated portrait of Trudeau in the Parliament Buildings, just outside the House of Commons, he wears, as a final homage, Charles's black cape, which he had kept for over half a century.[32] Clearly there was intense grief, but did he also feel "ambivalence" towards his father, thus

---

* Charles Trudeau's death attracted considerable attention in the Montreal press, with similar responses. *The Montreal Star*, April 12, 1935, mourned the death of a major sports figure, the owner of Belmont Park and the major investor in the Montreal Royals, while *La Patrie*, April 11, lamented, in a key editorial, the loss of a French-Canadian businessman who had attained "the prestige and influence of the rich," yet did not lose his friends even when he reached the highest steps on the ladder of success. Trudeau, *Le Devoir* claimed, had served superbly on its board as a financial consultant. The April 11–12 issue even speculated that although Charles Trudeau had become disillusioned with politics, he might some day have entered politics as a reformer.

complicating the grief, as some have suggested? That is less certain. I will return to the psychological impact of Charles's life
and death on Pierre later. The documentary records of the time
support his sister Suzette's comment that "[Pierre] didn't shock or
disturb us or react in a way that I would think was because my
father was gone . . . Perhaps he took on a certain responsibility."[33]
He never ceased to miss him profoundly, however.*

Camillien Houde, the Conservative and nationalist mayor
of Montreal; J.-A. Bernier, the president of the nationalist Société
Saint-Jean-Baptiste; and Georges Pelletier, the editor of Le Devoir,
joined the family as Charles's remains arrived in Windsor Station
early on the following Saturday morning. At the funeral there
were thirteen priests, several judges, and seven cars carrying
the flowers.[34] The funeral became etched forever in Pierre's
memory, but he was away from school only briefly and his marks,
which were recorded weekly, remained remarkably high. He
wrote rather formally to his mother on April 28 and again on
May 2, less than a month after his father's death, saying in both
letters that he knew she was "in good health" and hoped that she

---

* On April 10, 1938, the third anniversary of Charles's death, Pierre went to
Mass and took communion for the sake of his father's soul. He wrote in his
diary: "Time heals all. Maybe it's true that you are able to become accustomed to an absence, but the more time passes, the more I miss his firm
but kind goodness, his advice so full of wisdom. Without doubt, he guides
me from Heaven still but it would be so good to be able to talk with him
and discuss things with him once again." He lamented that he had been
given only fifteen years to profit from his father's wisdom. He accepted that
it was God's will that Charles was with Him. The loss is expressed constantly in the diaries he kept from 1938 to 1940. Journal 1938, April 10, 1938, TP,
vol. 39, file 9.

remained so. Occasionally he stayed in school as a boarder and, in the first letter, he noted that he missed the charm of home and the caresses of his mother. In the second he reported that his marks were the highest in the class, a total of 292 out of 300. He then wrote out "April's fool" in Greek, Latin, English, French, and another script. It was a good academic year. He wrote again to his mother on June 10 and told her that he expected to win prizes. Thanks to his excellent teachers, "we have all had a good year." He ended by thanking his mother for sending him to such a fine school.[35]

Several of Pierre's classmates have said that it was a different boy who returned to the school after his father died. He became more nonconformist, more eager to shock teachers and students alike.[36] Certainly his father was missed at Brébeuf, where the Jesuit priests later remembered how "Charlie" would "offer to buy them Havana cigars to pass around at a college dinner in honour of a visiting papal delegate or to send them a case of whisky for their own pleasure any time they liked."[37] Small wonder so many of them attended his funeral. The atmosphere at home also changed. Trudeau said later: "When my father was around, there was a great deal of effusiveness and laughter and kissing and hugging. But after he died, it was a little bit more the English mores which took over, and we used to even joke about, or laugh at, some of our cousins or neighbours or friends— French Canadians—who'd always be very effusive within the family and towards their mother and so on."[38] Pierre began to use the hyphenated surname Elliott-Trudeau, suggesting a new orientation towards the English side of the family, though in 1931–32 he had briefly favoured J.P. Elliott Trudeau.[39] It seems that he became more rebellious in class, while, in the less playful atmosphere at home, he increasingly strove to please Grace. His letters and notebooks indicate a more complex pattern after his father's death: he became more like a stone whose colours radiated differently, depending on the angle from which it was viewed. He concealed more, but, paradoxically, what he did reveal briefly illuminated his core.

To be sure, Pierre doted on his mother, expressing constant concern for her health. Although we have no written records of what Grace thought, Charles's death profoundly affected her. Her life had focused on her husband's career and, most of all, the children. Years after, Grace Pitfield, who was related by birth or marriage to many of the British elite of Montreal (and was the mother of Trudeau's friend and later colleague Michael Pitfield), told a journalist how Grace Elliott, who had Loyalist roots and a minor inheritance, had simply disappeared. She had friends who "had been at school with Grace Elliott," she explained. "They heard later that she had married a Frenchman. But nobody knew who he was, and of course they never saw her afterwards."[40] It was not surprising, given this divide in Montreal society at the time, that Grace—having cut herself off from her background—craved the affection and attention of her children. And they responded. The reserve that had marked her when the exuberant and extroverted Charles was alive disappeared when she was the sole parent, and she became more assertive, more playful. But that was Grace's private side. "'Formidable' is the word Trudeau sometimes uses to describe his father," quipped the journalist Richard Gwyn. "Everyone else applies it to his mother." After Charles's death, Grace Trudeau gained presence.[41]

Pierre seemed to become both son and companion, an emotional combination that has its charms and its dangers. He took more responsibility for family affairs, according to both Suzette and Pierre himself. His father's death brought financial independence and security, and Pierre cherished this freedom. Each of the children apparently received $5,000 a year, more than the average annual income for doctors and lawyers in the late 1930s. And there were reserves if needed.[42] In his late teenage years, Pierre became directly involved in managing a large inheritance. For her part, Grace divided the long remainder of her life among travel, charitable work, and the Roman Catholic Church, and she paid little attention to the management of the funds. In 1939 she even managed to lose some of the many stock certificates the family possessed.[43] She loved music and played the piano very well, to the envy of Pierre, who did so in an amateur way. She seldom missed a classical concert and even brought some of the leading artists of the day to her home, to perform for friends and family. At one time she persuaded the great Artur Rubinstein to come to McCulloch and perform.[44] Some thought the Trudeau home darkened after Charles died; it did, her children sometimes joked, because Grace was on the road so much. She travelled frequently to New York, Florida, Europe, and her beloved Maine, occasionally with the children but, increasingly, with female friends. Suzette, an amiable and uncomplicated daughter, became a consolation and companion to her, but she doted on Pierre.

—

When Charles died, Pierre was a day student at the Collège Jean-de-Brébeuf on St. Catherine Street in Montreal. His parents had initially sent him when he was six years old to Académie Querbes, a Catholic school for both English and French Catholics, and he stayed there until 1932. He first enrolled in the English section "for reasons I do not know," he claimed in his memoir. He had forgotten: his father had once written that, in the world in which "they" lived, the advantages came to those who learned English.[45] And so his children did.

Querbes, which boasted both a bowling alley and a swimming pool, was located at 215 Bloomfield Street in Outremont, and Pierre had only seven classmates in his first year. His report gave him perfect marks for conduct, application, politeness, and cleanliness. He stood first in the class nearly every month except for March, when he was sick. The size of the class grew to sixteen by third year, when he stood second. The following year he began in English, but then changed to French. He stood first in his last month in English, and he retained that place in his first month in French. He again graduated at the top, overall, with a percentage of 92.5 in June 1930. Grace had signed the reports when the courses were in English; Charles signed most of them when Pierre switched to French.

In school, Pierre became immersed in the Catholic faith and in the debate about moral sin, while on the streets, he fought as boys seemed to do in those days. Michel Chartrand, a fellow Querbes student and future labour activist, recalled that Pierre got into brawls on the streets of Outremont, where the poorer kids liked to take on the precious sons of the well-to-do.[46] In his final year, when he stood first in a class of twenty-six students with a percentage of 95.4, his best classes were mathematics and religion—and that pattern continued throughout his academic career.[47] Several of his essays are preserved in his papers. They reflect both his mind and the times in which he lived. He received "Beau travail" for an essay on the fabled French soldier Dollard des Ormeaux, who, in 1660, held off the Iroquois on the Ottawa River. Pierre concluded that Dollard and his companions were martyrs and saints without whose sacrifices "the colony would have been completely destroyed" by the barbarians. In an essay on guns, he told how he had asked "Papa" if he could go hunting with him. His father replied, "No, Pierre, you are only eleven years old and not old enough." When Pierre persisted, Charles gave examples of how accidents happen with firearms, and Pierre finally agreed with him. In an essay on the polite child, Pierre emphasized kindness to others, including the servants. In church, no one should speak or shuffle about but simply pray. The overall lesson he derived from the exercise was that a polite child becomes popular in society.[48] For this essay, he received his highest mark: 9.5 out of 10.

From Querbes, Pierre moved to the new classical college, Collège Jean-de-Brébeuf, which was within walking distance of his home in Outremont. It had been established in 1928 as one of the five Jesuit colleges explicitly devoted to the education of a French elite in Quebec. Discipline was quick, short, and brutal. The priests frequently expelled troublesome students, and the strap and other forms of discipline were always available. Pierre soon established himself as an outstanding student, but he developed a sharp edge during his eight-year stay there. He brought friends with him from Querbes and the streets of Outremont, notably Pierre Vadeboncoeur, who would follow him through Brébeuf, law school, and political activities for three decades. Brébeuf was a decisive experience in Trudeau's life, endowing him with a remarkable self-discipline, a profound interest in ideas and politics, and a cadre of friends and acquaintances who would play major roles in his life and career. He later claimed that he had little interest in politics while he was at Brébeuf, but, again, his memory failed him.[49]

Trudeau's account of his involvement in contemporary politics during his Brébeuf years is contradictory. He also said on occasion that Father Robert Bernier, who was "the most culti-vated man I had met . . . talked politics to me."[50] His notebooks of the time are full of "politics," both in the sense of political theory, beginning with the classical tradition, and in the narrower sense of the political events of the 1930s. He entered Brébeuf at the height of the Great Depression, "la Grande Crise" in Quebec, just before Roosevelt's presidency and Hitler's chancel-lorship. Students disappeared from his class as their parents fell into abject poverty, and the Catholic Church in Quebec and elsewhere was in turmoil as it tried to understand what the collapse of democracy in Europe, and capitalism everywhere, meant for the faithful. In Quebec a critique of Canadian capitalism and democracy emerged most strongly in the writings of Abbé Lionel Groulx. In 1919, the year of Pierre's birth, Groulx had given a historic lecture, "If Dollard Were Alive Today." His argument already had a deep impact on the young Pierre when he wrote his essay on Dollard at Querbes. The Abbé held the first chair in Canadian history at the Montreal branch of Laval University and went on to edit the highly influential journal *L'Action française*. In short order it became the catalyst for a new nationalism that linked the Catholic faith, the French language, and the family, while calling for autonomous institutions that would protect these key elements from Anglicization, Americanization, secularization, and a corrupt political class.[51]

The Abbé responded to the conscription crisis and the First World War by turning to the past: the Conquest of New France in 1760 became a decisive event, God's test of Quebec's defeated people; the pact of Confederation, a broken promise. Dollard's first battles with the Iroquois, or, for that matter, Étienne Truteau's, led to the origins of the parish, where the germ of the nation appeared and where common institutions and memories formed. In his eyes, during the Conquest, the Rebellions of the French against the English in 1837–38, the betrayals of Confederation, and the conscription crisis of 1917, a Quebec nation was forged in a fire of constant struggle and within the enduring bond of Catholicism. According to Groulx, the nation had become a reality through this continual battle with "the others."[52] The aggressiveness of English Canada during wartime; the continuing flow of rural francophones to Montreal, where the symbols of power were English; the drop in the birthrate of francophones in the city and of the French population in Canada (31% in 1867, but only 27% in 1921); and the economic inferiority of the francophone professional class created "the call of the race," or *L'appel de la race*, the title of Groulx's bestselling novel of 1922, about the difficulties of a mixed marriage between a French Catholic lawyer and a converted Protestant English mother. The jacket of the first edition carried a quotation: "All of the descendants of the valiant 65,000 who were conquered must act as one."[53] It was a powerful nationalist argument, one that roiled Quebec society in the interwar years.

In the 1930s, with bourgeois liberal democracy in danger and Communism, socialism, and fascism contesting for dominance in Europe, the winds that blew strongly from Europe reached Quebec. For Quebec Catholics, Communism was simply evil, and liberalism was tainted with its anti-clerical past and enervated present. Within the Quebec church, an angry debate developed between those who believed that the first task was to "rechristianize" the population and others who, with Groulx, thought that "national action" must coincide with "Catholic action" and with what he termed the refrancization of Quebec. On his return from France in 1937, André Laurendeau, later the co-chair of the Royal Commission on Bilingualism and Biculturalism, attacked the supporters of bilingualism in Quebec. An admirer of Abbé Groulx, he warned: "When all French Canadians have become bilingual, they will all speak English . . . and French itself will soon be useless."[54] The debate raged within the numerous Catholic youth groups that proliferated in Quebec in the 1930s, especially in response to a report on the subject by the Dominican priest Georges-Henri Lévesque which said the first concern must be the individual in society, not the national question.[55] When these debates left the classrooms and church buildings and arrived on the streets, they sometimes took a vulgar form in the creation of a Quebec fascist movement, the National Socialist Christian Party (Parti national social chrétien), whose emblem was a swastika surrounded by maple leaves, with a curious beaver as its crown. Its leader, Adrien Arcand, was a vicious anti-Semite who condoned attacks on Jewish businesses in Montreal and urged the deportation of Jews to Hudson Bay.

The times were clearly important in the formation of Pierre Trudeau, with the breakdown of the European order, the emergence of new nationalist movements in Quebec (especially the Action libérale nationale, or ALN), and the continuing economic crisis. Although there is no direct evidence that Charles Trudeau had urged political beliefs on his son, his own nationalism, as reflected in his association with Le Devoir and his friendship with men such as Camillien Houde, surely left its mark. And Pierre, until he turned twenty-one in 1940, was sheltered within the cocoon of Brébeuf, where the atmosphere was decidedly nationalist. In his first years there, Pierre concentrated on his studies and on sports. He usually began in the morning with prayers at 5:30, followed by early morning Mass. He did not shirk his religious duties, sometimes participating in Mass three times in one day. He attended retreats frequently, although at times he complained about the number of religious observances offered there.

About sports, he never complained. He became the captain of the hockey team, played lacrosse, and went on ski excursions.* And he exercised. In photographs, he is always lean and his body is hard, not in the fashion of modern weightlifters but similar to Clark Gable and other film stars of the time. His love

---

* Trudeau also liked to go to Montreal Royals' baseball games, and he tracked the scores. He won some popularity among the priests at Brébeuf by using the family interest in the Royals to get opening-day tickets. He was rewarded with a day off school when he accompanied Father Toupin to the game. Personal Journal, 1937–40, TP, vol. 39, file 9.

of competition was reflected in his academic work: he carefully followed his own marks along with those of his fellow students. He had to be first—in 1935, despite his father's death, he won numerous prizes and excelled. He also developed the reputation of being devilish in class: during a presentation on navigation, for example, he took a glass of water out of his inside coat pocket. He later interpreted these tricks as "opposing conventional wisdoms and challenging prevailing opinions," but they apparently did not greatly offend his teachers—or his mother, whom he regaled with some of the stories. And, it seems, they did not irritate fellow students as much as some of them later recalled. He was elected to several positions, including vice-president of the student assembly, and chosen to be editor of the student newspaper.[56] He was disappointed that he was not elected president but counted himself lucky, considering he had no particular group of friends, to finish second in the vote out of a class of fifty.[57]

Pierre's pranks and mocking comments were forgiven by his teachers because he became increasingly committed to the school, to the Catholic faith, and to understanding the "national question." The commitment intensified after the death of his father. Trudeau's son Alexandre (Sacha) believes that one major consequence of Charles-Émile's death on Trudeau was a distrust of business and commercial life and a suspicion of law. He came to identify business with late nights, heavy drinking, smoking, and boozy argument. In Alexandre's words, Pierre thought business killed his father. He never smoked, drank to excess, swore vigorously, or argued long into the night, even though he adored his father, who did.[58]

Oddly, although several Brébeuf priests influenced Pierre, notably Father Robert Bernier, the one who would have the strongest impact never taught him. Father Rodolphe Dubé, a Jesuit priest and novelist, wrote under the pen name François Hertel—the actual name of a ferocious and brutal opponent of the English and the Aboriginal enemies of New France. Trudeau's papers suggest that Hertel was probably the major intellectual influence in his life until the mid-1940s—explaining, perhaps, the lavish but oblique praise for him in his memoirs. However, the priest was a remarkably charismatic leader of the young, and his views on politics and the arts deeply influenced Catholic youth in the late thirties and early forties. He first attracted attention when he wrote a study in 1936 entitled *Leur inquiétude,* in which he talked about the restlessness of youth in Quebec, with their "desire to evade reality, their dissatisfaction with the present, their dolorous focus on the past, and their anxious view of the future."[59] Later scholars have reinforced Hertel's views and have argued that the anxiety that marked students in the classical colleges in the thirties—in the form of pranks, demonstrations, and misbehaviour—was a response to the colleges' emphasis on chastity, asceticism, and submission. In these male institutions, such teachings represented a threat to the sexual identity of the students at a time when modern attitudes provided so many distractions and temptations.[60]

Pierre was never dolorous, like the students Hertel describes, but he was increasingly restless. In February 1935 the fifteen-year-old wrote a spirited but juvenile essay for his English class, "My Interview with King George of England," in which he went to visit the monarch because there was so much disorder in his class at school. Arriving at the court, he was escorted in:

> Then amidst the sounds of trumpets and cries of "The King! The King!" a dignified old gentleman entered, escorted by many brilliantly colored soldiers.
>
> "How do you do Sir?" I said.
>
> "Fine, thank you, except for a little trouble with my teeth," he answered. "I am pleased to meet you."

"The pleasure is all mine," said I, "but come let us get down to business, and I would like to see you alone."

"Very well, you may leave, Captain," and after a brief argument in which the King proved he could take care of himself, the captain left. [An increasingly angry teacher writes, "Nonsense."]

Seeing the gentleman was beginning to sweat under his uniform, I bade him take off his coat; having done so I began. [Teacher: "Nonsense."]

Pierre went on to say that Governor General Lord Bessborough had urged him to see the King because the teacher was "English." He described the total disorder in his classroom at home:

"They are even setting off matches, no doubt to burn the college, and also stink bombs, the odors of which are very disagreeable. Now our professor, M. Gosling, being from England, I thought you might have some sympathy for him (for he finds it trying on his nerves)."

King George replied that he was very sad, for he "thought that all the boys in the British Empire on which the sun never sets were perfect gentlemen. It must be looked after at once." He promised to come down to speak to the class at Brébeuf. Then Pierre concluded:

"Thanks very much, George, I knew you would do it. Well, so long, I will be seeing you."

"Good-bye, Pierre."

"Good-bye. I think I shall go to Rome now and see if I can convince Pope Pius to come up and see us over in Canada too."

The teacher wrote: "As a writer of nonsense you may achieve fame but try to become a little more serious and do not use slang." A gentle caution, but more criticism would follow.[61]

As Pierre Trudeau became increasingly nationalist in his views, along with his classmates and teachers, his growing enthusiasm was reflected both in his academic work and in the books he read. He focused in particular on Abbé Groulx, apparently finding some of his interpretations congenial. On a copy of an article the Abbé published in L'Action nationale, he underlined a passage stating that some men dream for Canada of "total independence; for their province [Quebec] total autonomy; and for their nationality, a noble future." He also read one of Groulx's pamphlets and declared it "very interesting," adding, "It is necessary to make total preparations," although it is unclear what those preparations might have been.[62]

At the same time that he became more interested in national questions, his conservative Catholicism also deepened. The two commitments became inextricably intertwined for him, as they did for many other students too. While he had earlier complained to his parents about the frequency of religious observances, he now began to seek out retreats and discussions about the faith. Still, probably because of his independent spirit and Brébeuf's elitist ways, he did not become involved in the Jeunesse étudiante catholique, the best-known Catholic youth group of the day. When he edited the school newspaper, Brébeuf, he took strong issue with a request that all student newspapers take a common view. Rather, he read widely in Catholic literature and became especially interested in the Catholic revival in France in the twenties. In the fashion of the times, he vigorously condemned Communists: for example, he denounced André Gide as a Communist who, from a moral point of view, was "one of the most pernicious authors who ever existed." It was "a matter of life," of how Catholic faith penetrated all thought.[63]

In his notebooks, the adolescent Pierre reflected his times and his environment as he groped to understand a complex world. He blamed the Treaty of Versailles and, bizarrely, the British insistence on Germany giving up its colonies for the troubles of the 1930s. And his father's views found a place with his son. He expressed a traditional view of the difference between men and women: "God made the sexes, that of woman for the work in the house and that of man for the things outside." Men's robust bodies suited them for war and voyages, but women's weaker physique meant that "God has destined them to work at home and bear children."[64] In an October 1937 story he described a soapbox orator who talked about the conscription of twenty years before and warned that another war would mean automatic conscription.[65] In a Brébeuf debate he argued against intervention in the Sino-Japanese conflict because "China is infested with strangers, so Japan has a noble aim wanting the yellow race to survive." He also blamed the "Reds" for causing troubles in China.[66]

He wrote a short story in Father Robert Bernier's class in 1936 in which he deplored the isolation of the college and dreamed of what he might do as a sailor on some future adventure. In his fantasy, he travelled the world, joined the air force, engaged in "numerous dangerous exploits, blew up some enemy factories," and won the war. He then returned to Montreal "about 1976, when the time was ripe to declare Quebec independence." The Maritimes and Manitoba joined with Quebec to confront the enemies, and "at the head of the troops, I lead the army to victory" over the English Protestant infidels. "I live now," he fantasized, "in a Catholic and Canadian country."[67] He was the modern Dollard of the fabled "Laurentie" of Groulx and other nationalists of the day.

Like many of Pierre's intellectual meanderings at this time, this fantasy—that he would lead an army that won independence for Quebec in the same year that the Parti Québécois actually came to power—is simply juvenile trivia. In some essays, he favoured anti-Semitic, elitist, and conservative Catholic writers. In others, he merely took positions in a school where debate was strongly encouraged. He even praised the misogynist and elitist *L'homme, cet inconnu* by Alexis Carrel, as well as other works of a similar conservative Catholic character.[68] And, in a speech he gave on the survival of French Canadians in November 1937, he took his approach directly from nationalists like Groulx. "To save our French civilization," he said, "we must keep our language and flee American civilization." The "revenge of the cradle," he predicted, whereby French Catholics had large familes while English Protestants had few children, would soon allow the French population to exceed the English. He attacked immigration, because it tended to increase the English population, but rejoiced that the government had cut off most immigrants during the Great Depression. French Canada, he said, had a precise and even divine role—to propagate "French and Catholic ideas in the New World."

Yet the young Trudeau was also inconsistent at this time. In his 1936–37 notes, he made favourable references to Jacques Maritain, an eminent Catholic philosopher who opposed fascism and supported liberal democracy. He paraphrased his idea that "if the author is good, he will spontaneously criticize vice and approve good," and he strongly agreed with this liberal sentiment. He also proudly reported to his mother that he joined with other students in honouring not only the nationalist hero Dollard but also May 24, "la fête de la reine," the Queen's birthday, which was "another excellent occasion to display patriotism."[69] Contradictions abound.

Trudeau attended a "semaine sociale" at Brébeuf from November 28 to December 4, 1937, where they discussed a variety of social questions. The diet was strongly nationalist and

conservative, and he learned about the "error of economic liberalism," "the necessity of corporatism," and "the illusion of communism and socialism."* To his nationalist teachers and friends
there, he could deny strongly that he was "Americanized." Yet in
1937 he tried to establish a liaison between the student newspaper *Brébeuf* and its counterpart at the New York Catholic
Fordham College. He told the U.S. editors that "you will come
more directly in contact with the French and French Canadians,
and the object of Mr. Roosevelt in establishing relations of goodwill and friendship between the American people will be greatly
helped."[70] And, on the language question generally, unlike André
Laurendeau, Trudeau rejected the popular nationalist cause of
unilingualism, following, instead, his father's view that "because of
the advantages which knowledge of the English language presents,
the majority of 'Canadiens' are compelled to learn English. Far
from blaming them, I find them to be perfectly reasonable"—
except when they introduced anglicisms into French.[71]

Pierre could never identify with the element of extreme
nationalism that attacked the brothels and nightclubs of Montreal
and detested American music and movies. He continued to visit

---

* While the fare was highly nationalist and, in economics, corporatist in the
fashion of Catholic economic thought at the time, there was some diversity
and balance. André Laurendeau, for example, condemned Communism
strongly, but said that all collective property—"propriété collective"—was not
bad, giving the examples of electricity and railways. Father Omer Jenest, SJ,
said that the church's support for corporatism distinguished it from fascism. He
argued that the imposition by force of corporatism in Italy must be condemned.
Gérard Filion, the future editor of *Le Devoir*, spoke on cooperatives and said
they were most advanced in the Nordic countries. He added that Italy, because
of fascism, was better off than France. Trudeau's notes are in TP, vol. 4, file 6.

New York, go to the theatre, and adore the Marx Brothers and the sirens of Hollywood. He made a pledge to himself in 1937: "I don't want to go out with girls before I am twenty years old because they would distract me," especially frivolous American girls.[72] But that summer at Old Orchard he met an American student, Camille Corriveau, "whose beauty I had admired for 4 years."[73] She finally spoke to him on August 18, his resolve melted, and within a week he fell in love. In October she told him he should choose any profession except the priesthood. "Even the life of a policeman would be more exciting," she thought. Then he returned to Brébeuf.

It was a different world. Father Brossard taught him Canadian history. He was, said Pierre, a patriot but not a fanatic. On October 20 the young Trudeau shaved for the first time. The next day he stood for the "autonomists" in the student parliament and heard Henri Bourassa, the nationalist founder of Le Devoir, speak in the evening. On October 22 he and other students demonstrated against "Communists." Then he joined the family at Christmas, went skiing for a week before New Year's, and refused an invitation from his sister, Suzette, to attend a New Year's Eve dance with her and her friends. The profferred date, "Olga Zabler," was very pretty, but he was still shy. "I am always timid around women," he mused, though that reserve frequently made him exaggerate his self-assurance in their presence. In short, he was awkward. Reflecting his frustrations, he made a New Year's resolution to "cultivate the strongest possible sense of honour" and to avoid any act that would cause him embarrassment. Without doubt, the "exalted patriots," as Pierre called the fervent nationalists, would not have thought much of his ideas and activities during this holiday season.

Tip tagged along with his brother on a trip to New York on January 2, 1938. They went immediately to a Broadway musical, the next day to see the American Jewish comedian Ed Wynn, the following day to Rockefeller Center—"c'est colossal!" Pierre wrote—and, in the evening, to the fabled Cotton Club. There, "the orchestra and the comedians were good," but there was a touch of Brébeuf in his comment that "the review was rather immoral and vulgar." Far more satisfying was Radio City Music Hall, where he saw the Rockettes kick their legs high. They were "very good," and the theatre itself "a marvel." When he got home, he continued to go to movies and to write to Camille, all the while trying to resist his strong urges to approach attractive young women.[74]

When Pierre returned to Montreal on January 8, Brébeuf enclosed him within its capacious bosom. He was ambitious academically and athletically, although he remarked that a pretty girl could capture his attention "despite my coldness and independence."[75] His ambitions included standing for the school elections and participating in a drama contest. He worried about his popularity because of his shyness and his tendency to be "contrary." At times he was troubled. He wrote to his mother: "Temperature uncertain, like adolescence." And, in his notebooks, there is a draft of what is perhaps a poem: "My adolescent heart is like nature / Everything is upset. The temperature of sadness."[76]

Father Bernier had reassured him in the fall of 1937 that he had "a Canadien mentality mixed with English," a combination, in Pierre's own view, that was "not bad for broadening one's outlook." Brébeuf was French, however, and he resolved to improve his French diction, to read more widely, and to attend Mass often. Still, he had pride in his bicultural background, even if many critics of the time deplored the mixing of French and English. He determined that he would continue to sign "Elliott" as part of his name: it was an indication of "good stock and distinction."[77]

Then came a brutal blow to this bicultural calm. Just after the early February 1938 elections for the Academic Council, where his great rival Jean de Grandpré narrowly beat him for the presidency, "Laurin" told Pierre that a fellow student had declared he had no confidence in him—"that I was mediocre, Americanized, and Anglicized, in short, I would betray my race. I made it seem that I wasn't bothered, but it was a profound shock." "Perhaps I seem superficial about certain things," Pierre wrote in his journal. "But the truth is that I work. And I would never betray the French Canadians." If he was accused directly, he would punch the accuser in his face. Then he paused: "However, I am proud of my English blood, which comes from my mother. At least it tempers my boiling French blood. It leaves me calmer and more insightful and perspicacious." The incident made him more determined than ever to finish first at Brébeuf, the educational jewel of French education in Montreal.[78]

Four days later, on February 9, the results of yet another election were announced, this time for the Conventum—the class council. Pierre had initially not wanted to run but did so when he discovered that his father had been on the secretariat of the Conventum at his school. He again ran behind Jean de Grandpré, but he won the run-off election and became vice-president. "Oh, inexpressible happiness!" he exclaimed in his diary. He added that he was very pleased that his bilingual name, Pierre Elliott Trudeau, had not hurt him much in the election. In March the issue still bothered him. In English class he pretended to be Irish and, "for a joke," dared other students to take him on. No battle followed, although Father Landry threatened him with expulsion. However, he wrote in his diary after the class that he was content to have his English blood mixed with his French blood. The blend, he concluded, made him less fearful of going against "the popular spirit."

Some have claimed that Trudeau was the model for François Hertel's 1939 novel, *Le beau risque*—a story about "Pierre Martel," a young student at a classical college who loses his restlessness as his "soul" becomes thoroughly French. The novel takes the form of a memoir by a priest-professor who is going to Asia. He says that Pierre lacks confidence, despite his intelligence and a successful surgeon father he admires. The narrator, Father Berthier, soon discovers that the father is empty and lacks depth, concerned as he is only with appearance. Like Pierre Trudeau, Pierre Martel has acne, lives in a large house in Outremont, has a wealthy father, takes trips to New York, gratuitously irritates his teachers, prefers individual sports to team sports, loves poetry, and, most tellingly perhaps, spends his summers at Old Orchard Beach. The novel traces how Pierre turns away from the materialist and Americanized world of his father and finds strength in Boucherville, in the traditional world of his grandparents. He confronts his father for his scepticism, his Anglicisms, and his materialism, while, at the same time, he comes to admire his grandfather's respect for the past and, in particular, the way he has retained the spirit of the 1837 Rebellions. Pierre senses the call of the blood and angrily refuses to go to Old Orchard or to visit a Quebec "inn," which, he tells his father, must be called an "auberge." He takes up the continuing struggles of his people, becomes devoted to a renewed Catholicism, and expresses commitment to a world where "we will be more ourselves."[79] Trudeau read the book when it appeared, as did many young Quebecers, but his short review in his journal does not indicate that he identified himself with Martel. Nevertheless, the evidence suggests that Pierre Trudeau, like Martel, was a divided soul in those troubled times.

In the spring of 1938, while Pierre contemplated the comments about his "Americanization and Anglicization," he wrote a play entitled *Dupés*, about a Montreal tailor. In itself a disappointing, slight confection, it won a competition at Brébeuf and was performed there, with Pierre as one of the actors. Jean de Grandpré, Trudeau's greatest academic rival and a future prominent business executive, played the lead. At the time it was written, nationalists in Quebec were urging a "Buy from our own" campaign, which the Jewish community in Montreal condemned as anti-Semitic. Trudeau's "comedy of manners" is laced with sarcasm and some bitterness. The main character is a tailor, Jean-Baptiste Couture, who, in the first draft, is described as a good father of a French-Canadian family, honest but sometimes violent. Another character, Jean Ditreau, is interested in Couture's daughter, Camille, a name Trudeau devilishly chose in honour of his American girlfriend. Others in the play include a few customers, notably the dubious Paul Shick.

Ditreau has a diploma in "commercial psychology" from McKill University, and he offers to help Couture assess his clients. "Your business," he explains, is in a French-Canadian area, but francophones "prefer to buy from Jews, firstly because they don't want to enrich one of their own and then because they believe they will get a better price." His solution: Put up the sign "Goldenburg, tailor" in place of "Chez Couture." He also advises Couture to sell "American magazines" and to install a "soda-fountain"; people will then come after Mass to drink "Coke." While he is speaking, Ditreau tears down a sign that reads "Help our own" and replaces it with a new English sign that says: "We sell for less—Goldenburg, fine goods. Open for business."

Once all the signs have been changed, Couture tells his first customer, in the "manner of a Jew," that he has the latest fashions from Paris, New York, and London and then whispers, "in spite of our repugnance [for Hitler] we even follow the fashions of Berlin."[80] The deals continue—and the confusion mounts. Ditreau is finally rejected as a suitor by Camille because he is a politician, the lowest of all professions. The evil ways of politicians are also demonstrated by another customer, Maurice Lesoufflé, clearly modelled on Quebec premier Maurice Duplessis, who proposes having six "heroic" Canadians split the vote so a "Hebrew" candidate can win an election.

Dupés was a great triumph for Pierre Trudeau at Brébeuf, and the priests, parents, and students who attended the performance vigorously applauded its young author—youthful but complicated. It reflected not only the mood of Outremont but also a time when the Canadian prime minister could compare Hitler to Joan of Arc; when his major adviser, O.D. Skelton, an eminent liberal, could fret about the "Jewish" influence that was pushing Britain towards war; and when Vincent Massey, the high commissioner to Britain and future governor general, could declare that Canada needed no Jewish immigrants.

Like most students, Pierre Trudeau responded to what his teachers, his peers, and his family wanted of him—most of the time. But certain unresolved contradictions appear in his personal journal, where his private activities and views are expressed. On the surface, he seemed to conform to the nationalist, anti-Semitic, and anti-English environment of the time. Yet, just a few days before *Dupés* was performed, after careful supervision by the Brébeuf staff, Trudeau had his "encounter" with Laurin about his mixed blood and his American and English ways. Without doubt, this incident made the final text of *Dupés* more reflective of the general mood at Brébeuf. Pierre had written to his mother on January 24, 1938: "One of the qualities of the letter is tact. That is to say that when one writes, one should take account of the circumstances and adapt the letter to the one who will read it."[81] It was meant to apply to a specific letter, but the comment describes well how Trudeau believed he must adapt to particular circumstances. Yet, as he told his mother, he found it a "complex" task. He conformed, yes, but in his heart he often rebelled, and in his acts he sometimes contradicted.[82]

Three days before Pierre wrote *Dupés*, he made some notes about the "pros and cons" of the religious life. Here doubt and belief abound. The pro side emphasized how the priest-hood would always lead him towards perfection and closer to Christ. It would grant him a better place in heaven and, more generally, make him a better man. But the cons won. He was not much attracted to the vocation. He was not humble enough; he was too proud and too independent. He liked an active life, and he would not be good at confessions because he lacked the necessary spirit. Moreover, he would not be a good teacher: "I'm not open enough," he concluded. It was a shrewd assessment.[83] Pierre Trudeau was a good Catholic, but he would have made a poor priest.

—

CHAPTER 2

LA GUERRE, NO SIR!

I n the late spring of 1938, after the success of *Dupés* with the students and their parents at Brébeuf and his decision not to enter the priesthood, Pierre Trudeau began to wonder, as older adolescents often do, what his fate might be. He disliked business, and his father's career and death had left him ambivalent towards law. He wrote in his diary as the school year came to an end in June 1938: "I wonder whether I will be able to do something for my God and my country. I would like so much to be a great politician and to guide my nation."[1] This dream never died, though his conception of both his nation and its politics certainly changed.

When Pierre began the quest for his destiny at Brébeuf in the 1930s, the stream of world events quickly turned into rapids. The Great Depression altered its direction, Hitler's Germany disrupted its flow, and the confluence of war in China and in Spain created a torrent that crested in September 1939 when the world burst apart once more. Like others, Canadians became immersed in the flood of current events. Some were swept away by the martial spirit. Farley Mowat, the son of a soldier who gloried in memories of the First World War, saw his gleeful father come down the country lane bearing news of war, and the dutiful son set out to fight through six cruel years of war.[2] In the poor parts of Montreal, recruiting centres were clogged as the unemployed and the young with few prospects (including the future hockey star Maurice Richard) viewed the dangers of war as more alluring than the pain of their present plight. Among Pierre's classmates at Brébeuf, however, few answered the call, and most of this young elite probably opposed the war as a British imperial conflict that would spill Canadian blood and bitterly divide the country. Charles Trudeau's close friend Mayor Camillien Houde did not hide his agreement with that view.

Pierre was nineteen years old when the Germans stormed across the German-Polish border that September. His own attitude towards the war was not predictable, and he understood its bloodiness. In the debate at school on the Sino-Japanese conflict in which he took the Japanese side, he admitted they were ruthless: "But in war can such things be avoided?" he asked. "Did not Germany use gas in 1914 and bomb the Red Cross of the Allies? Did not Italy use very crude means in Ethiopia, did not China massacre Europeans in the Boxer rebellion, did not Franco render thousands of Spanish children orphans, did not France execute unscrupulously certain of her enemies in the last war, did not Great Britain herself use the inhuman explosive bullets against the Boer?"[3] Trudeau obviously knew much about war, but he displayed none of the generous views towards Mussolini's Italy and Franco's Spain that were common among the clergy and the commentators in Quebec at the time.

Camille Corriveau, his American girlfriend, wrote to him at the outbreak of war, begging him not to enlist. He did not answer directly but described the immediate signs of war in Montreal: "Soldiers guard the Jacques Cartier bridge; airplanes often survey the city. The regiments hunt for recruits. Parliament is now sitting to decide if there will be conscription.

There are some anti-conscription gatherings across the city. One hears some threats." He admitted he had not read any newspapers and was not well informed, but he confided that he personally believed Hitler was near the end.[4] Many who had read the newspapers shared this view when Hitler's war machine halted during the "phony war" of that first winter. But they were wrong.

Pierre could have enlisted, but he did not. There was no military tradition in his family, despite Étienne Truteau's celebrated seventeenth-century triumph over the Iroquois, and he later recalled that only one of his cousins enlisted.[5] In general, francophones were poorly represented within the Canadian military. French was spoken only in the famed Royal 22e Régiment, and military administration in Quebec was conducted in English despite the controversies of the First World War. Among the higher ranks, francophones were scarce, and not one of the brigade commanders of the First Canadian Division was francophone.[6] In Pierre's last year at Brébeuf, 1939–40, he concentrated on his studies for his bachelor's degree, on editing the school newspaper, and on his future plans. Meanwhile, he carefully guarded his opinions about the war.

"I'm not open enough," he had decided when pondering a religious life in his future. Certainly, Pierre had become less open as his teenage years progressed and as his own sense of identity reacted to his understanding of external events. He told his mother in the fall of 1935 that the priests at Brébeuf might be worried about the election results, but he expanded no further and passed quickly on to another subject.[7] He also grumbled that there were three Masses each day and no fewer than fifty-six religious exercises of various kinds in the Brébeuf regimen. But despite his complaints, his Catholic piety was increasingly and devoutly expressed: with exhilaration he told her how the lights were turned out at a retreat so they could

better see the magnificent cross that loomed above them on
Mount Royal. At another retreat house, in modest rooms near
a quiet river, he told her he enjoyed the sermons but valued
most the silence during meals—and, after the experience of
those few days, he began his lifelong practice of meditation.

Pierre wrote this letter to his mother on November 26, one
day after Quebec politics changed completely with the near
defeat of the corrupt and capitalist Liberal government of Louis-
Alexandre Taschereau; six weeks after the victory of Mackenzie
King's Liberals in Ottawa; three months after Mussolini's dive
bombers, in attacking Abyssinia, demolished the fragile hopes of
collective security through the League of Nations; and nine
months after Germany denounced the disarmament clauses of
the Treaty of Versailles and introduced conscription. It was also
only eight months after the death of Charles Trudeau. Quebec
turned inward as it confronted the new realities; so, for a while,
did Pierre.[8]

Although he turned inward, Pierre, contrary to his frequent later statements, remained deeply immersed in politics
in two important ways: in the sense, set out by Aristotle, that
the end of the science of politics must be human good; and in
the specific Quebec context where the rights of francophone
and Catholic citizens must be upheld. The cross on Mount
Royal, after all, symbolically linked Roman Catholicism with
the national mission of the descendants of New France in
North America. Pierre's Jesuit education mediated his understanding of contemporary politics in the 1930s, and his youthful play *Dupés* illustrates how closely he followed political
events despite his later claims of ignorance. His views, as
expressed publicly, were conventionally nationalist—what one
would expect of an adolescent Brébeuf student in 1938. He
supported the "Buy from our own" movement that arose as
Jewish shopkeepers proliferated in the francophone districts of

Montreal. He deplored the tendency to create constituency
boundaries so that Jews could have electoral representation,
although he wrongly blamed Maurice Duplessis rather than
the federal Liberals for that chicanery. In common with most
Quebec nationalists of the time, he portrayed active politicians
as corrupt and craven, a view that he expressed bluntly in a
Brébeuf essay that year where he said that anyone who entered
politics risked acquiring "the reputation of an imbecile." Yet he
and many others dreamed of a new kind of politics, not so corrupt, and he fancied a future political career for himself.[9]

Much later, in minimizing his nationalist views, Trudeau
recalled that he had joined students at a demonstration against
the French writer André Malraux, who was touring Canada to
advocate the Republican cause in the Spanish Civil War.[10]
Similarly, his views on international affairs, as expressed in his
schoolbooks—which the priests read—followed the line taken
by Quebec Catholic nationalists. For an English rhetoric class,
he wrote in October 1937: "Do we want to go to war? We do not.
Ask those who have been if they enjoyed the horrors, if they
enjoyed the terrors, the misery and the uncertainty of war."[11]
The memories of the last war and the bitter divisions it caused
were still strong in the province.

The anti-Semitism of *Dupés* was as conventional in its
time as it seems deplorable today. It lacks the ferocity of
Quebec fascist leader Adrien Arcand or, for that matter, the
Canadian-born Catholic priest Father Charles Coughlin, who
spread hatred and fear of Jews in Roosevelt's America—a fear
that grew rapidly as he denounced American Jews for drawing
the United States into a European war. It was less extreme than
the exaggerated view of Jewish economic power expressed in
1933 by Les Jeunes-Canada, a Quebec Catholic youth group
that in a famous April rally, "Politicians and Jews," heard
speakers denounce the "Jewish plutocracy" and argue that

Canadian politicians were quicker to condemn discrimination against Jews in distant Germany than against French Canadians in Ontario or the West.[12]

Pierre's anti-war sentiments echoed the strong isolationist sentiment not only in Quebec but also among English-Canadian intellectuals in the 1930s. His rhetoric pales beside that of University of Toronto history professor and war veteran Frank Underhill, who called on the Canadian government to make clear to the world, "and especially to Great Britain, that poppies blooming in Flanders fields have no further interest for us . . . European troubles are not worth the bones of a Toronto grenadier"—or, Pierre would have added, a Brébeuf student.[13] The conventional, history reminds us, is frequently badly wrong. The moral quandaries of the time lay elsewhere, and Pierre's manuscript for *Dupés* was revised several times not for its anti-Semitism but for its suspected sexual nuance.*

After 1935, Pierre began that period of adolescence when, in psychologist Erik Erikson's well-known phrase, individuals ask, "Who am I?" The voices he most often heard after the death of his father were those within Brébeuf—his teachers and

---

* The revisions were made at the insistence of Father Brossard, who was the censor for the occasion. After the play, leading Outremont figures such as "le juge Thouin" and Mesdames de Grandpré and Vaillancourt congratulated Pierre. The play was, Pierre wrote, "a great success," judging by "the congratulations and the laughter." The only objection was to a section of the play where Jean Couture speaks to his daughter, Camille, and uses the word *grosse* to describe her. One of the priests thought it might mean "pregnant" and condemned the "double sense." Pierre wrote in his diary that it was not his intention at all. When the hint of sex brought horror to the hallways of Brébeuf, he noted: "One can't please everyone." Journal 1938, May 17, 1938, TP, vol. 39, file 9.

his classmates. He immersed himself in books, especially in the Catholic religion, French literature, and Catholic philosophy. In a more general sense, he followed the outline, or *ratio*, established by the Jesuit founder Ignatius of Loyola in the sixteenth century. It laid out the first international system of education, one whose method and content were similar in Peru, Poland, or Quebec. For its time, it was utilitarian, a method to provide the human resources for good government and to create a Catholic elite. Its design was "intended to ensure an immersion into classical culture, mastery of material, quickness of mind, sensitivity to individual ability, and personal discipline."[14]

In this sense, Pierre Trudeau was an exceptional student. His discipline, a quality that Jesuit education inculcated, was extraordinary, and it remained so throughout his life. His notebooks are remarkable in their detail and conscientiousness; even when he was writing the compulsory letter to his mother, he made numerous corrections to individual phrases so as to find exactly the right word. He wrote reviews of every book he read while at Brébeuf, and the commentaries were perceptive beyond his adolescent years. He maintained his enthusiasm as he studied the differences between Aristotle and Plato, Rome and Athens, Jerusalem and Rome. He mastered his academic material in every class, whether classical Greek or, in 1939, political economy. His record was outstanding: in competition with an elite student body, he stood first in most of his classes, won more prizes than anyone else (to his delight, they were often in cash), and, in his final year, he bested his strongest competition, Jean de Grandpré, and stood first overall. He was extremely ambitious, a quality Ignatius of Loyola also valued: he carefully recorded de Grandpré's marks and cheered those occasions when his rival finished second.

In the world of the later 1930s, as Pierre contemplated the question of his identity, Brébeuf created the context where he found most of the answers. It differed from some of the other classical colleges, which concentrated on producing priests, and self-consciously viewed itself as the vanguard of intellectual Catholicism in Quebec. It already stood at the apex of a structure of classical colleges that Maurice Duplessis regarded as "our fortresses, indispensable bastions that are essential to preserve our patriotic and religious traditions."[15] As he remarked in one of his school essays, the "fortress" of Brébeuf was a closed world where daily rituals and duties defined his days.[16] Among his teachers, Father Robert Bernier, a Franco-Manitoban, was important in inspiring Pierre's literary interest, and they certainly had great respect for each other. At one Easter retreat, the priest advised him to develop a broader cultural interest, which, he said, most Canadians lacked. Above all, he added, "you must avoid all contact with the vulgar, even if it is under the pretext of a distraction." Pierre apologized for raising the subject but told Bernier he had no intimate friend who could give such advice.[17]

Bernier continued to counsel Pierre so long as he was at Brébeuf, but he was traditional in his views and self-effacing in manner. Gradually, Father Rodolphe Dubé, better known as the author François Hertel, became the greater influence. Hertel, Trudeau wrote later, "naturally gravitated towards everything that was new or contrary to the tastes of the day" and carried his students far beyond the thick stone walls of the fortress and the classroom.[18] In the words of one of Pierre's closest Brébeuf friends, Hertel was "a truly revolutionary force" among the sons of the bourgeoisie who predominated at the college, and he saved them from "the mediocrity and congenital folly of our condition."[19] Hertel's biographer has argued convincingly that the success of this charismatic and humorous priest derived in large part from the solemn atmosphere and rigorous discipline of Brébeuf in those times. A brilliant teacher and a clever comedian, he would begin his classes with a joke that often shocked the students and dramatically pierced the greyness in the classrooms.[20]

Deeply anti-capitalist, profoundly distrustful of the influence of Britain and the United States, but also a critic of racism in Germany and of "British imperialism," François Hertel admired the nationalist interpretation of history put forward by Abbé Groulx. In a 1939 article in *L'Action nationale*, the Abbé, in turn, responded with enthusiasm to Hertel's novel, *Le beau risque*. He said it provided a penetrating exposé of the empty soul of bourgeois French Canadians, who had cut themselves off from their nationalist roots, and he focused on one short passage which noted that the francophone bourgeoisie always raised the "national question" hesitantly with their children. In his view, the new generation had to break away from the compromises of earlier generations if the national question was to be seriously addressed.[21] Then a true democracy could exist, one based on a national faith that resided in the hearts and minds of the people.[22]

Pierre made no mention of this article in his journal, but his school writings contain similar anti-bourgeois and nationalist sentiments. Although there are several references in his papers to works by the Abbé, he seems to have had only one personal encounter with him during his Brébeuf years. On February 18, 1938, he went to a lecture Groulx gave on the intendant Jean Talon, who, in the latter seventeenth century, had tried to consolidate the prosperity of New France, and he reported: "The subject is interesting and was treated well, but the poor Abbé does not have a good voice or oratorical talent." Moreover, whether or not Trudeau was the model for the character Pierre Martel in Hertel's *Le beau risque*, the message of the novel—the dangers of Americanization and Anglicization, the obligations to the past, the limitations of bourgeois capitalism, the importance of national sentiment among youth—resonated loudly for him, despite his later denials in interviews that they did.*

Like Hertel and the other Brébeuf teachers, Pierre Trudeau shared the excitement that came from the reinvigoration of French Catholicism in the twentieth century, especially after the First World War. France, so secular and revolutionary in the nineteenth century, had become the centre of a remarkable revival of Catholic faith in the twentieth century. Leading Catholic thinkers and theologians such as the liberal Jacques Maritain, the "personalist" Emmanuel Mounier, and the conservative, elitist Charles Maurras came to dominate French intellectual life in the interwar years and began a process of seeking to "bare the human condition utterly."[23] Among the subjects they bared was the relationship between the citizen and the state. "Personalism"—a philosophical approach to the Catholic faith that emphasized the individual while linking individual action with broader purposes within society—would have a profound impact on Trudeau and on Quebec intellectual life.

---

* In an interview with Ron Graham in 1992, Trudeau gave this answer to a question about Groulx's influence on him. "I used to get some of his books as prizes at the end of the year when I'd get a first or something like that. He was quite revered as a historian. I don't think any of us at the time understood some of the analysis which has been made later that he was perhaps somewhat inclined to racism or fascism and so on, so I don't remember him as that, but he used to be talked about and he had quite a few disciples and followers, of which I was not one as I say; he wouldn't have liked me for applauding the defeat of the French at the Plains of Abraham." Although Trudeau encountered Groulx only once while he was at Brébeuf, the Abbé's work formed the basis of Canadian history teaching at the college. Interview between Pierre Trudeau and Ron Graham, April 28, 1992, TP, vol. 23, file 3.

Son of a bourgeois father and an English-speaking mother, rich, charmed by the New York theatre, at ease with American wealth, intrigued by American women, and infatuated with the movies, Trudeau's words and convictions as a Brébeuf student seem to belie his own past, present, and future actions and beliefs. And it is precisely these contradictions that shape the emotional and intellectual growth of Pierre Trudeau. He had internalized deeply the death of his father, but the source of his inquietude seems to have been the tension between the Catholic nationalism of Brébeuf and his own personal experience and developing convictions. Brébeuf was immersed in nationalism from the mid-thirties on. The college priests detested the Liberal government of Premier Louis-Alexandre Taschereau, who had compromised with the Americans and the capitalists, and they welcomed the rise of the Action libérale nationale—a rebel group that expressed the nationalism and social action which they and the Catholic youth groups found attractive as a response to the Depression and the discontents of the time. However, after the ALN formed a coalition with the Conservatives to form a new party, the Union nationale, the ALN's leader, Paul Gouin, lost the leadership to Maurice Duplessis, a conservative nationalist tied to rural Quebec. And, in 1936, the Union nationale won the election. In *Dupés*, Pierre had revealed his politics and those of the play's audience when he mocked Duplessis as Maurice Lesoufflé. Nationalism in itself was not enough.

—

In 1938 Pierre Trudeau began a journal, which he continued through his last two years in school. It is detailed, frank, and extraordinarily revealing. It is the only diary in his papers, apart from less personal travel diaries and an agenda for 1937 that contains some commentary, and it expresses his own need to chronicle the moments of late adolescence as he tried to find his identity. It begins on New Year's Day 1938 with the intriguing advice: "If you want to know my thoughts, read between the lines!"

The lines themselves tell a great deal about this tumultuous time in his life. He recounts how he lamented his father's absence on the third anniversary of his death; at other times, he says that things would be different and, presumably, better if his father were still with him. He does not mean that the Trudeaus would be wealthier. Here the pages abound with evidence of the Trudeau family's considerable wealth—a Buick for Suzette, who enjoyed bourgeois pleasures; a grand Packard that bears Pierre, Tip, and some priests to a retreat; the chauffeur, Grenier; the tickets for friends and teachers for Royals' games and the Belmont amusement park; and the good hotels and restaurants the family frequented when they visited New York City. Above all, the entries reveal two aspects of his character: first, his goals, as his ambition for a public life at the highest level becomes a constant refrain; and, second, his extraordinary intellectual curiosity and commitment to hard work. On February 17, 1938, the eighteen-year-old student even thanks God for the good health that allows him to work to midnight almost every night on his studies. Rarely does God receive such thanks from schoolboys.

His mother encouraged but did not direct. Grace Trudeau continued to spend summers at Lac Tremblant and Old Orchard Beach in Maine, while travelling frequently to New York in the fall and spring and to Florida in the winter. Grace, though a strong personality, gave her children surprising freedom. In his journal, it is the "eyes" of Brébeuf that watch the young Trudeau throughout these pages. He complained about this constant attention not only in the diary pages but even in an article he wrote in May 1939 for *Brébeuf*, the student newspaper, where he suggested that the departing class will rejoice at the end of the constant "surveillance" and the need to ask, "Father, may I . . . ?"[24] There were endless permissions, perpetual denials, and eclectic censorship. In March 1938 the censor forbade the presentation of a play after Trudeau and others had rehearsed it many times. And a few of the priests used the threat of expulsion for even trivial misdemeanours. Pierre was always diligent and fundamentally shy, but he sought popularity and gained attention by clever, rebellious distractions that infuriated some of his teachers. After a snowball fight and a couple of other incidents, Father Landry warned him in a menacing fashion that he was a millimetre from being kicked out of the college: the rector would no longer tolerate the "insolence of Pierre Elliott Trudeau," he said, and the next offence would mean a trip to the rector's office. Throughout the reprimand, Pierre smiled, to the certain annoyance of Landry. The next day the clever student found "an excuse" to call upon the rector, and there he discovered that everything was fine so far as the top man was concerned. Pierre already possessed political wiles.

Landry continued to pester him, but Pierre found allies in other teachers, notably Fathers Bernier, Sauvé, d'Anjou, and Toupin. Despite their counsel to avoid jazz, movies, and American popular culture, he travelled to New York in the spring of 1939 in his sister's Buick, which his mother agreed he could drive after an excellent academic year. Suzette had spent four months in France and, very much the young sophisticate, was returning on June 16 on the art deco gem the *Normandie*. Grace and the boys stayed on Central Park South at the elegant Barbizon Plaza, attended the New York World's Fair, and, with a friend of Suzette's, Pierre danced the night away at the Rainbow Grill on the roof of Rockefeller Center. The fair initially disappointed Pierre: "The first good effect is spoiled by all the common people, the crowd, and especially because nearly all the buildings are made of beaver board and the columns are of cardboard. And inside you see only a bunch of merchandise." It was, he concluded in best Brébeuf fashion, too vulgar. He found the Soviet pavilion an impressive exception with its marble, but he deplored the "marvellous Communist propaganda" it represented. He approved of the monumental Italian pavilion, however, though he made no political comments about it or Mussolini. On another evening he was deeply moved when he saw Raymond Massey star in *Abraham Lincoln in Illinois*. The aspiring politician was no doubt assured to discover that young Lincoln had been "troubled, timid, overwhelmed, and a misanthrope."[25]

The world beckoned, yet Brébeuf's pull persisted. There, Pierre increasingly wrestled with questions of faith, nationality, and vocation. Outside the college walls, he enjoyed experiences that his school notebooks often condemn. The tensions between experience and education, belief and practice, nationalism and cosmopolitanism, ambition and timidity created the dynamic that drove his personal growth in these critical years. As the international situation worsened and nationalist currents flowed more strongly, he built up his own internal protections against the pressures that suddenly confronted him. The eminent psychologist Jerome Kagan has explained that adolescents tend to categorize people and endow them with certain characteristics. If an adolescent who believes he belongs to a particular category suddenly behaves in ways that violate those expectations, he experiences considerable uncertainty.[26] Discontinuities compel resolution. In the late 1930s and early 1940s, Pierre Trudeau sensed such discontinuities, and he, too, sought their resolution.

One huge discontinuity occurred when Grace Trudeau registered both her sons at Camp Ahmek, the Taylor Statten summer camp on the shore of Canoe Lake in Algonquin Park, which was a favourite of the Ontario English elite. When he arrived on July 2, 1938, Pierre discovered that he had four English-Canadian roommates. Since he had left Querbes, his companions had been almost exclusively French. Sensing the foreign environment, he promised his diary that he would seize every occasion to declare that he was a "French Canadian and a Catholic." He quickly made his mark, not least in boxing, where his skills and well-developed body resulted in bloody noses for several of the other campers. He also excelled in acting, receiving the highest marks for performances that were, of course, entirely in English. In the sole English entry in his diary that summer he wrote: "It's good to hear 'He is Pierre Trudeau, the best actor in camp!'"[27]

—

The Brébeuf priests would also have been upset to learn that their prize eighteen-year-old student had fallen in love. Camille Corriveau, one year older than Trudeau, was a student at Smith College, and photographs indicate she was very pretty, with a full figure. Certainly Trudeau found her as attractive as Vivien Leigh and Jean Harlow, the actresses he admired in the movies. He was annoyed when the photograph she sent did not catch her stunning beauty. As he opened the envelope, he wrote in reply, the radio began to play the song "You must have been a beautiful baby." He wanted more than this unsatisfactory photo, he complained, "so I keep thinking of the beautiful soft hair that was left out of the picture, the delicate ear [he stroked out 'I am kissing'], a feminine shoulder, a graceful arm, a few charming curves, here and there [stroked out 'a lovely leg'], and so many other things I am missing. Truly, you have been holding out on me, you little iconoclast you!" We cannot be sure Camille received exactly the words in this draft letter, but it does convey the allure she held for him.[28]

A Franco-American, Camille vacationed in Orchard Beach every year with the many other francophones who gathered on the Maine beaches. Although a good dancer, Pierre was still shy with women, and he often turned down invitations thrust at him by his sister. When Suzette was presented as a debutante at Rideau Hall in Ottawa on January 28, 1938, he described himself, as he reflected on the occasion, as a bit of a misogynist. Still, he admitted that, for "esthetic" reasons, he could admire a beautiful woman. That would suffice for now, he concluded. It didn't.[29]

A few days after they met, Camille sent him a warm letter that stirred him despite his "coldness and . . . independence." At least, he opined, Camille was more serious than the majority of women he encountered in Montreal. The memory of her lingered and he was soon looking forward with anticipation to their coming summer meeting. There was a moment of doubt in April when he went to a religious retreat. Father Tobin, the American priest for whom he had procured Montreal Royals tickets, took him aside to talk about universities in the United States. Pierre had been considering American schools for graduate work himself, but Father Tobin was firm in rejecting this option. The universities, he declared, were mostly co-educational and had become veritable dens of immorality. The male-only universities were equally bad because students would sneak women into their rooms. Worst of all were women's colleges such as Vassar and Smith, which were "schools of immorality." Indeed, the mother of a Smith student had confessed to Tobin that contraceptives were to be found everywhere at the school. The reason—the immoral cinema. But even more influential were the professors who openly professed free love.

A shocked Pierre apparently did not argue with Tobin, who was his "guardian angel" for the retreat, but in his diary he wrote: "I am convinced that my Camille is an exception.

However, the atmosphere can have an influence." Fortunately, "she is Catholic," a commitment that was, in his still innocent mind, an impregnable shield against the forces of lust and the availability of condoms.[30]

The conversation lingered in the recesses of Pierre's conscience as the summer of 1938 and Camille's presence approached. Unfortunately, Pierre and Camille had not connived to make their stays coincident, and he went off to Camp Ahmek again in July. After lamenting to his diary that Camille was in Old Orchard while he was in the wilds of Ontario, he broke down in tears when he finished reading Edmond Rostand's 1897 play *Cyrano de Bergerac*. Cyrano spoke to his sense of romance and became his model. The greatest compliment, he wrote to Camille, would be to hear someone say, "You have won because you are Cyrano!"[31] Throughout his life Trudeau identified with Cyrano, who appealed to his romantic spirit. The daring seventeenth-century swordsman believed that, because of his ugly nose, the beautiful Roxane would never accept him — and, in the end, his handsome but dull friend Christian won her heart.[32] Pierre, who constantly worried about his acne and thought women did not find him appealing, clearly identified with the brilliant poet but tragic lover Cyrano. Four decades later, Trudeau also recalled the importance for him of Cyrano's famous "tirade" about walking alone to the heights: "I found there an expression of who I was and what I wanted to be: I don't care if I don't make it, providing I don't need anyone else's help, providing what I do make I make alone."[33]

Pierre enjoyed Camp Ahmek, but when the month was up on July 29, he was impatient to get to Old Orchard Beach.[34] The family chauffeur immediately drove him and Tip to Maine to join Grace and Suzette. Camille had agreed to stay a few more days. Alas, when he arrived, he discovered that she had not been able to find a room and might have to leave. Grace and

Suzette quickly responded to the crisis with an invitation for Camille to stay with them. For Pierre, "utopia had arrived!"[35] They had five glorious days in which, like Cyrano with Roxane, he read poetry to Camille, they watched the stars at night on the pier, and they went to confession together. Then they parted sadly on August 6, vowing to stay in touch.

They met again the next year in August at Old Orchard Beach, and the external world that was falling apart was far distant from the young lovers. Camille had spent part of the academic year in France, and Pierre found her aloof at first, but soon enchantment returned. They went to Hollywood films almost every night, then walked on the pier and talked—he about law school, which he had begun to consider, and she about becoming a schoolteacher. On the 17th they had their first fight, when he wanted to pass the evening reading and she wanted him to spend it with her. He finally agreed, and, the following night, they went dancing with Suzette and her boyfriend to celebrate the second anniversary of their meeting. Afterwards, the moon over the water was especially bewitching and, for the first time, they kissed.

At month's end, however, they fought again. She sent him a note telling him to meet her on the pier if he was not tired; her tone was cold. Pierre noted in his journal: "I found the proposal comic and I would have responded to her in the same tone, but I wasn't able to do so because I was in the bath." Resentfully, he met her and reproached her for her bad mood. They went to Camille's summer place, where he told her that she was beautiful and enchanting but he would not be pulled along by "the end of the nose." He confessed to himself that his behaviour might have been impolite, but, he reasoned, "it seems to me that the woman should not push the man around."[36] The next evening, as the Second World War began, she begged him not to do anything dangerous. Rather, she asked him to visit her at Smith in the autumn and to attend her graduation the following June. As she wept, he kissed her tears and whispered poetry in her ear before they finally parted at 2:45 a.m.[37]

The summer of 1939 was the best, he told his diary: "I read little, but I kissed a woman."[38] In September, school resumed: Pierre became the editor of the college newspaper, *Brébeuf,* and prepared to wrest class leadership away from Jean de Grandpré. He thought constantly of Camille, but among his peers the news of war incited considerable debate in the college corridors. He avoided the discussions and deliberately cloaked himself with ambiguity. On October 9 he wrote in his diary: "It's true that there is a certain charm to surrounding oneself with mystery." He preferred to have people say "Trudeau? No one knows him. Friend of all; intimate of none."

Pierre remained publicly aloof from the controversies about conscription. His journal provides convincing repudiation to anyone who argues that his nationalism made him an immediate opponent of the "British war." He found the declarations of many students—that they would resist conscription and flee into the bush—simply foolish. "Everyone is talking for and against conscription," he noted in one entry. "It is a sad thing but I would not do what many others are promising to do: hide themselves in the bush. I would sign up and go and come back for the sake of adventure." Then he hesitated: his own preference was to avoid the war and go to England—not as a soldier but as a Rhodes Scholar—or maybe to the States.[39]

Within the next months, war, as it so often does, changed everything, notably Canadian politics. Trudeau attended two election rallies in the fall as Duplessis challenged the federal government's war authority under the *War Measures Act.* On October 20 he went with his mother to the Montreal Forum for a Liberal rally. A family friend had given them tickets, but Pierre, whose father had been a Conservative, was offended by the Liberal crowd, which "cried like babies with each invective against the *bleus*."[40] Still, he found Mackenzie King's French lieutenant, Ernest Lapointe, very impressive. The federal Liberals had warned francophone Quebec that the re-election of Duplessis would mean the resignation of the Quebec Liberal ministers and, inevitably, the emergence of a conscription coalition, as in the First World War.

Six days later he attended yet another Liberal rally with his mother, where he heard the brilliant orator Athanase David speak. Pierre could not yet vote, but in his first *Brébeuf* article dealing with the war he cast a plague on all the older parties and expressed his belief that Quebec needed a new movement that was neither *bleu* nor *rouge*, conservative nor liberal. About the war, he was remarkably taciturn. He made no comments on the defeat of Poland or on the alliance of Communism and Nazism in its destruction. He attacked the tyranny of public opinion, where "soldiers dare not say they would like to halt war . . . and generals dare not call for peace."[41] Camille and plans for his future career preoccupied him more than politics, and he said nothing publicly when the provincial Liberals defeated Duplessis.

Camille had asked him to visit her at Smith. He hesitated, writing in his diary: "2,000 women. Ouf!" He admitted that he understood neither her nor women generally. He was jealous; he was suspicious. Perhaps recalling Father Tobin's warnings, he wondered about the summer day when Camille had revealed a "naughty" character. He finally decided that he would go to Smith, and he borrowed Suzette's impressive Buick for the occasion. Once again they went to the movies, where they saw *All Quiet on the Western Front*, the film based on Erich Maria Remarque's novel. Its anti-war message impressed Pierre, but this time Camille did not. She was too materialistic and too independent. She was, to be sure, charming and pretty, but "My God," he exclaimed, "I am too much an idealist and an intellectual for her." Although Catholic and French, she was, regrettably, too American.[42] He returned home, worried about the war, and with one goal in mind: to win the prestigious Rhodes Scholarship and go to Oxford.

—

If the Rhodes had been granted, Pierre Trudeau would have embarked on a path that took him away from his companions and the whirlwind of Quebec political life. His teachers at Brébeuf recommended him strongly for the award and, in January 1940, his chances seemed excellent. Indeed, the letter from Father Boulin, the head, or prefect, of the college, listed the astonishing number of prizes that Pierre had won (a hundred prizes and honourable mentions in seven years) and stated that he had performed with great distinction in all fields. Pierre was, he added, diligent and intelligent, though a bit timid and his own most severe critic. He was "a manly character, a desired companion, and a perfect gentleman." His determination was exceptional: in the past year, when he broke his leg in a skiing accident, Boulin continued, Pierre chose not to take a comfortable break at home; "instead, he became a boarder at the college, prepared for classes in the sick room and went to each course in a wheelchair. The decision was entirely his," he explained, "because his mother and his sister had not yet returned from a trip to Europe." He had demonstrated the manliness that Cecil Rhodes so prized, and he was developing a strong personality and character little by little. Boulin sent the letter to Grace, requesting that she not reveal its contents to Pierre. One suspects she did.

The family's Liberal friend Alex Gourd was asked to supply a letter of support for Trudeau's nomination for the scholarship. In it he listed the many awards Pierre had won and drew particular notice to *Dupés*, the work by the young playwright. After mentioning the numerous sports in which Pierre participated, he noted that he was fluently bilingual, his mother being "Scottish"—a description increasingly used by Pierre himself. Like Boulin, Gourd also suggested that the young man was "timid," but, in his view, the reserve derived from a lack of life experience. A final letter came from a Montreal city official, who emphasized the "affection mixed with respect" that Pierre showed towards his family, particularly his mother.

Pierre had to compose an essay for the Rhodes Committee. He offered to write it in English, but "being a French-Canadian student of a French-Canadian college," he thought the committee would prefer that he present it in French. He began by admitting the difficulty of writing about his interests and hopes, and then he continued with a defence of his education. First in his life came religion, which had universal application; then came study at Brébeuf, which had prepared him well for future public life. He pointed to the diversity of his studies and to his own tendency to grasp new experiences. He was, he noted in English, a "Jack of all trades." After listing an exhausting number of extracurricular activities, he said that this thirst for diversity had affected his career choice. Very simply, he stated, "I have chosen a political career." He defined politics broadly and indicated that both his own capacity and his particular circumstances would determine whether such a career was in politics itself, in the diplomatic service, or even in journalism. In any case, Pierre said that he was choosing his educational path so he might prepare quickly for public life.

To this end, he continued, he had studied public speaking and had published many articles in *Brébeuf*. He rejected demagoguery and political jobbery, arguing that the politician must have "a perfect understanding of men and a knowledge of their rights and duties." That was a tall order and good reason to study "Philosophy-Politics-Economics" at Oxford and, if it was not too much, modern history as well. His ultimate goal was a law degree. Finally, after raising the issue of what Oxford would mean for his "French self," he provided his own answer that the intimate contact with English culture would serve to broaden him. Rhodes himself had famously said, "So much to do, so little time in which to do it." Like Rhodes, Pierre Trudeau stated that he, too, possessed "an inextinguishable passion for action."[43]

But it was not to be. In January 1940 the Rhodes officials awarded the scholarship to another applicant. If Trudeau had won the Rhodes and gone to England, he would have become much less French and more a part of the Anglo-American world. He seemed to anticipate that fate. As editor of *Brébeuf*, he wrote that the journal had decided not to express any defined opinion on the subject of the war during the fall of 1939.[44] That public position echoed the private thoughts expressed in his diary. He did not initially oppose the war, reflecting the attitude of his church and probably that of most of his teachers. The archbishop of Quebec, Cardinal Villeneuve, took a clear stand for the Allies by asking God "to hear our supplications and that the forces of evil may be overthrown and peace restored to a distracted world."[45] Trudeau's presence at Liberal rallies with his mother and Liberal family friends suggests that he probably would have voted Liberal against Maurice Duplessis—as his mother surely did. But because he was not yet twenty-one, the voting age, he did not have to make that choice.

Everything changed in 1940. Jerome Kagan has noted how "adolescents, who are beginning to synthesize the assumptions they will rely on for the rest of their lives, are unusually receptive to historical events that challenge existing beliefs." Whether in Ireland at Easter 1916, Prague or Paris in spring 1968, or Montreal in 1940, adolescents are keen witnesses as history "tears a hole in the fabric of consensual assumptions." Young minds fly through that hole, Kagan wrote, "into a space free of hoary myth to invent a new conception of self, ethics, and society." With Pierre, some myths lingered, but in 1940 the conception changed.[46]

His contemporary and friend of the 1950s, the sociologist Marcel Rioux, later wrote that, for him and his generation, the war completely changed the direction of their lives. Their understanding of society and, especially, of the relationship between the economically dominant anglophone minority and the poorer francophone majority altered dramatically. Rebellion took many forms, whether at classical colleges or in the working-class areas of Montreal. For Pierre Trudeau, son of a French businessman and an English (now always termed Scottish) mother, this transformation was very turbulent.

—

The war made Trudeau into a Quebec nationalist. The ambiguities that had marked his writings and thought in the 1930s began slowly to disappear. He was well prepared: he knew the nationalist arguments and had repeated them to the nationalist priests at Brébeuf and to a broader audience in *Dupés*. Although he had serious reservations about the stronger nationalist arguments made by "our exalted patriots," he increasingly regarded his heritage as primarily French, and his education constantly strengthened that belief. When the Canadian government imposed the Defence of Canada Regulations that limited free speech and invoked conscription for Home Defence in 1940, Pierre suddenly saw history differently. He became, in his own phrase, deeply concerned about the fate of his "French self."

But the change came gradually, as he worked diligently to stand first at Brébeuf and as he edited, rather eccentrically, the student newspaper. As editor, he took a "hands-off" approach and put much energy into a "Tribune libre" edition where free expression was permitted. He was too busy to write to Camille very often, but at last on March 30, 1940, he sent her a long letter to fill her in on his activities. He wrote in English, even though Camille's French had improved after her time in Paris, but he took her to task for her earlier comment that his meanings were often obscure and his prose too complex. He admitted, however, that others at Brébeuf had made the same complaint. The letter gives the flavour of his life at the time and contrasts with the impression presented in his notebooks, where he concentrates on philosophical works and ignores the movies and concerts he attended and the popular books he read. After a long apology for the delay in writing, he began:

> And to make a long story less long, you find me with a pen in my hand, a happy Easter on my lips, and very little in the back of my head. But shall we get down to facts?
>
> During the past month I have done a great deal of most anything. Naturally we were overworked in school. As we finish a month ahead of the other classes, our teachers want to cram everything in at once.
>
> Then I have been reading quite a bit of "Dominique" by Eugène Fromentin [a French author and painter]. In the line of plays, I was at [Canadian director and actor] Maurice Evans' staging of Hamlet. It was a masterpiece of producing. I found his playing very comprehensive yet too declaratory. I saw Rostand's "Aiglon" which had some very high spots.

He went on to say that he had read Charles Péguy's *Notre jeunesse* and *Frivolimus '40*, a good example of Montreal low humour. He also saw French director Sacha Guitry's movie *Le roman d'un tricheur*, which he declared "insipid." He went to two concerts, one a Red Cross benefit which combined "the two Montreal Symphonic Orchestras," but "it was remarkable by its lack of anything remarkable." To all that, he told Camille, "you can add a few conferences [lectures] by the French philosopher [Jacques] Maritain," who strongly supported the Allied war effort. Given Trudeau's increasing nationalism and opposition to war, it's interesting that he listened carefully to the liberal and pro-Allied Maritain at this time.[47]

Pierre told Camille that his hockey team was in the play-offs and that he was simply "crazy" about skiing. He boasted that he had bought "jumping skis" (which, unhappily, were soon to break his leg). He said that the whole family had skied during the Christmas holiday and he and Tip had spent time together on the "superb" hills at Mont Tremblant. He went on to describe the controversies he had proudly stirred at Brébeuf:

> And now to end this one topic (myself conversation), I will please you by admitting that you are not alone to find my style obscure and incoherent: the last edition of "Brébeuf" had a "Tribune libre" in which several fellows took a few cracks at my essays. Evidently I could not let them have the last word, so I answered right back with good style . . .
>
> By the way I also published an article on Rut-thinking and standardized education that we have discussed together. It caused a scandal in the cloister, and I was called up to explain my views. It was even funnier because Tippy at the same time wrote an article on individualism. But I leave this to some other time for I am anxious to talk about you, my dear Camille.

After inquiring about her college, how she looked, and what she planned to do, he made a characteristically lame joke: "I think I'll have my graduation diploma pickled; that's because

I can't get stewed." In France, Camille had developed an interest in philosophy and in Freud and Proust.* Suddenly, Pierre,
in a pattern that he followed later in his relationships with
women, became earnest with her:

> Such deep thinking brings me to the subject of
> Philosophy and to your concept of philosophical ethics.
> Honestly, I think we could have a peach of an argument
> on the subject. Firstly, I would tell you to read [Alexis
> Carrel's] "L'homme, cet inconnu" to find out how bad it
> is to always do what pleases you. Secondly I should ask
> you to demonstrate, either by examples of metaphysics,
> your theory on how "one thing that might be wrong for
> the whole world to do, might be perfectly alright in one
> particular case." In other words, if all men are partici-
> pants of the human nature, why shouldn't all men obey
> one universal natural law? Thirdly, I should inquire why
> you say it took over 2000 years for society to catch on to

---

* Camille introduced Pierre to Proust in a serious way. He told her: I will
"always remain indebted to you for having set me under Proust's influence."
He had "heard much about him" but much "was naught in comparison with
what I found in reality. What power of expression, what penetration in his
observations, what suppleness of a style that can follow a concept into its most
subtle relations, explore the secrets of its development and verily track it down
to its birth in the proudest depths of the soul as surely as a hound will track a
bleeding prey." As this sentence indicates, Proust had affected his prose style,
and not for the better. The fact that Trudeau had not encountered the giant
Proust until he was almost twenty-one reflects upon the deficiencies in his
education—it had extensive French literary content, but only selectively so.
Trudeau to Corriveau, Oct. 29, 1940, TP, vol. 45, file 5.

itself. Do you mean that the birth of Christ marked the beginning of the period when society misunderstood itself, or of the period when it understood itself? But don't bother answering; true to your sex, you have probably changed your mind about everything in the past month, exchanging Freud's theories for Aristotle's.

Camille must have read Freud's *Civilization and Its Discontents*, a study that had its faults but was infinitely superior to Carrel's book. *L'homme, cet inconnu* is highly elitist and racist and, because of Carrel's repute as a Nobel Prize winner in medicine, his argument gave intellectual weight to Hitler's extermination policies. The book's "woman is weaker" strain is also reflected in Pierre's comments to Camille. He indicated no understanding of how Carrel conflicted with Jacques Maritain or, for that matter, Tip's article on individualism.

In an addendum to his letter, he signalled his confusion about himself and his beliefs. Apologizing for failing to write to an apparent mutual friend, Pierre wrote: "I should like to call it laziness; yet it truthfully is nothing but lack of genius. I, who always believed myself simple and 'like unto a little child,' have realized that I am, unfortunately, a complicated adult unable to speak a simple thought, without forethought and afterthought." He was, very slowly, becoming an adult, but a complicated one.[48] Given that Trudeau would turn twenty-one that year, he appears astonishingly adolescent in this letter. He wants to be a contrarian, to escape the "ruts," but his education seems to have left him adrift as powerful new waves swept over his world. He was well read but not yet well educated.

—

After he lost the Rhodes competition, Pierre Trudeau decided to stay in Quebec and to study law at the Université de Montréal—with the intention of entering politics. He had consulted widely, asking even Henri Bourassa for direction. Edmond Montpetit, the most prominent Quebec economist, advised him to study law, followed by economics and the social sciences. Father Bernier was involved in the final decision, in mid-June 1940. Trudeau told him that he had considered a career in chemistry or in medicine, with a psychiatric speciality, or, alternatively, in "politics," which he believed required a legal degree. When Pierre decided to rule out chemistry, on the grounds that it was "as good to govern men as atoms," Bernier accepted his final decision in favour of politics, but insisted that his former student should always maintain his interest in the arts. He explained, as Pierre noted in his journal: "So many worthy men, like Papa, had been compelled to work to earn their living" that they were unable to enjoy the fruits of their earlier studies. They both agreed that a man of principle should "have a mystique," and Pierre resolved to give fifteen to twenty minutes every day to "meditate on the goals of man, the Creator, the tasks to do, morality etc. and then conclude with a true prayer, a conversation with God." They also concurred on the need to maintain an ascetic life. Pierre recorded but did not comment on Bernier's advice that, in relationships with young women, one should not make "the least sensual concession." However, he agreed that "it was bad to work too much," no doubt recalling his father's early death. He concluded his entry on their discussion with a pledge to read literature more widely and to continue to study theology.[49]

A few weeks earlier, Pierre had expressed the same sentiments to a Camp Ahmek friend, Hugh Kenner, who, later, became an eminent literary critic. As he prepared to leave Brébeuf, Trudeau told Kenner that it had been "such fun probing into the mysteries uncovered by the study of metaphysics and ethics . . . Personally," he added, "it was with great awe that I came to the conclusion that space was only limited by God himself; that somewhere beyond our universe and all the universes, millions of light years away, out where matter ceased to be possible, there exists space conceivable, that is to say the Conceiver." Cosmology, Trudeau declared, would become his second focus; the first, of course, remained literature. And, as for so many others, literature would play a major role in making Trudeau a revolutionary nationalist at this time.[50]

In June, the same month Trudeau graduated, France fell. Immediately, the call for conscription echoed throughout English Canada as the British, the Free French, and a few Canadians fled Dunkirk in the famous defeat that became "their finest hour." In France itself many attributed the defeat to the secularism and socialism of the Republic and saw the creation of Vichy, the German puppet government under First World War hero Marshal Pétain, as a base from which to build a new France—one more Catholic and less corrupt than the previous regime. These views found strong support in conservative circles in Quebec, to the annoyance of many in Ottawa who were concentrating on the threat of invasion to Britain. Paul Gérin-Lajoie, the scion of one of Quebec's leading families, Trudeau's predecessor as editor of *Brébeuf*, and later an eminent public servant, wrote in the college newspaper in February 1941 that French democracy had been hopeless and that it must be replaced by a corporatist state based on the family—a system that recognized the French people's obvious need for authority. Drawing on the papal encyclical *Quadragesimo Anno* and, in Quebec, on traditional nationalist distrust of the impact of modernization, corporatism was a rejection of capitalism, socialism, and liberalism in favour of a more Catholic, authoritarian, and self-sufficient state. Mussolini's Italy, Salazar's Portugal, and, after 1940, Pétain's Vichy were sometimes cited as models of a corporatist state.* Trudeau came to share most of these views, and he kept Gérin-Lajoie's article among his papers.

The historian Esther Delisle has argued that, as early as 1937, Trudeau was secretly an ardent nationalist dedicated to Quebec independence, and that, while still at Brébeuf, he became a member of Les Frères Chausseurs, or LX, a secret revolutionary cell plotting the overthrow of the existing government. Although evidence of his early nationalism and even his sympathies for independence began to emerge before Trudeau wrote his own memoirs, he never responded to this charge. In the memoirs, he portrays himself as an anti-nationalist throughout the earlier period and depicts the war as a mild deviation from that path, one caused by the wrongs of wartime. "The war," he wrote, "was an undeniably important reality, but a very distant one. Moreover, it was part of current events, and, as I have explained, they did not interest me very much."

That account is disingenuous at best. The information about Trudeau's involvement in a secret revolutionary cell came initially

---

* Corporatist thought, the standard text on modern Quebec rightly declares, "is not easy to summarize." Essentially, "its vision was of all social groups, organized in 'corporations' or '[intermediate] bodies' dedicated to the pursuit of the common good, working together in harmony to ensure order and social peace. In this way, class 'collaboration would replace class struggle: employers and workers in the same economic sector would belong to the same corporation and work together for the advancement both of their sector and of the nation as a whole . . . Parliamentary democracy was a source of dissension, and corporatism would replace it with a unanimous society in which each person, imbued with the national mystique, would work towards—and at the same time benefit from—the general harmony and prosperity.'" Paul-André Linteau, René Durocher, Jean-Claude Robert, and François Ricard, *Quebec since 1930*, trans. Robert Chodos and Ellen Garmaise (Toronto: James Lorimer, 1991), 79.

from two sources: from his contemporary François-Joseph Lessard, an important member of Les Frères Chausseurs, who claimed in a book published in 1979 that Hertel had introduced Trudeau to the group in 1937 as the Simón Bolívar of French Canada; and from François Hertel himself, who said in 1977 that Trudeau was a founder of the group and, at that time, an angry nationalist who had battled with the police in 1937–38 during the centennial celebrations of the earlier Rebellions.[51] Trudeau did admit to interviewers that he was present at student protests against André Malraux and the representatives of the Spanish Republic, but he claimed it was the noise of the crowd that had attracted him to the event.[52] His journal clearly refutes that explanation.

Without doubt, Trudeau would later deceive interviewers who asked him where he was and what he believed when the Second World War was fought. Surprisingly, much of the evidence was already in the public domain, though Delisle was the first to put it all together: the testimony of Hertel and Lessard; press clippings about a speech and a trial following an anti-Semitic riot; and articles in the Université de Montréal student news-paper, Le Quartier Latin, where Trudeau's virulent opposition to the war was publicly expressed. There was even a question in the House of Commons from a Social Credit MP on April 5, 1977, when Trudeau seemed to admit that he had been a member of a "separatist" secret society. Yet before Delisle and, more recently, Max and Monique Nemni drew attention to this evidence, there was no public discussion about it, and, astonishingly, no journalist "followed up" on the question asked in the House.[53]

Based on Trudeau's complete personal papers, the evidence is overwhelming that Trudeau did become a strong Quebec nation-alist and that, during the war, he associated with supporters of "Laurentie," who espoused an independent French Catholic state. How did the fan of American movies, the participant in Liberal rallies in the 1939 Quebec election, the student who was suspicious of "exalted patriots" and proud of both his "English" blood and his "Elliott" name so quickly become a revolutionary separatist? The path, as always with Trudeau, has unexpected turns.

Trudeau's papers suggest that, in the pre-war years, because of his education and experience, Pierre was capable at certain moments of being strongly nationalist. Conversely, he reacted against that same nationalism when it touched on those of mixed English/French blood. He correctly told biographers that, at Brébeuf, he had shocked the priests and his classmates when he applauded Wolfe's victory over Montcalm on the Plains of Abraham. At other times, he was a strong defender of nationalist positions—on one occasion burning the Union Jack with a bunch of Brébeuf boys. In his own mind, he had established a sense of balance that occasionally tilted when, on the one hand, he attended an English-Canadian camp or, on the other, when a student accused him of betraying the French "race." Still, his heritage was primarily French and Catholic.

As France fell and the Canadian government introduced conscription for home defence, the Trudeau family was on its way to Old Orchard Beach. There they received a telegram from Grace's brother, Gordon, who lived in France and now asked for money to help him flee from the Nazis. Pierre recorded this "bad news" but, by the next morning, paid little attention to the crisis in Europe and the anti-conscription marches in Montreal as he slept in, did some oil painting, and remarked on the "perfect tranquility" with so few people on the beach. A few days later the full force of what was happening in Europe struck Pierre—perhaps because Camille was fiercely anti-Nazi and pro-Allies, even though she was an American. He wrote in his journal that the Germans were now in Paris. "Ah! the pigs," he exclaimed. He saw a newsreel on the fall of Paris that infuriated him; it was, he wrote, the work of "the dirty Boche." He decided he would join the Canadian Army to fight. In the meantime, he had to return for graduation.[54]

This evidence decisively disproves the claims made later by Hertel and some later historians that Trudeau had early anti-war or even pro-fascist sympathies. However, it is true that his attitude in June 1940 is surprising, given some of his notebook jottings on works by Alexis Carrel and others. Very simply, he is contradictory and conflicted.

—

Meanwhile, the Trudeau family had decided to take a train and car trip across Canada and down the west coast of the United States. It began on June 26, and Pierre's admiration for what he saw is clear in his notes. North of Superior, he wrote, "Quel pays admirable!" as he watched a splendid sunset. On arrival in Winnipeg, he described the city as "a drop of oil on the plains." As he surveyed the vastness of the land, he again pondered whether law and politics was the right career choice: "Would I be capable of leading the people of Canada," he asked, "or even the people of my own family?" In any event, he would follow where God led him, though, he added accurately, he would not be surprised if "the road has many forks, ditches and detours."

He had vowed to keep a psychological journal during the trip, but the demands of daily travel were too much. Still, he thought about what fate had in store for him. He worried about his timidity with women, in particular, and humanity, in general, and resolved to look people directly in the eye—something he apparently had found difficult earlier. But he did not lack self-confidence:

> I must become a great man. It's amusing to say that! I'm often surprised to think, as I walk alone, do others not see the signs, don't they sense that I bear within me, the makings of a future head of state or a well-known diplomat or an eminent lawyer? I am frankly astonished that those things

do not shine through. And I have compassion for those who will not be able to boast in ten or twenty years of having seen me a single time.

He believed he had made the right career choice but recognized that he might change course. For a man, he noted, career is essential. "In a young woman you admire what she is; in the case of a young man, you admire what he will become." He fretted about his strong attraction to women, although he admitted that the list of those he knew was "perplexingly short." Camille came first, followed by "Micheline, Myrna, and Alice Ann." Obviously, in his choice of women, Trudeau was—and remained—thoroughly multicultural. The danger, he warned himself, was that he would fall in love and marry before he completed his education. He concluded his self-assessment: "The moral of all this is that I must continually work for perfection and become likable, obliging, and gallant (what a word!)."

The trip continued, and, as he realized, it was as difficult to rule his family as Canada itself. In Edmonton they stayed at the grand Macdonald Hotel, where they met up with his Brébeuf friend Jean-Baptiste Boulanger and his family. The encounter was important because Jean-Baptiste, a Franco-Albertan, later became part of the secret society advocating a separatist state for Quebec. Together, they toured the cathedral at St. Albert, realizing, first hand, how far the French presence had extended. There was no talk of independence at that time, of course, and Trudeau passed on through the mountains at Jasper: "The first impression was profoundly moving," he wrote. He remained deeply impressed after they unloaded Suzette's Buick and drove through the Columbia Ice Fields to Lake Louise—where, on July 1, they celebrated Dominion Day.

There Suzette became sick, so Pierre had to drive through the mountains. It terrified him, not least because the car had faulty shock absorbers. Finally they reached Vancouver, where the natural setting impressed him but the university did not. Then, on July 9, they set off to drive down the Pacific Coast and have the car repaired. Pierre reflected upon the trip one day and pronounced it very worthwhile, especially from the point of view of the family. "We discussed a range of things," he noted in his journal, "assayed our faults, and recalled old times." He was more candid with Camille, telling her: "We are still having a riotous time, what with the scenery and the family arguments (some of them are honeys)." In his own case, he used the trip to develop "conversational arts," which he believed he lacked. He deliberately tried to draw strangers into conversation with him and looked them in the eye as he had planned. It was, of course, all good training for politics.

Finally, on July 22, they reached Los Angeles. The family went to the Hollywood Bowl, where they saw Paul Robeson in an "unforgettable" performance. But that was the best of Los Angeles for Pierre, who betrayed his Brébeuf training in his assessment of the entertainment capital: "I can't wait to escape this city," he complained. "I'm sweltering." There was no "ozone" in the air and too much carbon dioxide. "The people have the appearance of a dead fish," while the women did not look natural—all of them seemed to be waiting for a director to pass by. At this point in the trip he was tired of writing, so he brought his account to an end. At least, he noted, he had served "the needs of my biographers." Indeed, he had.

—

America was still neutral in the war, and the conflict seemed distant in Pierre's account as June turned into July. Still, he remained strongly opposed to the fascists, writing on July 19 that Gordon Elliott had finally reached England as the war continued "its hideous advance." Despite some later claims that Trudeau admired Hitler, he expressed loathing for him in his private journal. Hitler, he wrote, threatened to "exterminate the English," who were nevertheless putting up a brave fight. He had heard little of what had happened in France. "What an affair! But good night: that's my solution." He learned that there would be a "mobilization" on August 23 and wondered whether it would "spoil our trip."[55]

It did not spoil the trip, but Montreal was a changed city on his return. After the fall of France in June 1940 and the imposition of conscription for home defence, Camillien Houde, the Montreal mayor and his father's old friend, was interned for the duration of the war under the Defence of Canada Regulations because he had called for resistance to conscription. Before Charles Trudeau's death, when Houde, then the Quebec Conservative leader, had come to the Lac Tremblant cottage, Pierre would hear their loud voices complaining about the "Liberal machine." According to an accountant who had worked for Charles, Houde would drive into one of the Trudeau gas stations and say he needed "oxygen." The accountant would go to the safe and hand over one hundred dollars in cash.[56] The arrest of Houde and others shocked Pierre and his friends, and the war that had been so distant while he was on the Pacific shores became much closer.

It was not a war they wanted to fight. Of his 1939–40 class at Brébeuf, only one out of forty entered the Canadian military, in comparison with three who entered the priesthood, six who studied law, and nine who went into medicine.[57] At the Université de Montréal in March 1940, a poll showed that 900 opposed any form of conscription and only 35 approved; in the law school Trudeau entered that fall, the vote was 53 to 3. Daniel Johnson, a student leader (and future Quebec premier), had already declared in the student newspaper his strong opposition to a future war where Canada's interests were not involved. Now, with the "phony war" ending and conscription for home defence near, a young law student, Jean Drapeau, the future mayor of Montreal, also wrote an article in which he warned that another fight against conscription must begin, and he issued a call for vigilance.[58]

Once the *National Resources Mobilization Act* was passed, Trudeau and his friends were compelled to enrol in the Canadian Officers Training Corps and to engage in regular drill and summer training. He had been eager to join up as German tanks entered Paris, but things changed after he began law school. In the fall of 1940, when he entered the Université de Montréal, Trudeau immediately attended Abbé Groulx's history lectures. Of course, he had read Groulx's numerous books and articles, but his earlier comments did not suggest that the Abbé impressed him greatly. His decision to take this class reflected both his revived nationalism and the influence of Hertel, who was increasingly a guest at the family home. Trudeau never told interviewers later that he had studied with the Abbé, yet his detailed notes for the lectures exist among his papers. And, although his early encounter with Groulx had left him with the impression that the esteemed historian lacked oratorical skills, the content of the course intrigued him now. His notes indicate that Groulx was characteristically silent on questions such as separation and, seemingly, the war. Like any good historian, he provoked students to think about consequences — in his case, the consequences of the Conquest of New France. It was the will of God for the heirs of the defeated in 1760 to maintain French Catholic culture in North America.[59]

The Abbé left another clear mark on Trudeau: in his lectures, he emphasized the importance of the Statute of Westminster, giving it an exceptional constitutional significance in granting Canada freedom from the British Empire — an interpretation that went far beyond what the government of the day accepted. For many years afterwards, on December 11, Trudeau wrote "Statute of Westminster Day" on letters instead of the actual date. And, as he attended Groulx's lectures, his life at school became associated with nationalist causes. For example, in the fall of 1940 he took part in a satirical farce at the university that ridiculed politicians and denounced conscription. Among the players were Jean Drapeau and Jean-Jacques Bertrand, who later became premier of Quebec while Trudeau was prime minister.

Even his social life became buoyantly nationalist: Pierre kept a dance card from December 1940 on which he wrote, on the front, "Praise to liberty," and, on the back, "Long live liberty and the debutants."[60] To Camille, he wrote in French for the first time, thanking her for calling him "my dearest friend" and saying, "It is impossible to know fully the value of a friend, of someone who penetrates our inescapable solitude." But their romance was chilling, perhaps because of his new attitudes. He objected strongly when she ridiculed the decision of his friend "Roland" to become a monk, especially as she had always thought he was a "Don Juan." "The idea of getting up in the middle of the night to sing is perfectly ridiculous," Camille declared. An angry Trudeau found her remark "shocking."[61]

By the spring of 1941 he was complaining to her not only about law school—"A genuine lawyer is only supposed to study six times longer than what I have; no wonder most of them are idiots"—but also about the Officers Training Corps, which he had earlier told her he was eager to join. Now it would be "more thrilling to go to the Concentration Camp* or to the Front."[62] But he joined the Corps and, with resentment, did his service with many of his Brébeuf friends. Charles Lussier, a fellow nationalist then and a distinguished Canadian public servant later, remembered a revealing incident from that time: "One day our cadet captain marched us over to a depot where we were

---

* A camp for war protestors in Canada.

to move some shells. The officer in charge was English and gave instructions entirely in that language." The eight trainees were all French Canadians and all obeyed except one—Pierre Trudeau—who refused to move because, he said in French, he did not understand the command. After an officer repeated the order in very bad French, Trudeau replied in unaccented English, "Good, now I understand you."[63]

Liberty meant resistance, and resist Trudeau did, whether it was a unilingual officer or a bureaucratic directive. Yet his rebellion had limits. When, for example, he wanted to read Marx's *Das Kapital* and other works on "the Index" (the Catholic restricted list), including Rousseau's *Social Contract*, he dutifully asked the archbishop of Montreal for permission. After an initial refusal, he received the approval, although "His Excellency" urged him to treat the books with great care and guard them closely.[64] No doubt he did, but in other respects neither he nor some of his friends heeded the archbishop's counsel in 1941 and 1942 that French Catholics in Quebec should show restraint in opposing conscription and the war effort.

François Hertel was now openly separatist, and his 1942 study of personalism called for "men of action" who would make a free choice "to live." Trudeau took the advice. He became ever more drawn to the widening circle around the priest and wrote him several admiring letters. Hertel, who was an enthusiastic patron of modernism in the arts, introduced the Trudeau family to the surrealist and cubist artist Alfred Pellan, who had returned to Montreal from Paris after the Nazi invasion. Highly cultured, Hertel impressed Grace and her children, and they frequently invited him to their home and wisely took his advice on purchasing art. Hertel paid Grace the highest compliment in August 1941 when he wrote to Pierre that she was "the least bourgeois woman he had encountered in his life."[65] He encouraged Tip's growing interest in architecture and music, as well as Pierre's in literature. In this complex man, religion, literature, and politics mingled with romantic notions of revolution. Although he admired the French liberal philosopher Jacques Maritain, he did not follow his politics. Like many European personalists, including Emmanuel Mounier himself initially, Hertel saw much in Vichy to commend—particularly its "Catholic" sense of order, anti-capitalism, and corporatist rhetoric.

In 1941, when the Jesuit hierarchy exiled him to Sudbury for having a negative influence on the young, Hertel became Trudeau's confidant.* He encouraged Trudeau to work with a fellow student, Roger Rolland, to produce a literary review, while also expressing his firm opinions against conscription and the Catholic hierarchy and in favour of Pétain. Roger, the son of a major French-Canadian entrepreneur, had first captured Trudeau's attention when he lit a cigarette with a two-dollar bill, reminding him of the flamboyant ways of his father. He soon became Pierre's close friend (and, later, his speech writer when Trudeau was prime minister).[66] Hertel approved thoroughly of François-Joseph Lessard's "revolutionary" activities through his secret society, though he considered him a bit

---

* In July 1942 Hertel was told that his writings under his pseudonym did not bring credit to the Jesuit Order. While his influence on the young and his knowledge of theological doctrine were admitted to be great, his teaching was dangerous: "It is not by light talks on love or jokes or similar ways that one gives the young a taste for the serious, the profound, and the solid nor do they become aware of the gravity of the problems they face in their individual, family and social life." He threatened to quit the order but remained until 1946, when Trudeau encountered him once more in Paris. E. Papillon, sj, to Rodolphe Dubé, sj, July 18, 1942, Fonds Hertel, Archives Nationales du Québec-Montréal.

intense — as when Lessard suggested that Winston Churchill himself had intervened to send Hertel to Sudbury.[67]

The correspondence between Hertel and Trudeau began rather formally, with Hertel signing his name Rodolphe Dubé, SJ, but soon he developed a remarkable candour. Hertel was clearly Lessard's patron, and he asked Trudeau to be patient with his excitable colleague. Both men believed that Trudeau's major contribution to the revolutionary movement would be intellectual, and in October 1941 Trudeau mocked Lessard's political espionage in a letter to Hertel which clearly indicates that he was already a part of Lessard's secret society: "Meanwhile Lessard constantly has some missions of extreme delicacy to be undertaken, some deeply serious events to announce. I have some regret that he has taken me to be a confidant. I feel a certain embarrassment in displaying gushing enthusiasm when he reveals the exact number of fire hydrants in Ste-Hyacinthe." The revolutionary was well-meaning, the activities intriguing — but Lessard was too earnest.[68]

As their relationship developed, Trudeau flattered Hertel, calling him "un grand homme," a great man, while Hertel, in turn, told Pierre he now had the opportunity to be the man of action that Hertel himself had always wanted to be. In this sense, Lessard, however irritating, offered opportunity. In response to a letter from Pierre asking Hertel to explain who he really was, the priest wrote an extraordinary reply — distancing himself by using the third person:

> His friends are largely young men. And yet he's in no way homosexual. He differs in this respect from a certain number of the *Amérique française* [review established by Rolland and others] collaborators. Have no fear, it's not about the two Trudeaus and Père Bernier and [the unidentified] Jacqueline.
>
> And so this strange character is a softy deep down. He possesses a sensitivity that was once touchiness. He now

knows how to forgive and forget everything, and even fails to notice [insults] when it comes to his friends. The others he can forgive also. As often as possible he simply forgets. Above all, he has resolved to ignore petty reprisals.

Loving his friends is his life. Yet this love—and that's as far as it goes—however platonic and platonist, is demanding as Hell. To his friends, this "pilgrim of the Absolute" . . . desires the highest good more than anything. He would be much sorrier—I'm sincere here—to learn of Pierre Trudeau's death than to learn he was living common-law. And this is why, however broad-minded and tolerant of the tolerable he may be, the said Hertel's ears perk up when he foresees any potential danger that could be lethal to his friends' souls. That is why he doesn't like Gide [whose tolerance of homosexuality was controversial in Catholic circles], and dreads this elegant and naively perverse man because he may remove the fresh blossoms of those of his friends who are still blossoming. As far as a certain Pierre Trudeau is concerned, he believes his cynicism and maturity are sufficiently developed to keep him from being adversely affected by Gide. However, he would not like the said Trudeau to think that all his friends have reached the necessary degree of shamelessness to assimilate Gide without allowing themselves to be spoiled.

Hertel, in fact, doesn't like revolution the way Trudeau does. The latter loves it as one does a mistress. Hertel married revolution out of duty, because he had first given her children, and he does not wish to abandon them . . .

All in all, the moral portrait of the said Hertel—which we are currently sketching—is quite handsome. However, the hero is aware he is more handsome in his dreams than in reality. While on this subject, today this strange individual has chosen to add to this moral portrait his physical portrait. There are two. One for Pierre—which shows the tense, hardened Hertel, so fond of the "coups d'état" (although he has never himself seen or executed one); and [the other photo], Hertel, *par excellence*, the great Hertel.

Egads! I almost forgot the third: one for Madame Trudeau, in which she will easily recognize Hertel "à l'américaine," the one who offered to take her to a baseball game last year, while her two sons studied (the studious one) and tinkled away at the piano (the artistic one). A strong mother whose sons have been made effeminate by legal and literary hairsplitting was worthy to accompany the strong man from the Mauricie to these virile games.[69]

This letter makes several points clear. Whatever his faults, Lessard and his fellow revolutionaries were "Hertel's children," a fact the hierarchy recognized in moving him to Sudbury. The other references to homosexuality are obscure, but Hertel, though clearly regarding homosexuality as sinful, banters here and later about the physical appearance of young men. When he received a photograph of Trudeau in December, for instance, one he called a "physical photograph," he said it was "great. It could be Tahiti! Ah! If only Gauguin had known you." In the same letter his definition of his "revolutionary creed" had echoes of French Catholic thinkers of the thirties:

God is strong and pure and lucid. We are weak, carnal, and blind as bats. But do we blindly throw ourselves to God in order that he might give us all that we radically lack? The only great originality of my peculiar thinking is to have understood this: the close alliance between Christianity and Revolution. The all-embracing Christian revolutionary, practising and devout, this is the product I am striving to create and protect. This, because I have understood that he who may give his life is he, he alone, who knows how to give

it without losing [its essence]; that he who is completely
sincere, he alone can free himself of anti-revolutionary and
bourgeois prejudices . . . The church is, at the present
moment, the only possible source of revolution.

"Revolution" was a term used very casually at the time not only
by the political left and right and but also by the Protestant and
Catholic churches.* The Quebec Catholic hierarchy certainly did
not share Hertel's views on "revolution," but the priest had allies.

Father Marie d'Anjou—one of Trudeau's four favourite
teachers at Brébeuf—was even more supportive of the "revolution."
The Catholic hierarchy had removed him too from Montreal, and
his resentment was profound. Hertel believed that his fellow
priest was his closest ally in confronting these church leaders. In his
correspondence, d'Anjou always called Montreal "Ville-Marie,"
and he cherished the dream of Laurentie, the independent French
Catholic state.[70] During his absence from Montreal, he wrote often

---

* French intellectual debates had a great influence during these years on the
rhetoric of revolution in Quebec. In his history of postwar Europe, the historian
Tony Judt has emphasized how the "bipolar" politics of France, along with the
myth of revolution and the acceptance of "violence," was at the centre of public
policy. He cites the postwar example of the radical politician Edouard Herriot,
who announced in 1944 that normal politics could not be re-established until
France passed through a "bloodbath." His language, Judt adds, "did not sound
out of the ordinary to French ears, even coming as it did from a pot-bellied
provincial parliamentarian of the political center." Within French intellectual
and political circles, there was general if vague acceptance of the idea that "historical change and purgative bloodshed go hand in hand." Hertel clearly was part
of this heritage in both his language and his concept of historical change. Tony
Judt, *Postwar: A History of Europe since 1945* (New York: Penguin, 2005), 211.

to Lessard, and he recommended young Trudeau as the one most able to undertake various tasks for his "group."[71]

In his papers for the 1941–42 period, Pierre Trudeau has copies of a "plan" that describes a secret society which had been created some years before by three "guys" who were tired of half measures while "the people" slid downwards into the crevasse. They had read "Groulx, Péguy, Blois, Hertel, Istrati, Savard," and they believed in the immortal lessons of both history and Catholicism. The glories of New France must live beyond the granite of the monuments, they said, and the fearful, the down and out, the prostitutes, the blasphemers, and the drunkards who besmirch that tradition must be destroyed. Revolution is the daughter of "the Fatherland," the plan writers noted:

> Political and military revolution is but a stage, an accident of Revolution, as wars are but cataclysms of history. This is what the revolutionaries are, philosophers and doctrinaires. Of the philosophers of the Laurentian Revolution, one preached to the people the dogma of homeland, the other promulgated the dogma of hope to the desperate. Revolution, in this common view, of which we are the proof, is mankind who, in spite of everything, his selfishness, his cowardice, his passions, his flaws, the number and power of his adversaries, his failures, his mistakes, advances relentlessly. He, in the midst of all, sword in hand, despite obstacles, strikes again and again, until they fall.[72]

The plan identifies three "types" who had met together and organized this revolutionary cell. They were Lessard, Trudeau, and Jean-Baptiste Boulanger, the Brébeuf friend Trudeau had met on his cross-Canada tour in Edmonton. In his memoirs, Trudeau says that Boulanger and he "decided together to read over one summer the great works of political writing—Aristotle,

Plato, Rousseau's *Social Contract*, Montesquieu, and others . . . Boulanger knew more than me in this field, and that was why I hung around with him." In fact, Boulanger's course of studies included Georges Sorel, Leon Trotsky, and other theorists of revolution. Both also read the French authoritarian Charles Maurras, whose works became the pillars of Vichy.[73]

The barricades beckoned—and Trudeau rushed to the defence of the cause. The first battle came with the referendum on conscription. After the Japanese attack on Pearl Harbor on December 7, the Canadian government moved quickly to full mobilization. Ernest Lapointe, who had promised no conscription, had died, and the English newspapers demanded that Canada now respond as America and Britain already had. The wily Prime Minister Mackenzie King decided he should call for a referendum that would ask Canadians not a direct question on conscription itself but whether they would release the government from the pledge that there would be no conscription for overseas service. The date was set for April 27, 1942.

In Quebec, André Laurendeau organized the No side quickly under the banner of the significantly named Ligue pour la défense du Canada. Trudeau's anger was deep. He had written some rough notes twelve days after Pearl Harbor. "Is it necessary to be pro-British or anti-?" The answer was clear. He boasted to Camille about a "revolution" he was planning and, in 1942, asked her to obtain for him a copy of Malaparte's *Coup d'Etat: The Technique of Revolution*. Fearing censorship at the border, he cautioned: "I am anxious to read it as soon as possible; but I doubt it would be wise to mail it to me. I seriously wonder if the officials of this pharisaic puritan government would let the thing be delivered." He concluded with the words, "Thanks for your trouble, and long live liberty."[74] Out of Trotsky and other revolutionary theorists, Trudeau, Boulanger, and Lessard took the lesson that a small cell could carry out revolution effectively if it was cohesive and its plans were clear. It was, Trudeau suggested, the wave of the future. The old were the imperialists; the young, the separatists. The old did not belong to the future; they sought a solution that would maintain the status quo and allow them to play out their hand. It was already too late for that.[75]

Trudeau wrote to Hertel in January 1942 to say that the plan was moving forward, although not so effectively as he would have liked. As he had indicated earlier, he thought he could serve best intellectually—a position Hertel strongly supported. The anti-conscription movement continued to unite behind André Laurendeau, who, Hertel wrote in December 1941, was "a good man. Lots of sangfroid and vision." However, being too cerebral, he was "not a leader." Trudeau perhaps took the advice and told Hertel that "we" are trying to organize a study circle, which, under Laurendeau's direction, will examine social questions. Then he continued in a passage that, while illustrating his participation in a secret cell, revealed his doubts:

> I've told Arsenault, who is very understanding. He agrees that my work should be almost exclusively one of study . . . (with a touch of the spectacular anarchy I find indispensable). Lessard doesn't understand quite so well and is more inclined to have me play the role of mailman.
>
> I think the whole business is going badly in all respects. Too few are believers. Too weak an organization to fortify the tottering. Missed demonstrations. Too many clergy from the meek bourgeoisie . . . If it is impossible to make them see good sense and understand what's important, there must be some other way to force their hand. We'll have to see about that.

And so the "revolution" tottered forward, with Trudeau reading furiously, demonstrating regularly, and somehow crowding in his legal studies.[76]

Montreal seethed with discontent. Mayor Houde wore his prison garb; the Italians, whose main church honoured Mussolini, were adrift; the sailors fought furious battles over women in the bars near the port; and restaurants could serve only one cup of coffee or tea to each patron. On March 24, 1942, anti-conscriptionists gathered for a rally where the dissident Liberal Jean-François Pouliot was to speak with the support of the Université de Montréal student association at Jean-Talon market.[77] After the rally, a group of forty students got together at the corner of Saint-Laurent and Napoléon, in the centre of the city. Suddenly, windows shattered as young demonstrators threw stones, shouting, "Down with the Jews! Down with conscription!" The police quickly appeared and the demonstrators fled, but one fell and could not escape. In April this arrested demonstrator, Maurice Riel, a law student at the Université de Montréal, appeared in court charged with vagrancy—a favourite of Canadian police in those times. Trudeau spoke as a witness for the defence, and Riel—a Trudeau appointment to the Senate of Canada in 1973—was acquitted.[78] Meanwhile, the plan for an uprising went forward.

There were protests, even riots, and overwhelming francophone opposition to conscription. To Trudeau's despair on referendum day, Outremont stood out among the francophone population, with 15,746 voting Yes and only 9,957, No. There is no record whether Grace voted No with her son.

In his reading at this time, Trudeau focused on biographies of mystics and individuals who had confronted danger in support of Christ.[79] And many of his friends noted this sudden abstraction and mysticism in him. Already in the spring of 1941, Camille had told him that he was avoiding reality. A year later, ten days before the plebiscite, "your friend, the Great Hertel" wrote to him warning that he was becoming too abstract:

You are definitely a difficult guy to fit into day-to-day life. It seems that you are frightened to death of coming close to the quotidian and, therefore, the banal. Would you not, by chance, be some type of misunderstood romantic? Like Julien Sorel. Yet you haven't read, o chaste young man, [Stendhal's] *Le Rouge et le Noir.* Misunderstood romantic means, according to my worthy pen, unbalanced by choice, in love with tension. Don't you try to avoid, through energy and resolve, anything that could turn you away from your beautiful spirit? Do you not seek to escape to the higher levels than the barn floor upon which we must keep, at whatever cost, one foot of our being?

Hertel says he [Trudeau] has both feet in the blue skies: from time to time you come down to where mortals live to attend embryonic riots.[80]

Through the summer, the plan continued to spin out, with the hope that there would soon be a decisive event. Trudeau signed his letters to Hertel "Citoyen" and to Boulanger "Anarchiste," and he used the language of the French Revolution. During those warm months, even his travels testified to his nationalism. In 1941 he had joined his Brébeuf classmate Guy Viau and two others in retracing the path by canoe of the great coureurs du bois, Pierre-Esprit Radisson and Médard Des Groseilliers. They went along the Ottawa River, crossed Lake Timiskaming, and eventually reached Moosonee. The journey through the wilds of the Canadian Shield was described by a journalist as a group of students on a "planned trip." Trudeau was enraged: he wrote to Hertel, "Imagine then my mood when I learned that this 'arranged excursion' about which I had long dreamed, and which was a little *my* plan . . . should take on a thoroughly bourgeois allure. Merde!" In his description of his voyage, he emphasized the challenge and his brave response—a pattern he followed throughout his life. He emphasized how he ran the rapids while others portaged. As dangers mounted, rain poured, and harsh winds blew, he became stronger. "In fact, life began to be beautiful."[81]

By the following summer, Trudeau had a Harley-Davidson motorbike—already a symbol of youthful rebellion and reckless-ness long before the Hell's Angels and Marlon Brando gave the machine its swagger. Its speed was legendary; its exhaust explo-sive. For the timid Trudeau, it was the perfect accessory. He even wrote a short tribute, "Pritt Zoum Bing," for the Université de Montréal student newspaper, Le Quartier Latin, to the freedom motorcycles offered. During the long vacation, he decided to take two trips between sessions for his compulsory COTC training. Gabriel Filion, who accompanied him on the Harley, recalls that, on the first, they travelled "some five thousand kilometres through New Brunswick, Nova Scotia, and Prince Edward Island, sleeping in barns at night and sometimes in churches, or in houses that were being built. Most often, however, we slept in the countryside, pitching our tent in the fields or in the forest. We ate in small restaurants, and Pierre always paid the bill." On the other, they "retraced the route taken by François Paradis, the hero of Maria Chapdelaine." Here the nationalist motivation seems clear as Trudeau, Filion, and another friend, Carl Dubuc, followed the path of Paradis—in the novel, he left La Tuque and sought to join his love, Maria, on the shore of Lac St-Jean, only to die of exposure. The travellers escaped this tragic fate, but Filion injured his right leg badly on the second day. They decided to carry on and, in Filion's words, "every day, Pierre tended to my injured leg."[82]

When the trio returned to Montreal, Mackenzie King's Liberal government decided not to impose conscription imme-diately. But that did not still the anti-conscriptionist sentiment. In November 1942 a law-school classmate, Jean Drapeau, became an independent candidate in a by-election in Outremont, supported by both the Ligue and the Bloc populaire canadien, a new nationalist party that had supplanted the weak Action libérale nationale. At twenty-six, he was a fiery orator with strong connections to Catholic and other nationalist groups. It was Trudeau's own constituency, and he fought the battle furiously on streets he knew well. The Liberal candidate was General Léo Laflèche, who was endorsed not only by the English papers but also by L'Action catholique and several major French papers. Le Devoir, however, dissented and supported Drapeau. Trudeau spent most of his time in the fall of 1942 on that campaign, so much so that he told a business colleague that he had little time for other activities.

At a major rally during the campaign's last week, Trudeau gave such a spirited speech for Drapeau that Le Devoir published almost all of it. He began by denouncing the Liberals for running a military officer as their candidate; in a democracy, the military had no place in politics. He minimized the German threat, ridiculed the King government, and, according to Le Devoir, said that "he feared the peaceful invasion of immigrants more than the armed invasion by the enemy." The French of North America would fight when threatened, just as they had against the Iroquois; "today," he scorned, "it is against other savages." Then Trudeau stated dramatically: the government had irresponsibly declared war even though North America faced no direct threat of an invasion, "at the moment when Hitler had not yet had his lightning victories." The newspaper quoted his dramatic conclusion in full: "Citizens of Quebec, don't be content to whine. Long live the flag [drapeau] of liberty. Enough of Band-Aids; bring on the revolution."[83]

Two days after this demagogic speech, which seemed to equate the King government with savages, minimized the Nazi threat, and attacked immigrants (who, in Montreal, were mainly Jewish), Le Devoir ran another story about a polite heckler at a Laflèche rally who had been beaten by a thug. Trudeau kept the clipping and identified the heckler as his friend Pierre

Vaillancourt.[84] After the election, which Drapeau lost, Trudeau explained the reasons for the Liberal victory to a friend. There was no need for "lamentations," he said: "We know that in a constituency two-thirds Jewish and English, a nationalist and anti-bourgeois candidate would not have great appeal. Drapeau did not lose his deposit. And especially if Mr. King gives consideration to the polling statistics, he will understand that the votes for Laflèche are owed [?] almost uniquely to the Jewish and English areas and . . . to a powerful Liberal machine." He concluded by arguing that they had not really lost the election; rather, he blamed the "dishonesty" of what would later be called the "ethnic vote." The Bloc could well take the riding the next time.[85]

Trudeau's dramatic contribution to the Drapeau campaign contrasts with his relative silence at the university, where he published only one article in Le Quartier Latin that dealt directly with the war. This article, "Nothing Matters Save the Victory," mocked war propaganda and dripped with sarcasm about the rights the British were fighting to preserve. Although no fan of Hitler, Trudeau ridiculed the British regard for the rights of minorities. The Nazi hordes, he declared, would take away language rights, deny the rights of minorities in other provinces, capture the economic heights, and make the French population hewers of wood and drawers of water. Not even the dullest reader could miss Trudeau's comparison with the English treatment of the French after 1763. The editors indicated that its publication in the fateful month of November 1942 barely escaped the censors.[86]

One incident that has continually stirred controversy occurred in the summer of 1943 and involved Roger Rolland. In The Secret Mulroney Tapes, journalist Peter Newman complains that "journalists . . . seldom [mentioned] the fact that during the Second World War he [Trudeau] had cruised around Montreal on a motorcycle wearing a German helmet." The cruising was not in

Montreal, and the helmet was probably French, not German. In his memoirs, Trudeau explained how he and Roger had found some old German uniforms from the Franco-Prussian War of 1870 in the Rolland attic. Rolland's wealthy father had collected military souvenirs, including memorabilia from both the French and the Prussian side in this conflict. According to Rolland, Trudeau chose a French helmet when they decided to don the ancient military gear and surprise their friends, Jean-Louis Roux and Jean Gascon, who were members of the comedy troupe Les Compagnons de Saint-Laurent. The troupe was spending the summer season at a chalet at Saint-Adolphe-de-Howard in the Laurentians, quite some distance from Montreal.

As the pranksters headed north on their Harleys, Trudeau caught up to Rolland near Sainte-Agathe and told him that a villager had hailed him down to inform him that "a German soldier had just gone by heading north." That dramatic reaction spurred them on to even more tricks. They stopped at an imposing house and knocked on the back door. When a servant answered, Pierre demanded water, and the terrified woman brought a large glass out to him. But he signalled his suspicion of the contents, handed the glass to Roger, and demanded that he drink his share of it first. Once Roger had taken a few sips, he suddenly collapsed, screaming with pain. The servant quickly bolted the door, and the "soldiers" fled. When they reached their friends, they found only one of the actors there. He was "petrified" as he encountered the bizarre invaders and thought he was hallucinating. It took him a few minutes and a strong shot of cognac "to recover his senses." Trudeau later dismissed the whole incident as simply a prank, but, when interviewer Jean Lépine told him in the early 1990s that Rolland had admitted that they scared some people, Trudeau agreed.[87]

Curiously, the *Quartier Latin* article (although not the motorbike incident) escaped the attention of Canadian journalists, politicians, and writers when Trudeau was prime minister, even though it contained political dynamite. In 1972 a clever opposition party could have used Trudeau's angry anti-British rhetoric to win a few Ontario seats where "Queen and country" still mattered. Rumours constantly swirled around Trudeau, but surprisingly little effort was made to clear away the mists when, in some cases, they could have been easily dispersed. Jean-Louis Roux was not so lucky. After a brilliant career as one of Quebec's finest actors, he was appointed lieutenant-governor of Quebec. When the press revealed that he had worn a swastika on his lab coat five decades earlier at the Université de Montréal, he responded that, like other students fiercely opposed to conscription, he had simply wanted to be noticed. He apologized for his youthful deeds and explained that the context of the time had skewed his understanding of evil.[88] The appointment, however, was aborted.[89]

Trudeau, too, was a clever actor. In the summer of 1942, for example, he took part alongside Roux and Gascon in a play, *Le Jeu de Dollard*, in front of the statue of Cartier at the base of Mount Royal. And throughout this period, he changed roles quickly. The bland young essayist of Brébeuf became a biting polemicist at the Université de Montréal, as the caution that had marked his adolescent escapades disappeared. He was daring. In a debate on gallantry that took place the following January 8 in the presence of the federal minister of fisheries, Ernest Bertrand, Trudeau was outrageous, just as everyone expected him to be. The program romantically described him as "chevalier des nobles causes." Pierre, it declared, "cuts the figure of a revolutionary in our time." He told George Radwanski that, in his defence of gallantry, he pulled a gun, pointed it at one of the judges, and fired it. A puff of smoke appeared, but it was a blank. The judge ducked; the crowd was stunned. Not surprisingly, Trudeau and his partner lost the debate, in which they argued that gallantry belonged to the past, not the present, where gallantry was a fake.[90]

That winter night Trudeau received poor marks for gallantry—and common sense—from many in the crowd.

—

What are we to make of Trudeau in these exuberant, troubled times? His correspondence with François Hertel leaves no doubt that he was deeply involved with François-Joseph Lessard's revolutionary activity and that his politics were not only anti-war and anti-Liberal but also clandestine, highly nationalist, and, at least momentarily, separatist and even violent. Hertel was, as Lessard himself said, the major recruiter for the secret cell, and Trudeau was involved with Lessard well before the summer of 1942. His letter after the Drapeau defeat in which he blamed the Jews and the English, and the speech in favour of Drapeau where he announced his fear of immigrants, are both appalling. So too are some of the comments he made in his notebooks on works that were anti-Semitic or racist. After he read Charles Maurras's pro-Pétain and anti-Semitic volume *La seule France*, for instance, he told Hertel it pleased him very much, just as the "political jobbery" of Canada in 1942 disgusted him.

Trudeau's education, his friendships, and even more his participation in the summer military training exercises took him briefly to the barricades in 1941 and 1942. He deeply resented the military training, and his colleagues shared that resentment. Their attitude is clear in the remarkable photograph of the commandos "without zeal," and it's easy to imagine the pranks they contemplated as they "trained" together—pranks such as stealing their military kit and weapons.

Trudeau's opposition to conscription is understandable, and his political activities in the referendum campaign and in campaigning for Drapeau are expressions of his democratic rights. Under Hertel's spell, however, when he was bored with law school, entranced with the mystique of revolution, and freed by fortune to make his own choices, Trudeau did and said some foolish things. Yet perspective is needed.* He regarded Les Frères Chausseurs, or LX, as hopelessly disorganized and François-Joseph Lessard as a great bother. He did read Charles Maurras, Alexis Carrel, and others, but Hertel also introduced him to Alfred Pellan and Paul-Émile Borduas, and he spent far more time in salons listening to symphonies than in the streets calling for revolution. He, Lessard, and Jean-Baptiste Boulanger, who later became a prominent psychiatrist and disapproved strongly of Trudeau's dismissal of their separatist activities in his memoirs, seem strikingly immature. But then, many are in wartime.

Throughout this period, Trudeau lived at the family home, with its chauffeur and servants, while denouncing the bourgeois life. He invited his fellow students there for evenings of classical music, where his mother graciously entertained them. It seems

----

* In his memoir, Trudeau's friend and political colleague Gérard Pelletier describes their future colleague Jean Marchand's disillusionment with violent political nationalism in the forties in terms that could also apply to Trudeau: "[Marchand] had been recruited into one of the innumerable leagues that existed at the time (each one with twelve or fifteen members), all of which wanted to overthrow the government and put an end to democracy. That was the spirit of the age. Of course, the half-baked leaders of these little groups had no precise notion of what political action meant. They dreamed, they grew intoxicated with words, and in the basements of middle-class houses they cooked up heady plots which no one ever dreamt of acting on." Trudeau was far from alone in "trying out" these "heady" plots, but he later treated them with the disdain that Marchand and Pelletier did. Pelletier, *Years of Impatience, 1950–1960*, trans. Alan Brown (Toronto: Methuen, 1984), 9.

that he told her nothing about his nights on the streets or his notorious motorbike jaunt. These secrets he kept from her, and it surely would have jarred and distressed her had she known. And that, most assuredly, he was loath to do. It was a troubled time, and, as Camille Corriveau and even Hertel recognized, Pierre Trudeau, who had dreamed of being Canadian prime minister as he travelled across the country in the summer of 1940, had become a troubled young man.

Despite the daring of his political involvement (which was mentioned in the Université de Montréal debate program) and the boredom of his legal studies, Trudeau once again excelled in the classroom. He stood first at university even more often than he had at Brébeuf. Sure, he complained about the drill of law classes, but his remarkable discipline prevailed. His marks in civil law, for example, were 40 out of 40 in January 1941; 38 out of 40 in June 1941; and 38.5 out of 40 in June 1942, when he received 28 out of 30 in criminal law, 20 out of 20 for constitutional law, 17.5 out of 20 for international law, and 24.8 out of 25 for notarial procedure. Evidently, the plebiscite and politics made little difference to his grades.

The following year, in June 1943, Trudeau graduated first in law "with great distinction." He won the Governor General's Medal for overall excellence as well as the Lieutenant-Governor's Medal for standing first in the licensing examination. He personally wrote a letter of thanks to Their Excellencies for the medals. The response from the office of the Governor General thanked him for the information that he had won the medal—a gesture that surely confirmed Trudeau's contempt for the British nobles who then occupied the office.[91] When his sister, Suzette, read the results in La Presse, she wrote from Old Orchard Beach and congratulated him on "his latest achievements." She hoped he could use the publicity "in obtaining what you would like for next year."[92]

Trudeau, however, was still unsure what he liked. The five years between 1938 and 1943 were, nonetheless, decisive for him and, most historians argue, for Canada and Quebec too. He had to make a choice: Would he be a French or an English Canadian?[93] When he lost the Rhodes Scholarship and chose the Université de Montréal, Trudeau became Québécois. The term itself had no meaning in 1940, apart from being a resident of Quebec City. But Trudeau decided during those years that he was "French," a choice that was almost inevitable given the intensity of his education and the great events of the time. In making that choice, he became entangled in those events. And there was another factor: as Brébeuf's top student in a period when French-Canadian excellence was prized, he became a magnet for those who sought a leader for difficult times.

The debates, the battles fought by the young, and the relationships that were forged in the early 1940s echoed loudly in Quebec and Canadian political life for the next half century. The bodies aged and nuances emerged, but the names endured: Daniel Johnson, Jean-Jacques Bertrand, Jean Drapeau, Jean-Louis Roux, Paul Gérin-Lajoie, Charles Lussier, and so many more. When Trudeau spoke in the Outremont by-election, the other speakers for future mayor Drapeau's candidacy were Michel Chartrand, later a prominent labour leader and separatist in Quebec, and D'Iberville Fortier, one of the most eminent federal public servants forty years later. André Laurendeau, who worked closely with Trudeau in these battles, became the most respected Quebec journalist of his age. His best friend in the 1930s, Pierre Vadeboncoeur, became a major literary figure in Quebec; and Jean-Louis Roux and Jean Gascon were among the key personalities in the French and English theatre in the last half of the twentieth century. Most of these principal actors in the "revolutionary" moments of the early 1940s kept their silence about themselves—and about Pierre Trudeau.

At Brébeuf, Trudeau had stood a resented second to Jean de Grandpré until his final year. In another fateful decision, his rival chose to attend McGill University. As he explained:

> [Trudeau] could afford to search for his identity. People like me . . . were forced by economic necessity to get on with our careers, to go to McGill to improve our English because English was the language of business, to get a law degree and enter a practice immediately. Most of us married fairly early and started to raise a family and you had to earn money for that. As a rich bachelor, Pierre was able to spend years "finding himself."[94]

De Grandpré, whom Trudeau himself thought the most polished and articulate among his classmates at Brébeuf, rose to the top of the business world and became wealthy as the head of Bell Canada. There is much resentment in de Grandpré's comment, but also some truth in his charge that Trudeau, because of his personal wealth and independent circumstances, could search for his identity, experience adventure, try out anarchy, and delay finding himself. It was easier to be anti-bourgeois when your circumstances were thoroughly bourgeois.

Because Trudeau chose Université de Montréal for law and because he became involved in the conscription crisis as a leading opponent, he was immersed in the debate about the future of French-speaking Canadians in a way that he never could or would have been had he won the Rhodes Scholarship or gone to McGill. In a particular sense, he was correct in stating that the politics of wartime passed him by. Those great tides that turned in 1942 and 1943 did not sweep over his life, his classroom, or his friends as the Americans won the Battle of Midway, the Soviets held their ground at Stalingrad, and the Allies—with Canadians among them—set out on a bloody path

up the boot of Italy. Trudeau and his associates stood on separate ground, avoiding the battles in Europe while furiously
debating what their future as francophone professionals would
be in a modern North America. They knew that there could be
no return to the past, but in the early 1940s they saw the outline
of their future only dimly. Yet the debate that dominated
Canadian politics from the 1960s through the 1990s began
among Trudeau's classmates in the university corridors and the
Montreal streets in the 1940s. Those times cast the die.

For Trudeau, the times were exhilarating, confusing, and
dangerous. He swam in the same stream as others, opposing conscription, favouring Vichy and Pétain, outrageously equating
Hitler's Reich with British policy towards Quebec, and even
contemplating and plotting Quebec independence. Yet, in some
important personal ways, he remained apart, a self-declared
independent who often donned a cloak of mystery. He wrote to
his mother in English about how well he worked with his military superiors, and he vacationed at Old Orchard, enjoyed
American nightlife, and thought about a future political career.
What career, and even what country, remained an open question in 1943 as democracy, so threatened in the 1930s, began its
march forward towards its greatest victories. Despite his later
denials, he swam with the currents that flowed strongly through
his university. Yet, because of his background—his mother, his
wealth, and his intense search for free intellectual choice—he
sometimes took refuge on the shore, as when he apparently told
Gabriel Filion, his travelling companion on the *Maria
Chapdelaine* route, that he dreamed of a united Canada, or
when he told his diary that he was proud that his English blood
tempered his boiling French blood.

In the 1940s, as conscription loomed, Pierre Trudeau's
French blood boiled; as times changed, so would the man. He
would forget much of his youth, as all of us do. Yet in the attic

CHAPTER 3

—

IDENTITY AND ITS
DISCONTENTS

Twenty-one can be the cruellest year. Pierre Trudeau had drifted away from infatuation with Camille Corriveau by the spring of 1941, but, as with other significant women in his life, he clung to the intimacy they once had shared. With her and several women who followed, he peeled away the layers of hardened bark that enclosed the core where emotions flow. With men, he consistently refused to show weakness, whether in the classroom, the canoe, or the political forum. Among men, he sought uniqueness or, as he put it in his Brébeuf diary, to stand apart. This impulse created its greatest tension for him as he passed from adolescence to adulthood, that period when friendship is deeply craved and when, in twentieth-century North American society, identity becomes a pre-eminent concern. For Trudeau, the times were particularly difficult because he was determined to shape his own identity and to make choices freely, away from the direction of others.

In 1940 Pierre sent Camille a list of nine authors he felt he should master: it included René Descartes and Adam Smith, as well as Aristotle, Pascal, Montesquieu, Kant, Marx, and Bergson.[1] Many years later, in 1962, Germain Lesage, a Quebec journalist, asked ninety-seven Quebec clergy, writers, academics, and dramatic and visual artists to identify those who had influenced them most. Overwhelmingly, they chose French writers or philosophers, with Blaise Pascal and Paul Claudel—the French diplomat-writer—receiving the most mentions (thirteen times). Out of step with the others, Pierre Trudeau chose only one French author, Descartes, who appeared on no other list. His other choices were Adam Smith, Cardinal Newman, Sigmund Freud, and Harold Laski. Three were British, two were Jewish, and only Freud was mentioned by more than two of the others questioned.[2] Was Trudeau being playful in challenging the contemporary ethos or was he reflecting the unusual diversity of his intellectual mentors—particularly with his selection of Descartes and Smith? Still, it's worth remembering that 1962 was the year when the Quebec Liberal government stoked nationalist fires by nationalizing Quebec's private electricity companies. Descartes, of course, represented reason, and Smith the case for minimalist government intervention. At that moment Descartes and Smith made more sense to Trudeau than the passionate arguments for nationalization put forward by his friend the Quebec Cabinet minister René Lévesque. His choice of British thinkers was also provocative, a deliberate attempt to "shock the intellectuals" in Quebec. They also represented Trudeau's cosmopolitanism, a value and a term he had actively embraced as he matured intellectually in the mid-forties.

Because of his restricted education up to that point, Freud and Laski were virtually unknown to Trudeau when he graduated in law from the Université de Montréal in 1943. Like his peers, he had had his mind crammed with Jacques Maritain, Abbé Groulx, Paul Claudel, and the other names on the lists. Freud had already begun to interest him, and that prepared him for the intense personal encounter he had with Freudianism later in the decade. Harold Laski, a professor at the London School of Economics and a socialist thinker of renown and influence in

those times, would also profoundly influence Trudeau's conception of the state and public life.³ In the details of his playfulness
with the poll lay some truths, however, the major one being the
fundamental importance of the period 1943 to 1948 in the intellectual, personal, and public life of Pierre Trudeau. Let us begin,
as Trudeau would have preferred, with his mind.

When Trudeau was denied the Rhodes Scholarship and
forced to remain at the Université de Montréal in 1940, he gained
an enduring voice in the long debate among French Canadians
about their place in Canada. When he left Canada to study
abroad, first at Harvard in 1944–46, then in Paris in 1946–47, and
finally in London in 1947–48, Trudeau, to use one of his best-
known metaphors, opened the windows to fresh currents of thought
and action. Like many others, he unloaded some baggage that
had become offensive or superfluous: the former included the
casual anti-Semitism of his youth; the latter his close study of religious thought. As Father Bernier had counselled, he continued to
read theological works, but religious references quickly disappeared from his prose. Unlike many other Quebecers, such as the
eminent journalist and sometime politician André Laurendeau,
Trudeau would remain a believer, deeply interested in debates
about the character of faith and observant of Roman Catholic
sacraments. In this respect, his mention of Cardinal Newman
rather than Jacques Maritain, Teilhard de Chardin, or Emmanuel
Mounier is fascinating.

At Harvard and later at the London School of Economics,
Trudeau participated in the Newman societies that were the centre of Catholic life in the Protestant milieus of those universities
and, typically, immersed himself in Newman's life and thought.
What attracted him to Newman, the great Anglican intellectual of
the early nineteenth century? In part it was surely Newman's intellectual passage that he had detailed so brilliantly in *Apologia pro
vita sua*. When the English theologian sought to dispute the

legitimacy of the Roman Catholic Church, he concluded that, contrary to his task and his own beliefs, the church "had preserved unbroken her continuity with the Primitive Church, the Church set up by Christ, and founded on the Twelve."[4] At a moment in British history when anti-Catholicism was intense, Newman followed his conscience and converted to the Roman Catholic Church. He was no social reformer, but his intellect guided his actions, and his faith emerged from reason. An individualist, Newman chafed at the emerging doctrine of papal infallibility. Always, though, he found truth through reason, and Trudeau searched for the same grail. Trudeau's growing focus on individual choice within the structure of the Catholic faith stems directly from Newman, as does his willingness to challenge orthodoxies.

In commenting on the choices of the Quebec intellectuals he interviewed, Germain Lesage made two significant points: first, the fact that Paul Claudel and Georges Bernanos trumped Aquinas (named by only six of the ninety-seven interviewed) indicated that the intellectuals chose those who had influenced them most "beyond their formal academic training"; and, second, the choices reflected "loyalty to France" and "devotion to Christianity."[5] In this respect, Trudeau's political activism and his attacks on clericalism were not a rejection of Catholicism or religion itself; rather, like Quebec's Quiet Revolution in the sixties more generally, they were deeply rooted in "the grand ideas of European Christian renewal" among Catholics such as Jacques Maritain and Emmanuel Mounier.[6] Revolutions once begun find their own paths, and Trudeau eventually found the taste bitter. In the 1940s, however, he frequently savoured its flavour.

Trudeau consciously fashioned his identity in this decade, creating a recognizable shape from the elements provided by his past, his family, and his education. In his study of the "sources of the self" in modern times, Trudeau's friend and, later, political opponent, the philosopher Charles Taylor, emphasized how the modern Western quest for self differs from earlier Christian and other traditions in which "what I want and where I stand" is defined by others and by a set of beliefs and practices. In contrast, he said, the modern search for identity requires "leaving home"; it stresses self-reliance and, above all else, individualism. As we strive to orient ourselves to the good, however, we must try to "understand our lives in narrative form, as a 'quest.'"[7] In these words, Taylor, who was also a Catholic Montrealer, captures the sense of "quest" that pervades Trudeau's own understanding of his identity.

Trudeau was indelibly shaped by his childhood and adolescence, but he also exhibited a profound sense of individualism. "Ah! Liberty, independence," he wrote in his diary in February 1940. "Don't bend [your] knees before anyone; keep [your] head high before the powerful."[8] We see this spirit in his choice of intellectual influences, especially Newman and Freud. We understand its romantic origins in the tears that flowed from his eyes when he read how Cyrano de Bergerac strove to break free of the restraints of time and place. Yet, like the great nineteenth-century romantics, Trudeau had to bring his individualist instinct in line with his well-defined ambitions, which could be realized only within a mannered and ordered society. For Trudeau, writing that life narrative was an enduring struggle, one that brought periodic silences and curious forays, but never malingering.

There were delays: Stephen Clarkson and Christina McCall turn to psychology when they discuss Trudeau in the forties and conclude that he was a *puer,* a condition marked by delayed adulthood and prolonged adolescence. It's true that Trudeau did prolong the ease of adolescence and delay the trappings of adulthood, but he did so not only because he could, in material terms, but because he struggled continually with his past, his beliefs, and his quest.

In a very real sense, Trudeau mirrored Quebec itself in the forties as it wrestled with modern technology and politics and its relationship to its past and its traditions. The parallels are striking. Women in Quebec obtained the vote in April 1940, the same spring that Trudeau was wrestling with his strong sexual urges and his traditional Catholic conception of female chastity. Trudeau chose law over philosophy or the priesthood because he wanted to have an active part in public life, just as his province similarly came to terms with modern industrial capitalism despite the enormous impact it would have on traditional ways. When Trudeau talked in the forties about becoming a leader in his country, there was an ambiguity that is familiar to students of Quebec history in the twentieth century. He deeply resented British domination and was unsure what "la patrie," the fatherland, meant, but he did not commit fully to the concept of a separate Quebec state even while musing of revolution. It's a curious but common tradition at the time in Quebec, one that's reflected in the name of the nationalist groups Ligue pour la défense du *Canada* and the Bloc populaire *canadien*. Finally, he sought validation through external recognition—study at Harvard, Paris, and London—much as Quebec itself did, first by engaging in the "renewal" of Catholicism in the thirties and forties and in the lively European debates, and then by injecting modernism into culture and government in the fifties and the sixties. Trudeau was very much "a Québécois" Catholic; but, as with Cardinal Newman, his quest took unexpected turns.

When Pierre first began to ask, "Who am I?" at Brébeuf, he turned to his clerical teachers, notably Fathers Robert Bernier and Marie d'Anjou, for guidance. After many intense conversations, he took their advice very seriously and began to read the classics, to learn about art, and to listen to the finest classical music; in short, he immersed himself in the Western canon, though with a strongly European flavour. When he left Brébeuf for the Université de Montréal, he brought an extraordinary foundation of linguistic skills, knowledge of philosophy and religious thought, and, above all, intellectual discipline. At Montréal he quickly discovered that he was bored by law. He studied only what was "barely necessary" and despised lawyers but not his classmates. Instead, he devoted his time to politics and the arts and immersed himself in culture: reading books, attending concerts, studying the piano, painting in oil, and learning ballet, his favourite art. Still he stood first in his class. More than anything, he wrote to Camille earlier, he felt that his task in his early twenties was to "master" Pierre Trudeau.[9]

The correspondence continued mostly in English despite Camille's Parisian stay, and in March 1941 he reiterated that he was "still aiming to be accomplished in every field." This enormous goal meant constant challenges and tension, introspection, and even isolation as he tried to figure out his future:

> I seem to be slowly, surely and peacefully drifting away from the human world. I have forsaken every possible organization which might rob me of my time, and although I make an effort once in a while to go to a dance or a movie they profoundly bore me for the most part. Most of my law professors nauseate me, so I just study as much as is barely necessary . . .
>
> These different circumstances cause me to envelope myself in a world apart, where I crazily read and wrote, and dreamt about music and beauty and revolutions and blood and dynamite. It was most contradictory this combined desire of action and thought.[10]

His intensity frightened Camille, who, now in love with another man, warned him that he had fallen into "a terrible rut . . . You have shut yourself up in a room, and you are brooding and meditating on the future, and wondering how it will all come out." He should learn patience, she wisely counselled: "My dear Pierre, do you realize that 99% of the people with whom you will come into contact will be much more stupid and unintelligent, and you shall have to be patient with them because they will be the people on whom you will depend. You want and shall be successful, and whatever you do, either in law or the political field, you will find that people are not of your mental caliber." Still, she advised, he must learn to be patient with those "who are less fortunate and less endowed than you are."[11]

He infuriated her and others when they tried to grow close, yet at the same time he worked constantly to make himself ever more intriguing and attractive. In his notebooks, complaints about his appearance became fewer as excitement about women glancing his way grew. His graduation photograph captures the deep blue eyes and the fashionably parted dark wavy hair. He claimed that it was "brown" on a passport application in June 1940 and that he stood 5 foot 10—probably an exaggeration. At the university he honed the acting skills he had first developed at Camp Ahmek and Brébeuf and became a brilliant debater. He kept reminding himself that he must lose his timidity and always seek originality. He knew that humility was a virtue, but, he admitted to his journal, it was "sometimes difficult to reconcile ambition with such humility."[12] He practised different ways of relating with others, carefully noting their reactions to him. He committed himself to the healthy life, engaging in a variety of fitness exercises and testing his physical prowess on ski hills and, even more ambitiously, on wilderness trips.

In his confessional correspondence with François Hertel, he responded to the priest's observation that the "man of action" was a special and valued type.[13] Hertel ended an October 1941 letter with the words "Long live the France of Pétain. There was a man of action"—one who was undertaking challenging but necessary deeds even though he was over eighty years old. "Act, act, act," he counselled, advice that the young Trudeau believed he must heed.[14] Already acutely aware of his physicality, his presence as an actor and athlete, his attraction to women and beauty, he desperately tried to efface the acne blemishes on his face. His mother urged him to go to a chiropractor in the hope of finding a cure.[15] Time did end the acne, but the youthful affliction left him with mild scars that did not detract from the compelling intensity of his narrow face, piercing eyes, and remarkably high cheekbones. When he graduated from the Université de Montréal in the spring of 1943, he was very much an original and, to a large extent, his own creation.

But what to do? The war had disrupted all his plans to study abroad when he graduated from Brébeuf. Now, as he was completing his law degree, he applied to Harvard, Columbia, and Georgetown universities. The law school, apparently unaware of Trudeau's opinion that the professors were idiots, tried to secure a scholarship for its best student. He was, the dean wrote, "particularly outstanding, not only by his academic excellence but also by his assiduity and application."[16] Trudeau, however, could not get permission to leave Canada and his military obligations.

Fearing correctly that the practice of law would bore him, he sought other escapes, ones that suggest his revolutionary activities of 1942 were somewhat more playful than seriously considered. He wrote to a friend who had become a Canadian diplomat in South America and asked if he could get a diplomatic position in Rio de Janeiro: "I will be a lawyer within two months, old friend; that is to say, I'm almost a diplomat." The friend offered him little hope. He applied to the Experiment in International Living for a study trip to Mexico, but once again permission was denied. He spent part of the summer at a military camp in the Maritimes, after which he went on a trip "with his moto," telling his worried mother that, whatever happened, "be reassured, I will be prudent."[17]

The motorbike liberated him from the routine of practising law and released a side of him that his friends knew well—his playfulness and love of adventure. His close friend Jacques Hébert says that these were his most endearing qualities and that they redeemed his seriousness. In his article "Pritt Zoum Bing" in *Le Quartier Latin*, Trudeau claimed that the human species was made for the motorbike: "Man was conceived with the motorcycle already in mind: the nostrils open towards the back, the ears push back against the head, allowing the greatest acceleration without being overwhelmed by wind and dust." Above all, the roar of the bike as it swept through the countryside and crowded city streets served to "liberate the spirit; the body is turned over to its own resources and you think new thoughts again."[18]

Indeed, Trudeau was thinking new thoughts once more.

—

On his return to Montreal in the fall, he became a lawyer at 112 St. James Street West. He joined the firm of Hyde and Ahern, where he was paid $2.50 a day. For those apprentice wages, Trudeau handled simple files, most of them involving car accidents and evictions from apartments. As a landlord himself of a property at 1247 Bishop Street in central Montreal, which earned him $50 a month, Trudeau had no fondness for deadbeat tenants. He pursued one particular delinquent mercilessly through the courts that year.[19] Gordon Hyde and John Ahern were both King's Counsel, and Ahern was the grandson of Charles Marcil, a Liberal MP for thirty-seven years. In typical bicultural fashion, he was a member of the Reform Club as well as the francophone Club St-Denis, Charles Trudeau's old favourite.[20] Trudeau's rough files, still retained in his personal papers, reveal him to be a careful lawyer, extremely attentive to detail and thorough in his approach to cases. But however much his work pleased his employers, his politics in 1943–44 surely did not.

Trudeau remained active in politics, still firmly opposing Canadian war policy and the possibility of conscription—as did his friends.[21] The whiff of revolution quickly passed in 1943, leaving behind the nationalist and anti-conscriptionist Bloc populaire canadien. Trudeau participated in Bloc affairs, as did many of the other activists from Jean Drapeau's by-election and the conscription plebiscite. He sat on the organizational committee of the Bloc and agreed to be the secretary of the committee on education and policy. He even saved his badge from the Bloc Congress at the Windsor Hotel on February 3–6, 1944. It was signed by André Laurendeau, the man chosen because of his earlier role in the anti-conscription campaign to lead the Bloc in the upcoming provincial election.[22] Laurendeau denounced the federal and provincial Liberals and took his stand on the left. The Liberals, he declared in his inaugural speech, "gave us hypocritical governments which taught the proletariat much more effectively than any Marxist that the only way to triumph over a liberal capitalist state is through revolution."[23] The term "revolution" was used frequently by Quebec nationalists at this time, including Trudeau. Its meaning was broad and remarkably imprecise. So was the Bloc, which included right-wing Catholics, social reform Catholics, and others who simply despised both the Liberals and the Union nationale. Trudeau did not run in the election that summer, but he contributed financially to the impoverished party. Despite early hopes, however, it won only four seats. Maurice Duplessis used the nationalism card effectively during the campaign and defeated the Liberal government.

Trudeau remained loyal to the Bloc, but the fires of nationalism had begun to burn less intensely for him. Unlike Jean Drapeau, Michel Chartrand, and others who cast themselves energetically into the summer 1944 provincial election, Trudeau disappeared. He had applied again to the Mexican program of the Experiment in International Living and had spent the year studying Spanish. When he learned of certain restrictions the Experiment faced, he attached himself to a group of Canadian students who left Montreal on June 15 on a forty-day "goodwill" trip to Mexico. On June 7 Trudeau gave notice to his law firm and to the National Service registration. On the National Service form he first wrote "lawyer," then stroked it out and wrote "avocat," and provocatively added that the reason he was leaving was "La Bohème."[24]

Bohemian life in Montreal revealed itself to Trudeau in the late 1940s, mainly through Hertel. A mutual interest in the arts had initially brought him close to the Trudeau family, and he began introducing Grace and her children to some of the leading young artists of the time. Grace's brother Gordon Elliott had long been a friend and neighbour of the great French painter Georges Braque, and the Trudeau home already possessed one of his works. When the Canadian abstract painter Alfred Pellan returned to Canada after fourteen years in Paris, determined to break the shackles of traditionalism in Quebec artistic circles, Hertel became his champion. He arranged to hang a few modern paintings in the Trudeau home, which became, in effect, a salon where artists mingled with potential patrons in a time of political and artistic ferment. Pierre himself purchased three paintings—including a Pellan—from Hertel, who acted as an intermediary for some of the artists. He told a friend to pick up "a very fine [Léon] Bellefleur . . . from Pierre's room" which, he confirmed, Madame Trudeau would give to him.[25] Hertel, who occasionally wrote art critiques for Le Devoir, enthusiastically welcomed the European influences that Pellan brought back with him. He also encouraged Paul-Émile Borduas in 1941 as he moved from religiously centred representational art and portraiture to abstraction, when "the echo of an ideology more global" was first heard in Montreal salons—and in Pierre's bedroom, where the walls became adorned with modernism.[26]

Trudeau met Borduas through Hertel, and, in 1942, he often visited Paul-Émile and his wife, Gabrielle, and mesmerized

them—especially Gabrielle. She apparently went to a performance by Pierre in a play and was captivated by the younger man's
comic sensibility and dramatic presence. Like her husband, she
saw Pierre as a young revolutionary, albeit a peculiar one who
signed his entirely proper letters, addressed to "Madame Borduas,"
with "Citoyen." The following year her attraction moved to a
different level. "Good evening, my dear Pierre," she wrote most
familiarly on December 14, 1943, offering him "le plus grand
amour de la terre," the greatest love on earth. She was jealous, she
told him openly, adding that she hoped other women "would know
how to love you as fully as I could." She would not write more
for several reasons, one truly essential: "I deeply fear that I would
trouble your mother and, through her, Hertel, who is probably
her counsellor." She loved Grace because Pierre was her son,
because her son had her qualities, and because she had allowed
"an almost impossible friendship between us." However bohemian
he aspired to be, such a love affair—or such a future for the two of
them—surely was impossible. The relationship remained platonic
yet adoring.[27]

As Gabrielle knew, Trudeau had to take other paths. He
applied to Harvard, got his military service deferred, and went off
to Mexico for most of the summer. Camille had married Bill
Aubuchon Junior, a Franco-American businessman, in May 1943.
His family business was hardware, and the stores were found in
most cities and towns in the American Northeast. She invited
Pierre to the wedding. He did not go but replied, elegantly, that
he hoped "the man with whom you have agreed to share your
destiny . . . will show you all the concern that your tenderness
deserves." Over the years, he and other members of the Trudeau
family kept up some connection with the Aubuchons. Still,
although they had parted ways, Camille understood Pierre and,
as early as 1941, she had told him that he, too, needed to find
someone he could confide in and trust.[28] Obviously, Gabrielle

Borduas was not the answer, but, as she had recognized, he had begun to fall in love again.

Pierre had met Thérèse Gouin, the daughter of the eminent Liberal senator, Léon-Mercier Gouin, in 1943, when his friend Roger Rolland brought her to one of the classical music gatherings which Grace Trudeau held during the war years. Sometimes there would be a pianist; most often, young friends of Pierre, Tip, and Suzette would come to hear the best records on the expensive phonograph. Four years younger than Pierre, Thérèse, with her quick mind and glowing face, immediately caught Pierre's competitive eye, and he began to court her. When he left for Mexico in the summer of 1944, she was in second place on the list of people with whom he intended to correspond. There he wrote his first missive to her, in which he posed a question: Which was the greater civilization, the one Cortés founded or the one he destroyed? The brief postcard ended, "Amitiés du citoyen," Regards of the citizen. The language of revolution still persisted; so did Pierre's pranks.

In the late summer of 1944 as Canada faced a conscription crisis, the impish Pierre tried to attach a "No to conscription" label to the back of her father's jacket, just before he went off to his office. Thérèse stopped Pierre before he comitted this possibly fatal joke very early in their romance. That same summer, when Thérèse and Pierre were out together in a rowboat, he suddenly bolted to his feet and proclaimed, "I want to be the prime minister of Quebec."[29]

As Pierre courted Thérèse, he was attending plays and concerts and reading books in an eclectic fashion. Although his proposed course of study at Harvard was Political Economy, he read mainly literature, notably Paul Claudel, Stéphane Mallarmé, Arthur Rimbaud, Feodor Dostoevsky, and G.K. Chesterton. He also read and enjoyed James Hilton's *Lost Horizon*, whose exotic Shangri-La intrigued the adventurous

Trudeau. Law practice interested him little, military training irritated him, and political passions had waned despite his continued association with the Bloc populaire. In response to drift, Trudeau wrote a brilliant and revealing essay in 1943, "The Ascetic in a Canoe."

First published in the journal of the Jeunesse étudiante catholique , the essay was profoundly biographical and is a wonderful blend of descriptive writing and cultural analysis:

> I would not know how to instil a taste for adventure in those who have not acquired it. (Anyway, who can ever prove the necessity for the gypsy life?) And yet there are people who suddenly tear themselves away from their comfortable existence and, using the energy of their bodies as an example to their brains, apply themselves to the discovery of unsuspected pleasures and places.

A canoeing expedition is a beginning more than a parting, he said. Recalling his own search for the trails of the voyageurs between Montreal and Hudson Bay, Trudeau declared that "its purpose is not to destroy the past, but to lay a foundation for the future." He insisted that a canoeing expedition purifies one more than any other experience: "Travel a thousand miles by train and you are a brute; pedal five hundred on a bicycle and you remain basically a bourgeois; paddle a hundred in a canoe and you are already a child of nature . . . Canoe and paddle, blanket and knife, salt pork and flour, fishing rod and rifle; that is about the extent of your wealth."

On a trip by canoe, he wrote, there is a new morality, one where God can be gently chided, where one's best friend is not a rifle but the person who shares a night's sleep after ten hours of paddling. How does it affect the personality? The mind works in the way that nature intended, and the body, "by demonstrating the true meaning of sensual pleasure," serves the mind. "You feel the beauty of animal pleasure when you draw a deep breath of rich morning air right through your body, which has been carried by the cold night, curled up like an unborn child." Sometimes exhaustion triumphs over reason, and the mumbled verses of the first hours "become brutal grunts of 'uh! uh! uh!'" The humility one gains becomes a future treasure when one confronts the great moral and philosophical questions. He concluded, significantly: "I know a man who had never learned 'nationalism' in school, but who contracted this virtue when he felt the immensity of his country ('patrie') and saw how great the country's creators had been."

That man was Pierre Trudeau, and in 1944 that country, or "patrie," was Quebec, or "Laurentie."* His loyalty to its "founders" remained strong when he left Quebec in 1944 at the age of twenty-four. That October, before he embarked by train for Harvard and Boston, Thérèse visited him at home. She discovered

---

* The translation of this concluding sentence is by Professor Ramsay Cook. In the famous translation in Border Spears, ed., *Wilderness in Canada* (Toronto: Clarke Irwin, 1970), reprinted in Gérard Pelletier, ed., *Against the Current: Selected Writings, 1939–1996* (Toronto: McClelland & Stewart, 1996), 12, the nationalism vanishes: "I know a man whose school could never teach him patriotism, but who acquired the virtue when he felt in his bones the vastness of his land and the greatness of its founders." Professors Ramsay and Eleanor Cook had translated the original French for the Spears book, but when it was published, "nationalism" became "patriotism" and the "patrie" vanished. The Prime Minister's Office made the change, reflecting the Trudeau of the seventies, not of the fifties. Trudeau told Cook that he was the "man" who had not learned "nationalism" in school. Thanks to Ramsay Cook for this fascinating information.

that his strong sense of the past resonated deeply. He asked her to come to his bedroom, where he guided her towards a portrait of his father. Then, before his image, they prayed.[30]

—

Harvard University was an entirely different environment for Trudeau when he arrived in Cambridge, Massachusetts, that fall. A citadel of the English Puritan tradition, it had become a refuge for some of the finest Central European minds as they escaped fascist persecution. The university was filled with the wounded, the weak, and the foreign—but there were few women, except at the distant Radcliffe College. Yet it remained profoundly American, the self-confident expression of the swelling American sense of superiority in the late war years. Liberal democracy, after its failures in the 1930s, was winning a second chance on the battlefields of Western Europe and the islands of the South Pacific.

Trudeau, whose teachers in the late thirties had been frequent critics of bourgeois democracy, was now exposed to new arguments that profoundly challenged him. Although he had a law degree and a year of legal practice, he felt adrift. "The majors in political science at Harvard had read more about Roman law and Montesquieu than I had as a lawyer," he explained later. "I realized then that we were being taught law as a trade in Quebec and not as a discipline."[31] If his legal training was deficient, his knowledge of economics was pathetic. He knew nothing of John Maynard Keynes, whose economic theories were transforming not only the discipline of economics but also the role of the state in postwar economic life. Quebec academics and leading journalists knew that the province desperately needed a better knowledge of the revolution in economics that was occurring. In his memoirs, Trudeau says that his decision to study economics at Harvard followed a conversation with André Laurendeau, who told him that there were only two economists in Quebec and that the province lacked economic expertise. Trudeau had already met both of them, the academics Édouard Montpetit and Esdras Minville, and they, too, had strongly encouraged him in this direction, particularly when he told them that he wanted to enter public life.[32]

The great intellectual migration of the 1930s and 1940s from a disintegrating Europe recreated Harvard from a Protestant American cradle of the economic and political elite into a major intellectual centre through which flowed the stormy yet stimulating currents of twentieth-century thought. Very soon, and for the first time, Trudeau encountered Jewish intellectuals. Other professors, including Heinrich Brüning, the last German chancellor before Hitler, possessed thick European accents and deep wounds. Far more than the outer limits of the Canadian Shield, this new environment tested Trudeau. Domesticity and Montreal tempted him often. Suzette was marrying; his young brother, Tip, was soon to follow.[33] Fortunately, Thérèse, as she gradually captured his heart, helped him to endure Harvard.

Trudeau's Harvard experience was, in retrospect, intellectually rich; in his own words, Harvard was "an extraordinary window on the world" in which "he felt like being in symbiosis with the five continents."[34] He began his study of economics with the future Nobel laureate Wassily Leontief, who recalled bullets whizzing by his head in St. Petersburg in 1917 as the Russian Revolution began, who had studied in Weimar Germany, and who, in his twenties, had worked as an adviser to China's national railways before taking refuge in the United States in 1932. Within a decade he developed the first input-output tables for the American economy and made early use of a computer for economic research. He was a generation ahead of what passed for the discipline of economics in Canada in the early forties. In his class, Trudeau read Keynes, Kenneth Boulding, John Hicks, and Joan Robinson, although he remained respectful of Catholic practice when he asked the Boston archbishop if he could read books proscribed on the Index for his academic courses.[35] He learned quickly what was old (J.M. Clark and his long-winded descriptions) and what was new, notably Keynes's theory of general equilibrium.

But if some were charmed by Keynes, Trudeau's course in economic theory taught by the Austrian Gottfried Haberler clearly set out the case for the other side. Haberler, later a leading scholar at the conservative American Enterprise Institute, introduced him to more traditional views of what the state could and should do. The professor who left the most indelible impression was the Austrian Joseph Schumpeter, who fitted no categories but dominated a brilliant group of scholars at Harvard at the time. The gifted writer's 1942 classic, *Capitalism, Socialism, and Democracy*, argued that democracy's success, particularly its creation of an intellectual class, assured its doom, as the entrepreneurial spirit so essential for capitalistic renewal drowned in the doubting footnotes of intellectual debate in an advanced capitalist society.

Trudeau did well in his economics courses. His note-books reveal that he was a serious student of economics: he soon mastered both the new approaches that were transforming the profession and the increasingly high mathematical requirements of the field. Harvard economist John Kenneth Galbraith, who met frequently with Trudeau later, described him as a "first-rate economics mind of postwar vintage," a judgment his Harvard marks confirmed.[36] And here lies an enigma: Trudeau rarely reflected his economics training in his writings and, once he became prime minister, not only his enemies on Bay Street but also many of his colleagues and friends complained that he paid no attention to economics. Yet his training and even the lectures he gave to trade unionists in the fifties show clearly that he had a solid graduate education in economics. What he said was not original, but he was thoroughly aware of what the best students must know. Indeed, among Canadian politicians of his time, he ranked at the peak in terms of formal academic training in economics. Why, then, did he seem to put it to the side?

There are probably several reasons. First, Trudeau's Harvard training reflected a diversity of approach to economics that made the discipline much less confident than it had been earlier and than it was to become later. Keynes had created a tempest at Harvard, but traditionalists and the Austrian School, notably Schumpeter and Haberler, had battened down and resisted. From these two men he learned, in his own words, that Keynes had "expressed himself too vaguely, and can't be fitted to everyone's particular needs." Haberler, a strong personality ("Thus spake Haberler, May 3, 1946," Trudeau wrote on his notes), introduced Trudeau to Friedrich Hayek's conservative opposition to political Keynesianism.

Trudeau's comments on the texts he read reveal his intellectual excitement but also a growing understanding that economics was a debate, not a science, one that is grounded in political positions, economic circumstances, and the psychology of the crowd. "From Sept '29 to Aug '33 great losses were incurred," he wrote in his notes about Schumpeter's course. "Capitalists themselves lost faith in the system to a contemptible extent, and the Roosevelt administration had to cope with this psychological attitude." No fan of Schumpeter, John Kenneth Galbraith later reflected on the views he shared with Trudeau, notably "a consistent view of the inadequacy of those qualified simply by their possession of money or motivated only by the hope of pecuniary reward." Economics was, for Trudeau, not a mystical wand that

the wealthy could wave before the politician. Economic judgments were not the product of a science but more often the
result of special interests. It was a Harvard lesson he did not
forget. It moved Trudeau, who was himself a wealthy man, to
the political left.[37]

The second reason Trudeau moved away from economics
may seem paradoxical: by studying political economy, he finally
came to understand the significance of law. After his initial
encounter with the finest minds in economics, he moved on to
political science, which, initially for him, lacked the intellectual
excitement of economics. His course on comparative government offered by the distinguished British academic Samuel Finer
was, in Trudeau's view, too opinionated. More interesting was
Merle Fainsod's course on the Soviet Union, where he quickly
concluded that the British socialists Sidney and Beatrice Webb
were hopelessly naïve. Trudeau reached an important conclusion about political science and, perhaps, academic life: "The
more you read of [the Webbs'] seemingly thorough and detailed
analysis, the more you realize that respectable political scientists
can also indulge in pseudo-science."[38]

Trudeau also read several important contemporary works
on European fascism, and was profoundly troubled. He read
Franz Neumann's *Behemoth* sometime in 1945 and realized what
horrors Hitler had wrought. "Powerful work," Trudeau wrote in
his diary, "by an honest scientist, exceedingly well documented;
though written by a violent anti-Nazi, there is remarkably little
prejudice. The book in consequence is all the more convincing.
Shows all the power of Nazism, its awe-inspiring accomplishments; and yet analyses so thoroughly its cynicism, its militarism,
its fundamental, irrefutable irrationality." From Neumann's
work, Trudeau took an important lesson: liberal democracies
must prove that "efficiency" is compatible with liberty and that
"democracy is not synonymous with capitalistic exploitation."[39]

This important conclusion was the germ of his later beliefs that politics in a democracy must be "functional" and that romantic and unrealistic notions such as nationalism could be deeply damaging. Law is important not in the landlord-tenant disputes he had worked on in Montreal but in establishing the covenant between a ruler and a people. Positivist social science itself was insufficient because statistics cannot establish values. After reading Auguste Comte, he concluded: "The spiritual should have a decisive voice in education, but it should be only consultative in action."[40] This assessment marked a profound break with some of his earlier assumptions, and it remained a belief that was to animate his future public life.

Harvard and its professors made Trudeau rethink what he had learned and done. His past suddenly seemed parochial; all the excitement of Jean Drapeau's by-election, the plebiscite, and the debates in *Quartier Latin* seemed very different viewed through the prism of the violent history of the twentieth century. He realized, just as the Third Reich fell in the spring 1945, that he had been wrong.

> Will this be my great regret? In all my life, never to have raised my eyes from work of questionable value, tied to a hypothetical future, when the greatest cataclysm of all time was occurring ten hours from my desk. Or, does listening to one's conscience bring its own compensations for the losses it inflicts? And incidentally, what is true conscience, that which comes from reason or that which one feels intuitively?

Pierre had written these words to Thérèse Gouin in Montreal, and she asked for clarification: What cataclysm do you mean? He curtly answered on May 25, 1945, just as the Third Reich fell: "PS–The cataclysm? It was the war, the war, the WAR!"[41]

This exchange had a long life. George Radwanski was troubled when Trudeau spoke to him in the seventies about the war. He said, simply, that he had been "taught to keep away from imperialistic wars"—an explanation Radwanski found not "entirely convincing."[42] More tellingly, in his own memoirs, Trudeau seems to have an almost exact memory of the exchange with Thérèse. "It was only at Harvard, in the autumn of 1944," he wrote, "that I came to appreciate fully the historic importance of the war that was ending." Of course, it was not in 1944 that he wrote his letter to Thérèse but in May 1945, which was the actual date for the end of the war in Europe. He continued: "In that super-informed environment, it was impossible for me not to grasp the true dimensions of the war, despite my continued indifference towards the news media." Again, in almost exact parallel to his comment in May 1945, he wrote: "I realized then that I had, as it were, missed one of the major events of the century in which I was living."

Thérèse Gouin later recalled accurately that Trudeau had expressed doubts to her about the way the war had passed him by, but he never raised the issue again in his more than two hundred letters to her. Moreover, in his memoirs he refused to express any regrets for "missing" the "historic importance" of the war. "I have always regarded regret as a useless emotion," he said. At Harvard, he had "no time to indulge such moods."[43] The exchange reveals much about Trudeau: his exceptional memory, which retained exact details of his earlier thoughts and actions; his quick reactions to great events and his tendency to cast them in terms of his own personal narrative; and his willingness to change his views without pausing to admit he had been wrong. He had little patience with those who remained mired in the past, and, despite his great memory for detail, he could also close his mind to events and experiences that he deemed "chaff," a waste of time.[44]

In one powerful way, Trudeau's memory is correct: he did change at Harvard. From the debris he found around him in 1945, Trudeau, like the West itself, began a process of reconstruction. He realized that the law was not what he had learned in the "horrible" civil procedure class at the Université de Montréal or in the landlord-tenant tiffs he had handled in his practice. Rather, it was a conceptual framework through which he could understand change and help to shape it. His notes, particularly in his classes on political thought with constitutional scholar Carl Friedrich* and legal historian Charles McIlwain, reveal a curious and exceptional intelligence actively engaged in organizing his experience and his previous learning into categories of modern legal and political thought.[45]

The courses in general celebrated liberal democracy and were very different from what Trudeau had heard at Brébeuf. He recognized the contrast in intellectual climate and was sometimes uncomfortable. He "did not see the traces of fanaticism and ultra-democratic sentiment" in Samuel Finer's textbook, he said, that were sometimes present in his course.[46] Similarly, he had reservations about Friedrich's support of the Nuremberg trials, saying that "the present trials only give more legal appearance to things that could be done without them." Friedrich argued that the trials were important, even if "they deny positive law," because when a new "community" is created "it often overrules legal concepts." Trudeau was not convinced: "But if the emerging community imposed duties on the Germans, it did too on the

---

* On one occasion Trudeau took issue with Carl Friedrich on a question of philosophical definition. Friedrich apparently dismissed his comments, but then asked to see him and apologized for his brusqueness. Trudeau, as he told Thérèse, appreciated the gesture. Trudeau to Thérèse Gouin, Feb. 14, 1946, TP, vol. 48, file 17.

Allies. Shouldn't they be punished for having created a state of affairs conducive to war? Etc."* He himself was sceptical of the positivist and secular tone he found in many of his professors.

Trudeau did not become an American liberal democrat, but neither was he any longer the corporatist Catholic of Brébeuf days. Harvard, along with the success of the democracies in wartime, greatly altered his political thinking. Moreover, it focused his mind on the importance of the rule of law and its embodiment in constitutions—documents that could be used to protect minority rights. He remained deeply sceptical of the celebrations of British tradition at Harvard. He also retained a Quebec nationalist's resentment of the British impact on his people.

One professor, William Yandell Elliott, an anglophile, deeply offended him, and he responded by challenging him, at one time murmuring "son of a bitch" in class. When Elliott said that Robert Borden seemed an imperialist to French Canadians but a liberal to foreigners, and that R.B. Bennett put

---

* Trudeau was deeply troubled by another book, *The Day of Reckoning* (New York: Knopf, 1943), by Max Radin, a law professor, who had argued for international war-crimes courts. "Far from realizing its goal of making the trials for war criminals seem justified," Trudeau argued, "it raises a great many doubts—if not on humane grounds—surely on legal ones. I think it certain that if the (hypothetical) accusation was of an individual crime-murder-the trial should have been before ordinary tribunals of the state where the crime was committed. Before an international court, you can only try international crimes, e.g., who caused the war? But such a question can only be answered by history. The court's refusal of trial before German courts on grounds that it would take too much time is surely spurious." Trudeau continued to hold these views as prime minister when he argued against "correcting" history by compensating Japanese Canadians and in favour of trials of war criminals in Canadian courts. TP, vol. 7, file 21.

Canada first, Trudeau wrote: "But both would rush to defend Britain! . . . maybe their Canada First was Canadian pockets first." He put an exclamation mark in Elliott's statement that "G.B. prestige [came] as center of spiritual values[!] of freedom and toleration." The course profoundly annoyed him, as did the required readings. On one work he wrote: "There are any number of tedious repetitions and re-repetitions. But this seems to be the English way . . . Rather poor style; and many boring precautions, introductions, forewarnings etc. that the author thinks marks of a conscientious thinker."[47] Alas, Trudeau had the ill fortune to have two courses with Elliott and to write his major paper for him. One of these courses had considerable Canadian content, including F.R. Scott, J.B Brebner, and Stephen Leacock. Scott had impressed Trudeau very much when he spoke at the Université de Montréal in 1943 in opposition to conscription and the infringement of civil liberties in Quebec, but he was only a brief respite from Trudeau's general irritation with the course. Elliott assigned his own book on the British Empire as a text, even though it had been published in 1932. Trudeau was rightly contemptuous: "The Chapters were originally delivered as lectures, it seems. Which would account for the loose structure and loose style throughout. For all the rest would be forgiven, even a certain supercilious humor, if facts were not 14 years old."[48]

Trudeau submitted his major essay, "A Theory of Political Violence," to Elliott on January 20, 1940. He had consulted with him about sources several times, as well as with a new friend, Louis Hartz, who was to become a major theorist of American liberalism. Hartz, who was Jewish, had suggested that Trudeau study Mussolini, and Elliott had recommended, sensibly, that Trudeau look at Harold Laski, Tolstoy, and Gandhi. The essay, it seems, was written deliberately to offend Elliott. Trudeau, for example, said that the 1837 Rebellions should not be called by that term because "the 'Canadiens' were too realistic to believe their shooting would have much more effect than scaring the rulers into being a little less iniquitous." He wrote also of "our North-west Rebellion" as an uprising that aimed only "at getting a little more justice out of the Federal Government." One sees traces here of the debates in 1942 and Trudeau's flirtation with violent protest and demonstrations. He returned to Brébeuf form when he denounced the "liberal bourgeoisie" as "lovers of vicarious experience." Then came a remarkable paragraph:

> So I will say very little of [propaganda], else that I always feel a touch of hypochondria when I see how propaganda of a stupid sort can succeed in making people swear by absurdities one day, and die for the contrary absurdities the next day. "The sacred and worthless Atlantic Charter. The impossibility and necessity of conscription. Roosevelt for peace and for war too. Our friend Russia, the arch fiend. Beloved, execrable Finland Etc." Where mendacity in former times had to be whispered from mouth to ear, now that it is coupled with propaganda, every one in the land can be made to change his mind quicker than his shirt.

On the returned paper, Trudeau wrote beside this paragraph: "Probably the reason for my mark 'B.'"[49] Surely it was, but only in part. There were other reasons too. The essay, apart from its eccentricities, is weak. It drips with contempt for Elliott's anglophile views and for the man himself. Elliott was pompous but not entirely a fool. The paper merits his complaint that "it misses the systematic analysis and application of concepts." Too often it prefers the quip and the rhetorical flourish to the sustained development of its thoughts.

In Harvard's inflated mark system, the B meant trouble for Trudeau just before his general examinations, which, if passed successfully, would permit him to continue for a doctorate. He had done well in other courses, notably Merle Fainsod's course on Russia. Typically, he responded to the challenge. In May 1946 Trudeau passed his examinations with distinction—and left with an "A.M.," as Harvard eccentrically abbreviates its master's degree.

—

Trudeau did not like Harvard, even though he recognized that the experience and the education were intellectually valuable. Several of his classmates from his Harvard years have described him as "holed up in his room at Perkins Hall [the drab graduate residence], working ceaselessly to master the mysteries of economics and to cope with the heavy readings and essay assignments prescribed by his professors."[50] Unlike earlier student days, he did not participate in extracurricular events, and he made few friends. Traces of his Brébeuf flamboyance remained: the sign that he posted on the door of his room read "Pierre Trudeau, Citizen of the World"—though at Harvard its meaning was very different from what it would have meant at Brébeuf. His values were now increasingly cosmopolitan, a concept shunned by many of his teachers in the 1930s. His outlook changed. In many ways, Trudeau later minimized Harvard's influence. In an interview for the New Yorker in 1969, he spoke barely of Harvard but said, "I have probably read more of Dostoevski, Stendhal, and Tolstoy than the average statesman, and less of Keynes, Mill, and Marx."[51] The statement is absurdly modest and untrue.

Politics or, more accurately, the relationship between political action and political thought preoccupied him at Harvard. In his letters to Thérèse Gouin, he spoke almost never of literature but frequently of politics and, obsessively, of himself.* Trudeau, as Camille Corriveau earlier sensed, considered himself a loner and found intimacy difficult. Whether consciously or not, he took her advice that he must find someone he could trust and, with her, share his fears and hopes. He and his friends were invariably flirtatious in their relations with women, a trait that was common among young males at the time. Trudeau himself had become congenitally flirtatious, much like Clark Gable and Humphrey Bogart, the current movie stars. Yet proprieties were still often rigorous. After Tip's marriage, his wife, Andrée, wrote to Trudeau: "Pierre you are not supposed to write Xs to me because I'm married. They are for your girlfriends. Besides, they make me shy."[52]

In his isolation at Harvard, Thérèse Gouin seemed the ideal answer to his prayers. She had an eminent political lineage. Her

---

* The remarkable collection of letters between Thérèse Gouin and Pierre Trudeau is an archival treasure that reveals brilliantly two extraordinary young people as they fall in love and debate their times, dreams, and future. When their relationship ended, Thérèse returned his letters to Pierre, and he kept them in his personal archive. Madame Gouin Décarie did not expect that these letters would become available to any researcher during her lifetime. Pierre promised her they would not when they met during the 1970s. At that time he told her he had recently re-read the letters, and his comments about the war in his memoirs suggest that he also read them again in the early 1990s.

When the Trudeau private archive was transferred to Library and Archives Canada, the Gouin-Trudeau correspondence formed part of the donation. Because I had full access to the papers, I was able to consult the correspondence. I immediately recognized that, for a Trudeau biographer, it was the most significant portion of the entire archive. Moreover, Madame Gouin Décarie was one of the two or three most important influences on the young Trudeau. When I met with her to discuss these letters and her relationship great-grandfather Honoré Mercier was the founder of the Parti national and had become premier of Quebec in 1887 after a nationalist campaign that followed the hanging of Louis Riel. His son-in-law Sir Lomer Gouin, Thérèse's grandfather, became premier in 1905 and steered Quebec through the difficult war years; he opposed conscription in 1917 but then, in 1918, eloquently defended Confederation in a historic debate on a Quebec legislative resolution which stated that Quebec should leave Canada. After retiring in 1920, he became a minister in Mackenzie King's federal government from 1921 to 1924. His son Paul Gouin formed the radical Action libérale nationale in the thirties, the party that was popular with Brébeuf students, including Pierre

---

with Trudeau, she stated that she never expected that the letters would be read by anyone except Trudeau before her death. She had always refused to speak about her relationship with Pierre except with her husband, who admired Pierre. She said her reticence was, in part, a reflection of the agreement she had made with Pierre years before.

Once she became aware that her letters were in Library and Archives Canada, she travelled to Ottawa to read them. She wants them to remain private, but she recognizes the great significance of the correspondence for a biographer and has graciously allowed me to use the information I found in them. Her extraordinary generosity and warmth became evident as soon as I met her, and I immediately grasped why Pierre had become enthralled with this highly intelligent and sensitive woman. She and her husband, the distinguished philosopher Vianney Décarie, spoke freely of their enduring affection for "Pierre." They laughed easily about his pranks, complexity, and zest for experience. Of course, the "break-up" between Thérèse and Pierre created initial distance, but, eventually, both Thérèse and Pierre came to recognize that her decision in 1947 was correct, even though they retained deep affection for each other. When the Gouin-Trudeau correspondence does become public, readers will understand well why they did.

First baby picture, Pierre with his mother, Grace Elliott Trudeau.

On the boat to Europe. Front to back: Charles-Émile, "Tippy," Grace, and Pierre.

Grace Elliott Trudeau,
Pierre's beloved mother.

Pierre and his brother, Tip, already liked fast cars.

Pierre's last class at Querbes. Pierre is fourth from the right in second row; Pierre Vandeboncoeur is between the two priests on the left.

Class photo of the Belles-Lettres class at Brébeuf in 1936: Father Bernier is in the middle, front row; Jean de Grandpré is fourth from the right in the fourth row from the back, Pierre stands fourth from the left in the third row from the back and his face is turned away from the camera.

"Pour Pierre." The photograph that François Hertel, the influential mentor at Brébeuf, sent the young Trudeau.

The young Brébeuf scholar with his school badge in his lapel.

Throwing snowballs.
Winter, Montreal, 1935.

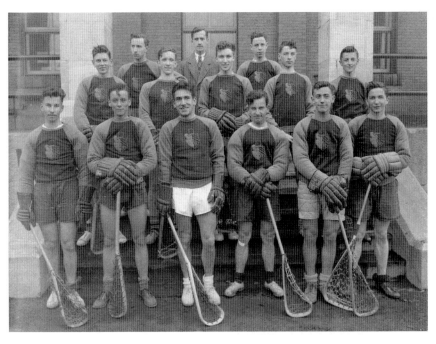

Pierre the team captain. Lacrosse, 1936. He stands in the middle of the second row.

Pierre (at back) at Old Orchard Beach. He had told his father he was not interested in girls!

Pierre with his first love, Camille Corriveau, at Old Orchard Beach, Maine.

Camille in 1940. Pierre found her as attractive as Vivien Leigh and Jean Harlow, his favourite movie stars, but this demure portrait disappointed him.

Camille and Pierre on the beach again. Camille introduced Pierre to both Proust and the kiss.

Trudeau, at the time. Pierre had heard him speak at the college in 1937, where he told the students and priests that he thought it his duty to battle Communism. He ended with the words "We are the sons of heroic Canadians and do not retreat before the sons of Stalin."[53] Lomer Gouin's other son, Léon-Mercier Gouin, a prominent Montreal lawyer and Thérèse's father, accepted an appointment to the Senate as a Liberal in 1940 and served as a deliberate Liberal contrast to Paul, who opposed the war and became associated with the Bloc populaire canadien in 1942. Rich, brilliant, attractive, and a student of psychology, Thérèse responded to Pierre's loneliness. She was a godsend to him during his two years in Cambridge, Massachusetts.

In the spring of 1945, just as his despair about Harvard deepened, Thérèse replied to a despondent letter from Pierre by telling him that she would see him in Boston on a study trip in early June. He was always careful when he wrote to her and sometimes produced multiple drafts of his letter. In his letter of response, he told her that, although he could speak to her more honestly than to other women, he had hesitated to write openly for several months.[54] That summer in Montreal, Pierre's springtime invitation to become "a friend" deepened into love. "Forgive me," he wrote on July 5, 1945, "for having slipped away without a gesture, Thursday evening. You appeared to be sleeping, and why should I awaken you?"[55] The formal *vous* became the personal *tu* by September, when he wrote from Boston, "this city of strangers," asking her for a photograph or a letter. He even attended some lectures on psychology so he could report to her on Harvard's Psychology Department.[56] She turned twenty-two that September; Pierre, twenty-six in October.

He began to write letters of remarkable intensity to her. The previous year, he wrote on September 26, 1945, he did not wish her happy birthday because of his natural reserve. But in 1945 he would wish her happy birthday knowing that she was ready to accept the joy and the worries and this strange being that was called Pierre Elliott Trudeau. And that was how he ended this early love letter.[57]

They soon became deeply affectionate, but the price for Thérèse was bitter complaints about his Harvard life. All was going badly, he wrote in October:

> I'm a misanthrope. I hate the Americans, their jazz, their cigarettes, their elevators.
>
> For almost three weeks now I've been trying to learn the virtue you recommended: flexibility.
>
> One has to be as flexible in life . . . Well, damn it, madam! I'm now in a room where you can hear all the neighbours' noises, the radios across the hall, the pianos downstairs, the elevators next door, the bands in the night-club, the kids in the street, the pacing upstairs, and the racket of the garbage men.[58]

The complaints continued: his work was "going to hell." In restaurants, thoughtless women sitting beside him blew hated cigarette smoke; in seminars, there were the abominable pipes. "I embrace you," he concludes this very long letter of complaint.

A few days later, on the eve of his birthday, his mood was better: "And so I am Pierre, I am 26 years old, I have passed my quarter-century, and for the first time [on a birthday] I have received an extraordinary and almost frightening gift." Her love had saved him from the arid and lifeless atmosphere in which he was imprisoned.[59] Yet, he protested, she did not write as often as she should. And there was the matter of the photograph. It was rather strange, he wrote on November 15, 1945, that almost every-one had a photo of his girlfriend except for him: "I who is—or you pretend is—one of your favourite admirers."[60] In reply, she play-fully dismissed his doubts and declared her love. In their letters, she became "Tess"; he, "my love" or, sometimes, "my little one."

He was demanding, complaining in one letter that she did not care enough about her physical health and that she should "work out" and not breathe the bad air on St. Catherine Street. Among his laments about his work and school, there were boasts about his own physical prowess, such as when he noted that he alone at the Harvard pool could do the swan half-twist.[61]

Despite his doubts about Harvard, he encouraged Tip to study architecture there with the German exile Walter Gropius. Tip, who clearly deferred to his older brother, took his advice after his marriage in June 1945.[62] The many contradictions in Pierre sometimes troubled Thérèse, and she chastised him often for being evasive. Their caution and Catholicism mixed oddly with the Freudian psychology that Thérèse studied and Pierre found intriguing. In planning their Christmas together in 1945, he wrote: "It would be so charming if we could celebrate the Nativity side by side." He dreamed of a midnight Mass together in the northern countryside, "but such plans perhaps assume an intimacy that is not appropriate or correct for us in the circumstances. Alas!"[63] He asked that his mother be involved in their plans together. And so she was.

Grace was, probably, present too often. Trudeau would later say that she "was a great respecter of the freedom of her children and was always prepared to take a chance." She allowed them to make their own decisions and did not impose her wishes.[64] Yet we sense in the letters how powerful her presence was to Pierre and how he yearned for her approval. Clarkson and McCall comment astutely that Thérèse "seemed eligible even to Grace Trudeau, who was notoriously sniffy about her son's female friends."[65] The freedom she granted created its own constraints. And she could be so intimidating. Thérèse told Pierre that she found Grace formidable. She said they talked often on the telephone, but "in front of your mother, I'm always afraid to show affection and to tell her how much I like her."[66] Yet neither her presence nor the eminence of Thérèse's father (whose Liberal politics Trudeau certainly did not share) inhibited the growth of their love. After he returned to Boston, he yearned for her presence:

> I've read your letter which had been waiting for me [in Boston] since before Christmas. I've found new reasons to love you, and thus to be even sadder. I don't yet dare take out your photograph because your real face is still freshly imprinted on my memory. But I think despairingly that just a few days will erase these ineffable features, that the taste of your mouth will elude me, that your heartbeat will vanish along with the soft warmth of your body. And so will begin my meditation before your image.

In conclusion, he quoted Walt Whitman:

> Passage, immediate passage! The blood burns in my veins
> Have we not darken'd and dazed ourselves with books
>   long enough?
> Sail forth—steer for the deep waters only
> Reckless O soul, exploring, I with thee, and thou with me.[67]

Trudeau desperately wanted to see her in the latter half of January, but his schoolwork was overwhelming; moreover, his mother wanted him to join her, Tip, and Andrée in New York at the end of the month. Thérèse also had school work, but he told her not to worry so much about her thesis. It was a means, not an end: "I want you to be a woman, Thérèse," he pleaded; "I don't want you to be an intellectual." Moreover, he was jealous of her associates at the psychology clinic who were allowed to dissect her soul, who knew more of "*my* Thérèse" than he, who talked with her about sex, masturbation, and other matters that he and she did not dare to raise. He was jealous of the way she turned herself over to "those who didn't truly care about her," while to him, who loved her, she pretended to "pacify" him with the assurance that he was "not neurotic." And she, he continued his rant, carried the blood of the daughter of a senator "and of the great Mercier! O shame, shame, shame!"[68] The tensions in this exchange — about her career, his ambitions, psychology, politics, and sex — intruded on the deep affection developing between Thérèse and Pierre. The strain reflected their place and their era.

Despite his desire for her presence, Trudeau had already begun applying to European universities for the fall term in 1946. He would attend classes abroad while continuing to work on a dissertation for Harvard, although he had not established a supervisor there for the work. In the end, he won two scholarships, one from the Quebec government to go to Oxford and one from the French government to study in Paris. With the war's end, the plans he had long ago made for study in Europe could finally be fulfilled, and he chose Paris. The French capital attracted him because he believed, correctly, that its spirit was markedly different from Harvard. Just before his general examinations, he complained to Thérèse: "The method of instruction at Harvard is the worst you can imagine. Everybody complains but nobody rebels. The teaching staff is recruited nearly exclusively of tyrants or megalomaniacs, with the result being a servile student body. Everyone simply follows the course because otherwise the professors will punish you. One does not study to learn something useful but simply to get the grades." He admitted that many of the professors were brilliant but deplored the fact that equally brilliant students were so servile.[69] Happily, his close friend Roger Rolland was also heading to Paris.

Thérèse and Pierre had begun to dream of touring the world, of transforming Quebec, of spending their lives together. She told him she would come to Boston at Easter with a friend. Her letter, with its news and its vision of a shared life, delighted

him, "for [he wrote in English] it was not the letter of the intellectual, nor of the psychologist, nor of the mystic, nor even of the
childish romanticist; but that of the *woman I love*." He found a
place for the two girls for thirty-five cents a day, near Perkins Hall,
and warned her that if she arrived with any of her "far-fetched,
incongruous, high-sounding and unconvincing complications of
the soul," he would have no patience.[70] At Harvard he showed her
off, and she was "wonderful advertising for Canada." Her sweet
presence still graced Harvard, the restaurant where they dined,
and his room after she left. Yet there were some problems among
the rush of expressions of love. It seemed to him that there was a
part of her that remained closed to him.[71] He admitted he was
often rude, complaining about her supervisor Father Mailloux,
snapping at her over dinner, but, then, "Thérèse, understand me,
I ask you on bended knee and with wet eyes to stop me from
becoming someone 'who loved not wisely, but too well.' I love
you too much to love you wisely."[72]

In May, after successfully passing his general examinations,
Trudeau delayed his return to Montreal for several days because
his mother had decided to come to Boston, which meant that
Thérèse and Pierre would see each other for but one week in
June. He had to return to Boston to receive his degree on June 26,
and she had to leave on a study trip. Although both their sched-
ules caused the problem, he said she was too caught up in her
psychology courses.[73] Just before he went to Harvard for graduation, he and Thérèse went to the annual meeting of the Quebec
bar, which was held, serendipitously, at the Manoir Richelieu,
close to the Gouin summer home. Along with her mother, they
all dressed up for the grand banquet. He returned to Montreal on
his fabled Harley-Davidson late on a Sunday night.

Surprisingly, after graduation, he went to work in the
Sullivan gold mines at Val d'Or, Abitibi—the company Charles
Trudeau had invested in after he sold his garages to Imperial

Oil. There Pierre truly went underground for a short time, and emerged with stories of hard labour that he used thereafter as the occasion arose, particularly with his sons.[74] His pay book indicates that he began on July 9 and ended on August 2, sufficient time to dirty his hands. "The work is hard," he wrote Thérèse, "the men tough, the food plentiful, the night cold, the flies bad . . . and," he added suggestively, "my arms are empty every night."[75] His pay was $5.65 for an eight-hour day, more than he had been paid as a very junior lawyer. His fellow miners probably did not know that the Trudeau family owned many shares in the company.[76] He concluded that, despite his hopes of getting to know and understand the workers, he remained different from them: "I am not assimilable. I don't speak like them, I don't think like them." Their drinking habits bothered the young ascetic, but he was more troubled, he said, by the emotional distance between him and the other men.[77]

The brief and solitary experience of hard manual labour does not seem to fit with the young intellectual he had become. What took him underground as a miner in the summer of 1946? He gave no answers then or later, but we can surmise that the purpose was similar to the journeys to the wilds of earlier summers. He possessed a profound desire to know "the other," and in the postwar world where labour and socialist parties thrived, the "worker" was an "other" that Trudeau believed he must know. In this instance, his disappointment was keen when he discovered that he stood apart.

That summer, before he left for Paris, Thérèse and Pierre talked often about marriage and about going to Paris together. Thérèse's mother whispered in her ear that Pierre was "a strange man," but Thérèse reassured her that even though he was, she still loved him madly. Moreover, the mother had come to adore her daughter's brilliant and rich beau, however strange he sometimes could be.[78] Pierre tried to get Thérèse more interested in politics, and he gave her a recent book by Harold Laski to read—agreeing, in return, to read one on psychology.[79] While he worked in the mine, she travelled to the Gaspé. In the end, they spent only a few weeks together in this summer they had long dreamed of sharing.

—

Trudeau left Montreal in September and arrived in France on the 29th, Thérèse's birthday. She wrote to him the previous day, asking where he was: "Today, I am 22 years old and I love you; tomorrow I will be 23 and I will love you still."[80] He did not respond until October 9, his excuse being that he had no paper and had lost some of his considerable baggage. Among the items he took to France were a beret, a Grenfell parka, a tuxedo, five suits, five sports jackets, eleven "chemises de ville," eight sport shirts, four sweaters, eleven jockey shorts, skis, his Harley (a treasured machine on Paris boulevards after the war), chocolate, jam, sugar, coffee—and cigarettes for his uncle, Gordon Elliott, who had returned to France after the Liberation.[81] Mocking himself and Thérèse's psychology studies, he said he had already lost his analism in Paris. In truth, he admitted he had lost himself in the quartiers, the courtyards, the grand boulevards, and the bistros of Paris.[82] In those times, so did many others.

Perhaps there was, in fact, no paper on which Pierre could have written. There was still rationing in Paris in the early fall of 1946, and the streets had few taxis, many military vehicles, and an emptiness that allowed a rich young Canadian student to race his Harley "across Paris at speeds that under other circumstances would have cost me my life—or at least my freedom."[83] Pétain, whom Trudeau had defended at Harvard, was in jail, his death sentence for treason having been commuted to life imprisonment. Charles de Gaulle, France's president after the Liberation, had resigned dramatically in January 1946, leaving an uneasy provisional government, including Communists, Socialists, and the right-wing group, over which the socialist Félix Gouin briefly presided. Soon after Trudeau's arrival, the French narrowly approved a draft constitution that gave women the vote. In the elections that followed on November 10, the Communists came first, but the third party, the Socialists, again provided the premier because the right quarrelled with the Communists. In the grand hotels, diplomats and journalists gossiped long into the nights as the Allies tried to agree on the shape of the postwar world, while prostitutes outside the peace conference offered delegates "an atomic bomb" experience.

Paris came alive after the Liberation. The clash of ideas between East and West, left and right, the modern and the traditional played out on a front along the Left Bank of the Seine, around the dining tables of the Café de Flore, or in cramped apartments crammed with books and Picassos. Jean-Paul Sartre, Albert Camus, Simone de Beauvoir, Maurice Merleau-Ponty, and others who came to dominate the footnotes of postwar Western academic journals created one of the great moments of the intellectual life of the twentieth century in Paris in these years. For Trudeau, the atmosphere was familiar in its uniquely French blend of the literary with the philosophical. As a Catholic, he became intellectually engaged in the attempt to reconcile Catholicism, modernism, and Communism, and this endeavour left a lasting intellectual imprint upon him. He was present, as one critic later said, in Paris during its "heyday."[84]

After staying at the Maison des étudiants canadiens, a student residence built in 1926 at the initiative of Canadians, Trudeau and Roger Rolland moved in the spring into L'Hôtel Square, a small but charming Left Bank hotel on St-Julien-le-Pauvre. There François Hertel, Pierre's former mentor and confidant, soon joined them. They had, as the hotel correctly advertises, "the finest view" of the magnificent Notre Dame Cathedral, and they all enjoyed their proximity to the intellectual and social turmoil of St-Germain-des-Près. The church on their street had become a Greek Orthodox Church late in the nineteenth century when secularism thrived in Paris.[85] Unlike Harvard, where Trudeau had no friends from Montreal, Paris had attracted seven other students from his years at Brébeuf, including Guy Viau, with whom he had canoed the Canadian Shield. Most of them, like Rolland, were studying literature and the arts, but Trudeau alone among former Brébeuf students opted for political science at the École libre des sciences politiques.[86] Other Montrealers, notably Jean Gascon and Jean-Louis Roux, guided their compatriots through the experimental theatre of Paris, while a future Trudeau minister, Jean-Luc Pepin, also studied politics.[87]

Aware of his presence in the city at a remarkable moment in the arts, Trudeau retained a pile of ticket stubs that indicate he saw, among other performances, Jean-Paul Sartre's *Huis-Clos*, Paul Claudel's *L'échange*, a private "Hommage à Jean Cocteau," as well as events with Walter Damrosrch, Artur Rubinstein, Jascha Heifetz, Leopold Stokowski, and Harry James. He also attended the opening of the celebrated Automatism exhibit at the Galerie du Luxembourg which featured Paul-Émile Borduas, Jean-Paul Riopelle, and other Quebec artists.[88]

With relatively light academic requirements, given his limited goal of gaining background information for his proposed Harvard dissertation on the vaguely defined but important theme of Communism and Christianity, Trudeau had freedom to indulge once again his love of the arts and, simply, to enjoy Paris. Now that Trudeau was united with François Hertel and Roger Rolland, the three quickly recalled an old trick they had learned together in Montreal. "Les Agonisants," or "The Dying," as Hertel, Rolland, and Trudeau dubbed themselves, performed their remarkable feat of suddenly going rigid, falling forward, and catching themselves with their hands only at the last second. In the salons and cafés of Paris they would appear to drop dead, one after another, before astonished Parisian innocents.[89] Trudeau comes alive in the photos from France, most tellingly in the images sent back to Canada by the French information service. Trudeau's brilliant eyes begin to dominate photos, and his physicality is obvious in the lithe contortions evident even in the still photography.

After his immersion in contemporary liberal democratic theory at Harvard, France took him back to familiar subjects in his personal history—most notably, religion. The postwar period proved to be a turning point in French Catholicism, and most of the contemporary French theologians Trudeau had encountered earlier at Brébeuf were themselves coming to terms with the war and its aftermath. In the lecture halls and churches of Paris during those years, the historic path to Vatican II was being paved as the Catholic Church modernized its liturgy, broke down barriers to dialogue with other faiths, and created a greater role for the laity. In early 1947 Trudeau attended lectures with Étienne Gilson, the great neo-Thomist philosopher, and, within a period of five weeks, he met the personalist Emmanuel Mounier, the Christian existentialist Gabriel Marcel, and the Jesuit Teilhard de Chardin, whose visionary linkage of evolution with Christianity deeply influenced modern Catholic thought.[90] He reported to Thérèse that he had met Teilhard, whom he found "formidable," but added that "Hertel was also formidable in his own way."[91] However, it was Mounier who left the deepest mark on Trudeau as the student linked his religious beliefs with his own sense of individual identity.

"It was [in Paris]," Trudeau later wrote, "that I became a follower of personalism, a philosophy that reconciles the individual and society. The person . . . is the individual enriched with a social conscience, integrated into the life of the communities around him and the economic context of his time." Although he had encountered personalism through Hertel and Maritain in the late thirties and forties, the war had fundamentally affected the concept of what personalism meant. In the courses he chose and the lectures and conferences he attended in Paris in 1946–47, Trudeau began to shape his personalist approach to religion.[92] He was, as always, a diligent student and, as before, he received permission from the church to read some proscribed books on the Index, so long as he kept them to himself. Among his courses, he studied with the renowned historian Pierre Renouvin and the sociologist André Siegfried, who had written two major works on Canada. He went on a student pilgrimage to Chartres in May 1947 and attended many other lectures on religious thought, especially with Hertel.[93]

These interests and activities captured the attention of his earlier acquaintance Gérard Pelletier, who was travelling through Europe for a Catholic fund for student victims of war. He had asked Trudeau in March to head a seminar on American civilization at Salzburg, Austria, that summer and to take an active part in the international Catholic youth movement.[94] Though Trudeau refused, he, Pelletier, and the other young Quebec students in France had begun to contrast the intellectual atmosphere in Canada with the passionate and open debates among Catholics, socialists, existentialists, and Communists that occurred in France and Europe more generally. Together, a group of these students wrote a bitter letter of protest home objecting to Premier Duplessis's banning of the celebrated French film *Les enfants du paradis*,[95] whose frank treatment of sexuality offended the church, but only one newspaper published it. Marcel Rioux, one of the Canadian students in Paris, recalls that "a negative unanimity" developed among these young intellectuals in this period against both the political regime and the hardened and ritualistic

Catholicism in Quebec.[96] It was a negativity that created the passion of positive commitment.

—

While Trudeau was wrestling successfully with his problems of religious and intellectual identity, his absence was creating difficulties in his relationship with Thérèse, problems that made him seek help to understand why he acted as he did. Paradoxically, Montreal seemed far away from Paris, despite the presence of many, like Guy Viau and Roger Rolland, who were part of the circle of friends they had shared in Montreal. Paris, where the left and especially the Communists occupied the postwar intellectual mainstream, radicalized Trudeau, who, like Emmanuel Mounier, sought to discover the intersection between Catholic thought and the egalitarianism of Communism. In these circumstances, Trudeau made little apparent use of the letters of introduction written by Senator Gouin to important Paris friends in which he described Trudeau as "a little like an adopted son."[97] Thérèse began to sense quickly that Paris was changing Pierre and that the rush of emotion that had overflowed in his letters from his lonely Harvard room did not flow quite so freely in Paris. Still, he began a letter on October 21, 1946: "This morning just before I woke up, I dreamt that you came into my bedroom and, to make me wake up, kissed me warmly on the mouth . . . it was so real, so beautiful, so good."[98]

But it was only a dream. He wrote less frequently than she expected; he asked how she found the time to write so often. He worried that she did too much, for "you are weak, a woman, delicate, precious and so petite. How are you able to prepare your course, your thesis, and the conference presentation and the evening course and [simultaneously] go through psychoanalysis, go to Mass, and do your exercises?"[99] But the bonds between them remained very strong: although he loved Paris, he said he loved her more. He wrote her on November 6 after looking at her latest photos: "Your last photo is stunning; with your hair swept back and your open mouth, you have a fire around you with the style of an Irish lass—and I love you always with all my heart."[100]

Thérèse expressed some doubt when she replied, indicating that their friend "D.D." (Andrée Desautels) thought Pierre should have a woman who was tall, thin, and fair, not one with the dark complexion and full figure that Thérèse possessed. She missed his presence profoundly, but with the reserve that marked young Quebec Catholics of their station, she added: "No, what I have to say has no sense and maybe cannot be said. I just feel like loving you. I think that if you were near me tonight, my darling, I would be 'coy,' resist you, play with you, evade you and then kiss you so hard and so well that you would feel faint. Therefore it is much better, my darling, that you are not near me."[101] How, after only two months apart, could they endure ten months? But for conservative young Roman Catholics of the time, the sexual revolution was far in the future. Courtship was prolonged, restricted, and titillating simply because sexual intercourse itself was inconceivable.

Despite their yearnings, they continued to disagree about her work and about the psychoanalysis she was undergoing as part of her academic course. He went to hear the psychologist Anna Freud, Sigmund Freud's daughter, speak at UNESCO and attended a seminar on love and marriage as a mark of his good will.[102] She told him—helpfully, she hoped—that her psychoanalysis made her realize that she was guilty because she had concealed some things from him. She did so, she added perhaps unhelpfully, because she felt in him "an insatiable curiosity" to know everything about her. She had no desire to live with Pierre "under a system of rules with exchanges and obligations," an attitude that obviously ruled out marriage soon. They should rather maintain an "essential" friendship.[103] Pierre responded to her in

early December, saying he was not really bothered by the suggestion that she should keep some of what occurred in her psycho-
analytic sessions private. However, he did not like her letter: "It's
the tone in which you speak to me, a tone that is cold, strange,
and even defiant." He admitted to being possessive, but added
that being together meant sharing thoughts, hopes, and events.[104]

Then, on December 10, Trudeau was rushed to the
American hospital in Paris for an emergency appendectomy.
The cost of the stay was meagre, about the price of a stay in a
modest Paris hotel at the time, but the anaesthetic was in short
supply. The operation was painful and the food scarce. On
December 13 he had to eat meat on a Friday, probably for the
first time in his life.[105]

From his hospital bed he wrote to Thérèse. He had
thought about their love and had come to realize that jealousy
was a deadly emotion. He apologized. Moreover, she should
now become his fiancée. On his back in the hospital, he had
realized that life without her would be impossible. He signed
off, "Poor Pierre."[106] She sent a message of love at Christmas, but
he had already left for Mégève, in the Alps, to recuperate. There,
his mood changed. He wrote her a letter a few days later in
which he returned to her earlier letter that had irritated him. He
again questioned her course of psychoanalysis. Once more he
was jealous, apparently because their mutual friend Pierre
Vadeboncoeur had passed on some news that displeased him
about the company she was keeping. He hinted that "André
Lussier" is more than "a friend"—but only the draft of this letter
remains; he never sent the final copy. However, in a letter he did
send on December 29 he admitted what he had intended to
write: "At this morning's Mass, I prayed for you. And I was
ashamed of myself, profoundly ashamed because yesterday I wrote
you a harsh letter that I knew would deeply hurt my 'Katsi,'" a
pet name for her. He apologized, but he remained anxious

about her associates and asked specifically about a friend with whom she went to a concert.[107] These fits of jealousy occurred even though Pierre and Thérèse had agreed that both could go to social events with others during their separation.[108]

The worm had entered the bud. Their letters alternated between abundant expressions of love and querulous doubts. On February 15 she was exasperated, not least because he had hinted he was enjoying the presence of a blonde. Indeed, he was. He had met Sylvia Priestley, and his agenda reveals that he saw her often that month. Thérèse called Pierre "cette étrange construction," this strange construction, and recommended that he consider psychoanalysis himself. In fact, he had already begun to visit a Paris psychoanalyst. He told her it was "cette dernière concession," his last concession.[109]

What survives of the consultations are the bills, which are high; the hours of consultation, which modern psychoanalysts tell me are unusually long; and Trudeau's transcript of his dream diary and his own notes of the sessions where he associated freely.* Psychoanalysis in the postwar period was thoroughly grounded in Freudian theory, and Trudeau's psychoanalyst, Georges Parcheminey, used Freudian categories to describe the process of

---

* I deliberately chose not to read these notes in full until I reached this point in my story of Trudeau's life, fearing they would influence the earlier chapters and sharing, I admit, some of Trudeau's doubts about overdependence on Freudian psychoanalysis for understanding the formation of identity. Once I did read them, I decided that the notes have great value, particularly because they confirm much of what Trudeau's teachers, school friends, and some scholars have surmised about him. But they also reveal subtle and even major amendments to the standard version of Trudeau presented in his own memoirs and in other studies of him. Still, there are problems with the document.

IDENTITY AND ITS DISCONTENTS   153

identity formation. Though a poor empiricist himself, Freud believed that psychoanalysis required a series of sustained sessions, and Trudeau's psychoanalysis reflected that belief. He went three or more times each week for appointments that sometimes lasted several hours. Fortunately, he found a psychoanalyst who mixed solid common sense with the heavy doses of Freudianism. He often told Trudeau not to take himself, his problems, or psychoanalysis as a science too seriously. Trudeau grew fond of the fifty-nine-year-old psychiatrist, whose commitment to Freud was so strong that he had courageously paid tribute to the Viennese Jew during the German occupation of Paris, and before German officers.[110]

The notes on the psychiatric sessions provide a snapshot of Trudeau at a particular and emotional time, February to June 1947.[111] They reflect those circumstances, particularly in their many references to his closest friend at that moment, Roger Rolland, and to Hertel, who lived in the same hotel room. They confirm Rolland's penchant for pranks and excursions but suggest little else about him. They substantiate Trudeau's close relationship with Hertel, but also his doubts about Hertel's fights with the church. He mentions Pierre Vadeboncoeur (nicknamed "the Pott") frequently, though in the context of his fondness for a friend whom he regarded as wonderfully eccentric. Unfortunately, some of the document is illegible, especially the part where Trudeau was scribbling down his psychiatrist's interpretation of his dreams or free associations.

The first dream, the night of February 11–12, sees him at the gold mine where he had worked the previous summer. A worker speaks to him about a nationalist book, which has been reissued in a deluxe edition. The worker explains that such writings displease the company management. Trudeau says he will buy the book, but not in the deluxe edition. The doctor gave this sensible interpretation to the dream: Trudeau's nationalism conflicts with his professional ambitions. In another dream that describes a speech by Henri Bourassa, Trudeau becomes troubled when someone he did not invite shows up. Similarly, when someone tells him that a Co-operative Commonwealth Federation candidate lost an election, he says, "Too bad," but then, when told that this candidate "got beaten in King's constituency," he approves, even though, earlier, he seems to have the contrary view. Ambition, nationalism, and socialism clearly clashed. There was, however, surprisingly little politics in his dreams.

In many dreams, his father was strikingly present and was regarded fondly and rather sweetly, such as when "Papa, on his return from Europe, ordered a 'frou-frou' cake, but a 'Canadien' brought him a half 'tarte' with whipped cream." In one session of free association with the doctor, he spoke of "great admiration" for his father but of impatience with certain of his mother's characteristics. His brother, Tip, and sister, Suzette, appear often in the dreams, without particular comments, but Parcheminey told Trudeau, who agreed, that he envied their more settled state, especially the fact they were married. Throughout the sessions, Trudeau talked about his fear of choice and the conflict between his wishes to tour the world and to have a "place." He saw a contention between his desire to be independent, which sometimes led to aggressiveness, and the contrary quality of caring about what other people think. Parcheminey told him it was a response to his timidity—a normal reaction when growing up.

On another occasion Trudeau described a dream in which he was walking along a beach with his mother when her brother Gordon appeared. Trudeau left them and went off with a young woman who was somewhat common and who told him he was good for nothing except skiing—a comment that pleased him. He then took a taxi, but the driver annoyed him by speaking English. He refused to pay him because he had not put on the meter. He concluded that this dream showed his dependency towards familial duty, his possessiveness towards money, and his sense of inferiority, which he manifested in his reaction to the skiing comment and his aggressiveness with the driver. In psychiatric terms, he wrote: "It is the combination of timidity and aggressiveness. I was not able to reveal myself openly in the genital phase because of restrictions. We saw, therefore, a regression towards the preceding phase, the anal phase. This frustration causes timidity and aggressiveness. [I show] possessiveness in the case of some things (money, adventures, and reputation, etc.) And these compensate for a genital phase that had not been achieved." When Parcheminey heard this interpretation, he warned Trudeau not to make too much of his own analysis and to avoid so much self-criticism—surely good advice.

When Trudeau talked about the development of his religious convictions, Parcheminey explained that they had become a restraint made even stronger by the sense of duty instilled during his childhood. He said that he had not found any particular castration complex in Trudeau which had been traumatizing, though there was "a certain blockage at the doorstep to virility" that had created compensation mechanisms through regression. In one of Trudeau's early dreams he leaves his friends to go in a car that has some beautiful women as passengers; another dream has him at a church, dressed in a bathing suit; and yet another has him finding a crucifix on a table and removing the linen that covers it. The psychiatrist explained that these dreams revealed how his religion conflicted with his "élan vital" and how he sublimated his strong sexual desires through his religious and intellectual activities as well as through sports and adventures. In the story of the cross, Parcheminey found a tendency to "asexuer le Christ." The genitals in these dreams are "dirty, unacceptable things."

Trudeau's mind whirled with these different comments. At that moment, he received a letter from Thérèse, who was at a retreat and fasting for Lent. Psychoanalysis, she told him, helps an individual to understand the self but not to change the self.[112] Pierre appeared to agree: after his many hesitations on the value of Thérèse's own psychoanalysis, he now seemed to develop a belief that the process could be helpful in fathoming himself.

Despite the costs in money and time, Trudeau persisted in his frequent trips to the psychiatric couch, where, his notes indicate, he hoped to gain insight into his timidity, aggressiveness, and sexuality. Parcheminey and Trudeau talked about homosexuality (which the psychiatrist said was curable, unlike schizophrenia), and he assured Trudeau that his absence of sexual intercourse with women did not mean that he had homosexual tendencies. He agreed with Trudeau, to use Freudian terms, that he often "regressed" to the anal phase, with its characteristic timidity, possessiveness, and occasional aggressiveness. Still, in Parcheminey's view, Trudeau's sexuality, although he remained a virgin at twenty-seven, was "normal." He had sublimated his strong sexual drive successfully because he was a believing Catholic, and marriage therefore had a special importance for him. In his own observations, Trudeau noted that abstinence and marital fidelity were much less common in France than in Quebec, even among believers.[113]

After a break at Easter, where patient and doctor agreed that Trudeau had no neurosis but that the sessions were nonetheless helpful, he returned for the final set that began in mid-May and ended on June 14, just before he left France. On his return, Trudeau said he wanted to focus on career and personal development, and both Parcheminey and Trudeau agreed that controlling his aggressiveness and impetuosity were important in that respect. They were, in the doctor's view, perhaps the result of his timidity and his lack of "visibility." The psychiatrist reassured him, after further discussion of a series of dreams, that there were mechanisms to cope: in Trudeau's case, marriage. "One or two years of married life, where the vital spirits would be able to find expression, where your virility would find its expression in the responsibility of the marital home, the contact with feminine softness, and the satisfaction of your sexual appetite."

After this discussion, the meetings continued for two more weeks, with marriage a central topic. Trudeau had a dream where a friend described a marriage gone bad, and another where his father confided in him how he had proposed to his mother. Parcheminey told Trudeau that it was probably true that his school and the strong moral authority of his home and his father were barriers to an "affirmation of self," but, step by step, adolescence and adulthood would lead to the solution of his problem, especially when he finally had intercourse within marriage. And so, to end the sense of inferiority and to achieve his desired virility, he must become "a man with a wife." The alternative was sublimation of his sexuality.

Parcheminey advised Trudeau that he considered the analysis ended. "One or two years after marriage, all should go well," he said.[114]

It would not be so easy.

CHAPTER 4

COMING HOME

During the winter months, Pierre and Thérèse had begun to consider spending their lives together. Senator Léon-Mercier Gouin, Thérèse's father, had even raised the question of a possible journalistic career for Trudeau in discussion with some publishers; and, in early March, Thérèse overcame her timidity in the presence of Grace Trudeau and attended a concert with her.[1] It appeared that, in Parcheminey's parting words, all would work out. And, sometimes, it seemed it would.

Thérèse finished her thesis, graduating *summa cum laude* and winning the major prize. Pierre rejected Gérard Pelletier's tempting invitation to lead a Harvard summer school in Salzburg and instead made plans for the summer with Thérèse in Quebec.[2] Yet jealousies stirred in Pierre, and doubts arose with Thérèse. Pierre went to dances in Paris; Thérèse, to concerts in Montreal. He yearned for her presence, but there were lapses in the letters and too many abject apologies. Although he complained about Thérèse's many friends and what he termed her silences, his own life was filled with parties, dances, and some other women in the spring of 1947. "If I wanted to make you jealous," he wrote to her in March, "I would tell you of a certain American or of Sylvia,* the daughter of the English writer [J.B.] Priestley."[3]

Grace Trudeau met up with Pierre in Paris in April, and mother and son toured the French Riviera together, sometimes on his Harley-Davidson, with the grande dame of Outremont riding behind her daredevil son. They saw the Ballets russes at the Casino de Monaco during the Easter break. She remained in France until June 6, only a few days before Pierre himself embarked for Canada.[4]

In Montreal's dreary spring, Thérèse dreamed that she, too, was in Paris, walking with Pierre along the Champs Élysées in the night, guided by the light of the fountains and the monuments while the fragrance of spring blossoms lingered in the air. As their hands softly embraced, she turned towards him, "his clear profile lost in the stars." She told him that she loved him and, she whispered, "I believe that you, too, are stepping towards love." In this letter, written shortly after Easter, she thanked Pierre for the chocolate rabbit he had sent but even more for his "love letter" and, above all, for his "great love."[5] On May 21 he told her of the romantic hotel where he dwelt and added: "If you would be my mistress, we would share the room together beneath the garret, between the dusty walls. The bed is low and rough, but your arms would be soft and your mouth welcoming . . . Every morning we would find a lost corner of Notre Dame and ask for pardon."[6] His desires were clear.

Yet tensions abounded. In his sessions with Parcheminey, Trudeau spoke surprisingly seldom about Thérèse but did have

---

* Priestley was second only to Churchill in his influence on the BBC in wartime. His broadcasts appealed enormously to the British working class. Trudeau told Thérèse that her father would not approve of Priestley's socialism.

visions of other women, including Thérèse's friend Andrée
Desautels, or D.D., who herself came to Paris in the spring. The
correspondence became intense yet less frequent, especially from
Thérèse. He wrote to her on April 16, begging her to write more
often, but before he sent the letter, he received one from her in
which she yearned for his return, while promising to meet him
wearing a hat of flowers when he arrived in July on the *Empress
of Canada*. Soon they quarrelled again about psychoanalysis,
and he protested strongly that she had revealed in Catholic confession that he was seeing a psychoanalyst: "a secret ought to
remain a secret," he bitterly complained.[7] On June 1, 1947, the
mood was different when he wrote to "My love Therese, my love-
able child, my crazy wise virgin." Still doubts persisted. He said
that "D.D." had spoken with difficulty about Thérèse. What did
D.D.'s silences mean? Why should he learn about her academic
success from others? A week later, after a bad dream about
Thérèse and an odd dream about "D.D.,"[8] he wrote an angry
letter, addressing her ambivalently as "My foolish love."[9]

> My very difficult darling, I have to rebuke you for being so
> worried, for being so full of fear and anguish. I pray for you
> often, as you have asked; but God is not pleased with you.
> He has told me that you were somewhat idolatrous and
> that you now find yourself being punished for worship-
> ping science above Him. You are playing God, and are
> becoming caught up in your own game. Beware that your
> game does not first trap you and, then, strangle you.
>
> My love, continue with your analysis, pursue it seriously
> and honestly. But don't take *tragically* that which should
> only be taken *seriously*. Believe me, Péguy's advice is impor-
> tant for you. Out of love for me—if you still have any such
> love left—do not try to do too much good. Remember that
> the arrival of this letter precedes my own arrival by only

three weeks; be tamer in those few days that remain. Your soul is peaceful; your spirit should be so as well. Do not fight, do not yell (I am using your own expressions). Do not inquire so persistently: you have not lost anything and you are not yet lost yourself. You are in my heart, I am holding your heart; yet I cannot embrace your spirit; it should be a more calm and more loving one.

Believe me, out of love for me I ask you to believe me; can you do so out of love for me? Don't take your analysis or [your analyst Father Noël] Mailloux so seriously in these few remaining days. You are so sad, and I hate myself because I am not there with you now. But give me only one half-moon, and I will be with you in Montreal. In the meantime, I urge you, at any cost, don't finish the analysis. You will have all summer and all of next year, and your whole life to do what you wish. But right now, ask Mailloux for permission not to worry so much: perhaps you can go to Malbaie for a few days, and, then, maybe you will see my ship go by in the distance, past the whistling buoy.

Parch[eminey] often warns against needless fears, against unscientific inductions, and against generalizations and systematizations. One must be calm and patient. You shouldn't believe in the bogeyman. Apparently, psychology students [like you] don't heed such advice.

We must not destroy all that time has slowly created. Above all, we must not systematize. My friend, my friend, my love, I wish so dearly that you would not be so sad.

~~Pierre~~ Me

P.S. I am leaving Paris on the 21st; you have time to send me a letter if you feel up to it.

Thérèse, I have just reread my letter, and I fear you will ignore all my words, instead choosing to portray me as ill-disposed towards psychoanalysis. You should not read my letter as such; I like your psychoanalysis, but I want you to do it better, in a way that is less caricatured. Either stop, or move forward "very cautiously."

The letter arrived just before Pierre reached Montreal, not on the *Empress of Canada* to be greeted by Thérèse in her hat of flowers but by air from Paris at 6 a.m. on June 22. They met again nine days later, and their love affair began to end. Years later Thérèse reminisced that, in the spring of 1947, she had decided that "if she and Pierre were to marry, they would have endured marital misery of a monumental order, 'un grand malheur.'"[10] Perhaps. Certainly, if the two privileged and brilliant children of the francophone elite had wed, their lives together would have been very different from the lives they did in fact lead.[11] Thérèse became an eminent psychologist.* Pierre would probably have become a university professor, a lawyer, or even a rich businessman. Again, perhaps.

What we do know is that he was most willing to marry Thérèse in the fall of 1946 and the spring of 1947 and that their relationship soured because of his jealousy, their professional ambitions, his suspicion of her psychiatric analysis—and his demand that she prematurely end it. We also know that, for a long time, they loved each other intensely in the peculiar fashion

---

* Thérèse became one of Canada's best-known psychologists, the author of several important works on the psychology of children, and an interpreter of the experimental psychology of Jean Piaget. An outstanding researcher and academic, she became an Officer of the Order of Canada in 1977 and served as president of several psychology associations.

of their different time and place. Theirs was not a physical relationship but it was intensely emotional. For that reason, we know
that when Thérèse ended their love affair, the disappointment
shattered Trudeau more than any other event since the loss of
his father. He wrote to her brother Lomer on July 10: "It is exactly
24 hours ago that your sister removed all reason for me to live."
Men, he said, cannot survive such deep wounds. And because he
sensed there was a certain empathy between Lomer and himself,
he asked him to discover whether Thérèse could even "bear my
presence." Could they meet just once more? He ended with the
signature, "Your lamentable, etc. Pierre."[12]

Brothers, of course, are seldom useful in such cases, but
Pierre did try to meet "Tess" once more at the Gouins' summer
home in Malbaie on the St. Lawrence, but Thérèse, to her mother's
distress, would not see him. Trudeau stayed the night but left the
morning of July 27, without talking to her. The next year she fell
in love with Trudeau's friend Vianney Décarie, a young philosopher. In the late spring of 1948, as Vianney and Thérèse were
dining at the apartment of Jean-Luc Pepin in Paris, there was a
knock at the door. It was Pierre, Jean-Luc's former classmate, but
he had come to see Thérèse. This time they did speak, but when
Thérèse told him she was now engaged, he simply shrugged. In
that case, he said, he would tour the world alone.[13]

Their paths crossed often in the future, Trudeau saved
press clippings about the increasingly eminent psychologist
Thérèse Décarie,[14] and Vianney published in *Cité libre*—the
journal Trudeau edited for several years. In 1968 the Décaries,
both then professors at the Université de Montréal, circulated a
petition soliciting support for the candidacy of Pierre Trudeau
for the leadership of the Liberal Party.[15] There's also a story,
repeated by Stephen Clarkson and Christina McCall, that, after
Trudeau became prime minister, Thérèse went to Ottawa and
asked a staff member in the Prime Minister's Office if she could

see him and offer her congratulations. Trudeau was not there, but she asked for a sheet of paper, wrote *Thérèse* on it, kissed it, and left the lipstick-stained note on the desk.

Madame Gouin Décarie laughs when asked about the story. There was neither the visit nor the lipstick on the paper: it was a prank by their mutual friend and congenital prankster, Roger Rolland, who was then a speechwriter for Trudeau. There is only one note from Thérèse in Trudeau's papers after their love affair ended. It is undated, but was surely written in 1969 when his political fortunes began to fall after the triumphant election of 1968. "Pierre, our Pierre, what has happened to you? You always seem angry. Your eyes are spiteful, and you appear mean." She cautioned him that those around him and those he must rely on would not understand. She ended gracefully: "We think so often of you. Thérèse."[17] The note lacks lipstick but not affection and dignity.

Thoroughly romantic, Trudeau deeply mourned the end of their relationship. It was, admittedly, an affair that seemed to flourish best when they were apart and one that faced many constraints. Still, its end was a decisive moment in the career of Pierre Trudeau. That summer in Montreal he seemed adrift. He saw a few old friends, including some women. In his quest for solitude, he journeyed by foot the hundred miles from Montreal to Lac St-Jean, experiencing the rough charms of La Mauricie, its surging rapids, deep forests, and high waterfalls.[18] In early August he took his first flying lesson, and continued the classes every day for two weeks in a Curtiss-Reid plane. He managed to fly solo on September 3, but he does not appear to have earned a permanent flying licence, although in the early fifties he did take up gliding.

During the remaining few weeks of the summer and early fall, Trudeau did not sulk as jilted lovers sometimes do. His calendar was full and interesting. On July 7 he had lunch with his friend Gérard Pelletier, and he spent the evening with his erstwhile revolutionary companion François Lessard and his wife. In mid-August he went to Toronto with Catholic youth leader Claude Ryan, who would later become a rival and a Quebec Liberal leader— they were hoping to found a coordinating committee of Canadian Catholic associations. Pelletier, a key organizer, was unable to accompany them because he lost his train ticket. In Toronto, Trudeau met Ted McNichols, whom he described as a Protestant and a Communist. The meeting featured "lively discussions on democracy and the possibility of reconciling [democratic] life with Communism." On his return, he went north on his motorbike, where he met an acquaintance whose girlfriend reminded him poignantly of Thérèse. He spent an evening with François Hertel, who was also back in Montreal, and visited Abbé Groulx. He spoke to Claude Ryan on Hertel's behalf, probably to explore whether his old mentor, who had by now left the Jesuits but not the church, could find work with the groups Ryan was organizing.

—

In September, Trudeau left Montreal once more for study abroad, this time at the London School of Economics (LSE). Within a month he would celebrate his twenty-eighth birthday. He travelled in a first-class berth on the *Empress of Canada*, and among his fellow passengers were Allan Blakeney, the future Saskatchewan premier, and Marcel Lambert, later Speaker of the House of Commons, both in tourist class.[19] Significantly, before he departed, he made certain that his Quebec links were strong. On September 8 he had lunch with Lomer Gouin; met at 3:30 with Gérard Filion, who became editor of *Le Devoir* in 1947; and followed with a call on the conservative nationalist Léopold Richer, with whom he spoke about possible articles for the journal *Notre Temps*. The following day he saw Claude Ryan again and had dinner with Hertel in the evening. Hertel was, in that month, his closest companion. He also had lunch with his classmate

Charles Lussier, now a promising lawyer, at the home of Paul Gouin, Thérèse's uncle, the former radical Liberal politician. And just before his departure, he met with the eminent civil libertarian, law professor, and poet F.R. Scott at the McGill Faculty Club.[20] Altogether, Trudeau's agenda for the summer of 1947 confirms his strong political interests and his continuing links with Catholic youth groups (Pelletier and Ryan), with Liberals (Gouin), with socialists (Scott), and with older and more traditional Quebec nationalists (Groulx, Hertel, Lessard, and Richer). Already he was preparing for his future. He was keeping many options open.

What did he discuss at these meetings? Career most likely, his education probably, politics certainly. Some hint of Trudeau's mood in these times is given in a letter to him from Lomer Gouin in the fall. Lomer, who had begun practising law, told Trudeau that he reminded him of "a bit of champagne that had turned into vinegar: you are full of effervescence, of young courage, but the taste is bitter." He would never make a good saint, but he was "ripe" for politics, a profession where saints, apparently, did not thrive. Gouin encouraged him to halt his travelling and his studies and return home. There would be elections in the spring, and Pierre should run, presumably as a Liberal candidate.[21]

Confusion and contradiction more than emptiness seemed to mark Trudeau's life in late 1947. He entered a doctoral program in political science at LSE in October, even though his Harvard doctoral thesis remained undone. And London, he soon found, was not Paris. The cluster of intense, madcap Brébeuf and Montreal friends was missing, and Trudeau stayed aloof, just as he had at Harvard. Paul Fox, a classmate and later an eminent Canadian political scientist, recalled that Trudeau seemed like a "young nobleman on a Grand Tour, very intelligent but quite disengaged."[22] As at Brébeuf, Trudeau deliberately concealed parts of himself, revealing only what seemed appropriate to the circumstances. His past, however, had made him, and the traces were clear: some he followed fitfully; others he began systematically to efface.

One trace was indelible: his commitment to Roman Catholic Christianity. But the nature of that commitment was changing. He could still write a letter that would have satisfied the most traditional of his Brébeuf teachers. At Easter 1947, for example, he had written to Thérèse about "the Christ of the Passion," who had come to represent for him the fundamental humanity of Christ. Christ's last days, he continued, were filled with uncertainty, betrayal, and defeat. He was no more than a poor fisher, and that humility bore His essential message to us. To the ever devout François Lessard, he sent a postcard that same Easter that ended with the words "Christ is King!"[23] In Paris he had paid scant attention to the atheist existentialism of Jean-Paul Sartre, Albert Camus, and Simone de Beauvoir, but Paris had nevertheless jolted him loose from the restraints on behaviour that Catholic devotion had previously entailed. In particular, his extended encounter with Freudian psychology at the dawn of the age of Kinsey began to loosen the religious bindings on his sexual behaviour.* Trudeau's faith was becoming more personal and less responsive to ecclesiastical authority and tradition, and in this respect he reflected his more fully defined personalist approach to religion and Catholic belief. While remaining a believer, he was

---

* The Toronto conference of young leaders that Trudeau, Claude Ryan, and others attended in August 1947 indicates that most Canadian young people were conservative in their personal behaviour. The meeting discussed a poll taken in 1945 of 57 Catholics, 56 of whom went to church every week. They were all opposed to gambling; 40 were opposed to drinking; and only 26 were supportive of "kisses and caresses" between unmarried men and women. All said they were opposed to going further than kisses and caresses — a frontier Trudeau was soon to cross. TP, vol. 8, file 16.

becoming a sceptic towards the Quebec Catholic Church, which, in his opinion, lacked the breath of contemporary life.

Some critics have pointed to contradictions in Trudeau's beliefs at this time. They certainly exist, as is to be expected in a man of his age, though his papers make it clear that they derived less from uncertainty on his part than from the influence of old friendships and relationships. He maintained close ties with the increasingly conservative and nationalist Quebec journal *Notre Temps*, in which he had invested the considerable sum of $1,000 in 1945. It had emerged from the rubble of the Bloc populaire canadien, where conservative and leftist nationalists had briefly embraced during the war. Subsequently, it had become increasingly supportive of the conservative provincial government of Maurice Duplessis and his Union nationale party.[24]

In the spring of 1947, Trudeau had told Thérèse that he felt angry with Canada and that he intended to write a critical essay about his country. And, soon after he arrived in London, he produced a long article, "Citadelles d'orthodoxie," which *Notre Temps* published in its October issue. As the title implies, Trudeau attacked the "orthodoxies" of contemporary Quebec society. While acknowledging that the conservatism of Quebec society had been essential in the resistance to assimilation, he deplored the way religion and nationalism had become stale "orthodoxies" that suffocated citizens who sought to be free, "without a system." The article is curiously vague and refers to only two individuals, the nationalists Henri Bourassa and Paul Gouin. Trudeau linked both of them with the "courageous" initiatives of the Bloc populaire. On the whole, the article lacks clarity, detail, and force; it reflects a mind in motion, but one whose direction is still unclear.[25]

Another major change came in Trudeau's political understanding and outlook. Both the classrooms and the streets of Paris had taken him on paths that led towards the political left. At

Harvard he had attended a couple of "socialist" gatherings, mainly out of curiosity. In Paris the Communists carried the cachet of wartime resistance and the promise of a revolutionary future. Trudeau was intrigued, particularly by the attempts of French Catholics to come to terms with the challenge of Communism. The eminent philosopher Emmanuel Mounier cast away the remnants of corporatist thought, which Vichy and wartime Belgium had discredited, and took up the cause of Christian socialism and opposition to the role of American capitalism in the postwar world. In his journal, *Esprit,* he linked personalism and Marxism, pointing out that both were concerned with alienation in modern industrial society. He saw the Communist revolution that was stirring in postwar France as a means of rejuvenating Christianity itself.[26]

These thoughts intrigued Trudeau. When the excitement of the Parisian streets drew him into the mass movements of the left, he had related to Thérèse how a demonstration had carried over from the revolutionary cafés of the Left Bank to the government institutions on the Right Bank; how he had been surrounded by police but managed to escape, then waved "bye-bye" in the depths of a Métro station.[27] More seriously, he listened attentively as Mounier and other French Catholics turned to socialism to reinvigorate Christianity.

While still in Paris, Trudeau had begun to tell friends that the thesis he would finally write would not focus on a narrow academic subject but would make a major contribution to the grand debate about the reconciliation of Catholicism and Communism. Long into the nights that year he debated with Gérard Pelletier whether anyone could reconcile Communism and the Catholic faith. Later, before the Iron Curtain crumbled, Pelletier candidly admitted the attraction Communism offered in those years. His French friend at the time, Jean Chesneaux, said that the logic of Christianity compelled a Christian to be a Communist in the postwar years. Trudeau, Pelletier continued, was more informed, more rational, yet in those times, in "the pile of rubble Europe had become . . . with neighbourhoods . . . flattened by bombs, and where Auschwitz and Dachau were horrible testimony to the bankruptcy not only of fascism but also of pre-war conservatism, Communism was a temptation or, at the very least, intriguing to a young practising Catholic."[28]

The London School of Economics was poorly suited for the study of Catholicism but ideal for academic work on Communism. Although it already had some eminent conservative thinkers, notably Friedrich Hayek, whose 1944 classic, *The Road to Serfdom*, was a brilliant attack on state planning, the school was rightly identified with the British Labour Party and with socialism. Sidney Webb, whose admiring work on the Soviet Union Trudeau had scorned at Harvard, had founded the LSE in 1896 to advance "socialist" education. Britain's postwar Labour prime minister, Clement Attlee, had taught there, but its most noted faculty member when Trudeau arrived was Harold Laski, a political scientist and Labour Party adviser. Laski had taught at McGill during the First World War, knew the United States well, and was a highly controversial public figure because of his continued praise for the Soviet Union as the Cold War began. He was, moreover, a brilliant lecturer—Trudeau described him as having an "absolutely outstanding mind"—who encouraged debate among his adoring students. Ralph Miliband, a British Marxist political scientist, recalled how Laski came up by train during the war to lecture in Cambridge:

> The winter was bitter and train carriages unheated. He would appear in his blue overcoat and grotesquely shaped black hat, his cheeks blue with cold, teeth chattering, and queue up with the rest of us for a cup of foul but hot coffee, go up to the seminar room, crack a joke at the gathering of students who were waiting for him, sit down, light a cigarette

and plunge into controversy and argument; and a dreary
stuffy room would come to life and there would only be a
group of people bent on the elucidation of ideas. We did not
feel overwhelmed by his knowledge and learning, and we
did not feel so because he did not know the meaning of
condescension. We never felt compelled to agree with him,
because it was so obvious that he loved a good fight and did
not hide behind his years and experience.[29]

Trudeau cared little for London but very much for Laski. He
became a major intellectual and, to a lesser degree, personal
influence on the young Canadian. A decade after Trudeau had
written the anti-Semitic *Dupés*, only five years after he had questioned Jewish immigration and participated in a riot where Jewish
windows were smashed, his mentor was a Jew and a socialist.
    In the formal ways of even the socialist English, Laski
required students to send him a letter requesting their first
appointment. Trudeau saw him at 3:15 on October 8, and he
asked Laski to be his thesis supervisor and told him he would
like to research the relationship between Communism and
Christianity. Trudeau, it seems, impressed Laski immediately:
he agreed to supervise his thesis and allowed him to attend several of his seminars. Trudeau's schedule indicates that he had
classes with Laski on "Democracy and the British Constitution"
for over three hours every Monday afternoon, another seminar
on "Liberalism" every Tuesday, and a final one on "Revolution"
every Thursday.[30] Trudeau claimed later that, when he left
London, "everything I had learned until then of law, economics,
political science, and political philosophy came together for
me."[31] Certainly it was not "together" when he arrived, as the
prolix and opaque "Citadelles" article demonstrates. Harold
Laski became, for Trudeau, a model: an engaged intellectual
whose philosophical and political thought had influenced one

of the major movements of the twentieth century—the British socialist movement as embodied in the Labour Party. Laski and the experience of the postwar Labour government was, he wrote to a friend, "excellent training" that made him anxious to return to Canada and to play his own part in politics.[32]

Laski may have influenced Trudeau in another way. He wrote superb accessible prose that Labour backbenchers, trade unionists, and Oxford dons could all appreciate. He began his work on the state with this gem: "We argue, as with Aristotle, that the state exists to promote the good life. We insist, as with Hobbes, that there can be no civilization without the security it provides by its power over life and death. We agree, as with Locke, that only a common rule-making organ, to the operations of which men consent, can give us those rights to life and liberty and property without the peaceful enjoyment of which we are condemned to a miserable existence."[33] In London, Trudeau's mind became clearer, his prose sharper, and his political ambitions more strongly defined.

Trudeau brought from France his interest in the reconciliation of Christianity and Communism. But as the Labour Party under Foreign Minister Ernest Bevin joined the Western alliance against the Soviet Union, Laski became a critic of his own party, believing that it was Labour's first interest to come to terms with Soviet Communism, which, even though corrupted by power, represented the ideal of economic equality and justice without which there could be no true democracy. These views influenced Trudeau deeply, and he quickly moved outside the North American liberal mainstream represented by men such as Arthur Schlesinger and Lester Pearson, both of whom argued that Soviet Communism represented a fundamental threat to the principles of individual liberty and the practice of democracy. Laski's views on the Soviet Union and his later writings have aged badly; indeed, critics at the time said that his work seemed "very old-fashioned," especially in his insistence, after the Nazi catastrophe and the evidence of Soviet imperialism, that capitalism was the greatest enemy of human freedom.[34] Still, Laski's views found echoes on the French Catholic left, where Communism was a political force, and they resonated with the young Trudeau, who followed those debates closely.

Laski also influenced Trudeau's interest in federalism, a topic of paramount importance in his later writings. He was a major theorist on federalism who argued, much like the later Trudeau, that authority should reside where "it can be most wisely exercised for social purposes." Later he shifted to the view that the central government should have primacy because of broader social needs.[35] In this respect, trade unions have a fundamental obligation to become directly involved in political activity, both for the workers as individuals and for the working class in a pluralist democracy. Laski lamented the fact that American unions stood apart from the political process.

Trudeau had demonstrated little interest previously in the Canadian labour movement, which had advanced quickly in wartime, but in France and now in Britain he was witnessing first hand a different model, one he came to believe could be adapted to the political circumstances of Quebec. When he eventually returned to Canada, he immediately sought out labour leaders and spoke to the leaders of the Co-operative Commonwealth Federation, Canada's socialist party, which was slowly moving towards a close embrace of the Canadian labour movement.[36]

The impact of his work with Laski was already evident in an article he wrote for Notre Temps in November 1947. He followed his professor in emphasizing that a system of law bestows "a certain order of things that guarantees sufficient justice that no revolution occurs." Similarly, he criticized the previous Liberal government of Joseph-Adélard Godbout because it had relied on the federal government to correct social and economic abuses, but in a way that abused the distribution of powers set out in the

Canadian Constitution. The present Duplessis government, in contrast, abused the people of Quebec by refusing to enact social reforms, arguing that the Constitution prevented it from acting in these areas. Still, there was a chance for Quebec to act. It was not too late if Quebec rejected orthodoxy and if the people showed their disgust for the elites and their rigidity. If they did not, he would not hold much hope "for our Christian and French civilization which our ancestors created with so many hopes." However, if Trudeau came to agree with Laski on the importance of a politicized and active trade union movement, he disagreed on one major item.

Unlike the atheist Laski, Trudeau was very active in Catholic circles in England. In early January he attended a conference on "Existentialism and Personalism" in which the French intellectuals Emmanuel Mounier and Gabriel Marcel participated. It was also at this time that he began to study the works of Cardinal Newman and to participate in Catholic youth discussion groups. He joined the Union of Catholic Students and helped to collect books to ship to Catholic universities in Germany.[37]

Otherwise, he fraternized little with other Canadian students, who mostly lived in crammed student rooms. He, in contrast, could afford better accommodation—he lived at 48 Leith Manor in the tony Kensington section of London, met with the great names of academic life,* and raced his motorbike around

---

* Modern students can only envy Trudeau, because it is unusual for students to meet the great names of academic life. In London, Trudeau met with the famed Fabian socialist G.D.H. Cole (an "anti-papist") and Harold Laski on October 8, soon after his arrival. The next morning he met with Ritchie Calder, a celebrated journalist and politician. Within two months, he had attended lectures by the Labour intellectual Richard Crossman, the historian Arnold Toynbee, and the philosopher Bertrand Russell.

the city and through the narrow trails of the British country-side.[38] On the Harley-Davidson, he travelled 1,725 miles through England and Scotland, apparently following the shoreline as much as possible and staying in youth hostels when he could. On some weekends he disappeared to Paris, memorably when his wild, good-looking friend Roger Rolland married there on March 20, 1948. Suzette, who had a taste for gossip, reported to her brother that Madame Rolland had told her she was astonished at the marriage because she did not know her son was interested in women.* Pierre, the best man, was overcome at the wedding and could not find the words he wanted to say at the reception after-wards.[39] It was an unusual lapse, but, given his own recent loss of Thérèse, completely understandable.

The spring brought uncertainty and illness. In February, he contracted a virus, accompanied by diarrhea, which led to several trips to a Harley Street doctor and a stay in the Charing Cross Hospital. He thought about returning home, and his family, partic-ularly Suzette, who fretted about Pierre as older sisters often do, urged him to do so. He wrote to a "Monsieur Caron" about a teach-ing position at the Université de Montréal, adding in his letter that he had always aspired to be in "active politics one day or another."[40]

At the same time, unknown countries far away from home still beckoned. Trudeau had dreamed of a world tour while at Brébeuf, had tantalized Thérèse with the romance of travelling together around the globe, and had developed contacts with diverse people in several countries who might assist his passage. He had met the young Jacques Hébert at a Catholic gathering in

---

* Roger Rolland denies Suzette's tale, pointing out that his mother knew of his many girlfriends (including Thérèse Gouin). She was upset that she had not met Roger's fiancée. Letter from M. Rolland, June 7, 2006.

the summer of 1946, and the two quickly became friends after Hébert regaled Trudeau with tales of his travels to exotic locales. A rebellious student like Trudeau, Hébert, four years his junior, had been sent by his father to Prince Edward Island to learn English after he was expelled from a classical college. Hébert then began a life of travel, and his tales intrigued Trudeau.[41] After he had recovered from the intestinal illness in June, Trudeau went to Harold Laski and asked for a letter of recommendation, telling him he wanted to finish his thesis on Christianity and Communism by travelling through Communist lands as well as the birthplaces of the great religions in the Middle East and Asia.[42] Jules Léger, later the Governor General of Canada but now a first secretary at the High Commission in London, and Paul Beaulieu, the Canadian cultural attaché in Paris, provided Canadian government letters of reference for Trudeau's wanderings.[43]

He was only twenty-eight, but his family remained troubled about his failure to "settle down." Suzette had complained to him even before he went to Paris in 1946 that he "had enough studying for one lifetime: that's what your friends and I have decided anyhow!" He should, she warned, not force himself to occupy every minute of his life with a "studied program—Learn to live and let yourself go," she advised, "otherwise it will soon be too late." More than two years later, in the fall of 1948, Tip gave the same message to his brother, urging him to settle down as he and Suzette had done earlier. Trudeau replied candidly, mildly rebuking his younger brother for the criticism:

> You have chosen marriage, a home, the quiet life, the work you enjoy, and moderation. I'm a nomad by inclination, but also by necessity, for academic pursuits alone haven't brought me wisdom. As I discover the world, I discover myself. This no doubt seems terribly trite, but I now accept the trite along with all the rest.[44]

Trudeau wanted to strip down to the essentials. He would travel like "Everyman: on foot with a backpack, in third-class coaches on trains, on buses in China and elsewhere, and aboard cargo boats on rivers and seas." Then, he would rebuild, taking the strongest materials he had found in his education and experience, and bonding them to the enduring pillars of his heritage.[45]

—

Trudeau left London on a fine summer day in 1948 and headed east, determined to pierce the darkness that had fallen over Eastern Europe. Despite letters of introduction from Canadian officials, he encountered sullen border guards, machine guns, and barriers as he passed through Poland, Czechoslovakia, Austria, Hungary, Yugoslavia, and Bulgaria. Soot darkened the elegant mansions of the Hapsburg Empire, and the remains of war were everywhere. In Poland he saw Auschwitz, where, he wrote not entirely accurately, "5 million were killed by the Nazis (1/2 being Jews)." He seemed not to ponder then what Auschwitz meant, but he had long ago left behind the casual anti-Semitism of his adolescence.[46]

What he retained was his intense curiosity, his sharp blue eyes that scrutinized all he encountered, and his lean, muscled physique. He sometimes shaped himself to his environment, wearing a full, albeit thin beard through the Middle East and donning native garb when appropriate. At other times, he was defiant, wearing North American shorts where none had been seen before. When he failed in his plan to visit the Soviet Union, he passed in the company of some students from Bulgaria into Turkey and the Middle East, where stability had been shattered first by war and then by the establishment of the State of Israel. In May 1948 five Arab armies had attacked Israel, but the better-disciplined Israelis defeated them and seized most of the lands the British had held as Palestine under the League of Nations

mandate. When Trudeau came in the fall of 1948, the war had not
officially ended, and tensions and suspicions abounded. Borders
were in doubt; gunfire sounded throughout the nights.

After he was told in Amman, Jordan, that all the roads to
Jerusalem were closed, Trudeau joined a group of Arab soldiers
and crossed over the Allenby Bridge to Israel, making his way
up to the Old City of Jerusalem.. Through gunfire, he sought
refuge in a Dominican monastery. As he left, however, the pale-
skinned, bearded Trudeau attracted the attention of Arab Legion
soldiers, who promptly arrested him as a spy. He was briefly
imprisoned in the Antonina Tower, where Pontius Pilate supposedly judged Christ. Fortunately, a Dominican priest, who, like
most Arab Christians, probably sympathized with the Arab cause,
convinced the jailers that Trudeau was simply a Canadian student, not a Jewish spy. A group of Arab soldiers returned him to
Amman, no doubt convinced that the peculiar Canadian student
was certainly a spy. In Jordan, where the government remained
closely linked with Great Britain, the British passport that
Trudeau had wisely procured in Turkey convinced the local
authorities that he should be released.[47]

In the turbulent Middle East, Trudeau constantly encountered new adventures and troubles of one sort or another. From
Jordan he travelled to Iraq to visit Ur, Abraham's birthplace, and
the fabled Babylon. When he stepped off the train, he asked to
be directed to Ur and was immediately sent to the great ziggurat.
He left his baggage at the station and wandered through the ruins
of the city, collecting a few shattered tiles inscribed with
Sumerian characters before climbing to the top of the ziggurat.
As he did so, he encountered some bandits:

> They made it clear that they wanted money. One of them
> indicated by gesture: "Let's see your watch." Since I wasn't
> wearing one, I replied, "Let's see your knife"—and

snatched it from his belt. They persisted: "We want whatever you've got. Hand it all over."

But Trudeau now had the knife, and he persuaded them to
go down the stairs to discuss matters. Meanwhile, he tricked them
and stayed at the top, shouting down: "Now come and get me."
They stood transfixed while he began to scream "to the skies all
the poems I have memorized, beginning with Cocteau's verse
about antiquity. I spewed octosyllables and alexandrines by the
dozens. I accompanied them with dramatic gestures." They
quickly and understandably concluded he was "dangerously
deranged." He descended the stairs, "still yelling." As the brigands
disappeared into the desert, Trudeau suddenly realized that his
study of poetry had brought him unimagined benefits.[48] He was
alone in Ur, which was surprisingly pristine. After seeing the vast
mausoleum, he climbed the ziggurat once again and reflected on
the history that surrounded him and what it meant. To be sure, he
wrote to his mother, some of the greatest treasures were now in the
museums of the many conquerors:

> But digging will always obsess archaeologists, and the compul-
> sive ritual of the dig will continue to reward them mainly with
> frustration. Every bump may hide treasures, but every pit may
> also. Nothing is ever finished, even if you have to keep digging
> another six inches. And by removing soil, they make other
> mounds, and forget a shovel here and there, leading archaeol-
> ogists of the year 10,000 to establish that 20th-century man had
> made little progress since his Paleolithic ancestor . . .
>
> Having reached the top of the ziggurat, I saw an enor-
> mous black bird fly slowly away after defecating on the
> column whose offerings had once been made to the moon
> goddess . . . *Vanitas vanitatum, et omnia vanitas.*

Alone, five days after his twenty-ninth birthday, he saw the burning sun create his shadow, the only human form where once a great civilization had thrived.[49] He felt mortality.

With his prized British passport, Trudeau set off on the fabled Silk Road that carried him through Samarkand to India and Afghanistan. He had already developed a lifelong dislike of Canada's Department of External Affairs, whose representatives, he claimed, had treated the bearded backpacker with disdain — in sharp contrast with the friendly reception given by British diplomats. He wrote to his mother and sister on December 2 that, in India, the "people at the Canadian High Commission were quite nice for a change."[50] In general, however, he sought out priests when he needed counsel and refuge, and they welcomed the ascetic of New Testament appearance who knocked on their doors. Curiously, although he had made no formal arrangements with any Harvard professor to supervise his proposed thesis on Communism and Christianity, he used the pretext of thesis research for Harvard to gain entry to political offices and to journalists and professors.[51] As a result, the letters he wrote to his family from Asia present a remarkable portrait of a continent in turmoil and a young man in the process of finding himself.

Although Trudeau gloried the scantness of possessions and in the meagre cost of his trip ($800, he later claimed), he mingled with the mighty as well as the derelict and the desperate as he passed through the Middle East and on to India, China, and Japan, before returning to Canada in the spring of 1949, after almost a year on the road. He wrote several letters to his family as his adventure progressed. What they reveal is his fondness for his mother, whose travelling passion he inherited; his keen eye for the variety of human experiences; and his passion for understanding the basis of political action. In their own right, the letters are important as descriptions of Asia at this critical time, as the

British Raj dissolved, India divided violently into separate pieces, and a new united China bloodily emerged.

He wrote from Kabul in early December, having passed through the Punjab, where he saw the Golden Temple at Amritsar. There he discovered few who spoke English and concluded that the Indians "seem to be getting even against all foreigners for 150 years of foreign domination." Imperialism became a constant theme in his writings home. Stranded with only his knapsack, Trudeau found himself in the no man's land between India and the new state of Pakistan. He was rescued from a walk of twenty miles to the Pakistani frontier by "a Muslim Punjab Police Captain," who whisked him through police cordons in a private car. That night he went "to bed with a huge glass of sweetened warm buffalo milk" and "slept like an angel." The next morning, he continued, "I bid this hospitable family good-bye, despite the invitation to remain longer; for the wife had to remain in purda all the time a foreign man was in the house, and I couldn't bear keeping the man from his wife all the time I was there."[52]

He moved on to Peshawar in new Pakistan, which had a fascinating bazaar, "by no means pretty, and a hopeless jumble, but [with] the atmosphere of a frontier town, various races seem to mingle, the Mongolian with the Indian and with the white." As he watched, "a troop of frontier tribesmen marched down the street, beating their tumtums obviously on their way to the fight in Kashmir, blowing their bagpipes and shooting in the air, something out of a movie." Trudeau said he "wandered about at random," and "dusk found me lost in the maze of lanes. I was too enchanted to be disturbed, except that my eyes stung with the heavy acrid smoke which hung about the place, smoke of that particular kind which comes from cooking over cow dung fuel." Once again, the police picked him up, but his British passport secured his release.

He finally managed to get a ride with an American diplomat who took him through the Khyber Pass, where he saw on the mountainsides the plaques commemorating British battles long ago in the great game to win Asia. He reported the stories of refugees who were fleeing their ancestral homes as Hindus and Muslims set upon each other in the bloody aftermath to Indian independence:

> We had a welcome breakfast at the outpost of the famous Khyber Rifles, high up in the pass. Wild honey was on the menu. Then on to Jahalabad: all along the way we passed endless caravans; these were the nomads of the heartland which I had thought had ceased to exist, but here they were, hundreds, thousands of them, men, women and children, all trekking south into Pakistan, through the Khyber Pass, coming from way beyond Kabul, whence the cold of the winter had driven them. The newborn babes ride on top of the camels with the chickens, perched high up on top of the huge load. I could write a book on these people, so much was I impressed by their features, their dress, their behaviours, their beasts of burden, their history, their inner mind; however I won't write it now for I would never get you to Kabul, the city a mile above sea level . . . We crossed the final pass at sunset and the pink and purple mountains, stretching away to infinity, is something to behold. And as a cadre, on either side, higher mountains snowcapped and formidable. Then the descent into the valley of Kabul, where the crisp winter air and smell of wood fires awakened many longings within me; despite my crude room in the only hotel in the place, I slept happily. Here was a taste of winter, and of Laurentian air, a change from the six months of summer I had enjoyed by going gradually south all the way from England, as I went east.

In Kabul, time seemed frozen. The bazaars stood "as they

have stood for centuries, all selling the same spices, silver jew-
ellery, colourful silks, beautiful cloths, artistically worked shoes
with pointed upturned toes, heavy woollens and brightly designed
skullcaps, to wear under turbans, as they have done for centuries."
But he could see clearly that the twentieth century would bring
changes as no other century ever had.

Later in December he returned to India, where he took a
boat through the twisted bayous at the mouth of the Ganges. He
passed through "lush jungles where tigers hunt the deer and
gazelle, betwixt banks with their many villages of grass houses,
whence primitive natives drive their sacred bulls and water buffalo towards rich prairies." Surrounded by Hindus and some
Muslims, Trudeau spent a pious Christmas Day: "I read the
masses, sang the hymns and generally spent the day in deep
meditation." It was, he claimed, "good for the inners." Then he
discovered a priest from Quebec who had been in India since
1922 and was overjoyed, he told Suzette, to encounter a young
guy from Montreal—a "petit gars de Montréal."[53]

"Do you remember the song we used to sing around you at
the piano?" Trudeau wrote to his mother from Bangkok on January
18, 1949. The song included the lines "North to Mandalay . . .
South to Singapore," and, thanks to the Dutch and "their outrageous imperialistic policy" in Indonesia, Trudeau was forced to go
north to Mandalay and, then, to China. Bangkok beckoned,
because Trudeau believed it was the best "listening post" in the
area. In Indochina, too, French colonial policy was "undergoing a
very critical test," though Trudeau was more sympathetic to it than
to the British brand. He quickly passed through Burma, where
"armed bandits" were everywhere. "I have seen no country," he
told his mother, "where chaos, bribery, looting, smuggling, insur-
rection and political assassination have been so prevalent and to so
little avail. There is perhaps no weaker government in the world
today; but there is no more divided and purposeless opposition, so

the government still stands. But that is all it does, it stands . . . at a standstill." He stayed, as so often, with priests and even gave a lecture to Catholic girls in a convent.[54]

Then he arrived in Siam (now Thailand), a country that bewitched him and from which he drew important lessons. "If any-one ever called upon me in argument to give him evidence of the beneficial effects of Freedom upon the evolution of a nation," he wrote to his mother on January 28, "I should suggest that he settle in Siam awhile." There he found cordiality, grace, and a basic truth:

> Practically alone in the East, this country ignores the vicis-situdes of domination by an imperialistic power (the Japanese stay was too short-lived to have left an imprint). In consequence, hate, suspicion, envy and arrogance, which follow from the inferiority complex of colonies, or former ones, are entirely absent from the psychological make up of the Siamese; instead you find a good-natured curiosity and a genuine desire to live and let live—at worst, add a dose of disguised condescendence. The spoken word is superfluous here, you can smile and gesticulate your way to anything, bow, clasp your hands before your face and you are at peace with everyone.

As an added benefit, he said, "tipping, soaking the foreigner, begging, shoe shining, 'guiding,' and other forms of disguised ser-vility are practically unknown here."* In Siam, he admired the way

---

* Tipping was a practice Trudeau despised. Some of his later dinner com-panions sometimes discreetly left additional cash on the table as Trudeau walked out of the restaurant.

everyone went his own way in a population that was "hybrid, part Thai (ancient Chinese), part Laotian, part indigenous (of the same ethnical branch as the Polynesian)." He regretted that he had brought no camera to record the "fairy-like splendour, the stupendous colour, the tireless worship, the unthinkable shapes," though the "very abundance of exotic form could not possibly fit into a camera." Oh, he exclaimed to his mother, "that I could blindfold you and instantly transport you within some sacred precinct, and leave you sitting on the matting of some pagoda; you would find no single familiar form with which to gauge reality, and you would swear you were dreaming."[55] Pierre, truly, had become his mother's son; there is a warm, settled, and satisfying quality in their banter.

He also took a trip to the old Siamese capital of Chiang Mai with an unexpectedly distinguished group, including a Thai prince and princess, the American cultural attaché, the French military attaché, and assorted judges, bankers, and other dignitaries. His own attention, he admitted, was fully diverted between "a pretty fraulein and a jolie demoiselle," although he did manage to talk to some missionaries and one of the "rare Communists" for the purposes of his thesis.[56] From Thailand he went to French Indochina, then in the first battles of a thirty years' war. In Saigon he found "hate, strife and inevitable waste of men, money and morals." Once again the youth of France were in uniform, fighting a war that was going "nowhere fast." Soldiers were everywhere, and people could travel only in convoys. The French held the towns and main highways, the rebels ruled the countryside, and "nobody holds the peace, though on both sides men die, [are] wounded, suffer and atrocities are committed in the name of elusive righteousness and honor." On the one side were patriots, "coupled together with cynical Stalinists and bloodthirsty thieves." On the other side, "you find bewildered idealists joined together with greedy Imperialists and disgusting knaves." Politics, Trudeau concluded, "thy name is mud."

He managed to find a bus to the legendary Angkor Wat, but he thought it such "a disgusting trip" that "at times [he] was hoping that the convoy would be attacked and a few of us killed off, to make room for the rest." Angkor, by chance, proved to be safe thanks to the presence of a *Life* photographer for whom French troops cleared out the beggars and bandits who normally lurked nearby. The grandeur and scale seemed to Trudeau to represent the "confused aspirations of an awesome builder, obsessed by the need to accumulate idol upon idol, height upon height, hallway upon hallway, in endless and fearful mountains of stone." Surrounded by French troops, the photographer and sundry others toured the ruins by torchlight and listened to an aged conservator tell the history of the monuments and how, among other things, the French novelist and future culture minister André Malraux, against whose "Communist" presence in Montreal Trudeau had protested in 1937, had stolen some of the artifacts.

Trudeau returned in an all-day convoy to Saigon, where he managed to get an admission card to an elite private club. There, enjoying the swimming pool, were women whose "bathing suits have gone one better" than those in France. At this "Club sportif," Trudeau sipped the forbidden absinthe and supped in regal splendour. The city itself was crammed, and he dwelt "in a make-shift dormitory, hot, noisy and crowded, only bearable because there are a few other shifty fellows like myself, foreign legionnaires, etc." He asked his mother to tell his friends that he would eventually write, but, he concluded, "when I settle down on a side-walk café, I don't seem to get much work done."[57]

From Saigon, Trudeau went to China, just as Mao's Long March was ending in triumph. At the edge of chaos and conflict, he saw a society and a polity in the throes of death. From the safety of British-ruled Hong Kong, Trudeau went to Canton, a city crammed with "all types," from "the escapists to the hard-boiled sewers of mankind." Then he set out for Shanghai. Refugees and wounded soldiers were everywhere, and the value of money changed by the hour. There were still many missionaries, and they frequently gave the wandering Canadian refuge. The devout Catholic also found welcome in the Protestant YMCA, and, thereafter, he always had great admiration for it as an institution. The road to Shanghai was unforgettable:

> I saw something of the real China; rambling mountains, wide rivers, endless rice fields in tiers along the hillsides or into gulches, poor villages, walled hamlets. I shivered at the poor peasant plowing his paddy fields with water buffalo, knee deep in the cold water. I slept in a tiny Chinese hotel and helped the daughter of the house with her English home work. I sat on a stool at a round table with many other famished travellers and learned to warm my fingers, numbed, on the boiling teacup, that I might be more agile with the chop sticks. Indeed, agility was an essential if I were not to go hungry; for there is no time to lose when everyone begins digging in at the common bowls.

When Trudeau left the crowded bus for a final journey by train to Shanghai, he noticed signs of a brilliant spring all around:

> A warm breeze rolls through the mountain gaps, and sweeps along the broad valleys, carrying the fragrance of the exquisite peach blossoms. Flooded paddy fields alternate with Yu-tsai crops in flower. The shimmering silver and pure gold squares form a heavenly checkerboard. Broad rivers and swift streams chase wildly through lush green expanses, young wheat under quaint, steep, Chinese stone bridges. Peasant women in bright blue pajamas stand on the threshold of their mud or brick houses. Old men in their long blue gowns and silver chin beards, smoke their silver pipes.

Coolies with conical straw hats bustle along with that quaint gait, synchronized with the oscillation of a double load dangling at either end of their bamboo yoke. Rolly-polly children in their over stuffed clothes look as wide as they are high. With mitigated attention, the sun beams benevolently on the glistening world. Yes it is truly great to be alive![58]

He told Grace on March 10 that he dreamed of being home for the three great events the next month: "your birthday, Easter and the sugar shack—la cabane à sucre." China, however, delayed him. The ancient city of Hangzhou, the "noblest city in the world" to Marco Polo, so intrigued him that he decided to return to it one late afternoon by climbing a mountain rather than following the valley. With the earth drenched by rain, he climbed into the dark towards a Taoist monastery but, on reaching it, he discovered its entry heavily barred:

I pounded on the doors, exchanged foreign words with voices inside, but to no avail. They would not risk unbarring their gates to any weird devil of the stormy night. So I turned away, quite downcast. However I had discounted oriental curiosity, and when they heard my heavy boots begin to clang down the steep, flag-stoned path, a monk and several servants opened the gates to get a peep at the marauder. I brazenly (but with appearance of dignity) walked through the monastery, caught a glimpse of the Taoist monks in black silken gowns and silken cornered head-dress, sipping their tea, made my way to the temple where I was guided by the pounding of a drum. There I stood, shielded by a few candles against impending, incense laden darkness, and as I peered through the shadows towards the eerie idols, the drum beats quickened and suddenly gave away to a weird rhythm tapped out on loud gongs, against a background of howling wind and beating rain. I stood there

as in a trance, feet together and hands joined, with a feeling
of many eyes peering at me, hardly daring to bat an eyelid.
Slowly the realization came to me that my hands had begun
to tremble, and I awoke to the thought: enough of this foolish-
ness. I hastened (walk, don't run) through the halls and courtyards to the door of the domain, and out into the rainy but
familiar night.

After this disturbing escape, Trudeau met the dean of the
law faculty at the university in Hangzhou and discussed "politics at great length with the professors," some of whom had
attended Harvard or London in earlier and better days. He then
left for Shanghai, where he immediately got into a fight "with a
gang of rickshaw coolies." He soon learned how to deal with the
throng of "swindlers, pimps, coolies, rickshaw coolies, shoe-shine
boys, down-and-outers, thugs and pests" that abounded in that
city. Refusing to speak French or English, he broke silence only
to shriek a few "ominous Russian words," to which they immediately responded by slinking away.[59]

In Shanghai he once more sought the company of Jesuit
priests, with whom he had "several jolly get-togethers." Refugees
from nearby battles were flowing into the city with tales of the
Communist army's approach. "I sure would like to be here for
the kill and see their operations first hand," Trudeau wrote, no
doubt to his family's despair. As hundreds of thousands fled the
looming battles, space was scarce on the ships leaving Shanghai,
but Trudeau managed to find passage to Yokohama in Japan. There
the Canadian government official* initially barred the bearded

---

* Likely Herbert Norman, who was later accused by the Americans of being
a Communist agent of influence and driven to suicide.

backpacker from leaving the ship and further increased his animosity towards Canadian diplomats. Once released, Trudeau asked Grace if she wanted to join him on a tour through Japan, as she had the previous spring, when they travelled through Provence and the French Riviera on his motorbike. She apparently declined, so he left Japan on a ship crowded with refugees, most of them Eastern Europeans, who were once again fleeing Communist revolution.[60]

—

At the age of twenty-nine, Trudeau returned to a home that he anticipated with uncertainty and ambivalence. He wrote much later in his memoirs that his return "threatened to be a nasty shock. It was."[61] In this respect he was referring to politics in the province of Quebec, but to others he also emphasized the personal doubts he had at the time. "But what did the wanderlust correspond to? Was it a basic loneliness? . . . I think the best answer would be that I was really completing the pedagogy of Pierre Trudeau, the growing up of Pierre Trudeau."[62] But had he yet grown up? Did Trudeau finally know who he was?

George Radwanski speculated that the trip and its deliberate "risk-taking" and "self-imposed hardships" reflected, on the one hand, his asceticism and, on the other, his desire to experience poverty, a "reality" that had eluded the wealthy young man.[63] Gérard Pelletier credited Trudeau's travels with developing an "international" sense that others then lacked. He deliberately sought out political ideas that could be applied to Canada and Quebec.[64] Trudeau's own letters and documents provide new answers to some of these questions. He did "miss" the war; and, during his political years, he expressed some regrets; he had told Thérèse Gouin in 1945 that he was too lost in his books as the war ended to understand the great "cataclysm" that had exploded around him. Yet there is little in his writings of 1948–49 to confirm that he regretted he had not fought in the war. In *Notre Temps* on Valentine's Day, 1948, he wrote a scathing attack on the policies of the King government in wartime, indicating that his views had not changed since the war. There he listed the multitudinous sins of the King government:

> Government by decree; suspension of habeas corpus, the Arcand, Houde, and Chaloult incidents. The lies of [Ernest] Lapointe. The joke of moderate participation. The farce of bilingualism and French-Canadian advancement in the army. The forced "voluntary" enrolment. The Drew letter and the scandal of Hong Kong. The fraud of the plebiscite, featuring the king of the frauds, Mackenzie King, the intimidating propaganda, and the no that meant yes.

The war, he said, had brought "the end of civil liberty" in Canada, and he vigorously denounced the wartime incarceration of fascist leader Adrien Arcand. This support led Arcand to write to Trudeau's mother praising the article and asking for Trudeau's address.[65] Probably shocked, she appears not to have replied. If some old grievances endured, others vanished, however, as Trudeau completed what he perceptively termed his "pedagogy."

What is striking is how deliberately and systematically he sought perfection in himself. The Jesuits and the classics rightly received credit for this emphasis on excellence in all parts of his person. He was demanding of himself and, very often, too demanding of others. In terms of education, he was fully "grown up" by the third decade of his life. Whether on the steps of the ziggurat at Ur, where he hurled unending stanzas of poetry at bandits, or on the streets of Shanghai, where he shouted abusive Russian phrases to repel street thugs, or in Harold Laski's office at LSE, where he defended his views, Trudeau demonstrated that he had an extraordinary range of knowledge. Fluently bilingual in French and English, comfortable in Spanish, understood in German, and with reading and writing knowledge of Latin and Greek, he knew the classics of Western thought in literature, economics, political science, and history. His travel writing drew on a deep understanding of historical and societal change, and his learning derived from his diligence in the classroom and in his private study. His receptive mind, with its unusually good memory, contained a deep reservoir from which he could draw as few others of his time could do.*

But to what end? In the late 1940s, Trudeau was still not clear about his destiny. Rather, he was wrestling with the direction his erudition and experience would lead him in and what his future public career might be. His article in *Notre Temps* illustrates the contradictions that existed in his understanding of the future of Quebec. The journal was a conservative and nationalist publication, and Trudeau's bitter attack on the wartime policies of Mackenzie King undoubtedly pleased most of its readers. At the

---

* John Crosbie, who possessed both a Newfoundlander's gift of gab and a fine education, had a grudging respect for Trudeau which transcended their profound political differences. He wrote in his memoirs that Trudeau "was a worthy adversary. Duelling with him was always risky, but it was very tempting." On one occasion, Trudeau was challenged about corruption in government and responded: "Quad semper, quad ubique, quad ab omnibus." Crosbie heckled, "That's the Jesuit coming out in you," to which Trudeau replied that Crosbie clearly did not understand what he had said. Crosbie replied with the lawyer's standard "Res ipsa loquitur," to which Trudeau replied in Greek. A frustrated Crosbie could only mouth the Greek motto of St. Andrew's College, the private school he had attended in Ontario. John Crosbie with Geoffrey Stevens, *No Holds Barred: My Life in Politics* (Toronto: McClelland & Stewart, 1997), 236–37.

same time, he also maintained some of his friendships from the days when he and others, enraged by the incarceration of Camillien Houde during the war and the betrayal on conscription, mused about revolution and separation. To two such friends, François and Lise Lessard, he sent a postcard on October 19, 1948, from Mesopotamia. Striking a strongly nationalist note, he wrote: "Here is a place which has known a bit more history than the island at the confluence of the Ottawa and the St. Lawrence. But what's five thousand years; perhaps the next five thousand will belong to us. Mesopotamia, the birthplace of the human race; Laurentie, the birthplace of the new world." He ended with a request that best wishes be sent to other nationalist friends.[66] It was a strangely discordant note for one who styled himself a "citizen of the world," but it was a reminder of how much had changed since Lessard and Trudeau had dreamed of revolution in the streets of wartime Montreal. His chords were not yet in tune.

Some friends and themes persisted, but much had changed in Pierre Trudeau during his absence from Quebec. His *Notre Temps* article uneasily combined a defence of the rights of fascists and nationalists with a strong defence of liberal and popular democracy, one that had rarely been heard earlier. He argued that the governors believed in government for the people but not by the people. Some might object that, in wartime, democratic rights can be suspended. "Quite the contrary," he asserted; "if there is any law upon which the individual citizen has the right to pass judgment, it is one that would expose him to death." What is more important in the article is evidence that he had rejected the corporatism that he had learnt at Brébeuf in favour of popular democracy. Similarly, he had rejected the formalist approach to law in favour of the emerging American positivist approach: that law must express changes within society, "for the world marching forward continuously creates new needs."[67] Among those needs in Canada was a more explicit understanding of human rights—a term that was becoming increasingly current in the postwar world.[68] These rights were to be grounded in a democratic society—"no other form of government safeguards those values better"—where the dignity of the individual person was most completely fulfilled.

Although the absence of ideology based on religion is striking here, Trudeau found grounds for his argument in a passage from Saint Paul that held that each human being was justified in obeying his own conscience. The study of Cardinal Newman had left a clear mark, as had Emmanuel Mounier and the French personalists, who stressed the role of lay Catholics as opposed to the clergy. In this case, diverse streams met and formed a stronger current in Trudeau in the wake of his travels, one that began to swell after he returned to Quebec and confronted the conservative government of Maurice Duplessis. Although he had become liberal, however, he was certainly not a Canadian Liberal—he believed the party had, among other sins, too poorly defended the rights of minorities.

In his letter to his mother from Siam, Trudeau's comments on the absence of "domination by an imperialistic power" are significant, particularly because they illuminate his detestation of colonial rule and minority intimidation. The result of colonial imperialism was, he claimed, "hate, suspicion, envy, and arrogance," all the product of the "inferiority complex of colonies, or former ones." Colonialism breeds suspicion and envy, qualities that are fundamentally destructive. From his travels and studies, Trudeau adapted this lesson to Canadian circumstances, as he and others began to draw parallels between the sullen anger of the Indians and the Indochinese emerging from colonial rule and the resentments of French Canadians. The killing of millions in the break-up of India, some of which he witnessed at close range, had an impact. Separation had brought massive bloodshed, and a federal solution was obviously the better alternative. Trudeau's fascination with the emergence of former colonies remained in his later writings. It was also reflected in his approach to international politics after he became prime minister, when he regarded the end of the colonial empires and the establishment of new states as the most significant historical event of the second half of the twentieth century.

Most of the world Trudeau saw on his travels was poor beyond his expectations. His decision to strip himself of worldly goods on his trip derived only in part from asceticism; it also reflected a rich man's attempt to enter into the life around him in all its facets. Like George Orwell's ventures into the world of the down and out, Trudeau linked his experiences with his education, which both in Paris and in London had awakened him to egalitarian philosophies. In postwar France, he gravitated naturally towards the socialist left and, like Emmanuel Mounier, recognized that Communism's greatest appeal came from its assertion of economic equality. His proposed thesis was based on the premise that the egalitarian character of Communism found echoes in the papal encyclicals that had long deplored the great material inequalities in modern industrial capitalism.

In Britain he encountered Laski, a controversial figure because of his defence of the Soviet system as one that attempted to create the economic equality he believed was the foundation of true democracy. Laski struggled both with Stalinism and with the obvious strengths and attractions of postwar American democracy. He prompted Trudeau to look at federalism, a subject Laski had long studied as a means of finding a balance between minority interests and an active central state that would be the strongest force in achieving the economic justice he regarded as essential. When he left London, Trudeau told a Harvard friend, he was "more and more preoccupied with problems of authority, obedience, the foundations of law etc." Harold Laski had left his mark.[69]

So had politics in Britain, where the Labour Party was creating a modern welfare state—something yet to take form in Canada. The importance of the trade-union movement in the Labour Party and, in a broader sense, in drawing workers into politics affected Trudeau's perception of how change might occur in Quebec. No doubt recalling the workers in the Abitibi gold mines with whom he had shared so little in 1946, he determined to focus more closely on what trade unions did. He began to see the trade-union movement as a highly effective method of expressing the workers' voice in politics. It was, he wrote in 1948, "the duty of all to participate in the body politic and to express one's conscience in guarding the common good and in all things to bear full witness to the truth."[70] The Welsh labour politician Aneurin Bevan, whom Trudeau came to admire during his year in Britain, would have strongly agreed.

Wearing a thin beard, Trudeau returned to Montreal in May 1949 with traces of the intense Middle Eastern and Asian sun on his hardened and lean body. He had acquired a broad knowledge of international politics and, through his education, of contemporary political economy. That knowledge formed the basis for political views that had become more secular, liberal, and egalitarian, and that co-existed with a renewed yet different Roman Catholic faith. He was less interested in nationalism and, indeed, in history and more concerned with what he was beginning to describe as "effective" and "rational" approaches to politics. He had, most definitely, grown up in respect to his "pedagogy" and his social and political views, although there remained an unpredictability and elusiveness about him.

And had he matured emotionally? He had outgrown the sophomoric hyperbole that he displayed in his major essay for the despised William Yandell Elliott at Harvard. His encounter with Freudian psychiatry seemed to be helpful in clarifying his adolescent fears about women and sex and in fortifying his belief in the importance of individualism. Freudian terms pervaded his prose over the next few years; and, although there is no definite evidence, it appears that the restraints on sex outside of marriage disappeared for Trudeau. Freud, personalism, and probably impatience apparently combined to do the trick. However, other restraints were accepted. The cascade of emotionalism and the regular outbursts of anger that had marked Trudeau in the early forties and, indeed, in his letters to Thérèse Gouin were tempered. Although he became a superb polemicist, his pen accepted limits, ones that eliminated the anti-American rants while at Harvard or the anti-English tirades whenever he had encountered the Union Jack. In fact, soon after his return he wrote a letter to the editor of *Le Devoir*, Gérard Filion, in which he dismissed Filion's call for a republican "social" movement. Republicanism, Trudeau declared, would be a waste of scarce political time; the "social" revolution must come first.[71]

Trudeau had changed; but, despite his claims that, in Quebec, "nothing had changed," it had, in fact, altered a lot.* He recognized that change on May 19, when he bought a painting

---

* In his *Memoirs*, written in the early 1990s, Trudeau makes this claim and adds that "Quebec had stayed provincial in every sense of the word, that is to say marginal, isolated, out of step with the evolution of the world." He quotes the chansonnier Jacques Norman, who predicted that "when the Soviets invade, they'll rename Montreal; they'll call it Retrograd" (61). Scholars now tend to emphasize the forces of change that were strongly felt in Quebec in the 1940s. Social and economic historians stress the impact of war on even relatively isolated areas of Quebec. In *Quelques arpents d'Amérique: Population, économie, famille au Saguenay, 1838-1971* (Montreal: Les Éditions du Boréal, 1996), Gérard Bouchard indicates that the period after 1941 saw decisive shifts in major indicators such as the use of contraception, age of marriage, and,

by Paul-Émile Borduas for $200.[72] In August 1948 Borduas, then an instructor at the École du meuble, wrote a scathing indictment of Quebec society and its major institutions, *Refus global*, which he and fifteen other younger artists signed. Decades later, its anger still erupts from the page as Borduas attacks a society where feelings were "shamefully smothered and repressed by the most wretched among us." The past could no longer beat down the present and the future: "To hell with Church blessings and parochial life! They have been repaid a hundredfold for what they originally granted." Now was the moment for magic, for love, for passionate action, and a world where "the ways of society must be abandoned once and for all."[73] Borduas set off a firestorm of criticism for his negativism and his tone. He lost his job and left Quebec within a few years, but the artist who had begun as a church painter had signalled the fundamental changes in Quebec society that were taking place. So had Trudeau, by his purchase of a Borduas canvas.

Gérard Pelletier did not approve of Borduas's statement. Returning to Quebec to become a journalist at *Le Devoir*, he

---

most important, literacy, where the rise was dramatic (455). In the area of intellectual history, Michael Behiels published a study of Quebec liberalism and nationalism which stressed how much change had occurred before 1949. Writing of the impact of war and depression in *Prelude to Quebec's Quiet Revolution: Liberalism versus Neo-nationalism, 1945–1960* (Montreal and Kingston: McGill-Queen's University Press, 1985), he argued: "Shattered beyond repair was the belief that Quebec was a society where nothing changed or would change." Despite the book's extensive and largely favourable treatment of him, Trudeau did not acknowledge its arguments in his memoirs. He did admit, however, that there was "a bubbling of ideas that already, in a very timid way, presaged the changes to come" (62).

condemned the document as adolescent, adding that "Mr. Borduas is not a young man. This is a mature man."[74] Yet Pelletier, too, was caught up in the sudden changes in Quebec society, and, when Trudeau sought out his old friend shortly after his return, Pelletier persuaded him to join the cause of the asbestos workers, who had been on strike since mid-February.

—

Trudeau had paid little attention to trade unions before his departure from Quebec in 1944, even though Thérèse's father was the author of the major text on labour law in Quebec. Now, however, he was interested in the potential of trade unionism to effect political and economic change and, even before his return, he had contacted Canadian Labour Congress officials about a possible job with them in Ottawa. Nothing eventuated, so, still uncertain of his own future, he quickly accepted Gérard Pelletier's invitation to join him in the Asbestos Strike, in the town of Asbestos, in the Eastern Townships.

This strike is a fabled moment in Quebec history because it illuminates the class and ethnic differences that fuelled the resentment and dissent in the province. The companies were overwhelmingly foreign-owned, and the managers spoke only English. The miners simply took the asbestos from the ground, loaded it on freight cars, and shipped it away. Less than 5 percent was processed in Canada. On the great rolling hills of the Eastern Townships where it was extracted, large gaping holes remained as testimony to their work. Although the postwar boom benefited the industry, and workers' wages rose, they knew the rewards went mainly to the foreign owners and the English-speaking managers. Gradually, too, the miners became aware that the material they extracted daily was destroying their lungs. All this knowledge gave force to the strike that exploded when Jean

Marchand, the secretary-treasurer of the Confédération des travailleurs Catholiques du Canada (CTCC or Canadian Catholic Confederation of Labour), first met with the workers about their grievances in February 1949. Spontaneously, the workers in their caps took to the streets, along with Marchand in his beret. The strike was illegal, passionate, and immediately controversial.

Trudeau and Pelletier set out to drive from Montreal to the strike sites in Pelletier's decrepit British-made Singer. Along the way, the police stopped this suspicious-looking vehicle and took both occupants to the police station for questioning. When the officer asked Trudeau, who had been sitting in the left front seat, for his licence, he replied, defiantly, "I have none," even though he had it in his pocket. The police were set to arrest him when Pelletier, in his typically calm fashion, asked the officers to come to the car. There they saw that the Singer's controls were on the right, in the British fashion. After an exchange of barbed words, the police resentfully let them go.

Once they arrived at Asbestos, Trudeau met Jean Marchand, a social scientist who had become a brilliant labour organizer in the fashion of the American Walter Reuther. Personally striking, with an uncontrollable thatch of dark hair and a voice that easily reached the back of union halls, Marchand was an impassioned orator who moved to action the men (and the few women) who came to hear him talk. Four decades later, Trudeau's boyhood friend Pierre Vadeboncoeur recalled Marchand in those days. "He had qualities that were truly exceptional," he said: "a lively intelligence, sure judgement, a critical spirit, a passionate temperament, obvious sincerity, combined with the extraordinary eloquence of a popular champion that one encounters only two or three times in a century in a single country."[75]

Trudeau's role in the strike was minor. He marched with the strikers, who called him Saint Joseph because of the oriental headgear, North American shorts, and straggly dark beard he still wore. But he made his mark when he gave a fiery speech attacking the Quebec police to five thousand miners. Jacques Hébert thought he spoke emotionally and well about the importance "of democracy, justice, and liberty in language they understood,"[76] but Marchand, more experienced with crowds, had a different take on the event. "Miners are not schoolchildren," he warned, "and while students might steal pencils, the miners steal dynamite. I had managed to defuse two or three cute little plots by the boys which would have blown up the mine manager and most of his staff. So you can imagine that when Trudeau urged physical resistance by the strikers, I got a little worried." All calmed down, but Marchand had discovered a valuable new colleague, and Trudeau had discovered where he belonged.[77]

At Asbestos, Trudeau, Pelletier, and Marchand bonded together—and they stayed together for the rest of their lives. They seemed to understand their mutual strengths, interests, and beliefs. Jean Marchand was the organizer, who travelled the highways and backroads of Quebec and became one of the workers' own. He slept in their bedrooms and spoke in their church basements, where he thrilled them as his emotions boiled on the tip of his tongue. He never had notes, but his thoughts suddenly exploded into the air. Sometimes, he would break into song, as he did in an Asbestos café one evening with "Les lumières de ma ville," a ballad made famous that year by the young Quebec chanteuse Monique Leyrac in the film of the same name.[78] Gérard Pelletier was not a singer or even much of an orator, but he listened well, as the finest journalists do. He quickly provided stories for the press that helped to make Marchand's case in the dailies.

Initially, Pierre Trudeau struck both Pelletier and Marchand as different but also remarkable, a man who brought the intellectual depth and international experience that Quebec labour badly needed in the forties. Pelletier's father was a stationmaster, Marchand's a worker, while Trudeau's had been a millionaire businessman. Both Pelletier and Marchand had developed a contempt for the sons of Brébeuf and Outremont, with their "smart" clothes and special banter, but when they saw Trudeau speak directly to the workers about justice and democracy in ways that the workers listened to and understood, they realized he possessed the gifts and commitment they needed. As Pelletier remarked later, Trudeau "made no show either of his money or his muscles. Nor of his intelligence. But despite a strange shyness that [would] never leave him, and which made him less than talkative on first acquaintance, he aroused one's curiosity."[79] Beginning at Asbestos, Trudeau began to link the world of Christian personalism he had discovered in Paris, and the socialism he had encountered in Laski's classrooms, with the needs of the Quebec working class. The workers became for him the best hope in a Quebec that had disappointed him on his return.

What Trudeau found there was, in his later words, "a Quebec I did not really know, that of workers exploited by management, denounced by government, clubbed by police, and yet burning with fervent militancy." It was, in many ways, a new Quebec, a fact he recognized in his finest publication—the introduction and conclusion to a 1956 book he edited on the strike. Although there had been other strikes, he wrote, the Asbestos Strike "was significant because it occurred at a time when we were witnessing the passing of a world, precisely at a moment when our social framework—the worm-eaten remnants of a bygone age—were ready to come apart."[80]

Trudeau did not forget the smoke-filled union halls or the workers in checked flannel shirts, their faces lined from years of hard and unhealthy work. After he went back to Montreal, he took on their case against the provincial government and the police, who had broken into workers' homes, falsely imprisoned many of them, and generally intimidated their towns and villages. He did not charge his clients a penny.[81]

But the strike was illegal and the workers were violent, destroying the property of the "scabs" who replaced them. The Duplessis government opposed the strikers on the legitimate basis of illegality, but it went much too far, breaking its own laws with impunity. The Catholic Church was divided on the strike, with parish priests rallying to their parishioners while most of the hierarchy backed the government—as they normally did. There were, however, notable exceptions: Archbishop Charbonneau of Montreal strongly supported the strikers' cause, and dozens of truckloads of food went from working-class Montreal parishes to feed the miners' families. Charbonneau's vigorous support of the strike became a principal factor in Duplessis's decision to have "a showdown with elements of the Church that he considered were subverting his authority and working iniquity with his constituents."[82] With prodding from conservative elements of the church and from the government of Quebec, the Vatican persuaded Charbonneau to resign his archbishopric on the grounds of "ill health," and he spent the rest of his life in Victoria, British Columbia. Pelletier realized that he and the others who had supported the strikers so vociferously had also become "marked men." Trudeau could no longer get a university job. Jean Marchand therefore offered him a position with the labour movement in Quebec, where he could continue to fight Duplessis.

But, in one of the surprising moves that mark Trudeau's life, he left Quebec just when, in his own words, the strike brought "a turning point in the entire religious, political, social, and economic history of the Province of Quebec."[83] To the shock of Pelletier and other friends, Pierre Trudeau departed for Ottawa and became a civil servant.

—

CHAPTER 5

HEARTH, HOME, AND NATION

Pierre Trudeau's decision to go to Ottawa perplexed some of his friends, who sought a rational explanation for this sudden change in direction. Gérard Pelletier, for example, later claimed that he never understood why Trudeau became a federal public servant when the challenges in Quebec were so great.[1] But when people make a choice, the rational and the emotional, the private and the public normally mingle together, and there were profound reasons why Trudeau found working in Montreal difficult in 1949. Several are obvious.

First, he had not liked his student experience at the Université de Montréal and probably had little desire to teach there, even if clerical and political conservatives had permitted him to do so. After his involvement with the Asbestos Strike, they would not. Second, many friends had married, including his closest male companion of the time, Roger Rolland, and Thérèse had married another friend, Vianney Décarie. Third, his brother and sister were married, and Suzette now lived close by her mother and could keep an eye on her, so he could leave secure in the knowledge that she would be cared for. Then again, the swarm of family and old friends must have seemed overwhelming after his solitary wanderings of the previous year.

Moreover, in the five years Trudeau had essentially been abroad, the world had changed. Liberal democracy, so troubled in the 1930s, had risen to the challenge of fascism during the Second World War, and Canadians now eagerly entered what *Time* magazine publisher Henry Luce had named the American century. In the stones and the forests of Quebec, American enterprise extended its claims, and church, state, and citizens responded to both its energy and its consequences. Some of Trudeau's former classmates, including his greatest Brébeuf rival, Jean de Grandpré, began to find their place within the Canadian corporate world, which was moving rapidly from its traditional link with the British-Canadian imperial tradition to welcome the flow of precious American dollars available to Canadians in the postwar years. Other classmates, such as Pierre Vadeboncoeur, were deeply suspicious of the impact of American economic and cultural influence on Quebec society, even though they recognized that the future world imagined in the Catholic classrooms of their childhood was undeniably lost.[2]

Outside Canada, a Cold War was emerging in the confrontation between the Soviet Union and the West or, as it was more often expressed, between Communism and democracy. In 1949 a new chill appeared in international affairs as the Soviet Union exploded an atomic bomb, thus ending the American monopoly, and Mao Tse-tung's armies passed through Peking's Gate of Heavenly Peace in triumph, not long after Trudeau left Shanghai. In the 1949 Canadian election, Conservative leader George Drew campaigned in Quebec on a strong anti-Communist platform, but he convinced few that Prime Minister Louis St. Laurent was "soft" on Communists. Both St. Laurent and his popular foreign minister, Lester Pearson, joined in stern jeremiads against the Communists. Indeed, even at the height of the Second World War, many Catholic leaders in Quebec had attacked the alliance with the Soviet Union. When Cardinal

Villeneuve and Premier Joseph-Adélard Godbout had called for assistance to Russia after Hitler's attack, the great nationalist Henri Bourassa had bitterly complained: "How can they not see that, some years from now, Russia will be the nightmare of the world?"[3] In 1949, for most people in Canada and Quebec, it was.

Pierre Trudeau, in many ways, was a bad fit for Quebec in the spring of 1949. During his long educational absence and world travels, he had carefully maintained links through correspondence with friends, family, and other individuals who kept him informed about events at home. The articles he published in *Notre Temps* clearly reflected this aim, as did an article in *Le Devoir* which appeared just as he returned: "Five minutes with Pierre Trudeau — Around the world in 580 days."[4] He immediately re-established old links and made pronouncements on a range of issues both in private and in public. His exchange on republicanism in *Le Devoir* attracted attention among the intellectual elite, for whom the nationalist newspaper was essential daily reading.

After the Asbestos Strike, Trudeau and Pelletier began to discuss the creation of an intellectual journal, which would be modelled on Emmanuel Mounier's *Esprit*. At the invitation of Claude Ryan, now the general secretary of Action catholique canadienne, Trudeau also spoke to a group of students on June 20. The West, he lamented, lacked economic liberty and was too materialistic. Marxism failed because it restricted liberty, but a better alternative lay in the blend of socialism and Christianity. He echoed the French diplomat-writer Paul Claudel in calling on students "to be sensitive to the world which surrounds us, the international community."[5] At a time when both the Canadian press and politicians were issuing clarion calls to confront global Communism, Trudeau's comments reflected his profound doubts about such a crusade.

The state of Quebec nationalism similarly made him

uneasy. His own public and private writings in the late 1940s possessed ambiguities that confused readers about what he actually believed. His old friend Pierre Vadeboncoeur, with whom he had re-established a close relationship, even wrote to *Le Devoir* on July 14, 1949, in an effort to clarify what Trudeau had meant in a letter he had written attacking Gérard Filion's call for a new nationalist political party. With considerable presumption, Vadeboncoeur stated that any party that he "and Pierre Trudeau" founded would not emerge in a nationalist cradle. "The nationalist should not integrate the social but the social should integrate nationalism, which currently has a traditional character."[6]

Trudeau knew that Quebec nationalism had a traditional, or conservative, character; reflecting that character, the Duplessis government rejected the social needs of society. Yet the Liberal Party in both Quebec and Ottawa represented neither the national nor the social needs of French-speaking Canadians. The federal CCF had no provincial counterpart, and its attentiveness to the demands of workers and economic inequality was not accompanied by a sensitivity to Quebec's heritage and postwar cultural challenges. Later, Trudeau told an interviewer that he had not looked for an active political career on his return because, very simply, "I did not agree with any of the major parties." He probably would have fitted well into a British Labour Party or a French Socialist Party, where the temptations of power balanced a commitment to social programs based on economic equality and progressive social action. In Canada, however, he found no defined political channel through which he could express the ideas he held and the facts he had learned in his five years of absence from Quebec.[7]

He was not alone. Many other Canadians, including the sociologist John Porter, the novelist Norman Levine, and the painter Paul-Émile Borduas, found Canada unresponsive to the dynamics of postwar progressive currents, whether in the arts or in politics.

In 1949 Canada remained distant from the ideal society that postwar social thought offered and economic prosperity seemed to secure.[8] What had begun with thunderous election declarations in 1944 and 1945 promising national health care and new social programs had ended with the conservative nationalism of Maurice Duplessis in Quebec and the business-oriented liberalism of Louis St. Laurent's Liberals in Ottawa. Despite some changes, Trudeau believed that the Old Regime still prevailed in Canada and Quebec, just as it did in the Roman Catholic Church.

A political career, then, was not an option in 1949, and Trudeau found his old friends adrift in a world where the mists of past debates too often clouded the form of the future. Other young intellectuals shared his alienation and uncertainty. When the sociologist Marcel Rioux returned to Quebec from Paris, he discovered no professional opportunities and took employment with the National Museum of Canada in Ottawa, a city which became, in his own words, "a refuge for the opponents to the [Duplessis] regime" in Quebec.[9] Trudeau, similarly, had no polit-ical outlet in Montreal, detested the regime in Quebec City, had limited professional opportunities as an academic in Quebec, and did not want to practise law.

No sooner was he back, it seemed, than others prepared to leave. For Trudeau and many of his friends, the most upsetting departure was that of François Hertel. In the spring of 1949, Hertel began, in his own words, his "exile" in France. He believed that his readers in the new world could no longer respond to what he taught and wrote, and, for that reason, "it became essential, almost a duty . . . to disown or leave that milieu."[10] Grace had warned Pierre that his friend was disconsolate. After a dinner with Hertel as he prepared to leave the priesthood and Canada, she reported that he said: "I'm returning to the new world because I'm weary of the old one, and contrary to geological and geographical opinion, I claim that America is the old world." The cultural renewal in France in particular, but in Europe more generally, he told Grace Trudeau, "makes America look old and decayed."[11] For the Quebec intellectuals of the postwar period, "troubled by the future of their own land, the ideological landscape of Paris was seductive."[12] For Trudeau, however, a return to Paris would have been exile from family, friends, and, not least, his own ambition. Ottawa, then, offered a convenient detour.*

—

Grace Trudeau was another factor in her son's decision to go to Ottawa. If Trudeau was to consolidate his new-found independence, he no doubt sensed that he should not return to live in the family home. He and his mother had always had an exceptionally close relationship. In the spring of 1947 she had clung to him like a youthful date while his Harley-Davidson careered at high speed through the corniche roads above Monte Carlo. In other photographs, the middle-aged matron and her adult son cavort on the beach just as they had done as young mother

---

* On his return in 1949, Trudeau spoke to two lawyers who were fast-rising francophones in External Affairs—Marcel Cadieux and Michel Gauvin. Both men were conservative Roman Catholics who had served with distinction in the war—the former as a public servant; the latter as a Canadian officer on the battlefields of Western Europe. Both were blunt. Cadieux said he would do everything to prevent the iconoclastic and capricious Trudeau from entering the department. Trudeau himself recalled that Cadieux was upset with his beard, which was not considered proper for young men in "External in those days." Interestingly, in 1968, when Trudeau became prime minister, Cadieux was undersecretary of state for external affairs; the

and child. When they were apart, they both wrote or phoned often. Her home was always his. Sometimes they misunderstood each other, but they shared their thoughts, their impressions, and, occasionally, their decisions. In 1949, when Trudeau returned, Grace was understandably relieved and welcoming, but she knew her son was more fraught than he would admit. More than anyone else, she was aware of the difficulties Pierre faced in Montreal that spring.

"Every time the postman comes I make a rush for the letters, hoping to hear from you," she had written to Pierre in January 1947 during his Paris sojourn. Pierre had been ill but had sought recuperation in the French Alps. How much better his boldness, she told him, than the complaints of Suzette's husband, Pierre Rouleau, who stayed in bed after a minor hemorrhoid operation. He is not, she declared, "of the Elliott stock! As Aunt Annie used to say." Constantly she worried whether Pierre had enough "cash" and regularly enclosed British pounds or treasured American dollars to "help out." As mothers do, she worried about his health and appearance, writing to him on January 17: "Be good to yourself—take the pills. How is your hair behaving, losing any?

---

less guilty Gauvin was ambassador to Ethiopia. But Trudeau bore no grudges: he made Cadieux the first francophone ambassador to the United States, Canada's most important diplomatic position, and he gave Gauvin several choice assignments, including ambassador to China. Interview with Michel Gauvin, May 1995. Cadieux's strong personal views on Canadian politicians can be glimpsed in John Bosher, *The Gaullist Attack on Canada, 1967–1977* (Montreal and Kingston: McGill-Queen's University Press, 1999), in which Bosher quotes extensively from Cadieux's very opinionated diary. Interview with Michel Gauvin, April 1994; interview of Pierre Trudeau by Jean Lépine, April 27, 1992, TP, vol. 23, file 2.

Beware of hard soap on it." The hair became a lasting concern, and photographs of Pierre as he aged provide genuine grounds for her worries. She regularly sent news of his friends, past and present. While visiting Tip at Harvard, she called on Pierre's past love, Camille Corriveau, and reported that she was "kept busy all day with two young ones." Even worse, she has "no help from outside—does all her own work"—as most American mothers did.

In response to Pierre's letters about Paris, she wrote: "You are in a social whirl, as much, if not more than your mom." She always shared his enthusiasm for French ways, although both were thoroughly North American in most of their tastes. A friend of hers had a guest from France who behaved badly and burnt a hole in a treasured Persian rug. "I can't but think," Grace wrote, "there is something French in this way of acting, giving one the impression they are our lords and masters." If her faith in the French was lacking, she had much confidence in her son. On February 20, 1947, she asked what Pierre thought of the world "upside down," with the British leaving India and the "Jews in Jerusalem [wanting] to get out and return to Germany." Concerned, she wrote: "It will take some intelligent people and strong minds to unravel the future. Will you be amongst them?"[13] Perhaps even more than Pierre, she was determined he would be.

In late February 1947, as Trudeau was in the midst of psychoanalysis, Grace was preparing for her trip to France. "Dear big boy," she wrote from the "Land of Snow": "Hurray! You are coming to meet me I heard today—what fun—provided I don't look all washed up when I step off the ship." To her son, if no one else, she did not. When she met up with Pierre again in April, she brought copious amounts of food to a France where heavy rationing still prevailed.[14] She had first visited her brother in Normandy and then rejoined Pierre, to sweep through the south of France on the Harley-Davidson as spring warmed the Côte d'Azur. There is no suggestion that he told her of his psychiatric sessions in Paris, and she appears not to have been aware of the intense correspondence between him and Thérèse in those weeks. Yet, as a mother, she surely knew something had gone badly wrong.

On her—and Pierre's—return to Montreal, Grace learned that Thérèse, great-granddaughter and granddaughter of premiers, niece of a political giant, daughter of a senator, and, in the view of many of the leaders of Montreal society, the ideal life partner for her brilliant son, had decided not to marry him. On July 16 she reacted with distress and concern to the news as Pierre began his trek by foot to the remote parts of Quebec. "My dear coureur des bois," she wrote:

> It was a good opportunity to get away and clear the sombre thoughts that have haunted you for the past few days. If I could only have consoled my poor boy in *those* moments—you know a mother's heart is much upset when she sees the unhappy situations that often arise in the course of her children's lives. It was something of a shock to me as well as to you. When I realized how serious was the rift, especially as I had begun to take the girl to heart— which requires time for such an adjustment! Blood is thicker than water you know I often say.
>
> However, I still believe that perhaps within a short time all may be well again between you two. I'm sure the girl must be unhappy—it is impossible to think otherwise. Since she had led you to believe—or I can imagine so— that you were the only man in her life—just be patient— she will have time to think things over and no doubt one of these days you may receive a note asking to meet her half way—I can speak from experience my dear—and when both parties concerned are proud and unwilling to make the first step—it means unhappiness for two people who are

really in love. Are you quite sure that you are *not* to blame
in showing any lack of affection? Or in being brusque? I know
that when a man makes up his mind to marry the woman of
his choice he can't stand or comprehend why there should
be any delay or seeming hesitation on the girl's side—of
course I'm surmising incidents which may have no bearing
on the whole situation. I feel so sorry for you my dear boy
that I can only pray the dear Lord may console and be your
guide and always mom will be there by your side to give
what comfort she can. All my love to you, Mom.[15]

It was, from a mother to a distraught son, a sensitive and
wonderful letter.

As with most sons, some parts of Pierre Trudeau's life
remained closed to his mother, but most did not. She had gently
chided him about the "tricks" that he and Roger Rolland were up
to in Paris and wondered, when Pierre was in London, whether
he missed the "street fighting" in which he and Roger had par-
taken. She anxiously worried whether he was healthy and
whether he had friends. In November 1947 she told him that
when people inquired about him, she replied that he was making
the most of his stay in London, "getting about to listen in on lectures, conferences as well as communist meetings." Perhaps, she
speculated, he was "freer to go about not having many friends or
am I wrong and do you have a circle? You never mention anyone." For good reason, of course, Grace had quickly realized that,
in London, there was no "circle."[16]

As Trudeau published his articles in *Notre Temps*, Grace
carefully monitored reactions. She told him that some of "the
clergy" said that one article was a "deep and well-sounding
piece," although she did seem a bit troubled that the former
Quebec fascist leader Adrien Arcand "wanted to write to" him with
compliments about the other article. However, "Dr. Turgeon

was tickled that you knocked [Prime Minister Mackenzie] King" in yet another essay. Surely, she remarked, "by the time you enter journalism in this town your name will be a byword." Wherever she went she heard praise for her exceptional son. Madame Décarie predicted a great future for Pierre, "just as we all think! Naturally—me especially."[17]

She fretted that he lacked money and, occasionally, operated on the black market for him, especially when postwar Canadian currency restrictions were put in place in 1947. In February 1948 she offered to get some funds in Boston if he ran short during his studies at the London School of Economics. And she made certain that he was well prepared for his adventures. Later, when he was short of funds after a trip to Africa, she sent him $500 by cable immediately and, when she heard nothing, sent $200 more a month later and told him not to "wait until the last minute" for further requests.[18] These were large sums for the time, equal to almost $6,000 today; in 1948 a decent meal could be had in a Left Bank bistro for twenty-five cents. When he proposed to tour Britain, she wrote: "I shall send you socks, army ones? Also shirt, long sleeves? I bought one a khaki color, perhaps it is not heavy enough—a gabardine cotton would be best, I shall look around altho' for hiking it might be the right weight. I also bought a short sleeved cotton jersey—dark blue—you could use for underwear— instead of wearing pyjamas if you get cold." Then she concluded, typically: "Thinking of you every day dear boy and praying the Lord to keep you safely. My love to you and God bless you. Mom. Enclosing $10." When he sent her saris from India, she proudly showed them off to her friends. She wore them for Pierre on his return, and the two of them hosted an "Oriental afternoon." She also reassured some priests, who wondered about his articles, that he was, most definitely, a strong Roman Catholic.[19]

Grace understood well his urge to wander. She even quoted Whitman to him: "O farther, farther, farther sail!" and told him that she, like him, "early in life . . . felt imbued with the desire to forever seek unknown worlds." Yet she advised him that he must come home and forget the wounds he bore, though she knew they would not heal soon.[20] She was wary as he began once again to introduce new female friends to his family. When she received a few photographs from a woman whom he had spent some time with after the relationship with Thérèse ended, Grace wrote to Pierre about his great love affair. Like mothers generally, she was unfair to the one who had rejected her son:

> I sincerely hope—and I am much in earnest, that you won't go out of your way for her—from things I learned in the *past year* my sympathy for her has completely turned . . . Perhaps I shouldn't have said so much—but you know how mothers feel when they could fight for their children's happiness—and I don't want you going through once more—the agony of last summer—we were all very much affected, in spite of saying little about the episode.

Grace worried about these strong words she had written to her son, concluding, "I hope you won't take offence at all this."[21]

Trudeau did not, but Grace's letters now lacked the sensitivity of her letter a year earlier when she had first learned of the break-up with Thérèse. Gone are the hints that Trudeau may have been "brusque" or that he was not always "affectionate." Grace, as always, came down strongly on her son's side. Trudeau likely believed that his mother's words reflected the continuing gossip in Montreal about what had happened between the couple. Many of his old friendships must have been affected by the end of his close relationship with Thérèse. In one letter Grace reflected on his future after he told her he had danced "socially" in Asia. "By the time you return and begin looking about for a 'wife,' many comparisons will be made — certain standards must be met — but then you have your ideal no doubt — the older one grows the more difficult one becomes — but I couldn't say or accuse you of having those bachelor ways which are hard to deal with — you still are the young enthusiastic youth I am sure."[22]

Grace Trudeau deeply affected her son, not least because he lived with her for most of her adult years. After his move to Ottawa, when he returned to Montreal on weekends, he brought his laundry. "I noticed you didn't bring your towel along this time," she wrote in October 1950, telling him that he should not send it to the laundry.[23] She became an authority on foreign currency rates as she made certain that he had the necessary funds for travel and study. She supervised cooking in their home — a skill that her epicure son, who cultivated his knowledge of fine wines and restaurants, never mastered. A later female companion recalled that, after several elegant dinners together, she visited his country home in the Laurentians, where she discovered that, if a meal was not cooked by someone else, dinner was spaghetti out of a can.[24] In his mother's home, Grace or her staff served him.

On a more positive side, they travelled together often and maintained into the sixties their custom of attending concerts and gallery openings. "My dear boy," she wrote in 1951, "once more we had to say good-bye — after such an enjoyable trip in Italy — for myself at any rate. It will remain one of the highlights in my late life."[25] Her support for him was generous financially and emotionally, and their relationship had an astonishing familiarity. For his thirty-first birthday, for example, she sent him a card with an attractive woman on it and wrote: "Hurrah — it's Pierre's birthday — many happy returns of the day dear boy. We must celebrate over the weekend. All my love, Mom." Then in a small note that could be detached, she wrote: "Happy birthday to the best son in all the world." She did, after all, have two sons.

When Pierre despaired, Grace, more than anyone else, was the rock upon which he built his hopes.

But she may also have been the reef on which his romances sometimes foundered. Certainly, Thérèse came to believe that she was, even though, like Madeleine Gobeil, she admired the way Trudeau softened in Grace's presence, and the devotion mother and son felt for each other.[26] In his psychiatric sessions in Paris, he portrayed his father, Charles, as almost Apollonian, distant and heroic, but, like the Greek gods, indifferent to the world in which humans live. Grace, however, troubled Trudeau. He required her approval; and, because of her strong presence, she represented forces such as the church and the social approval he occasionally and impetuously struck out against in a way that others found puzzling or inconsistent. Although, on the surface, his mother often had good relationships with Pierre's female companions, the women themselves, beginning with Camille Corriveau, came to believe, first, that she was a formidable individual not easily challenged and, second, that she had an enormous, perhaps decisive, influence on her son. In this respect, it is noteworthy that her letters to Pierre often complain about the various faults she found in her son-in-law. Interestingly, Pierre Trudeau delayed marriage until he moved out of his mother's house and, indeed, until she was virtually an invalid, no longer fully aware of events around her.

In her memoirs, Margaret Trudeau wrote that, for her husband, women fell into three categories: "There were his female colleagues, and these he saw only as working companions and not as women, though many were also close friends. Then there were possible dates and here, like Edward VIII, he preferred actresses and starlets, glamorous women who were perfect for flirtations and candlelight dinners. Then there was his wife, and she had to be dependent, at home, and available." The last of these roles, she and others suggest, was an impossible one played most effectively by Pierre's own mother. Trudeau, Henry Kissinger once quipped to Richard Nixon, was best understood as a "mommy's boy."[27]

In a very real sense he was, but Kissinger's dismissal is a cheap shot. To her timid son, Grace Trudeau brought confidence and a belief that he had few limits on what he could accomplish. He adored her because of her exceptional combination of playfulness and discipline, both qualities he inherited, and the strong sense of family that carried her children through first the turbulence of Charles's death and then the religious and social change in Quebec. She introduced him gracefully to the arts and provided stability as he moved into different worlds. She wrote to Pierre on May 11, 1948, her thirty-third anniversary:

> Tuesday, May 11, 1915—our wedding day, your father and I—strange that I happened to write it down just to-night— Since 13 years I like to think I have forgotten or at least overlook it—and you three children helped me carry on. What a blessing you have been to me—what would I have become without you—looking after your needs when you were young filled my life and now that you are all older and capable of carrying on without me—I still like to think I can be of help somehow.[28]

And in so many ways, she surely was.

Grace influenced Trudeau's relationships in two key ways. Obviously, she was a model of the domesticity he championed from the forties, when he quarrelled with Thérèse about her plans for a career and further study, to the seventies, when he opposed Margaret Trudeau's decision to work or return to school. His attitude troubled not only Thérèse and Margaret but also the other women to whom he talked of marriage. More subtly, and also more positively, his close relationship with his mother, their easy bantering and affectionate exchanges, made him seek out women as his confidantes. In his early days at Brébeuf he had resolved to stand apart from his classmates, and his correspondence with even his closest male friends tends to be brief, impersonal, and surprisingly rare. Always the disciplined correspondent, he kept lists of those with whom he corresponded while he was absent, and women were consistently at the top. Moreover, with male friends he tended to write about public or even philosophical matters; with women, he blended these topics with intimate discussions of his own feelings and ambitions—just as he did with his mother.

Anecdotes bear out the same impression presented in his private papers. Jacques Hébert, with whom he travelled frequently, said that Trudeau never spoke with him about religion, a view echoed by the devout Catholic Allan MacEachen, his House of Commons seatmate. MacEachen also reported a conversation with Jean Marchand in which he indicated, to MacEachen's surprise, that he and Trudeau had not spoken for several months. Marc Lalonde, Trudeau's closest adviser, said in the early 1970s that Trudeau spoke to him only once about a personal matter— the break-up of his marriage. He was, Lalonde added, like an oyster that opened with great difficulty. Yet with women, from Camille Corriveau in the early forties to the celebrity Kim Cattrall in the late eighties, he often bared his soul. To Cattrall, Trudeau was "epicurean." The actor Margot Kidder, with whom he later had an affair, described him as "the gentlest, sweetest little boy you'd ever known . . . When you realized this (as he eagerly handed you the simple-minded dinner of pork and beans and bacon out of a can that he'd cooked; or when he held you in his arms in the morning, beaming and enormously pleased with himself), it felt as if you knew a secret no one else knew, and in knowing it, you'd been anointed keeper of his flame."[29]

From de Grandpré at school in 1940, through his closest male colleagues in succeeding decades—Pelletier, Hébert, and

Lalonde—the private Trudeau remained a secret they never really knew.

—

Trudeau kept many secrets in Ottawa after he arrived in the late summer of 1949. After briefly considering External Affairs and the Finance Department, he opted for the Privy Council Office because, he later wrote, it was "the key decision-making centre, and because I wanted to observe in practice what I had just been studying in theory." His initial salary was a decent $2,880 per year, with a 5 percent deduction for his pension, and his office was in the historic abode of prime ministers, the East Block of the Parliament Buildings. A Victorian Gothic classic with high ceilings, impressive vaulted windows, and elegant fireplaces in the major offices but cubbyholes for junior clerks like Trudeau, the edifice was sufficiently small for Trudeau to encounter the "key decision-makers," including External Affairs Minister Lester Pearson and Prime Minister St. Laurent. In those days, however, to encounter was not to meet. The British traditions of formality and rank had formed a hardened crust around the so-called mandarins, whose sway in Ottawa was decisive in the postwar years. Even though St. Laurent was a francophone, he brought the manners of Quebec City's Grande Allée to an Ottawa that warmly embraced his almost regal bearing. His style contrasted strongly with the rough *bonhomie* of Premier Maurice Duplessis in Quebec. Despite their propinquity, there is no evidence that Trudeau and St. Laurent ever had a conversation during his time in Ottawa. Trudeau had considerable respect for St. Laurent, however, particularly for his work when, as justice minister, he made the Canadian Supreme Court the final court of appeal for Canadians.[30]

Ottawa at mid-century was very different from London or Paris. In contrast to London's West End, where the great thespians performed nightly, there was only sporadic amateur theatre in Ottawa. Paris bistros, with their excellent cheap Chablis and fine fare, were another distant fantasy. Junior civil servants normally brought bag lunches to work, while senior officials dined at the cafeteria of the Château Laurier. Across the river in Hull, alcohol flowed more freely, but few bureaucrats dared risk any hint of the bohemian life. Trudeau correctly described mid-twentieth-century Ottawa as "an English capital" where English was the only working language.

Later studies confirmed this view; the Royal Commission on Bilingualism and Biculturalism pointed out that the recruitment of francophones actually decreased considerably in the Department of External Affairs after the Second World War. In his account of Ottawa's mandarins at the time, historian J.L. Granatstein is scathing in his description of the "cultural blindness" that "has to be seen as an unconscious expression of the English-Canadian view of Quebec as a land of happy (if slightly disloyal) peasants, notaries, and priests." Pauline Vanier, the wife of the pre-eminent francophone Canadian diplomat of the time, told him that her husband's francophone compatriots were treated no better than "natives." Trudeau's experiences as a public servant testify to these criticisms: most of his lunches were with the relatively few francophones in Ottawa, while his memoranda are nearly all in English.* His most frequent luncheon partner was his old friend Marcel Rioux.[31] However, he was completely bicultural—indeed, multicultural—in his choice of female companions in Ottawa.

---

* Recruitment of francophones after the war brought the francophone percentage of the public service to the lowest level in Canadian history, even though the prime minister was francophone. The Interdepartmental Committee on External Trade, of which Trudeau was a member, had

As always, Trudeau was extraordinarily diligent. Although he was eligible for twenty days of leave in his first sixteen months, he took only seven of them. His supervisor was the similarly industrious Gordon Robertson, perhaps the finest Canadian public servant of his generation. Robertson, who was only two years older than Trudeau, recognized that a well-educated young francophone was a precious asset in federal-provincial relations and assigned Trudeau major responsibilities in that area. Trudeau, in turn, approached the arcane details of the Canadian Constitution with a zest for the subject that he retained until his death. In a climate where the correction of grammar and prose style was usual, Robertson rarely found fault with Trudeau, and in most cases he responded with such comments as "Thanks, very interesting."[32]

Both the quality and the quantity of Trudeau's work were remarkable, even though some of it was surely not congenial. As in law school, Trudeau may have resented the unimaginative tasks, such as the list of over fifty pages of federal-provincial agreements he was asked to compile, but he completed it quickly and thoroughly. When he finally went on vacation in October 1950, he described how all his major responsibilities were being fulfilled. His duties included such diverse subjects as civil aviation, territorial waters, peace treaty implementation, loans to immigrants, and the Sub-Committee on Coastal Trade. He gently chided Norman Robertson, the clerk of the Privy Council, over this last project, indicating in a note to his supervisor— Gordon Robertson—that the most senior public servant had

---

only two francophones among twenty-two members. Frequently, as the sole bilingual member, he became the secretary to various committees— in case some committee member momentarily lapsed into French. TP, vol. 9, file 13.

not responded to Trudeau's memorandum on the subject: "Presumably there is no urgent business."[33]

Trudeau himself attended promptly to business, a quality that impressed and sometimes surprised his superiors. Obviously, they did not expect the opinionated and spirited intellectual to carry out menial tasks with dispatch. Like a seasoned lawyer, he could argue a case where his own opinions were different. This fierce foe of conscription and wartime registration dispassion-ately analyzed "national registration" between 1940 and 1946, concluding that it might serve to "locate individuals who had been separated from one another during an evacuation."

He even asked Gordon Robertson whether he should draw up a summary of arguments for and against banning Communists.* His memoranda reflected the government's con-cern that foreign-language publications were often Communist in sympathy, but he concluded by pointing to Prime Minister St. Laurent's view that legislating against opinion was wrong. While noting Conservative leader George Drew's stern anti-Communism, he also observed the young Saskatchewan MP John Diefenbaker's strong attachment to the principles of human rights. In the tradition of the public service, he presented choices objectively, carefully analyzing the impact of decisions. It is small wonder that Gordon Robertson wrote to him: "Your note outlining government and opposition statements . . . is just what

---

* On matters relating to the Catholic Church, however, he was less open-minded and still observant of certain restrictions. On January 20, 1950, he wrote to Archbishop Vachon of Ottawa indicating that, because of his pro-fessional responsibilities, it was necessary for him to read Marxist works that were on the Index. The archbishop gave him the permission he sought eight days later. TP, vol. 14, file 12.

I wanted and should be very helpful"—helpful, of course, to the Liberal government of Louis St. Laurent.[34]

Although Trudeau's Ottawa memoranda fit the requisite blend of clear prose and well-reasoned argument, occasionally his strong streak of independence and caustic impishness broke through bureaucratic restraint, as when he wrote about national registration: "Having done very little to prevent man from being anything but a number in a series of numbers, we have no right to object when the government institutionalizes that philosophy through national registration." His advice, though carefully measured, normally expressed his own views. National registration, he suggested, might be appropriate in wartime but not in peacetime. Communism was a threat, but existing legislation was sufficient to meet it. Only on one subject—federalism—did his own opinions break through the usual official Ottawa wisdom.[35]

Trudeau's time in Ottawa made him extremely interested in the character of federalism, in both the theoretical and the practical sense. His far-ranging education had often dealt with the subject, and Emmanuel Mounier, Harold Laski, and Frank Scott had probably become the pre-eminent influences on him, despite their own very different approaches. Still, until he began working in the Privy Council Office, Trudeau was more likely to write about democracy or economic and political equality than about federalism.

Ottawa clinched his fascination with the various theories of federalism and its application in Canada. Pierre Vadeboncoeur, one of his closest friends at the time, later described Trudeau as one who approached political questions "through his legalistic side." François Hertel similarly emphasized that, to understand Pierre, you had to realize that he was essentially "a lawyer." While it is true that both men were bitterly estranged from Trudeau when they made these remarks, their comments have validity.[36] Once in Ottawa, Trudeau drew increasingly on his legal training and his conception of the importance of law, statutes, legislation, and, implicitly, political order. The legal structures of Canadian federalism began to fascinate him—in the way that a young pianist experiences his first lessons in counterpoint and harmony and finally understands how beautiful chords are made. In a setting where surprisingly few officials had a legal education, Trudeau's training in the law and in philosophy gave him advantages, especially in debate.

There was one additional legacy of his Ottawa years: he became much more interested in Canada, in how it worked and how it could fail. He attended the Dominion-Provincial Conference of 1950 and took copious notes on the discussions of possible constitutional change. He also revised official documents, as the government took advantage of his fluent bilingualism. To his superior's delight, he used his lawyer's skills to undermine provincial arguments. His views on Maurice Duplessis did not echo the harsh opinions of his superiors, who thought the Quebec premier a destructive and devious boor in federal-provincial meetings. In his opinion, Duplessis did not represent his province well because he was too narrowly nationalist and too blind to the forces of change. After one exchange, Trudeau remarked that Duplessis's intervention was "interesting but Supreme Court would have to be changed." F.R. Scott, then an adviser to the Saskatchewan CCF government, impressed him most with his arguments that the best way to break through constitutional impasses was to begin with fiscal issues and social security. It was the same view that Pierre Vadeboncoeur had expressed on Trudeau's behalf the previous summer in *Le Devoir*.

Throughout the next decade, Trudeau developed this position more precisely.[37] His Ottawa experience began to persuade him that the problems he observed in Quebec could be confronted through a more effective Canadian federalism:

But there is yet another reason why co-operation is indispensable to a federation. What is popularly referred to as
division of powers is in reality division of legislative jurisdiction. And since legislative jurisdiction does not always ide-
ally correspond to divisions of administrative jurisdiction, it
so happens that very often the government most apt to leg-
islate on a given subject cannot be relied upon to adminis-
ter the laws most efficiently. Thus the legislative power of
one government will have to seek co-operation with the
executive or judicial power of another; which in short
means that federal and provincial governments, far from
seeking efficiency through complete independence in their
spheres, will resort to agreement and understanding.[38]

While increasingly persuaded that federal government initiative in social and fiscal realms was essential, Trudeau argued
that the provinces should maintain authority where they had clear
constitutional responsibilities. He therefore vigorously attacked a
bill on civil defence that came forward in 1951. "The most offensive provisions," he told his supervisor, Gordon Robertson, were
"those which appear to be based on a fantastic conception of
federalism." Some parts of the bill extend the "peace, order, and
good government" clause of the *British North America Act* far
beyond what its drafters intended. "It is preposterous," he declared,
for the federal government "to claim jurisdiction over the provincial governments *themselves*." Cooperation, he wrote in another
memorandum, "is indispensable to a federation," and neither jurisdiction can proceed "with complete disregard" of the other.[39] His
view of the federation differed from that of some Canadian officials
who were, in the postwar era, strongly centralist. Those views
derived from his past—and they would affect the future.

If Trudeau was dutiful and restrained in his first year in
Ottawa, he nevertheless chafed at the restraints that the government

of Canada placed on its civil servants. He impatiently drafted a letter to *Le Devoir* in May 1950, complaining that "public servants do not have the right to have opinions." He never sent it. However, his differences with the St. Laurent government became significantly greater when Canada decided to enter the Korean War during the summer of 1950, after the North Koreans invaded the South, and the United Nations, through the General Assembly, authorized an America-led intervention.

Trudeau disapproved of that decision and, especially, of Lester Pearson's strong advocacy of Canadian participation. Pearson believed that the North Korean attack represented the same threat to the young United Nations as the Italian attack on Abyssinia (Ethiopia) had been in 1935 to the League of Nations. Just as Canada announced an expansion of its earlier participation, Trudeau wrote hastily to Jules Léger, who was then a middle-rank officer in External Affairs:

> Dear Jules,
> I've just heard Pearson's speech on Korea in the House. Not a single original thought. A little current history, a lot of propaganda . . . Asia is heading down hill. There is still time to save Europe, at least by introducing the European division [of External Affairs] to that study on neutralism you spoke to me about.[40]

Trudeau was a rare dissenter on Canadian foreign policy at a time when even the socialist CCF had joined the Cold War consensus on the need to confront the Soviet Union in Europe and in Asia. Grace Trudeau was also caught up in the fervour. She had written to her son during his world travels in February 1949:

> Does world news reach you fresh? What do you think of Cardinal Mindszenty's trial, Hungarian. It is the talk of the

whole world. Prayers have been recited in all churches; now it is the Protestants who are being persecuted, those Reds are infiltrating themselves at an alarming rate, and no doubt we Americans of this continent are too willing to close our eyes, and not be on guard to the subtleness of their smooth ways. Everyone repeats that there exists a large number of communists in Canada. Are you going to be able to exterminate them with all your knowledge?[41]

In this case, Trudeau did not heed Grace's advice or share her views.

On a copy of one of Pearson's speeches on December 5, 1950, in which he claimed that Canada had urged moderation and a sense of global strategy, Trudeau scrawled: "Not very really."[42] Five months later he sent private notes to Douglas LePan and Pierre Trottier, both of External Affairs, attacking another of Pearson's speeches. In his note to LePan deploring Pearson's attack on the "hard-faced despots in the Kremlin," Trudeau pointed out that the cultured Canadian diplomat John Watkins* had "pictured Soviet Russia as a country of war-weary, peace-loving people, naïvely proud of their primitively democratic institutions; whose government was mainly engaged in improving the civilian economy, and was even proceeding with a certain amount of demobilization." Similarly, Trudeau said that the Canadian mission head in China, Chester Ronning, who sympathized with Mao's side, had indicated that "progress is being made in their solution for the benefit of the Chinese

---

* John Watkins was later accused of being compromised by his close personal friendship with a Soviet agent, but he died of a heart attack during the long and secret RCMP interrogation in Montreal.

people as a whole." Given these reports, Trudeau concluded (in somewhat flawed English):

> Either Mr. Pearson is unacquainted with such reports, then he is not doing his job; or, being acquainted with them, he discounts their veracity, then he is guilty of retaining the services of two foreign service officers who are gullible soviet stooges; or, believing in their veracity, he still prefers to spread the belief that the Communists are intent on starting a war, then he is misleading the people. Wars are fought with physical courage, but in these times courage of a finer temper is required to affirm one's belief in truth and justice. If Mr. Pearson had that courage, would he not acquaint the public with facts which might tend to open an avenue of comprehension and sympathy towards the potential enemy?

He wickedly signed the letter "Comrade Trudeau."[43]

In his note to Jules Léger complaining about Pearson, Trudeau had recommended that Léger read the latest *Esprit*, some articles by Étienne Gilson in *Le Monde*, and a piece by Hubert Beuve-Méry of *Le Monde* which pondered neutralism in Europe. He did not hide his dissent from the consensus, and his colleagues began to mock his stance in a friendly way, calling him "Citizen" as a mark of his left-wing rebelliousness.

While Trudeau remained cordial, it soon became clear that neither his opinions on international affairs nor his personality were suited to the puritanical and earnest ways of St. Laurent's Ottawa. Still, he continued to work on his files and did not turn down social invitations. "It was very kind of you to have me in for dinner last Monday," he wrote to Norman Robertson a couple of months later, on June 5, adding, "Wine excellent."[44] At this dinner, his host apparently gave him an article that had appeared in the *Partisan Review* by Lionel

Trilling, the Columbia University English professor who had abandoned earlier Marxist and radical left positions during the first stages of the Cold War. Clearly, Robertson wanted to draw the clever young francophone away from the European temptation of neutralism in the increasingly fierce battle between the West and the East.* Trudeau, however, held tightly to the arguments against both the Korean War and the rapid strengthening of North Atlantic Treaty Organization troops in Europe—forces that included a significant Canadian presence. In both cases, he believed that Canada was simply following American policy towards the Soviet Union and China—policy he deemed too uncompromising and aggressive.

—

Although there was a cadre of talented young francophones in External Affairs, there were few in the Privy Council Office where Trudeau worked. Moreover, the women in the office

---

* Trudeau did not often attend dinner parties, mainly because he spent many weekends in Montreal. However, the family of the eminent journalist Blair Fraser was linked with the Trudeau family through a mutual acquaintance, and they entertained him several times while he was in Ottawa. He responded gracefully after one such dinner. "That was an extremely pleasant evening I spent at your house on Thursday. Not only was the dinner excellent, the sherry stimulating, and the conversation informative, but I was able to confirm by scientific experience a principle which had long been laid down, 'the Frasers are very nice.'" He claimed that he was fortunate to meet all the family and felt "privileged that even little Graham [later another eminent Canadian journalist] should have condescended to see us after the ominous interest of the tam-tam." Trudeau to Mrs. Fraser, nd [1950], TP, vol. 9, file 12.

were exclusively secretaries. As Margaret Trudeau commented, he treated these women professionally, as working colleagues; and they responded to his charm and invariable courtesy with an admiration that is still quickly evident when they speak of him. He was considerate, familiar yet respectful, and polite. When some of these female employees were interviewed shortly after his death, they expressed deep admiration mingled with fondness. Words like "gracious," "thoughtful," "shy and charming" were frequently used.[45] Yet Margaret mentioned another category—"the dates"—who were often "celebrities" in the seventies and the eighties.

In the fifties, Ottawa had few celebrities, but Trudeau's attention was captured one September morning in 1950 by a front-page article in the *Ottawa Citizen* which featured a large photograph of Helen Segerstrale. "Your attention Men," the article began. "May we introduce Miss Helen Segerstrale, 20 years of age, accomplished and beautiful. She's just out from Sweden to take over a clerk's job in the Swedish Embassy." She had studied at Lausanne, where she specialized in French literature, and spoke five languages. The dark blonde, strong-featured Swede would, the *Citizen* proclaimed, be "Sweden's antidote to the 'crisis blues.'" Interestingly, Trudeau, a relatively small, very thin, though strongly muscled man, was attracted to beautiful, full-figured, and tall women. He kept photographs of most of the women in his life, and they usually fit this description. He clipped out the newspaper column, quickly forgetting his "blues" as Canadian troops prepared to go to Korea, and began his pursuit of Ottawa's newest celebrity.[46]

By Christmas, Trudeau had managed an introduction and set out, intensely, to win her heart. No doubt Helen, who became Hélène to Pierre as they became more intimate, was immediately intrigued by the unlikely civil servant who drove a Harley-Davidson and a Jaguar, dived and swam like the Olympian movie star Johnny Weissmuller, bought expensive Italian-tailored suits and wore them elegantly (in a town where Eaton's department store set the fashion standard), and could converse about a Rodgers and Hammerstein opening in New York and a recent performance of Sartre's *Huis Clos* in Paris.* Their letters mingle polylingual banter (including some Swedish), ceaseless repetition of love's language, tales of travel planned or finished, and philosophical reflections.

In diplomatic mail delivered "by hand" to the East Block from the Swedish Embassy the following summer, notes arrived bearing such unofficial messages as "You made me sooooo happy . . . you are the most wonderful person on this side of the globe . . . no, even on both sides (though I don't know any Chinese yet, I'll have to find out." And, on another occasion: "I feel like a young debutante, who has the love of a young man who must write sentimental things to the object of his great desire." She signed her letters "Puss." Beaches beckoned, and candlelight dinners at twilight were followed by intimacy. His Catholic commitment to chastity had disappeared sometime in the fifties, as it apparently did for many others of the faith. Yet he, like many who wavered from the official teachings, remained committed to the church.

Pierre and Helen began to talk about spending their lives together. Grace Trudeau had come to know her well during her frequent weekend visits to Montreal with Pierre, and she began

---

* In February 1950 he bought two suits for $183, and, in June, a sports jacket for $35, at Tobia Felli, a Montreal Italian bespoke tailor. He had another suit made for $74 in November 1949. A suit at Eaton's in 1950 cost about $20. TP, vol. 9, file 5. Before he resigned, his salary had increased to $3,696, a reflection more of the rise in the cost of living than of a generous government.

The coureur de bois on the canoe trip to Hudson Bay, 1941.

At the officers training camp at Farnham, "21 juin au 4 juillet" 1942. "Les guerres commanos de la tente 'sans-zèle.'" This revealing photo was taken at the exact time when Jean-Baptiste Boulanger and Trudeau were musing about a coup. The rifles may have been taken from the base by these soldiers "without zeal." From left to right: Charles Lussier (future director of the Canada Council); Gaby Filion (prominent artist and Trudeau boarder); Robert Pager; Jean-Baptiste Boulanger (member of the LX with Trudeau); Trudeau; Jean Gascon (future Companion of the Order of Canada and artistic director of the Stratford Festival); and Jacques Lavigne, who apparently was in a neighbouring tent.

At twenty-two, stylish on the boulevard, May 1942.

The archer, 1944, the year after Pierre graduated in law.

Grace and Suzette skiing at Ste-Adèle, May 1945.

Pierre and his friends get a moose, 1946–47.

Harvard, jeudi soir, 3 janvier, 1946.

Thérèse bien-aimée,

Les chevaliers d'antan saluaient leurs Belle avant de chevaucher au combat, et je pitoyable contre-façon ne me sens pas le courage de m'engager dans cette longue et morne étape qui s'ouvre sans t'avoir préalablement adressé un dernier mot.

J'ai pu prendre l'avion ce midi, et ce n'est pas Mozart mais toi que j'ai vue là-haut. Je me suis endormi dans les airs, et j'ai rêvé à toi, non seulement de toi "... Belle, ô Mortels, comme un rêve de Pierre". Les premières heures dans Cambridge sont très dures. J'ai l'âme égarée, un creux au cœur, et les jambes un peu molles.

An example of Pierre's romantic correspondence with Thérèse Gouin, 1946.

Pierre and Thérèse just before their "engagement,"
at Samovar, a Russian restaurant in Montreal, 1946.

Pierre recovering from his appendix operation in Mégève, Switzerland, December 1946.

Pierre "studying" in Paris. This photograph, and the next three, were commissioned by the French government educational office to show how Canadian students enjoyed Paris.

Pierre awakening Roger Rolland in Paris, 1947.

Pierre scaling Parisian Heights as Canadian students look on. His future Cabinet colleague Jean-Luc Pepin is at the back, apparently ready to catch him.

Dinner at a Paris restaurant: "Pierre, D.D. (Andrée Désautels), Hertel, 'Chanteuse,' Roger Rolland, 'Chanteur.'"

In 1949 Pierre visited the Middle East and adopted the area's traditional garb.

Pierre often stayed with priests on his world tour. Here he resists their attentions, 1949.

"He used to go from country to country with only a packsack on his back," said his brother, Charles. He was once arrested by the Arabs as an Israeli spy.

Pierre brought home a sari for his mother. This was, he wrote, their Oriental moment, 1949.

Hélène Segerstrale: It was a photograph of her in the *Ottawa Citizen*
that first attracted Pierre.

Pierre and Hélène at "Ottawa's only
caberet," the Copacabana, 1950.

Malaga, Spain, 1952. Trudeau on a roadtrip with his glamorous motorcyle.

to guide Helen on a critical path towards marriage: her conversion to Roman Catholicism. Like most Swedes, Helen wore her
traditional Lutheran faith lightly and did not resist change. The
process, however, became complicated when she received different messages from the parish priests and from Pierre's
Montreal friends. She told him how she had explained to her
own mother that it was not he who was imposing Catholicism
on her, but that she was finding Catholicism an attractive way
to live:

> On the contrary, you always told me how important it is
> to be free, to follow your nature, and that religion is a
> question between oneself and God. And then I told her
> [her mother] that the clerical atmosphere in Quebec
> could hardly have led me to Catholicism, on the con-
> trary; I explained how you and your Cité-Libre friends at
> the meetings made me understand the problems and
> trouble the Catholic priests can cause. But it's always the
> same thing that is difficult for us, "free Vikings of the
> north": to feel humble and to keep faith precious and
> essential, and to disregard man's imperfections as having
> nothing to do with faith.

With Pierre's help, Helen wrote several times over the following
few months, she would find the humility that was the prerequisite
to Catholic belief, commitment, and marriage.[47]

Now over thirty, Pierre was anxious to marry. Still, he was
an exacting lover, demanding in the attention he craved yet
fiercely independent in his own allocation of time. And, to
complicate matters, by the late summer of 1951 he had decided to leave the civil service, travel in Europe and other exotic
places, and then return to find his future in Montreal. Ottawa,
he realized, was not a congenial place for him to accomplish

his goals, and he craved the freedom he had earlier possessed. Amid Pierre and Helen's declarations of profound love that fall, there were frequent arguments. Still, they continued making plans to marry.

Then, in December, Trudeau wrote Helen a brusque letter complaining about her "manner." Baffled at his anger, she responded: "My love, I love you, I always have and always will to the end of the world. My love, is this itself not enough? Evidently not, because you seem to say that I don't express my love well enough or often enough." He apologized and asked her to meet him in Gibraltar in January 1952, enclosing with his letter a collection of Rimbaud's poems.[48]

Like Thérèse, Helen had decided that the relationship would not work. On January 26, 1952, she wrote and told him she had decided they should not marry. There were, very simply, too many crises and too much torment in their relationship. It was now necessary to "see things as they are." Among the problems was religion, which had concerned her "constantly during your absence." The leap of faith required to become Catholic was proving to be difficult. His absence had not made her love stronger. Indeed, she had met someone shortly after Trudeau left on his trip the previous October, someone he probably knew. In one week with him she had found more "harmony and peace" than she had ever known before.[49]

Trudeau was deeply wounded, especially when she refused to meet him in Europe in the spring of 1952. He begged to see her, accused her of being cruel, and promised to silently withdraw from her life forever if she so desired. Later, he begged forgiveness for his conduct: "I cannot take leave of you without adding that my present grief has permitted me to fully understand the anguish beyond endurance that in the past year I have inflicted upon one who loved me more deeply than seems humanly possible, and one whose pardon I can at last

most humbly seek . . . Fare thee well, sweet, sweet Hélène."[50]
The old pattern was repeating itself.*

—

Once Trudeau had decided to leave Ottawa by October 1951,
he openly chafed against the restrictions of the Canadian public service, just as he had earlier reacted against the transat-
lantic alliance of Britain, the United States, and Canada in
which Lester Pearson's foreign policy fitted so well. Against the
conventional views followed in Ottawa, he presented those
proclaimed by the French Catholic left in *Esprit* and *Le
Monde*—ideas that argued for conciliation rather than confrontation in the Cold War and that supported decolonization
in countries such as Indochina, where smouldering embers
had become raging flames.

In keeping with this contentious mood, he had an interesting exchange with Norman Robertson when he returned the
magazine in which Lionel Trilling had argued the liberal case

---

* Grace Trudeau had liked Helen, whom she too called "Hélène," and she
comforted Trudeau: "My dear boy it is needless to say how I feel about the
turn of events—my heart aches for you–Why oh why, are you put to such
suffering? I shall keep on praying that the future holds promise of happiness
for you who are so kind and good—but these are God's people whom He
puts to severe tests." In a letter a month later, Grace pointed to religious
beliefs as the major difficulty: "It is always necessary to meet and iron out
various opinions during the normal span of married life—let alone religious
beliefs which are principles and foundations one should share." Grace to
Pierre Trudeau, Feb. 24 and March 9, 1952, TP, vol. 46, file 20. Trudeau did
not write to his mother for several weeks at this time.

against Soviet Communism. He told Robertson that the article did not impress him, although he did agree that it was an anachronism to look at "labour as an oppressed cause." He objected strongly to Trilling's description of the idealist as "someone who finds virtue only where he is not." Far more convincing to Trudeau would be the definition "someone who finds not only virtue where he is." To the rather intellectually pretentious Robertson, Trudeau responded in kind: "Both these brands of idealists are poor material for totalitarianism of either extreme. The true totalitarian is an idealist who finds only virtue where he is, or a realist or an agnostic* who pretends to do so in order to avoid the fate of Buridan's ass." This medieval ass faced starvation when he could not choose between two equally attractive piles of hay. Trudeau continued: "Incidentally the ass might not have starved had there been more than two hay stacks to sway between. Which makes me feel that if free men ever let the world be divided in two, they will have to die like asses to avoid living like slaves. Another argument for the third force!"[51] The "third force" was a popular concept in *Esprit* and *Le Monde* in which Europe, under French leadership, stood aside from the Soviet-American confrontation and established an alternative social democratic society. Robertson, a former socialist himself, had little patience with such views, but he and Trudeau parted on good terms.

---

* Robertson was an atheist, which Trudeau probably knew. In pious Ottawa, Robertson insisted that the census record him as "atheist," a category which the Canadian census did not then have. On Robertson, see J.L. Granatstein, *A Man of Influence: Norman A. Robertson and Canadian Statecraft, 1939-1968* (Ottawa: Deneau, 1981).

Trudeau invited Norman Robertson and his wife, Jetty, to drop in on Saturday night, and then he drafted his letter of resignation, which he sent on September 28. His first draft began with "Dear Great Man," which eventually became, in mock revolutionary fashion, "Dear Citizen." His secretary told him he had to send a written resignation, and he did so in a letter that mixed polite sarcasm with a modest degree of gratefulness for an experience where he had been able to put his ample learning into practice:

> My work with the Privy Council has been to me a constant source of satisfaction, and not infrequently of delight. As for fellow workers, I cannot imagine a more sympathetic lot. I have never ceased to be aware of the precedence in your mind of human beings over institutions, and this in itself has been a valuable lesson . . .
>
> I dare to hope that the structure of the central government will not be too badly shattered by my departure. But however that may be, any sense of despair should be tempered by the knowledge that I will probably return to the Bar from which I once so impetuously resigned.

He departed from Ottawa on October 6, 1951, took five days of statutory leave, and formally left the civil service on October 14, 1951.[52]

—

While Trudeau was still in Ottawa working as a civil servant, he had become intrigued by discussions with his friend Gérard Pelletier, who had now left journalism to work for the Catholic trade-union movement. During these talks, the idea came up of a Canadian journal, to be called *Cité libre*, similar to the review *Esprit* published by the French philosopher Emmanuel Mounier. It would link progressive Catholic faith with analysis of contemporary political and social issues, just as *Esprit* had done in France.

According to Pelletier, *Cité libre* emerged from the Catholic youth movement and his own admiration for Mounier. In 1950 he took the lead, because of Trudeau's absence in Ottawa, and worked with others, notably the teacher Guy Cormier and the trade-unionist Jean-Paul Geoffroy, to create a journal that would be Catholic yet dissident. Another *Cité libre* founder, the literary critic and notary Maurice Blain, has perceptively noted the impact that the Great Depression and the Second World War made on the generation that founded the journal: "This generation without masters is seeking a humanism," he said, "and is anxiously asking on what kind of spiritual foundation this humanism should be based."[53] Those were the central questions that Trudeau, too, had asked himself in the forties, although he, as a Brébeuf student, had not done so within the Catholic youth movement.

After riding his motorbike to Montreal, Trudeau would join in the long night debates about the shape the journal should take. Pelletier cemented Trudeau's participation with the suggestion that *Cité libre* would fundamentally challenge the status quo in Quebec. But, he recalled, he had to convince others to accept Trudeau:

> On the one hand, he really was a novice among us, still grudgingly accepted by our team, several of whom barely knew him. On the other hand, he was vitally interested in our undertaking, which was to allow him, after several years' absence, to find his place in his generation, and in a circle that was broader than the one to which he belonged.

Neither his personality nor his wealth* (or his continuing references to Cardinal Newman as a source of inspiration) made Trudeau popular among some of Pelletier's colleagues, and they told Pelletier their complaints:

> Four or five of us were standing in the middle of the large kitchen, glasses in hand. It was well past midnight, closer, in fact, to dawn. We were having a quiet post-mortem on the evening's discussion when, suddenly, the thing that had been incubating for months gave the conversation an unexpected turn. It was not Trudeau's ideas that were questioned by my friends, but his origins, his circle, his society connections.

Although fascinated by his intelligence and strength, many found him, in Pelletier's words, "a disturbing influence." And, as Pelletier added wryly in the 1980s, "he has continued to be throughout his life."[54]

---

* In 1992 Ron Graham asked Trudeau whether it was true that Claude Ryan had once told him to give up his wealth and that he had considered renouncing his inheritance at Harvard. He dismissed the rumour, though he added that, at Brébeuf, he had realized it was unfair that some students "were doing their homework . . . on the kitchen table with mother cooking the food and the rest of the family milling around and so on. And I felt it was a bit unfair that I should have a private room in my house to do work." Citing a story by Antoine de Saint Exupéry, Trudeau said that it was wrong that a Mozart could not have a piano because of poverty. "So," he concluded, "I think there's more sense of fairness than of guilt on my part." Interview between Pierre Trudeau and Ron Graham, May 4, 1992, TP, vol. 23, file 7.

Guy Cormier, reporting the same conversation, said that when the first issue of *Cité libre* was passed around on the evening of July 14, 1950, at a cottage on Île Perrot, the editors had a "courteous but very lively discussion" about Trudeau's participation. The former Young Catholics were especially critical, with one of them saying: "I don't want to see Trudeau on the team. He's not with our people; he never will be with our people." On that and so many other occasions, Pelletier strongly defended his friend.[55]

This account is unconvincing, not because of the details of the discussion but because the first issue was ready well before Bastille Day, 1950, and because Trudeau was essential to its production. While it is undoubtedly true that his wealth caused hesitations, Trudeau is probably wrong to think it was the major source of the opposition to him. His financial support was, in fact, a large ingredient in the journal's success. Pelletier's Young Catholics predominated and Pelletier's wife, Alec, not Trudeau, signed the bank note to guarantee funding, but Trudeau and his friends brought resources and relationships that were crucial for its early success. The journal depended on money from nine people: Réginald Boisvert, Maurice Blain, Guy Cormier, Jean-Paul Geoffroy, Pierre Juneau, Charles Lussier, Pelletier, Roger Rolland, and Trudeau. Pelletier and Trudeau gave the largest contributions, $250.32, while the others gave much less. Cormier contributed only $31.09, and Geoffroy, $47.09. Trudeau covered debts when necessary, and he regularly paid the costs for the impecunious Pierre Vadeboncoeur and for Geoffroy.[56] He was, admirably, always silent about his private charity.

Moreover, Trudeau's meticulous address book provided buyers for the journal, which had only 225 subscriptions on its second issue. Among the names on Trudeau's list are female friends (including Jacqueline Côté, later the wife of Professor Blair Neatby, Mackenzie King's biographer, and his sister, Suzette), the great Catholic philosopher Étienne Gilson, and

Marcel Cadieux, Jean-Louis Delisle, Mario Lavoie, Georges Charpentier, and Jean Langlois of the Department of External Affairs. Trudeau's reach, both financial and personal, considerably exceeded his colleagues' grasp. He also bought up thirty-three copies to send to François Hertel to distribute in France, in the hope of increasing their readers abroad.[57] The initial price asked of subscribers was a lofty $2, at a time when the popular weekly *Le Petit Journal* sold for 10 cents.

Trudeau's presence was dominant from the first issue on. And, significantly, Trudeau began to find his place among his generation in Quebec through *Cité libre*. In the June 1950 premier issue, Trudeau wrote tributes to three giants who had recently died: the French socialist leader Léon Blum and his own intellectual mentors Emmanuel Mounier and Harold Laski. "Emmanuel Mounier has gone," he began his tribute to the founder of *Esprit*, whose influence touched every page of *Cité libre*'s first issue. So great was his impact that the journal's founders had hoped to give him the first copy of the new review. The other obituaries have more substance, and they also indicate why Trudeau did not share the opinions of Lester Pearson and the Ottawa mandarins in the summer of 1950 as Canada joined the United States and the United Nations in responding to the invasion of South Korea by the Communist North.

There were, Trudeau wrote, two systems that divided humanity in a dangerous way, with each one able to annihilate the other. There were, however, some who had "refused to be signed up in one or the other of the totalitarianisms. They have instead devoted their lives to interpreting and acting upon a belief which holds that liberty, justice and peace must be pre-eminent. As is inevitable, they are hysterically denounced and hatefully censured by both orthodox Marxists and official Christianity." Among the "circle of the just" (to use Dante's phrase linking eternal and temporal justice) who maintain the principles of Christianity and

human dignity, Trudeau found it "astonishing" that "two Jewish
Marxists have without pause distinguished themselves by their
intelligence, their courage, and their unending generosity": Harold
Laski and Léon Blum. Laski, he wrote, received heads of states and
poor students with equal simplicity, and his work would endure
as humans built the "free city" where they were able to live in tolerance and eventually in love. That, he continued, was why both
capitalists and Stalinists were sworn enemies of the principled
Laski and of the admirable Blum.[58] And that was why Trudeau
was increasingly uncomfortable in Ottawa.

Trudeau did not sign his name to those tributes, understandably, given his civil service position. In the same issue, he
wrote a major article whose title became an emblem of his
approach to politics, one which, before that summer, had lacked
coherence. "Politique fonctionnelle" (functional politics) became
a term that he bore with him as he navigated the rapids of political change in Quebec in the fifties and sixties. Right from the
first issue of Cité libre, Trudeau demonstrated that his experience
with the practical side of politics in Ottawa had left a mark, while,
simultaneously, he recognized the uniqueness of the Quebec
Catholic experience of his past. A church, he wrote, "would be
an impostor if it stayed forever in the catacombs. Similarly, in
politics, you cannot stay below ground too long." French
Canada, it seemed, might be heading for a dead end where its
leaders exaggerated the dangers of religious and linguistic assimilation while brandishing threats from supposed enemies — "the
English, Jews, imperialists, centralizers, demons, free-thinkers,
and I don't know what else." While slaying imaginary enemies,
he cautioned, "our language has become so impoverished that
we no longer notice how badly we speak," and clerics discouraged students from going abroad lest their faith be challenged.

Another passage in the article became celebrated as
Trudeau's political credo:

We want to bear witness to the Christian and French fact in America. Fine; so be it. But let's get rid of all the rest. We should subject to methodical doubt all the political categories relegated to us by the previous generation; the strategy of resistance is no longer conducive to the fulfillment of our society. The time has come to borrow the "functional" discipline from architecture, to throw to the winds those many prejudices with which the past has encumbered the present, and to build for the new man. Let's batter down the totems, let's break the taboos. Better yet, let's consider them null and void. Let us be coolly intelligent.

It is, in retrospect, a remarkable paragraph. It gave no offence to his Ottawa superiors, yet it initiated the definition of a new program.* Indeed, although there were no senior public servants on *Cité libre*'s subscription list, Trudeau's criticism of the high-handed way the Duplessis government acted at the federal-provincial conference of January 1950 would have pleased them immensely. When presented with concrete offers, Quebec remained stupidly silent. In concluding, Trudeau argued that the nationalism of the past and its intimate link with the clergy

---

* Another unsigned article in June 1951 would certainly have offended his superiors. In it he argued strongly against Canadian participation in the Korean War. He complained, as Canadian diplomats themselves did, about American policy towards Formosa (Taiwan) and the decision of the American general, Douglas MacArthur, to cross the 38th parallel and enter North Korea. However, he went beyond those complaints to attack the policies of the West towards Asia more generally and those of the United States more specifically. Everywhere, he claimed, the hallucinating fear of socialism guided American policy. Can they not understand, he asked, that their free-enterprise policies protect the most

no longer served the interests of a Catholic and French people who must confront a new world where old barnacles had to be scraped away.[59]

The importance of *Cité libre* for Trudeau was enormous. When he left Ottawa, he asked Jean Marchand whether there was a position for him in the trade-union movement, but he took no permanent job.[60] Through *Cité libre* he developed close contacts with the emerging media, especially television, where several of his friends, including Alec Pelletier and Roger Rolland, were finding positions. Although the journal's subscription list remained small, its influence among the intellectual and political elite of Quebec was considerable. The conservative historian Robert Rumilly warned Maurice Duplessis that "the people at *Cité libre* are extremely dangerous; they have international affiliations with the review *Esprit* in France; they are subversives and you must be wary of them. In the long term, it is very dangerous for your government."[61] Duplessis accepted the advice, which had merit, and cast an increasingly suspicious eye on the "*Cité libre* crowd."

Historians more recently have criticized the oversimplification that *Cité libre* was the overwhelming centre of opposition

---

reactionary feudalism and that their evangelical promotion of democracy "refuses to the oppressed [Asians] the right to use their new liberty to create an economic system different from *the biggest and the best?*" "Positions sur la présente guerre," *Cité libre*, May 1951, 3–11 [English and italics in the original]. In the case of Canada, he pointed out that it was always faithful to its tradition of defending the strong against the weak and "in matters of external policy, it has followed, it does follow, and it will follow." It is not surprising that External Affairs was an early target of Prime Minister Pierre Trudeau in 1968 or that Lester Pearson so strongly objected to Trudeau's Foreign Policy Review.

to Duplessis. It was not, but, in the words of the leading text on modern Quebec history, "*Cité libre,* despite its small circulation, represented a major gathering place and channel of expression for reform liberals."[62] It stood out because it championed two predominant themes that resonated widely at the time: traditionalist nationalism was outmoded, and the socioeconomic reality of Quebec required new approaches that emphasized democracy and individual freedom. In defining and refining those themes, Pierre Trudeau was to play a principal role in Quebec after the mid-century.

—

CHÁPTER 6

NATIONALISM AND SOCIALISM

T rudeau returned to Canada to play the part in public life he had long planned and for which he had conscientiously trained at Harvard and in Paris and London. He discovered that his legal and social scientific training had value in public policy debates within the national government, but Ottawa was then too distant from Quebec—the province where he wanted to play a part. He told a later interviewer: "I had searched for a way to put [intellectual change] in motion in Quebec in order to renew ideas, old habits of thought, and old cultural customs. *Cité libre* was a path. Ottawa was not."[1]

Those were grand hopes for a journal that had fewer than 250 subscribers, including some in Ottawa, girlfriends and relatives of the editorial team, and the former priest François Hertel, who peddled copies in Paris. Yet in Quebec in the 1950s the Catholic Index still survived, intellectual life among francophones remained centred within the church (which dominated both the colleges and the universities), and classical colleges like Brébeuf had created an elite whose members closely followed the activities of their peers. The debates occurred within this context—one Trudeau recognized in his article on functional politics in *Cité libre*'s first issue. Although he called there for demolition of the "totems," he still bore witness to the Catholic and French fact in North America. The church, according to the historian Michael Behiels, "remained, even in 1950, one of the most powerful social institutions in Quebec, sharing power with the predominantly anglophone commercial and industrial institutions and the francophone political institutions. Through its diocesan and parish administrations, educational institutions at all levels, farmers' and workers' organizations, social service institutions, national associations of every variety, and its enormous fiscal power, the Quebec Catholic Church permeated all of the conscious and unconscious social, cultural, and political behaviour of the vast majority of French Canadians."[2]

In this context the journal had attracted clerical attention almost immediately—something the editorial team had fully expected. Trudeau and Pelletier, the co-editors, shared a profound intellectual and emotional commitment to Roman Catholicism, but their criticism of the Catholic Church in Quebec was "that it preached an overly theocratic social and political philosophy which had spawned a corrupting form of clericalism." This clericalism brought a religious dogmatism and an authoritarianism that stifled intellectual freedom in the province. Young Catholics like Trudeau and Pelletier, who had thrilled to the intellectual openness of the church in France in the postwar years, were determined to challenge it, though they had to work within the well-defined and narrow world of Quebec Catholicism.

And so, from the beginning, *Cité libre* tested the limits. On international matters, where Trudeau's training and travels gained him immediate pre-eminence at the fortnightly editorial meetings, there was considerable freedom. His article opposing the Korean War, for example, reflected the opinion of many influential people in the church, the newspaper *Le Devoir*, and, according to the polls, the French-speaking population at large. Although it created a modest stir in Ottawa, it was largely ignored in Montreal. The real problems came for the journal when it touched on the power and the glory of the church within Quebec.[3]

Not surprisingly, Trudeau's combination of playful mischief and personal independence got him into trouble first. He wrote an article attacking clericalism and, in particular, interference by the Catholic Church in secular affairs where the opinion of the priest, he argued, should count for no more than anyone else's. He even referred mockingly to the "divine right of bishops." Trudeau's friends warned him that he had gone too far. Father Richard Arès, the eminent editor of the Jesuit journal *Relations*, indicated that Paul-Émile Léger, the archbishop of Montreal and brother of Trudeau's friend Jules, was very concerned about the orthodoxy of *Cité libre* and of Trudeau personally. Monsignor Lussier, whose brother Charles was active in *Cité libre*, was even more troubled.[4] In *Relations*, Trudeau's comments provoked a harsh attack from Father Marie d'Anjou which startled Trudeau. D'Anjou had been one of his four favourite teachers at Brébeuf and, in the extreme nationalism of the war years, d'Anjou had collaborated with him in the creation of the secret revolutionary cell and promoted Trudeau as the natural leader among the group. When Trudeau questioned why he had published the article without first telling him, d'Anjou sent this reply:

> But objectively, I think you deserved the criticism. Yet, I will always distinguish between your errors and you as a person. And you were very much mistaken when you wrote that prime ministers have no more divine right than do bishops. True as far as prime ministers are concerned but heresy when you apply it to bishops. You knew that, Pierre, I'm certain. Why did you risk this pointless and inappropriate bravado in your otherwise sound and dispassionate article?
>
> Perhaps you will think I am coming to the defence of a bad cause, that of the clergy you no longer trust. Pierre, this

needs to be qualified! You know me too well—even some aspects of my personal religious experiences—to suspect me of blind loyalty. If I intervene here, it is because there are principles at stake which go infinitely beyond the cause of certain members of the clergy (however many there may be). My despair would be that you not recognize my point of view. But that is not my fear.

Then, suddenly, he changed topic:

Have you given your alms for Lent? If not I have a proposition to make, similar to the one you sent me from London three or four years ago. Once again I am coming to the assistance of an unwed mother. You know what that means. My cashbox is empty. If your finances allow it, I wonder if you could make a contribution . . . You need not apologize if my request arrives at an inopportune time. Thanks in any event.[5]

Despite his anger, Trudeau responded to d'Anjou's request for the contribution. D'Anjou thanked him "in the name of the individual who has benefited from your wonderful charity" and promised that he would say a Mass for him during Easter week. However, he added that he had chatted with Archbishop Léger, who expressed his concerns about *Cité libre*.[6]

In the spring of 1951, Archbishop Léger summoned Gérard Pelletier and Trudeau to his office. Trudeau was still working in Ottawa and had to make a special trip to Montreal for the appointment, which finally took place in the late summer. Pelletier had already warned him that Léger had told Claude Ryan, a prominent official in the Catholic Church and then an admirer of Trudeau, that he was concerned—and that it had something to do with *Cité libre*.* The mood was tense for the early evening meeting.

The Archbishop made his entrance. There were the usual greetings and handshakes, then . . . nothing. An embarrassed silence on both sides. A bad start. Why was our host, normally at no loss for words, sitting there and smiling at us? Was he expecting explanations from us before they were even asked for? As Trudeau didn't let out a peep, I screwed up my courage and said:

"You called us in, your Grace . . ."

He shifted in his chair.

"I invited you," he corrected me. "This is not a summons, I invited you, first of all to make your acquaintance and then to draw your attention to certain points . . . of doctrine raised by your articles."

After some discussion, it became clear that Trudeau had been the main offender by his comments about the "divine right of bishops," but he did not back down. He even said that if he and *Cité libre* were condemned, "we would appeal to the universal Church, as is our right." The archbishop, in response, "stared strangely" at Trudeau. Then, he passed to the next point. In "those few seconds," Pelletier wrote later, "the fate of *Cité libre* was decided in the incredible atmosphere of a medieval dispute."[7]

---

* Ryan reported that he said to Léger that "the group at *Cité libre* are Christians and their intentions are sound," that they were among his friends. He advised the archbishop to see Trudeau and Pelletier before he acted, but nothing happened. When Ryan next met Léger, the archbishop asked why they had not come. Ryan replied that "they were probably waiting for their invitation." After some time sorting out how it should be handled, the meeting was arranged. Pelletier to Trudeau, Feb. 28, 1951, TP, vol. 21, file 21.

But Quebec in the fifties was no longer medieval, even if some knights of the church and state wished it to be.

—

When Trudeau returned to Canada in 1949 after his world trip, he found that the Quebec nationalism that had thrust him towards the barricades earlier in the decade was no longer intellectually compelling or emotionally consuming. The Quebec Catholic Church, which had absorbed him earlier, now seemed marginalized from the engrossing debates he had encountered on his travels, particularly in France. There was, for him, a striking dissonance in his home province. In many ways Quebec was part of the general North American prosperity, with its new highways, stores crammed with merchandise, telephones that worked, and electricity that no longer flickered or disappeared. Yet in other ways it lagged, and, for Trudeau and his colleagues at *Cité libre*, the church had become the barrier not only to progress but to a richer spiritual life. In the diverse countries he visited, Trudeau had seen the boundaries changing, and he was becoming convinced that the essence of freedom for groups and individuals alike was the right to choose their identity.

Yet in defining his own identity he was still, at this time, pre-eminently French and Catholic, and he sought change within that mould. In his two years in Ottawa, his relationship with Helen Segerstrale is revealing: he wrote to her in French, they escaped to Montreal whenever they could, and his commitment to the Catholic faith became an obstacle between them. He did not wear British woollens or read the *New Yorker* magazine as his fellow mandarins did. Although he learned a lot about the Canadian political system through his work, his emotional and intellectual commitment to Canada's national political system remained weak.

As the 1950s progressed, however, Trudeau would develop an intellectual appreciation of Canada as a potentially successful state. Gradually this cerebral admiration would win over his emotional loyalty too. In these years he began to form the sense of Canadian identity that he later expressed eloquently in his political life, as both an author and an actor in the Quebec and the Canadian political process. The route he followed at this time, however, has perplexed scholars who objectively study his career, just as it did his closest personal friends.

In the fifties Trudeau often appeared to be aimless, if not dilettantish. The conservative nationalists with whom he had worked in the early forties, such as the Union nationale politician Daniel Johnson, dismissed him as a "dandy," a rich, unreliable playboy who made no serious contribution to the political scene. Even Pelletier became so frustrated by Trudeau's eclectic ways and frequent journeys to exotic destinations that he inquired: "Pierre, isn't it a catastrophe to be born rich?" Another friend bluntly asked, "What are you going to do when you grow up, Trudeau?" Thérèse Casgrain, the leading Quebec feminist and socialist who worked closely with him in the 1950s, also expressed impatience with his habit of "launching ideas or movements, only to lose interest or turn to something else." Reporters impressed by his quick intelligence and articulate arguments frequently qualified their praise by remarking on his lack of perseverance and sustained focus. An irritated Maurice Duplessis dismissed his old friend Charlie Trudeau's son as "lazy, spoiled, and subversive."[8]

True, Trudeau was single, and it did give him a freedom that Pelletier, for instance, who had a wife and children, did not possess. Some of his other colleagues, even if they were bachelors, had jobs at universities or colleges or with Catholic trade unions, and they feared losing positions and salaries because of clerical wrath. Trudeau also had the independence that wealth brings. His net worth in the early fifties remains unclear, but Belmont

Park, one of his principal investments, flourished, and the stock market and real estate provided handsome returns. His mother's money was available to him if he needed it, but, clearly, he did not. He derived enough from his trust, and, as the elder brother, he managed the estate with the assistance of an accountant and bankers. At that time, travellers needed banker's drafts for extended periods abroad. They were not automatic and most had limits placed on amounts that could be withdrawn. Trudeau, however, quickly obtained letters that allowed him to draw on funds in Canada, and most of them specified no limit.

To many observers, it seemed that Trudeau lived like a hedonist. Gérard Filion of *Le Devoir* called him a bohemian, but it was a peculiar bohemianism. He lived in his mother's gracious house, where she or the servants looked after all his daily needs. He wore expensive clothes, drove a Jaguar first and then a treasured Mercedes 300SL convertible, courted stunningly beautiful young women, and travelled to foreign locales whenever he felt like it. He frequented the bars on Crescent and the galleries on Sherbrooke, and, after his mother became president of the Montreal Symphony women's association in 1951, he often joined her in the finest seats at the concerts. With his colleagues, however, he often appeared indifferent to money—and understandably so, given that nearly all his youthful friends, except for Roger Rolland, lacked it.*

Yet Trudeau did not hesitate to appear ostentatious when the mood struck. Jean Fournier, a witty and charming External Affairs officer Trudeau sometimes socialized with in his Ottawa

---

* Rolland, whose family owned a large paper company, said later that they enjoyed being outrageous together, getting into pranks that made their families furious. Grace's letters reveal, however, that she, at least, enjoyed hearing about their escapades.

days, recalled that, one icy winter day, he and his wife urged Trudeau not to risk the motorbike trip to Montreal. Instead, Trudeau appeared at their house the following Monday morning "behind the wheel of a brand-new American car." Their young sons shrieked with pleasure when Trudeau scooped them up and drove them to school. The story reveals not only Trudeau's wealth and independence but his remarkable ways with children—who always loved his own childlike playfulness.[9]

Youngsters also appreciated his generosity. Tip's wife, Andrée, who adored Trudeau, gently chastised him for the abundance of gifts he bestowed on his nieces and nephews at Christmas and when he returned from exotic locales. A cottage neighbour said his five young daughters often heard complaints about Pierre's arrogance or distance but could not believe it of the older man, who charmed with his many tricks and listened to each of them as if there were no one else on earth. The stories about Trudeau's interaction with children are absolutely consistent.[10]

The criticism of the adults, however, left its mark. Deemed unreliable by some of his friends, lazy and ineffective by his enemies, Trudeau himself seemed to view the fifties later as a lost decade. When he published his memoirs in 1993, he allotted only five of the 368 pages to the period between his departure from the Privy Council Office in October 1951 and the election of Jean Lesage in 1960. He knew about the comments of his friends—Casgrain wrote in the early 1970s and Pelletier in the 1980s—yet he did not bother to refute them, much less the harsher comments of his enemies. He seemed to treat politics as a plaything, flirting with the Co-operative Commonwealth Federation (CCF), skewering Louis St. Laurent and Duplessis in the media, and periodically announcing a bold initiative for a new political grouping. It is hardly surprising that the blondes, the cars, the clothes, and the travel made even his friends wonder whether this extraordinarily gifted young man was truly "serious." But he was.

Trudeau's papers and writings indicate that the 1950s were fundamental in shaping the role he would later play so dramatically in both Quebec and Canada. That was the decade when he did become serious and consistent. Moreover, he began very ably to shape his adolescent thoughts of a public life into an adult reality. It was not an easy task. In his memoirs, he says that "people have often asked me whether, in the 1950s, I already had political ambitions. I have always answered in the negative, which was the truth."[11] It is a partial truth: only if you take an extremely narrow view of political ambition—specifically, election to a legislature—is the statement true. Even then, he did consider such a political career as early as 1952.

These personal papers also reveal a disconnect in this decade between the image of the brilliant but erratic bohemian and the reality of his life. Even more than the forties, when he moved from being a conservative Quebec Catholic nationalist to a cosmopolitan francophone on the left, the fifties was a transformative decade for him. He became deeply grounded within the political life of Quebec, and he gained political skills as he participated in the protracted assault by Quebec intellectuals and the liberal media on Maurice Duplessis's government. Simultaneously, he began his fateful encounters with the English-Canadian intellectuals in person and with the broader English-Canadian public through the media.

There are certainly moments of insouciant bohemianism in Trudeau's life in the fifties. But there is also great ambition, diligence, and a deliberate attempt to create a public presence that confronted not only Duplessis's Union nationale government but also Canada's lazy sense of conformity. Although Trudeau had no regular job, he worked hard on labour arbitration boards and on his journalistic writing, which appeared not only in *Cité libre* but also in *Vrai*, a newspaper edited by his crusading friend Jacques Hébert. There were letters to the editor, travel pieces for *Le Devoir*, attacks on various wrongs, and piles of handwritten letters to friends and foes. He was a painfully careful writer, revising drafts several times as he sought the perfect word. Usually, he found it. Pelletier later recalled how Trudeau would labour over a minor piece for *Vrai* and submit it at the last possible minute for publication. And he worked for several years on his major intellectual effort, an edited study of the Asbestos Strike. When it finally appeared in 1956, it immediately set off intellectual explosions in classrooms, editorial pages, and secular and religious chapels.

Books mattered, but Trudeau realized in the fifties that the new media—initially the radio, then television—were becoming fundamental to shaping public debate. On radio his quick repartee, distinctive voice, and immediate expression of emotion brought frequent invitations to participate in debates and discussions. Not so on television, where, initially, he was wary, hesitant, and not very good. Soon he mastered his presentation, however, and it became the medium that carried his message and personality far beyond the intellectual crowd at *Cité libre*. The proportion of Quebec homes with television grew from only 9.7 percent in 1953 to 38.6 percent in 1955, to 79.4 percent in 1957, and 88.0 percent in 1960—a higher number than for Canada as a whole. Very quickly, the audience that mattered most were the groups of people surrounding the black and white box every evening in Quebec homes.[12] Trudeau's face became familiar; his voice, compelling, as television aerials sprouted at astonishing speed above homes not only in Montreal and Quebec City but in the small towns and villages of Quebec. And he made sure he maintained close ties with television producers and personalities. Alec Pelletier was a producer; his former roommate Roger Rolland worked for Radio-Canada and his *Cité libre* colleague Pierre Juneau for the National Film Board; and several other acquaintances had employment or other ties in the field. He ceased to search for university jobs that would place him in classrooms rather than in living rooms.[13] He wanted a defined and carefully constructed public presence. He also wanted his independence and privacy. The tension between these competing desires remained until his death.

Trudeau learned to play to the camera. His compelling eyes, even white teeth, and high cheekbones captured the attention of his viewers, who became fascinated with his remarkable ability to shift his expression in an instant from withering contempt to an engaging, bashful smile. He used the debating skills he had honed so well at Brébeuf and in hundreds of evenings in Paris, in Pelletier's home, and "on the road." Marshall McLuhan, the celebrated Canadian media analyst and gifted phrase-maker, soon noticed this new talent on the "cool" medium of television and wrote to Trudeau, "You've got the cool image, the mask." There was an almost mystical link between Trudeau and television, he said: "The story of Pierre Trudeau is the story of the Man in the Mask. That is why he came into his own with TV."

McLuhan's comments intrigued Trudeau, and the ambitious young Quebecer struck up a friendship with the professor, often making unannounced visits to his home in Wychwood Park in Toronto. "The medium shapes the message," McLuhan quipped, and, in this electronic age, television was the medium for politics and campaigning—politicians, henceforth, would need to have charisma. Trudeau should not worry about possible contradictions in his developing ideas, he advised, but should "probe" wherever his thoughts led him. "It freed me up," Trudeau reminisced later, after this mentor's death. In McLuhan's view, Canada, and especially French Canada, possessed a profound "cultural gap." French Canada "leapt into the 20th century without ever having had a 19th century. Like all backward and tribal societies, it is very much 'turned on' or at home in the new electric world of the 20th century."[14] The statement oversimplifies, but it also emphasizes, rightly, the enormous impact television had on Quebec, as well as Trudeau's warm relationship with the camera.

The mystical mingled with simple good luck and crafty planning to make Trudeau's television presence so striking. He consciously created an aura of intrigue, adventure, and intellectual brilliance about him. The last came easily to Trudeau, although, characteristically, he sometimes had private doubts.*

---

* In 1954 Trudeau took an IQ test at the University of Ottawa. The Wechsler Test had seven categories and Trudeau was measured against the francophone population of Ottawa between the age of fifteen and sixty years. The results, interestingly, reflected his marks at Brébeuf. He ranked highest in mathematical and abstract reasoning (excellent) and lower in visual motor tasks (average and above average). His "average" ranking in attention and short-term memory was surely wrong. In any event, his overall ranking was the highest possible (excellent). Maurice Chagnon, University of Ottawa, to Pierre Trudeau, Feb. 1954, TP, vol.14, file 37.

He also had a "Miss Parsons," who appears to have been a female colleague, analyze his handwriting. She told him that his mind was "extraordinary. Brilliant, searching, certainly above the average." In a remarkably perceptive analysis, she wrote: "You are methodical in procedure, accurate and dependable . . . You may give the appearance of not noticing people and their actions, or what is going on around you to any great extent, but you intuitively understand and observe more, in five minutes, than the ordinary individual would observe in a day." She noted that he was shy but could also be "the life of any party." He had a quick temper and a tongue that could bite. He gave the appearance "for the most part of a gentle nature, and you probably are, but you can certainly be the opposite at will." She concluded, perhaps expressing a personal experience, that his interest in women was "nil." He admired beauty, "but it does not go any deeper, either by intent or nature." She concluded that there was "a great deal more to this writing of yours than meets the eye." One suspects that personal contact as much as Trudeau's unremarkable handwriting guided Ms. Parsons's analysis. D.L. Parsons to Trudeau, nd, ibid.

The mystery, so important to the culture of celebrity in the twentieth century, became part of the Trudeau image that he and others created in the fifties. Although his travels often inconvenienced his collaborators, they initially dominated the content of his public appearances on radio and television. As his critics noted, he romanticized his voyages.

On Radio-Canada on May 5, 1950, for example, the broadcaster Jean Sarrazin painted a "Portrait of Pierre Trudeau" that Trudeau corrected himself before the broadcast—one of the changes being his addition of "Elliott" to the title. Sarrazin began the broadcast by noting how "French Canadians like to travel." He then proceeded to describe how Trudeau had toured the world with only a backpack, a few dollars, and a beard. He "clandestinely" created "some ultra-official documents" that permitted him to penetrate the Iron Curtain. The most beautiful women in Europe were in Budapest, and he spent "voluptuous nights on the Danube!" The voyage continued in breathless prose as Trudeau became a postwar blend of Phileas Fogg and James Bond, fearing none, confronting evil, and meeting gorgeous women at unexpected moments. There was, for example, the time in Turkey when he was offered a bath: "Tragedy! He did not understand the sign and entered the women's section entirely nude . . . the beautiful Ottomans cried and sighed." Once again, he was expelled from the country.

The tale of dash and daring forged on, of the young Canadian with the backpack who went "behind the Iron Curtain . . . encountered Greek guerrillas, the war in Palestine, the troubles in Afghanistan, the war between India and Pakistan, the Burmese revolution, the battles in Indochina, and civil war in China. He was in prison ten times, shot at three times . . . And yet survived to tell the story." The last word on the broadcast belonged to Trudeau: no matter how perilous the journey, he said, it had been worthwhile because he "saw how human beings are good when you present yourself without pretension."[15] The story, of course, bore only passing resemblance to the accounts in his letters home. Altogether, it indicated that Pierre Trudeau had already learned how to make himself a lively story. He knew that presentation mattered as much as content.

Part of the presentation involved his clothes, hand tailored not at Eaton's or Holt Renfrew, but by an Italian tailor working with the finest imported cloth and sometimes even silk. Occasionally, he would wear his father's dramatic black cape. Accessories such as scarves or gloves he often bought on European trips, where he also purchased some vintage wines unknown in Quebec, even though he was abstemious where alcohol was concerned. In the photographs of the early fifties, Gérard Pelletier, Jean Marchand, and most of the others have cigarettes in their fingers, tousled hair, and jackets a bit askew. Trudeau, in contrast, has a short haircut, never a cigarette (although he had tried smoking in the early forties), and, even in casual wear, clothes that seem to fit perfectly. He bought the best but, as Marc Lalonde later pointed out, he kept it for a long time, depending on an excellent sense of personal style in his clothing.[16]

Certainly, he is fit himself: the enormous stock of photographs of Trudeau in a bathing suit, surprisingly bikini-like for the times, reveals an adolescent's lean, well-muscled body. He tended it carefully, to the point of taking ballet lessons to learn how artists control their movement.* Similarly, he supplemented the boxing skills learned from his father with the Japanese self-defence system of

---

* The ballet lessons he took with Sylvia Knelman, later the eminent economist Sylvia Ostry. Conversation with Dr. Ostry.

karate. All these acquired abilities created a shield, along with the personal self-confidence that sometimes seemed "swagger" to others. René Lévesque, for example, once said that Trudeau had an "inborn talent for making you want to slap his face." As Pelletier remarked, René would have "taken good care to avoid a dust-up with Pierre . . . because he [Lévesque] was gifted for boxing the way Muhammad Ali is for embroidery."[17] Despite his average stature, Trudeau intimidated physically.*

Once he returned to Montreal, Quebec politics quickly became his main preoccupation. His Ottawa experience had soured him on federal politics, though it had intrigued him in terms of the potential he now saw in federalism. Still, he was annoyed by the dull, anglophile style of the capital and by the government's integration of Canadian defence and foreign policy with that of the United States. He respected Louis St. Laurent, but the francophone prime minister disappointed him because he expected him to be another charismatic Laurier and not a "chairman of the board," while Lester Pearson, the external affairs minister and the most popular politician in the Canadian media, did not impress him much. He now also detested the Duplessis government and thought little of the Liberal opposition in Quebec City. He could not abide the anonymity of being a civil servant, particularly the requirement that he remain silent on public issues. Freed of such restraints and home in Montreal, he expressed his political interests through his pen and his media presentations and, to a much lesser extent, through membership in the CCF.

---

* Although the 5'10" height he always listed for his passports may be in doubt, his tailor's records indicate that, in 1955, at age thirty-six, his neck size was a well-muscled 15 inches, his chest 38, and his waist only 32. TP, vol. 14, file 1.

Among the *Cité libre* crowd, Trudeau's specialization quickly became politics and international affairs—areas that fitted in well with his desire to travel.*

But the team was not amused when, on October 24, 1951, just a few weeks after his return to Montreal from Ottawa, he set off on yet another grand tour for the winter and spring to Europe, Africa, and the Middle East—including a visit to the Soviet Union.

—

Trudeau's decision to attend the International Economic Conference in Moscow in the spring of 1952 so soon after his

---

* Trudeau had been deeply influenced by dreams of a "middle way" between Communism and capitalism. His experience around the world had made him sympathetic to national liberation movements in colonial empires—developments the Soviet Union ostensibly championed and many Western states opposed. In Ottawa there had already been an example of this interest.

During his world tour in 1949, French Indochina, as it then was, had charmed him. He admired the people and the mingling of French and Asian culture. Now a public servant, on October 2, 1950, he took two "Annamite gentlemen" to call on the External Affairs' Asian specialist, Arthur Menzies: Peter Martin Ngo Dinh Thuc, the archbishop in Hué, Indochina, and his brother Ngo Dinh Diem. Five years later, Ngo Dinh Diem would become president of an independent South Vietnam, only to be killed by the Central Intelligence Agency in 1963, just as the Vietnam War entered its bloodiest years and three weeks before the assassination of President John Kennedy. In the External Affairs memorandum on the meeting, Trudeau is reported as saying little, but he expressed scepticism in a later marginal note he wrote about "American weapons" being an appropriate response to the challenge of Vietnamese departure from the Privy Council Office troubled his former Ottawa colleagues. As a civil servant working in the Privy Council, he had been granted the highest security clearance and access to top-secret diplomatic dispatches. Meanwhile, in Washington, Senator Joe McCarthy and his henchmen were hounding suspected Communists, and, ever since the Gouzenko spy affair of 1945–46, Canada had been a favourite hunting ground. When Igor Gouzenko, a cipher clerk in the Soviet Embassy in Ottawa, defected, he revealed the existence of a spy network within the Canadian government. It was a dreadful time—one of paranoia and fear. The Canadian diplomat Herbert Norman, who had been linked with Asian Communists while

---

Communist leader Ho Chi Minh. "Like building up Chiang Kai Shek!" he scribbled. Although he believed deeply in decolonization, he knew that the process could be difficult, and he thought the Americans were usually clumsy in their attempt to preserve capitalist interests during the decolonization process. In his conversation that day, Diem was adamant that France should not fight to keep Indochina; indeed, he said that French culture, which the Vietnamese treasured, should be maintained through French Canada, whose missionaries were highly respected in Indochina. Trudeau agreed: whether in Algeria or Indochina, he opposed the French Empire but supported a French cultural presence.

This belief was ultimately the basis for later Canadian efforts to create a community of francophone-speaking countries. The incident reveals how Trudeau's international politics drew deeply on his European education and possessed neither the anti-Communism of the Catholic Church nor the American suspicion that led the United States into Indochina and the Vietnam War. "Visit of Monseigneur Thuc and Mr. Ngo-Dinh-Diem," Oct. 2, 1950, TP, vol. 10, file 11. Dr. Greg Donaghy, the Foreign Affairs historian, informs me that the record of this meeting is missing in departmental papers.

a student and teacher at Harvard, was already in McCarthy's sights, and FBI director J. Edgar Hoover even expressed doubts about Lester Pearson. Trudeau, moreover, had made no secret of his strong opposition to American foreign policy.

When Norman Robertson, the clerk of the Privy Council, heard about Trudeau's imminent departure, he recalled his former officer's arguments against the Korean War and in favour of reconciliation with the Communists.[18] He was concerned that Trudeau was setting off to Moscow just as the Soviet Union was imposing even greater restrictions on the freedom of Canadian diplomats in the capital. As a result, Trudeau's path was carefully followed by External Affairs personnel, and they assured Canada's allies that Trudeau had guaranteed them he would reveal no secrets.

After an initial disagreement with Robertson about his even attending the conference, Trudeau obtained credentials as a reporter for *Le Devoir*. The other members of the Canadian delegation were well-known figures on the left, including Morris Miller, who had been a classmate at Harvard and at the London School of Economics. As Trudeau departed from Prague on his way to Moscow, he told journalists (according to a report from a Canadian Embassy official) that the conference "would provide the first step for the establishment of economic and trade relations between capitalist states and countries with planned economies." It did not. He also claimed that the conference had attracted "lively interest" in Canada. Again it had not, except, perhaps, in the East Block and the Communist Party of Canada.

On March 31, 1952, *Pravda* announced the arrival in Moscow of Pierre Trudeau, "lawyer and adviser on trade-union questions." The Canadian Embassy contacted him and he met the chargé d'affaires, Robert Ford—a poet and perhaps the shrewdest diplomat ever to serve in Moscow during the Cold

War. Ford dismissed the conference as propaganda and paid little attention to Canadian delegation members apart from Trudeau. He reported to Ottawa that Trudeau, unlike the other delegates, continued to check into the embassy "for advice and also to inform us of what was going on." He was "useful" as he gave them copies of the conference proceedings. Ford soon realized that Trudeau was not the usual "fellow traveller" from the West. He quickly irritated his Russian "guide," for example, by asking why there were so many portraits of Stalin and none of Trotsky. The two men seem to have had fun together: Ford introduced him to caviar at the embassy, where Trudeau spent more and more of his time as he quickly became fed up with the conference itself. Still, Ford found him "puzzling" and wondered what "his real attitude to this country is."

There, in the darkest days of the Cold War, with madness insinuating its effects even more deeply into Stalin's aged mind, Ford and Trudeau argued about the meaning of Soviet Communism. Trudeau, according to Ford's memoranda to Ottawa, had been greatly impressed by the conference sessions on Soviet living conditions. He described conversations with three Soviet academic economists, and he took those exchanges as support for his belief that people could associate freely in Moscow. Trudeau, Ford continued, "claims his position is that of a neutralist-idealist and that it is possible for men of good will to try to act as a centre group which will gradually widen and prevent the two extremes from clashing." Ford strongly disagreed: "I am willing to believe that his feelings on this subject are genuinely idealistic, but I am afraid that he fails to realize that being neutral in the present struggle seems inevitably to involve leaning over backward to justify Russian actions, on the one hand, and to criticize the Western position, and particularly the United States, on the other." This idealistic strain was, in Ford's words, accompanied by "a kind of infantile desire to shock"—one that would not matter in Montreal but did very much in Stalin's Moscow.*

Trudeau went to the American Embassy chapel to attend Easter Mass. There, at midnight, he met the wife of the American chargé. In a provocative mood, he told her, yes, he was Catholic but a Communist too, "after which he proceeded to heap praises on the U.S.S.R. and attack the United States." Or so the dispatch to Ottawa reported. Ford encountered an angry American diplomat the next day: "I thought you said Trudeau was not a Red?"

---

* In his memoirs published in 1989, Ford was forgetful, discreet, or exceedingly diplomatic about this incident. He said he met Trudeau when he "unexpectedly turned up in Moscow at a mysterious economic conference organized by the Soviets and attended mostly by representatives of communist front organizations," and that Trudeau also became fed up with Russian lodgings and food. Strangely, given the story told by the U.S. envoy, he concluded his account: "Nor did he hesitate to accompany my wife and myself to Easter mass in the impromptu chapel of the American embassy." Robert A.D. Ford, *Our Man in Moscow: A Diplomat's Reflections on the Soviet Union* (Toronto: University of Toronto Press, 1989), 113. However, he was more caustic in an interview with Professor Robert Bothwell on October 15, 1987. "Going off the record," Ford asked: "What should one make of a prime minister who in 1952 had visited Moscow to attend the conference of a front organization? He'd enjoyed Hotel Rossiya food for a week before he came to the embassy for relief dinners—after which he ate well enough and clung to the embassy. But no explanation of why he was there." Then he said to Professor Bothwell, at the embassy "he liked us and we liked him." He discovered caviar there and always contrasted the treatment in Moscow with the bad treatment he received at other Canadian missions. Really, Ford said, Trudeau was "one of the brightest and most attractive people" he had ever met. Interview with Robert Ford, Oct. 15, 1987, Robert Bothwell Papers, University of Toronto Archives.

Ford denied he was, but then the American repeated Trudeau's remarks to his wife. Ford responded that Trudeau was simply joking. Nevertheless, he told Ottawa that he was sure a report would "go back to the State Department that a man who only six months ago was employed in a confidential job in the Privy Council is now in Moscow . . . and has openly stated that he is a Communist."

Not for the first time, Trudeau knew he had gone too far. He sent a handwritten letter to Norman Robertson, copied to several desks in External Affairs, in which he said that he had "half heeded" his advice not to go by gaining his press credentials. Claiming he held "few men in higher regard" than Robertson, he defended his decision to attend because of his urge to travel. Then, unctuously, he concluded: "I trust that Spring is finding Mrs. Robertson and your daughters in the best of health, and that you are finding life in the Privy Council Office as pleasant and as stimulating as I always did." Indeed.[19]

Trudeau was subsequently denied a visa to travel to China via Tashkent, but he did manage to obtain permission to visit Tbilisi, Georgia, after obtaining some extra rubles from British economist Alex Cairncross. When he arrived at the train station in Moscow, he met a beautiful young woman who addressed him in excellent English and shared his mixed-sex compartment for the three-day journey. She was, of course, a spy, but a welcome one. To know a country, Trudeau later wrote, one must take a long voyage on a train . . .

Farther away from Moscow, the Soviets became "nice and friendly, they walk around in pyjamas every day, exchanging jibes with the vendors in the train stations, before buying their roast chicken and their cheap wine; they could not care less about the propaganda being spouted out all day, but rush in to hear the football scores. In short, it's a normal society, with the normal sampling of swindlers, drunks, beggars and loose women. They're human, in other words."[20] Trudeau visited the grave of Stalin's mother, where his interpreter wept. He returned to Moscow and tried to travel to Leningrad, but his activities, notably his throwing snowballs at Soviet monuments, had caught the attention of the authorities. One early morning there was a bang at the door and "these burly policemen came in," told him to go, packed his bags, took him to the airport, and placed him on a plane. Leningrad would await a later journey.[21]

On his return to Canada on July 23, 1952, Trudeau declared publicly what he had told Ford privately: "I felt that people must use every possible means to get to know each other better. For, on either side, it is precisely the fear of the stranger which is at the root of this pathological hatred that is bringing us relentlessly closer to the third and final world war. So at last I would be able to throw a little light on this stranger . . ."[22] And in a later broadcast he denied that the secret police were terrifying. He mentioned how a Bolshevik Party member told a joke that mocked the police and the military, who, Trudeau claimed, seemed too preoccupied with exchanging salutes "to have the time to terrorize the population." He also ridiculed those in the West who claimed he was "followed" at every moment when he was in the Soviet Union.[23]

Trudeau's reports quickly brought criticism, most notably from Father Léopold Braun. The priest had been in Moscow during the purges and famines of the 1930s and he now condemned Trudeau's articles in Le Devoir and other Catholic publications as hopelessly naïve, ill informed, and even dangerous. Trudeau reacted with surprising vigour. He told André Laurendeau at Le Devoir that Father Braun was "an imbecile" and demanded full right of reply. "If Le Devoir does not give me a half page, I will pay for it," he threatened.[24] Braun pointed out that he had lived in the Soviet Union, endured the persecution of the Catholic Church, and witnessed church members disappearing into the Gulag.[25]

Trudeau responded strongly, but his tone was too harsh. The editor of Le Droit told him that although Braun might be wrong, he should treat the issue seriously, not dismissively and crudely. In the journal *Nos Cours*, where Braun and Trudeau exchanged attacks, the editor, J.-B. Desrosiers, took Braun's side, telling Trudeau that if he had damaged his reputation, it was his own fault. Trudeau again demanded a right to respond and approached Archbishop Paul-Émile Léger (soon to become a cardinal) to assist him, even though his articles in *Cité libre*, quite apart from the Soviet trip, had upset the Catholic hierarchy. Others, including the respected Université de Montréal economist Esdras Minville, said the Braun attack on Trudeau was a "serious" matter. With some desperation, Trudeau wrote to a Father Florent, a priest with whom he had enjoyed long discussions about the Soviet Union in Paris in 1947, and enclosed his exchanges with Braun. He told Father Florent that his reputation had been hurt in Quebec, and he asked him to openly declare his support. It would, Trudeau declared, be "an act of charity and justice."[26]

Braun then went too far and labelled Trudeau a Stalinist mouthpiece, which he definitely was not. Trudeau's reaction to Braun reflects his deep opposition to clerics using their position to pronounce on political affairs. This reaction was consistent with his writings in the period. Yet Trudeau too readily dismissed Braun's descriptions of Stalinist atrocities. Solzhenitsyn, Khrushchev, scholars of the Soviet regime, and history itself have all revealed the enormity of Stalin's crimes. Appalled by the exaggerations and excesses of Senator Joe McCarthy and the use of anti-Communism by the Duplessis government against its opponents, Trudeau in response found some virtue on the streets of Moscow. In the Université de Montréal *Quartier Latin* report of his visit, he permitted himself to be called "Comrade Trudeau."

His writings and his associations with the many "fellow travellers" soon caught the eye of various intelligence agencies and their media colleagues.[27] In March 1954 Trudeau was denied entry to the United States—as were other eminent individuals at the time, including Graham Greene and Charlie Chaplin. He moved quickly to remedy the problem. Questioned about his visit to Moscow, he responded that he had gone to the conference to see if international trade would break down the Iron Curtain. On March 9 he learned that he was temporarily excluded because his entry might be "prejudicial to the interests of the United States." But after an appeal to American consular officials, the decision was soon reversed. He was allowed to travel through the United States on his way to a Commonwealth Conference in Pakistan, which he attended at the invitation of the Canadian Institute of International Affairs. Still, Trudeau's trip to Moscow, his favourable comments about the Soviet Union, and his other journeys behind the Iron Curtain and to China made him a target for extreme anti-Communist groups such as the Canadian Intelligence Service. Henceforth he also drew the ire of fierce nationalist journalists and writers such as Duplessis supporter Robert Rumilly in Quebec, and the militant anti-Communist Lubor Zink in the conservative *Toronto Telegram*.

A close reading of Trudeau's many reports on his visit reveals his scepticism about the Soviet system and its accomplishments and his commitment to Western democratic values. Unfortunately, his tendency to shock and to provide "colour" often grabbed the attention of his readers and distorted his meaning. As ever, he enjoyed being a contrarian and, when pushed, he would defend his position passionately. Still, the analytical portions of his travel accounts yield a more subtle and balanced view. For example, he probably attracted the attention of the student audience at the Université de Montréal when he praised the Soviet educational system and, bizarrely, Soviet architecture. Nevertheless, his remarks strongly criticized the "capitalism of the state" created by Soviet Communists, and he contrasted the proletariat's control of political parties and unions in the West with the closed system in the Soviet Union.[28] Although he lavished praise on the Bolshoi Ballet and on Soviet support for the arts, he recognized that the government there supported the "extérieur" of artistic expression but suppressed the internal spirit—the composers Shostakovich and Khachaturian, for instance, were reduced to writing mere melodies, while the great film director Eisenstein had simply been tossed aside. "Perhaps," he wrote, "it is not wise in the USSR to cast a glance inwards. There is a warning at the frontier of the world of the spirit: Do not enter."

Trudeau told a Soviet Communist acquaintance that he should not be surprised that the Catholic Church was opposed to Communism. He too was opposed to a system that was anti-religious. Although he ridiculed the claims of the extreme "anti-Soviet camp"—Rumilly and Zink—that the great Russian authors were banned in schools (he had seen Dostoevsky in the libraries, he said), he commented in his writings on the void at the core of the system, one where the brilliant Russian composer Stravinsky and the great Russian painter Chagall were as unknown as Maynard Keynes and Alfred Marshall. And, he said, there was no doubt in his mind that "the worker has, in effect, more importance and much more influence in our democratic countries than in the USSR."

The strongest indication of his views is Trudeau's description of the evening in a popular Moscow restaurant where he met three Russians. They recognized him as a foreigner, and two of the three spoke with him. They left, and the silent one remained for a moment. Then, in a voice "which did not tremble in spite of the danger, this perfect stranger told me that he was neither Bolshevik nor Communist but a democrat." The effect was electric: "He seemed to have released a truth that had long been buried in his heart, for he shot up and strode to the exit like a visionary. If poetry is this man's art, I thought, this evening he will write his greatest poem, because his inspiration has just been set free." In Russia as in Canada, Trudeau knew, liberty was the most precious individual good.[29] These were not the words of a duped fellow traveller.

—

Trudeau's travels were fundamental to his broader purposes throughout these tumultuous years, and reflected both his ambitions and his doubts. First, he believed, correctly, that his journeys—especially to remote and challenging regions—provided him with the intellectual capital on which he could draw for his analysis of his own society. In some ways he resembled other intellectuals in the early years of that decade who "welcomed the television rays that illuminated the integration of Quebec into North America."[30] While welcoming assimilation into a more "efficient" and "modern" society, Trudeau recognized that francophone Quebecers had to learn about the world beyond North America. More specifically, they had to locate their own experience within the context of the "winds of change" that were quickly sweeping away the old colonial empires in the postwar decades.

Although he later had a reputation for inattention to Canada's role in the world, his articles and media appearances in this period certainly focused more often on international than domestic events. He also realized that the rise to celebrity of René Lévesque came from *Point de mire*, a television series in which the irrepressible Lévesque, hands darting and smoke billowing, introduced viewers to the cascade of international changes in those times. The shrewd Gérard Pelletier, who knew Lévesque well because his wife also worked for Radio-Canada, recalled how, in their meetings together, Trudeau would cast a sceptical and mocking glance at Lévesque as he started "on one of his usual long tirades, riddled with hasty judgments, brilliant, profound or superficial."[31] Trudeau was convinced that his analysis of international affairs had a profundity that Lévesque's stream of consciousness lacked—yet both knew that events outside Quebec now mattered more than ever.

Second, Trudeau knew that his own comparative advantage in the intense debates among Quebec intellectuals came from his far-ranging education, now bolstered by the layers of exotic detail and intriguing anecdote he had gleaned through his travels. The stunning Russian on the train to Tbilisi, the mysterious dark monastery on a Chinese hill, the bandits on the ziggurat of Ur provided the colour that listeners and viewers would remember. His articles and Radio-Canada presentations are crammed with stories to illustrate his arguments, and, as radio broadcasts of his world tour indicate, he did not mind embellishing his tales for dramatic effect. In a remarkably insightful article on Trudeau, Jim Coutts, his long-time principal secretary, pointed out that, contrary to general opinion, Trudeau "did and said little publicly that was not carefully rehearsed in advance."[32] His presence and his charisma were carefully constructed; his "cosmopolitanism" was a fundamental building block. At times he went too far, secure, perhaps, in his wealth and independence. Gérard Filion, publisher of Le Devoir, believed that Trudeau occasionally hurt rather than helped his cause, and he sometimes refused to publish his letters, even though he had visited Moscow himself soon after Trudeau did, and they agreed on the need for reconciliation between East and West.

Third, Trudeau's cosmopolitanism reflected the unease he felt about Quebec and Canada in the early fifties. He felt more assured about his beliefs on international relations than on domestic Quebec and Canadian politics. And his return home brought a hard landing. His romance with Helen had burnt out suddenly, although he had tried to relight the flame during his months in Europe in the spring of 1952. Then he told her in late summer that he had no permanent work in Montreal. Tip, who was a precise but not very profitable architect, was leaving to live in Europe, and he would follow if things did not work out in Quebec. "Have you left Canada," she asked on December 18, 1952, or had he made a final commitment to "Quebec's social issues?" Trudeau was grumpy.[33] Things were not working out well in Quebec, he replied, especially for one who had "social causes."

On July 16, 1952, exactly a week before Trudeau returned to Canada, the Duplessis government had been re-elected, even though the Liberals under their new leader, Georges-Émile Lapalme, had initially led in the polls.[34] Duplessis, as always, had campaigned brilliantly, albeit often demagogically. His biographer Conrad Black describes the raucous election day, when the mayor of Quebec asked for the intervention of the Royal 22nd Regiment to protect a Liberal victor in Lévis from a mob and, later, to prevent the assault on Liberal committee rooms in Montreal by gangs armed with "bottles, brickbats and revolvers." In one case, hooligans threw a Liberal campaign worker and a police constable out of a first-storey window.[35] In a later broadcast on the election, Trudeau declared that democracy is a form of government that works when everyone agrees on counting heads, not breaking them. In *Cité libre*, he warned:

> Our deep-seated immorality must be explained. After all, we claim to be a Christian people. We subscribe to ethics that rigorously define our duties towards society and our neighbour. We do not fail to respect civil authority, and we generally live in a climate of obedience to law. We punish treason and assault in the name of the common weal and of natural law; we explain Communism in terms of the faltering of faith; we consider war to be the ransom of sin.

While "our ideas on the order of society are shaped by Catholic theology," Trudeau continued, there was one exception. In the case of the state, "we are really quite immoral; we corrupt bureaucrats, we blackmail members of the Assembly, we put pressure on the courts, we cheat the tax-collector, we turn a blind eye when it seems profitable to do so. And when it comes to electoral matters, our immoralism is absolutely appalling. The peasant who would be ashamed to enter a brothel sells his conscience." With a glance to his own experience only a decade earlier, perhaps, he wrote: "We have to admit that Catholics, collectively, have rarely been pillars of democracy. I say that to our shame, and without seeking to prejudge the future . . . In countries with a large Catholic majority . . . Catholics often avoid anarchy only by means of authoritarian rule." He went on to express a theme he expanded on continuously in future years: pluralist societies do not turn to authoritarianism, but there was a danger that they might devote too much of their civic energies "to the pursuit of the Catholic weal." The product of this pursuit was a narrow nationalism that created immorality and undermined the greater "public weal."[36] Trudeau had travelled far along the liberal democratic path since those nights on the streets in 1942.

Despite these views, Trudeau did not bother to rush back from Europe to work in the coming election campaign. His absence betrayed the weakness of the intellectuals opposed to Maurice Duplessis, and of the Quebec labour movement, which had failed to build politically on the Asbestos Strike. Gérard Pelletier, Jean Marchand, and others had briefly considered running labour candidates in working-class ridings in 1952, a policy that would have broken the traditional policy of formal neutrality espoused by the Confédération des travailleurs catholiques du Canada (CTCC) while, at the same time, "punishing our enemies and rewarding our friends." To that end, Pelletier wrote to Trudeau, asking him to consider being one of the labour candidates. Trudeau replied from Paris on March 16, 1952. Yes, he said, "it would interest me because I have never in my life felt so unattached, physically and morally; because I am ready to commit the greatest follies; and because, all in all, I am in a rather pitiable state." Perhaps he was still recovering from Helen's rejection. Whatever the cause, he told Pelletier that he had intended to "vegetate in the Sicilian sun," but he would consider a candidacy if certain conditions were met. His conditions were impossible but appropriate: such a "labour" campaign would need organization, money, a platform, and "total support of the unions." However, the unions were split; there was no platform; and no other candidates had yet been chosen. Wisely, Trudeau declined. Yet he was intrigued by the offer and, tellingly, asked if his candidacy would exclude "the possibility of my becoming a 'technical adviser' to the CTCC (the job Marchand offered me)?"[37]

Trudeau never took the job, but, the following year, he did become more directly involved in the labour movement. In a broader sense, his focus began to shift from international politics, the subject of most of his writings since 1949, towards domestic politics. He had proudly told Helen back in the summer of 1952 that he had been asked to speak at the prestigious annual Couchiching Conference of the Canadian Institute of International Affairs on the topic "The Adequacy of Canadian Foreign Policy." Of course, he found it inadequate.

What is striking is the self-confidence of his presentation at Couchiching, and the consistency of his views. With some revisions created by current events, the ideas he expressed on the shores of Lake Simcoe that summer remained his opinions throughout his life. He was publicly and scathingly critical of Lester Pearson, who, he said, thought the role of Canadian policy was to interpret "London to Washington & vice versa, as if they needed a despicable mouthpiece." To confirm his point, he mentioned a recent speech Pearson had given in New York where he said that Canada's tutors were the United Kingdom and the United States. He suggested that Pearson sounded like an Albanian speaking in Moscow. Trudeau agreed with Pearson that Canada's foreign policy should follow from Canada's "Anglo-Saxon political thoughts and institutions," but he held that it should also reflect our "bi-ethnical and bi-lingual character" and the fact that Canada was a young, small, but economically power-ful country. Yet Anglo-Saxonism "drowned" out everything else. There was no independent Canadian public opinion. Ottawa read and heard only American and, to a lesser extent, British news. Why not read *Le Monde* or even the Paris *Herald Tribune?* Canada needed to develop a public opinion that truly reflected its bicultural and bilingual character and to build a foreign service that could "construct" truly Canadian policies in those many areas where there was not "a determined U.S.–U.K. axis." How could that be done, he asked, when "we had not formulated polit-ical theory about Canada itself" and when Quebec was not inte-grated into Canada's international presence?[38]

—

Trudeau's journeyings became less frequent and earnest, even though he gave a long radio broadcast on "Techniques du voyage" in which he said he travelled not to bring home tales of three-star restaurants or, like diplomats, of meetings with kings and presi-dents, but to know humanity in its richness. To do so, he needed to mix with the people, travel light, and abandon airs and luxury— only then did he encounter the saints, the wandering philosophers, poets, and scoundrels who form the human fraternity.[39]

By the fall of 1952 he realized that his adventures in Palestine and Moscow were richer than his recent experiences in Quebec or in the remainder of Canada. If he was to fulfill his goals for a public life in Canada, he would have to change direction.

So he began to clarify his domestic political program. In personal terms, he identified three specific actions: deeper involvement in the trade-union movement in Quebec; more political activity in Quebec; and interaction with English-Canadian intellectuals who were "waking up" to Quebec and who shared many of his political ideas about civil liberties and the dangers of unbridled capitalism.

Trudeau's contact with anglophone intellectuals, notably his growing friendship with F.R. Scott, a McGill University law professor, CCF activist, and well-known poet, was undoubtedly a significant factor in his closer identification with liberal democratic thought—especially as it was embodied in the English-Canadian socialist tradition.[40] Yet Trudeau was always his own man, deriving his approach to domestic affairs from diverse influences ranging from personalism and *Le Monde* to Maynard Keynes and Paul Claudel. He reflected these varied streams in his involvement with *Cité libre*, and, during the fifties, his experience in teaching workers in the mine and mill towns of Quebec also influenced him strongly. As his address to the Couchiching Conference reveals, Trudeau knew and, in many ways, admired the Anglo-Saxon political tradition, but he had profound doubts about the manner in which it had developed in the former British North American colonies.

During his long absences in Europe and in Africa and Asia, Trudeau had remained in contact with his *Cité libre* colleagues, and he missed those nights where the group came with their wives, girlfriends, and manuscripts to obey, in the words of one of the members, Jean Le Moyne, "no orders of the day but only the disorders of the night."[41] He realized that he must immerse himself more deeply in the life of his city and his province or risk losing the influence his intellect and imagination had gained for him since those first gatherings in Gérard Pelletier's stone house on Lac des Deux Montagnes. The election of 1952 in

Quebec, which he had conspicuously missed, had stirred dissent and opposition to Maurice Duplessis among intellectuals and the professional classes in Montreal. *Le Devoir*, which had generally supported Duplessis in 1948, had become an opponent of the government by 1952, and it followed the election with ever stronger attacks on the ruling party. One rallying point was the dismissal of the reformist archbishop Joseph Charbonneau in Montreal (who actually controlled some shares of *Le Devoir*) and his replacement by Paul-Émile Léger. The new archbishop "sought to reassert the influence of the Church on the faithful and to stimulate religious faith while opposing the growing materialism of Montreal."[42] Yet the schools, the hospitals, and the social services that the church had controlled for so long were overwhelmed by the material and spiritual needs of the postwar flood of people to the factories and shops of Montreal, whose metropolitan population grew from 1,139,921 in 1941 to 1,620,758 in 1956. The Catholic urban voice in the Quebec capital was fainter than that of the rural counties where Duplessis's Union nationale held sway.

Tensions grew. In the fall of 1952 a strike of textile workers at Louiseville had brought police intervention, violence, and bloodshed. Duplessis declared the government response justified, arguing that society rested on two pillars—religious authority and civil authority—which must not erode. A threat to one undermined the other. In the pages of *Le Devoir*, André Laurendeau had already decided that the government no longer defended the common good and, in the eyes of the workers, had become no more than "the ally of the bosses." Laurendeau's niece later recalled that she had the impression that "the Laurendeau living room became the staging ground for the warriors on the left," gathering their forces to defeat Duplessis.[43] The CTCC, the Catholic union, called a meeting just before Christmas, 1952, to discuss a general strike, but it was a confession of weakness rather than strength. The CTCC was only part of organized labour in Quebec, where the Fédération des unions industrielles du Québec (FUIQ) and the Fédération provincial du travail du Québec (FPTQ) competed for membership and authority. Although the CTCC had grown faster than any other union, it lacked the financial support of international unionism that its rivals possessed. That financial weakness was one reason why the CTCC decided not to enter directly into politics.

That December, in *Cité libre*, Trudeau attacked the decision, claiming that Quebec workers would cleanse the political system and that the old parties offered no prospects of real change.[44] On a Radio-Canada broadcast early in the new year he explained his beliefs in more detail. In a democracy, he said, a police force must not be allowed to beat up a union member's family, blow up a bus, and break a legal strike. Yet a general strike was not an answer either. Equally ineffective were the solutions offered by some well-meaning church officials—a volley of prayers in one instance and, in another, a quasi-fascist dictatorship that would act against evil factory owners. These responses, he stated, betrayed the political illiteracy of French Canadians: "It is a notorious truth that the English Canadians have healthier political reflexes than we do. But this superiority has not come by chance: it derives from a civic education that is continuous from schooldays through daily life and is expressed by those English Canadians who think, write and discuss civic affairs." Quebec, he said, must first choose democracy; then social good would follow. If it did not, hatred for the "rules" would grow, civil disobedience would stir, and violence would follow that would make the "massacre" of the textile workers at Louiseville seem like a picnic.[45]

Some aspects of Trudeau's views were naïve, but his gibes about the excellence of English-Canadian democracy were deliberately provocative. Nevertheless, he was increasingly excited about Quebec, its future, and his participation in the debates that swirled around the changes taking place. Another participant in those debates, André Malavoy, recalled the "astonishing" intellectual clashes of the fifties:

> All shrewd observers sensed imminent change, a real upheaval in the structure of politics, our way of life and our thoughts. As in all pre-revolutionary periods, the intellectuals at last engaged and were drawn into political action. In truth, they were not numerous—perhaps no more than two hundred people who knew each other and met often.
>
> But how enriching were those meetings, those long nights of discussions, those projects and dreams.[46]

Emmanuel Mounier, the French Catholic personalist and founder of *Esprit*, had taught Trudeau to "see, judge, act." It was now the time to act.

That summer, Trudeau began to encounter workers directly for the first time since his brief stint in the Sullivan mines in Abitibi seven years previously and his 1949 foray to Asbestos. Yet, theoretically, he and the *Cité libre* group had decided it was the workers who, through democratic means, were the best hope to overthrow the Duplessis regime and give birth to a modern, secular Quebec state whose leaders would be young francophone intellectuals like themselves. Trudeau was well prepared to act as the major players took their place in the public forum. His training as a lawyer and an economist provided him with the tools to take apart many of the arguments of the Duplessis government and the conservative nationalists, and he did so with a rapier that often cut quickly and deeply.

—

Two events deeply affected Trudeau's activities in the mid-fifties, and defined his views of Quebec's place in Canada as well as his own position in Quebec and Canadian intellectual life. The first was the decision of the province of Ontario to accept a tax-rental agreement with the federal government, thereby breaking the alliance between Canada's two largest provinces against the federal government's assertive centralism. This decision caught Duplessis by surprise and forced him, and his opponents, to consider not only the revenue sources for the province but also Quebec's response to the federal government's increasing presence in the social and economic life of Canadians. In February 1953, when Maurice Duplessis created a Royal Commission on Federal-Provincial Relations, under Judge Thomas Tremblay, Trudeau was appointed to draft the brief of the Féderation des unions industrielles du Québec for the commission. The second event (as described in the next chapter) was the 1954 decision by Pelletier to pass over to his friend the long-delayed editing of a book on the Asbestos Strike. This task gave Trudeau a leadership role among a group of respected intellectuals and, most important, the opportunity to write the introduction and the conclusion to the book. Fate had made a choice.

Trudeau complained later that his acquaintances did not believe that he "worked" during the fifties. The comments angered him: "But, you know," he replied, "I'd be working bloody hard— at writing articles and preparing my dossiers for whatever conciliation procedure I had or at administering my father's estate, which my brother and sister had no inclination to do, or at receiving clients or visiting the labour groups."[47] His complaints are justified. His personal papers are crammed with arbitrations where he acted for the labour side. He carefully prepared notes for his summer visits to labour classes. He gave lectures or talks to labour groups in church basements or union halls. He would spend a week or a long weekend giving a more sustained series of presentations in educational sessions for workers. There are also numerous broadcasts, meetings, and articles that he drafted and redrafted.

The creation of the newspaper *Vrai* by his friend Jacques Hébert brought new deadlines. His agendas are full, and, when travelling, he brought his work with him.

Trudeau rode his motorbike to the labour colleges, wore open shirts under his leather jacket, and appeared very much the rural teacher. His presentations were conventional explanations of the operations of the economic system, with particular attention to the place of the worker and the union. Although he was a member of the CCF, his lectures lacked ideology, and he accepted the idea that owners should have their profits. Of course, he was an owner himself who carefully monitored the profits from his family's stake in the Belmont amusement park in Montreal. Even when dealing with trade unionism, he did not speak of nationalization—the subject that dominated British Labour Party Congresses in those times. In a course given at a school of metallurgy in January 1954, he neatly set out the principles of Keynesian economics without ever mentioning Keynes: budgetary surpluses in times of inflation compensate for deficits in times of unemployment, thus assuring the long-run prosperity of the nation. He was offered $25 for his course, but he returned the cheque—perhaps to the surprise of the organizers, who might have heard many stories about Trudeau's careful ways with money.[48] In another course in 1956 he spoke about politics rather than economics, although economics indirectly entered his discourse when he talked about the respective duties and jurisdictions of the federal and the provincial governments.

Trudeau's work for the Tremblay Royal Commission on Federal-Provincial Relations made him a major figure both in Quebec and in Canada, a recognized authority on the Canadian Constitution and the division of powers. Because he wrote the brief for the international Fédération des unions industrielles du Québec, he worked closely with the Canadian Congress of Labour and its research director, Eugene Forsey—a charming and influential labour historian. At the time he wrote the brief, the debate on the economics of Canadian federalism had been stirred by the publication of *Le fédéralisme canadien: Évolutions et problèmes*, by Maurice Lamontagne. Its message, coming from a leading Quebec economist, brought enthusiastic approval in Ottawa and denunciation from nationalists in Quebec. Accepting the Keynesian argument Trudeau had presented to the workers, Lamontagne argued that only a strong central government could assure the prosperity and economic security that postwar policies had produced. From this point, he concluded that only a fuller integration into Canadian society could assure Quebec of the fiscal resources needed to modernize its society and provide economic security to French Canadians.[49] Trudeau did not know Lamontagne, one of the organizers, with Father Georges-Henri Lévesque, of the Social Sciences faculty at the Université de Laval (which irritated Duplessis even more than *Cité libre* did), but he recognized the similarity of Lamontagne's views to his own.[50] So did Duplessis and traditional nationalists in Quebec. The battle formed around the Tremblay Commission.

Like Trudeau, Lamontagne called for a functional approach, one grounded in the new social sciences and in a better understanding of the way economic levels could be manipulated by experts to guarantee economic growth and equality. *Le Devoir*, so critical of Duplessis in many areas, nevertheless rejected Lamontagne's claims, arguing that an "Ottawa-inspired social welfare state would result in a technocratic and bureaucratic nightmare of statistics, reports, and programs all unsuitable to the complex and ever-changing socioeconomic realities at the regional and local level. Ottawa's social welfare state would lead to the regimentation of everyone, making them dependent upon a distant bureaucracy, 'not eager to come to life, grow, study, work, suffer, age and die.'"[51] For Trudeau, this attack on Lamontagne went too far, yet, despite similarities in language and approach, he disagreed with Lamontagne in many respects. In doing so, he drew on his own experience in Ottawa, where he had come to believe that the St. Laurent Liberal government was too careless about treading in provincial fields. That experience, along with his recognition as an economist, gave authority to his voice.

When the Fédération des unions industrielles du Québec presented its brief to the Tremblay Commission in March 1954, it attracted immediate attention because of its content and also because of its clear and sometimes eloquent prose: "The Federation is made up of men and women who use all of their earnings and energies to assure their material security and that of their family," Trudeau declared. "They know that they are influenced more by the imperious need to earn their daily bread than [by] constitutional guarantees of their religious, cultural, and political evolution, for it is necessary to live before philosophizing . . ." The survival of the French language and culture depended neither on the law nor on literary conferences; rather, in an industrial age, he continued, it rested on the hard work of, and proper rewards to, the working class. He followed with a detailed analysis of the economic condition of Quebec's working class and the economic inferiority of Quebec workers, compared with their Ontario counterparts.

The analysis, if not the approach, reflected Lamontagne. But when it came to specifics, the differences appeared. Trudeau believed that the federal government needed to possess adequate powers to secure economic stability and growth, but it did not require (as Lamontagne recommended) the replacement of tax-rental agreements with subsidies. Nor did the weakness of Quebec labour legislation justify a constitutional amendment transferring that authority to the federal government. In a federation, he said, such authority normally resided at the regional level. Closer cooperation among jurisdictions was essential, but each one should respect boundaries that were rational. Rather than reduce or eliminate areas where the provinces held responsibility, the provinces should make sure that they had the revenue necessary to carry out the services required at the regional level: "In effect, the unity of a political society depends on the will to assure the vital minimum to all members of the society, wherever they may live."

The role of the federal government was clear: it had responsibility for economic stability. At the same time, Trudeau stressed, the provincial governments had to have taxation power and responsibility for education and the family—areas that were strictly in the provincial jurisdiction. The federal government must cease payments to universities and direct grants to families; in such cases, the funds should pass to the provinces.[52]

Eugene Forsey scribbled large question marks on this passage of the draft Trudeau sent to him. Trudeau was never predictable. At a time when many reformers in Quebec, especially professors and college administrators, were ridiculing Duplessis's refusal to accept federal government grants to universities, Trudeau took his side, a stance that would have important repercussions later. His attitude surprised many, but it reflected his increasingly defined views on Canadian federalism and his wariness about Ottawa. Why, he asked, should Quebecers or other Canadians put "the future of Canadian federalism entirely into the hands of federal economists"? Other traces of his scepticism towards Ottawa in the 1950s came in a *Cité libre* article in which he attacked, along with André Laurendeau and traditional nationalists, Ottawa's refusal to consider tax deductibility for Quebec taxes on federal taxes: "The federal government and its clever civil servants accommodate themselves only too easily to a system that, at least until 1954, amounted to manifest defrauding of the Quebec taxpayer."[53]

By the mid-1950s Trudeau had become a close student of Canadian federalism and a defender of provincial rights. At the same time, he remained a social reformer who believed that the federal government was responsible for economic growth and stability and for promoting equity among regions and peoples. Nor surprisingly, he attracted the attention of English Canadians, who saw in him a perfectly bilingual and articulate opponent to the "reactionary" Duplessis government in Quebec. Through his friend Frank Scott, Trudeau met leading CCF intellectuals as well as Eugene Forsey and others associated with the Canadian Labour Congress. These English Canadians immediately recognized his political usefulness. Trudeau did not believe in a major constitutional revision and did not deprecate the influence of British institutions in the development of democratic habits. His attitudes infuriated conservative Quebec nationalists, such as the historian Robert Rumilly, who attacked him as a French Canadian who "goes to Toronto to hurl abuse against French Canadians, in English, before the English, for which he is celebrated as a grand spirit, a genius." Rumilly's harsh description of Trudeau's arguments did not greatly distort them: Trudeau believed that the French Canadians had foolishly subordinated their politics and economics to the defence of their ethnicity. Moreover, their strong Catholicism made them too respectful of hierarchy, resulting in an attitude, in his words, that "combines political superstition with social conservatism."[54]

Rumilly, a Duplessis supporter in Canada and a monarchist in France,[55] dismissed Trudeau as a leftist but did not deny the sincerity of his Catholic beliefs. Trudeau's writings, while reflective of the progressive social tradition of Catholic personalism, drew increasingly on contemporary social science as it was developing in the United States and, to a lesser extent, in Britain. For that reason, his voice and his sources resonated in English Canada. Yet Anglo-American social science alone does not explain the character of his analysis and discourse in the mid-1950s.

After the encounter with Archbishop Léger, the rebuke from Father d'Anjou, and his many quarrels with official Catholic voices, Trudeau became more determined to challenge the sway of the official Catholic Church in Quebec. His writing becomes more openly secular; his determination to challenge church conservatism more marked; the willingness to call himself anti-clerical much greater. He lost interest in debates within the church and concentrated on arguments about the church. Sylvia Ostry, then a young economist and later an eminent scholar and public servant, recalls how Trudeau would become animated and emotional in the mid-fifties when he spoke with her in cafés about the church's oppressive presence in Quebec.[56] When he was attacked in *L'Action catholique* because he said that clerics should withdraw entirely from politics, he repeated the argument at greater length in following issues of *Le Devoir*.[57] Increasingly, he became a public presence, along with his *Cité libre* colleagues. He loved debates on topics such as "Does Canada need other political parties?" (Trudeau feared a new nationalist party would be conservative); "Does Canada need a stronger military?" (No, said Trudeau, who pointed to "the futility of a good part of our military efforts"); or "Do Canadians need identity cards?" (Trudeau was firmly opposed). One television program, "Idées en marche," attracted Duplessis's wrath when Trudeau supported Louis St. Laurent's statement that Quebec was not a "different" province "from a constitutional point of view." Television captured attention, and so, increasingly, did Pierre Trudeau.[58]

These days, he had a new determination and direction. When he left on a trip in 1954, he took a long list of friends to whom he would write, many of them women. The despair he had expressed about himself and the future to Pelletier and, earlier, to Helen Segerstrale had disappeared. In August 1955 he wrote to Helen, who was now married in Europe. The tone was markedly different. "I have been doing the expected," he noted, "practising law with the trade unions in Canada, but I also manage to do a lot of writing, radio & television work. It is all very satisfying, especially because I can satisfy my wanderlust from time to time."[59]

Pierre Trudeau was finally home.

—

CHAPTER 7

EVE OF THE REVOLUTION

T he 1949 Asbestos Strike in the Eastern Townships was a decisive moment in the history of Quebec—and in the life of Pierre Trudeau. The strike actually defined Trudeau more than it changed the province. The victory of the Catholic unions, which was achieved through negotiation, was surprising, but it proved difficult to build upon. The Duplessis regime did not crumble, and the Catholic Church retained its dominance. Trudeau quickly discovered that he could not get a position at the Université de Montréal, but he at least had independence—the product of his inheritance and his own will. He remained determined to learn from the experience of the strike.

The international unions had strongly supported the strike and sought to take advantage of it. Some of the strike leaders, including Gérard Pelletier, Jean Marchand, and Canadian Labour Congress (CLC) activists, decided that a book should be written to describe the diverse experiences of the strikers, their clerical and intellectual supporters, and the labour unions—which, for the first time, had shown exceptional resolve in confronting the Duplessis government and the multinational companies connected with the mines. Two years later,

Recherches sociales, a group funded by the Canadian Labour Congress to strengthen socialist sentiment among francophones, commissioned a book that would analyze how the strike represented "a turning point in the social history of Quebec" and "inform the general public of the cruel or reassuring lessons we had learned."[1] F.R. Scott, the McGill law professor and socialist activist, was the director of the project, with Gérard Pelletier as editor. When Pelletier's schedule became too busy, his *Cité libre* co-editor, Pierre Trudeau, took on the task. Trudeau had not edited a book before, nor had he ever written a sustained analytical essay of the type needed here for the introduction and the conclusion. The project had significant potential — but would prove a challenge.

Trudeau was now thirty-two years old and arbitrating labour disputes, researching the brief for the Féderation des unions industrielles du Québec (FUIQ) for the Tremblay Commission on Federal-Provincial Relations, writing articles for *Cité libre* and various newspapers, teaching courses for little or no money to workers during the summer, and, of course, travelling.* Most of the authors who had agreed to write the other articles for the book on the Asbestos Strike worked closely with the labour movement: Maurice Sauvé was the technical

---

* Unfortunately, Trudeau did not keep detailed notebooks in the fifties as he had on earlier travels. Nevertheless, his brief notes show that he used travel to develop his political views. In Europe in the fall of 1951, he draws the lesson from the study of different party systems that bureaucrats should be more effective and concludes that Quebec's greatest need is an independent and competent public service. He did keep a laundry list of his extended 1951–52 travels that broke down items into nine fascinating categories: cities, architecture, adventure, national traits, theatre, music, art, antiquities, and

adviser for the Canadian and Catholic Confederation of Labour (CCCL); Pelletier edited *Le Travail* for the CCCL and was its director of public relations; Jean Gérin-Lajoie worked for the United Steel Workers; and Charles Lussier, like Trudeau, practised labour law. Other authors included Father Gérard Dion of Laval University, the editor of *Relations indus-trielles*; Réginald Boisvert, a television writer who specialized in working-class dramas; and the brilliant young Laval sociologist Fernand Dumont, who agreed to explore the historical forces that "prepared the scene for the Asbestos Strike."[2] F.R. Scott would write the foreword. A disciplined worker, Scott soon despaired as the editor and the authors continually missed their deadlines.[3] There was additional delay as Trudeau tried, unsuc-cessfully—and with the help of author Anne Hébert, on whom he had an unrequited "crush"—to find a French publisher in the fall of 1955. To his chagrin, he discovered there was little interest in contemporary Quebec in Paris.[4]

Progress on the book was further delayed when Trudeau departed for Europe in the winter of 1955–56, but he tried, with the assistance of Laval political scientist Jean-Charles Falardeau, to stitch the volume together while he was away. Still manu-scripts did not arrive, and promises went unkept. Falardeau himself

---

scenery. The architecture category was brief and peculiar: Italy's elegant Villa d'Este and Le Corbusier's work in Moscow and Paris. More interesting was music: *Der Rosenkavalier* at the Berlin Opera, Pablo Casals at the Prado, a Sudanese ensemble in the desert near Khartoum, and pygmy drums in the Congo. Adventure was typical and amusing: "sleeping outdoors in equatorial forest and raging baboons; tracking elephants & buffaloes; riots in Cairo; swimming [in the] Bosphorus; and contradicting Politbureau." Voyage 1951–1952, TP, vol.12, file 4.

apologized abjectly just before Christmas: "I repeat to you, Pierre, that I understand, that Frank [Scott] understands, that Gérard [Pelletier] understands your impatience, [we understand] even the disgust of which you spoke some time ago. You accepted, and you fulfilled your responsibility, to edit this volume to completion, you carried out these chores briskly and, with good reason, you already had enough of it in the summer." Falardeau was astonished that Trudeau "in these circumstances and despite all, remained so patient." When something mattered, however, Trudeau could be patient indeed.[5]

Finally, in 1956, a complete text came together, and the *Cité libre* press became the publisher. Trudeau wrote two major essays for the book: a long introduction describing the social, economic, and cultural context of the strike, and an epilogue reflecting on the effects of the strike and on developments in Quebec after 1949. Polemical, angry, eloquent, these essays remain his finest analytical writing.

Through the prism of the Asbestos Strike, he illuminated the calamity of Quebec in the twentieth century, a time of "servile and stupefied silence" in which the social doctrine of the Catholic Church was "invoked in support of authoritarianism and xenophobia" until, in Asbestos in 1949, "the worm-eaten remnants of a bygone age" finally came apart.[6] The many drafts among his personal papers and the delays confirm that Trudeau chose these and other inflammatory words and sentences carefully. What separates these essays from other of his writings is their detailed research, especially on the economic history of Quebec, and the extensive presentation of facts in support of his arguments. In social scientific terms, he sought to rearrange the "facts" of Quebec's historical experience and then establish new norms for behaviour in that society. Although nearly all the arguments had already appeared in Trudeau's earlier writings, they are presented here more clearly and consistently in a brilliant attempt to convince "a whole generation, [which] hesitates on the brink of commitment," to smash old totems and "examine the rich alternatives offered by the future."[7]

Trudeau organized his introduction meticulously, beginning with the "facts," followed by the "ideas," and then the "institutions." The facts established that Quebec had benefited from industrialization and modernization, although the riches had not flowed as bounteously to the francophone population as to others because "we fought [modernization] body and soul." Ideas had mattered: "In Quebec . . . during the first half of the twentieth century, our social thinking was so idealistic . . . so divorced from reality . . . that it was hardly ever able to find expression in living and dynamic institutions." Nationalism became a system of defence that "put a premium on all the contrary forces" to progress: "the French language, Catholicism, authoritarianism, idealism, rural life, and later a return to the land." At a time when French Canadians confronted a materialistic, commercial, and increasingly democratic North America, nationalism became a "system of thought" that rejected "the present in favour of an imagined past."[8]

The institutions of a modern state were either stunted or stillborn in Quebec, he argued, principally because of the predominance of the Roman Catholic Church, with its conservative and nationalist doctrine. Labour unions were feeble, the press servile, and political parties corrupt. The fault lay with the leaders, not the people, because the church had never encouraged the political education of the masses. Votes were sold on election day for a bottle of whisky by citizens who spoke righteously after Mass on Sunday about the common good of society. Yet these same leaders simply "rejected any political action likely to result in economic reforms" because "liberal economic reforms were proposed by the 'English'" and "socialist reforms by 'materialists.'" Instead, they pursued quixotic dreams of a return to the land and of corporatism, an economic philosophy "which had the advantage of *not requiring any critical reflection.*" Church and state combined to exclude or condemn those who challenged this consensus, whether they be Communists, the Co-operative Commonwealth Federation (CCF), the left, or the English. The universities, under the heavy hand of the clergy, also avoided not only critical reflection but also modern technology and social science. In these collective failures lay the importance of the Asbestos Strike, which "assumed the proportions of a social upheaval."[9]

Trudeau went on to make scathing attacks on the principal exponents of nationalism and Catholic social doctrine in Quebec. He condemned the Jesuit scholar Father Richard Arès and the Montreal economist Esdras Minville as ignorant of both modern social science and the contemporary world itself. He linked Abbé Groulx with authoritarianism and xenophobia. He accused André Laurendeau of fearing any social reform initiated by the federal government because of the threat it represented to "Catholic morality" and the dreams of corporatism, in which individualism would disappear and elites would be organized to manage society. He criticized the conservative and nationalist economist François-Albert Angers for his support of corporatism, his opposition to state action, and his condemnation of socialism. He attacked various church leaders for their opposition to socialism and the CCF, including Father Georges-Henri Lévesque, even though he admitted that Lévesque had recently demonstrated more liberal ways as the dean of the Faculty of Social Sciences at Laval. And he even condemned his earlier friend and mentor François Hertel for a 1945 essay that spoke wistfully of the need for corporatism.[10]

Although Maurice Duplessis remained the main target, few escaped Trudeau's relentless attack. Paul Gouin, Thérèse's uncle, merited praise for creating the Action libérale nationale in the 1930s, but he was also criticized for his alliance with Duplessis. The exile of Bishop Charbonneau to Victoria became a symbol of the oppressiveness of the church and its antipathy to free speech. Grudgingly, Trudeau gave credit to the church for its efforts in charitable associations, welfare organizations, and adoption agencies, but, in truth, he concluded, the church's "heart and mind were certainly not in it, but longed for the golden age when an obscure rural people was accustomed to hide behind the skirts of the clergy."[11] Not surprisingly, Jean-Charles Falardeau and Frank Scott worried about the impact Trudeau's comments on these individuals would have.*

The essay is an incisive, often bitter, social and political analysis that defines Trudeau's beliefs more sharply than ever before. It sets out the outline for what he would later term the "just society," one in which legal protections assure democratic participation in the development of public policy. He was firmly anti-nationalist—not simply an opponent of conservative Quebec nationalism but wary of a doctrine that closed borders to ideas, people, and goods. Because of the church's link with

---

* Falardeau wrote a long letter to Scott saying he had asked Trudeau to "make more accurate and historically objective his references to P. Lévesque and to the Faculty of Social Sciences [at Laval]" and to "tone down the aggravating accent of his statements concerning such people as M. Minville etc." Scott and Falardeau both emphasized editorial perfection because of the difficulty they had experienced in finding a publisher, and because they expected the book to be severely criticized. When it was finally finished, Falardeau wrote to Trudeau that they should learn important lessons from the whole affair: "That would require another book in itself." Falardeau to Scott, Sept. 7, 1955; and Falardeau to Trudeau, July 27, 1955, and April 13, 1956, TP, vol. 23, file 16.

conservative nationalism in Quebec and its opposition to "progress," he believed it should retreat from the socioeconomic realm and occupy only the spiritual heights, where its presence was fully justified.

Here Trudeau was very much a "modernizer," one who believed that material needs were important in a democratic society and that contemporary social science and Keynesian economics were essential to the creation of the "good life." He was also a socialist cast in a British-Canadian mould. The essay treated the CCF as a great opportunity lost. Despite later claims that Trudeau was never a party person, this piece made it clear that the CCF closely reflected his views, just as the receipts for CCF dues for 1955 in his papers prove his participation in CCF campaigns.* Indeed, at a conference sponsored by *Le Devoir* in February 1955, Trudeau—in elegant suit and tie, with pocket handkerchief perfectly placed—scandalized his listeners by strongly urging socialism for Quebec. "M. Elliot-Trudeau," as the newspaper wrongly named him, "reproached *Le Devoir* for having no philosophy of economics. A kind of schizophrenia," he declared, "exists among the editors of *Le Devoir* on these questions."[12]

Like many of its leaders, Trudeau thought that the best hope for the future of the CCF lay in the trade-union movement, whose earlier gains in the forties had not been built on during the Cold War fifties. He rejected the "proletarian messianism" of the

---

* So do the comments of CCF activist Thérèse Casgrain, who wrote to Saskatchewan premier Tommy Douglas on April 16, 1955, asking if "Pierre Trudeau, whom you have met and who is one of our extremely promising young Canadians," could attend the federal-provincial conference with the Saskatchewan delegation. Saskatchewan Archives, Douglas Papers, collection number 33.1, vol. 671.

Communist left, but he saw alternatives in the democratic socialism of Western Europe. He ended his epilogue to the book: "The only powerful medium of renewal is industrialization; we are also aware that this medium will not provide us with liberty and justice unless it is subject to the forces of an enlightened and powerful trade-union movement." Finally, Trudeau looked beyond the Quebec border with a generous description of North America and English Canada. Quebec, he argued, could not stop the world and seal itself off, just as "nationalistic countries like Spain, Mexico, Argentina, etc. have learned that bloody revolution eventually topples archaic structures." Fortunately, "we," the French Catholic people of Quebec, "have a safety-valve in a continental economy and in a federal constitution, where pragmatism, secularism, and an awareness of change are the predominant attitudes."[13] For the first time, Trudeau had clearly defined the value of Canada for himself and for his province.

Beneath the clarity of the vision, beyond the rhetoric of debate and the flow of statistical evidence, Trudeau's essays expressed a deep-seated anger. Not surprisingly, they generated anger in return, and they continue to do so as modern historians reassess the dramatic events of the fifties and sixties in Quebec. At the time, François-Albert Angers devoted six essays in *L'Action nationale* to Trudeau's attacks on nationalism and his promotion of socialism, fearing it would lead to homogeneity with English Canada. More troubling to Trudeau was the response of Father Jacques Cousineau, a highly respected Jesuit who had mediated the strike in 1949 and was considered a supporter of the rights of unions and workers. The priest pointed to the role of the Catholic-affiliated unions in the strike and the activity of some important elements of the church in its mediation and resolution—all of which Trudeau had ignored. It was a just criticism, but Cousineau went too far in claiming that Trudeau simply reflected the views of the CCF and its Quebec branch, the Parti

social démocratique (PSD). Father Richard Arès, the editor of
the Jesuits' *Relations*, refused to publish Trudeau's reply to Father
Cousineau or even a letter to the editor from him. If Trudeau was
disappointed, he was not surprised by his former Jesuit mentors'
disavowal of their prize student.

Trudeau expected the neo-nationalist André Laurendeau—
whom he had met in the thirties, fought with in the forties against
conscription and Canadian war policy, and debated in journals
and on television in the fifties—to attack him in *Le Devoir* for
his views. Laurendeau did, but indulgently. While agreeing that
the conservative nationalism of the Duplessis government and
the social thought of the church created a barrier to social reform
and essential change, he argued that Trudeau oversimplified
and ignored the genuine challenges to the survival of a French-
speaking people in a modern North America. Nevertheless, he
deemed the essay a brilliant and evocative ode to liberty: in its
argument, ideas, and prose, it presented "a remarkable personality"
to Quebec public life.[14] Still, Laurendeau rebuked his colleague
for his anger and for his personal attacks on those who had
fought the same battles and endured similar blows. At the very
least, he said, Trudeau was rude, especially to many of his early
mentors and teachers.

If Trudeau's essays on the Asbestos Strike are significant
for the intellectual history of Quebec, they are fundamentally
important in his own intellectual biography. In them we sense
that Trudeau, the student who fiercely cherished his individu-
ality, the adolescent who chafed against authority, and the young
lover who dreamed of a haven from the deadened hand of
Catholic morality, believes he has finally broken free. His own
past has become another country, one he has largely abandoned
and whose monuments he no longer honours. Those long nights
and days at Brébeuf College where he pored over the texts of
Abbé Groulx, French religious philosophers, and assorted papal

Trudeau's time in Ottawa had bred a strong resentment against the second-class status of French-speaking Canadians within the Canadian public service. The fifties in Montreal now provided him with a practical education that made him a bitter opponent of the conservative and nationalist government of Duplessis and a resentful critic of the church that tried to silence him and his colleagues. And, through Frank Scott, the CCF, the Canadian labour movement, and his participation in the Canadian Institute of International Affairs (through which he attended two international conferences in Africa and in Asia), Trudeau would increasingly develop relationships with English Canadians who had considerable respect for his credentials from Harvard and the London School of Economics.[16] With his effortless and often eloquent English and his liking for foreign travel, he was sought out for conferences and media appearances in English Canada. His striking appearance, whimsical yet elegant taste in clothes, and unpredictability of views made him a well-known figure in Montreal cultural and intellectual circles, and television carried his name and views to a broader audience. While some of his previous characteristics changed significantly in this decade, others remained constant. He was still elusive, a mystery to those around him. And he continued to pursue his ambition for public life, even if its object was not yet clear.

The Asbestos Strike [La Grève de l'amiante] appeared in the fateful fall of 1956, when Britain, France, and Israel conspired to attack Egypt and brought the world to the brink of war. Soviet troops, meanwhile, crushed the Hungarian uprising, exposing the brutal disregard of democratic and individual rights within the Communist bloc. In France and elsewhere, Communist intellectuals were abandoning the Communist Party, but they remained disillusioned with the West because of the conspiracy among the French, British, and Israeli governments to smash

Arab nationalism. By 1957 the United States, the Soviet Union, and the United Kingdom, which was clinging desperately to great-power status, had tested hydrogen bombs that had the capacity to destroy humanity in minutes. The Soviets tested an intercontinental ballistic missile that could not be intercepted, and President Nikita Khrushchev admitted the crimes of the Soviet past.

In Canada the Liberal government felt the changing winds of international politics, and Prime Minister Louis St. Laurent condemned the British-French collusion, declaring that the age of "supermen" had passed. Although his remarks offended many English Canadians, they recognized an important truth: the old colonial empires were quickly collapsing. At Bandung, Indonesia, in 1955, Prime Minister Jawaharlal Nehru and other leaders of new or emerging states declared a position of neutrality in the Cold War. "Sisters and Brothers," Indonesian president Achmad Sukarno intoned at the opening, "how terrifically dynamic is our time! . . . Nations and States have awoken from a sleep of centuries . . . We, the people of Asia and Africa, far more than half the human population of the world, we can mobilize what I have called the 'Moral Violence of Nations' in favour of peace."[17]

Trudeau quickly accepted the justice of this cause. His travels had made him suspect frontiers — the dangers they created and the damage they did to people who lived around them. He worried about nationalism in the developing countries as much as in Canada. In 1957 he joined a Commonwealth group under the auspices of the World University Service that travelled to Ghana, the first decolonized African member of the Commonwealth. While he welcomed the liberation, he worried about what the future held for Ghanaians. In discussions, he presented the case that "culture can exist only if people are able to provide themselves with [the] instruments of government."[18] He was already worried that those instruments in the developing world were weak. And he was right.

This onrush of world events stirred Trudeau and others like him in Quebec. Increasingly, the conservative nationalism of Duplessis and the leaders of the Roman Catholic Church was on the defensive, as Trudeau and his colleagues championed the concept and principles embodied in the United Nations 1948 Universal Declaration of Human Rights. These principles in turn influenced a series of important judicial decisions in Canada in the fifties. Trudeau, drawing on his legal training, began to work closely with the Canadian Civil Liberties Association and, especially, with F.R. Scott in asserting the importance of individual rights. In 1957 the Supreme Court of Canada finally struck down Duplessis's notorious 1937 Padlock Law, which permitted the state to "lock" down any facilities where it believed "Communist or Bolshevik" activity had occurred. Scott was the principal lawyer in that case as well as in the Roncarelli case. In 1946 Duplessis had denied Roncarelli's tavern a liquor licence because he had paid bail for some Jehovah's Witnesses who insisted on their right to free speech. Roncarelli sued Duplessis, and the case made its way through the courts and through the elections of 1952 and 1956, where Duplessis made effective use of it:

> The Liberals were not going to take the side of the Witnesses any more than they were ready to declare any partisanship for the Communists, so Duplessis was free to disport himself as the indispensable rampart of democracy and established Christianity . . . against enemies that had no audible spokesmen. It was like hunting; it was good sport. Duplessis was a great nimrod, hunting subversive rodents, and the federal game warden kept interfering with him.[19]

The Liberals remained silent when Duplessis passed a preposterous law in 1953 that authorized the provincial government to ban any religious movement that published "abusive or insulting attacks" on the established religions. Such legislation horrified and embarrassed Trudeau. In 1959 the "federal game warden"—the Supreme Court of Canada—finally decided in favour of Scott and Roncarelli and against Duplessis, who was ordered to pay damages of $46,132. That he did—not from his own pocket but from funds advanced by the Union nationale.

Although historians first treated the fifties as a "return to normalcy," much as the twenties had been, closer scrutiny has revealed the strong dynamic for change that emerged from unlikely places—from suburbs and urban slums, coffee houses and country music. Just as Jean Marchand had sung Monique Leyrac's "Les lumières de ma ville" during the 1949 Asbestos Strike, in the 1950s Félix Leclerc gained international celebrity as he spun his musical folk tales of Quebec life. As a popular Québécois musical culture developed, it faced powerful competition from the blues and the rock rhythms of Elvis Presley, Bill Haley, and the first Motown beats that bellowed from the Impala hardtops that "cruised" St. Catherine Street. Trudeau treasured Leclerc, Leyrac, and the other chansonniers, but he found rock an alien dialect, even though his lithe body followed its beat in the late fifties on the dance floor. And, when his mother sorted out some of the Trudeau real-estate holdings, she asked Pierre if he wanted to take over some space at 518 Sherbrooke West, in the heart of the new nightlife district. While he retained his Outremont home address with her, the downtown "pad" brought him close to the new excitement on Montreal streets as the sixties approached. It also gave him independence, just as his appeal to and interest in women was strong.

Madeleine Perron, for example, wrote a note praising *Cité libre*, but especially its editor. She asked if he had time between "two conquests" to send her a copy of the latest issue and concluded, "My admiration to the author, my hommage and respect to the prince, and my biggest peck to Pierre." Doris Lussier, who was gaining fame as an actor in the new television hit *La famille Plouffe/The Plouffe Family*, in both English and French Canada, supported his attack on clericalism in *Cité libre*, ending her message with the words "Long live your liberty! Sacred Pierre. You are peerless, like a Greek god." Lionel Tiger, a McGill professor who also enjoyed Montreal's nightlife, sent "regards to the exquisite woman with whom I occasionally see you living the good life with."

Carroll Guérin, an artist and occasional model to whom he likely referred, certainly was exquisitely beautiful, and she became one of Trudeau's most frequent companions in the late fifties. In her elegance, dress, and appearance, she strikingly resembled Grace Kelly, the American movie star who married Prince Rainier of Monaco and dominated the tabloids of the day. And indeed, Trudeau did pursue women very much as the Greek gods did—or, for that matter, Prince Rainier. When a student in England did not return his calls during one of his visits, he wrote:

> Perhaps I am beginning to look ridiculously like the running gentleman harassing the perfect woman . . . Still for a short while yet it remains that "spring is a 'perhaps' hand in a window," and as I am leaving for France shortly I will have one more go at this perhaps business. And I invite you to tea, or dinner, or to the theater, or to the cinema, or the concert on Wednesday, the 26th. If you want to bother refusing or accepting, you can phone me at Dominions Hotel . . . Otherwise I will be waiting for you outside the Academy, 65 Gower St., between 5:15 and 5:45 on Wednesday.

Alas, we don't know if she showed. But there were many others who did.[20]

In a time marked by conformity, Trudeau was different, and the difference charmed. He took a major role as a lawyer in the fifties in challenging orthodoxy, as the courts broke down the layers of prejudice that had formed around private clubs and social groups. This burst of "civil rights" cases reactivated Trudeau's legal instincts and recalled his outrage in the previous decade with the internment of both Camillien Houde (for his opposition to conscription) and Adrien Arcand (for his fascist sympathies). The dramatic 1954 United States Supreme Court decision on racial segregation in schools, *Brown vs. Board of Education*, raised the bar for previously smug Canadians who had criticized Americans at the same time as they ignored segregation in Halifax and southern Ontario schools or overlooked clubs and universities that barred Jews.*

The newspaper *Vrai* became a crusading voice for those whose rights were destroyed or undermined, whether Jehovah's Witnesses, mental patients, or Wilbert Coffin, a backwoods guide who, editor Jacques Hébert believed, had wrongfully been convicted of murdering three American hunters. Trudeau joined with his close friend Hébert in these campaigns and wrote long

---

* In his study of race and the Canadian courts, James Walker has clearly shown that Quebec was not out of step with other Canadian jurisdictions in restrictions on the rights of Asians, Jews, and Blacks. In 1954, when the federal government revised the *Immigration Act*, Minister of Finance Walter Harris explained that "the racial background of our people would be maintained within reasonable balance; and . . . we would avoid an influx of persons whose viewpoint differed substantially from that of the average, respectable, God-fearing Canadian." The *Globe and Mail* thought Harris went too far but, revealingly, dissented weakly: Who are we being protected from, it asked, "Arabs, Zulus, or what? No one seriously proposed taking immigrants from any part of the world save Western Europe." Quoted in James Walker, *"Race," Rights and the Law in the Supreme Court of Canada* (Waterloo: Wilfrid Laurier Press, 1997), 248.

306 CITIZEN OF THE WORLD

articles for him explaining the origins of democracy and liberty. When Duplessis called an election for June 20, 1956, Trudeau decided to stay in Quebec that spring to be an active participant in the campaign—active, but not Liberal. The Liberal Party was not yet a palatable alternative for him, even though its leader, Georges-Émile Lapalme, had restructured it and sought out better candidates. But the party was broke, while Duplessis's Union nationale was awash with funds that it used shamelessly to favour friendly newspapers, buy gifts for voters, and reward constituencies that elected its candidates. Duplessis's decisive victory seemed to confirm that, in Quebec, provincial election success could be bought. During the election, the sixty-six-year-old four-term premier faced a coalition of opponents ranging from the labour unions to the Social Credit "Créditiste" movement. Still, Duplessis managed to capture headlines, especially in his favoured rural areas, with inflammatory charges that the federal government, and Cabinet minister Jean Lesage in particular, had intervened by importing—of all things—"Communist eggs" from Poland to Quebec. By the time the Liberals recovered, the Union nationale "had already saturated the province with pamphlets and newspaper advertising conjuring up the lurid spectacle of the imminent arrival of a new communist armada flying the hammer and sickle, bringing more federally procured eggs for the unsuspecting breakfast tables of the province."[21]

Meanwhile, the CCF had remade itself into the Parti social démocratique (PSD) under the leadership of Trudeau's friend Thérèse Casgrain—the daughter of a millionaire French-Canadian stockbroker, and herself a remarkable and strikingly attractive woman—who had headed the campaign for women's suffrage in Quebec for many decades. Grace Trudeau reported the name change to Pierre in the late summer of 1955, while he was driving his Jaguar in Europe: "Did you know that the CCF party name had been changed? Mrs. Casgrain was invited on the

TV last week to give *her views*—as she remarked to me on the phone today—this was no doubt only because of changing the party's name." She also wrote in October that "Mrs. Casgrain" had called to discuss an article about her that had appeared in *Le Devoir*. She generally liked it, except for a "remark on her figure 'taille haute *et robuste.*'" In Grace's opinion, the photograph beside the article denied the adjective "robuste."[22] Trudeau supported Casgrain in her whimsical quest to reposition the party, but we do not know whether, in the privacy of the polling booth in Outremont, he voted for Lapalme (who stood for the Liberals in the riding and won overwhelmingly) or he was one of the 726 souls who cast their ballot for the PSD candidate (who finished last behind the Communist contender).

We do know that Trudeau joined with several other left-leaning personalities, including René Lévesque, in writing a letter to *Le Devoir* attacking the Liberal Party for its phoney "nationalist" attack on the PSD for being centralist and controlled by English Canadians.[23] Overall, the PSD won only 0.6 percent of the vote, while Duplessis triumphed with 51.8 percent and seventy-three seats—both figures slightly higher than in 1952.[24] It was a stunning defeat for the Liberals, who took only twenty seats, three fewer than before, with 45 percent of the vote. The results provided vivid testimony to the ineffectiveness of the opposition and the unfairness of the electoral system.

—

What did Duplessis's triumph mean? Did all those carefully crafted articles, those brilliant analyses of the inevitable emergence of Quebec from an authoritarian, priest-ridden past, and the engagement in opposition of so many of the finest minds of the media and the university count for so little? How did it all happen? In his first article in *Cité libre* in 1950, Trudeau had called on those who opposed the current regime in Quebec to be "coldly intelligent." Perhaps they were not.

The election results, as well as the refusal of the Liberals to integrate the *Cité libre* program into their own platform, suggest that Trudeau and his colleagues were sowing a lot of seed on very barren ground. *Cité libre* has loomed large in history because its principals later became eminent in Quebec and in Canadian public life. At the time, however, the journal merely exasperated Duplessis and was usually ignored. It was not compulsory reading among Quebec City politicians or officials.[25] Moreover, its range was surprisingly narrow and its publication irregular. In the final four years of the Union nationale, 1956 through 1959, *Cité libre* published a grand total of nine irregularly spaced issues. The subscription records also fail to impress. In February 1954 *Cité libre* had only 444 subscribers, of whom 115 had not paid or had disappeared. The remainder were sold by the directors or in bookshops. In 1957–58 the print run was approximately 1,500 copies, compared with almost 15,000 for the Jesuit-controlled *Relations* and over 2,000 for *L'Action nationale*.

In addition, *Cité libre*'s range and character of subscribers in the mid-fifties was disappointing. There were only six subscriptions from France, and few outside Ottawa or the province of Quebec. The grand hopes of a journal that would complement or even rival France's politically influential and socialist *Esprit* had been abandoned. The French, as happened too often, did not reciprocate the warm embrace of the *Cité libristes* and, by the end of the 1950s, Trudeau, Pelletier, and others grumbled about *Esprit*'s ignorance of Quebec. Members of the journal's editorial board constantly reminded friends to renew, carried issues to conferences, and extracted a few dollars from those who could afford it. Trudeau sent mocking letters to friends, saying that, if they were truly poor, they need not pay the $2 subscription cost; otherwise, they should pay up. Pierre Vadeboncoeur, whose "share"

Trudeau initially subsidized, compensated by enthusiastically selling copies wherever he went. For Guy Cormier, who had moved to New Brunswick, the pressure to peddle and personally subsidize the journal was too much, and he tried to resign in 1958. Maurice Blain attempted to escape as well. Finally, in 1960, after the fall of Duplessis, the review was reorganized under the leadership of Jacques Hébert, fully funded, and suddenly began to prosper. Ironically, its best times lay in the past.[26]

It's easy to mock a bunch of intellectuals talking to themselves, having long dinners and debates over wine in living rooms or basements furnished with cracked-leather couches, their wives and girlfriends mostly silent or pouring the drinks, and the men warily testing the newcomers or arguing over where commas belong.* Despite its infrequency and limitations, however, *Cité libre* mattered enormously to Trudeau at the time—and later. He had no university position, no regular

---

* The writer Jean Le Moyne was invited to one meeting with eighteen participants in Charles Lussier's basement. "In the dim light I could see two small bottles of wine at each end and a Dominican priest, a man both austere and paternalistic, sitting in their midst . . . The discussion was extremely mature but it was so solemn and ponderous I wanted to escape. Our meetings [at *Le Relève*] were very different. We would have a wonderful dinner with much laughter and talk about books. The end of the evening would find us under the table replete with good wine and great ideas. I was thinking about this [contrast] when the Dominican suddenly asked me where I was coming from, and I answered him facetiously, 'From under the table, Father.' Nobody knew what I was talking about, of course, but if they had known, I had the feeling they wouldn't have laughed." Jean Le Moyne, quoted in Stephen Clarkson and Christina McCall, *Trudeau and Our Times*, vol. 1: *The Magnificent Obsession* (Toronto: McClelland & Stewart, 1990), 64–65.

column in a newspaper, no affiliation with a major political party, no seat on corporate boards, and, unlike René Lévesque with his regular program, he appeared only intermittently on the sensational new medium of television.

Trudeau seemed to resent Lévesque's celebrity, particularly when he became the exciting new voice of the French-language media after his dramatic coverage of the Korean War. The anecdote about their first meeting in a CBC cafeteria is revealing. "Hi, guys!" Lévesque said as he spied Trudeau and Pelletier at a table planning a new issue of *Cité libre*. But before Lévesque could sit down, Trudeau retorted: "Hey, Lévesque, you're a hell of a good speaker, but I'm starting to wonder whether you can write." Lévesque had failed to deliver some promised piece for the journal. "How can I find the time?" Lévesque shot back. But Trudeau would not relent: "Television's all very well," he said, "but there's nothing solid about it, as you know . . . Now, if you knew how to write, maybe with a little effort now and then—" "If that's what you think, you can go peddle your potatoes, you bloody washout of an intellectual," Lévesque exploded.[27] *Cité libre* gave Trudeau the finest potatoes he could peddle at the time.

The subscribers might be few, but they talked a lot and eventually they mattered. Frank Scott congratulated the editors on the first issue, in which he found "the socialist spirit was present even if it was well hidden." Senator Charles "Chubby" Power, a powerful Quebec City minister in the King government, wrote to Trudeau in 1953 congratulating him on the journal but, interestingly, dissenting on his strong criticism of Quebec nationalism. Father Georges-Henri Lévesque took notice of Trudeau's ideas in *Cité libre*, as did young students who would later make their mark in Quebec intellectual and political life. Pelletier complained that although the journal had an enormous impact in religious colleges, that influence meant only two or three subscriptions because tattered and clandestine copies were passed around almost like sexy French postcards. The author Roch Carrier recalled how a young priest would quiz him about *Cité libre*, and he soon began to realize that it was not to rebuke him but to discover what the sensational but forbidden publication had recently said.[28] At a time when Trudeau's responses to criticisms of his writings were denied publication by Catholic reviews or newspapers, *Cité libre* provided him with a platform from which to respond.

The readers included Guy Favreau and Lucien Cardin, both future justice ministers in the Pearson government; Eugene Forsey, the research director of the Canadian Congress of Labour; many Canadian diplomats, including Jean Chapdelaine, Pierre Trottier, and Trudeau's future undersecretary of external affairs, Marcel Cadieux; as well as the Union nationale politician Daniel Johnson, the eminent journalist Blair Fraser, the poet Earle Birney, the young philosopher Charles Taylor, and Canada's renowned political philosopher C.B. Macpherson. As the editor, Trudeau dealt directly with submissions from authors, and he now had the opportunity to work closely with the finest young minds in Quebec, including the political scientist Léon Dion, the sociologist Guy Rocher, and the essayist Jean Le Moyne (who would be his French speech writer when he became prime minister). The relationships that he forged as editor lasted—and they mattered.[29]

Still, the criticisms of the journal stung. The 1956 devastating election results revealed how politically ineffectual not only *Cité libre* but also the other critics of the Duplessis government had been. The Liberal performance in Quebec deeply disappointed; and, alarmingly, the Liberal government in Ottawa had also begun to stumble. St. Laurent slumped in his Commons seat in depression as the Conservatives and others ferociously attacked his government for arrogance. Well past the biblical three score and ten, St. Laurent seemed incapable of reacting imaginatively to the challenges of Canada and Quebec. The government drifted and, in 1957, it was defeated by the Conservatives under John Diefenbaker. The Conservatives lost the popular vote because Quebec remained overwhelmingly loyal to the Liberals and St. Laurent, yet they won the most seats and formed the government on June 21, 1957. The unilingual Diefenbaker won only nine seats in Quebec but managed to take power by ignoring Quebec in his electoral strategy. St. Laurent soon resigned, and Pearson became his inevitable successor as Liberal Party leader. In Montreal, Jean Drapeau, who had been elected as mayor on a reform platform in 1954, lost his position in 1957. It was, for the reformers, a bitter loss and a bad year.

—

This rapid shift of the political terrain left Pierre Trudeau and his colleagues much less surefooted, so in the summer of 1956 he and others organized Le Rassemblement, a grouping of intellectuals, professionals, and labour officials with the specific goal of promoting democracy. It refused to affiliate with any party, but, instead, announced it would work for progressive approaches to Quebec politics. Trudeau had always admired popular movements and their leaders—men such as Paul Gouin, Henri Bourassa, and, in the city of Montreal, Jean Drapeau. They had rejected the special interests embedded in the traditional parties and set out to create their own parties—groupings based on a popular movement with a clear program. He hoped to do the same with the Rassemblement.

At its founding convention on September 8, the noted scientist and academic Pierre Dansereau from the Université de Montréal became its first president, with Trudeau as vice-president. Among the directors were his friends and colleagues André Laurendeau, Jacques Hébert, and Gérard Pelletier. The

Rassemblement mingled *Cité libre* modernizers with neo-nationalists like Laurendeau who believed that traditional nationalism's link with the church was dangerously misguided, and that Quebec's social and economic system needed rapid change. Few members had direct political experience, and most were suspicious of political involvement. The new organization existed uneasily somewhere between a lobbying group and a fledgling political party. Not surprisingly, it was politically ineffective.[30]

Laurendeau, who had worked with the Bloc populaire canadien in the forties, soon lost interest as the members began to bicker.* The Laval political scientist Gérard Bergeron, an early member, identified the problem in his 1957 description of the "Rassemblement type" as one who had originally disdained direct political action, then become involved in social action, and, suddenly, in the mid-fifties, realized that the solution to social problems must come through the "politics" he continued to despise. In his memoirs, Trudeau claimed that he turned to the Rassemblement because the major parties in Quebec remained unacceptable and the CCF's Parti social démocratique was weak, its policies too centralist and too reflective of the concerns of English Canada. The only alternative was the Rassemblement, a "fragile and short-lived body . . . [created] to defend and promote democracy in Quebec against the threats posed by corruption and authoritarianism."

---

* Trudeau regularly jousted with Laurendeau and *Le Devoir*. In 1957 he was invited to a conference of "Amis du Devoir" and asked to be a keynote speaker. He began by citing André Gide's response to the question, Who is the greatest French poet? "Hugo, hélas!" If one were asked what is the best French newspaper in Canada, he continued, the answer should be "Le Devoir, hélas!" *Le Devoir*, Feb. 4, 1957.

Throughout its brief history, its members quarrelled about membership, possible affiliation with the Parti social démocratique, and the role they should take in direct political action. Trudeau persisted in his belief that the Rassemblement was the best political choice available, and he became its third and final president in 1959. By then, Laurendeau had resigned, saying that he found the group's intellectualism too remote from the everyday voter, who, in the end, would decide the nature of social change.[31]

Laurendeau's complaints about the Rassemblement were cause for concern, but Jean Marchand's opposition was much more serious. After meeting with "Comrade Marchand" in late August 1957, Pelletier told Trudeau that Marchand wanted to reflect on matters before proceeding further with the group. He specifically wanted "a self-examination about what we are and what we are doing about the R and what the relationship between the R and the real world is." Marchand always insisted that Pelletier's and Trudeau's intellectual activities should have a direct connection to the "real" world, where workers woke at 6 a.m., earned barely enough to send their children to school, and lacked the pensions that would have protected them in their old age. The Confédération des travailleurs catholiques du Canada (CTCC) was divided on the usefulness of the Rassemblement, and the other unions had merged to become the Quebec Federation of Labour (QFL). This new organization was directly linked with the Canadian Labour Congress, and its leaders were urging workers to support the CCF. Where did that leave the Rassemblement?[32]

In the end, Marchand did abandon the Rassemblement, but it lingered on in political limbo. Although Trudeau remained active, the organization was feeble, with membership fees arriving intermittently and a bank balance of only $71.13 on August 15, 1958.[33] In *The Asbestos Strike* in 1956, Trudeau had argued for a just society based on socialist principles, but one year later he was already recoiling from the Parti social démocratique, the Quebec socialist party, and claiming that "democracy" must come before the social revolution. Quebec, he urged, must have democracy before it could change its social and economic institutions.

Despite his frustration with the political scene in Quebec, Trudeau split with his reformist colleagues on one provocative issue—his argument that Duplessis was correct to refuse federal grants for universities. Yet here, too, he was being consistent, for he had already expressed this view in the brief he had written in 1954 for the Tremblay Commission. He had been overruled by the research director, Eugene Forsey, so the draft was altered, but Trudeau's mind was not.[34] He had recommended a clear division of responsibilities between the federal and the provincial governments, along with restraint by the federal government in using its taxing authority to invade provincial fields. When, in 1956, Louis St. Laurent allowed Quebec's grants to be held in trust by the National Conference of Canadian Universities until Duplessis relented, Trudeau's opposition seemed inexplicable to some and infuriating to others.

Trudeau responded in *Cité libre* the following January, arguing that the federal government had no right to take excess tax revenues and create devices by which it could then invade provincial jurisdictions. The crisis of the universities, which, in the fifties, were becoming the motors of modernization, was real. Between 1945 and 1953, the enrolment at Laval had grown by 109.6 percent and, in the same period, the Quebec government's budget had increased by 194 percent. Yet the provincial grant to Laval had gone up only 7 percent. Professors, whose salaries had exceeded those of most other professionals in 1940, had, by 1951, seen their average earnings rise by only 17.4 percent to $3,850 per year, while other professionals saw an increase from $2,502 to $9,206 in the same period.[35]

Understandably, some university teachers who had fought the battle for increased funding in *Cité libre* now complained that the independently wealthy Trudeau did not understand their personal plight. As tempers flared, traditional nationalists and, of course, Duplessis warily accepted the support of their often bitter antagonist, but Trudeau shunned their embrace. If Quebec universities were poor, he said, the fault lay within Quebec, specifically within the provincial government that had refused to fund universities adequately. At a student congress at Laval in November 1957 he urged professors and students to begin a general strike to force Duplessis to become more generous.* An outraged editorial writer at *Le Soleil,* Quebec City's leading newspaper, countered with a lead editorial attacking his irresponsibility.[36]

—

Trudeau might be unpredictable, yet he was usually consistent as he carefully honed his political identity. In *Vrai* he wrote a series of articles on democracy, liberalism, politics, and political thought.[37] In other writings, principally in *Cité libre,* he defined his stand on particular themes. On radio and on television he took part in numerous debates on contemporary issues, often stirring criticism. One radio program caused much controversy: he asked when it was right to assassinate a tyrant. Given that many critics called Duplessis a tyrant, Trudeau surely knew he would provoke a response. In an article in *Vrai* he had already written that if the social order was perverse, citizens

---

*A year later, Trudeau debated the question on radio and argued that the grants were "against the constitution and the spirit of federalism." TP, vol. 25, file 4.

should follow their conscience rather than any authority: "And if the only sure means to re-establish a just order is to wage a revolution against a tyrannical and illegal authority, well, then, do it." On radio, the qualifications that appeared in print—"personally I dislike violence"—were lost. A municipal politician jumped into the debate and declared *Vrai* and Trudeau more dangerous than the "yellow press" that the religious authorities had condemned. Pierre Trudeau's article, he fumed, was "a direct call for sedition." It was a serious offence "to preach revolution."

Jacques Hébert, the editor, replied on Trudeau's behalf in the sarcastic and personal tone increasingly common in Quebec political debate in the mid-1950s: "Brave M. Lauriault, you thought you read: 'Is it necessary to assassinate an imbecile?' and you became terrified. But rest assured; it is only about tyrants. Therefore, you are not endangered. Sleep quietly. The revolutionaries won't waste their cannonballs on wet noodles like you."[38]

To escape this parochial and disputatious environment, Trudeau sought new intellectual outlets. In March 1957 the *University of Toronto Quarterly* had invited him to write an article on political parties in Quebec. He refused, saying that "the orientation of my actions within the next several months hinges upon a series of decisions which are still being collectively pondered and are still in the making. It is fundamentally a question of what is going to happen to a new democratic ["political" is crossed out] movement we have founded—the Rassemblement." He did, however, begin to prepare an article for a book to be edited by Mason Wade, author of the standard history textbook *The French Canadians*. When the book was delayed, Trudeau submitted his piece to the *Canadian Journal of Economics and Political Science (CJEPS)*, which published it in August 1958 under the title "Some Obstacles to Democracy in Quebec."

Trudeau's arguments flowed from a familiar stream of analysis of Quebec's political development, and echoed other voices, such as recent work by Michel Brunet, a nationalist historian at the Université de Montréal, which claimed there were three dominant themes in French-Canadian social and political thought: "l'agriculture, l'anti-étatisme et le messianisme." But to most English Canadians at the time, these views were new. *CJEPS* was read by virtually every economist, political scientist, and historian working in the English language, and some politicians and journalists also subscribed. In common rooms, cocktail parties, and even a few Muskoka cottages, Trudeau's article caused a stir.[39]

In forceful prose and polemical argument, Trudeau made his case that, "in the opinion of the French in Canada, government of the people by the people could not be *for* the people, but mainly for the English-speaking part of that people; such were the spoils of conquest." French Canadians had democracy but did not believe in it: "In all important aspects of national politics, guile, compromise, and a subtle kind of blackmail decide their course and determine their alliances. They appear to discount all political or social ideologies, save nationalism."

Although he criticized English Canadians who believed in democracy for themselves but not for others, his critique of the authoritarianism of the Quebec past, the corruption of contemporary Quebec politics, and the blend of nationalism with a conservative Roman Catholic Church and a weak Quebec state resonated widely in English Canada—too widely in some cases. John Stevenson, a veteran Ottawa journalist for *The Times* of London, praised the article generously in a letter to Trudeau: "For a French-Canadian to make such an arraignment of his racial compatriots required great moral courage, and you certainly showed it in your article." He even asked for some offprints to send to the Queen's private secretary.[40] The following year Trudeau's article won the prize sponsored by the president of the University of Western Ontario for the best scholarly article in English. Grace Trudeau reported that the award received prominent mention in the English press of Montreal but not in the French press.[41]

Wherever he could, Trudeau pressed his case for greater democracy in Quebec. He covered the provincial Liberal convention in May 1958 for both *Vrai* and the CBC and concluded that the party and the convention were anti-democratic:

> It would be unjust to impute to the Liberal Party alone an anti-democratic tendency which is the characteristic of our people as a whole. To be sure, a party that has dominated the political life of our province for so long bears a major responsibility for our political infancy. But other factors also make a significant contribution: the authoritarianism of our religious and social institutions, the insecurity complex deriving from the Conquest, the systematic degradation of our civic life under the Union nationale, and many other factors as well.

Trudeau condemned the Liberal Party Congress as undemocratic not because of party officials or even party rules but because the Liberal Party itself failed to realize that a party cannot be built from above. The congress had been given little time for policy discussion; its purpose, after all, had been to choose the leader. He recognized that the new leader, Jean Lesage, a federal MP for thirteen years, was "a fighter, an energetic organizer and a charming and ambitious man," but there was no evidence, he said, that he was a democrat or that a party under his leadership would become the mass-based political movement essential to obliterating the forces of reaction and authoritarianism in Quebec.[42]

On a copy of Lesage's acceptance speech, Trudeau underlined Lesage's call for the party to seek the active sympathy of "all honest citizens who want to serve the democratic ideal," and for those groups that wish to "pursue their action from the margins of existing political parties" to rally under the Liberal banner to defeat Duplessis. At this point in the document he scrawled, "Drapeau?"[43]

In 1954 Jean Drapeau had won the Montreal mayoralty as the head of the non-partisan Civic Action League. Might not the mayor and his movement be an alternative to Lesage if it were to spread its democratic embrace beyond Montreal? Drapeau, who perhaps shared the dream, invited Gérard Pelletier, Trudeau, and the activist Jean-Paul Lefebvre to the basement of his home in the Cité-Jardin. The talk went badly when, according to Pelletier, Trudeau and Drapeau fought over the nature of democracy and "Trudeau invoked principles that were very disturbing to the practical mind of Drapeau."[44] Trudeau truly believed a popular movement based on the young and an educated working class could achieve genuine social change in Quebec. Drapeau thought he was unrealistic.

Trudeau's consistency of views was becoming the enemy of compromise—and he increasingly antagonized his former colleagues and friends. In the minutes of meetings of the Rassemblement, he is central in defining its purpose and direction. He took the lead in steering the group away from the Parti social démocratique, to the distress of Thérèse Casgrain and its new leader, Michel Chartrand, who had hoped that Trudeau's social-ism would bring about his definite commitment to the party. He had worked closely with Chartrand in the anti-conscription campaigns of the early 1940s and through all the labour actions of the 1950s. Now they were becoming antagonists.

But if Trudeau disappointed Drapeau, Chartrand, and others, he thrilled an eighteen-year-old Ottawa student who met him at a Rassemblement meeting in Ottawa in April 1957. Madeleine Gobeil, who was to play a major part in his personal life, had read Cité libre and the book on the Asbestos Strike.

Now, she wrote, she would like to know more about the myths surrounding Pierre Trudeau.[45] He responded to her letter with a serious discussion about politics, but he remained elusive about himself. Nevertheless, her interest charmed him, and they stayed in contact with each other until his marriage in 1971.

Gradually, television also contributed to the myth that was developing about Pierre Trudeau. Although he appeared much less often on the magic screen than Lévesque or Laurendeau, sometimes, he stole the scene. On one occasion on his program *Pays et Merveilles*, Laurendeau taunted him about being a young millionaire touring the world. "Did you use a rickshaw, the Chinese vehicle where 'coolies' pull the rich?" he demanded, archly. "Yes," responded Trudeau, "but I put the coolie in the seat and pulled the rickshaw myself."[46] The quick repartee that was the mark of the public Trudeau was already apparent.

—

By the fall of 1958 it was clear that Jean Lesage was having some success in rallying the opponents of Duplessis behind him, but his arguments did not convince Trudeau. Rather, in the October 1958 issue of *Cité libre*, Trudeau announced the creation of yet another new grouping—the Union des forces démocratiques—a movement that aimed to bring together everyone who shared a belief in democratic principles. Those who committed themselves to its Democratic Manifesto were not allowed to be members of political parties that refused to support the new Union. With the lowest cards in the deck, the Union bluffed and pretended it had the highest trump. The Rassemblement continued to exist, but the Union became the new vehicle for popular political reform—primarily through the accumulation of signatures that were intended to indicate political strength.* Trudeau signed the document as the president of the Rassemblement, but there were few other prominent or inspiring new faces.[47]

Over at *Cité libre*, Gérard Pelletier was becoming uneasy regarding the finances, the gaps between issues, and, increasingly, the divisions within the group. The directors gathered on November 11, 1958, in the grand Outremont home Trudeau still shared with his mother—the first time since a sparsely attended meeting in May. The minutes bear a strained sense of humour: "Mr. Pierre Vadeboncoeur's absence was regretted by no one; Mr. Gilles Marcotte's, whose sympathy for *Cité libre* was notorious, was lamentable. The absence of two directors, Messieurs Charles Lussier and Roger Rolland, whose commitment to *Cité libre* has become more and more intermittent, has been noted." Trudeau began with a complaint about the funding of the journal, pointing out that, in the past, a few of the directors had been obliged to pay personally for the publication of some of the issues. How the other directors reacted as they sat in a room with a famed Braque and a startling Pellan painting on the walls, elegant china in a cabinet nearby, and Grenier, the chauffeur, outside was not recorded in the minutes. They agreed to prepare another issue, for which the missing Vadeboncoeur was given major responsibility. They did not accept Guy Cormier's

---

*Historian Michael Behiels was scathing in his criticism: "The procedural strategy had a bad taste of boy scout amateurism and a large dose of political naïveté. When a public manifesto was signed finally by twenty-one 'eminent' political personalities in April 1959, only one Liberal, Marc Brière, endorsed the document, and he had not been mandated by the party." See his *Prelude to Quebec's Quiet Revolution: Liberalism versus Neo-Nationalism, 1945–1960* (Montreal and Kingston: McGill-Queen's University Press, 1985), 254.

suggestion that the journal should add a statement on its cover page that "the articles published in the review do not reflect the opinions of *Cité libre* but only the authors themselves." Pelletier argued that such a statement would "separate" the journal too much from the opinions expressed in it.

The directors met again just before Christmas at Gérard Pelletier's more modest home at 2391 Benny: "One doesn't know whether it was the approaching Christmas season, the Jingle Bells on St. Catherine Street, the Santa Clauses in the store windows that stirred the spirits of the participants, but the assembly was a wild one." At one point, Pelletier, who was chairing the meeting, pointed his index finger at Trudeau and told him to shut up because, for once, he was not the chair, so couldn't talk whenever he wished.* Trudeau, the minutes recorded, refused to heed the chair's rebuke. Once again the meeting went badly. Pierre Vadeboncoeur, who was absent again, had told Trudeau that he had no time for an issue on "peace" that he had earlier proposed. They were left with a few potential articles, most of them already overdue. Trudeau would see if a December 1958 conference in Ottawa on the anniversary of the Universal Declaration of Human Rights had any useful material. Réginald Boisvert promised a piece on three university students who were protesting outside Duplessis's office, including Laurendeau's daughter Francine and the future Trudeau minister Jean-Pierre Goyer. Before long, however, Boisvert resigned from *Cité libre*, declaring he had lost interest.[48]

---

*A few weeks later Trudeau's garrulous behaviour caused one real loss. According to *Nouvelles illustrées* on December 27, 1958, Trudeau was an "excellent combatant" in a judo competition, but he was disqualified because he "talked too much"—a characteristic not expected of a brown belt in judo.

The two groups—the Rassemblement and the Union des forces démocratiques—had brought attention to Trudeau's belief that a broad democratic mass movement was necessary to defeat the Union nationale and the forces of reaction. Now another new argument became strongly identified with Trudeau in these years: that participation in the democratic process and individual rights took precedence over the collective rights of the group and the authority of leaders, whether of church or state. He became a crusading lawyer for the cause, taking on cases that supported the rights of aggrieved individuals against both the state and the church. His clients ranged from the Canadian Sunbathing Association, which was violently raided by Quebec provincial police officers bearing cameras as well as guns, to the inmates of asylums and hospitals. The sunbathers seemed to intrigue him—he spent considerable time researching their case. He also vigorously supported Jacques Hébert's defence of the accused murderer Wilbert Coffin and, after Hébert was convicted for contempt of court, he successfully took his appeal to the Quebec Court of Appeal. He became even closer to Frank Scott, after the law professor moved directly from the classroom into the courtroom to win victories in the Supreme Court in the Roncarelli case and the Padlock Law case. Trudeau made sure to attend some of the sittings for these historic cases.

These decisions, along with Prime Minister John Diefenbaker's announcement of a Canadian Bill of Rights, intrigued Trudeau and drew his attention to the courts outside Quebec. At the December 1958 conference on the Universal Declaration on Human Rights in Ottawa, he encountered Bora Laskin, the future chief justice, who was emerging as the major legal academic in English Canada. Laskin, like Frank Scott, had begun to argue strongly for a Canadian bill of rights in the mid-1950s—Laskin, in particular, believed that the debate over the bill raised fundamental issues of Canadian federalism. His approach was highly layered: "The most fundamental civil liberties (freedom of association, speech, and religion) were exclusively assigned to federal authorities," while others, including those associated with legal process or economic entitlements, might be either federal or provincial, depending on the precise right.

Scott differed from Laskin on this issue by arguing for the constitutional entrenchment of all important rights. Trudeau sided with Scott: he looked on the Constitution not only as a protector of political rights but as a means of placing limits on "the liberal idea of property" that was "hampering the march toward economic democracy." It was a debate in which Trudeau, who had already argued for a bill of rights encompassing "the most fundamental civil liberties" in his presentation to the Tremblay Commission four years earlier, was to become an important participant and, ultimately, the most significant one.[49] The debates linking federalism and civil liberties flowed directly into discussions about the future of Quebec—once Maurice Duplessis was out of the way. Moreover, Trudeau's increasing participation in these debates and the publication of his article in the *Canadian Journal of Economics and Political Science* made him much better known among English Canadians.

No person was more important in Trudeau's introduction to English Canada than Frank Scott—a foremost literary talent, legal scholar, and socialist political activist. Trudeau recalled first meeting Scott when he came to the Université de Montréal in 1943 to speak understandingly of French Canadians and their opposition to conscription. Scott, for his part, believed that he first saw Trudeau at an anti-Semitic and anti-Communist rally in the late thirties. He was deeply concerned by what he termed "fascism in Quebec" and became a leader in the transformation of Canadian socialism from the authoritarianism evident in the Regina Manifesto to a Western European democratic socialist party. Despite his loathing of fascism, he had initially been opposed to Canadian participation in the Second World War, and was the most prominent English-Canadian voice arguing the case of Quebec opposition to conscription.

Scott and Trudeau met each other frequently as they worked on civil liberty questions in the early fifties and became active in the Canadian Civil Liberties Association. Scott was Trudeau's anglophone ideal: a highly intellectual man whose ideas were balanced by the practical needs of everyday politics; a constitutional lawyer who sought to protect individual rights within a bill of rights; and a poet who was also an eminent social scientist. A large man whose ubiquitous pipe created a pensive presence, Scott intimidated gently. Women adored him, and he responded generously—to his artist wife Marian's considerable dismay. Trudeau welcomed invitations to Scott's parties at his country house in the Eastern Townships, where beautiful young anglophone students clustered about the professor. He also gained access to leading European socialists through Scott's introduction. Here was a man of considerable substance—and he intrigued Trudeau.[50]

In the late winter of 1956, just as the book on the Asbestos Strike was finally to be published, Trudeau heard that Scott was planning a trip to learn first hand about the North. As an experienced voyageur, Trudeau apparently called Scott to ask if he could join him on the adventure. Initially Scott was taken aback, but he respected Trudeau's ability in the wilds and, perhaps, Trudeau also intrigued him. Once in the canoe together, they got along well. Both were physically strong, although Trudeau, the smaller man, typically took on challenges that seemed reckless to Scott. Ever the poet, he described one occasion when Trudeau entered a tremendous surge of water at the point where the Peace River and Lake Athabasca merged. He yelled, "You can't go into that," but Trudeau ignored his pleas and forged on:

> Pierre, suddenly challenged,
> Stripped and walked into the rapids,
> Firming his feet against rock,
> Standing white, in white water,
> Leaning south up the current
> To stem the downward rush,
> A man testing his strength
> Against the strength of his country.[51]

Just as Trudeau's journeys in the early 1940s had traced the path of the nationalist hero, so the journey into the Canadian Northwest also seems to have been a nationalist experience, one that made Scott and Trudeau understand the vastness of the land, its harsh demands, and its endless rewards. In another of his poems on the trip, "Fort Providence," Scott wrote:

> We came out of Beaver Lake
> Into swift water,
> Past the Big Snye, past Providence Island
> And nosed our barges into shore
> Till they grated on stones and sand.
> Gang planks, thrown to the bank,
> Were all we had for dock
> To drop four tons of freight.
>
> A line of men were squatting
> Silently above us, straight
> Black hair, swarthy skins.
> Slavies they call them, who left
> Their name on Lake and River.

None of them spoke or moved
Just sat and watched, quietly,
While the white man heaved at his hardware.
Farther on, by themselves,
The women and girls were huddled.

They saw from far off the fortlike school where a Grey Nun from Montreal was in charge, and they spoke French to the priests and nuns who taught the native Slaveys in their own broken English.

We walked through the crowded classrooms.
No map of Canada or the Territories,
No library or workshop,
Everywhere religious scenes,
Christ and Saints, Stations of the Cross,
Beads hanging from nails, crucifixes,
And two kinds of secular art
Silk-screen prints of the Group of Seven,
And crayon drawings and masks
Made by the younger children,
The single visible expression
Of the soul of these broken people.

Upstairs on the second storey
Seventy little cots
Touching end to end
In a room 30 by 40
Housed the resident boys
In this firetrap mental gaol.

The natives learning English from French priests, the missing maps, and the haunting reference to the residential school

Carroll Guérin: Pierre admired her beauty and her unconventional lifestyle, 1959.

Carroll, an artist, sometimes
worked as a fashion model too.

Carroll and Pierre enjoyed an idyllic summer holiday in Europe.

Carroll often changed her hairstyle—blonde, dark, short, long.

The beautiful and intelligent Madeleine Gobeil was a close companion for well over a decade.

The young intellectual, 1950s.

In the fifties, Trudeau gave over much of his time to the labour movement in Quebec. Note the shirts and ties, typical of the quest for respectability at the time.

Pierre and Frank Scott with the aircraft that transported them for their Mackenzie River Valley trip. Even going into the wilderness, Frank wore a hat.

Pierre relaxes on the Mackenzie River trip, 1956.

The Canadian Delegation in Mao's China, 1960. From left to right: Pierre Trudeau, a Buddhist monk, and Jacques Hébert.

Three men in a boat: The Cuba Escapade, 1960.

Trudeau sets out to row to Cuba.

surely left a deep imprint on Pierre Trudeau's mind, one that would later influence his own and his country's future.[52] For now, however, the adventurers returned home safely, bonded by their challenge to the Canadian North and their common understanding of Canada's possibilities.* Just as he had at the Ontario camp long before, Trudeau had tested his strength against a foreign physical world and discovered he could conquer it easily.

—

Trudeau began to participate regularly in English-language television programs, including coverage of the 1958 election with his old family friend Blair Fraser on the CBC, and he took part in other activities organized by English-Canadian groups. In 1957, for example, at the World University Service of Canada summer program in Ghana, other delegates included Douglas Anglin, a Carleton University specialist on Africa; James Talman, from the University of Western Ontario; Don Johnston, Trudeau's future lawyer and Cabinet minister; Robert Kaplan, another Trudeau

---

* Scott's biographer Sandra Djwa says, correctly, that Scott had a considerable influence on Trudeau. She also suggests that Scott's use of the term "just society" was the source for Trudeau's later political slogan. She admits, however, that tracing the influence is difficult. She points out that in his memoirs, Trudeau refers to T.H. Green and Emmanuel Mounier as important influences in the forties but does not mention Scott. Moreover, she continues, "There is no reference to Scott's role in Quebec in the Memoirs, nor to their joint Mackenzie River trip. Scott's name appears only once in a brief paragraph on the CCF." Although Trudeau admired Scott, his papers suggest that Scott's influence was perhaps more personal than intellectual. Sandra Djwa, "'Nothing by halves': F.R. Scott," *Journal of Canadian Studies* 34 (winter 1999–2000), 52–69.

minister to be; Tim Porteous, a future Trudeau staff member; and Martin Robin, who was to teach Margaret Sinclair before Trudeau married her. In the discussions about Canada in Ghana, Anglin and others argued that federalism should be highly centralized, but Trudeau countered that federalism, even in an "industrial age" that needed strong government, should be seen as a counterweight to the deadening effect of bureaucracy and a tool to bring government "closer to the people." Porteous, who was one of the creators of the wildly successful McGill revue *Spring Thaw*, recalls that Trudeau was shy but completely unpredictable. He insisted on breaking the anglophone monotony by taking a side journey to neighbouring francophone states.[53]

Trudeau's activities among English Canadians attracted little notice at the time in the intense debates going on in Quebec, where the Rassemblement and the Union des forces démocratiques were now cast to the side as the forces of opposition to Maurice Duplessis gathered behind Jean Lesage. Trudeau's position became more difficult. Political scientist Léon Dion criticized the negative tone of Trudeau's analysis of Quebec politics and his excessive reliance on arguments about the past. Others were less polite. The *Nouvelles illustrées* began to make Trudeau a regular target. Its gossip column mocked his "election" to the presidency of the Rassemblement, implying with considerable truth that the organization was elitist and its elections meaningless. In an anonymous letter to the editor of the same journal on April 25, 1959, the author urged that Trudeau should be sent on the first interplanetary journey so he could establish his new party on the moon, where "it would be more useful."

Trudeau's efforts seemed increasingly quixotic and even a waste of his considerable talent. In the *McGill Daily* of October 31, 1958, "Jean David" commented on the Democratic Manifesto. "Generally," he wrote, "the author is considered to be a brilliant man but to many [he] still remains a dilettante. This means that Trudeau himself has a limited influence but his ideas are usually taken into account." The effect of the manifesto, he continued, would be tied to the reaction of Quebec political leaders. At McGill a few months later, Trudeau once again said that because the "people" have not been taught democracy, they should create a completely new party. It was, he said, "the only way out."[54] A few days later in a debate on Radio-Canada, Jean Drapeau firmly rejected the Union des forces démocratiques as an effective tool to bring down Duplessis.[55] Trudeau could brush off student complaints and even Drapeau, but now he received a blow that troubled him more: his friend from childhood, Pierre Vadeboncoeur, attacked his Democratic Manifesto.

Vadeboncoeur had worked closely with Trudeau on all his projects, hailing his return to Quebec in Le Devoir in 1949 as a giant step towards a new day in Quebec. His anti-nationalism was even stronger than Trudeau's in the early 1950s, and both spoke regularly, if vaguely, of revolution. He was the butt of Trudeau's pranks, which he fully reciprocated. You remain, he wrote in 1955, "the one guy in the world I love, with whom I love to laugh and be reckless." Although Vadeboncoeur was a lawyer by training, a labour activist by profession, and a successful essayist by nature, he was perpetually short of money. Trudeau lent him funds when he needed them, as he had since they had both begun classes at Académie Querbes decades before. From the beginning it had been a strong, mutually supportive friendship.

In 1959, however, Vadeboncoeur became exasperated with his old friend. First in a labour-socialist publication and then in Le Devoir, he gently attacked the Union des forces démocratiques and Trudeau. "You'll find," he began, "that the analysts who are too clear-sighted sometimes make the greatest errors. The famous options that are proposed by that deeply penetrating spirit—that is my oldest friend, Pierre-Elliott Trudeau—are of such a kind." Soon after, in Le Social Démocrate and then in Le Devoir on May 9, he denounced the Union as "le Club de M. Trudeau," an elitist bunch who were undermining the possibility of socialism while ineptly promoting the Liberal Party. It was a hard punch, and it hurt Trudeau.[56] However, old friends can take blows, and Trudeau took it in good spirit.

When Pierre Vadeboncoeur made his attack in Le Devoir, Trudeau was away on another long trip around the world. Then events in Quebec moved quickly in his absence: the strike by producers at Radio-Canada in mid-1959 resulted in a political earthquake that turned René Lévesque and others into neo-nationalists. Trudeau himself later identified Radio-Canada as the strongest force in breaking through the media monopoly and the elite's fears, both of which had protected Duplessis's autocracy. The strike, therefore, had dramatic implications for the flow of free political information in the province. During this crisis, on September 7, Maurice Duplessis died unexpectedly after a series of strokes. The tattered remnants of the Rassemblement, along with critics such as Vadeboncoeur and Casgrain, accused Trudeau of departing just as the battle lines formed, but, in truth, he was not ready for further battle. His letters and his papers at the time suggest that he was eager to escape the infighting and quarrels in Quebec as the various factions jostled for position and the old fortresses of church and tradition began to crumble. Moreover, he had not expected Duplessis to die. After all his years in power, few did.

—

When Trudeau left Quebec at Easter 1959, he hoped to enter China once again, though he also intended to revisit old haunts and discover new vistas. Unlike his journey a decade earlier, he did not set off this time to be a vagabond student wandering the world with a knapsack. He was forty years old now and he travelled first class most of the way, staying in fine hotels such as the St. James in Paris and Hotel Mount Everest in Darjeeling. Yet, in spirit, he remained a passionate observer and a curious student. In Vietnam he noted the presence of police on every corner and despaired that the country might remain forever divided. In India he discovered a passion for politics among the people, and the historic Hindu openness to sexuality. He visited the gorgeous, erotic friezes in Kathmandu, Nepal, where the women are portrayed with their limbs spread apart and their "sex open," and animals bear "the perfect replica of the human sexual organs of normal size." He marvelled at the "ménages à trois" or even four. The "glorification du sexe" was part of their life, he wrote, perhaps with some envy. On one street he saw men walking with their hands on their genitals and wondered what it meant. The secular Congress government of India was trying to promote birth control, but the Catholic Trudeau questioned whether it would "modernize" the country or simply create neuroses.

Moving on to Persia, he noted how the forces opposed to the Shah detested the Americans, whose discreet presence as consultants there was considerable among the military. But he was most impressed by the changes in Israel, a country he described as a miracle. From the deserts of the Middle East, the Israelis had created a land of "greenness, of gardens, flowers, wheat fields, cotton, and corn" and a society of healthy children and well-dressed citizens. Although he detected a touch of chauvinism among the Israelis, he compared them favourably with the surrounding Arabs. He noted in his diary that he believed they were not expansionist and were willing to accept the status quo.[57]

Trudeau later attended an International Socialist Congress in Hamburg, Germany, where he met Moshe Sharett of Israel and Guy Mollet of France. Throughout his trip he called on prominent individuals in business, politics, and academic life. Before he left, he had asked his numerous contacts for appropriate letters of

introduction. One of the most curious was a letter from Rex
Billings, the general manager of Belmont Park in Montreal, who,
on April 9, 1959, wrote: "The bearer of this letter, Mr. Pierre E.
Trudeau, is a director of Belmont Park, and is travelling abroad
on a combined business and pleasure trip. He will be visiting
various amusement parks in the course of his travels, and any
courtesy extended to him will be appreciated."[58] He was not able
to visit China, although two prominent English Canadians who
were sympathetic to Chinese Communism — Margaret Fairley, a
Toronto intellectual, and James Endicott, a controversial United
Church minister — attempted to obtain an invitation for him. His
mother was pleased they did not succeed. She worried throughout
the trip: Don't stick "out your neck to reach China — and have
your passport confiscated or get into an international mess," she
warned. "You have seen enough excitement in your life — besides
you won't be able to run as fast as you once could — remember
your sore foot."

In the end, he spent most of the time in Europe, where he
bought a new Mercedes 300SL convertible, a gem of a car. He
also bought gifts: pearl earrings for Carroll Guérin, amber earrings for "Alice," pearls for "Ada," a silver pin for "Nicole," an
unspecified gift for Mireille G., a pin and scarf for "Kline," and
some perfume and a "pin" for Grenier, the family chauffeur. He
bought a black and gold brocade jacket in Hong Kong for himself, and then spent 225 dollars or pounds for a suit made by
William Yu at the celebrated Peninsula Hotel. On September 9
his mother wrote to him that the Mercedes had arrived in
Montreal missing one door.[59]

Back home, his oldest friends were puzzled; his colleagues,
often frustrated. Who is Pierre Trudeau? they asked during the
political ferment of the summer and fall of 1959. Who were his
friends? What did he want? His mother knew how much he
wanted what she termed "success." She resented Alec Pelletier

when she told her in May how "*her* husband" kept Pierre informed during his absence—"not that I know of anything very important," she added, as "my entourage is the passive kind I suppose." In fact, Gérard Pelletier was rarely in touch with Trudeau* and seems not to have known what occurred in his personal life all that well.[60]

Meticulous as always, Trudeau kept a record of the letters he wrote during his long absence. It appears that he wrote ninety-two letters. Pelletier and Jacques Hébert received two each, one less than his mother and the same number as Suzette and her family. Carroll Guérin, his most frequent but far from exclusive female companion, received eleven. Numerous other women, including Nicole Morin, Micheline Legendre, Marie Sénécal, Madeleine Gobeil, and others whom he met in Europe, received a single letter. The rest of the list intrigues because it illustrates how Trudeau had forged new ties with English Canadians and Americans who were almost completely absent in his lists from the late forties and early fifties. Among them are John Stevenson of *The Times*, Morris Miller of Saskatchewan, Lionel Tiger of McGill University, Ron Dare of the University of British Columbia, and the historian Blair Neatby.[61]

Trudeau arrived home in the fall just before Maurice Duplessis's promising successor, Paul Sauvé, unexpectedly died. He was succeeded by the unimpressive Antonio Barrette, who set off a stampede among the reformers to support the Liberal banner. Trudeau seemed at a loss as René Lévesque, journalist Pierre

---

* In his memoirs, Pelletier says that Trudeau "barely read daily papers." Yet his papers are crammed with clippings from all the major newspapers, and he found even obscure references to himself in the tabloid press.

Laporte, constitutional lawyer Paul Gérin-Lajoie, and several reform leaders announced they were joining Jean Lesage to fight the next election. While others prepared for this stunning political change, Trudeau happily busied himself with plans for an astonishing canoe trip from Florida to Cuba. As Lesage began to electrify audiences, and René Lévesque dazzled viewers on television, Trudeau set off from Key West for Cuba with two friends. According to the Florida newspapers, Trudeau, Valmor Francoeur, and Alphonse Gagnon, a millionaire businessman from Chicoutimi, had developed "a unique method of propulsion. While one man paddles in conventional fashion, the second lies on his back and paddles with his feet. The third rests and they switch off after two-hour hitches." Unique it surely was, but wildly dangerous too: three-foot waves drenched them thirty miles out and a shrimp boat pulled them back to the Florida shore on May Day, 1960. Although the trip had no ideological connection, it became part of the lore of Trudeau's links with Fidel Castro, whose rebels had recently taken Havana. In interviews, Trudeau said nothing about politics, but he apparently told the *Miami Herald* he was thirty-nine, then dropped the age to thirty-six for the *Key West Citizen*. Like the trip, it was all good fun.[62]

But his absence was not whimsical—it may have been deliberate. The platform of the Lesage Liberals had become increasingly neo-nationalist during the first months of 1960. Jean Lesage's campaign emphasized provincial autonomy and began to speak of a special status for the province. Trudeau became very troubled as the rhetoric of nationalism, which he had so long deplored in *Cité libre*, became the lifeblood of the Liberal campaign, particularly in Lévesque's television appearances. The Liberals tried to woo Marchand, but there is no evidence they asked Trudeau—the president of the Rassemblement, the co-editor of *Cité libre*, the author of the Democratic Manifesto, and the founder of the Union des forces démocratiques—to become a candidate. He was, perhaps, wounded—or maybe he sensed it was wise to bide his time. Certainly, he made himself difficult to contact—a small canoe in the middle of the ocean could not have been more impossible to reach—as the forces of opposition to Duplessis swelled behind Lesage and his team.

Once the Cuban canoe escapade was over, Trudeau returned to Montreal and wrote an editorial in *Cité libre* that appeared just before the election of Jean Lesage on June 22, 1960. It argued, grudgingly, that the Liberals were to be preferred to the Union nationale, but he persisted in claiming that his Union des forces démocratiques would have been a better alternative than the Liberal Party in the creation of a new government. He was especially scornful of the Parti social démocratique and the Civic Action League for their refusal to join actively with the Union. He debated with his young friend Madeleine Gobeil whether it would be "complicity" to support the Liberals.[63]

On June 22 Lesage won a surprisingly narrow victory over the battered Union nationale. It was, and remains, a landmark in the recent history of Quebec, one that opened dams that had been long closed. Unlike most of his colleagues and friends, Trudeau was not taken at the flood.

—

CHAPTER 8

A DIFFERENT TURN

"I'm confident French Canadians will once again miss the turn," Pierre Trudeau wrote in *Le Devoir* at the beginning of 1960, the year of Quebec's historic "Quiet Revolution." "At least, they'll miss it if their political authorities continue to cultivate mediocrity, if their ecclesiastic authorities continue to fear progress, and if their university authorities continue to scorn knowledge."[1] Many in Quebec and elsewhere did miss the turn that, in the sixties, became a social and political revolution in the West. The decade began in North America with leaders who had been born in the nineteenth century. Canada's John Diefenbaker adored the monarchy, disdained alcohol, spoke fractured French, had served in the First World War, and was formed by the devastation of the Great Depression. President Dwight Eisenhower, whom he greatly admired, was, at seventy, older than Diefenbaker but, like Americans generally at that time, more modern in his tastes and demeanour. Yet both seemed old in 1960 as the American Democratic candidate for the presidency, John Kennedy, began his successful campaign, at the age of forty-two, with a call to pass the torch to a new generation of Americans who faced new challenges and dreamed new dreams.

Montreal had shared the remarkable prosperity enjoyed in this continent during the postwar years. Historian Paul-André Linteau ranks the period with the 1850s and the beginning of the twentieth century as the most prosperous in the city's history. And prosperity brought its physical and cultural rewards, such as the boulevard Métropolitain that channelled the expressway to the city's heart and allowed Trudeau's Mercedes to change lanes swiftly as he sped southwards to a party at Frank Scott's summer home in the Townships, or northwards to the sophisticated resorts of the Laurentians. The number of automobiles in Montreal more than quadrupled from 229,000 vehicles after the war to over a million in 1960—far beyond the wildest dreams of Charles Trudeau with his gas stations in the twenties. With its skyscrapers culminating in the symbolic cruciform of Place Ville Marie in 1962, Montreal seemed a thoroughly North American and modern city.

In the clubs of the city centre, Trudeau saw Oscar Peterson emerge as the finest jazz pianist of his age and Félix Leclerc as one of the great chansonniers. After the nationalist riot of 1955, when the National Hockey League commissioner suspended the local hero Maurice "the Rocket" Richard, the Montreal Canadiens inspired francophone pride by winning five consecutive Stanley Cups. By this time Trudeau cared less about hockey, which he had once played well, than about culture, but here, too, a new spirit appeared, with the creation at the end of the fifties of Gratien Gélinas's Comédie-Canadienne, a host of smaller theatres, and Ludmilla Chiriaeff's Les Grands Ballets Canadiens. Trudeau no longer had to rely on touring companies to bring him ballet, the art he treasured most. But prosperity assured that the best touring companies came as well, and he heard the great Maria Callas and the New York Metropolitan Opera, which performed in Montreal five times between 1952 and 1958.[2]

Trudeau savoured these changes, just as he did the new restaurants where he and his various dates—he seems to have had several companions at this time — enjoyed ever finer cuisine and wines.* Montreal was the international city he had dreamed it might be in the thirties. Yet there is a wistfulness to his tone at the time, a sense that the heavy hand of the past had not lifted after Duplessis's death in September 1959. He feared that Quebec would miss the turn essential to its competing success-fully in the North American economy and realizing its full human potential, if its francophone universities remained immersed in their sacramental heritage and if its political debates shunned the cosmopolitan flavour that marked other Western capitals at the beginning of the sixties. His own efforts to open the political system through the development of new political groupings had won little success, and that failure no doubt affected his vision as he watched the real changes occur-ring about him.

Trudeau, of course, was not alone in underestimating the changes in Quebec that had occurred in the fifties. By 1960 his voice was heard in the debates in *Le Devoir*, on television news programs, and in public meetings, especially those organized by the Institut canadien des affaires publiques. He also became a familiar figure at meetings where Laval or Montréal students protested against the meagre provincial government support for the universities, and the young filled the admittedly small ranks of the Rassemblement as well. At his best in debate, his scintillating, quick wit scored with an astonishing range of literary, philo-sophical, and exotic allusions. He was particularly active in

---

* His frequent companion of the 1960s, Madeleine Gobeil, describes Trudeau as a gourmand who, when in Paris, went to Michelin-starred restaurants and ordered Bordeaux from the fabled châteaux. However, he drank little and wine lingered long in his glass. Interview with Madeleine Gobeil, May 2006.

public debates on civil liberties issues, which often focused on the use of an identity card. Trudeau strongly opposed the idea.[3]

Despite all his political activity, his writing, his networking of the previous decade, Trudeau remained an outsider. He was both "the most fascinating and disappointing intellectual of the 1950s" in Quebec, according to the Laval University professor Léon Dion. There was a "bewitching magnetism" around him, an envy of his intellectual and physical prowess, and admiration for "his charm and his wealth. He had the reputation of possessing the most cultivated and the most progressive spirit of the times."[4] None of his contemporaries offered more, even though some, like René Lévesque, were better known. However, he chose to walk away when the Liberal troops stormed the barricades, and he was not a player in what Lévesque dubbed the "spring cleaning of the century" that began in June 1960. Lévesque was there with Jean Lesage as he assembled his team, took office, and began to sweep away the barriers to speech, thought, and social change. As others took up the brooms Trudeau had so long advocated, he, strangely, remained at the sidelines.

But was it so strange? By all accounts, Trudeau's feelings and his prospects were uncertain at this critical moment. Although Lévesque later claimed that Trudeau, Gérard Pelletier, and Jean Marchand all turned down the chance to become candidates in the 1960 election (Marchand certainly said no to Jean Lesage, who considered the celebrated labour leader a prize candidate), Lévesque's biographer Pierre Godin argues convincingly that Pelletier and Trudeau were not even asked. At the time, Trudeau welcomed Lévesque's last-minute decision to enter politics and, after the Liberal victory, his appointment to the Cabinet. Later, he admitted he was envious that Lévesque had "made a jump into politics at a time when it was crucial." "I felt a bit sorry for myself," he said, "because I'd never be asked to get into politics . . . I was against the party he had joined." But he also told Lévesque's

Liberal Cabinet colleague Paul Gérin-Lajoie that he was "lucky" to have "Liberal beliefs": "This permits you to get into politics," he said. For his own part, a wistful Trudeau believed he "would always be on the outside writing articles about what the politicians should be doing and weren't." It was the price he paid for trying to create viable new parties—the Rassemblement and the Union des forces démocratiques—and for condemning vigorously the traditional political parties. Still, for all his talk, he had never doubted that he should be on the inside. He had told a union meeting in 1957, for instance, that "it was much better to have men standing up in the legislature in Quebec than marching on it." But when the reformers finally took their place on the front benches in 1960, a disappointed Trudeau wasn't there.[5]

Yet bliss it was in that summer of 1960 to be alive, democratic, and liberal, even if not Liberal, in Quebec. Despite Trudeau's differences with the leaders of the new regime, he shared with them "a common understanding on a range of subjects such as the urgency for the modernization of Quebec or the sad awareness of the loss created by 25 years of Duplessisism in the province."[6] Trudeau's post-election article in Cité libre treated the Lesage election as heaven-sent—his mood contrasting sharply with his previous hesitations about the election and the Lesage Liberals. "We must first salute those who delivered us from the scourge of the Union nationale," he wrote. "It is the Liberal Party and none other which waged the decisive battle for our liberation, and it is to them that today I doff my hat." In particular, he saluted "the incorruptible Mr. Lapalme and . . . the indefatigable Mr. Lesage," who had built piece by piece an army from a group that, then years before, had only eight members in the legislature.[7]

But Georges-Émile Lapalme and Jean Lesage did not doff their hats to Trudeau for helping to build the army that triumphed in June 1960. In his superb memoirs of his political career, Lapalme dismissed the role of Cité libre in defeating

Duplessis. And the former premier, had he been alive in 1960, would surely have agreed. The reasons behind their grudging reservations were all too clear in that same article Trudeau published immediately after their election victory. Some of the new Liberal politicians had only recently begun to oppose the Union nationale, he said, and he still had doubts about the past, present, and future of the Quebec Liberal Party:

> For sixteen years, the Province has wallowed under an incompetent, tyrannical, and reactionary government. This regime, resting on lucre, ambition, and a fondness for the arbitrary, would not have been possible, however, without the cowardice and complacency of almost all those exercising authority, commanding influence, or leading public opinion . . .
>
> Whether chancellor of a university, principal of a school, union leader, director of a professional corps, head of a company, militant nationalist, or administrator of any institution, each used the particular arrangement he had come to with the power of government as a pretext to justify not denouncing this power when it systematically harmed the common good in the domain for which each was responsible: industrial relations, natural resources, well-ordered economic development, civic honour, respect of intelligence, education, autonomy, justice, and democracy.

Trudeau also defended his absence from the political front ranks in his article. He disingenuously omitted mention of his central role in the formation and leadership of the Union des forces démocratiques. He pointed to the close results in many constituencies as well as Lesage's narrow victory. He argued, accordingly, that if all anti-Duplessis forces had united behind a coalition such as the Union, the majority would have been larger and the mandate for change stronger. He criticized the socialist party—the Parti social démocratique (PSD)—which had joined the Liberals in refusing to rally behind his Union, and claimed that the dismal results it received were deserved. In Trudeau's view, the PSD would "probably disappear from the provincial scene for a long time." In this judgment he was correct. Finally, he pointed out that the Liberals had only recently united effectively against Duplessis: in the past, under the domination of Mackenzie King and Louis St. Laurent, they had acquiesced too often to Duplessis's anti-labour policies, on the one hand, and Ottawa's centralization, on the other. While the Liberals had remained in thrall to the forces of reaction, others had fought for justice "with vehemence, courage, and persistence."[8] In other words, he claimed, the editors and authors of *Cité libre* had been on the thin front lines when the Union nationale was intimidating almost all the others. Trudeau's argument fundamentally and correctly asserted that the party politicians had determined the outcome in the present, but that the thinkers and the students, the ones who cared about *Cité libre*, had been equally important in what French historians call the *longue durée*.

Trudeau had other reasons, too, for his reservations about the Liberal government. The Radio-Canada strike had made Lévesque into a nationalist angry with the government of Canada, though he remained a secularist modernizer and became part of a group identified as neo-nationalists—a group that included André Laurendeau, the journalist Pierre Laporte, and the academic Léon Dion. Trudeau dissented ever more strongly from the neo-nationalist position, and the presence of many neo-nationalists in the new Lesage government bothered him. These differences divided Trudeau and Gérard Pelletier, who tended to follow Trudeau's lead, from those who became the Quebec intellectual mainstream after June 1960.

There had been signs of the future division earlier in *Cité libre*. In 1957 Léon Dion had issued a mild dissent from the general tone of Trudeau's analysis of Quebec society. He criticized the "pessimistic nationalism" of Michel Brunet and the so-called Montreal school of historians in a *Cité libre* article that did not mention Trudeau. Correspondence makes clear, however, that Trudeau, who at the time shared some of Brunet's analysis, was also a target. Trudeau published the article after considerable editorial debate. The following year, in another journal, Dion criticized Trudeau in more detail, arguing that he ignored the existence of some democratic institutions within Quebec while being too vague about what democracy itself represented. He wrote that Trudeau's bleak assessment of the dominance of the clerical and conservative elite and of the obstacles to democracy in Quebec ignored moments in Quebec's history, such as the Rebellion in the 1830s and responsible government in the 1840s, when democratic tendencies were strengthened. Trudeau's focus on unions and democracy was too narrow, his despair too sterile, he charged.

Earlier, Pierre Laporte, *Le Devoir*'s senior political reporter, had also reproached Trudeau, "my good friend," for his pessimism after hearing a presentation he made to the Institut canadien des affaires publiques. Laporte claimed that Trudeau went too far when he said that "French Canada had produced nothing, not a thinker, a researcher, a man of letters or a professional worthy of the name." Trudeau, moreover, was dead wrong when he claimed that English Canadians had given democracy as a gift to French Canadians. Like Dion, Laporte asked what they should make of the blood spilt and the battles won by the patriots in the 1830s and 1840s once representative and responsible government came to Quebec.[9] "A gift from the English?" Hardly.

These emerging divisions were reflected within the *Cité libre* team itself. Although some of the younger writers and their supporters were at loggerheads with the founding fathers, the fall of the Union nationale suddenly drew enormous attention to the journal. Despite sporadic publication and limited circulation, they all knew it had played a major part in expressing and disseminating intellectual dissent throughout the 1950s. Dion might have had differences with Trudeau, the editor, but he recognized the journal's significance in a February 1958 letter to him: "It is here that I see the immense usefulness of 'Cité libre'—it allows us to express our thoughts with ease before and for our contemporaries."[10]

In the summer of 1960 *Cité libre* was reorganized under the business leadership of Jacques Hébert, who had experience running *Vrai* as well as a successful new publishing house, Éditions de l'homme. By broadening the journal's group of supporters, he turned it into a financial success: its subscriptions increased dramatically from under one thousand to over seven thousand at one point. English-Canadian subscriptions soared as the intelligentsia in the rest of Canada struggled to understand what was happening in Quebec. Yet, as so often occurs, this success bred even more dissension as Trudeau's hesitations about the Lesage government, on the one hand, and his criticisms of the Parti social démocratique, on the other, created friction with earlier sympathizers such as Paul Gérin-Lajoie and René Lévesque, who were themselves ministers in the new government, and Pierre Vadeboncoeur and Marcel Rioux, who were becoming ever more strongly socialist and nationalist.

Then, suddenly, the spectre of separatism began to disrupt their deliberations. The first but still minor explosion came on September 10, 1960, when about thirty mostly young Quebec francophones in a Rassemblement pour l'indépendance nationale (RIN) issued a manifesto that called for the "total" independence of Quebec.

—

As the newspapers reported the RIN manifesto, sometimes dismissively but often with curiosity, and the Lesage government began its fundamental reforms of Quebec's educational and social system, Pierre Trudeau and Jacques Hébert were flying over the

Atlantic with the hope of visiting China. Hébert and Trudeau obviously enjoyed each other's company, even though they were very different: Hébert, an extrovert who laced his life with wry but regular humour; Trudeau, essentially an introvert whose pranks were invariably ingenious. They shared a love of the unexpected and the mysterious and a distrust of the mighty and the meretricious. By the sixties, they had forged a partnership based on their love of exotic travel and their sometimes playful but often deadly serious attack on the establishment—whatever it might be.

Both men, but especially Hébert, were outraged when Wilbert Coffin was hanged on February 10, 1956, on questionable evidence, for the murder of three Pennsylvania hunters. The American secretary of state, John Foster Dulles, personally contacted Quebec authorities on the case, Duplessis responded as requested, and the conviction came quickly after the judge charged the jury with the words "I have faith that you will set an example for your district, for your province, and for the whole of your country before the eyes of America, which counts on you, and which has followed all the details of the trial." This disgraceful charge, the fawning government response to American intervention, and the flimsiness of the evidence outraged the lawyer Trudeau and the crusading civil libertarian Hébert. For a decade, their demand for posthumous justice for Coffin bonded them in their mission.[11]

This commitment also made them defiant in the face of American and conservative Canadian challenges. China intrigued them, both in itself and as a challenge to orthodoxy. Except for a photograph, Trudeau omitted mention of this six-week trip from his memoirs, even though he and Hébert had written a book, *Two Innocents in Red China*, describing it. Three others accompanied them: Denis Lazure, a psychiatrist and future separatist politician; Micheline Legendre, one of Canada's great puppeteers; and Madeleine Parent, a leftist union activist.

They were a peculiar quintet encountering an enigma. Although Canada had begun trading with Communist China in mild defiance of the Americans, there were no formal diplomatic ties between the two countries. The group formed a "delegation" whereby they all officially visited sites appropriate to their particular background. In Trudeau's case that meant courts and related institutions.

The Chinese had invited one hundred French Canadians to visit their country, but only twenty, according to Trudeau and Hébert, "dared to answer." Most of those invited feared for their reputations should they accept. The authors, however, felt they were "pretty well immune to reprisals." Both "had been generously reproved, knocked off, and abolished in the integralist and reactionary press in consequence of earlier journeys behind the iron curtain." Thus, "the prospect of being assassinated yet again on their return from China was hardly likely to impress" either of them.

In the Shanghai chapter, Trudeau ruefully complained that his mischievous companions had told his solicitous hosts that he loved sea slugs. As a result, every day they served him the "quite repulsive beast which lives in slime and looks like a fat, brownish worm covered with bumps." Trudeau had fled Shanghai in 1949 as Mao's armies neared. He found it "strange to come back after eleven years to a city that used to embody all the fascination, all the intrigue, all the violence and mystery that could arise from the collision of East and West." Now the beggars and wounded soldiers were gone; the streets were clean, and no one wore rags. The bars and brothels of earlier days had disappeared; the city went to bed at 11:30; and "Shanghai has become an industrious city." One night Trudeau escaped from his insistent and sometimes imperious guide, Mr. Hou, and wandered through the streets at midnight. He found nary a bar or a café but, in the city's parks, saw "several young couples

[with] their arms round each other's waists [who were] kissing." The sight appealed to his warm, romantic side and broke the monotony of the too "industrious" city.

On October 1, the anniversary of the Communist victory, the Canadians and the other guests stood atop the gate at Tiananmen Square in Beijing and witnessed tens of thousands dancing and celebrating below them while fireworks turned the heavens into daylight. As Mr. Hou began to escort the guests back to their hotel, Trudeau hid behind a pillar, then suddenly darted away into the crowd and disappeared. "What happened," Hébert wrote, "we shall never know exactly, nor are we convinced that Trudeau remembers it clearly himself. He took part in weird and frenzied dances, in impromptu skits, in delightful flirtations." Later, he described "exotic orchestras, costumes of the moon people, strange friendships and new scents . . . dark tresses, inquisitive children, laughing adolescents, brotherly and joyful men." The memory lingered of lights dimming and faint footsteps in dark alleys, and a long walk back to the hotel in the early dawn.[12]

In his epilogue, Trudeau said that his purpose in writing the book was to dispel the notion of "the Yellow Peril." The real threat, he concluded, is "not the Yellow Peril of our nightmares; it is the eventual threat of economic rivalry in the markets of the world, and the nearer threat of an ideological success that is already enabling China to help . . . the even poorer countries of Asia, Africa, and Latin America."[13] He said that the "two China" policy of recognizing China and Taiwan as sovereign entities was unacceptable and dangerous. It was American "prestige" that prevented the acceptance of China in the international arena, but, in a thermonuclear age, "innocents" must ask whether Taiwan is "worth the trouble of setting off the final thermonuclear holocaust." Trudeau himself did not worry about the "China threat" during his own lifetime. China had too much to do internally; its history was not that of an aggressor, unlike the nations of the West. Hébert and Trudeau did get to meet Mao, "one of the great men of the century," who possessed "a powerful head, an unlined face, and a look of wisdom tinged with melancholy. The eyes of that tranquil face are heavy with having seen too much of the misery of men."[14]

A largely handwritten draft of the book is preserved in Trudeau's papers, and it indicates that Hébert was the principal author and Trudeau mainly the editor. Trudeau's most substantial contribution is the chapter on Shanghai and the epilogue, although Hébert claimed that Trudeau made constant changes to drafts of other sections. Perhaps because of this shared authorship, the two friends wrote in the third person in their book.

Hébert published the volume and launched it at the Cercle Universitaire on Sherbrooke Street in Montreal on March 28, 1961. Fortunately for them, the anticipated attacks on their "innocent" presentation of "Red China" were few. Indeed, several priests came to the elegant book launch and eagerly sought the authors' autographs. In his speech that evening, Trudeau called for Canadian recognition of China and again predicted, accurately, that China would someday challenge the West not only in ideology but also in trade.[15]

Almost half a century later, Trudeau's prediction of the economic challenge of China is fulfilled. Yet today we also know that the misery the travellers saw in Mao's eyes was very often of his own dictatorial making. In their well-received biography of Mao, Jung Chang and Jon Halliday strongly criticized Trudeau and Hébert for their naïve views of China. The "starry-eyed" travellers, they wrote, ignored all the evidence of famine that refugees in Hong Kong reported in detail to anyone who would bother to listen. In their own book, Trudeau and Hébert did dismiss these reports. Pre-Communist China, they said, was a place "where unspeakable misery and deadly famine were the lot of the unemployed and their whole families. Unemployment meant death by hunger and cold." With Communism, in contrast, all Chinese had work: "This means precisely that it has been able to guarantee them the right to live. Before this fundamental fact, all our Western reflections on the arduous nature of work in China, on female labour, on the wretched standard of living, on the totalitarian régime, appear as ineffectual quibbles."*

Today, these reflections are clearly no longer "ineffectual quibbles." As Trudeau, Hébert, and the other Western guests participated in long banquets where wine flowed and food abounded, over twenty million Chinese died in the great famine of 1960. While Chinese starved, Mao showered funds on Indonesia, Africa, Cuba, and Albania, seeking to become the "model" for the post-colonial world that Trudeau and Hébert had heralded. But in the epilogue, Trudeau appeared to have some premonition of what was to come: "It is true that, if the authors . . . are guilty of anything, it is naïveté. We had the naïveté to believe that what we saw with our own eyes did exist; and the further naïveté to think our readers capable of

---

* Trudeau's enthusiasm for China pervaded his letter to his friend Carroll Guérin. She wrote when she received a note from him at the time: "It was fascinating to receive word from China, particularly since you praise it so much. Pierre, you are so lucky to have met Mao Tse-tung . . . I imagine everyone will react to your favourable reports as they did towards your previous ones about Russia in '52." Guérin to Trudeau, Oct. 18, 1960, TP, vol. 39, file 6. China continued to intrigue Trudeau. Years later, when asked by Thérèse Gouin Décarie and Vianney Décarie who had impressed him most among world leaders, Trudeau answered immediately, "Chou En-lai." Conversation with the Décaries, June 2006.

making the necessary adjustments in the often outrageous claims made by our Chinese informants."[16]

Indeed, the Canadians became part of a theatre directed by Mao without realizing that they were players. Yet Trudeau was perceptive in early recognizing that China was forming the base for a strong industrial society and correct in his assessment that the majority of Chinese themselves had more confidence in the regime than they had had in the ramshackle and corrupt quasi-democracy of 1949. Even if the travellers failed to learn about the horrible events in the countryside simply because they did not ask enough questions (and would likely not have received honest answers if they had), they were correct in their analysis that the increased literacy in the cities and in large areas of the country would be a powerful and positive force for future transformation.

Trudeau was not alone in his overly sanguine view of China. In a review of the book the following year, the writer Naim Kattan observed that the authors exhibited no ideological bias. "Some readers," he wrote, might find it "a negative description of China"; others might declare it uncritical. "It all depends on the colour of the glasses a person wears. Jacques Hébert and Pierre Trudeau did not wear any." They reported what they saw, and they did not know that so much was concealed from them—their myopia was shared by many others at the time. Chang and Halliday denounced not only Trudeau and Hébert but also the future French president François Mitterrand, and the former head of the Food and Agricultural Organization, John Boyd-Orr, who commented that China was feeding its people well. Even Field Marshal Bernard Montgomery, the hero of the Battle of El Alamein, denied reports of widespread famine and dismissed criticisms of Mao. China, he declared, "needs the chairman," who must not "abandon the ship."[17] Others followed in this same positive vein for many years, including the quintessential realist Henry

Kissinger, who bantered most banally with the Chinese leader about sexual appetites.*

Given Trudeau's response to other leaders and nations around this time, it's fair to ask a broader question: Was he generally too sympathetic to authoritarian regimes of the left? Trudeau's comments about China under Mao followed not long after his optimistic assessment of the Soviet Union during the last months of Stalin's madness. He also became an early advocate of Fidel Castro, visiting Havana after his failed canoe trip to Cuba. There he met "Che Guevara, with his cigar, mingling with the guests and everything else." He did not meet Castro, although he attended a huge rally where Castro "made a great speech . . . and

---

* Western views of China and Mao were much more generous than views of the Soviet Union and Stalin. Journalist Edgar Snow's book *Red Star over China* romanticized Chinese Communism, and, by the 1960s, Mao was a cult hero among the radical young who clung to his famous Red Book. By the 1970s even American Republicans had succumbed. Although Mao did not praise America, Nixon told Mao at their first meeting that "the Chairman's writings moved a nation and have changed the world." He said Mao was a "professional philosopher"; in return, Mao spoke admiringly of Kissinger's success with women. Unbelievably, the transcript reads: Mao—"There were some rumours that said you were about to collapse (laughter). And women folk seated here were all dissatisfied with that (laughter, especially pronounced among the women). They said if the Doctor is going to collapse, we would be out of work." The Chinese took extraordinary pains to cut off locals from foreigners. During the Nixon visit, which occurred at Chinese New Year, thousands of rural youth were sent back to their villages lest they encounter the American president—an encounter that security had already made impossible. Jung Chang and Jon Halliday, *Mao: The Unknown Story* (New York: Knopf, 2005), 584, 587–89.

people were just mesmerized by him."[18] And in 1976 he became the first NATO leader to visit Cuba. At home, in his long battle with Duplessis in Quebec, Trudeau had been a strong proponent of "democracy," "civil liberties," and "individual" rights—yet it was obvious that the Communist regimes of Stalin and Mao in particular were guilty of abundant human rights abuses. Trudeau did change his views of the Soviet Union and Stalin after Khrushchev's dramatic revelations in 1956. Yet even if he saw little state oppression in China, no objective observer would suggest that the values of democracy and human rights were cherished in the Chinese Communist state—or, for that matter, in the Soviet Union and Cuba. While acknowledging that many others failed to penetrate the thick curtains concealing famine, human rights abuses, and brutality, we have to admit that Trudeau, despite Kattan's review, did have some rose colour in his glasses.

There are a number of reasons for his seemingly contradictory approach. To begin with, Pierre Trudeau often reacted against conventional views, and, when he visited the Soviet Union in 1952 and China in 1960, stern anti-Communism was the dominant political current in North America. Already it had caused numerous abuses of civil rights in North America itself. Trudeau's travelling partner Madeleine Parent and her husband, Kent Rowley, had endured the fierce sting of irrational anti-Communism from the Quebec police, the RCMP, and the press. These events establish a context for Trudeau, who loathed the careless anti-Communism of Duplessis, the anti-Soviet diatribes of Conservative leader George Drew, and the McCarthyism that tainted American public life in the 1950s. They pricked him towards contrary actions. As Robert Ford, Canada's ambassador to the Soviet Union, later remarked, Trudeau was by nature "anti-establishment" and the Soviets were never the establishment—even on the left.[19]

A complex and peculiar incident that occurred during the 1960 Quebec election campaign illustrates Trudeau's sensitivities on this score. Abbé Gérard Saint-Pierre, in dismissing one of Trudeau's election comments, called him "the Canadian Karl Marx" in a Trois-Rivières newspaper sympathetic to the Union nationale. A Quebec court had recently held that calling someone a Communist was libellous. Trudeau decided to take action but, interestingly, followed Catholic canon law rather than pursuing the case in civil court. Accordingly, he asked Georges-Léon Pelletier, the bishop of Trois-Rivières, to demand a retraction from Saint-Pierre; otherwise, he threatened to turn to the secular courts. Bishop Pelletier answered on June 20, noting that Trudeau had once said that Lenin was "a remarkable sociologist." He added: "In common parlance, Karl Marx personifies socialism whether it be political or economic. It is difficult therefore to prove that one can associate this description with heresy, much less communism." Pelletier cleverly concluded that "the label 'communist' actually preceded Karl Marx." Trudeau therefore deserved no retraction.

On June 30 Trudeau appealed, although he agreed that the spirit of Bishop Pelletier's reply reflected certain papal encyclicals. When he received no apology, he wrote again on August 26. Pelletier quickly replied on September 3 and authorized Trudeau to go ahead with a suit in civil court. But it was too late. Quebec libel law required that any action had to proceed within three months of publication. The Pelletier letter had arrived precisely at the point when the legal remedies were exhausted.

A later debate on the issue took place in the pages of *Cité libre* and the conservative Catholic *Notre Temps*, in which "Jean-Paul Poitras" said that Trudeau had not needed to turn to canon law but could have gone directly to the courts. In a reply entitled "The Inconvenience of Being Catholic," Trudeau denounced Poitras for his ignorance, adding wryly that "for a long time, *Notre Temps* has accused *Cité libre* and its editors of being bad sons of the Church. Today *Notre Temps* and M. Poitras accuse me of holding the laws of the Church in too high regard."[20]

By the summer of 1961, however, when Trudeau wrote this attack on clericalism and the church's conservatism, he was tilting at windmills. The debate belonged to the past, not to the intense present of Quebec after June 1960. What remains remarkable is the time he spent on the matter when so much else of political significance was developing in Quebec. The denunciations of the "Soviet sympathies" of his LSE mentor Harold Laski, the Union nationale's use of the Padlock Law, and the wild exaggerations of the "menace" of Communism all played a part in his attitude, as did, perhaps, his long-forgotten thesis on the reconciliation of Communism and Catholicism. Trudeau rightly despised this McCarthyism of the North, especially when the church was involved. These experiences and this attitude formed part of the baggage he carried to China.

A second explanation for the authors' naïveté in their reaction to China lies in Trudeau's understanding of international politics, an area where Harold Laski, Emmanuel Mounier, and the eminent French newspaper *Le Monde* had all had considerable influence on him. He believed, like many other intellectuals of the time, that, in the nuclear age, all possible effort should be made to break down the differences between the East and the West. André Laurendeau and *Le Devoir* shared his views, as did Gérard Pelletier, particularly in the late fifties and early sixties when the superpowers began testing ever more potent hydrogen weapons and the Western anti-nuclear movement grew rapidly. On June 24, 1961, he clipped a piece from *Le Devoir* in which his former fiancée Thérèse Gouin, by then a highly regarded academic psychologist, wrote of the terror she felt for the fate of her children in the thermonuclear age. Trudeau shared Thérèse's fears, and his beliefs bonded him to the young, a tie he cherished. But it was not only the young: Maryon Pearson, Lester Pearson's wife, boldly joined the Canadian Voice of Women, an organization whose rallying call at the time was opposition to nuclear weapons. In those anxiety-filled times, Trudeau, like many of his students, wore a peace symbol on his lapel.

Furthermore, Trudeau reflected contemporary social science in its belief that, especially in recently decolonized countries, nations could achieve economic gains more quickly by central planning than by democratic means. He concluded a CBC "post-news talk" on Valentine's Day with some reservations, saying that what he saw in China "was not the neat economic planning of our textbooks," and he spoke of the "bottlenecks" that planning caused. But, he concluded, "only a fool would fail to see that . . . it was the clumsy awakening of what in years to come . . . may turn out to be the world's most powerful industrial giant."

For many observers in the late 1950s, the Soviets seemed to have grown economically at rates far beyond that of the United States and Canada. They had launched the first earth satellite and, according to John F. Kennedy in the 1960 presidential campaign, had managed to produce far more missiles than the United States had done. In a world where missiles counted, the Soviets had apparently become the greatest military power. China, for its part, seemed much superior at the time to its obvious democratic comparison, India, in terms of literacy, economic growth, and infant mortality. Eminent social scientists such as Samuel Huntington noticed the results and concluded that democracy might not be the best path for the newly independent African and Asian states to follow.

In 1959 Michael Oliver, the McGill professor and socialist activist, had asked Trudeau to comment on an article by George Grant, the well-known Canadian political philosopher. Grant was critical of contemporary capitalism but argued that social priorities were "more advanced" in North America than in the Soviet Union. Trudeau placed a question mark beside that claim, though he agreed with Grant that North American capitalism did not produce the "right services"—there were too many cars and garages and not enough classrooms.[21] Trudeau was willing to give the Soviets, the Chinese, and, later, the Cubans much credit for getting their "social priorities" correct. While acknowledging the limitations on civic rights in these authoritarian societies, he emphasized their social achievements, especially when others in the church and in Quebec and Canadian politics so vigorously denied them.

Finally, Trudeau and Hébert were more troubled about the intellectual and cultural development in China than their critics suggested. After one of the endless "factory" tours where they saw how "Soviet experts" had helped production—as an official delegation they had no choice but to go where their hosts took them to showcase the Chinese accomplishments—the Canadians longed

> to dream awhile before the tomb of an emperor, or the tranquil Buddha of some pagoda lost in the mountains. But that's the past, and Mr. Hou, like all the Mr. Hous in China, thinks only of the present, dreams only of the future. When we ask our hosts to identify some modern building, they reply enthusiastically: "It's a hospital, it's a library—built *after* the Liberation."
>
> "And that lovely temple, on that little hill over there?"
> "I don't know—some temple . . ."
> "Buddhist?'
> "Perhaps."
> It doesn't interest them.[22]

The earnestness and ignorance of the Chinese universities also bothered them: "Trudeau asks the economists if they know some of the Western economists who have studied socialist economics: Schumpeter and Lerner, for instance, or even the Polish economist Lange? They don't know them." The Canadians "can't help wondering" if the students "ever take time for a little fun." Apparently they don't, and if a foreign student from a "brother"

Marxist country is caught redhanded in a "harmless flirtation," he will be considered a "degenerate, a bad Marxist," and sent home. As one who flirted constantly, Trudeau's condemnation was severe![23]

—

When Trudeau returned home from China in November 1960, he found that Quebec's politics and classrooms were becoming very different from those he had excoriated in the fifties. His fears that the Lesage government would be hesitant and too beholden to traditional political interests had been unwarranted. The "team of thunder," as the Liberals called their government, moved forward with breathtaking speed as it secularized education, began to redefine social security, and even considered an international role for Quebec. René Lévesque became a symbol of this dynamism and, increasingly, its nationalism. The Catholic Church reeled from the impact of change, and its priests began to notice that the faithful now came much less often to mass. Cardinal Paul-Émile Léger, as he had now been promoted, struggled to meet the forces of modernization. He implored *Le Devoir* not to break its historical link with the Roman Catholic Church and agreed to restrict church interference in the universities—a decision that opened academic positions to church critics such as Marcel Rioux and, of course, Pierre Trudeau. In Trudeau's case, the cardinal personally intervened to remove the ban, and Vianney Décarie played a major part in securing a position for his wife's great admirer.[24]

In January 1961—a decade after the historic meeting between Léger, Trudeau, and Pelletier over Trudeau's article questioning the "divine right" of priests—the cardinal once again invited them in for a discussion—this time to his home in Lachine. It was, Pelletier recalled, "a friendly encounter"—a mood that would colour their relationship through the momentous Vatican II reform process and in many other meetings until 1967. Then Léger, the prince of the

Quebec church, left his province for Cameroon, to become once again a simple parish priest.[25]

What had happened in Quebec was that the positions of Pelletier and Trudeau, on the one hand, and the cardinal, on the other, had converged. True, there were still some flourishes from the past, as in Trudeau's battle with the bishop of Trois-Rivières. Another occurred when Jean-Paul Desbiens anonymously published *Les insolences de frère Untel*, a strong condemnation of Catholic education in Quebec. André Laurendeau wrote the preface and, in the fall of 1960, he received a severe rebuke from Cardinal Léger for his efforts. The book sold an astonishing 150,000 copies, but, by then, Desbiens had been excommunicated by the church. Here was a cause Trudeau and his colleagues could champion, as in the dark days of the fifties, and *Cité libre* gave Desbiens its "prix de la liberté" to express its solidarity with him.[26]

Unlike many of their now openly agnostic or atheist colleagues, however, Trudeau and Pelletier remained believers. Pelletier admitted as early as October 1960 that he had not realized how weak the Quebec church had become behind its imposing physical structures and powerful traditions. In *Cité libre*, where Quebec Catholic ways were often deplored, Pelletier lamented that "we are proceeding, I believe, towards a spiritual void and a religion without a soul similar to North American Protestantism." Pelletier and Trudeau were not admirers of Abbé Groulx, but they shared his opinion, to some degree, that the spiritual aridity of the Quiet Revolution had created a confusion of ideas and an aggressive secularism.[27]

Trudeau also shared with Pelletier a growing admiration for the reform movement in the Roman Catholic Church that began with the election of Pope John XXIII in 1958.[28] The historic encyclical *Mater et Magistra*, issued on May 15, 1961, reflected many of the intellectual streams, including personalism, which had animated the first meetings between Pelletier and Trudeau as young men in postwar Paris. The Pope's own rhetoric, including his references to the importance of the individual within society and, above all, his call to "open the windows" of Catholicism to the world, bore a strong resemblance to Trudeau's beliefs and writing. And Trudeau found little humour in the mocking of the church that became increasingly common in Quebec in the sixties. However, it was not the blasphemy of the artist or the young, with whom he was otherwise closely allied in spirit and style and concern, that perturbed him most during the winter of 1960–61: it was the increasingly assertive nationalism of Quebec political debate, a nationalism that he came to regard as a substitute for the religious zealotry of the past.

—

Since its November 1960 reorganization under Jacques Hébert, *Cité libre* had become a monthly publication. It had been refinanced with seventy-five shareholders and had created a large administrative committee, including an auditor and an archivist. The larger grouping meant, of course, greater diversity of views. Trudeau and Pelletier, as editors, were troubled as neo-nationalists and separatists on the committee became increasingly vocal and, they believed, too influential.

Curious about what the young thought, they organized a gathering of the "friends" of *Cité libre* at the Université de Montréal on a Saturday morning in the fall that year. The crowd looked much different from those of earlier days. The suits were few, the women far more numerous, beards were everywhere, and separatist slogans were on the notice boards. The students challenged directly, showed little regard for formalities, and clearly demonstrated that the sixties belonged to the young and that those over forty, like Trudeau, would have to prove themselves before they got any respect. His own turtlenecks, sandals, open shirts, and casual jackets no longer seemed bohemian and shocking—even though he often asked his young companion, Madeleine Gobeil, for sartorial advice.[29] There, at the university, Pelletier immediately "noticed the first unequivocal signs of a nationalist renaissance among our juniors." One young woman heckled him and accused *Cité libre* of disregarding French culture in Quebec. He replied that the journal had been culturally nationalist from its first issue but had rejected political nationalism as retrogressive.

Pelletier and Trudeau responded quickly to the charges against them in the pages of *Cité libre* and elsewhere. After he returned from a holiday in Europe, Trudeau drafted an article on nationalist alienation, "L'aliénation nationaliste," which appeared in March 1961 as the lead. He began by declaring that the journal had always displayed a tendency to consider Quebec nationalists as alienated. He replied, at least implicitly, to the young woman at the university that memorable Saturday morning:

> The friends of *Cité libre* were suffering—as much as anyone else, I guess—from the humiliations which afflicted our ethnic group. But as great as the external attack on our rights may have been, still greater was our own incapacity to exercise those rights. For example, the contempt shown by "les Anglais" for the French language never seemed to rival either in extent or in stupidity that very contempt shown by our own people in speaking and teaching French in such an abominable way! Or again, the violations of educational rights of French Canadians in other provinces never seemed as blameworthy or odious as the narrow-mindedness, incompetence, and lack of foresight that have always characterized education policy in the province of Quebec, where our rights were all nevertheless respected. The same could be said for areas where we claimed we were being wronged: religion, finance, elections, officialdom and so forth.

Trudeau went on to castigate separatists who, in the past, "called on the people for acts of heroism . . . on the very people who did not even have the courage to stop reading American comics or to go see French movies." Separatists wanted to close the borders and hand back power to the same elites who were responsible for the "abject state from which separatists were boldly offering to free us." The young separatists might "make fun of the cowards at *Cité libre*" who would not endorse separatism or extreme nationalism. Yet it was they who were unrealistic in not recognizing that they were aligning themselves with the most conservative "interests in the heart of the French-Canadian community." Separatism and neo-nationalism would close off that community, cut off the breath of true freedom. In a conclusion that became a later slogan, Trudeau declared ringingly: "Open up the borders, our people are suffocating to death."[30]

—

In the spring and summer of 1961 the atmosphere in Quebec and in Canada worried Trudeau, especially the attraction of separatism to the young. Even his most frequent female companion, Carroll Guérin, wrote to him: "What do you think of the separatist motion? Do you think it will eventually succeed. You probably will disagree, but I have a feeling that it might—so necessary is it for the French Canadians to find an identity and so strong is their conviction that this identity cannot exist interspersed with the English factor." Disagree they did, but on nuclear disarmament they shared the view that it was the greatest problem of all. The times might be exciting, but crisis loomed close by.

In Ottawa, John Diefenbaker's Conservatives were beginning to stumble badly, and they seemed particularly inept in facing the challenge of the new Quebec Liberal government. Diefenbaker's stunning electoral victory in 1958 (in which he won 208 seats, the

Liberals 48, and the CCF 8) had forced the other parties to serious reconsideration of their own position. The Liberals began a policy review in 1960 in which Maurice Lamontagne played a major part and Jean Marchand a minor one.

Trudeau, however, was not drawn to those discussions; his ties on the federal level were far closer to the Co-operative Commonwealth Federation, which had now decided to re-establish itself as the New Democratic Party. Trudeau's ties with English Canada politically were almost exclusively with CCF intellectuals, notably Frank Scott, Eugene Forsey, Michael Oliver, and, in the 1960s, the philosopher Charles Taylor. He developed further links after he met the historian Ramsay Cook at a friend's wedding, and Cook soon invited him to contribute to the CCF-leaning *Canadian Forum*. The purpose in creating the NDP was to connect the party more closely with organized labour, an objective Trudeau had supported in both the Quebec and the Canadian context throughout the fifties. Yet, when that merger occurred, he hesitated to make an open commitment to the new socialist party.[31]

Jean Marchand later claimed that he had dissuaded Trudeau from this tie in the fifties because there were more immediate problems, such as "to get rid of Duplessis." After Maurice Duplessis fell and the CCF transformed itself into the more urban NDP, Marchand said it became a problem of conscience for them. Normally, he and Trudeau, as labour champions on the left, would support the CCF-NDP, but, he explained: "It's useless to start building a party with your neigh-bour and say, 'Well, maybe someday in twenty or twenty-five years we'll have a good party representing exactly our ideolo-gies.' We thought that the NDP could not achieve power even if we had joined the party because a large portion of Quebec would have been opposed to us." He was pragmatic—and no doubt correct.[32]

Trudeau, like Marchand, also knew that Tommy Douglas, the pioneering socialist premier of Saskatchewan and the first NDP leader, was not likely to attract Quebec voters. Moreover, although he admired the intellect and ethics of his fellow voyageur Frank Scott, there were real differences in their approach to the Canadian Constitution and in their understanding of the role of Quebec within Canada. Trudeau was always most generous in acknowledging Scott's influence on him, but, after analyzing some of Scott's theories, he often reached his own, sometimes opposite conclusions. For his part, Scott, much as he respected Trudeau, did not like his acclaimed article "Some Obstacles to Democracy in Quebec."[33] Trudeau was too much a decentralist for Scott's very centralist taste, and his criticisms of the British tradition did not have the approval of the professor—a man of proud Anglo-Canadian heritage and bearing. In debates with Scott in which other francophones participated, Trudeau rejected nationalism in the same breath that he expressed doubts about the centralizing policies of Canada's socialists.

Despite these disagreements, Frank Scott and Michael Oliver had asked Trudeau to contribute an article to A Social Purpose for Canada, a book sponsored by the CCF.[34] Trudeau joined the editorial committee of the project in 1958, along with Frank Scott; Eugene Forsey, the research director for the Canadian Congress of Labour; George Grube, a University of Toronto professor; and David Lewis, an official with the CCF. Like the Asbestos project, the book dragged on; Trudeau was the laggard this time, with his essay on the practice and theory of federalism finally arriving in May 1960.

Michael Oliver, who was the editor for the volume, did not like the essay and commented harshly. He accused Trudeau of overstating his argument and of being imprecise, because he often "used" politics rather than political science.

The complaint has some merit, for Trudeau's writings are not those of the academic political scientist or university intellectual. He wrote for broader audiences and avoided the heavy apparatus of scholarship, a fact that his academic foes often criticized.[35] Moreover, Oliver claimed that Trudeau's argument in favour of decentralization was contradicted by his call for an activist state. He was especially puzzled by Trudeau's statement that he was an "outside observer" of the CCF. In fact Trudeau was,* even though he participated in campaigns and, occasionally, held party membership cards. He regarded the CCF, correctly, as the federal party that had consistently advanced civil liberties and argued for greater economic equality. Those views he shared. Yet the party was too English, and his approach to federalism was different, particularly after the NDP began to flirt with Quebec nationalism and the "two nations" approach to Canadian federalism in 1963.[36]

The NDP was one example of how, in 1961, Trudeau was generally wary of committing to any binding ties. His *Cité libre* articles betrayed his general discontents. He was now over forty years old—in a decade that the young tried to dominate. Most of his friends were married with children. His hair was thinning, and his worried mother told him to try the remedy of

---

* Trudeau, along with Frank Scott's son Peter, did not demonstrate the earnestness of many socialists in the fifties. Their efforts in one of Thérèse Casgrain's campaigns consisted of "driving recklessly around Montreal in Trudeau's open sports car with a bull horn. They regaled passers-by with CCF slogans in two languages, vying with each other in a public display of witty bilingualism, with Scott concocting the French sentences and Trudeau embellishing the English." Stephen Clarkson and Christina McCall, *Trudeau and Our Times.* vol. 1: *The Magnificent Obsession* (Toronto: McClelland & Stewart, 1990), 88.

standing on his head.[37] His plans for the political role he had so long desired seemed to have misfired, while others among his friends, such as René Lévesque and Paul Gérin-Lajoie, were dominating headlines as political actors and changing their society. He often felt disenchanted and at loose ends.

In the winter of 1961 he busied himself with publication of the book on the China trip. He dithered over the invitation list to the March launch and personally wrote out the addresses of more than two hundred people he and Hébert invited. This invitation list provides insight into his connections and friendships at the time.[38] The invitees were overwhelmingly francophone, with a few anglophones such as Michael Oliver of McGill University and the writer Scott Symons. Frank Scott, interestingly, was missing. René Lévesque was the major politician invited, but apparently he did not come. Thérèse Gouin Décarie and Vianney Décarie did. The old *Cité libre* crowd, including Réginald Boisvert, Maurice Blain, and Guy Cormier, were on the list, and most of them attended. There were new names associated with television and the cultural community. And there were also many single women.

Carroll Guérin, the hopeful artist and occasional model who was now Trudeau's most frequent companion, was there for the celebration. Her candour and liberal lifestyle had immediately attracted Trudeau when he met her in the late 1950s. He was encouraging her to go to Europe to study, promising to join her there in the summer. (When she went to England and applied to the London School of Economics, however, she was turned down — much to Trudeau's chagrin.) At the book launch, Trudeau also spent time with another invitee, Madeleine Gobeil, who had matured into a brilliant young woman in the four years since Trudeau first encountered her as a teenage student at a meeting of the Rassemblement in Ottawa. Ambitious, forthright, and visibly young, her beauty, sometimes blonde, at other moments darker, impressed Trudeau's friends whether they saw her on a beach or at the symphony.[39] Their friendship developed into a romantic relationship that endured for well over a decade.*

As the sexual revolution began in the early sixties, women were becoming a preoccupation for Trudeau, but now he shunned the intense relationships of earlier years in favour of multiple involvements. He preferred, in the jargon of the age, "to play the field" or, in Jean-Paul Sartre's description of his own involvement with women, "the theatre of seduction." His female friends complained that he still held back much of himself. One of them said his "interior" was closed, but, to

---

* Madeleine Gobeil, who would become Trudeau's most frequent companion until his marriage to Margaret Sinclair in 1971, took part in a *Maclean's* roundtable chaired by Gérard Pelletier in the spring of 1963. The young journalist Peter Gzowski described her on that occasion as fitting "neither the cliché about the shy, family-dominated young *canadienne* who wants only to be married and have a dozen children or the one about the gay, champagne-drinking flirt. She is serious, clever, frank and, above all, emancipated. She is, for example, unafraid to say publicly that she no longer believes in her church." She was, however, the most unambiguously "Canadian" in her comments, saying: "Maybe it's because I come from Ottawa, but I feel I'm more Canadian." However, when asked how they "felt" about English Canadians, she agreed with another participant: "I find [English Canadians] boring too. They have nothing interesting to present. They aren't really very good conversationalists." Peter Gzowski, "What Young French Canadians Have on Their Minds," *Maclean's*, April 6, 1963, 21–23, 39–40. Madeleine claims that she and Pierre rarely discussed religion. He insisted that his faith was a private matter. Interview with Madeleine Gobeil, May 2006.

Carroll, the shyness that was in itself so attractive made him "emotionally withdrawn."*

Trudeau still officially lived with his mother in the Outremont family home, though he kept his "pad" on Sherbrooke Street. Grace was becoming forgetful and, when he was away, their letters were fewer than they once had been. Her decline had begun, and it saddened Pierre even more than the state of politics in Quebec. They celebrated Christmas and other festive times together with Tip, Suzette, and their families, and, as always, Trudeau entranced the children with his shy charm and endless athletic tricks—jackknife dives, headstands, and dramatic leaps. Suzette still lived close to her mother and was devoted to the family.

The summer of 1961 brought huge changes in their careers for Trudeau and his friends. A surprised Gérard Pelletier eagerly accepted an offer to become the editor of *La Presse*, and Jean Marchand agreed to become the head of his union, the Confédération des syndicats nationaux (CSN). The outsiders were moving inside. While Trudeau had been in China, the rector of the Université de Montréal had called Grace, "terribly anxious" to speak with him about a teaching position there. Ironically, although he had long complained about his enforced exile from the Université de Montréal by the Catholic Church and now had the opportunity he craved, he did not

---

* Carroll herself was not shy, and her lively exchanges with Pierre capture his charm for women as well as his weaknesses. After she called him in Montreal, she wrote to him on June 18, 1962: "How thrilled I was to speak to you a couple of hours ago! I am still under the effect, and practically phoned you back to tell you how glad I was but thought that you probably would not appreciate it if I reversed the charges again."[40]

really welcome it. The times had changed. The classroom, which had earlier beckoned, no longer seemed an attractive haven. Initially he turned down an appointment to the Institute on Public Law there, but then half-heartedly accepted an associate professorship at the law school itself (with a cross-appointment to the Institute)—an institution he had scorned as a student and as a lawyer. Once the arrangements were in place, he promptly left for Europe.

Trudeau ran with the bulls in Pamplona—a mad and daring act—met Carroll Guérin in Rome, and went to the jazz festival at Juan-les-Pins on the Riviera, where he and Carroll heard the young star Ray Charles and the jazz legend Count Basie.* They stayed in a small hotel somewhere on the Mediterranean. The days were unforgettable; the parting difficult. "When you said goodbye to me this morning," she wrote later that day, "do forgive me for asking you to go, but as you know, I felt so very sad at the thought we were going to be separated again that I did my best to avoid a scene on the street—without too much success. Funnily enough, the little maid who opened the door was in tears herself, so we happily skipped the ladida." After giving Carroll some funds for her return to student life on a part-time basis in London, Trudeau travelled eastwards alone and visited

---

* In 1968 the celebrated Canadian artists Michael Snow and Joyce Wieland organized a "Canadians in New York for Trudeau" meeting in that city, where they were living. They had a jazz trio with the drummer Milford Graves. Snow introduced Graves to Trudeau as "the greatest drummer in jazz today." Trudeau shook Graves's hand, saying, "Oh! Well, what about Max Roach." Graves was not insulted but astonished at Trudeau's knowledge of jazz. Michael Snow in Nancy Southam, ed., *Pierre* (Toronto: McClelland & Stewart, 2005), 125.

the massive palace in Split, Yugoslavia, where Diocletian went to escape the declining, decadent Rome. Like Diocletian, he grumbled to others about the state of his homeland and even mused about staying in Europe.[41]

Back at home, Grace Trudeau worried about her son. On September 5, 1961, she wrote: "By now your peregrinations are finished, or coming to an end—it was labor day yesterday—schools reopening—so the professors are expected to take their duties." On September 25 she wrote again, pleading for him to come home: "Four months is a long stretch! Your Mercedes is raring to go."[42]

Obviously, Trudeau had prepared little for his classes, with the inevitable result that he had to work very hard when they began. George Radwanski later described Trudeau's work habits in his pre-political years: "He laboured intensely at whatever he happened to be doing and he did quite a variety of things, but—with the exception of *Cité libre*—he always gave the impression of doing it with one foot in and one foot out, poised to move on to something else."[43] Certainly Trudeau was not ready to settle in the classroom. A few years later he said that when he arrived at the university, he "found a rather sterile atmosphere; the terminology of the Left was now serving to conceal a single preoccupation: the separatist counter-revolution."[44]

Through the winter of 1961–62 he began to seethe as the Lesage government became more neo-nationalist and the young called the founders of *Cité libre* dinosaurs. *Cité libre* itself was not immune, as both the younger and older members of its expanded board challenged its traditional aversion to nationalism, its criticism of socialism, and its virulent opposition to separatism. In April Trudeau complained to a friend that he was often working till midnight at the university and was mostly unhappy. He wanted to be in a warm country in the sun with the sea nearby: "Truly," he said, "everything is detestable in Quebec."[45]

That spring Peter Gzowski came to Montreal to experience

the new excitement and discovered the remarkable "engaged intellectual" Pierre Trudeau. (The photograph on this book's cover was included with the article.) In a profile of Trudeau that he published in the French- and English-language *Maclean's*, he described him as an "angry young man" who directed his eloquent scorn at the separatists' "dead causes." Trudeau gave credit to the reforms of the Lesage government, he said, but declared how much better it would be if they had more government members like René Lévesque with energy and talent. And, Gzowski continued: "He was caught tossing snowballs at Stalin's statue—*before* stoning Stalin was fashionable." Here Trudeau becomes a turtle-necked, intellectual celebrity: a millionaire professor with an exquisite sense of fashion, a classic Mercedes sports car, an apartment on elegant Sherbrooke, and a pied-à-terre at his mother's "large house" in Outremont. Trudeau was also an excellent athlete, orator, and "a connoisseur of fine wines and women. He created a sensation," Gzowski continued, "when he decided to swim in the pool when it snowed at one of the meetings of the Institut des affaires publiques at Ste-Adèle." The articles attracted considerable public attention to Trudeau in Quebec and in English Canada. He later claimed that he was offered an English CBC television position at this time, perhaps as a result of the article.[46]

—

That same month, Trudeau published another article in *Cité libre*, "The New Treason of the Intellectuals"—probably the most influential essay he wrote in the 1960s. His target was direct: Quebec separatism and nationalism and their prophets, "the clerks"—the Quebec intellectuals. He took his title from a 1927 polemic by Julien Benda, who had fought the trend towards conservatism and nationalism in the 1920s in France, as Benda opposed Maurras and other authoritarians Trudeau had once admired. His anger spilled over as he made five fundamental arguments that became central to his stance in political debates in the 1960s.

First, he wrote, "it is not the concept of *nation* that is retrograde; it is the idea that the nation must necessarily be sovereign." Second, he responded to the best-selling 1961 book *Pourquoi je suis séparatiste* by Marcel Chaput, a federal government employee, which resulted in Chaput's dismissal and a political fury among Quebec nationalists. Chaput, Trudeau argued, was dead wrong in suggesting that the experience of decolonization in Africa and Asia had relevance for Quebec. Chaput himself had admitted that "French Canada enjoys rights these people never did." Many of these newly independent states were poly-ethnic, as was Canada. They were not homogeneous nations but multi-ethnic countries where minorities dreamed of the rights French-speaking Canadians had long possessed. Woodrow Wilson's "Principle of Nationality," just like the decolonization movement itself, had never been intended to create a wave of nationalist secessions.

Third, Trudeau continued, for most of history there had been no nations; however, since the rise of the nation-states in the previous two hundred years, the world had witnessed "the most devastating wars, the worst atrocities, and the most degrading collective hatred." There would be no end to wars "until in some fashion the nation ceases to be the basis of the state." Fourth, history taught that "to insist that a particular nationality must have complete sovereign power is to pursue a self-destructive end . . . every national minority will find, at the very moment of liberation, a new minority within its bosom which in turn must be allowed the right to demand its freedom." Fifth, Anglo-Canadians "have been strong by virtue of our weakness," not only in Ottawa but also in Quebec City. In both places, the politicians had been marked by political cynicism and the political system by "the pestilence of corruption." Had English-speaking Canadians "applied themselves to learning French with a quarter the diligence they have shown in refusing to do so, Canada would have been effectively bilingual long ago."

Too much energy had therefore been wasted on worthless quarrels. The "treason of the intellectuals" arose from their propensity to fight such quarrels and to waste hours of each day discussing separatism. These discussions amounted to no more than an aimless flapping of the arms in the wind. Nationalism in Quebec was reactionary. In a battle, the right-wing nationalists, from the village notary through the small businessman to the members of the Ordre de Jacques Cartier, would always triumph over the new left-wing nationalists, who dreamed of nationalizing and using the state to secure benefits for the emerging French-Canadian bourgeoisie. The existing Canadian Constitution already gave full scope to Chaput, or the young separatists, to carry out the reforms they wanted and to have the "inspiration" they craved. To a young poet who had said that a new state of Quebec would make him "capable of doing great things," Trudeau replied: "If he fails to find within himself, in the world about him and in the stars above, the dignity, pride and other well-springs of poetry, I wonder why and how he will find them in a 'free' Quebec."

The "nation" guards a heritage, he continued; it does so principally through a Constitution and a federal system that protect a pluralistic and "poly-ethnic society." Those matters with "ethnic" relevance—education, language, property, and civil rights—were already within the power of the province of Quebec under the existing Constitution. So, he concluded, "French Canadians have all the powers they need to make Quebec a political society affording due respect for nationalist aspirations and at the same time giving unprecedented scope for human potential in the broadest sense."[47]

These arguments remained at the core of Trudeau's response to Quebec separatism and neo-nationalism for the next three decades. Some items changed: he moved away, for example, from his status quo approach to the Constitution. But most fundamentals—bilingualism, a reverence for the role of law, more franco-phone presence in Ottawa, a suspicion of nationalism attached to economic policies, and a stronger state at provincial and federal levels—endured in his speeches, his writings, and his actions. In the spring of 1962 he reiterated them publicly in a debate among André Laurendeau, René Lévesque, Frank Scott, and Jean-Jacques Bertrand, the Union nationale politician and future premier. When Bertrand asked whether Trudeau opposed a project to open up the Constitution and create a "special status" for Quebec, Trudeau answered quickly and unambiguously, "Yes." He believed that the Constitution should be patriated, but he opposed any special status for Quebec that would diminish the other provinces and ultimately lead to the break-up of the federation. In his interview with Peter Gzowski he was scathing: "A nation or people has only so much intellectual energy to spend on a revolution. If the intellectual energy of French Canada is spent on such a futile and foolish cause as separatism, the revolution that is just beginning here can never be brought about."[48]

Trudeau's argument that nationalism reflects bourgeois aspirations at the expense of broader working-class economic interests developed partly from conversations with two young brothers, the sociologist Raymond Breton and the economist Albert Breton—ideas they went on to present in *Cité libre* and elsewhere. Trudeau became particularly attracted to their claim that the new Quebec must focus not on nationalist diversions but on "real" solutions to economic problems—reforms that would improve the lot of all, and not the bourgeois elite alone.

—

Trudeau's anger was real, and his ideas had become more focused. That focus intensified in the course of regular debates that began in the fall of 1961 when René Lévesque, now minister of natural resources in the Lesage government, asked André Laurendeau to organize a group to meet with him every second Friday over the winter (which in Montreal stretches from October into May). Laurendeau in turn invited Jean Marchand, Gérard Pelletier, and Trudeau. Pelletier's Westmount home was the usual meeting place; there, dinner was casual and incidental to the conversation. Trudeau and Marchand usually departed first and left the voluble Lévesque and Laurendeau arguing long into the smoke-filled night. The meetings began with René Lévesque describing events that had occurred during the previous two weeks in Quebec City. Trudeau would await his moment, then pounce on the errors in the stream of consciousness that flowed from Lévesque.

Nevertheless, Trudeau and Lévesque shared many views on the need for Quebec's modernization and, by the mid-winter of 1962, Trudeau had come to respect what Lévesque was doing as a member of the government. However, this amity shattered quickly when Lévesque pressed forward with his campaign to nationalize the hydroelectricity companies, which had long been the symbol of English-Canadian economic dominance in Quebec.[49]

The issue was old; its political impact, new. Neighbouring Ontario had state-owned hydroelectricity, but the rich water resources of Quebec were still largely in private hands. The case to nationalize private electricity production and distribution outside Montreal was clear: rates would be made more uniform throughout the province and the ever-growing needs of industry and consumers would be met. The enormous cost to meet these demands would be shifted to the government, to the society as a whole. Nationalization had both political and economic significance. Even though it had been mentioned briefly in the elaborate Liberal platform of 1960, it had remained dormant. Lévesque became impatient with the constant divisions within the Cabinet over the issue and, in February 1962, went out on his own and launched "Electricity Week"—a public campaign in favour of nationalization. Laurendeau enthusiastically supported it; Lesage, however, was wary and at one point stopped speaking to Lévesque because he had breached Cabinet solidarity. Lévesque became "René the red," a role he played brilliantly during the summer as he struck out against the economic elite. His antagonists inevitably became the Anglo-Canadian business barons, and his arguments ever more nationalist.

In exasperation, Lesage finally organized a Liberal retreat at a chalet at Lac à l'Épaule. He asked George Marler, a minister without portfolio who, in Lévesque's words, spoke "French as well if not better than us . . . [and] represented with exquisite courtesy the most upper-crust of the dominant minority," to put forward the case against nationalization. In striking emotional and physical contrast, the excitable and passionate Lévesque presented the opposite view, with cigarette and hand gestures animating his talk. When they finished, "all eyes were on the premier, only the twiddling of his pencil belying his air of quiet composure." To the astonishment of all, Lesage decided to call an election to settle the issue. The election slogan quickly and historically became "maîtres chez nous"—masters in our own house.[50]

Trudeau immediately dissented on the policy and, especially, the nationalist slogan. At their Friday night meetings, he strongly attacked Lévesque's plans. Both have left an account of their confrontation. Lévesque reconstructed the exchange in his memoirs:

"You say it's going to cost something like $600 million," Trudeau would argue, inviting others to register the enormity of the thing. "$600 million, and what for? To take over a business that already exists. It's just nationalist suspender-snapping. When you think of all the real economic and social progress you could buy with a sum like that!"

"Yes," I'd reply, "but a sum like that doesn't just drop out of the sky for any old project. In the case of electricity, the present assets and the perpetual productivity stand as security. Try to find an equivalent to that."[51]

Lévesque further argued that the control of "such a vast sector of activity" would be "a training ground for the builders and administrators we so urgently needed."

Trudeau's memories are similar. He recalled one night when Lévesque launched into his dream of nationalizing Shawinigan Power just as Premier Godbout had nationalized Montreal Light, Heat and Power during the war years. "I asked," Trudeau recalled, whether it would not be better to spend the money on education: "He said that it would allow us to create managers and to double employment. But I told him I saw the priorities differently, and the argument began about the use of the term nationalization and I said, at least if you can do it, you ought to speak of socialization, not nationalization." Trudeau, unlike Marler and the capitalists, did not object to state ownership of hydroelectricity. Indeed, an article he published that June in the *McGill Law Journal* on "economic rights" went far beyond any of Lévesque's "socialist" appeals in his campaign that summer to have state ownership in the hydro-electricity sector. Trudeau's problem was the nationalist rhetoric surrounding the hydro debate. "What he was afraid of," Lévesque later wrote, "was the mobilizing potential of the word and its power of acceleration, a force one felt might be able to go very far in a society that took a stormy turn." Lévesque had a point.[52]

But Trudeau did too. Trudeau also believed that the highly emotional arguments of the Lesage government were increasingly diminishing both the social scientific and rational analysis of what was best for all citizens in Quebec. Maurice Lamontagne, probably the best-known Quebec economist of the time, shared Trudeau's views: education was a far better investment than the bricks and mortar of a power plant. Albert and Raymond Breton were also opponents who did not accept Lévesque's arguments about the creation of a "cadre" of franco-phone professionals. In their view, the poor, the workers, the shopkeepers, and the widows who also spoke French would pay the price for the creation of that cadre—and so would their children. Nor, in Trudeau's view, was the Lesage government's "politics of grandeur," with its "red carpets in Paris" and pretentious titles and trips, more than a diversion from its proper tasks in improving Quebec's education and infrastructure. Trudeau looked on anxiously as Lesage welcomed the French culture minister, André Malraux, to Quebec like a princely emissary and, in return, accepted invitations to the French president's palace, where de Gaulle treated him as a honoured and cherished head of state. Trudeau knew Lord Acton's maxim well, and he saw again how power could corrupt.[53]

When Trudeau was asked whether these arguments with René Lévesque broke up the Friday night meetings, he replied, "No, because I was the only one who made them." Gérard Pelletier and Jean Marchand apparently were largely silent. André Laurendeau, the neo-nationalist who had called for similar nationalization two decades earlier, supported Lévesque. The meetings came to an end after two years in November 1963, but, as Pelletier later wrote, it was not because of any particular contention at the time. The differences were fundamental, and they had been present at the creation of the meetings in the fall of 1961. But as Lévesque's nationalist fervour grew, the gap became too great to bridge.[54]

In discussing their different points of view, Lévesque's biographer has argued that Trudeau's heart was on the left but his stock portfolio made him fall on the right.* Others, including Frank Scott, Stephen Clarkson, and Christina McCall, believe that Trudeau moved towards free-market liberalism in the 1960s in reaction to nationalism, pointing to the fact that Albert Breton's "public goods" arguments are associated with the free-market neo-classical Chicago school economists. However, Trudeau's public and private writings at the time as well as Breton's contemporary association with the federal NDP undermine such claims. Trudeau's article in the *McGill Law Journal* was a vigorous attack on the liberal concepts of property, and drew on the economist John Kenneth Galbraith and even the Marxist C.B. Macpherson, not on Milton Friedman and Gary Becker of the University of Chicago. Moreover, based on Trudeau's own comments, Gzowski called him a "millionaire

---

* Pierre Godin raised the charge in support of his belief that Trudeau's "portfolio" affected his actions. He pointed out that Trudeau was, frankly, a cheapskate when it came to paying entertainment bills or tipping. Evidence suggests the charge has some validity. Margot Kidder, who dated Trudeau in the 1980s, recalled how she pretended she was going to the washroom after the dinner ended so she could return to the table and leave some additional cash for the waiters—to whom Trudeau had given just a couple of dollars. The bartender at the upscale Troika Restaurant in Montreal in the 1960s remembered an evening when Trudeau came in alone. An apparent friend joined him at the bar. When they appeared ready to leave, the bartender gave the bill to Trudeau, assuming that he was the host. He paid, and both customers left. However, Trudeau quickly returned and rebuked the bartender: "Never again give me a bill unless I ask for it." Yet there are also abundant examples of Trudeau generosity, from his treatment of "poor boy"

socialist." In November 1962 in *Cité libre*, Trudeau described himself as a "man of the left," but one who deplored the lack of realism of the NDP. In the upcoming crucial election, he said, the provincial party was not uniting behind the Liberals and was even considering a candidate to oppose René Lévesque, the voice of the left in the provincial government.

Despite his own opposition to the nationalization of electricity, Trudeau could not understand how any democrat could consider voting against the Liberals, given the unthinkable reactionary alternative. Indeed, he was more supportive of the Liberals in 1962 than he had been in 1960. His major regret after the election was that Lesage would have no "man of the left" to reinforce René Lévesque. He ended with the hope that, after the election, a new Liberal government would express, with more "realism," a genuine politics of the left in Quebec.[55]

—

Gaby Filion in the early forties at school, through François Hertel and Pierre Vadeboncoeur in the fifties, to the impecunious student Carroll Guérin in the sixties. This mixed behaviour does not seem unusual. In a television docudrama aired later, Pelletier asked Trudeau why he was so parsimonious. Trudeau replied that, even when he was a schoolboy at Brébeuf, kids wanted him to pay because they knew he was rich. Trudeau's defensive analysis was almost certainly correct. The biographies of millionaires are replete with similar stories, such as the payphones for guests in Jean Paul Getty's castle. Thérèse Gouin Décarie describes Trudeau's attitude towards money as "confusing," while Madeleine Gobeil says he was an intellectual who was troubled by his millionaire status. Pierre Godin, *René Lévesque: Héros malgré lui* (Montreal: Les Éditions du Boréal, 1994), 118 ; interviews with Margot Kidder and Jacques Eindiguer; and "Trudeau, the Movie," CBC Television, Oct. 2005.

On November 14, 1962, René Lévesque won his gamble, and Jean Lesage his election. These were fateful, terrifying months. In October the world probably came closest to its destruction when John Kennedy and Nikita Khrushchev went "eyeball to eyeball" over the presence of Soviet missiles in Cuba. When Khrushchev "blinked" and backed down, the Canadian federal government began to come undone. Not a minute too soon, thought Trudeau, Marchand, and Pelletier. Marchand had considered joining the Lesage team for the 1962 election, but, unlike in 1960, Lesage did not extend an invitation this time. One reason may have been an angry televised debate between Marchand and Réal Caouette, the Quebec Social Credit / Créditiste leader, who, in the June 1962 federal election, had won an astonishing twenty-six seats in Quebec and reduced John Diefenbaker's Conservative government to minority status. Jacques Flynn, the Quebec Conservative organizer, correctly analyzed the Social Credit success: "No one had foreseen it . . . it was a protest, period—a vote against."[56] Caouette's success was the strongest pillar in Trudeau's argument that every democrat must vote Liberal in the Quebec election: Caouette represented the broader forces of reaction that threatened to undo the Quiet Revolution that had begun in 1960.*

---

* Indeed, Trudeau's fears were justified. The Gallup polls showed strong Social Credit support in Quebec. Union nationale politician Daniel Johnson wrote to Diefenbaker at the height of the 1963 election on March 8, 1963, predicting that if an election were held that day, the Social Credit party would win "50–55 seats." The letter suggested the continuing support of some Union nationale politicians for Diefenbaker, on the one hand, and Caouette, on the other. Johnson to Diefenbaker, March 8, 1963, Diefenbaker Papers, XII/115/F/281, Diefenbaker Library, University of Saskatchewan.

In the fall of 1962, Jean Marchand, perhaps wounded by Lesage's failure to enlist him for the November election, began to talk quietly with Trudeau and Pelletier about running for the Liberals in the next federal election. It would not be long in coming. John Diefenbaker had quarrelled with Douglas Harkness, his defence minister, who had upbraided him for his hesitation as prime minister to support President Kennedy during the Cuban Missile Crisis. Harkness then set off a Cabinet revolt that, at a meeting around the dining-room table at 24 Sussex Drive, nearly forced Diefenbaker from office. Instead, the government fell, an election followed, and Lester Pearson became prime minister—though in a Liberal minority government.[57]

Lester Pearson's government took office on April 22, 1963, but Jean Marchand, Gérard Pelletier, and Pierre Trudeau were not part of it. In the election, Trudeau had firmly supported the federal NDP because of Pearson's January statement that Canada should respect its previous commitments and accept nuclear warheads from the United States. This stand probably won seats for the Liberals in Ontario and accelerated the demise of Diefenbaker, but it hurt the Liberal cause in Quebec. In Ontario, the historically Tory *Globe and Mail* and Toronto *Telegram* swung behind the Liberals. In Quebec, however, *Le Devoir* and *La Presse* (which Pelletier edited) both supported the NDP opposition to nuclear weapons.

The most vitriolic attacks, however, came in *Cité libre*, where Jean Pellerin, Pierre Vadeboncoeur, and Trudeau condemned Pearson's stand "as part of a nefarious scheme to sell Canada down the river in return for American campaign funds." Trudeau's attack has become legendary, and its virulence has not been exaggerated. Contrary to popular lore, however, he was not the first to describe Pearson as "the defrocked prince of peace." That derisory gem mocking Pearson's Nobel Prize for Peace had been coined by his friend Vadeboncoeur, but Trudeau

used it to begin his own essay. "Pope Pearson," he wrote, had
decided one morning when eating his breakfast to embrace a
pro-nuclear policy and thereby defrocked his own party:

> It mattered little that such a policy had been renounced
> by the party congress and excluded from its program; it
> mattered little that the leader acted without consulting
> with the national council of the Liberal federation, or its
> executive committee; it mattered little that the Leader for-
> got to speak to the parliamentary caucus about it, or even
> to his main advisors. The Pope had spoken; it only
> remained for the believers to believe.

The nuclear policy itself was contemptible; the "anti-democratic"
character of the Pearson decision, intolerable.[58]

Trudeau came close to a conspiracy thesis in interpreting
the Pearson action and the fall of the Diefenbaker government.
The "hipsters of Mr. Kennedy" had decided that "Diefenbaker
must go." You think I dramatize? Trudeau asked.

> But then how do you think politics are done? Do you think
> it's as a mere tourist that General Norstad, the erstwhile
> supreme commander of the allied forces in Europe, came
> to Ottawa on January 3 to publicly summon the Canadian
> government to respect its commitments? Do you think it's
> by chance that Mr. Pearson, in his speech on January 12,
> was able to rely on General Norstad's authority? Do you
> believe it was by mistake that the State Department passed
> on to the newspapers, on January 30, a communiqué rein-
> forcing Mr. Pearson's position, in which Mr. Diefenbaker
> was bluntly treated as a liar? Do you think it's by chance
> that this communiqué provided the leader of the opposition
> with arguments he liberally peppered throughout his

speech in Parliament on January 31? Do you believe it was
by coincidence that this series of events ended in the fall of
the government, on February 5? Well then, why do you
think the United States would proceed any differently with
Canada than with Guatemala, when reasons of state
required it, and circumstances lent themselves to it?

Although Diefenbaker largely supported this interpretation, neither
Basil Robinson, his foreign policy assistant at the time, nor Denis
Smith, his definitive biographer, agrees. As so often, coincidence
and error explain most of what happened. But not all.[59]

The Kennedy administration made its detestation of
Diefenbaker known publicly. The contempt for the prime minister's hesitation to endorse Kennedy's ultimatum to the Soviets—
a response that was, in Smith's words, "honestly ambiguous in the
Canadian tradition"—pervades the reports sent from Ottawa by
the American ambassador, W.W. Butterworth. When Trudeau
wrote his attack on Pearson, he was troubled about the American
influence on Canada. Vadeboncoeur was horrified: he identified
"Americanization" with the deadening impact of modern technology on the human spirit. In the April 1963 issue of Cité libre,
he and Trudeau joined in a virulent attack on the Liberals and,
in particular, on Lester Pearson. Trudeau had long considered
the prime minister a too willing supporter of American international arrogance.

—

On the nuclear issue, Trudeau's views were shared by Pierre
Vadeboncoeur, André Laurendeau, Claude Ryan, René Lévesque,
Michel Chartrand, and virtually all his allies and friends of the
forties and early fifties. But nationalism and separatism were
another matter. In the early sixties, different attitudes on the

"national" question were fraying and ending many old friendships. Trudeau's correspondence and writings of the period reveal
an erosion of the shared confidences and principles that had
long marked good friendships. Sometimes, however, separatist
sentiments did not break off relationships. When Carroll Guérin,
for example, told Trudeau she thought the "French people" (she
was "half French") had an innate need to separate, her views did
not affect their summer weeks of cherished intimacy. With men,
however, it was different, and Trudeau remained troubled about
the number of break-ups that occurred.

On Remembrance Day 1992, Trudeau met with Camille
Laurin, an old friend and an Outremont neighbour with whom
he had shared long walks in the fifties. Laurin, a psychiatrist, had
been the "father" in the 1970s of the Quebec language legislation
that made Quebec officially unilingual and deeply offended
Quebec federalists. Now, as they sat together again, Laurin
recalled that he and Trudeau had once shared "the same goals of
modernization and declericalization" and had fought a common
"battle for liberty against dictatorship, cynicism, and political
immorality." As late as November 1961, Laurin had described
separatism in *Le Devoir* as an illness. Using Freudian terms, he
claimed that French Canadians saw the English as fathers and,
thus, separatism was a form of revenge. Trudeau now asked
Laurin what had made him change his mind. Lesage's "revolution," he answered. It had made him realize that federalism would
not give Quebec the necessary tools to modernize. Trudeau
replied that a strong team in Ottawa would open Quebec to the
world while assuring modernization at home. Laurin demurred
and pointed to the fate of the francophones in other provinces.[60] It
was an old debate, but one that was largely stilled among the
young professionals and intellectuals in the fifties by the common
political cause they pursued. In the sixties, their common goals
dissolved in political difference.

Pierre Vadeboncoeur and François Hertel had been closer friends to Trudeau than either Pelletier or Marchand. Their increasing disagreements on the "national" issue, however, shattered the ties of friendship as Vadeboncoeur began to embrace nationalism, then separatism, and an ever more militant socialism. Vadeboncoeur placed the break in 1963–64, as the slogans of Quebec separatism burst out of university classrooms and bars, where students and fringe politicians met, and exploded into the mainstream of public debate. He recalled the moment when he decided that Trudeau and Pelletier were blind to the forces animating the young and the future. They were, he wrote, not "brutes" but simply blind: "Mr. Pelletier responded to me when I spoke of the existence of a current leading to independence: 'But what current?'"[61]

Vadeboncoeur believed that he and Trudeau took different paths mainly because Trudeau's approach to political understanding drew so much on the law. In the 1940s, at law school, they had both regarded the law as a conservative force. They despised the law even as they dreamed of revolution, staged political theatre, and searched the streets at night for poetry and romance. Trudeau, he said, failed to understand the new world after 1960, one that was infected with "a massive contagion of political ideas, notably among the poets, the artists, and the best intellectuals of the country," a contagion so powerful that the general population caught its exceptional strain. As they drifted apart, Vadeboncoeur was initially sad, wistful, and respectful of his friend's integrity.

In 1970, as criticism of Trudeau's intellectual honesty abounded, Vadeboncoeur came to his defence, stating that he "did not have the least hesitation in affirming that Trudeau had not betrayed his beliefs . . . but, to the contrary, he had remained scrupulously faithful to his beliefs." Inevitably some bitterness came later, when he began to write bluntly about Trudeau, the destroyer of so many dreams. Trudeau himself was mostly silent, but he placed exclamation marks beside a 1963 press clipping that described Vadeboncoeur as by far the most radical member of a panel on separatism and socialism. As they parted ways, Vadeboncoeur paid back the money his closest friend had lent him over the years. Two middle-aged men were left with their memories of a shared childhood on the streets and alleys of Outremont, of the terrifying first days at Brébeuf, of the hilarious moment when Vadeboncoeur threw his law notes into the air and declared he was free, and of the secrets they shared when Trudeau came back from Europe in 1949. Thirty years after they separated, Trudeau paid a final personal tribute to his old friend, by then a major literary figure. He wrote in his memoirs that it was Vadeboncoeur who had taught him to write good French.[62] It was a lasting gift that estrangement could never efface.

If Vadeboncoeur had been one of Trudeau's closest male friend of adolescence and youth, François Hertel was his principal mentor in those days. Later, they had met frequently in Paris, where Hertel edited a journal on the writings of the French diaspora to which even Grace Trudeau subscribed. The rise of separatism after 1960 stirred Hertel's old sympathies and aroused new hopes. In the winter of 1963 he wrote an essay, "Du séparatisme Québécois," in which he recalled for readers his statement in 1936 that "one day, separation will come." Now, finally, Quebec was preparing to leave Canada and was creating "a solid bloc" in which its intellectual, artistic, and social life would flourish "in a rediscovered security and serenity." There was no serenity as Trudeau marked the essay with nine exclamation marks, one question mark, numerous underlined passages, and one illegible comment that reacted to Hertel's statement that even a Swiss-style decentralization, which he had held out as a last option thirty years before, was no longer possible.

The essay displeased Trudeau immensely, but he was outraged when students at the Université de Montréal published an article by Hertel in *Le Quartier Latin* in April 1964. André Laurendeau, a nationalist but also an eloquent opponent of separatism, had agreed to co-chair the Royal Commission on Bilingualism and Biculturalism that Pearson established soon after he took office. Laurendeau's new role was too much for Hertel. He wrote: "If you want to assassinate someone, assassinate a traitor, someone who is celebrated among us—that would be the perfect blow. For example, deliver from existence poor, bored Laurendeau, a prematurely old man who is also obscene." In *Cité libre* in May 1964, Trudeau lashed out against Hertel. He accused him, in a biting comment, of being a Torquemada about to begin an inquisition. He profoundly regretted that Hertel, whom he had long respected for his refusal to conform, had chosen to enter "into the separatist chapel." In a Quebec where terrorists were becoming heroes and the collectivity was once again being idolized, Hertel's words were thoroughly "irresponsible," as was *Le Quartier Latin* for publishing them.[63]

Hertel protested to Trudeau and others—ingenuously, given the tensions of the times—that he was being metaphorical and that he actually detested violence. Yet a chill had entered his relationship with Trudeau and, eventually, it froze nearly all contact. Like Pierre Vadeboncoeur, Hertel later came to Trudeau's defence when others questioned his sincerity. While dismissing Pelletier derisively as a "boy scout," Hertel echoed Vadeboncoeur in suggesting that Trudeau's failure to share their beliefs derived from his excessive focus on the law: "In the case of Trudeau, whom I know well, it's another matter. He's a jurist, one who, in my view, has become imprisoned in a formula that he would do well to enlarge. A little British by birth too."

The last comment no doubt further infuriated Trudeau. In fact, while favouring independence, Hertel did later became concerned about some of its violent physical and verbal expressions, and he loathed the "Communism" of some of its most vociferous supporters. As they drifted apart, he and Trudeau still apparently exchanged casual notes. When Hertel returned to Canada in the eighties, he was wistful about the past and suspicious of the direction the young had taken in the 1960s in literature and in life. He died in 1985 and, to the surprise of all, had a religious funeral, which Camille Laurin and Pierre Trudeau attended together.[64]

Hertel and Vadeboncoeur were correct in their sense that Trudeau's interests were no longer strongly literary, as they had been in his early forties.[*] The strong literary preoccupation of his youth had waned. As a professor at the Université de Montréal he had joined the Groupes des Recherches Sociales, and his own writings reflected his increasing interest in social science and law, especially the intersections between the two. In June 1963 he wrote to an Ontario friend in reply to a letter sent a year earlier. The delay, he said, resulted from the strain he had been under. He declined the friend's request to "tour" Canada to explain the "French-Canadian point of view" because he was leaving for Europe and North Africa: "The past year has been a mad one: lectures & research at the University, my office, *Cité libre*, civil

---

[*] Trudeau and Vadeboncoeur continued to share their enthusiasm for labour matters. Although Trudeau, unlike Vadeboncoeur, was not a full-time labour organizer in the 1960s, he spent untold hours drafting a brief that incorporated labour's views for the constitutional committee established by the Quebec National Assembly in May 1963. The brief reflected Trudeau's hesitation about "opening up" the Constitution as well as his support for instituting a bill of rights. This work prepared him exceedingly well for the debates about the Constitution in the following decade. For his overall opinions on these issues, see his essays "We Need a Bill of Rights" and "Quebec and the Constitutional Problem" in Gérard Pelletier, ed., *Against the Current: Selected Writings, 1939–1996* (Toronto: McClelland & Stewart, 1996), 214–16, 219–28.

liberties, peace research, and all that. It is not too serious that I do not answer letters; but it is serious when I find no little time for legal studies. I hope to find a way next fall to barricade myself up in the University."[65]

He did not barricade himself, not least because it was the leftist and separatist students who were building barricades he wanted to tear down. Far more satisfying was the time he spent at cafés near his Sherbrooke apartment with Madeleine Gobeil, who was now teaching at a Montreal classical college where she found, to her dismay but not to Trudeau's surprise, "a whole generation of people my age who, instead of working and becoming competent in their own field, sit around discussing things like separatism." Albert Breton, the most impressive young francophone economist of his generation, with links to some of the leading international economists of the age, was present when Madeleine made that comment. Now, when asked whether his first allegiance was to Canada or to Quebec, he always described himself as a "North American." And although Trudeau was critical of American politicians, he was increasingly attracted to American social science and intellectual debates. In the early 1960s his social thought increasingly reflected the arguments about countervailing powers and the poverty of the public sector set out by John Kenneth Galbraith, whose book *The Affluent Society* was a bestseller.

Over the winter of 1963–64, Trudeau joined with the Breton brothers, Montreal lawyer Marc Lalonde, sociologist Maurice Pinard, lawyer Claude Bruneau (who had worked for Conservative Justice Minister Davie Fulton), and psychoanalyst Yvon Gauthier to investigate why, in Trudeau's words, separatists wanted "the whole tribe [to] return to the wigwams." That, Trudeau further argued, "will not prevent the world outside from progressing by giant's strides; it will not change the rules and facts of history, nor the real power relationship in North America."

In May 1964 *Cité libre* published their manifesto "Pour une politique fonctionelle," which appeared simultaneously in a translation by Montreal lawyer Michael Pitfield in the *Canadian Forum* under the title "An Appeal for Realism in Politics." The authors revealed their legal and social scientific training as they deplored the lack of realism in Quebec politics, the absence of political leadership, and the government's refusal to deal with economic problems. In making their case for "the free flow of economic and cultural life," they rejected "the idea of a 'national state' as obsolete" and announced their refusal "to let ourselves be locked into a constitutional frame smaller than Canada." Trudeau's new friends helped him find a different approach through "functional politics." As so many old friends marched off under a new nationalist banner, Trudeau took a different turn.[66]

CHAPTER 9

—

POLITICAL MAN

On an early spring morning in Westmount in 1963, René Lévesque, Gérard Pelletier, and André Laurendeau were still at the Pelletiers' table at 2 a.m. Trudeau and Jean Le Moyne had left earlier. Out of cigarettes but still brimming with thoughts, Laurendeau and Lévesque had a last cup of coffee. Suddenly, an explosion ripped through the silence outside. "It's a FLQ bomb," said Laurendeau, blaming the Front de libération du Québec, a loose organization created earlier that year to bring about an independent Marxist state through violence. "No, no," Lévesque retorted, "it's an explosion in the Métro," the subway system then under construction in Montreal. Laurendeau disagreed: "I recognize the sound. They planted one not far from my place last month." Alec Pelletier descended the stairs and was decisive: "It's a bomb." Another explosion, and this time even Lévesque began to doubt his Métro explanation. The FLQ found mailboxes an easy target—where else could they drop a package and not look suspicious?

The three journalists—one now a Cabinet minister, another an eminent editor, the third a political and media icon—set out in search of a big story. With Alec still cloaked in her

elegant dressing gown, they soon found a grocery store whose
windows had shattered, leaving a wall of cigarette packages
completely exposed: "What luck, René," Alec declared. "Just
help yourself."

With the scent of smoke and the thrill of the chase intense,
the men set off to find the source of the other explosion.
Oblivious to danger, they drove close to a mailbox where another
bomb lay, but, fortunately, that explosion would come later in
the morning. As crowds milled around the splintered glass,
Pelletier kept an astonished silence. Lévesque was divided in
his response, critical, yet admiring: "You've got to hand it to
them—they're courageous, those guys." Laurendeau became
reflective: "It's incredible," he mused. "When I was twenty I used
to call on a girlfriend in this part of town. I never dreamed that
such things could happen here. Absurd, isn't it?"[1]

In fact, 1963 was often an astounding year—of mailbox
bombs, the rising FLQ, and the assassination of John F.
Kennedy. After Kennedy's death in the Dallas afternoon of
November 22, Laurendeau, Trudeau, Pelletier, Lévesque, and
Marchand had the last of their meetings that evening. Lévesque
mourned the president's death profoundly, "as if the crime had
wiped out a member of *his* family." Trudeau was analytical,
pondering other American presidential assassinations, while
Laurendeau deplored the violence that, in the argot of the
1960s, seemed as American as apple pie. Their different reactions to Kennedy's death reflected their varying reaction to the
equally stunning changes in Quebec. Throughout the year,
René Lévesque had been making explosive comments about the
future of Quebec within Canada. He had begun to reflect publicly about Canada being composed not of ten provinces but of
two nations. He often mused about the possibility of separation
if the federation failed to reform itself. He startled an admiring
Toronto audience when he described Confederation as an "old

cow" that had to change or Quebec would leave. When asked by the television host Pierre Berton whether he would be greatly troubled if Quebec left the Confederation, Lévesque replied: "No, I wouldn't cry long." The controversial comments and casual quips that boldly flirted with separation did not escape the notice of Laurendeau and Trudeau.[2]

Laurendeau was deeply troubled. Though nationalist in his views, he was nevertheless becoming identified as a "federalist" committed to the reshaping of the Canadian Confederation. In September 1961 he had bluntly stated his position in *Le Devoir*: "Independence? No: a strong Quebec in a new federal Canada." Soon after, as John Diefenbaker's Conservative government crumbled in Ottawa, Laurendeau called for the creation of a commission that would study and report on the creation of a new bilingual and bicultural federation. Diefenbaker said no, but Liberal opposition leader Lester Pearson endorsed Laurendeau's proposal in one of his speeches.

When Pearson took office in April 1963, he moved quickly to create the commission. After some fumbling, as his weak Quebec colleagues recommended people who commanded no support in Quebec, Pearson turned to Laurendeau and asked him to co-chair the commission he had originally proposed. Laurendeau hesitated at first but consulted widely. Lévesque gave him many reasons to refuse and one odd reason to accept—the "big bang" that Laurendeau's quick resignation from the commission would cause. Still, after a shouting exchange in which Laurendeau declared he was not a separatist and Lévesque replied, "Neither am I," Quebec's most popular politician resigned himself to Laurendeau's chairmanship. In July, Laurendeau met Pearson and accepted the position. He also convinced Jean Marchand to join him as one of the commissioners.[3] The commission hired Michael Oliver of McGill University and Léon Dion of Université Laval as co-directors of research, and they created an ever-swelling

research team* for, perhaps, the most significant royal commission in Canadian history.[4]

Trudeau watched these events warily, particularly since he
worried about Laurendeau's avowed nationalism. The commission asked him to undertake a study of the role of a "Bill of
Rights" in protecting cultural interests.[5] He accepted initially but
put it aside as the demands of his university courses, his journalism, and the family business increased after 1963. His mother's
health was deteriorating, the manager of the family's business
had died, and Tip was now often absent abroad or at his country
retreat. He had developed a reputation as a fine architect, but he
and Pierre do not seem to have been close after they left Brébeuf.
When Trudeau was abroad, his list of correspondents indicates
that he seldom wrote to Tip. He saw Suzette often at their childhood home in Outremont, and they bantered as they always had.
She was a shrewd financial manager, and Grace and Pierre both
valued her advice. Her role at the centre of the family intensified
as her mother's health began to fail quickly in the sixties. Trudeau

---

* By the fall of 1964, the Royal Commission on Bilingualism and Biculturalism,
chaired by André Laurendeau and Carleton University president Davidson Dunton,
was, in historian Jack Granatstein's words, "far and away the largest research organization in the country," with eight divisions, forty-eight full- or part-time researchers,
and a small army of consultants and students. Besides Marchand and Laurendeau,
Trudeau knew well Frank Scott and journalist Jean-Louis Gagnon, who were committee members. The commission's eight members were evenly balanced between
francophones and anglophones and included one francophone and one anglophone "ethnic," Professors J.B. Rudnyckyj and Paul Wyczynski (who is, coinciden-
tally, the father of the archivist directly responsible for the Trudeau archive). There
was one female member, Gertrude Laing of Alberta, but no Aboriginal member—
the cause of much complaint during committee hearings.

took over more responsibility for the management of finances and, when he was in Montreal, met weekly with his advisers. They included the lawyer Don Johnston, who later joined his Cabinet. Trudeau's "office" was a spare room with a metal desk, filing cabinets, and bare floors located on the burgeoning rue St-Denis. No doubt Trudeau enjoyed lunch in the nearby bistros much more than the accounting details.[6]

Pelletier's demanding work as editor of La Presse meant that he had less time to devote to Cité libre. And the journal's troubles were many. In the 1950s Trudeau had been a rare voice on the left; now many others had leapt over him, shouting Marxist slogans and scrawling revolutionary mottoes on school corridors and street signs. The intellectual boundaries that Cité libre had established in the early 1950s expanded quickly in the early 1960s, to the great distress of the founding editors. In 1963 these boundaries burst. Young members of the Cité libre team quit to establish the strongly leftist and nationalist journal Parti pris, but not without bitter farewells. In Cité libre itself, the twenty-five-year-old journalist Pierre Vallières argued that the founders should realize that the torch should be passed to a younger generation. The original team recognized the strength of the sentiment and, despite Jacques Hébert's doubts, made Vallières "editor" of Cité libre in 1963.[7] In the summer issue, not long after the night of the mailbox bombs, Vallières wrote an article on Cité libre and his generation. He began with the journal's stirring 1950 declaration of purpose. Those once-young men who had made that declaration were, he cruelly pointed out, "now forty or over." They had fought worthy battles against Duplessis and for the workers in the dark 1950s, but now they felt no need to engage in a "dialogue with the younger group."[8]

In February 1964 Pierre Vallières published another article in Cité libre which discussed a speech Walter Gordon, the federal finance minister, had given in Toronto alerting the audience to the "revolution" in Quebec. Vallières scorned this term as a description of events in the province since 1960 because, he argued, there could be no revolution without the destruction of bourgeois capitalism. It was time to choose the streets instead of the salons of Westmount, to prefer action to dreams. Gérard Pelletier, who had known Vallières in 1960 when he was "a member of the Little Brothers of Jesus, a mystic, something of a dreamer," deplored this revolutionary rhetoric. He recognized the creativeness of the revolutionaries, the seriousness of their work, and the important literary efflorescence occurring on the left. Their aims, however, were unacceptable: "a separatism wholly secular and anti-religious, a totalitarian socialism installed by violence, with the inevitable civil war provoked by the systematic agitation of a revolutionary party."[9]

Trudeau was not as polite as Pelletier in his rejection of the incendiary new dreams of youth. A generation earlier, he had mused about revolution himself. When the Catholic Church and Senator Joseph McCarthy excoriated and pursued Communists with terrifying and destructive zeal, he had dared to visit Russia and China and to declare himself a socialist. Now, in May 1964, he rejected any link with the Parti pris editors, who had, in their first issue, declared the founders of Cité libre "our fathers." He refused to acknowledge these self-declared offspring and attacked Vallières and the new nationalist socialists as separatist "counter-revolutionaries." Deep "upheaval" was characteristic not only of revolutions but also of counter-revolutions, he warned. Think of fascism and Nazism, of Hitler, Mussolini, Stalin, Franco, and Salazar:

> It cannot be denied that they all claimed to be serving the
> destiny of their respective national communities; further,
> three of them called themselves socialists. But who would
> call the whole of their work revolutionary? They upset a

great many institutions, they even opened the way for some material progress; but they abolished personal freedom, or at least prevented it from growing; that is why history classes them as counter-revolutionaries.

And so I get fed up when I hear our nationalist brood calling itself revolutionary. Quebec's revolution, if it had taken place, would first have consisted in freeing man from collective coercions: freeing the citizens brutalized by reactionary and arbitrary governments; freeing consciences bullied by a clericalized and obscurantist Church; freeing workers exploited by an oligarchic capitalism; freeing men crushed by authoritarian and outdated traditions.

That revolution had never occurred, although "around 1960, it seemed that freedom was going to triumph in the end." There were the victories of Roncarelli in the freedom-of-speech case, the retreat of the church from dogmatism, and the entry of previously barred professors into universities. In 1960, he exulted, "everything was becoming possible in Quebec."

A whole generation was free at last to apply all its creative energies to bringing this backward province up to date. Only it required boldness, intelligence, and work. Alas, freedom proved to be too heady a drink to pour for the French-Canadian youth of 1960. Almost at the first sip it went at top speed in search of some more soothing milk, some new dogmatism. It reproached my generation with not having offered it any "doctrine" —we who had spent the best part of our youth demolishing servile doctrinairism—and it took refuge in the bosom of its mother, the Holy Nation.

But the dogmatism of the cleric was giving way to the "zealots in the Temple of the Nation," who, like the authoritarians of the past, "already point their fingers at the non-worshipper." Indeed, in its April 1964 issue, *Parti pris* had acknowledged that there was "a necessary totalitarianism," while attacking Trudeau not for his ideas but because he was rich. Trudeau responded angrily.

He began with a discussion of his own previous and contemporary writings that had praised revolutionary figures in Russia, Algeria, and Cuba. "Genuine revolutionaries" such as Lenin, Ben Bella, and Castro had stressed "collective freedom as a preliminary to personal freedom" in situations where personal freedom had "scarcely been protected at all by established institutions." That was not the case in Quebec: "True, personal freedom has not always been honoured in Quebec. But, I repeat, we had pretty well reached it around 1960." Those who now talked of revolution had not been in the vanguard: "Thanks to English and Jewish lawyers (ah, yes!), thanks to the Supreme Court in Ottawa, personal freedom had at last triumphed over the obscurantism of Quebec's legislators and the authoritarianism of our courts."

Every week, Trudeau complained, "a handful of separatist students" told him they were "against democracy and for a single-party system; for a certain totalitarianism and against the freedom of the individual." Like the most traditional and reactionary individuals, they believed that they possessed "the truth" and all others must follow them. When others didn't, they turned to violence, all the while claiming persecution. In their privileged places "in the editorial rooms of our newspapers . . . at the CBC and the National Film Board," he said, "they lean with all their weight on the mass media." Others went underground to plant bombs and became "fugitives from reality." The separatist "counter-revolution" served mainly to protect the interests of the francophone "petit-bourgeoisie" and the professional classes, who would have diplomatic limousines, offices in the new national bank towers, and tariffs to protect their fragile businesses. "Rather than carving themselves out a place in [twentieth-century industrial society]

had become a champion of the literary separatists, upset the founders. Then, in March 1964 Vallières and other new voices used *Cité libre* to attack the journal's former editors directly. Some articles mocked them, including a clever satire by the poet and future separatist politician Gérald Godin comparing federalists and separatists to Hurons and Iroquois. In Vallières's opinion, Trudeau and Pelletier believed they had created "a monster." The young, for their part, suddenly realized that "their former idols had become old so quickly." Vallières and several others resigned immediately after this issue appeared. He founded a new review, *Révolution québécoise*, that embraced socialism, separatism, and violence. Two years later, he was in jail charged with terrorism.[11]

Trudeau might quarrel with the young, but he himself remained youthful in his taste and demeanour. He wore turtlenecks at the university, raced his Mercedes through the streets, and sought out younger friends. He was an active member of the anti-nuclear movement and an early opponent of the Vietnam War. On campus, he wore the dove peace symbol as early as 1962, long before it became ubiquitous. Yet he did not share the eccentric François Hertel's fascination with, and approval of, those "who play with dangerous and different ideas" because he believed that the ideas of Vallières and his colleagues were irresponsible and destructive. Perhaps he had once had such notions, as Hertel insinuated in his reply to Trudeau's 1964 attack on him in *Cité libre* after the priest seemed to call for the assassination of André Laurendeau. But the mingling of separatism with nationalism and, more recently, with violence represented to Trudeau a horrid return to an earlier world of extreme nationalism that had thankfully disappeared. Where Vallières saw echoes of the streets of Algiers or Hanoi, Trudeau saw the Munich beer halls of the twenties and the Nuremberg rallies of the thirties. The gulf between them widened quickly in 1964. His long-time companion Madeleine Gobeil, now living in Paris but still fully engaged in Quebec debates and making a name as a writer, told Trudeau that she would publish in *Cité libre* because it would identify her as anti-separatist. To publish in *Parti pris*, which was much more strongly literary in character, would lead everyone to believe she was a separatist.

Both journals had drawn the line. Trudeau, along with Pelletier and others, once again reorganized *Cité libre* with the intention of making it a journal of opinion that was leftist, secularist, but most decidedly not separatist. The journalist Jean Pellerin remained as editor after Vallières left, and the McGill philosopher Charles Taylor, for whom Trudeau had worked in the 1963 federal election when Taylor was an NDP candidate, became very active in the journal. Yet serious divisions remained: Charles Taylor, Jean Pellerin, and others were sympathetic to nationalist arguments and to the NDP's support for the concept of "two nations." Pelletier and Trudeau were increasingly not.

—

These passionate debates and differences shaped later understandings of what happened in Quebec in the sixties. Was there a profound rupture from the past at the time? What happened to the French Canadian and when did the Québécois appear? What was the meaning of the Catholic past and the socio-political culture of the thirties and forties for the new society that emerged in the sixties? And, above all, what was Quebec's place in Canada?

On the last question, Trudeau had become increasingly clear: Quebec's place lay within a Canadian federal state where individual rights were well defined and the cultural rights of French-speaking Canadians were guaranteed. He differed from André Laurendeau and from his New Democrat friends in his vehement opposition to the concept of "two nations"; he, in contrast, emphasized constitutionally guaranteed individual rights.

While accepting the existence and importance of the French language and culture in North America, he rejected a political definition of "nation" based on "ethnicity." Toronto historian Ramsay Cook, who knew him well in the early sixties, recalled that Trudeau came to believe that democracy in Quebec—a goal he had long cherished—faced one huge danger after the Lesage victory: nationalism. "For Trudeau," Cook wrote, "nationalism was conformist force founded upon conservatism and insecurity. At worst it was totalitarian. Moreover, in the Quebec context, nationalism acted as an emotional substitute for reasoned solutions to real problems." It was, therefore, the young who would lose the future as they sought out some "imaginary Jerusalem" rather than more immediate and useful goals.[12]

In his study of memory and democracy in Quebec, social critic Joseph-Yvon Thériault insists that Trudeau, as an intellectual and a politician, must be understood in the context of Lord Durham's famous report that described two different "nations" in the 1830s. Of Trudeau, he wrote, "His thought as much as his political deeds is structured as a critique and a transcendence of French-Canadian nationalism." In this respect, Pierre Trudeau was very much "a Quebec man of his generation." Like Durham, he identified the quarrel of the French-Canadian people as "a debate about principles between the defence of nationality and liberal values." He believed that the "defence of nationality" had prevented the development of "a true political pluralism" among French Canadians.[13]

In the 1960s Trudeau's thinking on nationalism and politics was increasingly framed in the language and concepts of political science, although he resisted academic and intellectual straitjackets. He became even more interested in what a new friend, the French journalist Claude Julien, termed "the American challenge"—and, indeed, there were echoes of Julien and American social science in the call for functional politics that Trudeau and several other Montreal intellectuals issued in 1964. Julien, a foreign correspondent for *Le Monde* who had been educated at Notre Dame University in Indiana, believed that the technological achievements of contemporary America threatened to leave Europe a fading, second-class continent. On his frequent trips to Paris, Trudeau visited Julien, who—like him, a Catholic on the left—kept wondering what the leftist and statist doctrines would mean for economic progress.

In his attack on the "separatist counter-revolutionaries" that year, Trudeau lamented the price the young in Quebec had paid for ignoring "the sciences and the techniques of the day: automation, cybernetics, nuclear science, economic planning, and whatnot else." Instead of facing the future, a few built bombs, others wrote revolutionary poetry, and the world moved past them. The poets, painters, authors, and songwriters were once again raising the banners of revolution in the coffee houses, the clubs, the streets, and in literary reviews, but, Trudeau believed, many of the younger generation were dangerously closing both their borders and their minds. While he welcomed the progressive reforms of Vatican II, the youth around him mostly ignored the changes and rejected religion itself in favour of alternative secular substitutes.

To get a better perspective on what was happening, Trudeau sought out new voices. The University of Montreal economist Albert Breton shared the same concerns as he and Julien did. They had lunch almost every week in a campus restaurant, where Trudeau revealed a "sweet tooth" along with his extraordinary knowledge of federalism. He could quote *The Federalist Papers* verbatim. Breton, who went on to become one of the world's leading economists in the study of federalism, claims that he "first learned about federalism from [Trudeau] during those lunches." Trudeau began to attract other young intellectuals— such as the lawyer Marc Lalonde and the public servant Michael Pitfield—because of his generosity in expressing his own ideas.

They also had their good times and laughed easily together: on one occasion as a few of them journeyed to the annual meeting of the Canadian Political Science Association in the Maritimes, they decided to indulge in the local delicacy and ordered lobster at a roadside restaurant. Bitter was their disappointment when it came in sodden lumps from a can.[14]

Separatism itself did not lead immediately or always to a break in personal relations; when Trudeau visited Paris, for instance, he always saw François Hertel, who had openly embraced separatism at the beginning of the sixties. He even welcomed the new nonconformism of the youth in Quebec, which expressed itself in a riotous abundance of facial hair, T-shirts, and mini-skirts in Montreal's lively bars and bistros. Moreover, like the rebellious young, he retained a Parisian's disdain for American foreign policy and materialism, particularly the Vietnam War and nuclear policy. The problem was not the nonconformity of the young—he relished and personally represented individualism in taste—or the sixties amalgam of sex, drugs, and rock and roll. He much enjoyed the first, tolerated but did not participate in the second, and danced superbly to the third. Rather, it was the conformity of the young that bothered him enormously, particularly at the university, where the students were overwhelmingly separatist. Most serious, in his view, was their unwillingness to consider alternative views and, in the case of the FLQ, their deadly seriousness. "Would Quebec miss the turn?" he had asked in 1960 on the eve of the Liberal victory. As he listened to students with their dreams of an "imaginary Jerusalem," he feared that, once again, it had.

Trudeau therefore shared Julien's sense that American energy and technology were transformative and that Canada was fortunate to share a continent with such a dynamic force for change. In the same vein, Quebec was blessed to be part of the prosperous and vital Canadian federation. Despite doubts about the influence of

American investment that he had first expressed in the 1950s, he even accepted parts of Julien's strained argument that Canada, with its openness through that investment to American technology and creativity, was "Europe's last chance."[15]

Trudeau no longer read much Quebec fiction—which increasingly played to Quebec nationalism. Gérald Godin, Hubert Aquin, Michel Tremblay, Jacques Godbout, and others who formed the cultural base of the nationalist and separatist efflorescence of the mid-sixties all annoyed Trudeau in their use of the colloquial "joual," their polemical rejection of the past, and, above all, their profound political irresponsibility, as he saw it. Although chansonniers like Gilles Vigneault and Félix Leclerc touched his romantic core, he reacted uneasily to the marriage of the cultural avant-garde to separatism and its flirtation with violence. In a different sense, he opposed the attempt by academic sociologists, notably by his old friend Marcel Rioux (now a separatist), to treat francophone Quebec residents sociologically—a path that led directly to the distinctiveness that, in his view, found political expression in separation.[16]

Following the "purge" at Cité libre and the publication of the statement on functional politics, Trudeau became increasingly distressed about the more explicitly nationalist direction of the Lesage government. He simultaneously worried that Lester Pearson's government in Ottawa was badly advised on constitutional matters and too weak to respond to the aggressive demands for jurisdiction and dollars from Quebec City. In his articles and in letters or comments to some of his closest friends—Carroll Guérin and Madeleine Gobeil, both now in Europe, and Marc Lalonde and Jacques Hébert—he expressed despair about the state of Canadian affairs and fretted over the best way to respond. Although he had never much admired Pearson, he had come to believe that Lesage was actually a weak leader who had lost control of his government. What should he do in these circumstances?

Trudeau realized that columns in *Le Devoir* or rants in *Cité libre* reached few of the workers in shops, in factories, or on farms who would make the final choice on the issue. Confrontations with his students in the classroom were also unsatisfying. He began to place his hope in television, which was entering a golden age of public affairs broadcasting. In 1964 he tried to negotiate an agreement with the CBC to become a host for the *Inquiry* series. The negotiations failed. Carroll Guérin summarized his sad lot in the early winter of 1965: "Correcting exams must be a huge bore; but I guess it is part of the price one has to pay for teaching. What a pity the TV thing proved to be a flop. It goes to show that our apprehensions were not without reason. It is a pity that entertainment is placed before *ideas*—but what can you expect from Toronto."[17]

Laurier LaPierre, a McGill University historian, became the Quebec intellectual who charmed English Canadians in 1965, alongside Patrick Watson, on *This Hour Has Seven Days*, a Sunday night program that shocked both the government and its audience. But Trudeau became a frequent participant in seminars and other academic gatherings as Canadians tried to understand what the tempests of change would bring. In 1964 the federal Parliament bitterly debated a new flag for Canada, one that would not bear the traditional British symbols. Carroll Guérin detested the design; Trudeau dismissed it as a trifle. In October 1964 riots broke out as the Queen made the last royal visit to Quebec City, not long after another English institution, the Beatles, made a more successful imperial progress across North America. The times, the American folk artist Bob Dylan rightly declared, were "achangin.'" But not always happily, it sometimes seemed, for Trudeau. His enemies appeared to be multitudinous, and Malcolm Reid summarized their reasons in his book about the literary and political radicals of mid-sixties Montreal:

What *Partipristes* could not forgive Trudeau, what seemed to them false and treacherous in his demolition of theocracy, was his cool, assured tone. How could he live in the smothering of liberty and not cry, not scream, not scribble on walls, not take to drink or dynamite? Such calm could come only from a basic cosiness with the very English money which paid for this reign of darkness, an Anglo-Saxon confidence that all would be straightened out when the French-Canadians learned engineering, business administration and behaviorist labour relations.[18]

The critique was unfair, but not entirely incorrect. Even if Peter Gzowski had described him—admiringly—as an "angry young man," Trudeau had learned to control his internal rage and to present himself to the world with a "cool, assured tone." In his self and in his politics, he was determined to be "functional," just like the architectural style—lean, international, and modern. And that style increasingly impressed those who came into contact with him, in person, through the press, or on television. Trudeau, a leading francophone professor told Ramsay Cook in 1964, was "the most talented intellectual in Quebec," but, alas, one whose talents were not fully exploited.[19] That situation was about to change.

—

The fourth year of the Quiet Revolution began with the Armée pour la libération de Québec, one of the several fringe separatist groups, announcing its intention of liberating the province by force within two years—a declaration punctuated on January 30, 1964, when an ALQ group stole a truckload of arms and ammunition, including anti-tank missiles, from the armouries of the Fusiliers de Montréal. Further raids on defence installations occurred on February 15 and February 20.

Editorialists debated whether the Queen should stay home as rumours of a murder plot circulated. "Are we savages?" Lorenzo Paré asked in *L'Action*. During the royal visit, the police struck the separatists down with truncheons. The *Globe and Mail* reacted as the separatists hoped when it declared that "Canada has walked to the edge of crisis and in many ways its perform-ance has been appalling." Trudeau had no love for the British monarchy, but he agreed: events were spinning out of control.[20]

In 1964 Abbé Lionel Groulx, one of Trudeau's early men-tors, published *Chemin de l'avenir*, "the road to the future"—a future that he claimed lay somewhere between outright inde-pendence and associate-state status. Immediately, the Société Saint-Jean-Baptiste came out in support of an associate state in a document written by the well-known historian Michel Brunet. Such a tract would likely have gathered dust in the archives except for its endorsement on May 9, 1964, by René Lévesque, who declared that associate-state status should be negotiated "without rifles and dynamite as soon as possible." Lévesque did not back down, and soon even Jean Lesage seemed to affirm most of his arguments. Such demands can easily be dismissed today as empty political rhetoric, but Trudeau and others recognized that the Lesage government had gathered together an impressive group of bureaucrats who were more than a match for their federal counterparts. The Ottawa men were reeling under the continual expansion of Quebec City's demands.

The Pearson government had come to office committed to creating a European type of welfare state in Canada. Unlike Europe and even the United States, Canada had no "social secu-rity" system in 1963. Only a fraction of high school graduates went to university, compared with the system of mass university education that had developed in the United States after the Second World War. Pearson's ambitions, which were inscribed in the Liberal Party platform after the historic "Thinkers'

Conference" at Kingston, Ontario, in September 1960, directly challenged the distribution of powers in the *British North America Act*, in which health, education, and social welfare generally were the responsibility of the provinces. Despite the opposition of many provinces, including, of course, Quebec, the Pearson government, once elected, decided to press forward with a fundamental restructuring of the role of the state in Canadian life. The Lesage government proposed the same for Quebec.[21] Not surprisingly, the governments clashed.

The clash, however, was sometimes productive—in many ways a justification of Canadian federalism, as Trudeau argued at the time. The province of Quebec had independently developed a strong proposal for a social security or pension system. The federal government was compelled to react. After difficult and bitter negotiations, the Canada Pension Plan and the Quebec Pension Plan were created through a system in which Quebec was allowed to "opt out" and receive a larger share of "tax points." Judy LaMarsh, Pearson's minister of health and welfare, threatened to resign over the issue, but pleas to her that invoked "national unity" concerns obtained her silence—for a while.* Trudeau welcomed the new social spending, but was disconcerted by the clumsy and irregular character of the decision-making and by the precedents being set.

---

* Judy LaMarsh was excluded from the final meeting when the deal was made to create the pension plans. She wrote in her bitter memoirs: "I felt that I had been shamefully treated by my Leader. Pearson did not then, nor has he ever, even acknowledged what a dirty trick he played. I admit that circumstances may have forced his hand, but I will always maintain that he did not need to do it that way." Later, LaMarsh became a strong opponent of "special deals" for Quebec and, eventually, of Pierre Trudeau, even though he largely shared her opinion. Judy LaMarsh, *Memoirs of a Bird in a Gilded Cage* (Toronto: Pocket Books, 1970), 281.

What astonished Trudeau more were the moves by the Quebec government to obtain an independent presence in international affairs. What had begun, sensibly, as the creation of a francophone Canadian presence in the French world, with the establishment of Quebec offices in Paris and elsewhere, had become a path whereby Quebec would attain an independent right to sign treaties and to conduct international relations in areas of provincial competence. More troubling was the presence in Charles de Gaulle's government of numerous officials who encouraged Quebec in these ambitions. Trudeau's old acquaintance Paul Gérin-Lajoie, a leading constitutional scholar, was the political and intellectual leader of the Quebec foray onto the international stage, and others, notably *Le Devoir* journalist and nationalist Jean-Marc Léger, rallied intellectual opinion behind the government's ambitions.

In January 1965, while the two men were both relaxing in Florida, Lesage told Pearson he had lost control of his government: he felt like a man holding on to the tail of an enraged bear. Public opinion polls indicated that Quebec separatism was no longer an idle dream but, potentially, a political movement with the support of somewhere between one-fifth and one-third of Quebec voters. As the Royal Commission on Bilingualism and Biculturalism travelled through the country, commissioners heard tales of francophones who had lived in Ontario, Manitoba, or elsewhere who had been denied jobs and told to "speak white." These incidents sparked many comments and bred resentment. André Laurendeau's diary of the commission's tour included such details as the young francophone living near Windsor, Ontario, who told how her French accent caused her problems even in an area with a historic and substantial French presence. When she was trying to rent an apartment, a friend told her not to make the calls because of her accent. Across Canada, the Commission rubbed against old scar tissue from the earlier wounds of conscription during the war, school language battles, and the rebellion of Louis Riel. Laurendeau also recounted how one commission member, Gertrude Laing, spoke with a young "Anglo-Canadian" who admitted that "he hated the French, that several of his friends felt the same way," and that he did not "believe at all in the task we are involved in." When pressed why, he said he had the impression that Quebec was "destroying the Canada he loves."

Polls taken by the *Calgary Herald* and the *Winnipeg Free Press* indicated that their readers believed the commission's work was harmful—an opinion Conservative leader John Diefenbaker shared. Not surprisingly, the commissioners decided they must sound an alert by issuing a "preliminary" report. Published in February 1965, that report declared, memorably, that "Canada, without being fully conscious of the fact, is passing through the greatest crisis in its history."[22]

After the commissioners rang this alarm, *Cité libre* published an anonymous attack on the report and on Laurendeau himself. Laurendeau was convinced that Trudeau was its principal author. He learned his suspicions were correct when Jean Marchand confirmed them and Trudeau later "partially" agreed. Trudeau's papers do contain a draft of the text.[23] It was primarily the commission's method that concerned Trudeau. As historian J.L. Granatstein observed, "the commissioners had gone beyond the traditional role of a royal commission in collecting data and offering recommendations; instead, they had involved themselves in the process and had become, in fact, *animateurs*." Trudeau, Marc Lalonde, and the others who had called for a functional politics thought that Laurendeau remained trapped within the nationalist womb—especially given his musings about a special status for Quebec. They feared that the federal Liberals' Quebec representation was simply too weak to counter the challenge from Quebec City and, at the same time, deal with the commission's demands.

In the spring of 1965, however, national public opinion

polls began to shift towards the Liberals. John Diefenbaker's protracted and histrionic opposition to the maple-leaf flag had angered many Canadians, and the Quebec Conservative Party had disintegrated. Despite some doubts about the bi and bi commission, there was a general expectation that its report would work to the Liberals' advantage. Many in the party therefore pressured Pearson to call an election

Unfortunately, at this moment, scandals and corruption were dogging the Quebec Liberals.[24] The weak Quebec ministers were a problem in Ottawa. Guy Favreau, the minister of justice, had been unable to secure provincial acceptance for the Fulton-Favreau proposals on the reform of the Canadian Constitution. Now his health was quickly failing and, in the spring of 1965, he became embroiled in a scandal surrounding a notorious drug dealer, Lucien Rivard.* Pearson had already lost his parliamentary secretary, Guy Rouleau, because of the scandal and the firebrand Yvon Dupuis because of an apparent bribe.[25] Now two more Quebec ministers, Maurice Lamontagne and René Tremblay, had become major political liabilities because of their alleged failure to pay for furniture from a bankrupt Montreal furniture dealer. The scandals, the astute journalist Richard Gwyn wrote in 1965, "resulted from a series of compromises made in the name of political expedience, which

---

* Lucien Rivard was a drug dealer whom the United States wanted to extradite. In fighting the extradition, he managed to gain the assistance of Guy Masson, a prominent Liberal, and, more important, Guy Rouleau, the parliamentary secretary to the prime minister, as well as Raymond Denis, the executive assistant to the minister of citizenship and immigration and the executive assistant to Favreau himself. Denis, it appeared, offered a $25,000 bribe to the lawyer representing Rivard. Favreau should have submitted the case to Justice Department legal advisers rather than deciding himself that no charge should be laid.

permitted what *Le Devoir* memorably termed 'the Montreal Liberal trashcan' to stand outside the back door of Parliament a good half-decade after it should have been removed."[26]

At the very moment when Quebec had become the Liberal government's most challenging issue, its francophone voices were discredited. Gérard Pelletier declared that Pearson's path led him into a "perpetual cul-de-sac," no matter what direction he turned. Journalists in French and in English cruelly portrayed Lester Pearson, who had privately impressed André Laurendeau and the other commissioners with his sensitivity and shrewdness, as a hopeless bungler. In January 1965 Pearson had met with Lesage and implored him to come to Ottawa, suggesting that the post of prime minister would be his reward. Lesage told him the timing was wrong: he was in the third year of his mandate in Quebec, and an election would normally fall in the fourth year. Pearson knew that the federal Liberals could not wait so long. Their sophisticated American pollster Oliver Quayle told them they must call an election in the summer of 1965, while Diefenbaker was still the Conservative leader. Moreover, in July 1965 Pearson managed to get nearly all the premiers to agree to a "medicare" plan, thereby giving the Liberals the progressive issue they needed to attract NDP votes. Despite strong opposition from

---

Favreau offered his resignation, Pearson refused it, but then appointed him to a new portfolio. He remained bitter for the remaining few years of his life because so many had abandoned him. Tellingly, Pearson responded to a letter from the eminent historian A.R.M. Lower, who had complained that there was too much "rot" in Canadian politics, by saying: "I do not agree that the conduct of Mr. Favreau, Mr. Lamontagne, and Mr. Tremblay, however inept and ill advised, represents any form of corruption or lack of integrity on their part." Lower had neither mentioned the three ministers nor referred specifically to Quebec.

many prominent Liberals, including Defence Minister Paul Hellyer and the wily political veteran Paul Martin Sr., the Liberals had already raised expectations of an election.

Pearson, who stood accused of indecisiveness, could hold off no longer. After a late-summer tour of the West, he returned to Ottawa on September 7, 1965, and called an election. Three days later, at a Montreal press conference in the Windsor Hotel, the three friends Pierre Trudeau, Gérard Pelletier, and Jean Marchand together announced that they would stand as Liberal candidates. For the Liberals, it was a coup; for Quebec politics, a shock.

—

Jean Marchand was the prize: a trade union leader as Liberals battled with the NDP for labour votes; a bare-knuckled debater who could go "toe to toe" with Réal Caouette's Créditistes; and a popular figure with the Lesage government, including René Lévesque. But the fall of 1965 was Trudeau's time too, just as it was Marchand's and Pelletier's. Marchand's role in the labour movement had become more difficult, and he had resigned as the head of the Confederation of National Trade Unions (CNTU) in the spring, knowing that politics offered an alternative. In that same spring, the board of directors of La Presse had fired Pelletier as editor.[27] Politics beckoned all three men to the Liberal fold almost at once. Trudeau was elated—his mood reflected the excitement of his new venture, his sense of mission at this troubled time in Quebec's and Canada's history, and the realization, at last, of his plan to be a political man.

Jean Marchand had considered running provincially or federally with the Liberals since 1960. When he decided not to run in 1963 because of Pearson's stand on nuclear weapons, he stepped aside quietly. Such was not the case with Pelletier, whose editorial opinions at La Presse denounced the decision and continued to criticize the scandals that plagued Pearson's minority government.

It was Trudeau, however, who rankled Liberal veterans most. They forgot neither his bitter denunciation of Pearson's decision to accept nuclear weapons nor his frequent attacks on Liberal MPs as "imbeciles" or "trained donkeys." Accordingly, Pearson was informed that Vadeboncoeur, not Trudeau, was the author of the notorious phrase "the defrocked prince of peace." Technically, the explanation was valid, although Pearson apparently was not told that Trudeau liked the phrase so much that he had chosen it to introduce his own caustic essay on Pearson in *Cité libre*. Fortunately, there were no copies of the review in Pearson's library. According to Jean Marchand, the powerful national party organizer Keith Davey tried to convince him that he should run alone only days before the election was announced. But he stood firm and insisted that the others must run too. He had "great confidence," he told Davey, "in Mr. Trudeau's mind and in Pelletier's judgement."

On September 9 the decision could be delayed no longer. At Guy Favreau's request, Marchand, Pelletier, and Trudeau met with him at a suite in Montreal's Windsor Hotel, along with Maurice Lamontagne and party organizer Robert Giguère. Maurice Sauvé apparently came without invitation. The meeting began at 8:00 p.m. and lasted until 3:00 a.m. Lamontagne frankly argued against the candidacy of Trudeau and Pelletier, telling them that things would be "very tough" and they would receive a cold welcome in Ottawa. But Trudeau maintained his "jolly mood" through it all. At 4 p.m. the next day, September 10, the three, quickly dubbed the "Three Wise Men" by the English press and "Les trois colombes"—the Three Doves—in the French press, announced that they had suddenly become Liberals and would stand as candidates in the next election.[28]

Trudeau remained the coy political mistress and took some time to find a constituency. According to journalist Michel Vastel, Trudeau dreamed of representing Saint-Michel de Napierville, where his ancestors had dwelt. It provoked uproarious laughter in the editorial rooms as journalists pondered the image of "the intellectual of *Cité libre*, the bourgeois of Outremont" going from door to door among the farms on the South Shore of the St. Lawrence. More astutely, the young Liberal Eddie Goldenberg realized Trudeau's remarkable political appeal when he came just after the announcement to speak to students at McGill University. He reflected on Greek philosophy, analyzed democratic thought, and, to Goldenberg's initial consternation, spoke unlike any politician he had ever heard. But the students were entranced. With Trudeau, it seemed that politics at last might be different.[29]

After much commotion, the party finally found Trudeau a seat in Mount Royal, a constituency that was rich, strongly Liberal, largely anglophone, and with a significant Jewish population. McGill University law professor Maxwell Cohen had positioned himself to run there, so Pearson intervened himself to persuade a disappointed Cohen to step aside. The excellent House Speaker Alan Macnaughton, who had held the seat since 1949 with remarkable majorities in recent elections, gracefully made way for Trudeau. However, the popular physician and veteran Victor Goldbloom was unwilling to allow the party's favourite a clear run at the nomination. His reluctance may have emerged from Trudeau's casual appearance when he came to a meeting with Liberal organizers driving his Mercedes sports car and wearing "an open-collared sports shirt, a suede jacket, a beat-up old peaked hat, muddy corduroy slacks, and sandals." He was sent home to change before the sceptical party faithful could encounter this strange new political beast. Trudeau mused about dropping out, claiming he did not want to run against Goldbloom, who was a "good man." The result, Marchand said, was "the most awkward convention I have ever seen, with Goldbloom saying that Trudeau was the best candidate, and Trudeau saying that Goldbloom was the best candidate." At the insistence and with the blessing of Pearson's organizers, Trudeau became the candidate.[30]

Marchand had to calm Trudeau once more when he learned that his friend Charles Taylor, for whom he had campaigned in 1963, would be his NDP opponent. Taylor had participated in a joint attack in *Cité libre* in reply to Pelletier's and Trudeau's October 1965 explanations for their decision to run for the Liberals. Their argument for joining the Liberal Party amounted to a blunt statement that they wanted to be politicians to carry out their policy aims, and only the Liberal Party offered them the possibility of placing their hands on the levers of power. "There are two ways in which one can become involved in public life," they wrote: "from the outside by critically examining the ideas, institutions, and men who together create political reality; or from the inside itself by becoming a politician oneself."[31] It was, as Taylor pointed out, the type of expedient argument that Trudeau and Pelletier had so often condemned.

Moreover, they were both self-declared voices on the left, and their decision weakened the NDP, whose popular leader, Tommy Douglas, was attracting much new support. Their sudden switch to the Liberals stunned the Canadian left, but it also encouraged many. Ramsay Cook, who had been an eloquent voice interpreting Quebec politics and thought among English-Canadian intellectuals, wrote to Trudeau on September 10, 1965: "Today's announcement of your intention to seek a nomination in the next election astonished me . . . While my heart is with the NDP, I would gladly do anything I could to help you." He, too, had become disillusioned by the NDP's two-nation policy. Trudeau's old colleague Maurice Blain—not so willing to help—was disappointed that they had abandoned the political left to work in "a traditional party subservient to capitalism, identified with anti-democratic institutions, and committed to electoral opportunism."[32] These comments worried Trudeau, but Marchand convinced him he should not let them get to him and simply knock on doors to win the votes.

On November 8 Trudeau won Mount Royal with a margin

of 13,135 votes, less than half of Macnaughton's margin of 28,793 in 1963. It was not a smashing victory, but he had a safe seat for the remainder of his long political career, always with large margins of victory. The government also won re-election, but once again the cherished majority eluded Lester Pearson as Diefenbaker's campaign skills carved up the Liberal vote, especially in the West, and scandals continued to plague the Liberals in Quebec.* It was, Liberal organizer John Nichol later said, "a long, long way to go for nothing." Marchand entered the Cabinet immediately as the minister of citizenship and immigration, with the promise that he would soon become the minister of a new Department of Manpower. Once Pearson named him his senior Quebec minister, Marchand relished the task of "cleaning up" the Quebec wing of the Liberal Party.

Pelletier and Trudeau took their place on the back benches, probably because some penance was appropriate before the other Liberal MPs could be expected to accept the freshly minted Liberals. Politically, it was wise to dampen expectations because the trio had caused a whirlwind in Quebec, especially in intellectual circles where there was, in Blain's words, "an emotional reaction."

---

* The final results were 131 Liberal (129 in previous Parliament); 97 Conservative (95); 21 NDP (17); 9 Créditistes and 5 Social Credit (24 combined). There were two independents. The Liberals took 40 percent of the popular vote; the Conservatives, 32 percent. In the pre-election polls and election polls, the Liberals were in the 45 percent range and stood at 44 percent in early November, just before the election. The Liberals actually had a higher percentage of the popular vote (42%) in the April 1963 election. The Liberals did gain 12 seats in Quebec, but lost three to the Conservatives despite the party split before the election. The NDP, despite the leadership of the popular Robert Cliche, did poorly, increasing its vote to 11.9 percent only because it ran many more candidates in Quebec.

As he perceptively remarked just after the election, the three "had not so much embraced a new career as set out on a mission." Detested by separatists, distrusted by neo-nationalists and the left, they came to represent a shift in the political landscape in Quebec and, perhaps, in Canada. For Pierre Vadeboncoeur, this mission slowed the swelling momentum leading to an independent socialist Quebec. Laurendeau, who approved of their switch, nevertheless believed that "their decision dealt a major blow to 'democratic socialism' in Quebec, and killed a lot of hopes." Years later, Bob Rae, the former federal NDP member of parliament and Ontario premier, said that their emergence on the federal scene as Liberals "ended the dream of a socialist Canada under a New Democratic government."[33]

Such judgments belonged to the future in the fall of 1965 when, in Pelletier's words, "many people thought that Trudeau and I would cross the aisle in Parliament after a month." Of course, they did not. In 1992 Trudeau told Michael Ignatieff, who had supported his campaign for the leadership in 1968, that he had decided "not to make party options too soon." Rather, he advised, you should complete your philosophical formation first because, "once you join a party, it's hard to switch. You have the whole history of friendship and everything else."

Even before the supposedly decisive meeting on September 9, 1965, Trudeau had told Madeleine Gobeil that he was making "the big jump."* More tellingly, his confidante Carroll Guérin wrote to him in October, just before the election. She regretted leaving him at the airport, "though I am quite glad

---

* When Madeleine Gobeil met Grace Trudeau on election night, the proud mother declared: "Now he might amount to something." Interview with Madeleine Gobeil, May 2006.

that you are engrossed in politics now; probably because I'm safely removed from the front now! But I felt I was leaving you to something very vital (to put it mildly), and not walking off while you returned to a way of life that you must admit was something of a dead end." She summarized so many intimate conversations in those two brief sentences. Pierre, whom she loved profoundly, had found his place. "With hugs," she concluded her letter, "even if you are in the Liberal Party."[34]

—

The Liberal Party was scarcely congenial for a backbencher arriving in Ottawa in the winter of 1965–66. Walter Gordon, who had strongly urged Pearson to have an election, offered his resignation after the defeat. To Gordon's surprise, Pearson accepted it. With Gordon's departure, the left or reformist wing of the party was suddenly weak, particularly when the more conservative Mitchell Sharp became the new minister of finance and the decidedly conservative Robert Winters, after he had divested himself of his numerous company directorships, minister of trade and commerce.

What this reorganization meant, the eminent journalist and editor Claude Ryan wrote in *Le Devoir*, was that the Cabinet had "two tiers"—the first a group of senior ministers who were "the real masters," and the second a group of juniors, who would have to prove themselves. The "masters" came almost entirely from Ontario; in Quebec, only Marchand might be called upon "to enter the 'inner sanctum' where the big decisions are made." Ryan was correct in his assessment that nearly all the Quebec ministers were on the lower tier; what he did not realize was the extent of the mandate Pearson gave Marchand to "do that [clean-up] job" in Quebec they both deemed essential. Trudeau and Pelletier, in Marchand's words, supported him but "were not

directly involved or personally involved" in the political house-
cleaning. They were backbenchers "like the others," though
already an aura surrounded them.[35] There were also the doubters
and the believers.

The influential Toronto *Globe and Mail* greeted the entry
of Marchand, Pelletier, and Trudeau as potential bulls in a
Liberal store filled with fragile china. For his part, Pearson's lead
Quebec minister Guy Favreau, though willing to accept their
entry, was so upset that he took "a long ride on his motorcycle at
high speeds" to work off his frustration—no doubt something
Pierre had done in the past himself.[36] Of the three, Trudeau was
the least well known; the firing of Pelletier from *La Presse* amid
rumours of plots by Lesage and large business interests had
attracted attention even in English Canada. Trudeau was not listed in the English-language *Canadian Who's Who* for 1965, and
almost none of his writings were available in English. When he
first arrived in the fall, Ottawa reporters treated him as an exotic
species whose sartorial tastes as much as his intellectual prowess
set him apart from his parliamentary colleagues.* Not for the first
time, the media attributed to him a lower age.

Yet difference and mystery intrigue. In a book on
Canadian nationalism published in 1966, the well-known
University of Toronto historian Kenneth McNaught famously

---

* The young Albertan political assistant Joyce Fairbairn first met Trudeau at
the Parliamentary Restaurant, where he often had breakfast after the short
walk from his room at the Château Laurier Hotel. He brought, she claimed, a
reputation for being eccentric "because of his initial casual attitude toward
wearing apparel. In a House of Commons filled with suits and ties and socks
and laced shoes, he showed a shocking tendency toward sports jackets, cravats,
and sandals—sometimes worn without socks." After "a lengthy succession of

drew attention to Trudeau: "It was to stem the now common habit of looking upon and treating Ottawa as a foreign power that this brilliant and essentially non-political sophisticate plunged into the icy waters of federal politics in Quebec." McNaught, a leading socialist activist and the biographer of J.S. Woodsworth, feared Trudeau's impact on his NDP but welcomed his voice in Ottawa and Quebec:

> For his pains he has been smeared as a *vendu*, and there is little doubt that he shares what I have called the English-speaking view of Canada. His political fate will likely be the political fate of Canada. Nor should anyone question the agony of his decision, for it involved further crippling the struggling Quebec wing of the NDP, which is the party that best represents Trudeau's social thought. His decision that the Liberal party—the party which flirts most openly with American continentalism—is yet the party which alone might avert the imminent culmination of racial nationalism was the measure of his fears for Canada.[37]

In Quebec, Jean-Paul Desbiens, whom Trudeau and *Cité libre* had honoured in 1960 for the publication of his notorious attack on the Quebec education system, similarly declared in a letter to

---

boiled eggs," she warmed to Trudeau, who made little of the "light political conversation" that marks "the Hill," and she grew to respect him enormously. And to like him: "From the very beginning I sensed a shyness in him that was hooked on to an element of kindness that I came to know well over the years of work and friendship." The shyness sometimes came through—wrongly in her view—as arrogance or lack of interest. Joyce Fairbairn in Nancy Southam, ed., *Pierre* (Toronto: McClelland & Stewart, 2005), 39.

In 1962, as the international anti-nuclear movement spread, Gérard Pelletier and Trudeau read a peace movement pamphlet. Trudeau wears the "ban the bomb" lapel pin to identify his commitment.

"The Three Wise Men": Gérard Pelletier, Jean Marchand, Pierre Trudeau, 1965.

Pelletier, Trudeau, and Marchand announce their candidacy for the Liberal Party, September 10, 1965.

The Big Attraction.

The inevitable tea party for the new candidate in Mount Royal, 1965.

The candidate's storefront office: first campaign, Mount Royal, 1965.

Trudeau's first campaign poster, 1965.

Trudeau as a candidate in Mount Royal, 1965: note the
Fleur-de-lys and the Star of David in the background.

Lester Pearson and his successors: Pierre Trudeau,
John Turner, Jean Chrétien.

A forceful Trudeau at the Quebec Federal Liberal Party Conference, 1968.

Suddenly Everyone Looks a Little Older.

Pearson featured his minister of justice at the Federal-Provincial Conference in 1968.

A Mirage!

The Swinger.

The candidate surrounded by his supporters at the leadership convention.

The early gunslinger pose: Liberal Party leadership race, 1968.

Some members of the Trudeau team at the leadership convention, 1968. From left to right: Jean Marchand, Mitchell Sharp, Pierre Trudeau, and behind with a pipe, Edgar Benson.

Trudeau kissed women, not babies: leadership convention, 1968.

Playing with a flower to break the monotony during the four ballots of the leadership race. Edgar Benson looks on.

Candidate for the Liberal Party leadership, 1968: sliding down
the bannister at the Château Laurier Hotel, Ottawa.

Trudeau that he and his colleagues represented for Canada its "last hand of cards."[38]

Trudeau, wisely, appeared eager to lower expectations. During the election campaign he told reporters that when he became a candidate, he was not offered a Cabinet post. Moreover, he said, "I made it clear I did not want such a post before anyone had the chance to offer me one." Blair Fraser, the national reporter Trudeau had known well since his youth, wrote profiles of Trudeau, Pelletier, and Marchand shortly after the Cabinet was formed in December 1965. The article rightly identified Marchand as the key player. "Trudeau and Pelletier," Fraser wrote, "are quite content as backers of Marchand, with no special ambitions." He reported that Trudeau found the all-candidate debates surprisingly enjoyable and that "his wry humour went down well." He also rightly identified some of the baggage that Trudeau carried with him to Ottawa: he had "never been obliged to work for a living"; his "English-speaking mother (Le Devoir insists on spelling his name Elliott-Trudeau)"; and, "gravest of all . . . his habit of speaking his mind." Some details aside, the article, oddly, has one wildly-off-the-mark analytical flaw—Fraser's assertion that "the fact that he is a well-to-do bachelor" was something "which women voters seem to resent."[39]

Immediately after the election, while others flew to Ottawa to pursue positions, Trudeau, true to form, went off to Europe on a ski trip. While he was there, Pearson decided to offer him the post of parliamentary secretary to the prime minister. Trudeau promptly declined, probably because he was wary of working closely with Pearson when he had little knowledge of him and his office or simply because he worried—correctly—that too rapid promotion breeds jealousy.

Marchand was livid. He had promoted Trudeau for the position of parliamentary secretary to the minister of finance and was pleasantly surprised to learn that Pearson wanted him for the Prime Minister's Office. Never close personally to Trudeau and exasperated with his moral dithering about running against Victor Goldbloom for the Liberal nomination and then against Charles Taylor in the election, he called Trudeau in Europe. In the sanitized version of the heated conversation that appears in his memoirs, Trudeau says that he told Marchand: "Give me time to get settled, to do my homework. You know I don't like to go into anything unprepared." Marchand responded caustically: "We didn't come here to refuse to work, Pierre. What brought us here is that there's a job to be done, and we have to grab every opportunity to do it."[40] Trudeau could not refuse his colleague, and so he became parliamentary secretary to Lester Pearson—the man he had criticized regularly since his first encounters with him as a young bureaucrat in Ottawa in 1949.*

What he saw of Pearson in the first months of office confirmed some of these doubts. The failure to win a majority government profoundly depressed the prime minister: on election night his face seemed frozen when he spoke on television; he took no questions and told reporters, "It's been a hard two months—I think I'll go home and go to bed." Probably he slept little that early morning of

---

* When asked why he appointed Trudeau his parliamentary secretary, Pearson said: "I had read his pieces for years, and was impressed by them, particularly by his detailed technical knowledge of economics and constitutional law. We're into a period where that's very important, and we'll be dealing a lot with Quebec. Pierre is a Quebecer and seems the kind of qualified person we need." It is unlikely that Pearson had read his pieces for years, and Trudeau did not have "technical knowledge of economics." Yet, in a period when the Quebec government had many highly sophisticated constitutional specialists, such as Claude Morin, Paul Gérin-Lajoie, and Jacques-Yvan Morin, and "technical economists," such as Michel Bélanger and Jacques Parizeau, Trudeau was a precious asset in Ottawa.

November 9 as he contemplated the resignation he would offer to his Cabinet in the morning. It was, as expected, rejected, but he left the meeting determined to have a new team. Walter Gordon left quickly, along with prominent party officials such as Keith Davey and Jim Coutts. Tom Kent, a dominant intellectual presence in Pearson's office, became Jean Marchand's deputy minister in the new Manpower Department. Pearson insisted that different faces were essential, even if the old ones were, in some cases, those of friends or of politicians wrongly caricatured as corrupt. Maurice Lamontagne, who had been Pearson's major Quebec adviser since opposition days, was an early casualty as Pearson told him personally that it was time for him to "get out." René Tremblay suffered the same fate, and Guy Favreau was retained in the minor post of president of the Privy Council. There his health continued to weaken, his East Block office remained empty, and his secretaries rarely saw him until he died in 1967. Maurice Sauvé, correctly distrusted by his colleagues as the source of "leaks" to the press about the government's internal troubles, retained his minor Cabinet post of minister of forestry, but his influence was much diminished. Apart from Jean Marchand, the sole important francophone was Minister of Justice Lucien Cardin—and, as another scandal would soon reveal, his task was beyond his capabilities.[41]

Later, when asked about these times, Trudeau said that "what surprised our little gang . . . is how easy it was to get yourself in a position of importance in a . . . historically established party . . . We knew that if we could get the people to support our ideas, some of the old guard would say: 'Well, these guys can win with new ideas, so let's win.'"[42] What made their success possible were two major factors: the discrediting and disappearance of the "old guard" (Lamontagne dated from the St. Laurent era, and Favreau and Tremblay from 1963); and the priority that Pearson and the Canadian public gave to the Constitution and the Quebec issue after the election of 1965.

Trudeau sensed the opportunity immediately. André Laurendeau, who did not "feel" like congratulating Trudeau on his victory, met him at two cocktail parties in early January. He remained the jolly soul he had been in November in the Windsor Hotel, and Laurendeau "was struck by his good spirits, and his energy: it's been a long time since I've seen him so up." Marchand told Laurendeau that the Liberal MPs were finding it difficult to accept Pelletier, whose barbs they remembered well and whose column on being a candidate during the 1965 campaign reflected extremely poor political judgment. Trudeau was different: he was "wonderfully successful. He astounds English Canada." And, Marchand concluded, "I'm willing to bet my shirt that within a year Pierre will be their big man in French Canada, eclipsing all the others."[43]

—

Fortunately and fortuitously for Trudeau, the first big issue he had to address was the Constitution. Already, before he entered politics, he had worked intensely on constitutional questions with his friends Marc Lalonde, Michael Pitfield, and groups affiliated with the Canadian Labour Congress in Quebec. Now, the unwillingness of the Lesage government to support the Fulton-Favreau process for constitutional revision in 1965 and 1966 brought deadlock and crisis. For Lester Pearson, it was a bitter disappointment. In February 1965, for example, he had confided to his close friend the journalist Bruce Hutchison that his greatest accomplishment was in the area of "Canadian federalism" and that he was now "totally devoted to national unity." This issue became the bond between Trudeau and his political chief: he could grasp the bloom of fresh opportunity from this nettle of failure. And, as he gained success, his respect for Pearson slowly grew.

The opening came from Premier Jean Lesage, who, antici-
pating a provincial election, separated the provincial Liberals
from the federal Liberals. The federal Liberals immediately
arranged a convention for their Quebec branch, where constitutional policy became the central issue. Jean Marchand, realizing
he must establish his authority at this convention, turned to
Trudeau for assistance on policy questions. Already Lesage's hesitancy had cast doubt on the federal government's earlier
approach to Quebec, and the January 20, 1966, Throne Speech
in Ottawa had set out a "harder" line in its approach to constitutional revision and to provincial demands, stating that it would
"exercise great care in agreeing on joint programs with the
provinces in which all provinces do not participate."

Now, at the convention, Trudeau, under Marchand's tute-
lage, brought forward resolutions for the Quebec Liberal
Federation that reflected his own similar hesitations about "any
kind of special status for Quebec." Intellectually, he dominated
the gathering. His argument that no major revision of the *British
North America Act* was needed was generally accepted, as was his
rejection of "an independent Quebec, or associate status, or special status, or a Canadian common market, or a confederation of
states." He also argued for bilingualism within the federal government and the importance of a Bill of Rights that would enshrine
individual rights across the country. Although Claude Ryan in *Le
Devoir* dissented from Trudeau's "honest but dubious" proposi-
tions and his "cold logic," the power of Trudeau's ideas and the
centrality of his role in federal politics in Quebec were firmly
established within months of his arrival in Ottawa.[44]

Trudeau's early success in federal politics occurred at a time
of chaos in Ottawa. The CBC's popular television series *This
Hour Has Seven Days* (which had considered Trudeau as a host)
had introduced a confrontational form of interviewing that
caught most politicians unprepared. In one program just after

the election, Justice Minister Lucien Cardin revealed the name of George Victor Spencer, a postal clerk who had been fired because he was suspected of spying for the Soviet Union. Ruffled, he went on to say that Spencer would not be charged but would be under surveillance for the rest of his life.

With those careless words, Cardin upset both civil libertarians and anti-Communists and made himself a target for John Diefenbaker, who fancied himself, with some justice, as the advocate of both. When the House returned in January, Cardin faced Diefenbaker's relentless attack. Quebec Liberals already detested Diefenbaker and blamed him for the destruction of Favreau, Lamontagne, and Tremblay—again with some justice. The Cabinet had decided in January that there would be no inquiry into the charge, but Diefenbaker and the NDP demanded that George Victor Spencer's curious case required investigation. Some members of the Liberal caucus, including Trudeau and Pelletier, began to question the government's stand. Bryce Mackasey, an outspoken Montreal MP, rose in the Commons to call publicly for an inquiry. On the way to Pearson's office, apparently to offer his resignation as parliamentary secretary, Mackasey encountered Trudeau, who, in Mackasey's recollection, told him, "I'll go with you [to Pearson's office] and I'll resign as well, because I felt what you felt." Pearson gave them a "good tongue-lashing," telling them if he wanted their resignation he would ask for it.[45] It was, for Trudeau, a good lesson.

More lessons soon came as Spencer's case magnified the government's and the prime minister's weaknesses. On March 2 David Lewis of the NDP told the House that Spencer himself wanted an inquiry—a clear repudiation of Pearson's statement the previous day that no inquiry was needed. Diefenbaker went for the jugular as only he, the most effective parliamentary debater of his generation, could do. Two days later, sensing that the beleaguered justice minister stood alone, he pressed the attack, hinting that the government was concealing various security breaches in the past and the present. It was mudslinging at its worst, and Cardin responded in kind, warning Diefenbaker that he was the last person to give advice on security cases. Pearson, who had come into the House, strongly applauded his minister. Diefenbaker pointed at him and shouted: "Applause from the Prime Minister. I want that on the record." Cardin misunderstood, thinking that Diefenbaker was demanding the name of the security case, and he stupidly blurted out "Monseignor." He had meant to say "Munsinger." Gerda Munsinger was a German immigrant to Montreal who had carried on affairs simultaneously with a Soviet diplomatic official and Pierre Sévigny, the associate minister of national defence in Diefenbaker's government. Pearson and Favreau had threatened Diefenbaker earlier with revelation of the Munsinger affair if he persisted in his bitter personal attacks on Quebec ministers.* Thus began the only serious sex scandal in Canadian political history and, more significant, the departure of Lester Pearson from Canadian politics.[46]

In a minority government and with his major advisers of the past now absent, Pearson made the fatal error of reversing his position and agreeing to the inquiry, even though three senior ministers, including Marchand, had defended Cardin's stand against an inquiry in the House.[47] Once again it seemed that Pearson had abandoned a Quebec minister under siege. Jean

---

* In one disgraceful episode when Pearson repeated the threat, Diefenbaker responded by shaking his fists at Pearson and saying that "he had a scandal" on him. Diefenbaker, in Pearson's words, said that "he knew all about my days as a Communist." Pearson laughed in his face and said it was the testimony of a "deranged woman," Elizabeth Bentley, who had been a dubious but major source for J. Edgar Hoover and other Americans pursuing Communists.

Marchand, according to one account, went over to Pearson's desk after he announced the inquiry and said: "If you ever do to me what you've just done to Cardin, all hell will break loose." It soon did. Lucien Cardin went home to Sorel for the weekend, decided he must resign, returned to Ottawa, and handed a letter of resignation to the prime minister. Pearson refused to open it. On the Tuesday, Trudeau attended the Quebec caucus. The members were furious with this abandonment of Cardin and almost voted for a motion of censure directed against Pearson, an action that would force the prime minister to consider resignation. Marchand told Cardin that he would resign with him, as would some other francophone Quebec ministers. Under pressure, Cardin stayed on; and Pearson stumbled through a sordid inquiry into the security risks of Gerda Munsinger's lively sex life.[48]

Trudeau shared the anger of his Quebec colleagues. He drew important impressions from the political chaos he experienced during his first three months in Parliament. First, he confirmed his impression that Lester Pearson was a weak but well-meaning leader. Second, he agreed with his Quebec francophone colleagues that their ministers did not receive the support they needed to confront the challenges of Quebec nationalism and separatism. Third, he strengthened his opinion of the House of Commons as a chamber where "trained donkeys" brayed and "imbeciles" roared. One day when Trudeau appeared for a vote wearing leather sandals and a foulard, Diefenbaker thundered denunciations at him for showing such disrespect for the ancient sartorial rules. He paid little attention to the House in the remainder of his first year and never developed the affection for the Lower Chamber that parliamentarians ranging from Wilfrid Laurier to Henri Bourassa to John Diefenbaker had done. In later years, Trudeau made some memorable speeches in the House, and his quick repartee made him highly effective in Question Period. But he was not a born gladiator in the political arena of the House of Commons.

After Trudeau's death, Pierre Vadeboncoeur defended his old friend, with whom he had bitterly disagreed since the mid-1960s, against charges that he was haughty and conceited. Quite the contrary, he said, Trudeau was often unsure of himself and was not "a natural tribune." As a politician, he became successful through his talents, but even more through a determined will to control "with precision, his actions and his attitudes." Because he was not a natural in the political battle, he sometimes adopted a pugnacious approach that was "contrary to his own more simple and authentic character." These thoughtful comments illuminate Trudeau's unusual political persona when he went to Ottawa in 1966—one exuding strength while simultaneously retaining a deep reserve that could become a beguiling shyness or, unexpectedly, a burning anger.[49]

Although Trudeau became Pearson's parliamentary secretary, they seldom worked together that year. In his own memoirs, Pearson admits that "Trudeau had neither very much to do nor the opportunity to learn very much in my office." Trudeau, in his own memoirs, states that he expected "some modest parliamentary chores and some pencil-pushing." Instead, Pearson sent him "running around the world."* In April he attended a meeting in Paris of the newly created Canada-France Parliamentary Group, one of the forums that allow backbenchers to travel and be

---

* With a minority government, the House sat long into the summer of 1966. As a summer student working on Parliament Hill that year, I regularly saw Pearson and Paul Martin, whose External Affairs office was in the East Block. Even Guy Favreau made occasional appearances, but, except for a few votes in the House, Trudeau was rarely in Ottawa. I first learned about him when some friends of mine met him at a Laurentian resort in mid-summer. They found him serious with them but very flirtatious with the women.

rewarded. Herb Gray, a young MP from Windsor, also attended the Paris meetings, where, he recalls, Trudeau startled the Canadians and the French alike with his detailed knowledge of Paris, Europe, and Africa, and with the stunning blonde woman who accompanied him to some of the formal events. Trudeau seemed at home in Paris, a perception validated by the "contact" list from his 1963 trip, which bears over forty names, including such eminent intellectuals as Jean Domenach of *L'Esprit* and the distinguished and currently fashionable philosopher Paul Ricoeur—and, inevitably, numerous single women.[50]

This parliamentary association was important because of the French and, more particularly, President Charles de Gaulle's interest in Quebec nationalism and separatism. Many French journalists travelled to Quebec at this time, attracted by the liveliness of the political debate, the literary and musical efflorescence of Montreal and Quebec—Michel Tremblay and Marie-Claire Blais, Félix Leclerc and Monique Leyrac were suddenly receiving raves in the French press—and their own government's increasing willingness to deal directly with a Quebec administration that had completely lost its suspicion of republican and atheist France. Quebec responded warmly to this embrace, establishing a "délégation générale" in Paris and undertaking a series of ministerial visits where Lesage and his ministers received treatment normally reserved for representatives of the most important sovereign states. Meanwhile, the Canadian ambassador, Jules Léger, Trudeau's old friend from Ottawa days, was treated contemptuously by de Gaulle, whose government signed a Quebec-France cultural entente in February 1965 that *Le Magazine Maclean* termed "the entry of the state of Quebec on the international scene."

Although the struggle between Ottawa and Quebec City to limit Quebec's "international" activities had many comic aspects, including the measurement of flags and even battles between limousines to lead processions, there is no doubt that some French officials, principally in the president's office, joined in intrigues to promote the independence movement in Quebec. Just as Canada had gained independence through its signature on fishing treaties and its appointment of "ministers" to foreign countries, so Quebec's international activities in Paris and, increasingly, in the former French colonies could well have led to political sovereignty. On this matter, Pearson and Trudeau strongly agreed. Trudeau therefore represented Canada at an international convention of French jurists and, later, wandered through five African countries to promote Canadian interests in the new "Francophonie"—a French Commonwealth being promoted by Senegal president Léopold Senghor, a poet who very much impressed Trudeau.[51]

Before he entered politics, Trudeau had criticized Quebec's efforts in the international arena, and he agreed to chair a group of legal experts who were considering how Canada should respond to these challenges. Two Pearson advisers whom Trudeau admired greatly, Marc Lalonde and Michael Pitfield, were part of the group, along with the undersecretary of state for external affairs, Marcel Cadieux, and the head of the department's legal division, Allan Gotlieb. This brilliant group of lawyers tested Trudeau, honed his intellectual skills, and shaped his response to Ottawa as well as Quebec. They shared the fear that Quebec's international ambitions could cut away the legal ties that bind a nation together, and these fears intensified when the Lesage government endured a stunning defeat in the election of June 5, 1966.

The new premier, Daniel Johnson of the Union nationale, promised to be much more nationalistic than Lesage, who in the final weeks of the campaign had ferociously denounced separatism. Johnson, whom Trudeau had met in the 1940s and who had been an early subscriber to Cité libre, campaigned on the slogan of his 1965 book, "equality or independence," and promised in the first plank of his party's platform to make Quebec "a true national state" through an extension of the province's powers and its sovereignty, especially on the international level. On election night, Johnson ominously remarked that, when you subtracted the Jewish and English Liberal vote, 63 percent of the French "nation" had rejected the Liberals. "Too many people," Johnson opined, "treat the BNA Act like a sacred cow, even though it's been violated many times in closed committee sessions and even in hotel rooms. So why not get rid of it and draft a sixth constitution?"

Trudeau, of course, personally rejected all these premises: the need for a new Constitution, the equation of the French-speaking population of Quebec with a "nation," the need for special status for Quebec, and the right of Quebec to have separate international representation. His group, together with Al Johnson, who had joined the Department of Finance from the Saskatchewan bureaucracy, began to elaborate a strong federal response to Premier Johnson's demands, which were presented by Finance Minister Mitchell Sharp to the federal-provincial conference on tax and fiscal affairs in September. Firmly rejecting special status for Quebec and further "opting out" by Quebec alone, Sharp asserted the essential need for the federal government to maintain the taxing authority necessary to meet Canada's fiscal needs. Claude Ryan in Le Devoir accurately noted the influence of Trudeau and Marchand in the federal approach, particularly in the firm rejection of "special status for Quebec."[52]

For much of the fall of 1966, Trudeau himself was absent from Ottawa because he was a member of the Canadian delegation to the United Nations. There he infuriated Paul Martin Sr., Canada's minister of external affairs, who at the time was leading all the polls as the most likely successor to Lester Pearson. In the late 1940s Pearson had established the practice of sending promising MPs of all parties to the UN as a way of building support for his foreign policy, and it proved to be an effective tool. Trudeau, however, took an immediate dislike to the elaborate rituals of the UN and to the policies Canada espoused there, particularly its tortured approach to the admission of China. He openly dissented from Paul Martin's "two China" approach, which called for both mainland China and Taiwan to have representation and was doomed to failure.

The Vietnam War now dominated the headlines as American involvement deepened and international opposition to the war grew. Yet the UN was at the sidelines, unable to give leadership in ending the conflict. Gérard Pelletier later recalled that Trudeau often spoke about the war in these times and, like Ryan, Laurendeau, and most Quebec intellectuals, strongly opposed American involvement. Vietnam, which had charmed him so much on his 1949 voyage, disappointed him when he returned in 1959. It no longer had "charme" or "classe." He noticed the police everywhere and the presence of the International Control Commission members, including many Canadians. Sadly he noted: "The country will perhaps be divided forever." More disturbing was the evidence that the government in the South depended entirely on the support of the Americans, who were ubiquitous.[53] However, Marcel Cadieux from External Affairs, who had served in Vietnam in the 1950s and detested Communist North Vietnam, discouraged Martin from criticizing American war policy. Trudeau, therefore, cast an increasingly wary eye towards the External Affairs Department and its minister, especially after he learned from Cadieux that Paul Martin favoured a conciliatory approach to the romance blooming between the government of Daniel Johnson and France. With Lalonde and others, he became sharply critical of Martin and warmly welcomed the January re-entry to the Cabinet of Walter Gordon, a vocal critic of American foreign policy.[54]

Gordon's return would be fundamentally important to Trudeau's future, although he barely knew Gordon at the time. Gordon was an ardent economic nationalist, an outspoken opponent of the war in Vietnam, a critic of Canadian membership in

NATO and in NORAD, and an increasingly strong critic of Pearson, whose political career he had financed and nurtured more than anyone else.[55] And the times increasingly favoured the left. *Canadian Dimension,* a magazine founded by one of the Vietnam "draft dodgers" from the United States who took refuge in Canada, polled many leading intellectuals in the winter of 1967 and discovered that most expected a "nationalist and socialist" government to rule Canada very soon. Pearson sensed the change and—in an astute political move—began to tack to the left.[56]

Gordon had expected that Maurice Lamontagne would join him in the Cabinet. When he did not, Gordon asked Pearson for an explanation. Pearson replied that Jean Marchand had vetoed the appointment—information Gordon immediately passed on to Lamontagne, who then confronted Pearson. The prime minister confirmed the story and invited the two men to his residence to sort it out. There Marchand told Lamontagne that the Quebec caucus would not accept his reappointment to Cabinet. It was a brutal blow and pointed both to Marchand's pre-eminence in federal Quebec politics and to the opportunity open to new Cabinet members from Quebec. Not surprisingly, on April 4, 1967, Trudeau succeeded the battered Cardin as minister of justice. In a single, quite brilliant stroke, Pearson appointed the most outstanding constitutional specialist in the party just as Quebec and the Constitution were becoming the major issues facing the government, and he strengthened the left of the party just as the NDP threatened the Liberals in English Canada. On both fronts, Trudeau acted quickly to reinforce his strengths.[57]

The times appeared to be perfectly tailored to fit Pierre Trudeau. In 1967 the very foundations of tradition seemed to be collapsing as John Lennon declared the Beatles more popular than Jesus Christ, the pill broke down ancient sexual taboos, and the young cheered for revolution. Canada finally seemed ready to abandon its reserve as television broke through restrictions in its treatment of sex, politics, and religion. Above all, it was Canada's Centennial Year, which began quietly but, by late spring, had become a noisy celebration of a North American country that was suddenly and unexpectedly "cool." Expo 67 in Montreal became a wildly successful world's fair that gave a sophisticated and modern face both to Quebec and to Canada.[58]

In English Canada, even *Canadian Business* magazine welcomed Trudeau enthusiastically and declared that the "swinging millionaire from Montreal who drove sports cars and wore ascots into the House of Commons" represented "the best traditions of the *engagé* intellectual." The French press was more restrained, including Claude Ryan in *Le Devoir*, who complained that Trudeau did not reflect Quebec opinion in his constitutional orthodoxy. Trudeau brushed off the complaints, quickly organized his office, and embarked on an astonishingly ambitious agenda that would transform Canada. Justice Department officials who had heard of Trudeau's "playboy" reputation were astounded to encounter a remarkably disciplined worker with great intellectual ability and an unusually retentive memory. Years later, when asked what was most impressive about Trudeau, staff members matched each other with tales about his "elephantine" memory for detail, to the point where he could recall memoranda by date and even by paragraph. Nicole Sénécal, a press secretary, said she never had a "boss" so difficult yet so wonderful.[59]

Initially, he focused on two major items: the Canadian Constitution and the reform of the Criminal Code. It was the latter that attracted the public's interest as the forty-seven-year-old bachelor announced plans to legalize homosexual acts between consenting adults, permit abortion when a mother's health was endangered, and broaden greatly the grounds for divorce. "Justice," Trudeau told Peter Newman, then a journalist for the *Toronto Star*, "should be regarded more and more as a department planning for the society of tomorrow, not merely the government's legal advisor . . . Society is throwing up problems all the time—divorce, abortions, family planning, pollution, etc.—and it's no longer enough to review our statutes every 20 years."

Within six months, in the late fall of 1967, Trudeau introduced these historic amendments to Canada's Criminal Code, and just before Christmas the House unanimously approved the first divorce reforms in one hundred years. A senior NDP member, H.W. Herridge, praised Trudeau for creating a "precedent in Canadian history." Where other governments had avoided divorce reform as "politically dangerous," Trudeau himself had moved forward and had shown he was "a very sensitive, humanitarian individual." According to one correspondent, "Trudeau blushed."[60]

Lester Pearson had announced his resignation a week before Herridge spoke. The Centennial had brought much satisfaction but also considerable grief. In late July Charles de Gaulle made his official visit to Canada aboard the French warship *Colbert*. After landing at Quebec City, the French president made a royal progress along the historic North Shore to Montreal. There, on July 24, from the balcony of Montreal's Hôtel de Ville, the greatest French leader of the century made his infamous declaration, "Vive le Québec libre," before a huge and enthusiastic throng. Lester Pearson was livid; Paul Martin Sr., who was in Montreal, counselled caution. When the Cabinet met on July 25, both Jean Marchand and Robert Winters were reluctant to rebuke de Gaulle.

Trudeau disagreed: according to the Cabinet minutes, the minister of justice "said the people in France would think the Government was weak if it did not react." Moreover, he pointed out, de Gaulle did not have the support of French intellectuals, and the French press was opposed to him. Despite the hesitations of Martin, his most senior English Canadian minister, and Marchand, the leading Quebec minister, Pearson heeded Trudeau's advice and his own instincts. With the help of the Quebec ministers, he drafted a harsh rebuke to de Gaulle, who responded by cancelling his plans to go to Ottawa. The incident strengthened Trudeau's role within the Cabinet.[61] It also raised the debate about Quebec's future to a new intensity.

During the summer, Trudeau and Marchand consolidated their hold on the Quebec federal Liberals. The provincial party was debating a historic resolution that René Lévesque had placed before them, calling for Quebec independence followed by negotiations for an economic union with Canada. It was, Claude Ryan correctly wrote, "a new step towards the moment of truth." For Trudeau and many of his colleagues, it was proof that Lévesque had long been a closet separatist. When the resolution was defeated, Lévesque and others left the Liberal Party and formed the Mouvement souveraineté-association—the base from which the Parti Québécois took form. At the MSA's first meeting, Lévesque promised the triumph of a party committed to Quebec sovereignty, a party he would lead. The battle of Canada had begun.[62]

Lester Pearson had fought his last fight, and he knew his successor would face new battles on more difficult terrain where his skills were poor. So did Walter Gordon, whose influence in the party remained strong because he had mentored so many MPs and retained his close links with the *Toronto Star*. Gordon called Trudeau in mid-November and invited him to his Château Laurier suite to meet with two of his Cabinet allies, Edgar Benson and Larry Pennell. All four men agreed that they were not excited about "any of the leadership candidates."[63] Pearson had let it be known that the next leader should come from Quebec, and he initially turned towards Marchand. But Marchand's flaws were many: his English was not good; his voluble personality was attractive but politically risky; and his judgment was not always sound. During the de Gaulle incident, he had been offside with Cabinet opinion, and his plan to allow public servants to unionize and strike was unpopular on editorial pages and among many of his colleagues.

Trudeau, in contrast, was attracting increasing attention, which he shrewdly did not exploit. The plan he had developed in the late 1930s, when he first determined he wanted a public and political life, remained in place. He would cloak himself in mystery and be the friend of all and the intimate of none. Moreover, the extraordinary discipline he revealed in bringing the Criminal Code legislation forward while simultaneously acting as the federal leader on constitutional matters dispelled most of the criticisms about the swinging playboy who had never worked.

Many friends commented that they had never seen Trudeau as happy as in the summer of 1967. True, there were some disappointments. His mother, who had nurtured his dreams of a public career, was no longer able to appreciate his success. The last note from her in his papers is a couple of tragically broken sentences from Florida written in the spring of 1965 as Alzheimer's disease began to infiltrate her once lively, curious, and considerable mind. Her decline created a gap in his life that none could fill.

In Ottawa he was still frequently seen with Madeleine Gobeil, who taught at Carleton University and attracted great attention with an interview she did with Jean-Paul Sartre for *Playboy* magazine in 1966. They dined together regularly, talked long into the night, and shared their excitement about the new world unfolding before them. She introduced Trudeau to Sartre and Simone de Beauvoir, and, probably more meaningfully, to the first James Bond movies—which, not surprisingly, Pierre relished.

Pierre's most intense relationship during this decade appears to have been with Carroll Guérin, who now lived mostly in Britain. But after she and Trudeau spent that memorable summer together on the beach at St. Tropez, sharing an intense affair, she became ill with an incurable virus. He saw her the next summer, although she was, in her own words, no longer fully a woman. They met again in 1964, when she was confined to a wheelchair and any physical activity was impossible. It was, she wrote, "very generous of you to want to meet me under these circumstances. I realize only too well what a burden I am, even to myself."[64]

Guérin never forgot Trudeau's kindness. He also persuaded her mother, who regarded her artist daughter's European residence as expensive whimsy and her illness as primarily psychological, to become more generous. Like most of Trudeau's female friends, Guérin was emotionally voluble and poured out her feelings freely and passionately. She, too, found Trudeau "emotionally withdrawn" and sought to turn the keys that locked his core. In the summer of 1967 he disappointed her when she hoped to meet him in Corsica. Instead, he left the Buonaparte Hotel before she arrived for the rendezvous, without informing her and without leaving a forwarding address. She admitted he had not "really sounded very enthusiastic over the phone in Montreal" when they planned the meeting. But, she wrote, "maybe it was all for the best . . . Anything you do, Pierre, will always be very close to my heart; but it would seem that as far as living together is concerned we are not able to manage . . . With all my heart, dearest Pierre, I wish you all the success that you so rightly deserve." She would retain her deep affection for Trudeau despite being "stood up."[65]

At Christmas that same year, it was Trudeau's turn to be stood up. He decided that December to escape Canada's winter and the increasing attention of politicians and the press by flying with two friends, Tim Porteous and Jim Domville, to Tahiti's Club Méditerranée, where he intended to read Gibbon's *Rise and Fall of the Roman Empire* and think about whether to seek the leadership of the Liberal Party. There, one afternoon as he was waterskiing, he attracted the attention of an alluring nineteen-year-old college student who was lying on a raft. Stunning in her bathing suit and with eyes that immediately entranced, Margaret drew crowds around her. Pierre came over to her and began to talk about Plato and student revolution—Plato, he knew well, while she was intimate with student revolt. She told him that her name was Margaret Sinclair and she was attending the new Simon Fraser University in British Columbia, where student radicalism was in full flower. She was, in her words, drinking it all in—"the music, the drugs, the life." She "jibed only at opium, scared off by Coleridge." Yet she "did try mescaline one day, and spent hours sitting up a tree, wishing I were a bird."

Margaret's parents were holidaying at the Club Med with her. Her mother, the wife of the Honourable James Sinclair, a war veteran who had been a minister in the St. Laurent government, told her daughter that the man she had met was Pierre Trudeau, Canada's minister of justice and the "black sheep" of the Liberal Party. Entranced by Margaret, Pierre joined the family at the long Club Med table for dinner each night. Margaret remembers she was not "particularly impressed," even though her parents were increasingly aware of his growing attraction to their daughter. Later, when he, so very "shy" and polite, asked her to go deep-sea fishing, she initially said yes but went off instead with "Yves," a handsome young French waterski instructor who was also the grandson of the founder of Club Mediterranée. He danced like a Tahitian and loved long into the night. But Pierre persisted, "old and square" though he might be. Margaret's vitality, her astonishing beauty, and her refreshing candour left a deep impression on him as he flew home. When he next saw her, at the Liberal leadership convention three months later, the black sheep of the Liberal Party was about to become its "white knight." At that moment, suddenly, he recalled Tahiti.[66]

—

CHAPTER 10

A TALE OF TWO CITIES

érard Pelletier was grumpy as he arrived for dinner in a small private room at Montreal's Café Martin on a cold Sunday evening on January 14, 1968. Jean Marchand and Pierre Trudeau, his dinner companions, were "hale and hearty, in wonderful shape" after vacations in the sun, while he was "as pale as a grub." Marchand had summoned his colleagues to discuss the fate of the Liberal Party as it faced an imminent leadership contest. The three had met in mid-summer and decided that it would be best if there were no francophone candidate because "the man to govern Canada was inevitably a conciliator, and in the present situation, francophone Canadians were in no mood for compromise." But Marchand had changed his mind in December. There had been almost no francophone presence when the Progressive Conservatives chose Robert Stanfield as their new leader in September 1967. If there were no francophone candidates for the Liberal convention in April 1968, what would Quebec conclude? "That the Canadian government and the big federal parties are run by English Canadians, and we have nothing to do with it." The logic seemed impeccable, but the real surprise was Marchand's decision about his own future. He would not be a candidate—it must be Trudeau.[1]

Pelletier immediately realized that he would have "a ringside seat" for a historic political battle, and, the following day, he began a diary to record the Liberal leadership contest of 1968. Simultaneously Richard Stanbury, a newly appointed Toronto senator and the principal organizer of the leadership convention, also began a diary. Back in the fall, Lester Pearson had confided his intention to resign as prime minister to Stanbury and to John Nichol, the president of the Liberal Federation, and had correctly predicted that the leadership race would be hotly contested. Pearson hoped for a strong Quebec candidate — Marchand was his favourite — and he worried about Paul Martin Sr., the external affairs minister, who he believed belonged too much to the Liberal past at a time when new voices were essential.

As Richard Stanbury began preparations for the convention, he shared these worries. In early January, when he scheduled his meetings with the candidates, he began with Martin. "Who's your candidate?" Martin demanded. "Of course I'm impartial," Stanbury replied. "Oh, you and I know that, but who's your candidate?" Stanbury said he thought it was a "fine wide-open race and that anyone might win." Martin "harrumphed," and the conversation ended. Stanbury already knew that Martin, who had stood first in the polls, was failing to find his expected support. Toronto, which had been a Tory bastion for most of Canada's first century, was now a dynamic centre of Liberal intrigue, dreams, and fears.[2]

In the sixties, Toronto shucked off its conservative raiments and customs and donned the more colourful garb of its hundreds of thousands of immigrants. The formerly staid citizenry began to drink wine, open nightclubs, and play professional sports on Sunday. Stanbury still taught his Bible class every week, but the dense Protestant, British, and Conservative atmosphere surrounding the city was quickly lifting. Those traditional forces continued to hold sway on Bay Street, which, since the 1950s, had vanquished all its economic competitors. But Montreal remained Canada's largest city and a very sexy one too, as the elegant modernity of Expo 67 and the swinging new night life in the old city testified. Pierre Trudeau's path to 24 Sussex Drive would pass through the political heart of Canada's two largest cities. As they set out to persuade him to run, Pelletier and Marchand told Trudeau they would "handle" Quebec; the rest of Canada was his concern. He barely knew "the rest," but English Canada was quickly learning about Trudeau who the wily young political operative Keith Davey had not even considered as a possible candidate two months earlier.[3] He cleverly borrowed *Globe and Mail* editorialist Martin O'Malley's statement "The state has no place in the bedrooms of the nation" and, in a December 22, 1967, television interview made it famously his own.[4] It caught precisely the new spirit of the times.

On January 13, 1968, the Gallup Poll revealed that the Liberals had gained on the Conservatives, who had moved ahead in the polls after they chose the Nova Scotia premier, Robert Stanfield, in September. The Liberals now trailed by only six points. That same day Peter Newman reported that a group of Toronto academics were "rallying the forces" behind Pierre Trudeau. He described the instigators—Ramsay Cook, John Saywell, and William Kilbourn—as three of the academic community's brightest young men, although he wrongly described these historians as political scientists.* Their petition imploring Trudeau to consider the Liberal leadership quickly

---

* Ramsay Cook was instrumental in organizing these petitions, but William Kilbourn got only one signature: Pierre Berton's. Saywell, apparently, took little part in the campaign. At the University of Toronto, radical student activists Michael Ignatieff and his friend Bob Rae also rallied behind the Trudeau candidacy

gained signatures from hundreds of English-Canadian academics who were fascinated by the possibility of a Trudeau candidacy.[5] Peter Newman linked the petition and its "assault on smug old-line thinking" with the forthcoming publication of Pierre Berton's book *Smug Minority*, which, in Berton's words, asserted that "the kind of political leadership we've had has been the wrong leadership, because it has been restricted to a cosy little group." Trudeau, Berton claimed, would save Canada from this coterie:

> Trudeau is the guy who really excites me; Trudeau represents a new look at politics in this country; he is the swinging young man I think the country needs. What we need is a guy with ideas so fresh and so different that he [is] going to be able to view the country from a different point of view. He has many weaknesses—inexperience, inability to project on the platform and all this. But they said these things about Kennedy too.

These comments from Newman and Berton, English Canada's most influential journalists, appeared one day before Marchand, Pelletier, and Trudeau gathered for the fateful dinner at the Café Martin. Yet when Marchand said after the first aperitif that Trudeau should run, Trudeau was, in Pelletier's words, "stunned." He left his boeuf bourguignon untouched on the plate.

Why was Trudeau stunned? His close friend Jacques Hébert had been urging him to run for the leadership for months. In the fall he had met with Walter Gordon and other English-Canadian MPs and mused about leadership. Pelletier and Marchand were probably unaware of this meeting, but Trudeau surely recalled the important encounter. Pearson had told Marchand that there must be a Quebec "French" candidate, and there were only two possibilities—Marchand or Trudeau. In Montreal, Pearson's aide Marc Lalonde did not take a Christmas vacation because he was busy organizing the potential Trudeau candidacy. Trudeau's own assistants, Eddie Rubin and Pierre de Bané, helped Lalonde put the details in place—and Trudeau knew what they were doing. Just before New Year's Eve, Lalonde persuaded Rubin and Gordon Gibson, the executive assistant to BC minister Arthur Laing, to rent an Ottawa office for the campaign. Rubin found the office, gave Gibson $1,000 to pay for it, and Gibson signed the lease—all to conceal the office's true purpose. By that time Walter Gordon had told the *Toronto Star* that he favoured Marchand for the leadership, but, if Marchand did not run, Trudeau would be his choice.[6] All this had happened before the dinner at Café Martin.

As usual, Trudeau's coyness was deliberate and wise. He knew that Marchand's support was crucial, but he was not yet certain that his colleague did not want to run. In Tahiti, he told Tim Porteous that he believed Marchand would eventually run. When Trudeau, Pelletier, and Marchand met again on January 18, Trudeau said he would be a candidate if Marchand refused, and then he listed his own weaknesses. Pelletier, who was much closer to Marchand than was Trudeau, believed that Trudeau "really wanted to be sure that Marchand's refusal was final." It was. Marchand privately and publicly attributed his refusal to his health—a serious drinking problem was already developing—and to his limited English vocabulary and heavy French accent. In December he had already told André Laurendeau that he had no desire to succeed Pearson, as Davidson Dunton had suggested to him. He told Laurendeau that he didn't enjoy living in Ottawa: "I don't like to have to speak English all the time; it diminishes me by 50%. It's a crazy job, worse even than being a trade unionist— there at least you've got roots."[7]

A second reason for Trudeau's seeming reluctance was that he had several opportunities to gain exposure in the forthcoming few weeks, and they would be lost if he declared his candidacy.

The Quebec Liberal Federation was meeting in Montreal on January 28, and Trudeau could advance his views there on law reform and constitutional review. Even more important was the constitutional conference that Pearson had promised after the "Confederation of Tomorrow" conference organized by John Robarts, the Ontario premier, in the fall of 1966. Trudeau and Pearson had responded by expressing a new willingness to discuss constitutional change and, in particular, a Canadian Bill of Rights that would form part of a revised Canadian Constitution. Trudeau had promised that he would consult the premiers before the constitutional conference. If he was a candidate, he would have to resign as minister of justice, a move that would imperil the chances for a breakthrough at the constitutional talks.

Finally, Trudeau was genuinely fearful of the intense glare of media attention on his private life. As reporters began to cluster about him, and his photograph appeared regularly in newspapers, he recognized that celebrity brought political gains, but at the expense of the inner core he had long and jealously protected. Madeleine Gobeil, who saw him often, recalls his intense need for a private space, away from other people. Right from the start of his time in the spotlight, he never bothered to correct the many stories that stated his age as forty-six during the leadership race.[8] Moreover, he told Margaret Sinclair before they married that in recent years he had prayed every night for a wife and a family. He was now forty-eight, an age when fatherhood becomes difficult and a first marriage rare. Would the prime minister's office end those hopes forever?

—

On January 18 Trudeau set out on his tour to meet the provincial premiers, and an increasingly curious press followed him. Accompanied by Eddie Rubin, who openly promoted his minister, and the eminent constitutional specialist Carl Goldenberg, Trudeau's tour was unexpectedly eventful and successful. W.A.C. "Wacky" Bennett, British Columbia's Social Credit premier, ignored Trudeau's statement that the two of them would not meet the press during the course of their confidential discussions. To everyone's surprise, Bennett told the assembled journalists that Trudeau impressed him so much that "if he ever decides to move to British Columbia, there's a place for him in my Cabinet."

More important than Bennett's praise was the endorsement from the equally eccentric Liberal premier of Newfoundland, Joey Smallwood. Observers expected that Smallwood would support Trade Minister Robert Winters, whom he knew well and who came from the Atlantic provinces. However, Winters had dithered about his candidacy, and this indecision exasperated Smallwood. When Smallwood met Trudeau on January 25, he immediately took him and his party to his private dining room, brought out a vintage Chambertin, asked Trudeau how to pronounce Chambertin properly, demanded that his colleagues try to match Trudeau's elegant accent, and proceeded to entertain his guests with a breathless monologue ranging over many topics but centred on himself. When Trudeau's assistants became anxious because the late hour meant that Trudeau would miss his visit to Nova Scotia, Smallwood called Nova Scotia premier G.I. Smith and asked him to join the party, where the wine—Smallwood called it "syrup"—was flowing freely.

Smith refused, and eventually the federal party took its leave. As he was departing, Carl Goldenberg, who knew Smallwood well, told the premier that Trudeau was the finest political philosopher in Parliament. Smallwood no doubt fancied himself as the finest on "The Rock" and immediately called a press conference so that Trudeau and he could match thoughts and wits. There in the lobby of the Confederation Building in St. John's, a city Trudeau scarcely knew and with a premier he had never met before,

Smallwood appeared to endorse Trudeau. He was, Smallwood declared, "the perfect Canadian" and the "most brilliant" MP of all. This bizarre performance was of fundamental importance to Trudeau because Smallwood controlled the votes as no other provincial premier did. His support for Trudeau in the leadership race would eventually provide the margin needed for the victory of Pierre Trudeau and the defeat of Bob Winters.[9]

After a brief visit with Premier Louis Robichaud of New Brunswick, Trudeau went directly to the Quebec Liberal Federation meeting in Montreal, where Marchand and Lalonde made sure that Trudeau would play the central role. Even in the absence of the leadership contest, he would have attracted attention because of the constitutional issues that Lester Pearson and Quebec premier Daniel Johnson identified as the principal concerns of their governments. Moreover, the proposed Criminal Code revisions, particularly those respecting abortion and homosexuality, were causing increasing criticism in rural Quebec and within the Roman Catholic Church. Both the Constitution and the Criminal Code were Trudeau's responsibility, and both created dangers and opportunities for him in his bid to become the Canadian prime minister.

The "committee" to elect Trudeau met for the first time at the home of the thirty-seven-year-old Marc Lalonde on January 25, just as Smallwood was giving his major endorsement of the Trudeau campaign. Donald Macdonald, an Ontario MP three years younger than Lalonde but close to the powerful Walter Gordon, reported that seventy Ontario delegates were already assured. Pelletier said that Quebec would provide "at least 450." Trudeau's committee members were young, eager to bring their generation to the party's forefront. Seniors had long prevailed there—Louis St. Laurent was sixty-six when he was chosen in 1948, and Lester Pearson was sixty-one in 1958. The sixties were different: in the United States, John Kennedy called for the torch to be passed to a new generation, while in Quebec, forty-five-year-old René Lévesque was wooing the youth into a swelling separatist force. Trudeau's new voice needed to be heard to win this essential Quebec support. Lalonde and Marchand made sure that Trudeau was the only respondent to questions about "special status" on the panel on Canadian federalism sponsored by the Quebec Liberal Federation on Sunday, January 28—just in time for the Monday media.[10]

The newspapers the following morning reported how Trudeau had brilliantly outlined the federalist option and how the delegates jumped to their feet, applauded, and sang, "Il a gagné ses épaulettes." Even Claude Ryan of Le Devoir, who was increasingly critical of Trudeau's rejection of the concept of special status, admitted that Trudeau had been most impressive. Where delegates had expected a cold, distant, and abstract intellectual, they heard a remarkable communicator "capable, without oratorical artifice, of raising to a degree of lucidity and simplicity, an accomplishment that is perhaps the apex of eloquence in our times."[11] This surprising reaction, given Ryan's doubts about Trudeau's constitutional views, surely gave Trudeau more confidence, but he was not yet ready to declare.

Events were moving fast—too fast, it seemed to some. On January 30 the Canadian Press ran a story, which appeared across Canada, that "professional politicians" were asking, "Has Justice Minister Trudeau, without even declaring candidacy for the Liberal leadership, peaked too soon?" The next day a "Mrs. R.A. King" responded to the story in a letter to the Montreal Star: "Last summer, John Diefenbaker chided Mr. Trudeau for appearing in the House of Commons in casual clothes. As far as I am concerned, if this brilliant Canadian chooses to run for the Liberal leadership and becomes prime minister, he can preside over parliament in a bedsheet!" Such responses infuriated the other candidates, and the Canadian Press reported that there was "naturally some ill-feeling . . . at Mr. Trudeau's jet-propelled rise to national prominence."[12]

The reports were true. Convention organizer Richard Stanbury, who in his diary had described the Montreal meeting as a "good launching pad" for Trudeau, learned that Mel McInnes, the special assistant to Allan MacEachen, the minister of national health and welfare, was complaining that the party hierarchy favoured Trudeau. Stanbury wrote to MacEachen offering to resign if the minister truly believed he was not impartial. MacEachen accepted the reassurance. However, it did not help that his relative and close friend Bob Stanbury, a Toronto MP, announced at the end of January that he was organizing a committee to "draft" Trudeau. Moreover, Bob Stanbury told the press that a poll in his riding indicated that Trudeau was already the frontrunner, even though not formally a candidate.

Gérard Pelletier, who, unlike most journalists, had not been impressed by Trudeau's performance at the Quebec Liberal Federation,* now faced constant pressure from Paul Martin, to whom he was parliamentary secretary. First Martin demanded to know if Trudeau was running; then, within days, he was so obsessed with the subject that, four times, he called

---

* Pelletier believed that Trudeau spoke well, but he confided to his diary that Trudeau's "tasteless jokes about France-Quebec relations" irritated him. He wondered whether they indicated a broader problem: "Making jokes (and Lord knows they're easy to make) implies, after all, that France-Quebec relations are unimportant. Knowing what he actually thinks on the subject, I'd be happy if he spoke seriously. But I don't understand the lack of sensitivity he puts on this matter, nor his apparent lack of respect for others' feelings on the subject. Perhaps it's a sign of his impatience." Gérard Pelletier, *Years of Choice, 1960–1968* (Toronto: Methuen, 1987), 264–65.

Pelletier "Pierre." On January 23 he even sent his son, "Paul Martin *Junior*, as he calls himself," to tell Pelletier that his father wanted to be identified with the "leading wing of the [Quebec] party and not with the *old guard*." However, members of "the leading wing" refused to sign up with Martin because they were waiting for Trudeau. They would continue to wait.[13]

Trudeau had one more event he and his supporters did not want to miss: the opportunity to challenge Daniel Johnson at the constitutional conference of February 5–7, 1968, in Ottawa. There, Lester Pearson, barely concealing his preference for a francophone successor, seated Trudeau next to him. He had already ceded the intellectual ground to Trudeau, who, on February 1, had issued a booklet, in Pearson's name, entitled *Federalism for the Future*, which outlined the federal government's stance and Pearson's own views.[14] After its release, Trudeau gave interviews outlining how the federal government would approach both the conference and the demands from Quebec. The booklet rejected special status and the "two nations" policy espoused by Daniel Johnson, the federal Progressive Conservatives, and the NDP because Trudeau believed that special status would lead inevitably to separation. Instead, it emphasized the linguistic rights of francophones throughout Canada, placing them on an equal basis with anglophones in Quebec.

Trudeau had known Daniel Johnson since the 1940s, when they were both conservative young Catholic nationalists in Quebec who strongly opposed conscription and the war policies of the federal Liberals. In the close world of Montreal legal, religious, and academic circles, Johnson and Trudeau had frequently encountered each other, but their relationship soured after Johnson was appointed Maurice Duplessis's assistant. In that role he became the target of nasty cartoons by Hudon in *Le Devoir*, where he was depicted as a court jester, and of scurrilous jibes by opponents who labelled him "Danny Boy." As a Union nationale member of the National Assembly since 1946, however, Johnson was often underestimated, certainly by Lesage. It came as a shock, then, when he stunningly defeated the Quebec Liberals in 1966 and began to consolidate his victory.

Johnson was highly intelligent and a shrewd politician, yet he was not ready for Trudeau at the constitutional conference. He expected Pearson to lead the debate with his customary diplomatic skill, and the other premiers, who shared some of his doubts about the Trudeau program, to accept the recommendations on linguistic equality proposed by the Royal Commission on Bilingualism and Biculturalism. Indeed, he had welcomed the initiative in the preceding weeks. What he did not anticipate was the major role Trudeau would play. Before the conference, Trudeau spoke derisively of "the little empire" the Quebec provincial government sought to build. He told Peter Newman, his ever more enthusiastic promoter, that he wanted to "take the fuse out of explosive Quebec nationalism by making sure that Quebec is not a ghetto for French Canadians—that all of Canada is theirs."

To Johnson's satisfaction, on the Monday morning in the historic West Block, Pearson opened the conference in expansive, optimistic but dramatic words: "Here the road forks," he said. "If we choose wrongly, we will leave to our children and our children's children a country in fragments, and we ourselves will have become the failures of Confederation." Reassuring speeches followed from the other premiers. Johnson spoke third, after Pearson and Ontario's John Robarts. He was dour and direct in stating that only the "adamant few" denied that Canada was made up of "two nations." It was essential that a two-partner Canada be created to ensure the maintenance of the "ten-partner" Canada. Other premiers responded, some comically (W.A.C. Bennett and Joey Smallwood) and others icily (Alberta premier E.C. Manning, who warned of a constitutional "Munich" whereby Quebec would be appeased at the cost of Canadian unity). Outside the

West Block, a lonely protester took up this theme on a placard: "Another Munich. Another Appeasement."

On the Tuesday morning, Johnson lauded the premiers' general acceptance of linguistic equality but then reiterated his demand for fundamental constitutional change. As he listened, Trudeau was sitting beside the genial and casual Pearson. The intense television lights sharpened all the participants' features but were particularly favourable to Trudeau's chiselled face and striking eyes. Johnson, in contrast, appeared uncomfortable under the glare. In his response to the Quebec premier's speech, Trudeau bluntly expressed his strong opposition to special status and his belief that these proposed changes to the Canadian Constitution would only undermine the position of Quebec's MPs in Ottawa. He further emphasized the importance of a Canadian Charter of Human Rights to enshrine linguistic rights, a proposal that Manning and Johnson had dismissed the previous day. His tone ever more biting, his voice metallic, Trudeau responded to Johnson's reference to him as the "député de Mont-Royal" by describing the premier as the "député de Bagot."

Sensing the tension and worried himself about Trudeau's tone, Pearson called for a coffee break. During the break, Trudeau curtly nodded at Johnson and muttered that the Quebec premier was seeking to destroy the federal government. Johnson sneered that Trudeau was acting like a candidate, not a federal minister.

Reporters rushed from the room to file their stories. The federal government has finally found its own voice, they stated, as they ignored the complicated substance of federal-provincial relations and focused on Trudeau's articulate attack on Johnson. English Canadians who had been troubled by the weak federal response to Johnson's demands for equality or independence were impressed, perhaps because they were weary of the protracted debate about the Constitution and probably because Trudeau had confronted Johnson so effectively. French-speaking Canadians had been given a rare opportunity to hear an important national debate in Ottawa in French. More could have been achieved, but the conference did have two notable results: the acceptance of linguistic equality for both official languages in the government of Canada, and the creation of a formal structure for review of the Constitution through regular conferences. They were no small accomplishment.[15]

"At the beginning of February," Jean Marchand later recalled, "Pierre Trudeau was really created." After the hesitancy that had seemed to mark the response of the Pearson government to Quebec's demands for greater legislative powers, Trudeau came to represent clarity, novelty, and strength. While Claude Ryan and many Quebec editorialists lamented both the tone and the substance of Trudeau's remarks, English-Canadian editorialists welcomed his approach. Quebec sociologist Stéphane Kelly later described how Trudeau's "virile performance" at the conference made him a Hamiltonian candidate, "a strong and authoritative leader, capable of establishing order after ten years of political instability."[16]

After the conference ended, Trudeau joined his assistant Eddie Rubin and other members of his prospective campaign team. They were probably worried about the intensity of the exchange and its impact, but youthful organizer Jim Davey, who had been assessing Trudeau's support across Canada, reported that the effect was electric. He concluded: "Trudeau should be presented as he really was, as himself, both for his own personality and his own ideas about Canada, its problems and its great opportunities." Once the analysis was done, Trudeau walked down Parliament Hill to the Château Laurier, where he stayed when he was in Ottawa, and swam in the elegant art deco pool in the basement of the grand hotel. As he methodically did his laps, he realized the prize might be his. But it was not certain.

—

Trudeau's opponents were already in the field, and delegates were making commitments. Paul Martin began his phone calls before breakfast and continued late into the night, in complete disregard of Canada's varied time zones. Pelletier and Marchand thought that the bilingual Martin would take at least half the Quebec delegates if Trudeau did not run. Mitchell Sharp, Canada's finance minister, was constantly in the news, and his elegance and authority had considerable influence in both the Canadian public service and corporate boardrooms. Paul Hellyer, the defence minister, was already at forty-four a multi-millionaire and a seasoned political veteran. Through his historic if controversial unification of the defence forces during the Pearson government, he had stood up to the generals and never retreated. John Turner, at thirty-eight, was even younger and already a junior minister. He had grown up in British Columbia, won a Rhodes Scholarship to Oxford, danced with an enchanted Princess Margaret, learned French and practised law in Montreal, and had invited Trudeau to his wedding to Geills Kilgour, the daughter of a leading Winnipeg businessman. This impressive and handsome young politician, Peter Newman wrote, "jogged into the race . . . with a list of professional and personal attributes that made him sound like a story-book prime minister, or at least a story-book prince."

Other candidates included the brilliant albeit idiosyncratic Eric Kierans, who had been a minister in the Lesage government; Joe Greene, a lawyer from eastern Ontario, who consciously appealed to the boys and girls from back concessions; and the Nova Scotian Allan MacEachen, the craftiest parliamentarian of his times. It was already a remarkable field when Gérard Pelletier and Pierre Trudeau drove together to Ottawa on Sunday evening, February 11, 1968, and tried to sort out Trudeau's confused thoughts.[17]

Trudeau told Pelletier that he was close to a decision, but uncertainty persisted. Marchand was working hard in Quebec, but

Claude Ryan, the editor of *Le Devoir*, was preparing to endorse Sharp; Maurice Sauvé was leaning towards Martin; and Maurice Lamontagne had become a bitter opponent of Trudeau. After the constitutional conference, André Laurendeau criticized Trudeau and expressed his support for Johnson, while René Lévesque, now organizing a separatist party, dismissed Trudeau as the new Nigger King (roi-nègre) of Quebec. Jean Lesage also made known his displeasure with Trudeau. Two impressive young francophone ministers, Jean-Luc Pepin and Jean Chrétien, had committed to Sharp, as had the powerful C.M. "Bud" Drury, whom Trudeau much admired. Although Quebec Liberal Party president Claude Frenette, who had won a decisive victory over a Hellyer candidate in January, was an enthusiastic Trudeau supporter, he and Marchand needed a decision from Trudeau soon. But Trudeau refused to decide. He told Pelletier that Sunday evening that he had two major considerations, which Pelletier summarized in his diary:

> Has he the right to run for the highest position in the party after only two years in Parliament and barely ten months in the Cabinet? Why is it that no one thought of him in November, and two months later his name is all over the press? Why is there all this agitation in the party, by all those who want to see him leader?

Always wary of the press, Trudeau found it "ironic and disquieting to be hoisted onto the shoulders of the media." His second consideration followed from the first:

> Even if he was convinced of the legitimacy of becoming a candidate, he would still take into account a "visceral resistance," a diffuse anxiety, "something" in him that counselled himself against the undertaking.

Pelletier responded to Trudeau at length on the first point as they continued their drive to Ottawa. Trudeau should not worry about his hesitations, he advised. If he did not hesitate, he would be presumptuous, but presumptuous he had never been. He would have to trust the judgment of others about his capacity to govern and the risks it involved. In Pelletier's view, the media attention, which was already dubbed "Trudeaumanie" in French and "Trudeaumania" in English, was in some ways a "spinoff" of the Kennedy legend that had so profoundly affected North American politics—and would again, in March 1968, as Bobby Kennedy began his historic and tragic quest for the American presidency. Trudeau should not worry, Pelletier insisted. "If that myth settled on the shoulders of an incompetent, a candidate without vigour, he would be crushed. But it happened that Trudeau had a certain stature. He would never be crushed by the myth. On the contrary, he had what was needed to sustain the myth and make it reality. Chance, but not only chance, had chosen Trudeau."

Pelletier then turned to the second objection and asked Trudeau, "Do you sleep well?" Yes, he replied, "very well," but it was in the mornings that he began to worry about feeling unhappy as prime minister. He would lose the *joie de vivre* and "never accomplish anything worthwhile." Pelletier again rejected Trudeau's fears and said that this resistance would disappear once he made a decision. He had seen what had happened since the three friends came to Ottawa. Unlike Marchand and himself, Trudeau took to Parliament and government "like a duck to water—every minute of it, or almost." Then Pelletier made the crucial point that the press did not know: Pierre, he said, "your whole life has been a preparation for politics." The car became silent. When they arrived and Pelletier shut off the engine, Trudeau remained seated. Finally he spoke: "I think you've convinced me," he said quietly. "I'll see, tomorrow morning."[18]

Finally, the die seemed cast when Pelletier, Marchand, and Trudeau met for lunch on February 13 in Marchand's office. Yet Trudeau still refused to make a commitment and demanded reassurance. They met again in the evening, but "the conversation slipped into the same old ruts." Earlier, on the weekend of February 9, Trudeau had gone to the Ontario Liberal convention, where his brief appearance resembled that of a rock star as young women squealed and grabbed at him while reporters thrust microphones into his face. He told an insistent crowd that he would decide within ten days. Bob Stanbury, Donald Macdonald, and many others who organized the Toronto meeting were becoming increasingly impatient as their political futures became hostage to Trudeau's delays. The same was true of Marchand and Pelletier after they met Trudeau for dinner on that Tuesday night. The conversation convinced Marchand and Pelletier that Trudeau probably would not run. They then went to a meeting of the Trudeau "team" without Trudeau and, in Pelletier's words, felt as though they were living "in a bad dream" as Trudeau's many Ottawa supporters plotted a Trudeau campaign that would likely die before birth. Trudeau apparently did not tell Marchand and Pelletier that he had met with Pearson earlier, before the dinner with them, and that the prime minister, whose common sense he had come to admire, had encouraged him to run. Later, he shared his thoughts with Marc Lalonde and Michael Pitfield before he walked slowly back to the Château Laurier and decided his fate that cold winter night.[19]

The next morning, Valentine's Day, Trudeau surprised Marchand and Pelletier in the Parliamentary Restaurant by telling them he would run. Marchand immediately announced that he would step down as Quebec leader at the Wednesday morning caucus and that Jean-Pierre Goyer, a fervent Trudeau supporter, would help him organize the Quebec caucus for Trudeau. Trudeau was not yet ready to go public with his decision, and he wanted proof of support. Goyer, accordingly, promised a crowd of over fifty Quebec MPs and senators for a noontime gathering on Thursday, February 15, but only about twenty showed up. It was disappointing, and also an indication that Trudeaumania might have swept the media but had run into some resistance on Parliament Hill. Trudeau fretted; Marchand fumed. Pelletier and others worked the phones and determined that caucus support in Quebec was strong. At 6:30 that evening the Trudeau team of Marchand and MPs Edgar Benson, Jean-Pierre Goyer, and Russell Honey met with assistants Eddie Rubin, Pierre Levasseur, Jim Davey, and Gordon Gibson. They carefully counted the potential support and concluded that Trudeau already had 675–700 votes on the first ballot. That number was not enough to win, which required about 1,200 votes, but it was enough to convince Trudeau that he should announce his candidacy the following day.[20]

On February 16, 1968, Trudeau walked across the street from his West Block office to the National Press Club and declared himself a leadership candidate. It was a remarkable announcement, unlike that of any leadership hopeful before. He drew the press into the conspiracy that he and his friends had created, and it captured them—for a while:

> If I try to assess what happened in the past two months, I have a suspicion you people [the press] had a lot to do with it. If anybody's to blame, I suppose it's you collectively. If there's anybody to thank, it's you collectively. To be quite frank, if I try to analyze it, well, I think in the subconscious mind of the press . . . it started out like a huge practical joke on the Liberal Party. I mean that, because, in some sense, the decision that I made this morning and last night is in some ways similar to that I arrived at when I entered the Liberal Party. It seemed to me, reading the press in the early stages a couple of months ago, it seemed

to me as though many of you were saying, you know, "We
dare the Liberal Party to choose a guy like Trudeau. Of
course, we know they never will, but we'll just dare them
to do it and we'll show that this is the man they could have
had as leader if they had wanted. Here's how great he is."

The press, Trudeau continued, then said that the Liberals
did not have the guts to choose the "good guy." Now, the joke had
blown up in the media's many faces and in his own face:

You know, people took it seriously. I saw this when—not
when the press thought I had a chance, and that I should
go, and so on—but when I saw the response from political
people, from members of the party and responsible members of parliament. This is when I began to wonder if, oh,
you know, this whole thing was not a bit more serious than
you and I had intended. And when members of parliament formed committees to draft me, and when I got
responsible Liberals in responsible positions in different
parts of the country telling me seriously that I should run,
I think what happened is that the joke became serious . . .
So I was stuck with it. Well, you're stuck with me.

Stick to Trudeau they did, until he finally became prime minister
of Canada less than two months later.[21]

—

Trudeau's hesitations had irritated many friends and puzzled the
other candidates. The pattern was familiar to some, such as Pelletier
and Marchand, who recalled earlier examples of Trudeau's reluctance. Yet the stakes were higher and, as Pelletier told Trudeau,
he had spent a lifetime preparing for the political career now

within his grasp. This time Pelletier could not "guess what was going on in the conscience, the emotions, the inner depths of a friend, even when one had known him for twenty years." His friend had refused to peel away the carefully constructed layers that shielded his emotional core. But despite his supporters' concerns, Trudeau had good reason to consider his decision carefully.

To begin, the one person whose consent he valued most had fallen silent. On weekends he would return to the family home, see his mother with her polished nails, perfect coiffure, elegant but conservative dress, take her hand and speak softly, but now she had no answers. Alzheimer's disease or some other form of dementia had closed Grace Trudeau's excellent mind at the very moment when her fondest dream was about to be realized. Trudeau was more alone than ever before.

Moreover, he was rightly wary of the media enthusiasm for his campaign. He knew that this embrace could chill quickly, as it had for Diefenbaker or Lesage, whose charisma had lasted but a fleeting moment. Journalist Leslie Roberts, a supporter, feared that the media's "constantly repetitive use of that idiotic word 'charisma'" could cause a counter-reaction through which Trudeau "could easily be laughed back to seventh place in the twelve-man league of leadership contenders by his own best friends."[22] Trudeau himself worried that he was simply an "epiphenomenon," a phantom floating above the reality of Canadian politics—a reality he barely knew. He also knew that his past had secrets that could quickly capture the front pages of all the dailies. Already, the maverick Toronto Liberal Ralph Cowan was passing around translations of Trudeau's bitter 1963 attack on the "defrocked prince of peace" Lester Pearson, and he promised more revelations. Trudeau, the scourge of separatists and the most eloquent supporter of a secular state in the sixties, had endorsed an independent, Catholic "Laurentie" in the early 1940s. He had championed Pétain and urged violence.

Many who now loathed him knew his past. Would they reveal it? How would it affect him?

In fact, he didn't appear to care. When asked on a Radio-Canada late-night comedy show to name his favourite author, he answered "Niccolò Machiavelli"—a startling choice for a demo-cratic aspirant. But it amused him and, apparently, his audience.[23] Politics, he seemed to be saying to himself and to others, could be playful.

Finally, Trudeau valued his privacy and often reacted to attacks in a decidedly personal manner—as in his protracted dis-pute with Father Braun in the early fifties over his trip to the Soviet Union. When he became a political celebrity in the winter of 1968, the gossip, jealousy, and suspicion that invariably attach themselves to prominence quickly abounded. Christina McCall, who knew Ottawa well in those days, remembered the Conservative candidate in the Beauce who, in denouncing Trudeau's legislation regarding homosexuality, said that the bill was "for queers and fairies," adding, gratuitously, that Trudeau was a bachelor. Walter Gordon told McCall that, when he con-fronted Trudeau in the House of Commons lobby about the many rumours of his own homosexuality, Trudeau reacted angrily and suggested that the men making the charge should leave him alone with their wives for a couple of hours. According to one reli-able source, Pearson himself asked a close associate of Trudeau whether the justice minister was a homosexual. The infamous Canadian Intelligence Service, which had linked Pearson with Communist spy rings, began to transfer its attention to Trudeau, who had already made appearances in its pages.[24]

To these largely personal concerns, Trudeau now added a shrewd political assessment: it was by no means certain that he would win the leadership and the election to follow. The Progressive Conservative lead in the polls was 6 percent, and the Liberal leadership campaign was already proving divisive.

Moreover, the "draft Trudeau" campaign could identify only seven hundred supporters; he would need to attract about five hundred more to win the leadership. Neither he nor Marchand knew the party beyond Quebec, and they had to rely on the assessment of others to estimate his support. Surely all those church suppers, summer barbeques, and favours rendered over thirty-three years of Liberal service meant something for Paul Martin's candidacy! Was the party a largely hollow shell waiting to be filled with enthusiastic newcomers? Did it matter that his most eminent academic supporter in English Canada, the historian Ramsay Cook, had been a longtime supporter of the CCF-NDP and, in a 1965 private letter, had criticized Trudeau's affiliation with the Liberals while welcoming his presence in Ottawa? The political times were not normal or predictable. And it was fortunate for Trudeau they were not.

Trudeau announced his candidacy on Friday, February 16, and, three days later, the Liberal government was defeated on a budget item in the House of Commons. In the House, Finance Minister Mitchell Sharp and Acting Prime Minister Robert Winters had decided to go ahead on a third-reading vote against the advice of Allan MacEachen, the Liberal expert on House rules. The bells rang, the Conservatives rounded up members the Liberals thought were absent, and the Liberals lost the vote. Normally, that would mean the defeat of the government and an immediate election, presumably with Lester Pearson leading the Liberals in the campaign.

Pearson was holidaying in Jamaica, and three leadership candidates were absent. Pearson, "shocked and enraged," flew home and berated his colleagues for their irresponsible actions. He then persuaded Robert Stanfield to agree to a twenty-four-hour adjournment of the House. It was a fatal error for the Conservative leader, one the highly partisan John Diefenbaker would never have made. As Walter Gordon later said, all "Stanfield had to do . . . was to get up and walk out of the House [saying]: 'The Government is defeated; there is nothing more to do here.'" But Stanfield hesitated and lost. Pearson counterattacked, managed to delay the vote of confidence on the narrow item of the Monday night vote, and convinced the Créditistes to reverse their vote. Throughout the crisis, Trudeau gave constitutional law advice to Pearson and the Cabinet and performed coolly in the House of Commons in defending the government's stand. Immediately, he benefited most from the whole dramatic event.[25] The leadership race continued, but Mitchell Sharp's campaign had been mortally wounded.[26]

The press reacted sharply to the chaos in Liberal ranks. It confirmed for Trudeau the grumbling of his supporters Marc Lalonde and Michael Pitfield about the poor organization of the Pearson government and validated his belief that a more rational approach to politics was essential. Rationality in government became a major theme of the Trudeau campaign. The sudden weakness of the Sharp campaign caused a stir among conservative Liberal supporters, especially in the business community. At the 1966 Liberal policy convention, Sharp had successfully presented himself as the opponent of both Walter Gordon's nationalism and left-wing tendencies in the party. The rapid expansion of Canadian social programs in the mid-sixties had taken a toll on the government's finances, and Sharp had proposed postponing the inauguration of medicare for one more year. After the week of February 19, it was difficult to imagine Sharp becoming leader, and the conservative and business faction of the Liberal Party began to worry.

Suddenly a movement developed in the Senate to draft Robert Winters, who had dismissed a run for the leadership in early January and had himself been implicated in the disastrous decision to hold the vote. His role there appeared to be forgotten, and Winters responded to the draft, offering his resignation to Pearson on February 28 and announcing his candidacy the following day (February 29 in this leap year). He spoke in terms his supporters understood: "I have always believed that if you don't agree with the policies of a firm, you either get out or take it over."[27] He would be the candidate for fiscal rectitude and against government excess.

—

The first polls that appeared in early March were taken in early February. They showed Paul Martin in the lead, but Trudeau, who had not then even announced, stood a remarkable second. The results were very encouraging, but Martin had a strong organization, while Trudeau's was still informal. Trudeau's campaign team was decidedly amateurish, with Pelletier as the policy coordinator, Jean-Pierre Goyer in charge of convention arrangements, Jim Davey as leadership campaign coordinator, Pierre Levasseur as the Ottawa operations manager, and Gordon Gibson, the son of a wealthy British Columbia political legend, as Trudeau's handler and travelling companion. Though short on political experience, they were bright, ambitious, and willing to try novel approaches, in part because they didn't know the traditional ones. But who could be sure the new approaches would work? Moreover, on March 1 the Trudeau campaign fund had collected only $6,500.

After Winters's announcement, the characteristically pessimistic Pelletier wrote in his diary on March 6: "Trudeau's victory seems to me most uncertain." He was repelled by "the high degree of *fabrication* and mythology" that surrounded Trudeau as a candidate, a "personage" who bore "no resemblance to the fellow I've known for twenty years under the name of Pierre Trudeau." Yet what peeved Pelletier astounded and intrigued others. And there was another factor: the candidate Pierre Trudeau was not the man Pelletier had so long known.

Pelletier had worried about Trudeau's bitter sarcasm and unexpected cruelty in debate. What he saw once the campaign began was a "cool" Trudeau, slow to anger and amused and tolerant when journalists attacked. When television interviewers Pierre O'Neil and Louis Martin unfairly accused Trudeau of having no support in Quebec, he "stayed cool" and "replied that we should wait and see." When they rudely interrupted him before he answered, he simply smiled. Moreover, the timidity that Trudeau usually exhibited at social events disappeared in the midst of the adoring crowds that greeted him during the leadership tour. At the launches for the two books hastily assembled by his supporters from his previous writings, *Federalism and the French Canadians* and *Réponses,* Trudeau astounded both his old friends and reporters as he kissed the numerous beautiful women present as enthusiastically as traditional politicians bussed babies. At least, in this new political phenomenon of kissing adult women, he did bring much experience.

Out on the campaign trail, reporters vied with each other to spin the tastiest tales. A desk clerk at a Sudbury hotel was so stunned by Trudeau's handshake that she forgot to make change. A MacEachen supporter declared, on seeing Trudeau, that rather than meeting him she wanted to marry him, forgetting that her husband stood nearby. A middle-aged woman in a meeting at the National Library became so nervous in asking her question that she placed the microphone in her ear. A playful Trudeau answered with the microphone in his own ear. In British Columbia the wife of the president of the Liberal Federation, a Hellyer supporter, told reporters that the party needed a new leader who was not stodgy. "And anyway," she continued, "I think he's sexy." Everyone knew she meant Trudeau. Soon Trudeau was dubbed the candidate of the Age of Aquarius—he wore a rose in his lapel just as hippies wore flowers in their hair. He promised he'd open 24 Sussex Drive to parties and, when asked who would be the hostess, he replied: "Why should there be only one?"[28] Woodstock was not far away.

Trudeau's new "personage" carried the message that he would be different. He ran for office among the finest group of politicians ever to contest a party leadership in Canada, and he stood out above them all. The issues identified with him—specifically, the reform of the Criminal Code, the Constitution, and Quebec—reflected the spirit of a country that wanted to change and, in the case of Quebec, knew it must change. His high-contrast campaign posters, which, against the advice of the campaign executive, were commissioned by two remarkable young women, Alison Gordon and Jennifer Rae, were also strikingly different. Years later they were "the most coveted souvenirs of the leadership race."[29] In the *Toronto Star*, Peter Newman recognized the significance of Trudeau's announcement the very day it was made: "Two years ago, in pre-Expo Canada it would have been almost impossible to imagine [Trudeau] as a serious contender. Now, we don't have to go on muttering hopefully, 'the times they are achangin.' The times *have* changed."

Trudeau's Criminal Code amendments and, more important, his clear explanations of the reasons for the changes—"the state has no business in the bedrooms of the nation" and "what may be sin to some is not law for all"—contrasted strongly with the ambiguity with which his opponents approached the same issues. Norman Spector, then a left-leaning McGill student, expressed the view of youth and the spirit of change when he wrote a letter to the *Montreal Star* on January 12:

> The reforms which have been instituted in recent weeks by the Hon. Pierre Elliott Trudeau should meet with the approval of all thinking Canadians. Without a doubt our minister of justice is an intellectual of the first order.
>
> To those of us who have reached the conclusion that the Liberal party had grown staid and stodgy, the reforms of the Criminal Code come somewhat as a surprise. Is this the same Liberal party which is procrastinating so needlessly

before inaugurating medicare? Is this the party which ele-
vates Robert Winters and ostracizes Walter Gordon? Have
the Liberals finally seen the light?

For many of the young, the unorthodox and stylish challenge of Pierre Trudeau had become the light that illuminated a
new Canada.

—

For others, such as his old acquaintances Daniel Johnson and
Claude Ryan, Trudeau's accession to the Liberal leadership
would thrust Canada into a new darkness. The first spat came
with Johnson soon after Trudeau announced his candidacy. The
Quebec premier focused on a flippant comment Trudeau had
made that the French taught in Quebec was "lousy"—there was "a
state of emergency as regards language" in Quebec which its government ignored. This remark contrasted strongly with the politeness that Trudeau exhibited in challenging his Liberal leadership
opponents. Johnson replied acidly, claiming that the election of
Trudeau would mean the death of Canada. Trudeau encouraged
English Canadians to retain "backward and retrograde attitudes"
towards Quebec. He called Trudeau "Lord Elliott" and compared
his remarks to those of Lord Durham, who had famously encouraged the assimilation of French Canada in 1839.

Trudeau responded quickly and pointed out that his goal, in
contrast to Durham's, was to gain equality for the French language
throughout Canada. He challenged Johnson directly: "I think this
shows how afraid he is of the people of Quebec becoming interested in federal politics. If they do, then he knows he won't be lord
and master over all Quebec." For good measure, he added that
"calling me Lord Elliott when his name is Johnson is . . . a sticky
wicket." To another critic, he simply and effectively replied: "When

the king is naked, I say that the king is naked." Trudeau not only won the debate with Johnson but also gained attention and support in English Canada. A poll of Alberta delegates revealed a surge of support for Trudeau, who was increasingly seen as the best candidate to confront Quebec separatism and nationalism.[30]

The clarity of purpose that impressed many Albertans troubled others. Claude Ryan began to criticize him daily in *Le Devoir* for his rigidity. The dispute with Johnson infuriated Ryan, who warned English Canadians that they were mistaken in believing that Trudeau was a "Messiah" who would lead them out of the constitutional wilderness. He argued against Trudeau's constitutional stand and emphasized that the two provincial parties were united in their support for special status. Another international issue with serious implications for the special status of Quebec appeared with the invitation from the African state of Gabon for Quebec to participate in an educational conference among francophone states. Trudeau took a hard line, pointing out that foreign affairs was a federal responsibility, and he even provoked Pelletier, who wanted a compromise in which Quebec could form part of the Canadian delegation to the conference. Nevertheless, his strong statement against "French interference" so soon after Charles de Gaulle's "Vive le Québec libre" speech reinforced his image as the key opponent to special status and special rights for Quebec.

The other candidates noticed the swelling opposition to Trudeau in Quebec ranks and began to criticize him. Mitchell Sharp, for example, attacked Trudeau's harsh exchange with Johnson, while Paul Martin Sr. argued that a prime minister must be "a man who has not clouded relations with any prominent government or provincial premier." Once again, Trudeau benefited from the simplicity of his constitutional stand: linguistic equality enshrined in a charter of human rights. In the classic formulation of the French scientist and writer Comte de Buffon, the style became the political man.[31]

Gérard Pelletier was finally convinced of the political worth of Trudeau's new personage when his old friend visited his riding of Hochelaga. His previous appearances there had been listless, but this time Trudeau was confident, poised, and the object of adoration. It proved for Pelletier the "American" maxim that "nothing succeeds like success." The excitement in Hochelaga reminded him of what Trudeau had said to him after he was mobbed in Victoria. There, when his campaigners asked him how he managed to smile all day long, he did not dare tell them the truth. But he confided to Pelletier: "It would have been harder not to smile. I found it all so odd, grotesque, almost hilarious."

Odd and hilarious it may have been, but it was working. Thanks to the efforts of Marchand, the Quebec support finally materialized with thirty-one MPs agreeing to support him publicly after a March 6 meeting. In a confidential survey of MPs carried out in mid-March, Trudeau received support from thirty-eight of the eighty-seven MPs who replied. Hellyer, who had won the first delegate-selection meetings in Toronto, had the support of fifteen; Winters, thirteen; Martin, eleven; Turner and MacEachen, four each; and Sharp and Greene, one each. Trudeau, moreover, was the second choice of nineteen, followed by Winters, with fifteen. In the last week before the convention, the campaign became, very simply, Trudeau against the rest.[32]

Walter Gordon finally endorsed Trudeau on March 26, although he admitted he was troubled by Trudeau's opposition to economic nationalism. And Joey Smallwood officially supported Trudeau, a fact he had confided to almost every journalist in Newfoundland. Members of parliament Bryce Mackasey and Edgar Benson took the leadership in his campaign and provided valuable political experience for the last days. Then fortune fell unexpectedly in Trudeau's path: Mitchell Sharp withdrew from the campaign and threw his support to Trudeau.

A complex string of events lay behind this move. Sharp had tried to reinvigorate his campaign in the last half of March, but the crowds were meagre and his heart was weak. As his well-financed organization polled the delegates, it quickly learned that Sharp's support had evaporated. After the budget crisis in February, Sharp had spoken with Pearson about withdrawing and asked the prime minister what he thought of Trudeau. Pearson said he was impressed but puzzled, a factor that persuaded Sharp to stay in the race. Rumours of this discussion leaked to the Trudeau camp. Marchand, in a gesture that betrayed considerable naïveté, then approached Sharp to say that he and Trudeau should run a joint campaign, with the caucus deciding who should become leader. Although Sharp was identified with the conservative and business wing of the party, he had lost respect for Robert Winters. When Winters indicated in January 1968 that he had no intention of contesting the leadership, he gratuitously added that the finances of Canada were in bad shape and poorly handled. Sharp, as finance minister, took the remarks personally and asked for an apology. Winters apologized in a private letter, but then destroyed its political impact by refusing to allow Sharp to release it.

Sharp met Pearson again in late March and told him that he now had a higher opinion of Trudeau. Pearson said he did too. So, on April 3, the convention's eve, Sharp endorsed Trudeau, and Sharp's supporters Jean-Luc Pepin, Jean Chrétien, and Bud Drury also joined Trudeau's team. All three were political gems — Pepin because he was a powerful franco-Ontarian, Chrétien for his extraordinary campaign skills, and Drury for his ties with business.

The news fuelled a wild Trudeau rally at the cavernous Chaudière nightclub across the Ottawa River. There the irrepressible Joey Smallwood declared that "Pierre is better than medicare — the lame have only to touch his garments to walk again."[33]

—

On Thursday, April 4, the convention's first day, James Earl Ray shot Martin Luther King in a Memphis motel and riots swept through large American cities as his murderer fled to Toronto. The tragedy provoked sombre thoughts but did not deaden the excitement surrounding the policy workshops in Ottawa. Trudeau's crowds were the largest, crammed with mini-skirted youthful enthusiasm. The tribute to Lester Pearson that evening ended with the bizarre gift of a puppy and, to the retiring leader's embarrassment, Maryon Pearson's strong hint of affection for Trudeau.

The next day came the speeches. Ottawa's Civic Centre was crammed, television booms and cameras were everywhere, and streamers dangled from every rafter. Two fringe candidates, the Reverend Lloyd Henderson and Holocaust denier Ernst Zündel, were not permitted to speak in the regular workshops but were restricted to a short session in which the trilingual Zündel condemned the historic mistreatment of French and German Canadians. On Friday evening, Trudeau was the target of the other speakers, who largely disappointed except for Joe Greene, who gave a populist "barnburner." Paul Hellyer's poor performance had a major impact later as voting delegates remembered his bland words.

With a speech drafted mainly by Tim Porteous, with French translation by Gérard Pelletier, Trudeau spoke well; Richard Stanbury thought only Greene was better, and none doubted that the Trudeau crowd was the largest and noisiest. He spoke for only nineteen of the permitted thirty minutes because his supporters demonstrated so long and vigorously. They continued to cheer him as he declared: "Liberalism is the only philosophy for our time, because it does not try to conserve every tradition of the past; because it does not apply to new problems the old doctrinaire solutions; because it is prepared to experiment and innovate and because it knows that the past is less important than the future." The message was typically clear: the Liberal future lay with Trudeau. It was both a promise and a warning.[34]

Trudeau began Saturday, the final day, with a pancake and maple syrup breakfast at the Château Laurier which six hundred delegates attended. As he left, he slid down the hotel's grand staircase banister, to the delight of photographers and delegates alike.

Balloting began at 1:00 p.m. At 2:30 Senator John Nichol announced the results:

Greene	169
Hellyer	330
Kierans	103
MacEachen	165
Martin	277
Trudeau	752
Turner	277
Winters	293

Trudeau had met his team's expectations; Paul Hellyer's face began to drip with perspiration; Maurice Sauvé immediately bolted from his seat beside Paul Martin and pushed through the crowd towards Trudeau. Young historians Robert Bothwell and Norman Hillmer were shocked to see Claude Ryan begin to shake with rage in the press booth.[35]

Lloyd Henderson received no votes and was automatically eliminated, and Ernst Zündel had withdrawn before the ballot, but that meant the other candidates had to decide individually if they would step aside. Kierans and Paul Martin, who had led the leadership polls for so long, both withdrew graciously. MacEachen intended to withdraw but failed to notify Senator Nichol by the deadline, so, to the disappointment of the Trudeau camp, he remained on the second ballot. On that ballot, Trudeau moved up to 964, as he picked up most of MacEachen's left-wing support. Winters finished second with 473 votes, Hellyer won a disappointing 465, while Turner rose to 347 and Greene fell to 104. The beneficial impact on Trudeau's campaign of Mitchell Sharp's withdrawal suddenly became obvious.

The two successful businessmen Hellyer and Winters conferred on what they should do to stop Trudeau. Despite Winters's entreaties, Paul Hellyer refused to drop out—which would have cast the weight of his votes behind Winters. Winters then asked Judy LaMarsh, who supported Hellyer and loathed Trudeau, to have a word with Hellyer. Television and boom microphones were new to Canadian politicians at the time. Unaware she was being overheard, a tearful LaMarsh, now wearing a Winters button, shouted at Hellyer: "It's tough, Paul, but what the hell. Do you want that bastard taking over the party?" He didn't, but, crucially, he did not withdraw.[36]

On the third ballot, Winters took 621 votes; Hellyer, 377. Trudeau, at 1,051, was only fifty-three ahead of their combined vote. Turner held onto 279, and Greene, at 29, was dropped. Had Hellyer spoken better on Friday evening, had Sharp not endorsed Trudeau, Paul Hellyer probably would have become Liberal leader. These are the "what ifs" of history, which intrigue but remain wistful dreams for losers. Hellyer did keep his promise to Winters that he would endorse him if Winters moved ahead on the third ballot. Enthusiastically waving a Winters banner, he began to chant "Go, Bob, go." Joe Greene joined the crowded Trudeau box, where Trudeau coolly amused himself by tossing grapes in the air and catching them in his mouth as they fell. John Turner stubbornly refused to withdraw, and, as the final voting began at 8 p.m., most of the crowd erupted in shouts of "Trudeau. Canada. We want Trudeau."

When Nichol began to read out the final results—Trudeau 1,203—the crowd exploded, drowning out the announcement of

Winters, 954, and Turner, 195. Trudeau's face momentarily and exuberantly beamed, then froze in silent contemplation.

What images swirled in Pierre Trudeau's mind as the crowd swarmed around him as he moved slowly to the podium? Certainly he recalled the moment two days before when he spied in the crowd the beautiful young woman he had met on the beach in Tahiti, and he immediately broke away from his handlers to speak a few words to her. He probably thought of Thérèse Gouin Décarie, who, with her husband, had organized the academic petition for his candidacy at the Université de Montréal. And there were surely memories of those nights in Pelletier's basement, drafting tracts that few read and many resented; of days in Paris dreaming of a Quebec that might be, and of summers at Old Orchard Beach with the family; of long nights when Papa brought home his political friends who argued long into the night, and of a mother who, in silence, still radiated her endless love for him. He reached the stage at the front of the convention hall, mounted the steps—and, suddenly, he smiled.

NOTES

—

Unless otherwise specified, all references to the Trudeau Papers are found in MG 26 02 at Library and Archives Canada.

CHAPTER ONE: TWO WORLDS

1. Isaac Starr, "Influenza in 1918: Recollections of the Epidemic in Philadephia," *Annals of Internal Medicine*, Oct. 1976, 516.
2. Quoted in Jean-Claude Marsan, *Montreal in Evolution* (Montreal and Kingston: McGill-Queen's University Press, 1981), 256.
3. The population of Montreal in 1911 was only 25.7 percent English. The third largest group, the Jews, at 5.9 percent, tended to affiliate, nervously, with the English minority while building their own institutions to maintain their religious identity. See Paul-André Linteau, *Histoire de Montréal depuis la Confédération* (Montreal: Les Éditions du Boréal, 2000), 162. The English group had fallen from 33.7 percent to 25.7 percent between 1901 and 1911.
4. Zweig is quoted in Gérard Bouchard, *Les deux chanoines: Contradiction et ambivalence dans la pensée de Lionel Groulx* (Montreal: Les Éditions du Boréal, 2003), 38. Earlier, in 1904, the renowned French sociologist André Siegfried had visited Canada and declared Canadian politics corrupt, unable to rise above "the sordid preoccupations of patronage or connection." How long, he asked, could Canadian politicians suppress the crisis that loomed before them? André Siegfried, *The Race Question in Canada*, trans. E. Nash (1907; Toronto: McClelland & Stewart, 1966), 113.

5. Terry Copp, "Public Health in Montreal, 1870–1930," in S.E.D. Shortt, ed., *Medicine in Canadian Society: Historical Perspectives* (Montreal: McGill-Queen's University Press, 1981), 395–416; and Martin Tétrault, "Les maladies de la misère: Aspects de la santé publique à Montréal, 1880–1914," *Revue d'histoire de l'Amérique française* 36 (March 1983): 507–26.

6. Grace Trudeau to Pierre Trudeau, March 30, 1948, Trudeau Papers (TP), MG 26 02, vol. 46, file 16, Library and Archives Canada (LAC).

7. The Clio Collective, *Quebec Women: A History*, trans. Roger Gannon and Rosalind Gill (Toronto: The Women's Press, 1987), 254–55.

8. "Philip" was the surname of Trudeau's maternal grandfather. "Baby's Days," Baby Book 1919–1929, TP, vol. 1, file 14.

9. Ibid. In a contest in 1988 when members of the Prime Minister's Office were asked to give his full name, Trudeau wrote "Joseph Yves Pierre Elliott ? Trudeau"—and lost the prize. See Nancy Southam, ed., *Pierre* (Toronto: McClelland & Stewart, 2005), 64.

10. The Baby Book indicates that Trudeau held his head erect at two months, crept at eight months, and stood alone at eleven months. He had his first tooth on August 6, 1920, and his second on August 10. His first outing on a sleigh was on December 8, 1919, and his first trip to St-Rémi on December 13, 1919, when his grandfather, Joseph Trudeau, died. He had his tonsils removed on October 16, 1921. TP, vol. 1, file 14.

11. Charles Trudeau to Grace Trudeau, Aug. 17, 1921, TP, vol. 53, file 30.

12. Pierre Trudeau's assessment of Charles is found in George Radwanski, *Trudeau* (Toronto: Macmillan, 1978), ch. 4. Other notable biographies of Trudeau that contain important family material, often drawing on the interviews Trudeau gave to Radwanski, are Stephen Clarkson and Christina McCall, *Trudeau and Our Times*, vol. 1: *The Magnificent Obsession* (Toronto: McClelland & Stewart, 1990), vol. 2: *The Heroic Delusion* (Toronto: McClelland & Stewart, 1994); and Michel Vastel, *Trudeau: Le Québécois* 2nd ed. (Montreal: Les Éditions de l'Homme, 2000). See also Pierre Trudeau, *Memoirs* (Toronto: McClelland & Stewart, 1993).

13. Radwanski, *Trudeau*, 43.

14. Victor Barbeau, quoted in Claude Corbo, *La mémoire du cours classique: Les années aigres-douces des récits autobiographiques* (Outremont, Que.: Les Éditions Logiques, 2000), 33.

15. These comments and records are found in TP, vol. 1, files 1–6.

16. Trudeau, *Memoirs*, 6; Radwanski, *Trudeau*, 47.

17. Trudeau, *Memoirs*, 10–13.

18. Vastel, *Trudeau*, 22–23. Clarkson's recent comment is in John English, Richard Gwyn, and P. Whitney Lackenbauer, eds., *The Hidden Pierre Elliott Trudeau: The Faith behind the Politics* (Ottawa: Novalis, 2004), 33. For the friend's recollection, see Clarkson and McCall, *Trudeau and Our Times*, 1: 30. Max and Monique Nemni also doubt that Charles was abusive and paint a similar portrait to the one presented in this book. See Max and Monique Nemni, *Trudeau: Fils du Québec, père du Canada*, vol. 1: *Les années de jeunesse, 1919–1944* (Montreal: Les Éditions de l'Homme, 2006).

19. Paul-André Linteau, René Durocher, and Jean-Claude Robert, *Quebec: A History, 1867–1929*, trans. Robert Chodos and Ellen Garmaise (Toronto: James Lorimer, 1983), 345–47.

20. Charles Trudeau to Grace Trudeau, Aug. 17, 1921, TP, vol. 53, file 30.

21. Trudeau, *Memoirs*, 13. Also Radwanski, *Trudeau*, 44, and TP, vol. 53, file 31. On his club memberships and directorships, see *Le Devoir*, April 11, 1935.

22. Interview between Pierre Trudeau and Ron Graham, April 18, 1992, TP, vol. 23, file 3. In this interview, Trudeau said that he thought the majority of the customers were the French elite. That probably was not the case, although the evidence is elusive.

23. Pierre Trudeau to Charles Trudeau, nd, TP, vol. 53, file 33.

24. Charles Trudeau to Pierre Trudeau, Sept. 28, 1926, and Charles to Pierre, May 1930, ibid., file 31.

25. Pierre Trudeau to Charles Trudeau, nd, and Charles to Pierre, July 19, 1929, ibid.

26. Pierre Trudeau to Charles Trudeau, ibid.

27. Pierre Trudeau to Charles and Grace Trudeau, March 10, 1935, and Pierre to Charles, April 8, 1935, ibid., file 33.

28. Trudeau, *Memoirs*, 30; Radwanski, *Trudeau*, 54.

29. Radwanski, *Trudeau*, 55.

30. Trudeau, *Memoirs*, 30.

31. Père Jean Belanger to Pierre Trudeau, April [12?] 1935, TP, vol. 41, file 1.

32. Trudeau gave this information to the painter. TP, vol. 23, file 6.

33. Radwanski, *Trudeau*, 55.

34. *Le Devoir*, April 15, 1935. The names are overwhelmingly francophone.

35. Pierre Trudeau to Grace Trudeau, April 28, May 2, and June 10, 1935, TP, vol. 2, file 5.

36. Vastel, *Trudeau*, 27.

37. Clarkson and McCall, *Trudeau and Our Times*, 1: 31.

38. Ibid.; Radwanski, *Trudeau*, 55–56.

39. TP, vol. 1, file 22.

40. Grace Pitfield wrote these comments to Christina McCall-Newman on October 26, 1974. Quoted in McCall-Newman, *Grits: An Intimate Portrait of the Liberal Party* (Toronto: Macmillan, 1982), 65.

41. Richard Gwyn, *The Northern Magus: Pierre Trudeau and Canadians* (Toronto: McClelland & Stewart, 1980), 23.

42. "Notes sur la succession JCE Trudeau et la Cie Trudeau-Elliott," TP, vol. 5, file 17.

43. TP, vol. 1, file 25.

44. Conversation between Trudeau and Suzette, his sister, TP, vol. 23, file 5.

45. "Cahiers d'exercices," TP, vol. 2, file 8.

46. Fernand Foissy, *Michel Chartrand: Les vois d'un homme de parole* (Outremont, Que.: Lanctôt, 1999), 29.

47. The files on his Querbes period are found in TP, vol. 1, files 16–22.

48. The three essays are "Dévouement de Dollard," "Danger des armes à feu," and "L'enfant poli." Ibid., file 22.

49. Trudeau, *Memoirs*, 25, 31–32.

50. Radwanski, *Trudeau*, 36. Bernier confirms the character of the political discussion on page 37.

51. The best description of the origins of Groulx's nationalism is in Bouchard, *Les deux chanoines*, 38ff. Also, Pierre Hébert, *Lionel Groulx et L'appel de la race* (Montreal: Les Éditions Fides, 1996), 20–21.

52. Frédéric Boily, *La pensée nationaliste de Lionel Groulx* (Sillery, Que.: Les Éditions du Septentrion, 2003), 50.

53. Lionel Groulx, *L'appel de la race* (Montreal: Bibliothèque de l'Action française, 1922). See the account of the reception of the novel in Boily, *La pensée*, ch. 5.

54. Quoted in Donald Horton, *André Laurendeau: French-Canadian Nationalist, 1912–1968* (Toronto: Oxford University Press, 1992), 82.

55. See Louise Bienvenue, *Quand la jeunesse entre en scène: L'action catholique avant la révolution tranquille* (Montreal: Les Édition du Boréal, 2003), 42–44.

56. Trudeau, *Memoirs*, 21. For the water incident, see Trudeau to mother, April 14, 1937, TP, vol. 2, file 8. On friends, see Radwanski, *Trudeau*, 53; and Clarkson and McCall, *Trudeau and Our Times*, 1: 36–40.

57. Personal Journal 1938, June 8, 1938, TP, vol. 39, file 9.

58. Interview with Alexandre Trudeau, Feb. 2006.

59. François Hertel, *Leur inquiétude* (Montreal: Les Éditions de Vivre, 1936), 14.

60. See Louise Bienvenue et Christine Hudon, "'Pour devenir homme, tu transgresseras . . . ': Quelques enjeux de la socialisation masculine dans les collèges classiques québécois (1880–1939)," *Canadian Historical Review* 86 (Sept. 2005): 485–11. See also their "Entre franche camaraderie et amours socratiques: L'espace trouble et ténu des amitiés masculines dans les collèges classiques (1840–1960)," *Revue d'histoire de l'Amérique française* 57 (spring 2004): 481–508.

61. Trudeau, "My Interview with King George of England," Feb. 17, 1935, TP, vol. 2, file 5.

62. The comment is found ibid., file 10; for the underlining, see TP, vol. 37, file 9.

63. TP, vol. 2, file 8. On the incident with the other Catholic youth groups, see Nemni and Nemni, *Trudeau*, 131–32. This book indicates that Trudeau and Pelletier had not met at the time; however, his Journal entry for November 12, 1939, shows that he met Pelletier at a student conference in Quebec City. TP, vol. 39, file 9.

64. TP, vol. 2, file 8.

65. Ibid., file 10.

66. Ibid.

67. Ibid., file 8. Story "L'aventure."

68. Vastel makes the comment in his April 8, 2006 "blog": http://forums.lactualite.com/advansis/?mod=for&act=dis&eid=1&so=1&sb=1&ps=10. The Nemnis' account of the 1937 speech is found in their *Trudeau*, 83–85.

69. The comments on Maritain are in TP, vol. 2, file 8. See also Nemni and Nemni, *Trudeau*, 308ff.

70. The "Semaine sociale" program is in TP, vol. 4, file 6. The Fordham letter is in vol. 2, file 10.

71. TP, vol. 2, file 9.
72. Personal Journal, TP, vol. 39, file 9.
73. Ibid., Aug. 18, 1937.
74. Ibid., Jan. 2–5, 1938.
75. Ibid., Feb. 2, 1938.
76. Letter to mother, Dec. 19, 1936; undated poem, TP, vol. 2, file 8.
77. Ibid., Oct. 1937.
78. Ibid., Feb. 5, 1938.
79. François Hertel, *Le beau risque* (Montreal: Les Éditions Fides, 1942), 130.
80. The draft of the play is found in TP, vol. 1, file 29.
81. The original text reads: "Une des qualités du genre epistolaire est le tact. C'est à dire que celui qui écrit doit prendre ton proportionné aux circonstances et adapté aux sentiments de celui qui lira la lettre."
82. Pierre to Grace Trudeau, TP, vol. 2, file 10.
83. TP, vol. 39, file 9.

CHAPTER TWO: LA GUERRE, NO SIR!

1. Pierre Trudeau, Personal Journal, June 19, 1938, Trudeau Papers (TP), MG 26 02, vol. 39, file 9, Library and Archives Canada (LAC). The original French reads: "Je me demande quelque fois si je pourrai faire quelque chose pour mon Dieu et ma patrie. J'aimerais tant être un grand politique et guide mon pays."
2. See Farley Mowat, *And No Birds Sang* (Toronto: McClelland & Stewart, 1979).
3. Debate transcript in TP, vol. 2, file 10.
4. Corriveau to Trudeau, Sept. 7, 1939; Trudeau to Corriveau, Sept. 12, 1939, TP, vol. 45, file 4.
5. "Entrevue entre M. Trudeau et M. [Jean] Lépine, 27 avril 1992" [Lépine interview], Trudeau Papers, (TP), MG 26 03 vol. 23, file 2, Library and Archives Canada.
6. J.L. Granatstein, *Canada's Army: Waging War and Keeping the Peace* (Toronto: University of Toronto Press, 2002), 180. More detail is found in Jean-Yves Gravel, ed., *Le Québec et la Guerre* (Montreal: Les Éditions du Boréal, 1974), especially Gravel's own contribution, "Le Québec militaire," 77–108.

7. Trudeau to Grace Trudeau, Nov. 26, 1935, TP, vol. 2, file 5.
8. In an influential work on the mid-1930s, political scientist André Bélanger argued that the period is marked by the intellectuals' turning away from direct political action as they responded to the "mêlée" by concentrating on religion, nationalism, and economic organization through corporatism. There was, in his view, "a major turning" in 1934–36. Bélanger, *L'apolitisme des idéologies québécoises: Le grand tournant de 1934–1936* (Quebec: Les Presses de l'Université Laval, 1974). Of course, ideas do matter, and the political retreat of the intellectuals does not mean that their writings and thoughts failed to affect the actions of their students or their readers. Trudeau's claim that he paid little attention to politics is valid in the sense that he and his classmates apparently did not participate in elections.
9. "Propos d'éloquence politique," Feb. 10, 1938, TP, vol. 2, file 10.
10. Interview between Pierre Trudeau and Ron Graham, April 28, 1992, TP, vol. 23, file 3. Max and Monique Nemni have not seen this document or the reference to Trudeau's participation in demonstrations against Communists cited in chapter 1. They assume, correctly, that Trudeau did take part in the numerous demonstrations against Communism by Catholic students. See their *Trudeau, Fils du Québec, père du Canada*, vol. 1: *Les années de jeunesse, 1919–44* (Montreal: Les Éditions de l'Homme, 2006).
11. No title, note of Oct. 6, 1937, TP, vol. 2, file 10.
12. Lucienne Fortin, "Les Jeunes-Canada," in Fernand Dumont, Jean Hamelin, and Jean-Paul Montminy, eds., *Idéologies au Canada français* (Quebec: Les Presses de l'Université Laval, 1978), 219–20.
13. Quoted in John Herd Thompson with Allen Seager, *Canada 1922–1939: Decades of Discord* (Toronto: McClelland & Stewart, 1986), 313–14.
14. Douglas Letson and Michael Higgins, *The Jesuit Mystique* (Toronto: Macmillan, 1995), 143.
15. Quoted in Louis-P. Audet, *Bilan de la réforme scolaire au Québec, 1959–1969* (Montreal: Les Presses de l'Université de Montréal, 1969), 14.
16. "À l'aventure," nd [1936?], TP, vol. 3, file 8.
17. Personal Journal, entry of April 10, 1938, TP, vol. 39, file 9.
18. Pierre Trudeau, *Memoirs* (Toronto: McClelland & Stewart, 1993), 22. For a later appreciation of Hertel's impact on students, see J.-B. Boulanger, "François Hertel: Témoin de notre renaissance," *Le Quartier*

Latin, Feb. 14, 1947, 4. See also Trudeau, *Memoirs*, 23–24. On Hertel more generally, see Michael Oliver, *The Passionate Debate: The Social and Political Ideas of Quebec Nationalism, 1920–1945* (Montreal: Véhicule, 1991), 130–35; and Jean Tétreau, *Hertel: L'homme et l'oeuvre* (Montreal: P. Tisseyre, 1986).

19. Boulanger, "François Hertel: Témoin de notre renaissance," 4. Trudeau saved this article in his papers. TP, vol. 38, file 30.

20. Tétreau, *Hertel, L'homme et l'oeuvre*, 64–65.

21. Lionel Groulx, "La bourgeoisie et le national," *L'Action nationale* 12 (1939): 292–93.

22. On Groulx and democracy, see the discussion in Gérard Bouchard, *Les deux chanoines: Contradiction et ambivalence dans la pensée de Lionel Groulx* (Montreal: Les Éditions du Boréal, 2003), 91–93.

23. See H. Stuart Hughes, *The Obstructed Path: French Social Thought in the Years of Desperation, 1930–1960* (New York and Evanston: Harper and Row, 1968), 67.

24. *Brébeuf*, May 27, 1939.

25. TP, vol. 39, file 9.

26. Jerome Kagan, *Three Seductive Ideas* (Cambridge, Mass: Harvard University Press, 2000), 138.

27. TP, vol. 39, file 9, July 1939.

28. Trudeau to Camille Corriveau, Jan. 11, 1939, TP, vol. 45, file 4.

29. Personal Journal, Jan. 28, 1938, TP, vol. 39, file 9.

30. Ibid., April 12, 1938.

31. Ibid., July 7, 1938. Also in his notebooks, July 1, 1938, TP, vol. 2, file 10.

32. Clarkson and McCall argue that, throughout his life, Trudeau identified with Cyrano, the romantic poet and protector of the weak whose "life dream took on a particularly dramatic form . . . He would yearn, as he openly admitted, to climb alone to the heights." Stephen Clarkson and Christina McCall, *Trudeau and Our Times*, vol. 1: *The Magnificent Obsession* (Toronto: McClelland & Stewart, 1990), 44. Max and Monique Nemni disagree with the Clarkson-McCall interpretation and argue that Cyrano was a favourite of most French adolescents. However, the strength of Trudeau's admiration for Cyrano's individualism in 1938 is clear in the journal entry and seems to support the interpretation of Clarkson and McCall.

33. Interview quoted in George Radwanski, *Trudeau* (Toronto: Macmillan, 1978), 35. For a different view, see Nemni and Nemni, *Trudeau*, 89ff. They did not see the journal containing these remarks.

34. Personal Journal, July 29, 1938, TP, vol. 39, file 9.

35. Ibid., Aug. 1, 1938.

36. Ibid., Sept. 1, 1939.

37. Ibid., Sept. 3, 1939.

38. Ibid., Sept. 6, 1939: "J'ai peu lu, mais j'ai baisé une femme."

39. Ibid., Oct. 9, 1939.

40. Ibid., Oct. 20, 1939.

41. *Brébeuf*, Nov. 11, 1939.

42. Personal Journal, Oct. 9–31, 1939, TP, vol. 39, file 9.

43. Alex Gourd to Rhodes Committee, Jan. 8, 1940, with enclosure of Trudeau's record; "Recorder-en-chef de la cité de Montréal to Rhodes Committee," Jan. 10, 1940; and Trudeau, "Statement of General Interests and Activities," Jan. 7, 1940, TP, vol. 5, file 7.

44. Gérard Pelletier, then a leading figure in Jeunesse étudiante catholique, asked student journals to express their opinion on the war, but *Brébeuf* did not respond. See Michel Vastel, *Trudeau: Le Québécois*, 2nd. ed. (Montreal: Les Éditions de L'Homme, 2000), 34, for background on this incident.

45. Quoted in *Catholic Register*, May 30, 1940.

46. Kagan, *Three Seductive Ideas*, 145–46.

47. Max and Monique Nemni, who wrongly believe that Trudeau had not encountered Jacques Maritain, describe Maritain's liberal democratic view and indicate that Trudeau opposed them. In fact, both Hertel and Trudeau had expressed agreement with elements of Maritain's individualistic thought. It is a measure of the change during the Vichy years. Maritain was identified with the personalist movement, and it is clear that Trudeau, who first read Maritain in the mid-1930s, had learned about the personalist approach long before he studied in Paris—the time when the Nemnis assert he assumed its outlook as the core of his Catholicism. In his biography of Trudeau "le Québécois," Michel Vastel points to 1940 as the decisive year when Trudeau decided to go to law school in Montreal and to move more deeply into the "French" world. His argument, which was new when it was presented in 2000, is based on a careful and, to my mind,

accurate reading of Trudeau's pieces in the school newspapers: *Brébeuf* and *Le Quartier Latin*. Vastel, however, did not have access to the full evidence on Trudeau's political involvements—evidence that would have strengthened his argument. In their biography of Trudeau, Clarkson and McCall emphasize that Trudeau was "contradictory," but they argue, much too strongly in light of the evidence of Trudeau's own papers, that his father's death was the principal explanation for his behavioural patterns. His own record suggests that he was not so ambivalent towards his father but much more reflective of the nationalist ethos as it developed at his school— Brébeuf. See Nemni and Nemni, *Trudeau*, 308–13; Vastel, *Trudeau*, 27–41; and Clarkson and McCall, *Trudeau and Our Times*, 1: 39–46.

48. Trudeau to Corriveau, March 30, 1940, TP, vol. 45, file 5. The Nemnis describe Trudeau's favourable reception to Carrel and are justifiably critical. Nemni and Nemni, *Trudeau*, 98–103.

49. Personal Journal, June 19, 1940, TP, vol. 39, file 9.

50. Kenner to Trudeau, March 17, 1940; Trudeau to Kenner, May 1, 1940, TP, vol. 49, file 37.

51. Esther Delisle has argued that Trudeau became a strong nationalist in 1937 and pushed that agenda through membership in a secret society and, later, by intense political action with other strong nationalists during wartime. This account exaggerates Trudeau's nationalism, especially before 1940, although it does add much detail to the existing record. It also refutes Trudeau's own arguments that he stood outside politics and beyond the wartime controversies, except for a couple of eccentric interventions. See Esther Delisle, *Essais sur l'imprégnation fasciste au Québec* (Montreal: Les Éditions Varia, 2002), 20–50. The sources she uses are an interview with François Lessard and Lessard's book *Messages au "Frère" Trudeau* (Pointe-Fortune: Les Éditions de ma grand-mère, 1979), 122; and an interview with Hertel in *La Presse*, July 9, 1977. Dr. Delisle has kindly given me some of her original material, including Lessard-Trudeau correspondence.

52. Delisle, *Essais sur l'imprégnation fasciste au Québec*, 42; and Sandra Djwa, *A Life of F.R. Scott: The Politics of the Imagination* (Toronto and Vancouver: Douglas & McIntyre, 1987), 170–76.

53. The question was asked by René Matté on April 5, 1977. Trudeau did not

respond orally, but the Speaker indicated that Trudeau had nodded his agreement. Hansard, April 5, 1977.

54. Personal Journal, June 15, 1940, TP, vol. 39, file 9.

55. The trip is described in Personal Journal, June–July 1940, ibid. The draft of the letter to Camille in which he speaks about the family is found in his papers, vol. 41, file 2. It is undated but, obviously, July 1940.

56. *Toronto Daily Star*, April 8, 1968. Robert McKenzie and Lotta Dempsey interviewed Raymond Choquette, a Trudeau family accountant.

57. *Brébeuf*, Oct. 30, 1941.

58. *Le Quartier Latin*, March 3 and March 15, 1939.

59. He began classes on September 18, 1940. His notes indicate that Groulx was very detailed in his explanations and that he commented frequently on the physical attributes of the individuals he mentioned. TP, vol. 6, file 13.

60. TP, vol. 5, file 23.

61. Corriveau to Trudeau, Nov. 21, 1940; Corriveau to Trudeau, Dec. 30, 1940; and Trudeau to Corriveau, Dec. 31, 1940, TP, vol. 45, file 5.

62. Trudeau to Corriveau, Feb. 4, 1940 (1941 by content), and March 18, 1941, ibid., file 9.

63. This description comes from an interview with Charles Lussier. See Clarkson and McCall, *Trudeau and Our Times*, 1: 41.

64. Archibishop of Montreal to Trudeau, April 9 and April 17, 1941, TP, vol. 4, file 8.

65. Hertel to Trudeau, Aug. 27, 1941, TP, vol. 49, file 8.

66. Stephen Clarkson and Christina McCall, *Trudeau and Our Times*, vol. 2: *The Heroic Delusion* (Toronto: McClelland & Stewart, 1994), 35, based on an interview with Rolland.

67. Hertel to Trudeau, Aug. 25, 1941, TP, vol. 49, file 8.

68. Trudeau to Hertel, Oct. 18, 1941, ibid.

69. Ibid., Nov. 15, 1941.

70. Tétreau, *Hertel*, 70; Delisle, *Essais sur l'imprégnation fasciste au Québec*, 58–59.

71. Delisle has provided me with several letters from d'Anjou to Lessard which mention Trudeau. Most are referred to in her *Essais sur l'imprégnation fasciste au Québec*, 59.

72. TP, vol. 5, file 21.

73. Nemni and Nemni, *Trudeau*, 230ff. See Trudeau's comments in his *Memoirs*, 24.

74. Trudeau to Corriveau, Feb.17, 1942, TP, vol. 45, file 6.

75. TP, vol. 5, file 12.

76. Hertel to Trudeau, Dec. 1941, TP, vol. 49, file 8; Trudeau to Hertel, Jan. 13, 1942, ibid.

77. *Le Quartier Latin*, March 20, 1942.

78. *Montreal Daily Star*, April 8, 1942. Delisle, *Essais sur l'imprégnation fasciste au Québec*, 61. Trudeau has the clipping in his files. Riel did not remember that event when Delisle asked him about it. Lessard confirmed that Trudeau was a witness at the trial.

79. Nemni and Nemni, *Trudeau*, 243.

80. Hertel to Trudeau, April 17, 1942, TP, vol. 49, file 8.

81. Much of the letter is quoted in Nemni and Nemni, *Trudeau*, 216ff. The letters to Boulanger are in TP, vol. 44, file 6.

82. Trudeau, *Memoirs*, 26–27; Nancy Southam, ed., *Pierre* (Toronto: McClelland & Stewart, 2005), 66–67. A note in Trudeau's papers, vol. 3, file 5, describes what he took on the trip. He had $70 in traveller's cheques and $25 in cash—a fairly large sum for a motorbike trip.

83. *Le Devoir*, Nov. 26, 1942, found in TP, vol. 5, file 19.

84. Ibid., Nov. 28, 1942.

85. Trudeau to Roméo Turgeon, Dec. 9, 1942, TP, vol. 53, file 45.

86. *Le Quartier Latin*, Nov. 29, 1942.

87. Roger Rolland to John English, June 7, 2006.

88. Trudeau, *Memoirs*, 36–37; Lépine interview, TP, vol. 23, file 2; Claude Bélanger, "The Resignation of Jean-Louis Roux," Nov. 1996, www2.marianopolis.edu/quebechistory/events/roux.htm. See also Delisle, *Essais sur l'imprégnation fasciste au Québec*, 43; and, especially, Jean-Louis Roux, *Nous sommes tous des acteurs* (Montreal: Éditions Lescop, 1998), in which he describes his membership in a secret "cell."

89. Roux later said that he was a member of Les Frères Chausseurs but left the secret organization because of parental opposition. A personal letter sent to Father Marie d'Anjou indicates that he intended to pursue cultural projects for the future state. The letter, with the heading Ville-Marie rather than

Montreal, says he continues to share the goals. Delisle claims, with some supporting evidence, that the play *Le Jeu de Dollard* was organized by two Les Frères members. Trudeau appeared in numerous theatrical events during his university years, and his presence in this performance is not necessarily political. In the same sense, those who played in Brecht were often not Communists. Delisle, *Essais sur l'imprégnation fasciste au Québec*, 63; Roux to François-J. Lessard, Nov. 5 [nd], Lessard Papers, privately held.

90. Radwanski, *Trudeau*, 60. Program in TP, vol. 5, file 10. *La Presse* reported the debate on January 16, 1943. Delisle has another account of the debate, claiming that it occurred in 1942. Lessard says that he participated, but the program does not confirm his presence there. Delisle, *Essais sur l'imprégnation fasciste au Québec*, 60. See also the description in Nemni and Nemni, *Trudeau*, 344ff.

91. *La Presse*, June 25, 1943. File on results is found in TP, vol. 5, file 24. On the prizes and the medals, see ibid., file 25.

92. Suzette to Pierre, July 1, 1943, ibid.

93. Vastel, *Trudeau*, 56.

94. Clarkson and McCall, *Trudeau*, 1: 44–45.

CHAPTER THREE: IDENTITY AND ITS DISCONTENTS

1. Trudeau to Corriveau, Sept. 24, 1940, Trudeau Papers (TP), MG 26 02, vol. 45, file 5, Library and Archives Canada (LAC).

2. Freud received seven mentions, one more than Aquinas and, interestingly, Emmanuel Mounier, but fewer than eleven other individuals. No Canadian other than Groulx (9) exceeded three mentions. Although Groulx ranked higher than Freud, he stood below two other Catholic philosophers, Teilhard de Chardin and Jacques Maritain (11), two writers, Georges Bernanos and Dostoevsky (11), and the French Catholic writer Charles Péguy (10), and he tied with the existentialist and novelist Albert Camus and the novelist Honoré de Balzac. The choices of Trudeau's political colleagues Gérard Pelletier and Jean Marchand were typical of others of their generation: Pelletier—Pascal, Mounier, Bernanos, Malraux, and Claudel; Marchand—Pascal, Berdiaeff, Péguy, Dostoevsky, and his own contemporary and Trudeau speech writer Jean Le Moyne. The list and an excellent analysis are found in Germain Lesage, *Notre éveil culturel* (Montreal: Rayonnement, 1963), 135–48.

3. The original lists are found in "Qui avons-nous interrogés et qu'ont-ils répondu?" *Le nouveau journal*, April 7, 1962, III; but the lists and discussion in Lesage, *Notre éveil culturel*, are much more useful.

4. Louis Bouyer, *Newman: His Life and Spirituality*, trans. J. May (New York: Meridian, 1960), 226.

5. Lesage, *Notre éveil culturel*, 143–45.

6. E.-Martin Meunier and Jean-Philippe Warren, *Sortir de la "Grande noirceur": L'horizon "personnaliste" de la Révolution tranquille* (Sillery, Que.: Les Éditions du Septentrion, 2002), 108.

7. Charles Taylor, *Sources of the Self: The Making of the Modern Identity* (Cambridge, Mass.: Harvard University Press, 1989), 40, 51–52.

8. Personal Journal 1939–40, Feb. 5, 1940, TP, vol. 39, file 9.

9. Trudeau to Corriveau, Sept. 24, 1940, ibid., file 5.

10. Trudeau to Corriveau, March 18, 1941, ibid., file 9.

11. Corriveau to Trudeau, March 21, 1941, ibid.

12. Personal Journal 1939–40, Feb. 5, 1940, ibid.

13. Hertel to Trudeau, Sept. 1941, TP, vol. 49, file 8.

14. Hertel to Trudeau, Oct. 1941, ibid. The letter appears to have been sent with the previous one.

15. Grace Trudeau to Trudeau, Feb. 4, 1940, ibid.

16. Gustave Beaudoin to Honourable Hector Perrier, provincial secretary, May 25, 1943, TP, vol. 7, file 3.

17. Trudeau to Pierre Dumas, May 18, 1943; Dumas to Trudeau, July 30, 1943, TP, vol. 41, file 4; Trudeau to Donald Watt, director of Experiment in International Living, May 8, 1943, TP, vol. 15, file 7; and Trudeau to Grace Trudeau, nd [Aug. 1943], TP, vol. 53, file 34.

18. Pierre Trudeau, "Pritt Zoum Bing," *Le Quartier Latin*, March 10, 1944. See also Max and Monique Nemni, *Trudeau: Fils du Québec, père du Canada*, vol. 1: *Les années de jeunesse, 1919—1944* (Montreal: Les Éditions de l'Homme, 2006), 364–65.

19. For the lease and other documents, see TP, vol. 7, file 2.

20. For Marcil, who was Speaker in Laurier's last government (1909–11), see www.parl.gc.ca/information/about/people/key/SP"-BC/hoc-cdc/sp_hoc-e.asp?SP=2734.

21. The *Bulletin d'Histoire Politique* 3 (spring/summer 1995) devoted an entire

issue to "La participation des Canadiens français à la Deuxième Guerre mondiale." It remains the best account of the complex story of war participation. The essays by William Young, Robert Comeau, Béatrice Richard, and Jacques Michon are especially valuable.

22. The badge is found in TP, vol. 5, file 12. The file also has a press clipping from *Le Devoir* indicating that a speech by the pro-war Abbé Maheux had been disrupted by Bloc members. Trudeau underlined the part about the disruption, emphasis that may indicate his own participation.

23. "Inaugural Speech," in Michael Behiels and Ramsay Cook, eds., *The Essential Laurendeau*, trans. Joanne L'Heureux and Richard Howard (Toronto: Copp Clark, 1968), 123.

24. Trudeau to Donald Watt, May 25, 1944, TP, vol. 15, file 7; and National Service Separation Notice, ibid., file 12.

25. This information is found in the Hertel Papers held at the Archives nationales du Québec (Montreal), file P42.

26. François-Marc Gagnon, *Paul-Émile Borduas: Biographie critique et analyse de l'oeuvre* (Montreal: Les Éditions Fides, 1978), 108. Hertel's review, "L'actualité: Anatole Laplante au vernissage," is found in *Le Devoir*, May 19, 1941. Oddly, Gagnon identifies Trudeau as being present at only one Borduas exhibit—in October 1944. It is very unlikely he was there because he was then a student at Harvard. However, he did attend other openings, as the Borduas correspondence indicates. He also bought a Borduas painting.

27. Drafts of letters to Gabrielle Borduas, Sept. 1942, TP, vol. 43, file 31; and Gabrielle Borduas to Trudeau, Dec. 14, 1943, ibid. When I asked Senator Laurier LaPierre whether he knew Madame Borduas, he replied, unprompted, that he did and that she loved Pierre Trudeau.

28. Camille to Pierre, March 22, 1941, TP, vol. 45, file 6. Interview with Alexandre Trudeau.

29. Interview with Thérèse Gouin Décarie, June 2006.

30. Ibid.

31. George Radwanski, *Trudeau* (Toronto: Macmillan, 1978), 66.

32. Pierre Trudeau, *Memoirs* (Toronto: McClelland & Stewart, 1993), 38.

33. "Tip" to Pierre, April 18, 1945, TP, vol. 53, file 26.

34. Trudeau, *Memoirs*, 39.

35. He wrote to the vicar general, Monsignor Hickey, who replied that "in

view of the circumstances, [the archbishop] grants you permission to read even on vacation" whatever books were required. Hickey to Trudeau, Nov. 20, 1944, TP, vol. 7, file 5.

36. Interview with John Kenneth Galbraith, Feb. 28, 2005. See his similar remarks in Nancy Southam, ed., *Pierre* (Toronto: McClelland & Stewart, 2005), 208–9.

37. On Keynes, see TP, vol. 7, file 11; on Haberler, ibid.; on Schumpeter, ibid., file 13; on Galbraith, Southam, ed., *Pierre*, 208.

38. The comments are from Trudeau's notes on their writings in TP, vol. 7, file 16.

39. See ibid., for the comments and the details.

40. Ibid., file 21.

41. Trudeau to Thérèse Gouin, May 1, 1945; Gouin to Trudeau, May 24, 1945; and Trudeau to Gouin, May 25, 1945, TP, vol. 48, file 13.

42. Radwanski, *Trudeau*, 62.

43. Trudeau, *Memoirs*, 37.

44. Conversation with Gerald Butts, close family friend, April 2006. Trudeau used the word "chaff."

45. Friedrich was of German aristocratic background. He emigrated to the United States in the 1920s and became a leading authority on constitutions and democracy. He was an adviser to the American military government of Germany. McIlwain was a specialist in intellectual history, notably medieval political thought. His publications also had a strongly constitutionalist and institutionalist focus.

46. TP, vol. 7, file 18.

47. Ibid., files 19 and 22.

48. Ibid., file 19.

49. Trudeau, "A Theory of Political Violence," ibid., file 23.

50. Christina McCall and Stephen Clarkson, *Trudeau and Our Times*, vol. 2: *The Heroic Delusion* (Toronto: McClelland & Stewart, 1994), 42–44.

51. Edith Iglauer, "Prime Ministre/Premier Ministre," *New Yorker*, July 5, 1969, 41.

52. Andrée Trudeau to Pierre Trudeau, July 18, 1946, TP, vol. 53, file 26.

53. Pierre Trudeau, "College-Jean de Brébeuf—Notes prises durant la semaine sociale 1937," TP, vol. 4, file 6.

54. Trudeau to Gouin, April 19, 1945; Gouin to Trudeau, April 21, 1945, ibid., file 2.

55. Trudeau to Gouin, July 5, 1945, ibid., file 14.

56. Trudeau to Gouin, Sept. 26, 1945, ibid., file 15.

57. Ibid.

58. Trudeau to Gouin, Oct. 11, 1945, ibid.

59. Trudeau to Gouin, Oct. 17, 1945, ibid.

60. Trudeau to Gouin, Nov. 15, 1945, ibid.

61. Trudeau to Gouin, Nov. 19, 1945, file 3.

62. Charles Trudeau to Pierre Trudeau, April 18, 1945; and Wedding Invitation, June 20, 1945, TP, vol. 53, file 26.

63. Trudeau to Gouin, Dec. 8, 1945, TP, vol. 48, file 16.

64. Iglauer, "Prime Minister," 38. See also Radwanski, *Trudeau*, 48–49.

65. Clarkson and McCall, *Trudeau and Our Times*, 2: 36.

66. Gouin to Trudeau, Feb. 25, 1947, TP, vol. 48, file 10.

67. Trudeau to Gouin, Jan. 3, 1946, ibid., file 17.

68. Trudeau to Gouin, Jan. 23, 1946, ibid.

69. Trudeau to Gouin, March 15, 1946, ibid., file 18.

70. Trudeau to Gouin, April 1, 1946, ibid.

71. Trudeau to Gouin, April 29, 1946, ibid.

72. Trudeau to Gouin, April 25, 1946, ibid.

73. Trudeau to Gouin, May 22, 1946, ibid., file 19.

74. Conversation with Alexandre Trudeau, Feb. 2005.

75. Trudeau to Gouin, July 14, 1946, TP, vol. 48, file 8.

76. See TP, vol. 8, files 1 and 2.

77. Trudeau to Gouin, July 20, 1946, ibid., file 8.

78. Interview with Thérèse Gouin Décarie, June 2006.

79. Gouin to Trudeau, nd [July 1946], ibid., file 5.

80. Gouin to Trudeau, Sept. 29, 1946, ibid., file 8; and Agenda 1946, TP, vol. 39, file 1.

81. TP, vol. 8, file 11.

82. Trudeau to Gouin, Oct. 9, 1946, TP, vol. 48, file 20.

83. Trudeau, *Memoirs*, 42–43.

84. Antony Beevor and Artemis Cooper, *Paris: After the Liberation, 1944–1949*, rev. ed. (London: Penguin, 2004), np.

85. Hertel, "La quinzaine à Paris," *Le Devoir*, May 12, 1971. The hotel is currently the Esmeralda, a one-star hotel of considerable reputation which has attracted celebrities ranging from Serge Gainsbourg to Terence Stamp. The quotation is found in a review posted in the hotel window at 4 St-Julien-le-Pauvre.

86. *Brébeuf*, Oct. 7, 1946.

87. Linda Lapointe, *Maison des étudiants canadiens: Cité internationale universitaire de Paris. 75 ans d'histoire 1926–2001* (Saint-Lambert: Stromboli, 2001), 80–84; interview with Vianney Décarie, June 2006.

88. Found in TP, vol. 8, file 7. Viau wrote a review of the show "Reconnaissance de l'espace" in *Notre Temps*, July 12, 1947.

89. Trudeau, *Memoirs*, 23.

90. The evidence is in his Agenda 1947, TP, vol. 39, file 1.

91. Trudeau to Gouin, TP, nd [1947] vol. 48, file 11.

92. Trudeau, *Memoirs*, 40.

93. For Index letter, see TP, vol. 8, file 6; Chartres, ibid., file 7; Renouvin and Siegfried, ibid., file 13.

94. Trudeau, Agenda 1947, TP, vol. 39, file 1.

95. Trudeau had seen the great film by Marcel Carné soon after he arrived in France. Trudeau to Gouin, Oct. 9, 1946, TP, vol. 48, file 20.

96. Trudeau, *Memoirs*, 44–45; Marcel Rioux, *Un peuple dans le siècle* (Montreal: Les Éditions du Boréal, 1990), 49.

97. The letter is dated Sept. 16, 1946, and on Senate of Canada stationery. TP, vol. 8, file 6.

98. Trudeau to Gouin, Oct. 21, 1946, TP, vol. 48, file 20.

99. Ibid.

100. Trudeau to Gouin, Nov. 5, 1946, ibid., file 21.

101. Gouin to Trudeau, Nov. 14, 1946, ibid., file 9.

102. Trudeau to Gouin, Nov. 22, 1946, ibid., file 21.

103. Gouin to Trudeau, Nov. 24, 1946, ibid.

104. Trudeau to Gouin, Dec. 3, 1946, ibid.

105. Trudeau, Agenda 1946, TP, vol. 39, file 1; Gordon Elliott to Trudeau, Dec.16, 1946, TP, vol. 46, file 1.

106. Trudeau to Gouin, Dec. 12[?], 1946, TP, vol. 48, file 2.

107. Trudeau to Gouin, Dec. 29, 1946, ibid.

108. Interview with Thérèse Gouin Décarie, June 2006.

109. Gouin to Trudeau, Feb. 15, 1947, ibid., file 10; and Trudeau to Gouin, Feb. 22, 1947, ibid., file 22.

110. A brief biography can be found at www.aejcpp.free.fr/ psychanalysefrancaise5.htm. It contains this reference.

111. Trudeau's notes are found under the heading "Journal personnel thérapie, fév.–juin 1947," TP, vol. 39, file 10.

112. Gouin to Trudeau, Feb. 25, 1947, TP, vol. 48, file 10.

113. Journal personnel thérapie, TP, vol., 39, file 10.

114. Ibid.

CHAPTER FOUR: COMING HOME

1. Gouin to Trudeau, March 3, 1947, Trudeau Papers (TP), MG 26 02, vol. 48, file 10, Library and Archives Canada (LAC).

2. The school had an impressive budget of $50,000 and would draw 150 students from the broken European countries. Professors from Harvard would participate. Trudeau to Gouin, March 19, 1947, ibid., file 22.

3. Trudeau to Gouin, March 6, 1947, ibid.

4. The schedule is found in Trudeau's agenda. TP, vol. 39, file 1.

5. Gouin to Trudeau, nd [received in Paris apparently on May 1, 1947], TP, vol. 48, file 10.

6. Trudeau to Gouin, May 21, 1947, ibid., file 11.

7. Trudeau to Gouin, April 7, 1947, ibid.

8. He dreamed that Desautels, Rolland, and Hertel were at the table with him and he urinated. He was afraid that he had scandalized the others, but Desautels dismissed the thought, saying that she had already seen sailors in a similar predicament. TP, vol. 39, file 10.

9. Trudeau to Gouin, June 7, 1947, TP, vol. 48, file 23. Also, Journal personnel thérapie, fév.–juin 1947, ibid.

10. Christina McCall and Stephen Clarkson, *Trudeau and Our Times*, vol. 2: *The Heroic Delusion* (Toronto: McClelland & Stewart, 1994), 45.

11. Michel Vastel, *Trudeau: Le Québécois* (Montreal: Les Éditions de l'Homme, 2000), 47.

12. Trudeau to Lomer Gouin, July 10, 1947, TP, vol. 48, file 24.

13. Interview with the Décaries, June 2006.

14. In her acknowledgments to her *Intelligence and Affectivity in Early Childhood: An Experimental Study of Jean Piaget's Object Concept and Object Relations* (New York: International Universities Press, 1965), Thérèse Gouin generously thanked Father Noël Mailloux, who, in her words, "made her love Freud" (xvi). As her analyst, he had appeared frequently in the Trudeau-Gouin letters.

15. Vastel, *Trudeau*, 46–47.

16. McCall and Clarkson, *Trudeau and Our Times*, 2: 88–89.

17. Gouin to Trudeau, nd [1969], TP, vol. 48, file 1.

18. An account of the trip is in TP, vol. 11, file 12, including photographs.

19. For the note on the *Empress of Canada*, see TP, vol. 7, file 17.

20. Trudeau, Agenda 1947, TP, vol. 1, file 39.

21. Lomer Gouin to Trudeau, nd [Nov. 1947], TP, vol. 48, file 1.

22. Quoted in Clarkson and McCall, *Trudeau and Our Times*, 2: 47–48.

23. Trudeau to Thérèse Gouin, Good Friday 1947, TP, vol. 48, file 11; and Trudeau to Lessard, nd [April 1947], Lessard Papers, privately held.

24. On *Notre Temps*'s conservative and Catholic stance, see Jean Hamelin, *Histoire du catholicisme québécois: Le XXe siècle*, vol. 2: *De 1940 à nos jours* (Montreal: Les Éditions du Boréal, 1984), 138. According to Hamelin, the journal was inspired by the French rightist publications. Conrad Black wrote in his biography of Maurice Duplessis: "Léopold Richer, former Bloc Populaire hothead, had rallied to become one of the more obsequious members of Duplessis's journalistic clique. He became the editor of *Notre Temps*, which styled itself 'the social and cultural weekly' and was owned by Fides, the publishing house of the Pères de Ste. Croix in Montreal. Richer himself, a nationalist and hostile ab initio to the Liberals, once converted to Duplessism, did so with the passion of conversions." He was not fully converted when he dealt with Trudeau in 1947. Conrad Black, *Duplessis* (Toronto: McClelland & Stewart, 1977), 566.

25. *Notre Temps*, Nov. 15, 1947; and H.P. Garceau, *Notre Temps*, to Trudeau, Dec. 27, 1945, TP, vol. 22, file 28, in which Garceau asks Trudeau to send some articles and tells him that they miss him in Montreal and that the promoters of economic liberalism will soon get their just retribution.

He said he sees several of their "friends" who are trying to do their part, notably the nationalist historian Guy Frégault.

26. Emmanuel Mounier, "L'homme américain," *Esprit*, Nov. 1946, 138–40; and John Hellman, *Emmanuel Mounier and the New Catholic Left, 1930–1950* (Toronto: University of Toronto Press, 1981), ch. 10.

27. Trudeau to Gouin, April 1947, TP, vol. 48, file 11.

28. Gérard Pelletier, *Years of Impatience, 1950–60*, trans. Alan Brown (1983; Toronto: Methuen, 1984), 19.

29. Ralph Miliband, "Harold Laski," *Clare Market Review* (1950) on www.spartacus.schoolnet.co.uk/TUlaski.htm; Pierre Trudeau, *Memoirs* (Toronto: McClelland & Stewart, 1993), 46.

30. TP, vol. 2, file 26.

31. Trudeau, *Memoirs*, 47.

32. Letter from Trudeau to John Reshetar, quoted in Clarkson and McCall, *Trudeau and Our Times*, 2: 46.

33. Harold Laski, *The State in Theory and Practice* (1935; New York: Viking, 1947), 3.

34. Max Beloff, "The Age of Laski," *The Fortnightly*, June 1950, 378.

35. Harold Laski, *Authority in the Modern State* (New Haven, Conn.: Yale University Press, 1919), 74–75; and Bernard Zylstra, *From Pluralism to Collectivism: The Development of Harold Laski's Political Thought* (Assen, The Netherlands: Van Gorcum, 1968), 75.

36. Trudeau had met often with CCF intellectual and McGill law professor F.R. Scott. He was more interested in Scott's strong civil libertarian stance in wartime than in his CCF activity. He certainly voted CCF in the 1949 federal election when he was the agent for the CCF candidate in Jacques Cartier riding in Montreal. TP, vol. 2, file 6. Trudeau also met with Scott and Canadian Labour Congress (CLC) researcher Eugene Forsey in May 1949. TP, vol. 11, file 18. He applied for a job with the CLC in April 1949. One of his law professors at the Université de Montréal, Jacques Perrault, a prominent CCF activist as well as the brother-in-law of André Laurendeau, wrote a letter of introduction for Trudeau on April 28, 1949, to the CLC. He said that Trudeau had stood first in his class at law school and recommended him as "an ideal research man in general for your movement in Canada and more particularly for

the province of Quebec." Perrault to A. Andras, assistant research director, CLC, April 28, 1949, ibid., file 23. It is tempting to contemplate Trudeau's fate had he worked for the CLC in the early 1950s. He would have been more definitely linked with the CCF and, almost certainly, would have been a CCF candidate—probably a losing one in a Montreal constituency. Most likely, he would never have become a Liberal Party leader.

37. Claude Ryan to Trudeau, Sept. 25, 1947, TP, vol. 8, file 30. Other clippings in the same file indicate other activities.

38. Trudeau attended the LSE Canadian Association, which had its first meeting on February 19, 1948. Among the attendees were Robert McKenzie, later an eminent British political scientist; John Halstead, a future Canadian diplomat and writer; and John Porter, Canada's most celebrated sociologist when Trudeau entered politics in the 1960s. Ibid.

39. Trudeau Agenda, 1948. March 20, 1948, TP, vol. 22, file 20.

40. Trudeau to "M. Caron," nd, ibid., file 23.

41. Interview with Jacques Hébert, Feb. 2006.

42. Laski wrote: "The bearer of this letter, M. Pierre Trudeau, is well known to me. He has been a member of my seminar in this School, and has won both my regard and respect for his vigour and tenacity of mind, and for his power to arrive independently at his conclusions. I recommend him with warmth and respect." Trudeau later responded by naming Laski as one of the five greatest intellectual influences upon his life. He named no other teacher and, in this respect, Laski was a mentor as no professor at Paris, Harvard, or Montréal had been. TP, vol.11, file 23.

43. Léger letter, June 15, 1948; and Beaulieu letter, June 23, 1948, ibid. They said Trudeau was a journalist for Notre Temps and Le Petit Journal.

44. Suzette to Trudeau, March 10, 1946, TP, vol. 3, file 40; and Trudeau to Charles Trudeau, Oct. 20, 1948, TP, vol. 53, file 36.

45. Trudeau, Memoirs, 48.

46. Agenda 1948, Aug. 28, 1948, TP, vol. 11, file 20.

47. Trudeau, Memoirs, 49–51.

48. Ibid., 53–54. The journals of the trip are in TP, vol. 11, file 21.

49. Trudeau to family, Oct. 23, 1948, ibid., file 22.

50. Trudeau to family, Dec. 2, 1948, ibid.

51. The record is confused. Although Trudeau was enrolled in a doctoral program at LSE and had asked Laski to supervise his thesis, he now regularly said that the thesis was for Harvard. Having completed his general examinations at Harvard, he was eligible to proceed on to the thesis stage. However, there is no record at Harvard or in Trudeau's records that he had found the required supervisor or had undertaken the necessary registration of the thesis. Harvard was very loose in thesis supervision. As a student there in the 1960s, I learned of one Canadian academic who had been working on his thesis for twenty years. In any event, Trudeau's thesis was really a pretext for travel, and his journals of the trip are more appropriate for journalism than for thesis research.

52. Trudeau to family, Dec. 2, 1948, TP, vol. 11, file 22.

53. Trudeau to Suzette, Dec. 27, 1948, ibid.

54. Trudeau to Grace Trudeau, Jan. 18, 1949, ibid.

55. Trudeau to Grace Trudeau, Jan. 28, 1949, ibid.

56. Ibid.

57. Trudeau to Grace Trudeau, Feb. 11, 1949, ibid. Also, Agenda 1949, Feb. 11–12, 1949, ibid., file 18.

58. Trudeau to Grace Trudeau, March 10, 1949, ibid.

59. Trudeau to family, March 20, 1949, ibid.

60. Ibid.; Trudeau, *Memoirs*, 60. Norman had been contacted about Trudeau earlier and was the ranking Canadian official in Japan.

61. Trudeau, *Memoirs*, 61.

62. George Radwanski, *Trudeau* (Toronto: Macmillan, 1978), 69–70.

63. Ibid., 69–72.

64. Pelletier is quoted in Edith Iglauer, "Prime Minister/Premier Ministre," *New Yorker*, July 5, 1969, 44.

65. "Réflexions sur une démocratie et sa variante," *Notre Temps*, Feb. 14, 1948.

66. Trudeau to Lise and François Lessard, Oct. 19, 1948, Lessard Papers.

67. Trudeau, "Des avocats et des autres dans leurs rapports avec la justice," in TP, vol. 22, file 31.

68. See the Canadian John Humphrey's *Human Rights and the United Nations: A Great Adventure* (Dobbs Ferry, NY: Transnational, 1984), in which Humphrey, an author of the 1948 Declaration of Human Rights, points to the centrality of the 1940s in defining human rights.

69. Trudeau to John Reshetar, as quoted in Clarkson and McCall, *Trudeau and Our Times*, 2: 46.

70. *Notre Temps*, Feb. 14, 1948.

71. Letter to the editor, *Le Devoir*, July 6, 1949.

72. Agenda 1949, May 19, 1949, TP, vol. 11, file 18.

73. Paul-Émile Borduas, "1948 Refus Global," in Ramsay Cook, ed., *French-Canadian Nationalism* (Toronto: Macmillan, 1969), 276–84. Also, François-Marc Gagnon, *Paul-Émile Borduas: Biographie critique et analyse de l'oeuvre* (Montreal: Les Éditions Fides, 1978), ch. 13.

74. *Le Devoir*, Sept. 28, 1948.

75. Pierre Vadeboncoeur, "Jean Marchand, autrefois," www.scn.qc.ca/Connaitre/Histoire/Vad/Vad2.html.

76. Douglas Stuebing, John Marshall, Gary Oakes, *Trudeau, l'homme de demain!* trans. Hélène Gagnon (Montreal: HMH, 1969), 44. Interview with Jacques Hébert, Feb. 2006.

77. Marchand is quoted in Radwanski, *Trudeau*, 74.

78. Monique Leyrac and 1949 film in http://www.thecanadianencyclopedia.com/index.cfm?PgNm=TCE&Params=U1ARTU0002065.

79. Pelletier, *Years of Impatience*, 14–15, 76.

80. Trudeau, "Quebec at the Time of the Strike," in Pierre Trudeau, ed., *The Asbestos Strike*, trans. James Boake (1956; Toronto: James Lewis & Samuel, 1974), 66–67.

81. Pelletier, *Years of Impatience*, 86ff. On asbestos and its significance as a product in Quebec, see William Coleman, *The Independence Movement in Quebec, 1945–1990* (Toronto: University of Toronto Press, 1984), 113–15.

82. Black, *Duplessis*, 528.

83. Trudeau, ed., *The Asbestos Strike*, 329.

CHAPTER FIVE: HEARTH, HOME, AND NATION

1. Gérard Pelletier, *Years of Impatience, 1950–1960*, trans. Alan Brown (1983; Toronto: Methuen, 1984), 85–86.

2. See Paul-Emile Roy, *Pierre Vadeboncoeur: Un homme attentif* (Montreal: Éditions du Méridien, 1995).

3. Quoted in Robert Rumilly, *Henri Bourassa: La vie publique d'un grand canadien* (Montreal: Les Éditions Chantecler, 1953), 777.

4. *Le Devoir*, April 13, 1949.

5. The notes for "Où va le monde" are found in Trudeau Papers (TP), MG 26 02, vol. 12, file 1, Library and Archives Canada (LAC).

6. Pierre Vadeboncoeur, letter to the editor, *Le Devoir*, July 14, 1949.

7. "Entrevue entre M. Trudeau et M. [Jean] Lépine, 27 avril 1992 [Lépine interview]," Trudeau Papers (TP), MG 26 03, vol. 23, file 2, Library and Archives Canada.

8. Interestingly, in his history of the London School of Economics, the German sociologist Ralf Dahrendorf suggested that the school's influence had been great on the democratic and liberal left in the postwar era. Some would describe the influence as Fabianism, others as socialism, and a few as the welfare state, but what the diverse voices expressed was, in Dahrendorf's words, "the combination of Westminster-style democratic institutions with a benevolent interventionist government guided by a view of the good or just society." For much of the West and even the developing world, what it meant was "a little Laski, so to speak, a little Beveridge, some Tawney and a lot of Pierre Trudeau, the long-serving Canadian Prime Minister with an LSE past." Ralf Dahrendorf, *LSE: A History of the London School of Economics and Political Science, 1895–1995* (Oxford: Oxford University Press, 1995), 405.

9. Marcel Rioux, *Un peuple dans le siècle* (Montreal: Les Éditions du Boréal, 1990), 50.

10. François Hertel, *Méditations philosophiques* (Paris: Éditions de la Diaspora, 1963), 26. The continuing affection for Hertel is found in Roger Rolland's tribute to him in *Le Petit Journal* in 1948. Hertel possessed, Rolland claims, an extraordinary verve. The article, "François Hertel," is found in TP, vol. 38, file 61. Trudeau had learned from his mother about Hertel's discontents and his desire to return to Paris. Grace Trudeau to Pierre Trudeau, Oct. 31, 1948, TP, vol. 46, file 15. Hertel's own description is found in "Lettre à mes amis (15 août 1950, Paris, France)," *Cité libre*, Feb. 1951, 34–35.

11. Grace Trudeau to Pierre Trudeau, Feb. 20, 1948, TP, vol. 46, file 16.

12. E.-Martin Meunier and Jean-Philippe Warren, *Sortir de la "Grande noirceur": L'horizon "personnaliste" de la Révolution tranquille* (Sillery, Que: Les Éditions du Septentrion, 2002), 115; see also footnotes 27 and

28, which describe the appeal of Paris intellectual life to Gérard Pelletier and Jean-Charles Falardeau.

13. Grace Trudeau to Pierre Trudeau, Jan. 8, Jan. 13, Jan. 11, Jan. 17, Jan. 26, Feb. ?, and Feb. 20, 1947, TP, vol. 46, file 15.

14. Ibid., Feb. 27, 1947.

15. Ibid., July 16, 1947.

16. Ibid., Oct. 31 and Nov. 20, 1947.

17. Ibid, Feb. 1 and Feb. 20, 1947.

18. Ibid., file 20, Feb. 24 and March 28, 1952.

19. Ibid., June 4, 1948, and Feb. 4, 1949. The estimated conversion of $700 in 2005 dollars is $5,600.00. See http://www.eh.net/hmit/ppowerusd/dollar_answer.php.

20. Ibid., Nov. 6, 1948.

21. Ibid., July 2, 1948.

22. Ibid., file 17, Feb. 4, 1949.

23. Ibid., file 18, Oct. 18, 1950.

24. Kristin Bennett in Nancy Southam, ed., *Pierre* (Toronto: McClelland & Stewart, 2005), 253.

25. Grace Trudeau to Pierre Trudeau, Nov. 28, 1951, TP, vol. 46, file 18.

26. Interviews with Thérèse Gouin Décarie, June 2006; and Madeleine Gobeil, May 2006.

27. Margaret Trudeau, *Consequences* (Toronto: McClelland & Stewart, 1982), 77–78; and Henry Kissinger in Gerald Ford Papers, Gerald Ford Library, Memorandum, Dec. 4, 1974, MR 02-75.

28. Grace to Pierre Trudeau, May 11, 1948, TP, vol. 46, file 17.

29. On Hébert and MacEachen, see Allan MacEachen, "Reflections on Faith and Politics," in John English, Richard Gwyn, and P. Whitney Lackenbauer, eds., *The Hidden Pierre Elliott Trudeau: The Faith behind the Politics* (Ottawa: Novalis, 2004), 153–60. On Kidder, see her remarks in Southam, ed., *Pierre*, 256. On Cattrall, see Line Abrahamian, "Taking Choices, Making Choices," *Reader's Digest*, April 2005, 70–71. Also, conversations with Marc Lalonde, Margot Kidder, Allan MacEachen, and Margot Breton.

30. Pierre Trudeau, *Memoirs* (Toronto: McClelland & Stewart, 1993), 64. On the salary, see R. Gosselin to Trudeau, Aug. 31, 1949, TP, vol. 9, file 7.

31. Pierre Trudeau, *Federalism and the French Canadians* (Toronto: Macmillan, 1968), 5. On the Department of External Affairs and the Royal Commission, see Gilles Lalande, *The Department of External Affairs and Biculturalism,* Studies of the Royal Commission on Bilingualism and Biculturalism, Number 3 (Ottawa: Information Canada, 1970), 42–46; and J.L. Granatstein, *The Ottawa Men: The Civil Service Mandarins, 1935–1957* (Toronto: Oxford University Press, 1982), 6. For an excellent description of the character of Ottawa at the time, see Stephen Clarkson and Christina McCall, *Trudeau and Our Times,* vol. 2: *The Heroic Delusion* (Toronto: McClelland & Stewart, 1994), 59ff.

32. See, for example, TP, vol. 9, file 13. Gordon Robertson's later comments on Trudeau may be found in his autobiography, *Memoirs of a Very Civil Servant: Mackenzie King to Pierre Trudeau* (Toronto: University of Toronto Press, 2000), 88–89.

33. Trudeau to Gordon Robertson, Oct. 28, 1950, TP, vol. 9, file 23.

34. Robertson to Trudeau, Jan. 6, 1951, TP, vol. 10, file 4. The other documents referred to are found in this file, as is the reference to Diefenbaker. On January 24, 1951, the Cabinet considered the question of internal security controls which Trudeau had been studying. RG 2, PCO, Series A-5-a, vol. 2647, LAC.

35. Registration quotation is in a Memorandum to R.G. Robertson, March 17, 1951, with attachment to "Mr. Eberts." The comment is in the attachment, not in the memorandum, which would have received wider circulation. TP, vol. 10, file 27.

36. Vadeboncoeur's comments are in *Le Devoir,* Oct. 20, 1965; and Hertel's comments are in *La Presse,* Sept. 17, 1966.

37. Trudeau's comments are in TP, vol. 9, file 10. On the complexities of the fiscal and social security questions, see R.M. Burns, *The Acceptable Mean: The Tax Rental Agreements, 1941–1962* (Toronto: Canadian Tax Foundation, 1980), ch. 5.

38. Draft of "Theory and Practice of Federal-Provincial Cooperation," nd, TP, vol. 10, file 5.

39. Memorandum to R.G. Robertson, March 13, 1951, ibid., file 3.

40. Draft of letter to Léger of Aug. 31, 1950, ibid., file 11.

41. Grace Trudeau to Pierre Trudeau, Feb. 28, 1947, TP, vol. 46, file 17.

42. Marginalia on Pearson's speeches of Dec. 5, 1950, and April 10, 1951, TP, vol. 10, file 11.

43. Trudeau to LePan, April 28, 1951, ibid.

44. Trudeau to Robertson, June 6, 1951, ibid., file 1.

45. Interviews with Trudeau staff. Meeting organized by Library and Archives Canada.

46. He saved the clipping in TP, vol. 38, file 70.

47. Segerstrale to Trudeau, Nov. 6, 1951, TP, vol. 53, file 1; Trudeau to Segerstrale, nd [Jan. ? 1952], ibid.

48. The notes to the East Block have no dates. Letter about her mother is November 10, 1951, and letter responding to Trudeau complaints is December 21, 1951. Letter about Gibraltar is January 2, 1952. Ibid.

49. Helen Segerstale to Trudeau, Jan. 26, 1952, ibid.

50. Trudeau to Segerstrale, March 17 [?], 1952, ibid.

51. Trudeau to Norman Robertson, Sept. 24, 1951, TP, vol. 10, file 1.

52. Trudeau to Norman Robertson, Sept. 28, 1951, TP, vol. 9, file 2. Trudeau's immediate supervisor, Gordon Robertson, treats Trudeau's departure briefly and has not responded to the account of the final conversation between the two presented in Trudeau's memoirs. See Robertson, *A Very Civil Servant*, 88–89.

53. Quoted in Michael Behiels, *Prelude to Quebec's Quiet Revolution: Liberalism versus Neo-Nationalism, 1945–1960* (Montreal and Kingston: McGill-Queen's University Press, 1985), 62.

54. Pelletier, *Years of Impatience*, 114.

55. Ibid., 112–13.

56. Accounts are found in TP, vol. 20, file 2.

57. TP, vol. 21, file 2.

58. "Faites vos jeux," *Cité libre*, June 1950, 27–28.

59. Pierre Elliott Trudeau, *Against the Current: Selected Writings, 1939–1966*, ed. Gérard Pelletier, trans. G. Tombs (Toronto: McClelland & Stewart, 1996), 27–28. Original, "Politique fonctionnelle," *Cité libre*, June 1950, 20–24.

60. Draft of letter to Jean Marchand, nd [1951], TP, vol. 15, file 8.

61. Quoted in Pierre Godin, *Daniel Johnson, 1946–1964: La passion du pouvoir* (Montreal: Les Éditions de l'Homme, 1980), 77.

62. Paul-André Linteau, René Durocher, Jean-Claude Robert, and François Ricard, *Quebec since 1930* trans. Robert Chodos and Ellen Garmaise (Toronto: James Lorimer, 1991), 254–57.

CHAPTER SIX: NATIONALISM AND SOCIALISM

1. "Entrevue entre M. Trudeau et M. [Jean] Lépine, 27 avril 1992" [Lépine interview], Trudeau Papers (TP), MG 26 03, vol. 23, file 2, Library and Archives Canada.

2. Michael Behiels, *Prelude to Quebec's Quiet Revolution: Liberalism versus Neo-Nationalism, 1945–1960* (Montreal and Kingston: McGill-Queen's University Press, 1985), 70.

3. Ibid., 60. On Korea, only 21 percent of Quebecers (both French and English) approved of the proposal to send forces to Korea (41% in the rest of Canada) on August 3, 1950. On July 23, 1952, only 32 percent thought it was not a mistake to send troops to Korea (59% in the rest of Canada). See Mildred Schwartz, *Public Opinion and Canadian Identity* (Scarborough, Ont.: Fitzhenry and Whiteside, 1967), 80.

4. Arès to Trudeau, March 2, 1951, TP, vol. 21, file 9.

5. D'Anjou to Trudeau, Feb. 21, 1951, ibid.

6. Ibid., March 2, 1951.

7. Gérard Pelletier, *Years of Impatience, 1950–1960*, trans. Alan Brown (1983; Toronto: Methuen, 1984), 119.

8. On Johnson, see Pierre Godin, *Daniel Johnson, 1946–1964: La passion du pouvoir* (Montreal: Les Éditions de l'Homme, 1980); Pelletier is quoted in Michel Vastel, *Trudeau: Le Québécois* (Montreal: Les Éditions de l'Homme, 2000), 105; Pelletier quotes the critical friend in his *Years of Impatience*, 87; Thérèse Casgrain, *A Woman in a Man's World* (Toronto: McClelland & Stewart, 1972), 139; comments of Jean Marchand from an interview in Stephen Clarkson and Christina McCall, *Trudeau and Our Times*, vol. 1: *The Magnificent Obsession* (Toronto: McClelland & Stewart, 1990), 70; and Duplessis in Conrad Black, *Duplessis* (Toronto: McClelland & Stewart, 1977), 559. Vastel is especially good on the 1950s and spends considerable time dealing with the image and the reality of Trudeau in that decade.

9. Fournier in Stephen Clarkson and Christina McCall, *Trudeau and Our Times*, vol. 2; *The Heroic Delusion* (Toronto: McClelland & Stewart, 1994), 65.

10. Conversation with Sharon and David Johnston, Dec. 2004; interview with Donald Johnston, June 2004. Johnston, Trudeau's lawyer and a Cabinet minister in the eighties, describes Trudeau with the family in his memoir *Up the Hill* (Montreal: Opticum, 1996).

11. Pierre Trudeau, *Memoirs* (Toronto: McClelland & Stewart, 1993), 69.

12. Paul-André Linteau, René Durocher, Jean-Claude Robert, and François Ricard, *Quebec since 1930* (Toronto: James Lorimer, 1991), 287.

13. Curiously, Trudeau told Helen Segerstrale on August 21, 1952, that he had been offered a position in political science at the Université de Montréal but had turned it down. This information conflicts with various other accounts, but it does suggest that Trudeau did not believe then that Duplessis had blocked his appointment. It may be that he referred to an offer that had not been approved by senior university officials. TP, vol. 12, file 53.

14. *Marshall McLuhan: The Man and His Message*, co-production of CBC Television and McLuhan Productions produced and directed by Stephanie McLuhan, 1984; Marshall McLuhan, "The Man in the Mask," quoted in W. Terrence Gordon, *Marshall McLuhan: Escape into Understanding. A Biography* (Toronto: Stoddart, 1997), 235. McLuhan's enthusiasm for Trudeau was evident in a 1968 *New York Times* book review of Trudeau's essay collection *Federalism and the French Canadians* (Toronto: Macmillan, 1968).

15. "Portrait de P.E. Trudeau à Radio-Canada, 1950," TP, vol. 11, file 27.

16. Interview with Marc Lalonde, April 2004.

17. Pelletier, *Years of Impatience*, 27.

18. At the time he wrote the article opposing the Korean War, Trudeau had debated with his *Cité libre* colleagues whether he should use a pseudonym that could be easily recognized, such as "Pierre d'Ecbatane." "Trudeau, citoyen," to "citoyens libres," [1951], TP, vol. 21, file 28.

19. Ben Rogers to Under-Secretary of State for External Affairs, April 1, 1952; Robert Ford to Under-Secretary of State for External Affairs, April 3 and April 17, 1952; and Trudeau to Norman Robertson, dated March 17 but sent April 17, 1952, from Moscow. All are in Privy Council Records, RG 2, C-100–4, LAC. I would like to thank Paul Marsden for drawing my attention to these records.

20. "Au Sommet des Caucases," broadcast *CBF au réseau français*, Sept. 18, 1952, TP, vol. 12, file 16.

21. Interview between Pierre Trudeau and Ron Graham, May 12, 1992, TP, vol. 23, file 12.

22. "J'ai fait mes Pâques à Moscou," broadcast *Réseau français de Radio Canada*, Sept. 4, 1952, ibid.

23. "Aux prises avec le Politbureau [sic]," broadcast *CBF au réseau français*, Sept. 25, 1952, ibid.

24. Trudeau to Laurendeau, draft of letter, Nov. 17, 1952, TP, vol. 12, file 12.

25. Braun, "Apparences et réalités religieuses en U.R.S.S.," *L'Action catholique*, Nov. 19, 1952.

26. The articles in *Le Devoir* are June 14 and June 16–21, 1952. The Braun attack may be found in *L'Action catholique*, Nov. 17, 1952. Also, *Nos Cours* 14 (13) (Jan. 10, 1953): 19–32. Correspondence with J.-B. Desrosiers in TP, vol. 12, file 12, including Trudeau letter of Dec. 4, 1952; letter to Father Florent, Jan. 23, 1951, ibid., file 14.

27. TP, vol. 12, file 18.

28. "Retour d'URSS: Le camarade Trudeau," *Le Quartier Latin*, Oct. 23, 1952.

29. Ibid.; and "Staline est-il poète?" broadcast *CBF au réseau français*, Sept. 11, 1952, TP vol. 12, file 16. On the Moscow conference, see the report by the economist Alec Cairncross, "The Moscow Economic Conference," *Soviet Studies* 4 (Oct. 1952): 113–32. Cairncross saw value in the conference as an occasion for Western economists to meet their Eastern counterparts. He noted that "the delegations from the West were drawn mainly from left-wing or radical groups and no voice was raised at any time that could be said to be really representative of right-wing opinion. The speeches, therefore, gave a rather one-sided impression and were uniformly complimentary to the USSR, but often extremely hostile to the USA" (114).

30. Susan Trofimenkoff, *The Dream of Nation* (Toronto: Gage, 1983), 285. See also Gérard Laurence, "Les affaires publiques à la télévision, 1952–1957," *Revue d'histoire de l'Amérique française* 6 (Sept. 1952): 213–19.

31. For a description of Lévesque's.style, see Paul Rutherford, *When Television Was Young: Primetime Canada, 1952–1957* (Toronto: University of Toronto Press, 1990), 175–77; and Pelletier, *Years of Impatience*, 27–28.

32. Jim Coutts, "Trudeau in Power: A View from Inside the Prime Minister's Office," in Andrew Cohen and J.L. Granatstein, eds., *Trudeau's Shadow: The Life and Legacy of Pierre Elliott Trudeau* (Toronto: Random House Canada, 1998), 149.

33. Trudeau to Segerstrale, Aug. 21, 1952; and Segerstrale to Trudeau, Dec. 18, 1952, TP vol. 53, file 1.

34. The election was closer than the number of seats indicated. The Liberals won 46 percent of the vote compared with 50.5 percent for Duplessis, but they won only 23 seats compared with 68 for the Union nationale. This imbalance became a major political issue in Quebec in the 1950s, although it occurs frequently in the British parliamentary system.

35. Black, *Duplessis*, 362–63.

36. Pierre Eliott Trudeau, *Against the Current: Selected Writings, 1939–1996*, ed. Gérard Pelletier, trans. George Tombs (Toronto: McClelland & Stewart, 1996), 29–33. Also, "La Revue des Arts et des Lettres," broadcast *CBF au réseau français*, Jan. 27, 1953, TP, vol. 25, file 5.

37. Pelletier, *Years of Impatience*, 131–33. On the political neutrality, see Roch Denis, *Luttes de classes et question nationale au Québec, 1948–1968* (Montreal: Les Presses Socialistes Internationales, 1979), 157–58.

38. Draft of remarks to Couchiching Conference, 1952, TP, vol. 25, file 41.

39. Trudeau, "Techniques du voyage," "Moulin à vent," Jan. 17, 1954, TP, vol. 12, file 17.

40. See, for example, Clarkson and McCall, *Trudeau and Our Times*, 2: 69–71.

41. Quoted in Pelletier, *Years of Impatience*, 110.

42. Paul-André Linteau, *Histoire de Montréal depuis la Confédération* (Montreal: Les Éditions du Boréal, 2000), 483.

43. *Le Devoir*, Oct. 15, 1952; Denis, *Luttes des classes*, 136ff; Donald Horton, *André Laurendeau: French-Canadian Nationalist* (Toronto: Oxford, 1992), ch. 8; and, for the description of Laurendeau's anti-Duplessis sentiment as it developed within his family, see Chantal Perrault, "Oncle André," in Robert Comeau and Lucille Beaudry, eds., *André Laurendeau: un intellectuel d'ici* (Sillery, Que.: Les Presses de l'Université du Québec, 1990), 34.

44. Trudeau, "Réflexions sur la politique," *Cité libre*, Dec. 1952, 65–66. On unionism and the *Cité libre* group, see Behiels, *Prelude to Quebec's Quiet Revolution*, ch. 7.

45. Trudeau, "La Revue des Arts et des Lettres," broadcast *CBF au réseau français*, Jan. 2, 1953.

46. André Malavoy, "Une recontre mémorable," in Comeau and Beaudry, eds., *André Laurendeau*, 20.

47. George Radwanski, *Trudeau* (Toronto: Macmillan, 1978), 83.

48. "École de la metallurgie, Cours de P.E. Trudeau, le 23 janvier 1954," TP, vol. 15, file 6.

49. Maurice Lamontagne, *Le fédéralisme canadien: Évolutions et problèmes* (Quebec: Les Presses de l'Université Laval, 1954).

50. Father Lévesque made contact with Trudeau through Doris Lussier, a friend of Trudeau who worked with Lévesque. She had given Lévesque the text of one of Trudeau's speeches. He said it was a strong address "whose vehemence equals its truth." He hoped to meet Trudeau soon and to have him speak at Laval.

51. Behiels, *Prelude to Quebec's Quiet Revolution*, 191.

52. "Mémoire de la F.U.I.Q.," TP, vol. 16, file 2.

53. See Black, *Duplessis*, 485; and Trudeau, "De libro, tributo et quibusdam aliis," in Trudeau, *Federalism and the French Canadians*, 66–69. Original in *Cité libre*, Oct. 1954, 1–16. On the grants specifically, see Trudeau, "Les octrois fédéraux aux universités," *Cité libre*, Feb. 1957, 9–31.

54. Robert Rumilly, "Pierre E. Trudeau honoré pour avoir insulté les Can.-Français," TP, vol. 14, file 38.

55. On Rumilly's background and attitudes, see Jean-François Nadeau, "La divine surprise de Robert Rumilly," in Michel Sarra-Bournet and Jocelyn Saint-Pierre, eds., *Les Nationalismes au Québec du xix au xxi siècle* (Québec: Les Presses de l'Université Laval, 2001), 105–16.

56. Conversation with Sylvia Ostry, Feb. 2003.

57. Erasmus, "À propos de 'Cité Libre,'" *L'Action catholique*, June 22, 1953.

58. Accounts of these programs are found in TP, vol. 25, files 3 and 4. Confidential interview with female friend about the Roman Catholic Church.

59. Trudeau to Segerstrale, Aug. 6, 1955, TP, vol. 53, file 1.

CHAPTER SEVEN: EVE OF THE REVOLUTION

1. Frank Scott, "Foreword," in Pierre Trudeau, ed., *La Grève de l'amiante* (Montreal: Les Éditions Cité libre, 1956), ix. Further references are to the

English edition, *The Asbestos Strike*, trans. James Boake (Toronto: James
Lewis & Samuel, 1974). The background to Recherches sociales is
described in David Lewis, *The Good Fight: Political Memoirs, 1909–1958*
(Toronto: Macmillan, 1981), 456. Gérard Pelletier describes the financing
arrangements and the "foundation" that would finance it. Frank Scott,
Eugene Forsey, Jacques Perrault, and Jean-Charles Falardeau were the
trustees, and they met to finalize the arrangements on February 11, 1951.
Trudeau Papers (TP), MG 26 02, vol. 25, file 15, Library and Archives
Canada (LAC).

2. Fernand Dumont, "History of the Trade Union Movement in the Asbestos
Industry," in Trudeau, ed., *The Asbestos Strike*, 107. Gilles Beausoleil, then
a graduate student at the Massachusetts Institute of Technology, was the
other author. Many others were considered as possible authors, including
Jean Marchand.

3. The project was nearly abandoned in 1953 because of the delays. Jean
Gérin-Lajoie to Trudeau, March 11, 1953, TP, vol. 23, file 16.

4. Ibid., Nov. 23, 1955.

5. J.-C. Falardeau to Trudeau, Dec. 20, 1955, ibid., file 15. The problems
with the printers are discussed in Grace Trudeau to Pierre Trudeau, Oct.
6, 1955; she sympathized with his difficulty in finding a publisher on Dec.
1, 1955, TP, vol. 46, file 23. Falardeau strongly opposed trying to publish
in France in a letter of June 17, 1955, TP, vol. 23, file 16.

6. Trudeau, ed., *The Asbestos Strike*, 345, 14, 67.

7. Ibid., 348–49. Trudeau's earlier articles that contain the seeds of the essay
include "La démocratie est-elle viable au Canada français?" *L'Action
nationale*, Nov. 1954, 190–200, and "Une lettre sur la politique," *Le
Devoir*, Sept. 18, 1954. On the church, see his "Matériaux pour servir à
une enquête sur le cléricalisme," *Cité libre*, May 1953, 29–37.

8. Trudeau, ed., *The Asbestos Strike*, 6–9. An excellent analysis of Trudeau's
argument can be found in Michael Behiels, *Prelude to Quebec's Quiet
Revolution: Liberalism versus Neo-Nationalism, 1945–1960* (Montreal and
Kingston: McGill-Queen's University Press, 1985), especially chs. 4 and 5.

9. Trudeau, ed., *The Asbestos Strike*, 16–21, 25, 37, 64–65.

10. Trudeau said, correctly, that Hertel advocated a corporatist version of personalism in 1945. Ibid., 24. On the politicians, see ibid., 51.

11. Ibid., 44.
12. *Le Devoir*, Feb. 2, 1955; *Vrai*, Feb. 12, 1955.
13. Trudeau, ed., *The Asbestos Strike*, 346–49.
14. François-Albert Angers, "Pierre Elliott Trudeau et *La Grève de l'amiante*," *L'Action nationale*, Sept. 1957, 10–22, and Sept.–Oct. 1958, 45–56; Father Jacques Cousineau, *Réflexions en marge de "la Grève de l'amiante"* (Montreal: Les cahiers de l'Institut social populaire, 1958); and Pierre Trudeau, "Le père Cousineau, s.j., et *La grève de l'amiante*," *Cité libre*, May 1959, 34–48. Laurendeau's articles are found in *Le Devoir*, Oct. 6, 10–11, 1956. The files on the Cousineau case are in TP, vol. 20, files 20–21.
15. The dismissal of Catholic and nationalist thought was a characteristic of many of the *Cité libre* group. Trudeau's own comment that the strike was purely the product of industrial forces and that ideas such as those of nationalism and religion could play no part brought later rebuke from Fernand Dumont, Trudeau's collaborator in the fifties: "An event which bears historical meaning without an ideological character, one that is produced solely by the forces of production, isn't that the greatest marvel?" Trudeau's implicit dismissal of the value of his own education and, of course, his years in law school was not unusual on the part of his generation. Fernand Dumont, "Une révolution culturelle," in Dumont, Jean Hamelin, and Jean-Paul Montminy, eds., *Idéologies au Canada français, 1940–1976* (Quebec: Les Presses de l'Université Laval, 1981), 19.
16. On Scott and Trudeau, see Sandra Djwa, "Nothing by Halves: F.R. Scott," *Journal of Canadian Studies* 35 (winter 2000): 52–69.
17. Quoted in J.D. Legge, *Sukarno: A Political Biography* (London: Allen Lane, 1965), 264–65.
18. Report of World University Service of Canada tour, TP, vol. 13, file 4.
19. Conrad Black, *Duplessis* (Toronto: McClelland & Stewart, 1977), 389.
20. Perron to Trudeau, Sept. 9, 1950, TP, vol. 20, file 2; Doris Lussier to Trudeau, May 21, 1953, TP, vol. 21, file 12; Lionel Tiger to Trudeau, Aug. 28, 1958, TP, vol. 18, file 1; Trudeau to "Jennifer," nd [1954], TP, vol. 53, file 38.
21. Black, *Duplessis*, 372–73; Paul-André Linteau, René Durocher, Jean-Claude Robert, François Ricard, *Quebec since 1930* (Toronto: James Lorimer, 1991), 269–70.

22. Grace Trudeau to Pierre Trudeau, Sept. 6, 1955, and Oct. 22, 1955, TP, vol. 46, file 23. When Casgrain had stood as a candidate in Outremont in 1952, Trudeau had worked for her. Ibid., vol. 28, file 14.

23. *Le Devoir*, June 1, 1956. Trudeau's drafts are in TP, vol. 22, file 12.

24. These results are taken from the official site of the Quebec National Assembly: www.assnat.qc.ca/fra/patrimoine/votes.html.

25. André Carrier, "L'idéologie politique de la revue *Cité libre*," *Canadian Journal of Political Science* 1 (Dec. 1968): 414–28.

26. Trudeau had many files on *Cité libre*. See also Yvan Lamonde and Gérard Pelletier, eds., *Cité libre: une anthologie* (Montreal: Stanké, 1991), for a more general history. A comparison of the journal's circulation is found in Pierre Bourgault, *La Presse*, Nov. 11, 1961; he gives the figures. Cormier's attempt to resign is found in TP, vol. 21, file 5. For the general files, see TP, vol. 20, files 1–45. The exchange with Vadeboncoeur occurred on January 22, 1955, TP, vol. 21, file 29. See also *Time*, Jan. 19, 1953.

27. Quoted in Pelletier, *Years of Impatience*, 1950–1960, trans. Alan Brown (1983; Toronto: Methuen, 1984), 26.

28. Lamonde and Pelletier, eds., *Cité libre*, 16.

29. These lists are drawn from files in the Trudeau Papers, especially TP, vol. 21, file 36. Scott to "Reginald [Boisvert]," July 7, 1950, ibid., file 26; Léon Dion to Trudeau, April 26, 1957, ibid., file 12; Jean Le Moyne to Trudeau, March 9, 1955, ibid., file 12; Rocher to Jean-Paul Geoffroy, May 20, 1951, ibid., file 25; Blair Fraser to Trudeau, nd, ibid., file 3; and Rocher to Trudeau, Jan. 21, 1953, ibid., file 2.

30. See Behiels, *Prelude to Quebec's Quiet Revolution*, 250–51, for a description of the Rassemblement platform and organization. For the constitution and principles of the Rassemblement, see *Le Devoir*, Sept. 14, 1956.

31. Pierre Trudeau, *Memoirs* (Toronto: McClelland & Stewart, 1993), 70; Pierre Dansereau, "Témoinage," in Robert Comeau et Lucille Beaudry, eds., *André Laurendeau: Un intellectuel d'ici* (Sillery, Que.: Les Presses de l'Université du Québec, 1990), 184; Gérard Bergeron, *Du Duplessisme au Johnsonisme* (Montreal: Éditions Parti pris, 1967), 132–35; Behiels, *Prelude to Quebec's Quiet Revolution*, 253–56; and André Laurendeau, "Blocs-notes," *Le Devoir*, Dec. 3, 1957.

32. Pelletier to Trudeau, Aug. 29, 1957, TP, vol. 27, file 13.

33. Ibid., file 9.

34. Pierre Trudeau, "Les octrois fédéraux aux universités," *Cité libre*, Feb. 1957, 9–31; Forsey to Trudeau, Feb. 26, 1954, TP, vol. 16, file 7.

35. Figures from Jean-Louis Roy, *La marche des Québécois: Le temps des ruptures (1945–1960)* (Montreal: Éditions Leméac, 1976), 273.

36. *Le Soleil*, Nov. 6, 1957. Trudeau debated the question on October 10, 1958, on radio and argued that the grants were "against the constitution and the spirit of federalism." TP, vol. 25, file 4.

37. They were later published as Pierre Trudeau, *Approaches to Politics* (Toronto: Oxford University Press, 1970).

38. Ibid.; "Faut-il assassiner le tyran?" *Vrai*, March 15, 1958; and Hébert's defence in *Vrai*, March 22, 1958.

39. The correspondence with Wade began on November 3, 1955, and included letters of October 5, 1956, and October 30, 1956. The *University of Toronto Quarterly* letter was written on March 12, 1957, and Trudeau's draft reply was April 17, 1957. He wrote on January 13, 1958, to offer the article to the *Canadian Journal of Economics and Political Science*, TP, vol. 24, file 1. See Trudeau, "Some Obstacles to Democracy in Quebec," *CJEPS* 23 (Aug. 1958): 297–311, republished in Pierre Trudeau, *Federalism and the French Canadians* (Toronto: Macmillan, 1968), 103–23. See also John Dales to Trudeau, Feb. 11, 1958, TP, vol. 22, file 1.

40. John Stevenson to Trudeau, Oct. 15, 1958, TP, vol. 53, file 13. The quotation is from Trudeau, "Some Obstacles," 106–7.

41. Clippings and the notification of the prize from James Talman, a historian at the University of Western Ontario, are found in TP, vol. 22, file 1. *Le Devoir* did report it. Flavien Laplante to Trudeau, Dec. 26, 1959, vol. 13, file 8.

42. *Vrai*, June 14, 1958.

43. The Lesage speech with Trudeau's annotations is found in TP, vol. 22, file 38.

44. Pelletier, *Years of Impatience*, 168.

45. Madeleine Gobeil to Trudeau, April 7, 1957, TP, vol. 47, file 32.

46. *Le Petit Journal*, May 29, 1955.

47. Trudeau, "Un manifeste démocratique," Cité libre, Oct. 1958, 1–31; and Behiels, *Prelude to Quebec's Quiet Revolution*, 254.

48. "Rapport d'un assemblée de Cité Libre tenue le 11 novembre 1958," and "Rapport d'une assemblée de Cité Libre tenue le 6 décembre 1958," TP,

vol. 21, file 41. On the university protest, see Jacques Hébert, *Duplessis Non Merci!* (Montreal: Les Éditions du Boréal, 2000), ch. 7.

49. Edward Sommer to Jacques Hébert, Feb. 15, 1961, TP, vol. 14, file 5. On the sunbathers and other files, see ibid., file 2. Trudeau appears to have had a friend who was an American nudist. On Laskin, Scott, and the relationship of federalism and civil liberties, see the excellent account in Philip Girard, *Bora Laskin: Bringing Law to Life* (Toronto: University of Toronto Press, 2005), 210–21. On Trudeau's views, see his "Economic Rights," *McGill Law Journal* 8 (June 1962): 121, 123, 125.

50. Letters of introduction by Scott in TP, vol. 13, file1. On the anti-Semitic and anti-Communist presence, see Sandra Djwa, *The Politics of the Imagination: The Life of F.R. Scott* (Toronto: McClelland & Stewart, 1987), 173. On the effect of the 1930s, see Sean Mills, "When Democratic Socialists Discovered Democracy: The League for Social Reconstruction Confronts the 'Quebec Problem,'" *Canadian Historical Review* 86 (March 2005).

51. The account is drawn from Djwa, *The Politics of the Imagination,* 322–27. F.R. Scott, "Fort Smith," in *The Collected Poems of F.R. Scott* (Toronto: McClelland & Stewart, 1981), 226.

52. Scott, "Fort Providence," ibid., 230–31.

53. Interview with Tim Porteous, May 2006.

54. The clippings with these comments are found in TP, vol. 25, file 28.

55. The Drapeau-Trudeau debate is found in TP, vol. 28, file 9.

56. For the notes that indicate the close friendship, see TP, vol. 21, file 29. The copy of *Le Social Démocrate* is found in vol. 28, file 9. The description of Vadeboncoeur teaching Trudeau to write is in Trudeau, *Memoirs,* 20.

57. For Trudeau's notebook describing the trip, see TP, vol. 13, file 5.

58. The Trudeau family profited from Belmont during the fifties, and Trudeau took the major responsibility for handling family investments. Ibid., file 6.

59. Ibid., file 6; and Grace Trudeau to Pierre Trudeau, June 1 and Sept. 8, 1959, TP, vol. 46, file 26.

60. There is scarcely a reference to Trudeau in the newspapers I consulted that is not neatly clipped in his own papers. Pelletier also claims that Trudeau had to be "coaxed" into television. In fact, he sought out appearances, kept press clippings about them, and urged his mother to watch his

performances. Pelletier explains that "it was understood between us that friendship had its limits." In terms of personal feelings and ambitions, the limits were significant. Pelletier, *Years of Impatience*, 187–88; Grace to Pierre Trudeau, Nov. 24, 1958, TP, vol. 46, file 25; and *The Canadian Intelligence Service* (July 1959): 2.

61. Michel Vastel, *Trudeau: Le Québécois* (Montreal: Les Éditions de l'Homme, 2000), 109. The list of addresses is found in TP, vol. 13, file 7.

62. TP, vol. 13, file 11. The stories on the trip are found in *Miami Herald*, May 2, 1960; and *Key West Citizen*, April 29 and May 2, 1960. There is a long story in the Canadian *Star Weekly*, Jan. 14, 1961, about Gagnon and the canoe technique.

63. Gobeil to Trudeau, May 18[?], 1960, TP, vol. 47, file 32.

CHAPTER EIGHT: A DIFFERENT TURN

1. *Le Devoir*, Jan. 29, 1960.

2. The account comes mainly from Paul-André Linteau, *Histoire de Montréal depuis la Confédération* (Montreal: Les Éditions du Boréal, 2000), ch. 16. Comment on the Metropolitan Opera and other cultural matters is in Paul-André Linteau, René Durocher, Jean-Claude Robert, and François Ricard, *Quebec since 1930*, trans. Robert Chodos and Ellen Garmaise (Toronto: James Lorimer, 1991), 304–5.

3. Some of the debates on the subject are in Trudeau Papers (TP), MG 26 02, vol. 22, file 16, Library and Archives Canada (LAC), including a strong denunciation of his television efforts on identity cards by Dr. J.S. Lynch which appeared in *Le Devoir*, Nov. 20, 1959.

4. Léon Dion, *Québec, 1945–2000*, vol. 2: *Les intellectuels et le temps de Duplessis* (Sainte-Foy, Que.: Les Presses de l'Université Laval, 1993), 195ff.

5. On the Liberal victory in the political arena, see Pierre Godin, *René Lévesque*, vol. 1: *Un enfant du siècle, 1922–60* (Montreal: Les Éditions du Boréal, 1994), 403–5. The information is repeated in Dale Thomson, *Jean Lesage and the Quiet Revolution* (Toronto: Macmillan, 1984), 85–86. Trudeau's comments are from interviews with Ron Graham for his memoirs in TP, vol. 24, file 15. His statement on the need for men in the legislature is in *Le Travail*, Feb. 22, 1957.

6. Pierre Godin, *René Lévesque*, vol. 2: *Héros malgré lui, 1960–1976* (Montreal: Les Éditions du Boréal, 1997), 118.

7. Pierre-Elliott Trudeau, "L'élection du 22 juin 1960," *Cité libre*, Aug.-Sept. 1960, 3. The article was written in July. Trudeau occasionally used a hyphen in his name at this time.

8. Ibid., 6. Georges-Émile Lapalme, *Mémoires: Le vent de l'oubli* (Montreal: Éditions Leméac, 1971). On Duplessis, see Godin, *Lévesque*, 1: 290.

9. Dion, *Québec, 1945–2000*, 2: 195–96; Léon Dion, "Le nationalisme pessimiste: Sa source, sa signification, sa validité," *Cité libre*, Nov. 1957, 3–18; Léon Dion, "L'esprit démocratique chez les Canadiens de langue française," *Cahiers*, Nov. 1958, 34–43; and Pierre Laporte, "La démocratie et M. Trudeau," *L'Action nationale*, Dec. 1954, 293–96.

10. Dion to Trudeau, Feb. 27, 1958, TP, vol. 21, file 12.

11. The case continues to find its place on lists of major injustices. Prominent Canadian criminal lawyer Eddie Greenspan has cited it as an argument for the abolition of capital punishment. See http://www.injusticebusters.com/2003/Coffin_Wilbert.htm.

12. Jacques Hébert and Pierre Trudeau, *Two Innocents in Red China*, trans. Ivon Owen (Toronto: Oxford University Press, 1968), 71–72.

13. Ibid., 150.

14. Ibid., 150–52. The comment on Mao is on page 71.

15. On the launch, see TP, vol. 24, file 3. Also, *Montreal Star*, March 29, 1961, which has the photograph of Hébert with the priests.

16. Trudeau and Hébert, *Two Innocents in Red China*, 61, 152. Jung Chang and Jon Halliday, *Mao: The Unknown Story* (New York: Knopf, 2005), 460.

17. Chang and Halliday, *Mao: The Unknown Story*; and Naim Kattan in *The Montrealer*, June 1961, 4.

18. Interview between Pierre Trudeau and Ron Graham, May 12, 1992, TP, vol. 23, file 12.

19. Interview with Robert Ford, Oct. 15, 1987, Robert Bothwell Papers, University of Toronto Archives.

20. Pierre Trudeau, "De l'inconvénient d'être catholique," *Cité libre*, March 1961, 20–21; and Pierre Trudeau, "Note sur le parti cléricaliste," *Cité libre*, June/July 1961, 23. The correspondence is in TP, vol. 21, file 35.

21. On the Soviets and the perception of strength, see Michael Beschloss, *The*

Crisis Years: Kennedy and Khrushchev, 1960–1963 (New York: Edward Burlingame Books, 1991), ch. 2; Trudeau's broadcast "China's Economic Planning in Action" is found in TP, vol. 25, file 26; Samuel Huntington, *Political Order in Changing Societies* (New Haven: Yale University Press, 1968); Trudeau, "De l'inconvénient d'être catholique," 20–21; and Michael Oliver to Trudeau, Oct. 29, 1959, TP, vol. 24, file 4.

22. Trudeau and Hébert, *Two Innocents in Red China*, 47.

23. Ibid., 111, 113.

24. Interview with Thérèse Gouin Décarie and Vianney Décarie, June 2006.

25. Gérard Pelletier, *Years of Impatience, 1950–1960*, trans. Alan Brown (1983; Toronto: Methuen, 1984), 120n12.

26. Desbiens and Untel are described in Dion, *Quebec, 1945–2000*, 2: 224–25.

27. Gérard Pelletier, "Feu l'unanimité," *Cité libre*, Oct. 1960, 8. The section on Groulx draws from a list of objections taken from various writings of the fifties and sixties found in Gérard Bouchard, *Les deux chanoines: Contradiction et ambivalence dans la pensée de Lionel Groulx* (Montreal: Les Éditions du Boréal, 2003), 22–23. In a 1962 letter to Raymond Barbeau, Groulx strangely echoed Trudeau in suggesting that Quebec was not ready for democracy; quoted in Bouchard, *Les deux chanoines*, 222.

28. Trudeau, "De l'inconvénient d'être catholique," 20–21, in which he clearly asserted his Catholicism while criticizing its restrictive aspects.

29. Interview with Madeleine Gobeil, May 2006.

30. Gérard Pelletier, *Years of Choice, 1960–1968*, trans. Alan Brown (Toronto: Methuen, 1987), 56–62; Pierre Trudeau, *Against the Current: Selected Writings, 1939–1996* trans. George Tombs (Toronto: McClelland & Stewart, 1996), 143–49.

31. Ramsay Cook to Trudeau, April 1962, TP, vol. 21, file 3; Trudeau to Cook, April 19, 1962, Ramsay Cook Papers, privately held.

32. Marchand, quoted in George Radwanski, *Trudeau* (Toronto: Macmillan, 1978), 260.

33. Sandra Djwa, *The Politics of the Imagination: A Life of F.R. Scott* (Toronto: McClelland & Stewart, 1987), 332–37. Scott told Djwa that he considered refuting the article in a 1980 letter.

34. The file dealing with *A Social Purpose for Canada* is found in TP, vol. 24.

522 NOTES TO CHAPTER EIGHT

35. A collection of attacks on Trudeau's writings and actions was published in 1972. Among the authors are the erstwhile friends Marcel Rioux and Fernand Dumont. André Potvin, Michel Letourneux, and Robert Smith, *L'anti-Trudeau: Choix de textes* (Montreal: Éditions Parti pris, 1972).

36. "The Practice and Theory of Federalism" is republished in Pierre Trudeau, *Federalism and the French Canadians* (Toronto: Macmillan, 1968), 124–50.

37. Grace Trudeau to Pierre Trudeau, Sept. 14, 1960, TP, vol. 46, file 26.

38. The book launch list in in TP, vol. 24, file 5.

39. On Gobeil, see *La Presse*, April 6, 1966.

40. TP, vol. 39, file 6. Sept. 21, 1961.

41. Trudeau to Guérin, Sept. 21, 1961, TP, vol. 39, file 6.

42. The travel file with ticket stubs and bills and a few letters is found in TP, vol. 13, file 13. Also, Grace Trudeau to Pierre Trudeau, June 14, July 26, Sept. 5, and Sept. 26, 1961, vol. 46, file 26.

43. Radwanski, *Trudeau*, 83–84.

44. Trudeau, *Federalism and the French Canadians*, xxi.

45. Trudeau to Marie-Laure Falès, April 22, 1962, TP, vol. 53, file 39.

46. Peter Gzowski, "Portrait of an Intellectual in Action," *Maclean's*, Feb. 24, 1962, 23, 29–30; and "Un capitaliste socialist: Pierre-Elliott Trudeau," *Le Magazine Maclean*, March 1962, 25, 52–55. Note the considerable difference in title.

47. Pierre Trudeau, "The New Treason of the Intellectuals," in Trudeau, *Federalism and the French Canadians*, 151–81.

48. "Faut-il refaire la Confédération?" *Le Magazine Maclean*, June 1962, 19; Gzowski, "Portrait of an Intellectual in Action," 30.

49. Godin, *Lévesque*, 2: 118; René Lévesque, *Memoirs* (Toronto: McClelland & Stewart, 1986), 172–73; and Pelletier, *Years of Choice*, 128–30.

50. Paul-André Linteau, René Durocher, Jean-Claude Robert and François Ricard, *Quebec since 1930*, 340; Gérard Bergeron, *Notre miroir à deux faces* (Montreal: Québec/Amérique, 1985), 48–50, on the emergence of Lévesque in the public; Thomson, *Jean Lesage and the Quiet Revolution*, 117, for an account of the Cabinet meeting; and Lévesque, *Memoirs*, 172ff.

51. Lévesque, *Memoirs*, 173. In *Memoirs*, the footnote to this quotation states: "These quotations are not meant to be textually accurate but serve only to reconstitute the correct context."

52. Trudeau in "Entrevue entre M. Trudeau et M. [Jean] Lépine, 27 avril 1992" [Lépine interview], Trudeau Papers (TP), MG 26 03, vol. 23, file 2, Library and Archives Canada. It is interesting that Trudeau omitted these comments in his memoirs. Also, Pierre Trudeau, "Economic Rights," *McGill Law Journal* 12 (June 1962): 121–25.

53. Lépine interview, TP, vol. 23, file 2; Albert Breton, "The Economics of Nationalism," *Journal of Political Economy* 72 (Aug. 1964): 376–86.

54. Stephen Clarkson and Christina McCall, *Trudeau and Our Times*, vol. 2: *The Heroic Delusion* (Toronto: McClelland & Stewart, 1994), 79–81; and Pelletier, *Years of Choice*, 137–38.

55. Trudeau, "Economic Rights," 121–25; Clarkson and McCall, *Trudeau and Our Times*, 2: 79–81; Godin, *Lévesque*, 117–19; and Pierre Trudeau, "L'homme de gauche et les élections provinciales," *Cité libre*, Nov. 1962, 3–5.

56. Flynn's comments are quoted in Michael Stein, *The Dynamics of Right-Wing Protest: A Political Analysis of Social Credit in Quebec* (Toronto: University of Toronto Press, 1973), 87n33.

57. The account of Diefenbaker's dining-room revolt and the nuclear weapon issue is found in Denis Smith, *Rogue Tory: The Life and Legend of John Diefenbaker* (Toronto: Macfarlane Walter & Ross, 1995), ch. 12. Trudeau's views are found in Lépine interview, TP, vol. 23, file 2. Pelletier later claimed that Lévesque and Lesage blocked Marchand when an organizer's report indicated that his candidacy would result in Créditiste votes being lost in rural areas to the Union nationale. It was a reasonable assessment. Pelletier, *Years of Choice*, 138–39.

58. John Saywell, ed., *The Canadian Annual Review for 1963* (Toronto: University of Toronto Press, 1964), 31; and Pierre Trudeau, "Pearson ou l'abdication de l'esprit," *Cité libre*, April 1963, 7–12.

59. Trudeau, "Pearson ou l'abdication de l'esprit"; Smith, *Rogue Tory*, ch. 12; and Basil Robinson, *Diefenbaker's World: A Populist in Foreign Affairs* (Toronto: University of Toronto Press, 1989).

60. Interview with Laurin is found in TP, vol. 24, file 13. *Le Devoir*, Nov. 28, 1961, offers the Freudian analysis. Interview with Graham Fraser, April 2005.

61. Pierre Vadeboncoeur, "Les qui-perd-gagne," in his *To be or not to be: That is the question!* (Montreal: Les Éditions de l'Hexagone, 1980), 101.

62. Ibid., 102; and Pierre Vadeboncoeur, *La dernière heure et la première* (Montreal: Les Éditions de l'Hexagone, 1970), 53. See also Pierre Vadeboncoeur, "L'héritage Trudeau: La fracture," *L'Action nationale*, Nov. 2000 (http://www.action-nationale.qc.ca/00–11/dossier.html).

63. The essay is found in *Rythmes et Couleurs*, Feb.–March 1964, 1–13. Trudeau's comments are in TP, vol. 38, file 30. The remarks about Laurendeau are made in "Un extraordinaire document de François Hertel," *Le Quartier Latin*, April 9, 1964. Trudeau's comments are in "Les Séparatistes: Des contre-révolutionnaires," *Cité libre*, May 1964, 3–4.

64. Hertel's comment on Trudeau is found in *Le Devoir*, Sept. 18, 1966. The article is entitled "Le bilinguisme est un crime." Grace Trudeau to Pierre Trudeau, Sept. 13, 1961, TP, vol. 46, file 26; and Jean Tréteau, *Hertel, l'homme et l'oeuvre* (Montreal: Pierre Tisseyre, 1986), 131–32, 211, 223, 232, 258, 320. Tréteau indexes Trudeau under "Elliott Trudeau."

65. The correspondence with the Ontario friend is found in RG 32, file 4, Archives of Ontario.

66. Gobeil and Breton are quoted in Gzowski, "What Young French Canadians Have on Their Mind," *Maclean's*, April 6, 1963, 21–23, 39–40; "Pour une politique fonctionelle," *Cité libre*, May 1964, 11–17; "An appeal for Realism in Politics," *The Canadian Forum*, May 1964, 29–33.

CHAPTER NINE: POLITICAL MAN

1. The accounts are from Gérard Pelletier, *Years of Choice, 1960–1968*, trans. Alan Brown (Toronto: Methuen, 1987), 130–33; Patricia Smart, ed., *The Diary of André Laurendeau* (Toronto: James Lorimer, 1991), 21; and Trudeau's discussion with Pelletier, June 9, 1992, Trudeau Papers (TP), MG 26 02, vol. 23, file 16, Library and Archives Canada (LAC).

2. Pelletier, *Years of Choice*, 136–38. Lévesque's statements are taken from the account of his changing attitude in Pierre Godin, *René Lévesque*, vol.2: *Héros malgré lui, 1960–1976* (Montreal: Les Éditions du Boréal, 1997), 290–92.

3. Laurendeau, Sept. 1961, quoted by Pierre de Bellefeuille, "André Laurendeau face au séparatisme des années 60," in Robert Comeau and Lucille Beaudry, eds., *André Laurendeau: Un intellectuel d'ici* (Sillery, Que.: Les Presses de l'Université du Québec, 1990), 159; Smart, ed.,

Laurendeau, 24; and J.L. Granatstein, *Canada 1957–1967: The Years of Uncertainty and Innovation* (Toronto: McClelland & Stewart, 1986), ch. 10. The so-called language issue, which is at the core of the changes, is described in Paul-André Linteau, René Durocher, Jean-Claude Robert, and François Ricard, *Quebec since 1930* trans. Robert Chodos and Ellen Garmaise (Toronto: James Lorimer, 1991), ch. 41.

4. Members are described in Smart, ed., *Laurendeau*, 13–17. The founding and development of the commission are described well in Granatstein, *Canada 1957–1967*, ch. 10. Well-chosen excerpts of testimony and commentary are available on http://archives.cbc.ca/IDD-1–73–655/politics_economy/bilingualism/.

5. The commission of Trudeau's study is described in the Royal Commission files in Fonds Laurendeau, June 18, 1964, document 324E, Fondation Lionel Groulx, Montreal.There is no apparent evidence in Trudeau's own papers that he worked on the study.

6. Interviews with Donald Johnston, May 2004, and Sophie Trudeau, Feb. 2006.

7. Interview with Jacques Hébert, Feb. 2006.

8. Pierre Vallières, "*Cité libre* et ma génération," *Cité libre*, Aug.–Sept. 1963, 15–22.

9. Pierre Vallières, "Sommes-nous en révolution?" *Cité libre*, Feb. 1964, 7–11; and Gérard Pelletier, "*Parti pris* ou la grande illusion," *Cité libre*, April 1964, 3–8. On *Parti pris*, see Pierrette Bouchard-Saint-Amant, "L'idéologie de la revue *Parti-pris*: Le nationalisme socialiste," in Fernand Dumont, Jean Hamelin, and Jean-Paul Montminy, eds., *Idéologies au Canada français, 1940–1976* (Quebec: Les Presses de l'Université Laval, 1981), 315–53.

10. This text of "Separatist Counter-Revolutionaries" is taken from Pierre Trudeau, *Federalism and the French Canadians* (Toronto: Macmillan, 1968), 204–12. It was originally published as "Les séparatistes: Des contre-révolutionnaires" in *Cité libre*, May 1964, 2–6. The translation here is from the *Montreal Star*, which, along with other English-language outlets, published it in the late spring of 1964.

11. Pierre Vallières's account is found in his *Les Négres blancs d'Amérique: Autobiographie précoce d'un terroriste québécois* (Montreal: Éditions Parti pris, nd [1968]), 291–96.

12. Ramsay Cook, *The Maple Leaf Forever* (Toronto: Macmillan, 1971), 36.

13. Joseph-Yvon Thériault, *Critique de l'américanité: Mémoire et démocratie au Québec* (Montreal: Québec Amérique, 2005), 310–13; Trudeau to Hertel, Jan. 13, 1942, TP, vol. 49, file 19.

14. Breton in Nancy Southam, ed., *Pierre* (Toronto: McClelland & Stewart, 2005), 35. Many discussions with Breton about Trudeau.

15. Trudeau, "Separatist Counter-Revolutionaries," 206. See also Claude Julien, *Le Canada: Dernière chance de l'Europe* (Paris: Grasset, 1965); and Jean LeMoyne, *Convergences* (Montreal: Éditions Hurtubise, 1961), 26–27.

16. A good account of the cultural renaissance is found in Linteau et al., *Quebec since 1930*, ch. 53. See also Michel Vastel, *Trudeau: Le Québécois*, 2nd ed. (Montreal: Les Éditions de l'Homme, 2000), 123; and Guérin to Trudeau [Feb. 1965], TP, vol. 49, file 8.

17. On Trudeau and the CBC, see Eric Koch, *Inside This Hour Has Seven Days* (Toronto: Prentice-Hall, 1986), 45; and Carroll Guérin to Trudeau, Dec. 16, 1964, TP, vol. 49, file 8.

18. Malcolm Reid, *The Shouting Signpainters: A Literary and Political Account of Quebec Revolutionary Nationalism* (Toronto: McClelland & Stewart, 1972), 59–60.

19. Cook, *The Maple Leaf Forever*, 41.

20. John Saywell, ed., *The Canadian Annual Review for 1964* (Toronto: University of Toronto Press, 1965), 46–49, includes the Paré quotation; and *Globe and Mail*, Oct. 14, 1964.

21. Saywell, ed., *The Canadian Annual Review for 1964*, 52–54; *Le Devoir*, Sept. 18–19, 1964; and John English, *The Worldly Years: The Life of Lester Pearson, 1949–1972* (Toronto: Knopf, 1992), 218ff.

22. Smart, ed., *Laurendeau*, 73, 90. The polls are described in John Saywell, ed. *The Canadian Annual Review for 1965* (Toronto: University of Toronto Press, 1966), 44. See also A *Preliminary Report of the Royal Commission on Bilingualism and Biculturalism* (Ottawa: Queen's Printer, 1965), 13.

23. Patricia Smart's introduction discusses Laurendeau's discovery of Trudeau's authorship of the critical article. Trudeau admitted "partial paternity" to Laurendeau. Smart, ed., *Laurendeau*, 6–7, 154.

24. English, *The Worldly Years*, 300–4; Claude Morin, *Le pouvoir québécois en négociation* (Montreal: Les Éditions du Boréal, 1975), 137.

25. Pearson to Lower, Dec. 22, 1964, Pearson Papers, MG 26 N3, vol. 3, LAC.

26. Richard Gwyn, *The Shape of Scandal: A Study of a Government in Crisis* (Toronto: Clarke Irwin, 1965), 244. In *The Worldly Years*, 278ff, I discuss the reaction of Pearson to these scandals.

27. Vadeboncoeur described how unionists realized that Marchand had lost his earlier élan and how "many militants" believed that "he had become too uncompromising in his actions and beliefs." See the official site: www.csn.qc.ca/Connaitre/histoire/Vad/Vad2.html. Pelletier describes his firing in *Years of Choice*, 138–39; see also Saywell, ed., *The Canadian Annual Review for 1965*, 483.

28. For the best account of the negotiations, revealing the deep tensions among the Quebec Liberals, see the interviews conducted by Peter Stursberg in his *Lester Pearson and the Dream of Unity* (Toronto: Doubleday, 1978), 255–60. See also Vastel, *Trudeau*, 129–32, which draws on interviews with Marchand conducted later by Pierre Godin.

29. Interview with Eddie Goldenberg, Sept. 2004.

30. Lamontagne in Stursberg, *Lester Pearson and the Dream of Unity*, 258; Pelletier, *Years of Choice*, 176; Vastel, *Trudeau*, 130; Peter Newman, *The Distemper of Our Times: Canadian Politics in Transition* (1968; rev. ed. Toronto: McClelland & Stewart, 1990), 360, on Macnaughton's "skill" as a Speaker; and George Radwanski, *Trudeau* (Toronto: Macmillan, 1978), 90. On Cohen, see Pearson to Cohen, Aug. 5, 1965, Pearson Papers, MG 26 N5, vol. 45; interview with Robin Russell, Macnaughton's assistant, June 2001.

31. "Pelletier et Trudeau s'expliquent," *Cité libre*, Oct. 1965, 3–5.

32. Ramsay Cook to Trudeau, Sept. 10, 1965 (thanks to Ramsay Cook for this letter); and Maurice Blain, "Les colombes et le pouvoir politique: Observations sur une hypothèse," *Cité libre*, Dec. 1965, 7.

33. Election results from Pierre Normandin, ed., *The Canadian Parliamentary Guide 1972* (Ottawa: Normandin, 1972), 382. Nichol quoted in Stursberg, *Lester Pearson and the Dream of Unity*, 274; Blain, "Les colombes," 8; Smart, ed., *Laurendeau*, 153; Pierre Vadeboncoeur, *To be or not to be: That is the question* (Montreal: Les Éditions de l'Hexagone, 1980), 91–109; and interview with Bob Rae, July 2003.

34. Gobeil to Trudeau, Sept. 8, 1965, TP, MG 26 02, vol. 47, file 35, and Guérin to Trudeau, Oct. 25, 1965, vol. 49, file 8.

35. Ryan in *Le Devoir*, Dec. 18, 1965; and Marchand in Stursberg, *Pearson and the Dream of Unity*, 261.

36. *Globe and Mail*, Sept. 14, 1965. On Favreau's motorcycle, see Pelletier, *Years of Choice*, 177.

37. Kenneth McNaught, "The National Outlook of English-speaking Canadians," in Peter Russell, ed., *Nationalism in Canada* (Toronto: McGraw-Hill, 1966), 70.

38. Jean-Paul Desbiens (Frère Untel) is quoted in Newman, *The Distemper of Our Times*, 512.

39. *Montreal Gazette*, Oct. 23, 1965; and Blair Fraser, "The Three: Quebec's New Face in Ottawa," *Maclean's*, Jan. 22, 1966, 16–17, 37–38.

40. Pierre Trudeau, *Memoirs* (Toronto: McClelland & Stewart, 1993), 78. See also the account in Stephen Clarkson and Christina McCall, *Trudeau and Our Times*, vol. 1: *The Magnificent Obsession* (Toronto: McClelland & Stewart, 1990), 93–94; Smart, ed., *Laurendeau*, 154; and Pearson as quoted in Radwanski, *Trudeau*, 91.

41. *Globe and Mail*, Nov. 9, 1965; English, *The Worldly Years*, 310–12; and Lester Pearson, "Election Analysis," Dec. 10, 1965, Pearson Papers, MG 26 N5, vol. 45.

42. Interview between Pierre Trudeau and Ron Graham, April 29, 1992, TP, vol. 23, file 4.

43. Smart, ed., *Laurendeau*, 154.

44. Bruce Hutchison, "A Conversation with the Prime Minister," Feb. 11, 1965, Hutchison Papers, University of Calgary Library; John Saywell, ed., *The Canadian Annual Review for 1966* (Toronto: University of Toronto Press, 1967), 52–53; *Le Devoir*, March 29, 1966; and *Toronto Daily Star*, April 2, 1966.

45. On Spencer, see Newman, *The Distemper of Our Times*, 534–53; House of Commons, *Debates*, Feb. 25, 1965; Saywell, ed., *The Canadian Annual Review for 1966*, 9–11; and, especially, Stursberg, *Lester Pearson and the Dream of Unity*, 291–94.

46. Diefenbaker had the materials in his papers. J.G. Dienbaker Papers, box II 008386–92, Diefenbaker Centre, Saskatoon. Pearson's account is in an interview with Bruce Hutchison, Feb. 11, 1965, Hutchison Papers.

47. House of Commons, *Debates*, March 2–4, 1966; and Newman, *Distemper of Our Times*, 540–42.

48. Newman, *Distemper of Our Times*, 540–42; Marchand is quoted in Stursberg, *Lester Pearson and the Dream of Unity*, 294; his resignation threat is described on page 297. Interview with André Ouellet, May 2001.

49. Pierre Vadeboncoeur, "À propos de Pierre Elliott," *Le Devoir*, Dec. 8, 2005.

50. Newman, *The Distemper of Our Times*, 604; Trudeau, *Memoirs*, 78–79, where Pearson's comment in his own memoirs is quoted, presumably indicating agreement. Interview with Herb Gray, June 2005.

51. *Le Magazine Maclean*, Jan. 1965, 2; and English, *The Worldly Years*, 319ff. The fullest account is given in John Bosher, *The Gaullist Attack on Canada* (Montreal and Kingston: McGill-Queen's University Press, 1999). See also Trudeau, *Memoirs*, 78–79.

52. Clarkson and McCall, *Trudeau and Our Times* 1: 99–101; Johnson's quotation on the Constitution is in Newman, *The Distemper of Our Times*, 445; Saywell, ed., *The Canadian Annual Review for 1966*, 57–73; and *Le Devoir*, Sept. 15, 1966. Interview with Mitchell Sharp, Jan. 1994. Sharp first noticed Trudeau during a discussion of the proposed tax structure at a Cabinet committee meeting where he represented Pearson and where he expressed his strong opposition to special status. See Mitchell Sharp, *Which Reminds Me . . . : A Memoir* (Toronto: University of Toronto Press, 1994), 139.

53. Comments in notebook, April 25, 1959, in TP, vol. 13, file 5.

54. Interview with Paul Martin Sr., Sept. 1990; interview with Marc Lalonde, Oct. 1990. John Bosher had access to Marcel Cadieux's diary, in which he fiercely criticized Martin, particularly on the French issue. See Bosher, *The Gaullist Attack on Canada*. Before his death, Cadieux spoke to me about his strong feelings against Pearson for his criticisms of American policy on Vietnam and against Martin for his "gimmicks," which he believed were a means to use foreign policy for electoral gain.

55. Gordon took the lead in the late 1940s in creating a fund, the "Algoma Fishing and Conservation Society," in honour of Pearson's Northern Ontario constituency. He was also the principal organizer of his leadership campaign and of the party reorganization in the late 1950s and early 1960s. He introduced Pearson to Keith Davey, Richard O'Hagan, and

many others who played a major role in the Pearson governments, and he was an important recruiter of candidates in the Toronto area. His relationship with Pearson never recovered after the prime minister accepted his resignation after the 1965 election. He wrote angry memoranda about their relationship, claiming that he had raised $100,000 in private funds for Pearson, and he remained deeply distrustful of Pearson, who, he wrote after his meeting in January 1967, "will renege [on the deal] if he can." Walter Gordon, "LBP," Dec. 5, 1965, Gordon Papers, MG 26 B44, vol. 16, LAC; and Memorandum of Jan. 18, 1967, ibid.

56. Gad Horowitz, "A Dimension Survey: The Future of the NDP," *Canadian Dimension* 3 (July–Aug.): 23, 24.

57. Lamontagne and Gordon told their stories to Stursberg, *Lester Pearson and the Dream of Unity*, 374–76.

58. Clarkson and McCall, *Trudeau and Our Times*, 1: 102; and Saywell, ed., *The Canadian Annual Review for 1966*, 34, 52–53.

59. Interview, Library and Archives Canada, March 5, 2003.

60. William Robb, "Trudeau Up Front," *Canadian Business*, May 1967, 11–12. Newman in *Toronto Daily Star*, April 25, 1967. The correspondent who saw Trudeau blush is Robert Stall, *Montreal Star*, Dec. 20, 1967. On Trudeau's early argument that natural justice must be observed, see RG 2, Privy Council Office, Series A-5-a, vol. 6323, April 6, 1967.

61. RG 2, Privy Council Office, Series A-5-a, vol. 6323, July 25, 1967.

62. *Le Devoir*, Sept. 20, 1967. The text of the Lévesque address calling for sovereignty was published in *Le Devoir* between September 19 and 21, 1967.

63. Gordon, Memorandum, Nov. 17, 1967, Gordon Papers, MG 26, B44, vol. 16.

64. Guérin to Trudeau, July 4, 1964, TP, vol. 28, file 8; interview with Madeleine Gobeil.

65. Guérin to Trudeau, Sept. 15, 1967.

66. Margaret Trudeau, *Beyond Reason* (New York and London: Paddington, 1979), 28–29; interview with Margaret Sinclair Trudeau, Feb. 2006.

CHAPTER TEN: A TALE OF TWO CITIES

1. Gérard Pelletier, *Years of Choice, 1960–1968*, trans. Alan Brown (Toronto: Methuen, 1987), 254–55. Pelletier's account seems to suggest that the dinner took place on January 7, 1968, but Donald Peacock's

more contemporary *Journey to Power: The Story of a Canadian Election* (Toronto: Ryerson, 1968) has the accurate date and a fuller account of the meeting at Café Martin (185ff). Trudeau's own memory has Pelletier making the first remarks. "Entrevue entre M. Trudeau et M. [Jean] Lépine, 30 April 1992," [Lépine interview], Trudeau Papers (TP), MG 26 03, vol. 23, file 5, Library and Archives Canada.

2. Richard Stanbury Diary, property of the writer. Mr. Stanbury also responded to my questions about specific diary entries. The Martin exchange took place on January 31, 1968. The best account of the Toronto Liberals remains Christina McCall-Newman, *Grits: An Intimate Portrait of the Liberal Party* (Toronto: Macmillan, 1982). John Nichol's recollection that only he and Liberal Federation official Paul Lafond knew about Pearson's resignation before it happened is contradicted by Stanbury's diary and by other interviews on the subject conducted by Peter Stursberg. See his *Lester Pearson and the Dream of Unity* (Toronto: Doubleday, 1978), 405–6. Interview with John Nichol.

3. Minutes of the meeting of Sunday, October 22, at 580 Christie Street, Keith Davey Papers, box 17, file 15, Victoria University.

4. O'Malley had written the phrase in the *Globe and Mail* on December 12, 1967. Trudeau was obviously taken with it and repeated it in an interview ten days later. See Richard Gwyn, *The Northern Magus: Pierre Trudeau and Canadians* (Toronto: McClelland & Stewart, 1980), 64.

5. *The Montreal Star*, Jan. 13, 1968. To my knowledge, the French press did not report on the petition.

6. Peacock, *Journey to Power*, 183–85; Martin Sullivan, *Mandate '68* (Toronto: Doubleday, 1968), 274; interviews with Marc Lalonde and Jacques Hébert; and *Toronto Daily Star*, Jan. 3, 1968. See also the account in John Saywell, ed., *Canadian Annual Review for 1968* (Toronto: University of Toronto Press, 1969), 17ff.

7. Laurendeau's diary entry of Dec. 3, 1967, in Patricia Smart, ed., *The Diary of André Laurendeau* (Toronto: James Lorimer, 1991), 170. Marchand's drinking caused Trudeau personal concern and he raised it with him. Interview with Alexandre Trudeau. Also conversations with Pauline Bothwell and Tom Kent, who were, respectively, Marchand's assistant and deputy minister. Interview with Tim Porteous, May 2006.

8. In the *New York Times* story, April 7, 1968, reporting his leadership win, Trudeau is described as a "46-year-old Montreal lawyer." Later, Jean Lépine challenged Trudeau on the ambiguity about his age, but he denied that he had lied. He placed the blame on journalists who did not check the facts. Lépine interview, TP, vol. 23, file 5.

9. On Smallwood, see Peacock, *Journey to Power*, 190–92. Smallwood's own comments are found in Stursberg, *Lester Pearson and the Dream of Unity*, 421. J.W. Pickersgill, who had been the Liberals' principal Newfoundland minister, eventually left politics because he could no longer deal with the eccentricities of Smallwood. As his summer tenant in the mid-1970s, I was often regaled with tales of Smallwood's increasingly bizarre behaviour. He included this support for Trudeau as one of the examples of such behaviour.

10. Pelletier, *Years of Choice*, 264. Peacock describes the tortured negotiations with Lamontagne over the Sunday session in *Journey to Power*, 195–96. Interviews with Donald Macdonald and Marc Lalonde.

11. *Le Devoir*, Jan. 29, 1968. See also Saywell, ed., *Canadian Annual Review for 1968*, 18–19.

12. *Montreal Star*, Jan. 30–31, 1968.

13. Stanbury Diary, Feb. 9, 1968; *Globe and Mail*, Jan. 30, 1968; and Pelletier, *Years of Choice*, 261, 27.

14. L.B. Pearson, *Federalism for the Future* (Ottawa: The Queen's Printer, 1968).

15. Cook in Saywell, ed., *Canadian Annual Review for 1968*, 82.

16. Marchand quoted in Stursberg, *Lester Pearson and the Dream of Unity*, 425; Stéphane Kelly, *Les Fins du Canada selon Macdonald, Laurier, Mackenzie King et Trudeau* (Montreal: Les Éditions du Boréal, 2001), 205.

17. Peter Newman gives the best summary of the candidates in his *The Distemper of Our Times: Canadian Politics in Transition* (1968; rev. ed. Toronto: McClelland & Stewart, 1990), 596–601.

18. Pelletier, *Years of Choice*, 272–74.

19. Ibid., 274–76; and Peacock, *Journey to Power*, 222–24.

20. There are differences in the accounts of the meetings with Pelletier. Some claim that Trudeau told them on Valentine's Day, but others (Saywell, ed., *Canadian Annual Review for 1968* and Peacock, *Journey to Power*) suggest the 15th. Pelletier's account is based on his diary and therefore is probably correct. See his *Years of Choice*, 276.

21. The quotation is from Saywell, ed., *Canadian Annual Review for 1968*, 21.

22. *Montreal Star*, March 9, 1968.

23. Tim Porteous in Nancy Southam, ed., *Pierre* (Toronto: McClelland & Stewart, 2005), 65. The answer may have been serious. Trudeau, along with many academics, considered that Machiavelli had been misunderstood and distorted.

24. Christina McCall-Newman, *Grits*, 113–15. Confidential interview. Trudeau saved copies of the *Canadian Intelligence Service* in his papers. The March 1968 issue features "revelations" by a former RCMP intelligence officer about Trudeau's trips to China and Russia and his failed jaunt to Cuba.

25. However, some journalists criticized Trudeau for following "old-style politics" in so vociferously defending the government. The *Globe and Mail*, which had been friendly to his candidacy but was hostile to the government, pointed out that "that man of principle, Justice Minister Pierre Trudeau, fell obediently in line with party discipline and voted with the government. Or is that *erstwhile* man of principle?" Feb. 19, 1968. Peter Newman rightly said that Trudeau benefited most because he, Turner, and Kierans "alone project a new style that dissociates them from the blunders of the Pearson administration." *Toronto Daily Star*, March 3, 1968.

26. Gordon interview in Stursberg, *Lester Pearson and the Dream of Unity*; *Globe and Mail*, Feb. 20 and 28, 1968. An excellent account of the Liberal manoeuvres is found in *Toronto Daily Star*, Feb. 26, 1968. Constitutional authorities were divided on the question of whether the government had the right to bring forward a vote of confidence. Eugene Forsey, for example, believed that it did. See Saywell, ed., *Canadian Annual Review for 1968*, 12–13. Sharp's analysis is found in his *Which Reminds Me . . . : A Memoir* (Toronto: University of Toronto Press, 1994), 159ff. Trudeau's comments are in Hansard, Feb. 27, 1968.

27. On Winters, see Newman, *The Distemper of Our Times*, 602–3. The February polls are found in the record of the Canadian Institute of Public Opinion, MG 28 III 114, file 89, Poll 327, LAC.

28. Pelletier, *Years of Choice*, 290–91; Peacock, *Journey to Power*, 255–58. The hostess comment is in *Toronto Daily Star*, March 4, 1968.

29. Tim Porteous in Southam, ed., *Pierre* , 61.

30. There is a full account in Peacock, *Journey to Power*, 251–53. See also *Le Devoir*, Feb. 16–17, 1968.

31. *Le Devoir*, March 6–7, 1968. The criticisms of Trudeau are found in Saywell, ed., *The Canadian Annual Review for 1968*, 24–25. On Johnson and Gabon, see Pierre Godin, *Daniel Johnson, 1964–1968: La difficile recherche de l'égalité* (Montreal: Les Éditions de l'Homme, 1980), 329–33.

32. Pelletier, *Years of Choice*, 293–300; *Montreal Star*, March 23, 1968.

33. Sharp, *Which Reminds Me . . .* , 155–65; interview with Mitchell Sharp. The Smallwood quotation is found in Newman, *Distemper of Our Times*, 628.

34. Stanbury Diary; Peacock, *Journey to Power*, 283ff. Interview with Tim Porteous, May 2006.

35. Conversation with Robert Bothwell, Feb. 2006.

36. The account follows Peacock, *Journey to Power*. However, slightly different wording is found in Newman, *Distemper of Our Times*, 638. The substance is the same.

NOTE ON SOURCES

—

T he source for this volume is the remarkable collection
of personal papers that has been transferred from the
Trudeau home in Montreal to Library and Archives
Canada in Ottawa. These papers were assembled in minute
detail by Grace Trudeau and by Trudeau himself.

The most interesting item in the preserved papers is the
Gouin-Trudeau correspondence of the mid-1940s. When the relationship between Thérèse Gouin and Trudeau ended, she
returned his letters. They later discussed the correspondence,
and he promised it would not be released in her lifetime—
although he mentioned to Madame Gouin Décarie that he had
recently read the letters once again. Having now been privileged
to read the correspondence myself, I can understand Trudeau's
wish that the letters be kept complete. They are remarkable
and, eventually, when they are published, they will take their
place among the most illuminating and important exchanges in
Canadian letters.

Although Trudeau made little apparent use of his papers
for his memoirs, there is considerable indication he read much
of the collection later in his life. There are notations, question
marks, and identification of individuals whose full names are not

given in the originals. His papers also contain the excellent interviews conducted for the memoirs by Ron Graham and Jean Lépine, as well as some interviews with family members and others as diverse as Michael Ignatieff and Camille Laurin. Again, very little use was made of this material for the memoirs. We now know that Trudeau's memoirs concealed much of his private thoughts and activities, but he did maintain the integrity of his papers, which fully disclose them all. We can only speculate on his reasons, but there is evidence in the Trudeau papers that, as early as 1939, he expected that he would, one day, have a biographer. Moreover, he admired confessional literature, from Saint Augustine through to Proust. Ultimately, he has allowed others to bare the soul that he so carefully concealed in his lifetime, and he apparently did so deliberately.

Some documents seem to be missing in his papers. For example, there are almost no letters from Father Marie d'Anjou or François Lessard, although we know that both corresponded frequently with Trudeau about nationalist and religious matters in the forties. There are also few letters from Jean Marchand and Gérard Pelletier, and none of substance from Trudeau in their papers—all of which suggests (especially in the case of Pelletier) that the correspondence relating to their political and literary work in the fifties and sixties is either lost or in some abandoned filing cabinet. Still, Trudeau's private papers are an exceptionally rich lode for a biographer to mine, and valuable nuggets appear in virtually every box.

This book has full endnotes indicating primary sources and secondary works. The majority of the secondary works dealing with Trudeau will be relevant for the second volume of the biography, which will deal with his political career and its aftermath. It is impossible to separate the sources for the two volumes because interviews relating to his later life, for instance, can also be relevant in discussing his earlier years. A full bibliography, including manuscript sources and interviews, will be available on the web at www.theigloo.org after the publication of this volume, and it will grow as I write Volume Two. The site will also provide an opportunity for others—students, scholars, and all interested readers—to offer their own information that might be relevant for Trudeau's later life.

ACKNOWLEDGMENTS

—

I n the Preface to this book, I thank the Trudeau family and the executors of the Trudeau Estate—Alexandre Trudeau, Jim Coutts, Marc Lalonde, Roy Heenan, and Jacques Hébert—for their invitation to write this biography. I also thank them for issuing the invitation without, for a moment, thinking to impose restrictions on me, and for entrusting me to write a full and objective account of Pierre Elliott Trudeau's life. I would also like to thank the Trudeau family for their encouragement, not only Alexandre and Justin, of course, but my friends Margaret Sinclair Trudeau and Sophie Grégoire, who is married to Justin Trudeau, for their invaluable feminine view on Trudeau's family.

There are many others whom I must thank greatly for expanding my understanding of Pierre Trudeau. Three individuals in particular, who not only knew Trudeau well but also greatly affected his life in this period, offered me assistance in clarifying the story. The remarkable Thérèse Gouin Décarie, Trudeau's close companion over many of these years, agreed to cooperate with this biographical project and gave me access to material that was essential. (Her husband, Vianney Décarie, also provided important information about Trudeau's early years.) Roger Rolland, the friend

539

in many of Trudeau's early pranks (and later his speechwriter), corrected tales that had been told wrongly in the past and provided new ones. Madeleine Gobeil, who knew Trudeau intimately in the sixties, when his personal files are thinner, offered unique, intelligent insight into his habits, tastes, and friendships.

I met two of Pierre's close friends when I attended Harvard University. Ramsay and Eleanor Cook came to Boston in the fall of 1968, just after Pierre became prime minister—in part because of their efforts. After Ramsay's lecture on Canadian history to Harvard undergraduates, a few of us Canadian doctoral students ruminated with him about the fate of the Trudeau government, which had already begun to lose some of the aura that surrounded it during the summer months. The following year I met Albert Breton, Trudeau's former colleague at the Université de Montréal, who followed Ramsay as the Mackenzie King Professor at Harvard. I was Albert's teaching assistant, and, when my wife, Hilde, and I formed an enduring friendship with Albert and his wife, Margot, they gave me a view of Pierre that was marked by immense personal warmth and respect. Ramsay and Eleanor have read this manuscript, and both have saved me from many errors of fact and interpretation.

I have also benefited from interviews about Trudeau that I conducted when I wrote a biography of Lester Pearson and, with Robert Bothwell, a book on postwar Canadian history. The bulk of these interviews with leading political and bureaucratic figures of the sixties and seventies are in the Bothwell Papers at the University of Toronto Archives and at Library and Archives Canada, and in my own papers at the University of Waterloo Archives. Bob has shared research notes from his work on Canadian foreign policy and Quebec and, in the United States, in the Nixon and Ford Papers. I owe an enormous debt to him for his generosity. I also owe a debt to many who have written perceptive articles, books, and essays about Trudeau. A full critical bibliography will accompany Volume Two of this biography and, in the meantime, the titles will be listed on the website for this book.

Library and Archives Canada has provided extraordinary assistance for this work. Under the expert guidance of Christian Rioux, a team organized the Trudeau Papers quickly and wisely. Peter de Lottinville, Michel Wyczynski, and George Bolarenko were also helpful, and I would particularly like to thank Michel for responding at short notice to my requests for visits. Paul Marsden, now at the NATO archives in Brussels, pointed me towards some important documents on Trudeau's work at the Privy Council in the 1950s. At every stage, Ian Wilson, the national archivist, has assisted me in my work with his exceptional attentiveness to the record of Canadian political history. Through his auspices, I was able to interview in small groups during 2002 and 2003 the following individuals (all with Honourable in their titles) who served Trudeau well: Jack Austin, Jean-Jacques Blais, Charles Caccia, Judy Erola, Herb Gray, Otto Lang, Ed Lumley, Allan MacEachen, André Ouellet, John Reid, Mitchell Sharp, and David Smith. Other Trudeau assistants and colleagues who participated in these interviews were Gordon Ashworth, Jean-Marc Carisse, Denise Chong, Ralph Coleman, Marie-Hélène Fox, Bea Hertz, Ted Johnson, Michael Langille, Mary MacDonald, Bob Murdoch, Nicole Sénécal, Larry Smith, Jacques Shore, Courtney Tower, and George Wilson. These interviews will be made available on my website when permissions are given.

I received many letters from both opposition and government members of the Trudeau years after the Canadian Association of Former Parliamentarians placed a notice in its newsletter asking former parliamentary colleagues of Trudeau to contact me about their experiences. Edward McWhinney, the distinguished constitutional authority, had not been a parliamentary colleague of Trudeau, but he, too, sent me a very helpful and long letter.

The Social Sciences and Humanities Research Council has supported this project through its research grant program, principally through funding for graduate research assistants. Several of these assistants were my doctoral students at the University of Waterloo, and they have simultaneously worked on dissertations examining various public policy issues of the Trudeau years. Their efforts will make regular appearances in the notes to the second volume of this biography. They also assisted in research in the important collections at Library and Archives Canada relevant to Canadian public life in the 1950s and 1960s. For this invaluable help I would like to thank Stephen Azzi, Matthew Bunch, Jason Churchill, Andrew Thompson, and Ryan Touhey. My former student Greg Donaghy, now in the Department of Foreign Affairs, helped with many inquiries. Marc Nadeau carried out research in Quebec archives, at Brébeuf College, and the Université de Montréal. Esther Delisle shared with Marc and me the evidence of the young Trudeau's involvement in a nationalist cell. Her exceptional research skills first found the trail that pointed to the proof presented in the early chapters of this book. The Hon. Alistair Gillespie and his biographer, Irene Sage, have shared their research in British and American archives, and Mr. Gillespie allowed me to read his own notes, which begin with the leadership convention. I would also like to thank the Hon. Richard Stanbury for giving me copies of his diary, which I have used extensively in the final chapter.

The University of Waterloo and its Department of History have provided a highly supportive atmosphere for scholarship and collegial activity. The department's chair, my friend Pat Harrigan, was the first reader of many of the chapters of this book (and the first to report victories of the Detroit Tigers, a passion we share). There are too many colleagues to mention who have contributed in some way to the book, but I would like to thank Dean Bob Kerton and President David Johnston at the University of Waterloo for their assistance during the past few years. In particular, they negotiated an agreement whereby I became executive director of the Centre for International Governance Innovation, a Waterloo-based think tank studying international affairs, which resulted from the imagination and financial generosity of my friend and former neighbour Jim Balsillie.

At the centre, Lena Yost has been my superb assistant, with support from Jenn Beckermann in the summer months. Research director Daniel Schwanen has not only taken on many tasks I should have done but has put his flawless bilingualism to the task of translation. Kerry Lappin-Fortin translated many of the quotations in French, and Alison de Muy helped with translation and some other questions. Trudeau's friend and close collaborator on his memoirs, Ron Graham, also translated some of Trudeau's letters. I would like to thank several colleagues at the centre, especially Andy Cooper, who did the bulk of the work on some books we co-edited; Dan Latendre and his staff, who helped with technical questions; and Paul Heinbecker, whose affection for Brian Mulroney provided the countervailing influence that Trudeau always deemed essential. Balsillie fellow Victor Sautry has helped with many tasks, and several excellent undergraduate students also provided research assistance. Alex Lund and Eleni Crespi worked for me during the summer months; and Jonathan Minnes has been the major organizer of the papers, the assistant "on call" throughout the year, and a reliable sleuth when endnotes were missing. Joan Euler gave me some useful articles I would not otherwise have found. Nicolas Rouleau, a brilliant young lawyer, volunteered to help me with the project. He brought a lawyer's mind to the manuscript, a historian's skill to research, and his bilingual facility to the project.

Once again Gena Gorrell, a proofreader who has an excellent eye for detail, has saved me from many errors and omissions. At Knopf Canada, Michelle MacAleese has assisted with the illustrations, and, with constant cheerfulness, Deirdre Molina has sorted out the various drafts of the manuscript, maintained the bulging files, and brought the scattered parts together. However, my greatest debt is owed to two exceptional women in Canadian publishing: my publisher Louise Dennys and my editor Rosemary Shipton. Louise received the Order of Canada this year because of her extraordinary contribution to Canadian publishing. She has brought to this biography boundless enthusiasm, stylistic elegance, a keen wit, and a devotion to understanding Canada. Her award is richly deserved. Next spring Trinity College at the University of Toronto will bestow an honorary doctorate on Rosemary Shipton, a recognition of her outstanding work as an editor. Trudeau took over Rosemary's life this winter, and, through the spring and early summer, she has shaped this book with remarkable skill and care. Like all prose she so expertly and graciously touches, mine has become clearer and better. My faults remain, but they are fewer because of Louise and Rosemary.

On a late September afternoon in 2000, my fifteen-year-old son, Jonathan, came home from school and said, "Adam and I are going to Montreal tonight." Two French-immersion students who were born the year after Pierre Trudeau left office, they had decided they must go to Trudeau's funeral. As the coffin travelled by train from Ottawa to Montreal, they left the old Kitchener station for the long ride that ended, fortunately, with seats in a remote corner of Notre Dame Cathedral, where they were present for one of Canada's greatest state occasions. Jonathan and his mother, Hilde, have endured too many absences from me while I wrote this book. I thank them both for their generosity and support, especially Hilde, who wanted so much to fight off her cancer until this book was published. She could not. I now mourn her deeply and dedicate this life story to her.

PHOTO CREDITS/PERMISSIONS

—

If not otherwise specified, all photos and images come from the Trudeau Papers

CP
Pierre in Middle East, Peter Bregg; Canadian delegation in China; Trudeau slides down bannister, Ted Grant.

LIBRARY AND ARCHIVES CANADA
Trudeau in 1950s, Walter Curtin PA-144330; Pelletier, Trudeau and Marchand announce candidacy, Duncan Cameron PA-117502; Pearson and his successors, Duncan Cameron PA-117107; Trudeau speaking, Horst Ehricht PA-184613; Trudeau at Federal-Provincial Conference, Duncan Cameron PA-117463; Trudeau at leadership convention, Duncan Cameron PA-206324; Trudeau team, Duncan Cameron PA-206327.

McCORD MUSEUM
The Big Attraction, M965.199.1451; Suddenly Everyone Looks a Little Older, M965.199.6529; A Mirage!, M997.63.37; The Swinger, M965.199.6647.

DON NEWLANDS/KLIXPIX
Pierre Elliott Trudeau (cover); Three men in a boat; Rowing to Cuba. Early Gunslinger; A kiss for good luck; Flower in mouth.

TRUDEAU FAMILY
First baby picture; Grace Elliott Trudeau; Pierre with packsack.

PERMISSIONS
The author has made every effort to locate and contact all the holders of copy written material reproduced in this book, and expresses grateful acknowledgment for permission to reproduce from the following previously published material:

Lévesque, René. *Memoirs* (Toronto: McClelland & Stewart), 1986.

Pelletier, Gérard. *Years of Impatience, 1950–1960*, trans. Alan Brown (Toronto: Methuen), 1984.

Pelletier, Gérard. *Years of Choice, 1960–1968*, trans. Alan Brown (Toronto: Methuen), 1987.

Saywell, John and Donald Foster, eds. *Canadian Annual Review for 1968* (University of Toronto Press, Toronto), 1969.

Scott, F.R. *The Collected Poems of F.R. Scott* (Toronto: McClelland & Stewart), 1981.

Trudeau, Pierre Elliott. *Against the Current: Selected Writings, 1939–1996*, trans. G. Tombs (Toronto: McClelland & Stewart), 1996.

Trudeau, Pierre Elliott and Jacques Hébert. *Two Innocents in Red China* (Toronto: Oxford University Press), 1968.

INDEX

—

JOHN ENGLISH is the author of the award-winning two-volume biography of *Lester Pearson: Shadow of Heaven: 1897–1948,* and *The Worldly Years: 1949–1972.* A professor of history at the University of Waterloo, executive director of the Centre for International Governance Innovation, and co-editor of the *Dictionary of Canadian Biography,* English served as co-editor of the *Canadian Historical Review,* chair of the Canadian Museum of Civilization, and Member of Parliament for Kitchener, where he lives.